Introduction to Philosophy:
From Wonder to World View

INTRODUCTION

From Wonder to World View

PRENTICE-HALL, INC., Englewood Cliffs, New Jersey   07632

TO PHILOSOPHY

DONALD SCHERER

PETER A. FACIONE

Bowling Green State University

THOMAS ATTIG

FRED D. MILLER, JR.

Library of Congress Cataloging in Publication Data

Main entry under title:

Introduction to philosophy . . . from wonder to world view.

   Includes bibliographical references and index.
   1. Philosophy—Introductions.   I. Scherer, Donald.
BD21.I57   100   78-11375
ISBN 0-13-491860-6

INTRODUCTION TO PHILOSOPHY: From Wonder to World View
Scherer, Facione, Attig, and Miller

10   9   8   7   6   5   4   3   2   1

Editorial/production supervision: Hilda Tauber

Cover and interior design: Walter Behnke

Manufacturing buyers: Harry P. Baisley, John Hall

PRENTICE-HALL INTERNATIONAL, INC., *London*
PRENTICE-HALL OF AUSTRALIA PTY. LIMITED, *Sydney*
PRENTICE-HALL OF CANADA, LTD., *Toronto*
PRENTICE-HALL OF INDIA PRIVATE LIMITED, *New Delhi*
PRENTICE-HALL OF JAPAN, INC., *Tokyo*
PRENTICE-HALL OF SOUTHEAST ASIA PTE. LTD., *Singapore*
WHITEHALL BOOKS LIMITED, *Wellington, New Zealand*

Contents

v

Philosopher's Workshops

These brief workshops present biographical sketches, primary source citations, special terminology, important theories, key distinctions, or crucial arguments. They serve to highlight ideas that have become widely discussed and relied upon by other thinkers and to supplement the text with biographical and primary source materials.

Preface for Students and Instuctors

Philosophy sets out from wonder about the world and our place in it, and aims at the construction of a comprehensive world view.

What kind of being am I in contrast to my surroundings, and in what does my unique identity consist? Am I and are others free enough in our behavior to be reasonably held responsible for what we do? What is the nature of reality: Is it mental, physical, or both? What can I know? How can I know about the physical world and the mind of others? Are we alone in the universe, or is there a divine being whose existence has a bearing upon the meaning of our lives? What things are genuinely valuable and worth pursuing as I try to lead a good and meaningful life? Philosophy begins in that wonder we all experience as we reflect on our humanity, our individual and social lives, and the universe in which we live. Philosophers are people who carefully pursue reasoned answers to questions like those above. Philosophical methods enable people to move beyond wonder to serious reflection on and thoughtful examination of these questions. Seen as a discipline with a history and heritage, philosophy presents an imaginative array of perspectives on these questions. In your study of philosophy you will join with thinkers throughout the ages, share their wonder, and reflect philosophically in thinking about yourself, your life, and the world in which you live.

The first purpose of this book is to help students come to grips with philosophical questions like those above. It offers serious, philosophical reflections and analyses of the approaches and perspectives that the philosophers who shaped our Western culture and civilization have brought to bear upon these issues. Second, the book provides students with the philosophical concepts and skills necessary to understand the theories that have been developed in these areas and, more important, to rationally evaluate alternative approaches, including their own, to solving or resolving philosophical perplexities. Third, it provides an overview of five intellectually influential attempts to synthesize diverse philosophical insights into fully developed world views, world views with far-reaching implications for how we live and interact.

To accomplish this goal the book is divided into eight parts. Part One presents four preliminary chapters on the intellectual tools needed to deal effectively with philosophical problems. It discusses the purposes of philosophy, rudimentary logical thinking, and definitional skills, and two basic approaches philosophers have developed to address the problems they have posed. Parts Two through Seven present an array of the most central problems in Western philosophy. The main topic areas are ethics; theory of human nature and personal identity; the mind-body problem; the dilemma of determinism; the extent and nature of knowledge; and God, religion, and the meaning of life. Each discussion presents a clarification of the issues involved, a treatment of the major perspectives on the issue, and initial responses to those perspectives. Questions for further thought and discussion are raised as the positions of different philosophers with regard to the topics are presented and analyzed. Essentially these middle twenty-seven chapters are aimed at clarification and criticism of the thoughts dominating the philosophical tradition of Western civilization on each topic. Part Eight provides a chapter on the systematic development of one's philosophical perspectives on a variety of problems into a comprehensive, integrated world view. Then in the final five chapters the world views of five prominent and representative philosophers from the Western tradition are presented together with exploration of the relationships of their world views to their life styles and subsequent thought and action. Unfortunately, space prevents us from exploring the richness of Eastern philosophy or from presenting other influential world views.

Beyond presenting the basic philosophical approaches, issues, perspectives, theories, and selected world views, and beyond introducing logical thinking and definitional skills to further clarify and discuss these matters, the book includes several features that should make it more useful to both teachers and students. (1) Each chapter begins by stating its objectives; these goals should guide the study of the particular chapter. (2) All chapters, with the exception of the five on world views, present a case study or story illustrating the ideas or the techniques being developed in that chapter. (3) The explanatory text of the chapter draws out theoretical points and describes philosophical techniques both abstractly and by appeal to the case study and other examples. The case studies are good discussion starters. (4) Each chapter ends with a set of sequenced exercises that demand thoughtful application of the ideas and the tools presented in that chapter. These exercises are designed as learning aids to reinforce, clarify, and lead beyond the text. Selected answers to exercises are provided, as are directions referring students to specific sections of the chapter, so that those students having difficulty may immediately review the relevant portion of the text. (5) Most chapters contain at least one supplementary insert called "Philosopher's Workshop." Most of these present excerpts of original source materials and indicate the historical development of philosophical thought. Several of the exercises are designed to sharpen students' abilities to deal with philosophical material by asking them to explain the thinking in these excerpts. Other Workshops present definitions of special technical vocabulary or descriptions of particularly influential arguments that philosophers have used to justify a point of view.

We approach philosophy as both method and content because it is as valuable to learn to think philosophically as it is to have a functional understanding of what others have thought. The many pedagogical tools in this book are aimed collectively at both of these goals. In the instructor's manual we offer further teaching suggestions, classroom aids, and testing tools.

Although this book was designed for a variety of possible uses, its primary use is as the chief text of an introductory philosophy course. Because of the organization of the material in Parts Two through Seven an instructor might select any of a variety of paths through the text. May we suggest that Part One, which presents the purposes, basic tools, and philosophical approaches, be regarded as the place to start. As the course moves into the discussion of various problems in philosophy, different groupings of Parts Two through Seven are possible, because each is designed to be a self-contained discussion of an area or problem. After having treated a variety of philosophical problems, we encourage the move to Part Eight, in which we emphasize the concern to synthesize several perspectives into an integrated world view. In presenting the world views of five prominent philosophers, Part Eight illustrates how theories on a wide range of issues can be combined into a systematic philosophy and even a "way of life." Although we could not describe every important world view, we have endeavored to include philosophers representing diverse historical periods and world views that have been particularly influential.

This book is designed to be compatible with a variety of instructional approaches, ranging from the lecture-discussion format to any of a number of self-teaching or self-study methods. Although certainly not a "programmed" text, it provides students with sufficient feedback and direction to make possible a self-study or independent study of introductory philosophy.

In order to permit maximum flexibility to the instructor and maximum room for original thinking for students we have tried to maintain our neutrality. We have presumed that most readers will have had no previous experience with philosophy. Accordingly, this book is appropriate to a variety of typical undergraduate philosophy courses at both public and private institutions and also in such other settings as community colleges, continuing education programs, and college preparatory schools.

We are most grateful for the help so many people have given us with this project, including our students at Bowling Green and our colleagues at Bowling Green State University, University of Toledo, University of North Carolina at Charlotte, and elsewhere. We also thank our reviewers and editors at Prentice-Hall for their constructive and directive comments, and we thank our typists and proofreaders for their care and attention to detail.

We welcome, and would be most grateful for, any comments and suggestions that you as student or as instructor might wish to offer.

ACKNOWLEDGMENTS

B.C. CARTOONS on pp. 28, 48, 167, 326, 390, 460, used by permission of Johnny Hart and Field Enterprises, Inc.

CARTOONS on pp. 18, 96, 123, 201, 216, 226, 248, 289, 315, 379, from *Non-Being and Somethingness*, by Woody Allen, drawn by Stuart Hample. Copyright © 1978 by IWA Enterprises, Inc. and Hackenbush Productions, Inc. Reprinted by permission of Random House, Inc.

PHOTOS on pp. 7, 160, 178, 214, 311, courtesy of News Service, Bowling Green State University.

PHILOSOPHER'S PHOTOS from the Bettman Archive: *Spinoza* (p. 62), *Socrates* (p. 64), *Aristotle* (p. 83), *Mill* (p. 96), *Locke* (p. 200), *James* (p. 440), *Plato* (p. 481), *Aquinas* (p. 498). From the Granger Collection: *Wittgenstein* (p. 374). Courtesy of New York Public Library: *Kant* (p. 528) and *Descartes* (p. 328). Courtesy of French Embassy Press and Information: *Sartre* (p. 122). Courtesy of National Galleries of Scotland: *Hume* (p. 513). Courtesy of German Information Center: *Marx* (p. 540).

PAINTING REPRODUCTIONS: *Joseph Accused by Potiphar's Wife* (p. 280), *Both Members of This Club* (p. 283), *The Repentant Magdalen* (p. 303), and *The Adoration of the Magi* (p. 500) courtesy of the National Gallery of Art, Washington, D.C.

Introduction to Philosophy:
From Wonder to World View

WHAT PHILOSOPHERS DO

In Western culture philosophy is at least 2,700 years old. In Eastern cultures it goes back even further. Nothing with so rich and diverse a heritage could reasonably be encapsulated by a simple definition or be fully understood at first glance. It is like a musical composition with a theme of wonder, whose melodies and harmonies reveal greater depth and subtler richness at each hearing. Although no generalization about what philosophers do, what their intellectual purposes and tools are, or what methods they use can even hope to be completely accurate, some very useful general statements can be made. We can identify four goals or purposes that thinkers with widely divergent points of view have seemed to pursue. We can detect basic intellectual approaches or tools which many philosophers use to pursue these purposes. We can describe methods of combining beliefs regarding philosophical problems into relatively more comprehensive and systematic world views. This first part, then, is only our first look at philosophy, an overview of its purposes and of three of the basic tools that can serve them. Regard Part One as but a starting point. In later parts, your ideas about what philosophy is will become more refined, the melodies and harmonies will begin to emerge, and its richness and perhaps even some of its enchantment will become evident.

The relationships of the four chapters in this part are shown in the diagram. Chapters 2, 3, and 4 each discuss a basic intellectual tool that can be directed toward the purposes described in Chapter 1. The tools discussed in Chapters 2 and 3 are actually prephilosophical. They can be used to pursue not only the purposes of philosophy but several other intellectual purposes as well. They closely apply in any other field of study.

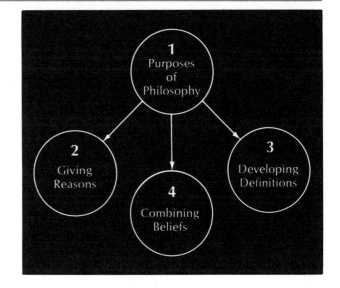

Purposes of Philosophy

Philosophy is the persistent attempt to think things through. This loose but useful definition captures both the serious intent and the reflective nature of the philosophical enterprise. However, you can be persistently thoughtful and yet remain unphilosophical in your thinking. Philosophical persistence in thought is not simply a matter of concentrating intensely or devoting a great deal of time to contemplation. Rather, what is distinctive about philosophical persistence in thought is its disciplined pursuit of purposes which have, historically, set philosophical thinking apart. This chapter introduces you to philosophy by describing those purposes: critical understanding, systematic articulation, precision and clarity, and reasoned evaluation. These four have been the hallmarks of philosophical thinking.

Different philosophers have emphasized different purposes. This difference in emphasis can influence decisively the selection of philosophical method and the identification of those problems deemed worthy of philosophical attention, as well as the development of a thinker's perspectives and world views.

After reading Chapter 1, you should be able to

- State the purposes philosophers have traditionally pursued.
- Distinguish a discussion pursuing one of those purposes from one pursuing another.

■ Provide examples of specific questions suggesting the pursuit of each of those purposes.

■ Explain how each of the four purposes distinguishes philosophy from other studies.

THE CASE OF SANDY AND THE KING

"Who does he think he is, anyway? He treats me like a kid. Sometimes he makes me so angry."

"Hi, Sandy. What's the matter?" It was Karen. She had come walking from the Science Building across to the far corner of the band's practice field where Sandy was sitting. Karen sat down on the grass next to Sandy, kicked off her shoes, and started to roll up the legs of her jeans. "Come on, tell me what's the matter? Did you flunk basketball or something?"

"No, it's my father. He thinks he's some kind of divine-right monarch or something. I want to live in an apartment near campus and he wants me to live at home. It makes me angry."

"Look, Sandy, don't let him bother you. He can't run your life. What's he going to do? Cut off your food or something? A father's power only goes so far, you know."

"Really, Karen! This is important to me. I can't defy him as if I were a little girl; that will make him think that he was right all along. Besides, he is my father, Karen, and that counts for something."

"Well sure he's your father, but that doesn't make him a god. He can make mistakes, too, you know."

"You're telling me! He makes decisions about my life and doesn't even explain the reasons. That's what really makes me angry. He thinks he can run my life for me. With him it's the kids-are-supposed-to-obey-their-parents routine. He says parents have the right to tell their kids what to do."

"Are you sure? Maybe — and I don't mean this as an insult — but, maybe he thinks you're immature. Or maybe he just doesn't want to accept the fact that you are no longer 'his little girl.' Maybe he still feels responsible for you."

"Are you kidding, Karen? It's just a simpleminded matter of raw authority. He says he's going to make the decisions until I'm eighteen. He says that's when I'm grown-up under the law. Isn't that just about the dumbest thing you've ever heard? As if they could pass a law and make people mature."

"Silly or not, it means you have two more months to go till freedom. Hey, let's forget this and go . . ."

"Karen, this is a problem! I wonder where my father thinks he gets all his so called 'authority' anyway. Maybe he thinks it's his legal right. But maybe he thinks he is so wise and experienced that he should decide everything. He keeps saying that he brought me into the world and he supplies the work and the money that support me. Maybe that's really all the justification he needs.''

"Nonsense, Sandy. You didn't ask to be born any more than I asked to be adopted. But once parents have kids or adopt them they are obligated to support them. It's your right to expect that support!"

"But if he's obligated to support me, doesn't that give him the right, or at least the authority, to tell me what to do? I mean, I just wish I knew what authority really was; you know, what does it really mean to have authority over somebody or something?"

"Well, I'll tell you. My dad has it all figured out. He says it's being in a position where your word counts — where you have the final say-so. Then he tells me his decision on this or that, and you know what I do?"

"No, what?"

"I ignore him!"

"Really, Karen! I already told you I'm *not* going to ignore my father. Can't you ever get serious?"

"Oh, all right, if you really want my advice I suggest you try to get your parents to look at family decisions a new way. You've been looking at them as if you father were 'the king of Baldwin Avenue' or something. But now that all the kids are older maybe you should look at your family more as a group of equal adults. If you did, then you would be more democratic about decision-making. At least you would be able to 'advise the king,' even if he refused to accept majority rule."

"Karen, that sounds great in theory but I doubt that it will work at all in my family. People don't just change their ways of looking at things — especially *my* parents."

"Well, *you* asked me to be serious. Both your other choices are poor. You're too old to just follow the king's orders; and you really shouldn't defy him either. That's how I see things. Look, Sandy, I've got to go now. Try my suggestion and tell me how things turn out between you and your father. I hope 'the king' doesn't put you in irons for treason."

"Well, thanks, Karen, I'll see you later."

1:1.1 *Reflection, wonder, and wisdom* The discussion between Sandy and Karen is an example of how everyday conversation on matters of importance frequently becomes philosophical. The discussion is dominated by reflection on the relationship between Sandy and her father, and ultimately upon the nature of authority. As is typical of philosophical reflections, neither Sandy nor Karen is willing to accept at face value the status quo, that Sandy's father is in charge of her life. Sandy senses the potential inadequacy of basing her actions on personal habit or social custom, as she would be if she were to follow her father's demands without a second thought. She is unwilling to accept her fa-

Philosophy begins in wonder . . .

. . . and grows into a disciplined search for fundamental truths.

ther's pronouncement unquestioningly, but she is also unwilling to openly defy him and thereby continue to behave in a childlike manner. Rather, she is determined to think things through in an effort to discover a course of action based upon sound reasoning.

It has often been said that philosophy begins in an attitude of wonder. Whereas everyday wonder about everyday matters may remain superficial and on the level of simple curiosity, the wonder in which philosophy takes root is different. The difference is that *philosophical wonder leads to serious reflection on the more fundamental or more general questions* that emerge in a variety of particular cases. Sandy and Karen push their thought beyond curiosity about what motivates Sandy's father to a consideration of the more fundamental, underlying issues of "What makes someone an authority?" or "What gives anyone a right to decide for another?" In pushing to this more fundamental issue or level of reflection, Sandy and Karen are entering the territory where others have been led to ask such philosophic questions as "What is the meaning of life?" "What is the nature of reality?" and "What are the limits of human knowledge?"

The wonder that leads to philosophical questioning also leads persons to prize the clear insight, sound perspective, and balanced judgment which may be taken as constituents of wisdom. Indeed the very term 'philosophy' comes from two Greek words: *philo* (I love or have a concern for) and *sophia* (wisdom). Thus philosophy is literally the *love of wisdom*. To claim to be a philosopher is to claim to be a seeker, and not necessarily a possessor, of wisdom. Sandy and Karen together pursue this ideal as they seek perspective and balanced judgment about the nature of authority and the relationship between father and daughter.

1:1.2 *Progress* It is important to emphasize that philosophy is a disciplined reflection with a definite sense of inquiry. Such reflections are not merely taken as pastimes for idling away spare moments. Rather, there is an active sense of discontent with not being able to answer the questions raised in reflection. This philosophical discontent is alleviated as the seeker of wisdom pursues the purposes of philosophical reflection discussed in sections to follow.

In this same connection it is important to consider the senses in which progress in philosophical reflection is possible. It is simply false that philosophy only goes around in circles. In the first place, progress is possible in the reflections of individuals. Each of the following sections describes a purpose of philosophy which may be pursued in progressively more sophisticated ways. As you pursue these purposes through philosophical inquiry, your own abilities to be critically circumspect, to think systematically, precisely, and clearly, and to assess or evaluate ideas may be improved.

Philosophical reflection does not occur in a historical vacuum. Your own reflections can benefit from your acquaintance with the richness of philosophical tradition. Within this tradition techniques have been developed to make possible more effective pursuit of the purposes described below. The historical progress in philosophy is not one of the gradual resolution of issues. Major philosophical questions are enduring questions. Rather, the historical progress in philosophy is one of refinement and deeper understanding of the issues together with increased sophistication in the articulation of positions and perspectives upon them. Even when more than one position remains open, many positions are shown to be deficient. Thus, both individual and historical progress in philosophy may be understood as spiral paths in pursuit of wisdom. Progress is also possible through dialogue with your fellow travelers on the path.

1:2.1 *The critical purpose*   The case study illustrates the critical spirit of philosophy. The authority of Sandy's father is not perceived as being beyond question. In the philosopher's view, everything is open to question; nothing, for reasons of religion or authority or anything else, is beyond criticism. Here philosophy can be distinguished from studies that rest on unproved, but unchallenged, assumptions.

This aspect does not mean that all views are to be rejected. To be critical does not mean to be negative or to be defeatist. Rather, it is to seek to discern the strength and cogency of a belief or position by subjecting it and the assumptions upon which it is based to close examination. One possible outcome is that the belief or position will be found to be seriously wanting. However, such examination can lead to your retaining and even deepening your convictions through increasing your understanding of them and their support. Thus, in the case study, Sandy and Karen's critical reflection on the authority of Sandy's father quickly becomes a more serious attempt to discover whether his claim to authority is well founded and precisely why it is or is not so.

The process of critical reflection may be understood as having three aspects, each of which is illustrated in the case study: (1) The meanings of words and questions, (2) the applications of concepts, and (3) the justifications of beliefs. These aspects are all susceptible to critical review, and much of philosophical reflection is devoted to this task.

1:2.2 *Meaning of terms*   In focusing on the real issue concerning Sandy's father, Karen and Sandy are duly critical of the meaning of the question they are raising. Initially they talk as if the issue were one of the extent of her father's *power*, or his sheer ability to force his way upon her. Sandy rightly dismisses this area as not really her concern. She has no interest in taking on her father in a power struggle. The question she finds worth pursuing is that of the *authority* of her father, or his right to exercise his power. The critical review of the meaning of a question defines the choice of issues that are to be addressed as reflection proceeds.

1:2.3 *Application of concepts*   After noting that the concept of authority extends both to persons who are in a position to know a great deal (perhaps through experience) as well as to those who have a right to make decisions, Karen and Sandy ask a different type of critical question. They wonder in what sense(s) the concept of authority can be correctly applied to Sandy's father. Is he in a position of greater knowledge? If he is, then he is an authority in that sense. But the critical question that is most pressing for Sandy is this: Even if it is reasonable to concede that he is an authority in the sense of being experienced, is it also true that he is an authority in the sense of his having a right to make decisions affecting Sandy's life? This critical question does not concern the meaning of words or questions but rather the appropriateness of applying a particular concept of authority in a given situation.

 PHILOSOPHER'S WORKSHOP

Philosophy as Liberation

Bertrand Russell (1872–1970) saw philosophy not as a stale academic discipline, but as a study that could both enrich our lives and liberate us from our biases, prejudices, unwarranted assumptions, and ethnocentricities.

The man who has no tincture of philosophy goes through life imprisoned in the prejudices derived from common sense, from the habitual beliefs of his age or his nation, and from convictions which have grown up in his mind without the cooperation or consent of his deliberate reason. . . . While diminishing our feeling of certainty as to what things are, [philosophy] greatly increases our knowledge as to what they may be; it removes the somewhat arrogant dogmatism of those who have never travelled into the region of liberating doubt and it keeps alive our sense of wonder by showing familiar things in an unfamiliar aspect.[1]

---

[1]Bertrand Russell, *Problems of Philosophy* (London: Oxford University Press, 1912), pp. 243–44.

1:2.4 *Justification for belief* Karen and Sandy don't simply wonder whether or not the concept of authority applies to Sandy's father in its various senses, but they ask one final critical question. They seek the possible justification of his supposed right to decide for her. Various reasons may be offered in defense of his claim. He may be thought to have a right to decide precisely because he is more experienced or because he is entitled according to the law or because of some biological privilege. On the other hand, he may have obligations simply by virtue of his being a parent. In any event, there is room for critical assessment of any such *reasons* that may be offered. It is, in general, always possible to be critical of the quality of reasons offered in support of positions or beliefs. You might ask yourself, however, whether it is always possible to give reasons for your beliefs. Should you be able to justify all your beliefs even if you could? What about the belief that rationality is a valuable characteristic? Can one rationally justify being rational? This, too, is a philosophical question worth pursuing.

Giving reasons and evaluating arguments are important skills in philosophy, as in other rational studies. We'll discuss these skills in Chapter 2. The broad question of the value of rationality recurs, especially in Parts Two, Three, Five, Six and Seven.

1:3.1 *The systematic purpose* As a persistent attempt to think things through, philosophical reflection tends also to be more than usually systematic. Minimally, what this statement means is that philosophers are concerned to (1) discover the connections between and implications of their concepts and beliefs, (2) develop concepts with extensive or comprehensive applicability, and (3) compare and contrast phenomena or develop models and analogies in order to substantiate the general applicability of the concepts they develop.

The case study illustrates each of these concerns. (1) Karen and Sandy can be seen as exploring together what follows from their belief that Sandy's father has no authority to decide for her, as well as Sandy's belief that her father is nevertheless worthy of respect. (2) In so reflecting, they discover that the concept of authority is one with wide applicability, both to persons who have gained knowledge through experience and to those who have a right to decide on particular matters. (3) Moreover, they see that it is no accident that the concept of authority extends to both groups; that is, there is a substantial similarity between them inasmuch as both types of persons are in a position in which their word counts for something. It is not simply a pun or semantic trick that allows for this general application of the concept. In the one case the person's word counts as he or she pronounces truths, and in the other case his or her word counts as decisions are made. It can be argued that there is a reasonable connection between these two senses of the concept: Persons may be entitled to decide on a given matter precisely because they are authorities in the sense of knowing more than others concerning that matter.

1:3.2 *Comprehensiveness* Philosophical thought is also systematic because it seeks to develop comprehensive understandings and perspectives concerning the world and the beings and experiences within it. In seeking such comprehensiveness, philosophers are interested in defining the relationships between groups of concepts while maintaining consistency and congruence within the group. In pursuing questions at ever more fundamental and general levels, philosophical reflection is almost inevitably comprehensive in this way.

In the case study, Karen and Sandy tend to reflect on authority comprehensively. They are not content with questions concerning the authority or nonauthority of Sandy's father. Rather, they push beyond specific cases to consider the more general level, where the authority of fathers, kings, and gods is compared and where one finds the underlying justifications for various claims to authority.

PHILOSOPHER'S WORKSHOP

Philosophy as Comprehensive

Baruch Spinoza (1632 – 1677) was one of the leading philosophers of the seventeenth century. In the following excerpt he insists on the importance of striving for a more comprehensive vision of reality.

Let us imagine, with your permission, a little worm, living in the blood, able to distinguish by sight the particles of blood, lymph, & c., and to reflect on the manner in which each particle, on meeting with another particle, either is repulsed, or communicates a portion of its own motion. This little worm would live in the blood, in the same way as we live in a part of the universe, and would consider each particle of blood, not as a part, but as a whole. He would be unable to determine, how all the parts are modified by the general nature of blood, and are compelled by it to adapt themselves, so as to stand in a fixed relation to one another. For, if we imagine that there are no causes external to the blood, which could communicate fresh movements to it, nor any space beyond the blood, nor any bodies whereto the particles of blood could communicate their motion, it is certain that the blood would always remain in the same state, and its particles would undergo no modifications, save those which may be conceived as arising from the relations of motion existing between the lymph, the chyle, &c. The blood would then always have to be considered as a whole, not as a part. But, as there exist, as a matter of fact, very many causes which modify, in a given manner, the nature of the blood, and are, in turn, modified thereby, it follows that other motions and other relations arise in the blood, springing not from the mutual relations of its parts only, but from the mutual relations between the blood as a whole and external causes. Thus the blood comes to be regarded as a part, not as a whole. So much for the whole and the part.

All natural bodies can and ought to be considered in the same way as we have here considered the blood, for all bodies are surrounded by others, and are mutually determined to exist and operate in a fixed and definite proportion, while the relations between motion and rest in the sum total of them, that is, in the whole universe, remain unchanged. Hence it follows that each body, in so far as it exists as modified in a particular manner, must be considered as a part of the whole universe, as agreeing with the whole, and associated with the remaining parts.[2]

---

[2]Baruch Spinoza, *Correspondence*, "Letter XV," trans. R. H. M. Elwes (New York: Dover Publications, Inc., 1955), pp. 291–92.

The comprehensiveness of philosophical reflection may also be seen if you consider the specialized disciplines that have devoted attention to the study of humankind. Each pursues study of a different aspect of human experience. Biochemists, physiologists, physicians, psychologists, sociologists, anthropologists, historians, and theologians all help us to understand humans, but often these specialists provide only fragmentary answers to basic human questions. Their insights need to be weighed, analyzed, and integrated. One purpose of philosophy is to undertake precisely this systematic task of integrating the knowledge developed in other fields of study so that when taken together their research and theories will make more sense. Comprehensive answers to questions as fundamental as "What is it to be human?" and "What is humankind's place in the universe?" can thus be pursued.

1:3.3 *Alternative understandings* The systematic grappling with fundamental questions can lead into realms of speculation where the bounds of knowledge are exceeded. This tendency is especially so, for example, when philosophers pose the question, "What kinds of things are there and how do these kinds of things relate to each other?" Many philosophers, for instance, have carefully scrutinized different models and analogies for conceiving of God. They have debated the appropriateness of and the relations between different metaphors, such as "king" and "father," for describing God. Similarly, in ancient times the philosophers Democritus and Empedocles developed, respectively, an atomic theory about the ultimate components of reality and an evolutionary theory about the origin and development of species of living things. They were thus developing means of conceiving, describing, and explaining what lay beyond the limits of the scientific knowledge of their day. Speculation on alternative ways of understanding things is of value because it meets our intellectual need for coherent and comprehensive views of what there is. As was the case with evolution and the atomic theory, these speculations may turn out to be scientifically applicable as well; but without any speculation at all the questions of truth or fruitfulness of our understandings of reality cannot even arise. This consideration, of course, raises the question of the role of speculation in contemporary science; and, too, how should one evaluate speculation? Must it be *true* or rather should it be *fruitful*? And what precisely does it mean for an idea to be fruitful?

1:4.1 *The goal of precision*   Throughout their reflections philosophers try to be as precise as their subject matter allows. Loose or sloppy thinking is to be replaced by clear and rigorous thinking wherever possible. This concern for precision and the clarity it brings is another element of discipline in philosophy. Here philosophy is distinguished from other studies in that the development of logic and of methods for framing definitions have been central to the philosophic enterprise.

One aspect of being precise is eliminating vagueness and ambiguity in stating positions and in asking questions. In the case study this consideration is illustrated as Karen and Sandy settle on just which question they shall discuss. Though Sandy is clearly concerned about her relationship with her father, there is initial vagueness about the exact nature of that concern. That vagueness is dispelled as the difference between concerns about power and about authority is sharply enunciated. Once this difference becomes clear and the issues are precisely formulated, it is possible for them to make the critical judgment that it is the matter of authority that warrants their attention. In Chapter 3 we will talk more about the ways in which you can use careful definitions to combat vagueness, ambiguity, and imprecision.

1:4.2 *Stating similarities and differences*   Your ideas will be more precise, also, to the extent that you are clear about the components of those ideas. In the case study, Karen and Sandy come to know the "components" of the idea of authority by knowing that if a person is an authority, then a person is either in a position to know or in a position to make decisions. In knowing these two components of the idea of authority, they have a more precise grasp of the applicability of the concept. In turn they are in a position to ask the critical question about whether, and in what sense(s), the concept is rightly applied to Sandy's father.

 PHILOSOPHER'S WORKSHOP

Imprecision and Ignorance

About three centuries ago John Locke (1632–1704) took his contemporaries to task for using vague words and non-sensical expressions. What some took to be signs of great wisdom, Locke saw as evidence of ignorance. His comments are not without relevance today.

Vague and insignificant forms of speech, and abuse of language, have so long passed for mysteries of science; and hard and misapplied words, with little or no meaning, have, by prescription, such a right to be mistaken for deep learning and height of speculation, that it will not be easy to persuade either those who speak or those who hear them, that they are but the covers of ignorance, and hindrance of true knowledge. To break in upon the sanctuary of vanity and ignorance will be, I suppose, some service to human understanding; though so few are apt to think they deceive or are deceived in the use of words; or that the language of the sect they are of has any faults in it which ought to be examined or corrected, that I hope I shall be pardoned if I have in the Third Book dwelt long on this subject, and endeavoured to make it so plain, that neither the inveterateness of the mischief, nor the prevalency of the fashion, shall be any excuse for those who will not take care about the meaning of their own words, and will not suffer the significancy of their expressions to be inquired into.[3]

---

[3]John Locke, *Essay Concerning Human Understanding*, ed. A. C. Fraser (London: Oxford University Press, 1959), vol. I, pp. 14–15.

In the area of systematic philosophical speculation, precision of this sort may be pursued as you speculate about the unknown in terms of models or analogies rooted in the known. You can eliminate imprecision in such thinking to the extent that you carefully clarify which components of the model or analogy are thought to be reflected in the reality conceived through it. Consider thinking about the God-humanity relationship on the model of the parent-child relationship. Your thinking would gain in precision if you noted, for example, that the relationships are thought to be alike to the extent that both God and parents are benevolent, and thought to be not alike to the extent that parents sometimes become indifferent to their children.

1:4.3 *Good reasoning*   The idea of precision also involves incorporating good reasoning into your thinking. If you start from an acceptable starting point (known truths), then good reasoning is reasoning that will, necessarily or probably, not lead you into error. Good reasoning tends to be *truth-preserving*; it allows you to accurately grasp what follows from what you know or assume to be true. Karen argues for the irrelevance of a biological standard of parental authority. She reasons that if such authority rested on a biological basis, it would extend only to biological, but not to adoptive, children. Yet since her father claims and she assumes he has the same authority as Sandy's, biology cannot be the basis, as she is adopted. The point about the truth-preserving character of good reasoning is that if Karen's premises are true (that she is adopted, that her father has the same authority as Sandy's father, and that similar authority has the same basis), then her conclusion (that the authority is not biologically based) must also be true. Note that if Karen's premises are not all true, her conclusion is not shown to be true. (The tool of good reasoning is discussed more in Chapter 2.)

1:5.1 *The evaluative purpose*   There are several senses in which one of the primary purposes of philosophy is evaluation. Ethics, social philosophy, political philosophy, and aesthetics are all branches of philosophy. All center on the quest for standards or principles in terms of which it is possible to evaluate what ought to be done or what objectives are worth pursuing. In seeking answers to questions such as "Is lying ever permissible?" or "Are persons always obligated to keep their promises?" or "Is suicide blameworthy?" ethics tries to evaluate alternative courses of action open to individuals. In seeking answers to questions such as "Are affirmative action guidelines in conformity with justice?" or "Do citizens ever have a right to resist the law?" or "Is democracy the best form of government?" social and political philosophy try to evaluate the purposes and operations of social and political institutions. In seeking answers to questions such as "What features make objects beautiful?" or "What makes a work of art good?" or "What makes one dramatic work better than another?" aesthetics tries to evaluate the purposes and products of artistic creation and the value of aesthetic experiences.

Dealing with Value Questions

The great American philosopher, John Dewey (1859–1952), saw philosophy as a tool for dealing with value conflicts that arise in making personal and social decisions. Value judgments are not only possible, but necessary. The issue becomes not how we do make value judgments, but how can we make value judgments wisely. In effect, the aim of philosophy becomes the resolution of today's value problems, whether they be individual or social.

When it is acknowledged that under disguise of dealing with ultimate reality, philosophy has been occupied with the precious values embedded in social traditions, that it has sprung from a clash of social ends and from a conflict of inherited institutions with incompatible contemporary tendencies, it will be seen that the task of future philosophy is to clarify men's ideas as to the social and moral strifes of their own day. Its aim is to become so far as is humanly possible an organ for dealing with these conflicts. That which may be pretentiously unreal when it is formulated in metaphysical distinctions becomes intensely significant when connected with the drama of the struggle of social beliefs and ideals. Philosophy which surrenders its somewhat barren monopoly of dealings with Ultimate and Absolute Reality will find a compensation in enlightening the moral forces which move mankind and in contributing to the aspirations of men to attain to a more ordered and intelligent happiness.[4]

[4]John Dewey, *Reconstruction in Philosophy* (Boston: Beacon Press, 1920), Chapter 1.

Reality and knowledge There are evaluative questions that arise also within other philosophical disciplines where the primary concern is with the nature of reality or the nature and extent of knowledge. On the one hand, where philosophy becomes metaphysics, the systematic study of what things there are and how they are related to one another, evaluative issues arise concerning the adequacy of alternative concepts, models, analogies, systems, or frameworks. On the other hand, where philosophy becomes epistemology, the study of the nature and limits of knowledge, evaluative issues arise concerning the standards for distinguishing knowledge from opinion. In general, all such questions about *adequacy* and *standards* are questions about what kind of thinking, or what kind of intellectual processes, we *should* subscribe to.

1:5.3 *Logic* Another branch of philosophy, logic, is concerned with how best to determine that arguments are valid, justified, and worthy of acceptance by reasonable people. At bottom even these concerns are evaluative. In its evaluative character philosophy is distinguished from all other studies that confine themselves to *descriptive*, rather than evaluative, questions.

1:6 *Thinking and doing* Earlier we suggested that philosophy may be understood as the love of wisdom. Those who prize wisdom, we said, prize clear insight, sound perspective, and balanced judgment. We can now say that the hope of philosophy is that as you approach wisdom through the pursuit of the philosophical purposes outlined here you will be led not merely to think more wisely but also to act wisely on the basis of your philosophical reflections. We hope that your study of philosophy will have what for you could be the biggest benefit of all, that it will enable you to more wisely evaluate the alternatives that life affords.

1:7 *Summary* In this chapter we have introduced philosophy as the disciplined attempt to think things through. Growing out of wonder, philosophy is the pursuit of wisdom. Philosophical reflection is marked by four distinctive purposes. First, it is undertaken in a critical spirit where everything is open to question. The meanings of terms and questions, the applicability of concepts, and the justification of beliefs are all subject to review. Second, philosophical reflection is systematic in seeking to understand the connections of concepts and beliefs, in seeking answers to the most fundamental and comprehensive of questions, and in seeking reasoned insight beyond the limits of knowledge. Third, philosophy seeks precision where it is possible, includ-

ing precision in the clear articulation of the meanings of concepts and questions, in the articulation of the components of ideas, and in the development of good reasoning. Fourth, philosophy is evaluative in that the disciplines of ethics, social and political philosophy, and aesthetics have evaluative questions as their principal concern, and in that systematic thought on reality and knowledge requires that the adequacy of modes of thought and the standards for distinguishing knowledge from opinion be evaluated. Moreover, the persistent attempt to think things through should make persons better able to evaluate wisely the alternatives presented to them as they give shape to their lives.

EXERCISES for Chapter 1

1. State the four purposes traditionally pursued by philosophers (refer to sections 1:2.1, 1:3.1, 1:4.1, 1:5.1).
2. Review the quotations in the four Philosopher's Workshops. In each passage determine the philosophical purpose that is being described. After checking your answers, underline the key words or phrases in the quotation that indicate which purpose is being described.
3. For each of the four philosophical purposes, make a list of words and phrases that could be used to signal clearly a philosopher's interest in pursuing that purpose.
4. Explain how the critical purpose, the systematic purpose, the goal of precision, and the evaluative purpose each distinguish philosophy from other organized studies (1:2.1, 1:3.2, 1:4.1, 1:5.3).

SELECTED ANSWERS for Chapter 1

2. Russell emphasizes the value of the critical spirit in the phrases "imprisoned in the prejudices," "habitual beliefs," "convictions . . . grown up . . . without the cooperation or consent of . . . deliberate reason," "arrogant dogmatism" and "liberating doubt." Spinoza compares human perception to that of the little worm. The worm needs to see things as "parts," not "wholes." The worm fails to imagine that there are "causes external to the blood." Spinoza also emphasizes comprehensiveness and focuses on interpreting concepts when he mentions parts of the "universe," "mutually determined" within the whole. Clearly he views things very generally. The ultimate or fundamental character of philosophical questions is not emphasized in this passage, even though it is part of the

systematic purpose. Locke's concern for precision is clear in his unhappiness with "vague and insignificant forms of speech, and abuse of language" and "hard and misapplied words, with little or no meaning" He is concerned about *deception* caused by words. He is concerned with "faults [in language] which ought to be examined and corrected." He is troubled by those who won't allow "the significancy [meaning] of their expressions to be inquired into." Dewey urges that philosophers are really concerned about "precious values." He sees them discussing "social ends," and by an *end* philsophers mean, roughly, a desirable goal or an ideal. In the future, he believes that philosophy should focus on "social and moral strifes," which will reward philosophers because they will be "enlightening the moral forces which move mankind and . . . contributing to the aspirations of men to attain to a more ordered and intelligent happiness." As noted in the chapter, the evaluative purpose of philosophy extends beyond moral and social evaluation to evaluation of all beliefs.

3. The *critical purpose* involves "criticizing" and making "doubt" a systematic habit. It opposes that which is "biased," "prejudiced," "unexamined," or "dogmatic." It encourages "care in reasoning" and believes only "in proportion to the evidence available," while tending to "suspend belief" entirely when little or no evidence is available or when the evidence available is confusing or contradictory. The *systematic purpose* involves forming a "comprehensive" view which "integrates" very divergent concepts. In order to form such a comprehensive view, philosophers pursuing this purpose attempt to ask questions that are very "fundamental," questions that need to be "settled first" before others can be reasonably discussed. They seek "general" terms broad enough to encompass any variety, and they pursue "ultimate" and "final" explanations by asking questions that go as far as it makes any sense to go. The *goal of precision* is a goal of "clarity." Our concepts should be "clear and distinct." If a term has two different meanings, then those meanings should be "identified and distinguished" from each other. Our concepts should not be "riddled with ambiguity," and "vague terms" may leave a person's meaning "obscure." The metaphor of "casting light" upon a subject or "seeking illumination" is frequently used to suggest the pursuit of clarity. The *evaluative purpose* is often signaled by terms such as "value," "worth," and "desirability," which indicate interest in an evaluation. Evaluation is a matter of "assessing" or "appraising" how "pertinent," "sound," or "acceptable" an observation, an argument, or a distinction may be. If you keep in mind the variety of things philosophers want to evaluate and if you recognize the great variety of terms ordinarily used for evaluating things, you will be able to recognize when a philosopher is interested in evaluation.

One final word: Philosophers very often combine two or more purposes. For example, a philosopher may be critical of a lack of precision. Another philosopher may evaluate a concept as less encompassing than others have claimed it to be. If you can understand and recognize these purposes of philosophy separately, then they should not trouble you when they appear in combination.

Giving Reasons

The Greek philosopher, Socrates (470 – 399 B.C.), made a career out of engaging people in discussions about topics in which they claimed expertise or great interest. His discussions usually revealed that their opinions on these topics were unfounded. Obviously this propensity hurt his popularity with the ruling class, but it showed the younger people the ideal of reason — to be able to prove the truth of what you believe. He taught the importance of having good reasons to support opinions. Opinions without reasons are no more secure than an art treasure left unguarded on the highway.

To make their opinions more secure, people give reasons. They try to show, in a logical way, why their opinions are true. All of us engage in reason-giving activity daily; we are also engaged in evaluating the reasons or demonstrations that others offer in support of their opinions. Our success in giving solid demonstrations and in accurately evaluating those presented to us depends on how well we have developed our skills in being logical. These skills are vitally important in our daily lives and they are among the chief tools philosophers use to develop their positions, perspectives, and world views. After reading Chapter 2, you should be able to

- Distinguish between arguments and nonarguments.
- Distinguish premises from conclusions within arguments.

- Make explicit the unstated assumptions of a given argument.
- Distinguish logically correct arguments from those not logically correct.
- Distinguish logically correct arguments that necessitate their conclusions from those that make their conclusions stongly probable.
- Distinguish arguments that beg the question from those that do not.
- Given a desired conclusion and an argument, determine whether the argument's stated premise(s) entail(s) the desired conclusion.

THE CASE OF OPPERST'S LETTER

Dr. Doplowski had been teaching critical thinking for twelve years. She had seen some very logical students. Ms. Klanton, whose turn it was today, was one of them. Ms. Klanton's assignment was to evaluate logically a letter to the editor that had appeared in the campus paper, *The State News*. The letter, about capital punishment, was written by Mr. Marv Opperst. Since the class had already read the letter, Dr. Doplowski decided to play the part of Opperst. The student, Klanton, was to try to demonstrate to the class how she would explain to Opperst why his position was not well argued. This assignment can be especially difficult when an illogical person is being criticized directly. A confrontation was possible.

"You see, Mr. Opperst, our aim here is to focus on how logical your position is. We are not interested in whether capital punishment is justifiable or not. Rather we want to look at the *reasons* you gave in support of your opinion. Is that clear?"

Klanton seems to understand her role and her material, thought Doplowski. *I think I'll try to cross her up.* "Yes, I think I follow you. You don't care about capital punishment. So if you don't care about it, why did you make me write about it?"

"I do care about capital punishment, I care very much. But our job here is to work on helping you think more clearly — or helping you be more logical. We can worry about specific issues later after we get our mental tools ready. Okay?"

"Yes, so what don't you like about my letter?"

"Well, first off you seem unable to express your reasons for your beliefs. For example, you say that the prison system in this country is rotten, but you do not say *why* you believe that, or *how* you know it."

"Fine, so you want my reasons. Here's why I think the prison system is thoroughly rotten: It's rotten because no matter what part of it you point to, it's rotten! That's the way it is."

Klanton refused to be put off by her professor's obviously poor reply. Calmly she continued, "As you have just demonstrated, Mr. Opperst, not all arguments are equally good. That leads me to my second point: When you do supply reasons for your conclusions you often are illogical. The last thing you said about why prisons are rotten is just one example. In the letter you tried to argue that capital punishment was *always* wrong because it is sometimes painful, but then you suggested that some methods were not painful. You said that using certain drugs, for example, was not painful. It would have been more acceptable reasoning to argue that we should use the relatively painless methods. Your premises do not imply that capital punishment is *always* wrong, only that *some* forms of capital punishment (the painful ones) are wrong. Do you follow me?"

"Yes. You want us to use capital punishment that's not painful."

"No, Mr. Opperst. Actually, I'm against *all* forms of capital punishment. But my reasons are rather different. Yet, if you want to argue that capital punishment is wrong because it's painful, you have to be prepared for the response that some forms are not painful. These then would not be wrong, at least for that reason."

"Yes, but what about the fact that capital punishment is killing people?"

"Okay, what about it? Are you now willing to offer a new argument?"

"Well, yes. If it's wrong to kill people, then capital punishment is wrong because it's a form of killing."

"That's about the most logical thing you have said so far, Mr. Opperst," Klanton said beginning to smile. "Now remember, though, it may not be true that killing people is always wrong. But at least we can separate the logic of what you just said from whether or not the beliefs upon which you base your arguments are true."

"What did you say?" replied Doplowski who by now had managed such an incredibly unenlightened expression that Klanton was almost unable to control her laughter.

"I said that we have two things to consider. One is how logical we are—that is, how well we use the tool of logic. The other thing is whether our beliefs are true—that is, whether we base our arguments on true or on false statements."

"Oh!. . . I'm not sure that I fully understand, Ms. Klanton, but maybe if you gave me another chance to write the letter I could . . .

"Mr. Opperst. . . if you want my advice, enroll in Doplowski's critical thinking course."

"Flattery works every time," said Doplowski. "Good job. Now, class, let's go over the issues Klanton brought to light."

2:1.1 *Arguments*

When you give reasons in order to demonstrate why an opinion is true, you are giving what philosophers call *an argument.* An argument is a group of written or spoken *statements.*[1] Some of the

---

[1]Statements are those sentences that we can reasonably evaluate as either true or false.

statements in the group are presented as grounds for, or reasons for, believing that one of the other statements in the group is true. In the case study, Ms. Klanton argues for the conclusion that Mr. Opperst's position is weak. She later enumerates two of her reasons for her belief: First, Mr. Opperst generally neglects to give reasons for his opinions; second, he often uses illogical argumentation. Her conclusion together with her two supporting statements constitute her argument.

You can think of an argument as a piece of reasoning that is revealed in, or expressed by, language. Your statements present your reasoning; they make your reasons public. Arguments thus become open to evaluation, and you can examine them to see if they are logical. You can assess the wisdom or the strength of the reasons people give on behalf of what they believe; that is, you can determine whether a person is logically basing his or her conclusion on true statements.

Viewing arguments as groups of statements presented as a proof or demonstration that one of the statements is true allows us to distinguish arguments from other kinds of language. For example, you can distinguish arguments from other groups of statements, such as reports, biographies, lists of truisms, creeds, and predictions. In these cases the statements are not being presented with a view toward using some as the grounds for proving the truth of another. You can also distinguish arguments from other groups of sentences, such as lists of questions, expressions of feelings, warnings, promises, or greetings. In such cases we not only miss the aspect of demonstration but also are dealing with sentences that cannot be considered *statements*. Sentences used to ask questions, greet, warn, promise, or express feelings are not evaluated as true or false. Because we are concerned to prove that a given point of view is true because it is logically based on true reasons, we must be sure that the point of view and the reasons are expressed as statements.

"Arguments," as we shall use the term, should not be thought of as quarrels or emotional debates. By "arguing" we shall mean trying to be rational, setting forth the reasons that show an opinion is true. Given this conception of argument, it can play an important role in everyday life. If it is true that "the unexamined life is not worth living," then the pursuit of truth is among the most important of human endeavors. Skills in constructing and evaluating arguments are essential components of that pursuit of truth.

2:1.2 *Premises and conclusions* You can call the statement that you are trying to prove true the *conclusion*. You can call those statements presented as demonstrating its truth the *premises*.

In the case study Ms. Klanton reviews one of the poor arguments that Mr. Opperst made: "Capital punishment is always wrong because it is sometimes painful, and whatever is painful is wrong." We can make his argument more explicit by presenting it in this way:

E.g. 1 (1) When something is painful it is wrong. (Premise)
 (2) Capital punishment is sometimes painful. (Premise)
 (3) So capital punishment is always wrong. (Conclusion)

As Ms. Klanton explains, this argument is not acceptable reasoning, but it is still an argument. Even a bad argument is an argument. As you examine various philosophical perspectives you will have two jobs: (1) You will have to reconstruct carefully the arguments given, and (2) you will have to assess the acceptability of those arguments. These jobs are quite distinct, as Ms. Klanton in the case study tries to show. Her first job is to reconstruct Mr. Opperst's arguments by identifying their premises and conclusion as in *E.g. 1*. Only then does she try to show why his arguments are weak.

There is no special number of premises that an argument must have so long as it has at least one. In the case study there is a very short argument with one premise offered by Mr. Opperst: "No matter what part of the prison system you point to, it's rotten. So, it's thoroughly rotten." There is also a rather long one implicit in the narrative that runs this way:

E.g. 2 (1) It is not easy to explain to an illogical person what is wrong about a given illogical argument. (Premise)
 (2) It is quite hard to explain what is wrong with a given illogical argument to an illogical person if that person authored the argument. (Premise)
 (3) Ms. Klanton knows Mr. Opperst is an illogical person. (Premise)
 (4) Ms. Klanton knows Mr. Opperst authored the illogical arguments in his letter. (Premise)
 (5) Ms. Klanton's job demands that she try to explain what is illogical about Opperst's arguments. (Premise)
 (6) Ms. Klanton is going to do her job. (Premise)
 (7) She is, therefore, going to simulate doing something that, in real life, involves a difficult interpersonal relationship. (Conclusion)

Arguments can also work in tandem. In the case study the conclusion statement expressed as (7) of *E.g. 2* operates as a premise in another argument.

E.g. 3 (1) Ms. Klanton is going to simulate doing something that, in real life, involves a difficult interpersonal relationship. (Premise)
 (2) Whatever involves a difficult interpersonal relationship will lead to a confrontation. (Premise)
 (3) So Ms. Klanton is going to simulate doing something that, in real life, will lead to a confrontation. (Conclusion)

You could challenge *E.g. 3* on the grounds that its second premise (statement 2) is false. Although a difficult interpersonal relationship makes conflict possible, that conflict need not become real all the
time. This observation shows that an argument can contain acceptable
reasoning (as *E.g. 3* does) even if it has false premises. The evaluation
of the truth of an argument's premises is separate from the evaluation
of the argument as acceptable or unacceptable reasoning. Let's look
more closely at evaluating arguments.

2:2.1 *Evaluating arguments: preliminary steps*   To be in a position to
evaluate an argument, you must first take two important preliminary
steps. Together they amount to reconstructing, or making as explicit as
possible, exactly what the argument is. First, you must identify the
parts, explicit or implicit, of the argument.

Step 1:   *Identifying Parts of the Argument.* Identify the conclusion intended by
the author to be demonstrated by the argument. Identify the premises
the author explicitly presents on behalf of that conclusion. Identify any
assumptions (usually unstated premises) the author intends to be taken
as additional components of the argument.

Most arguments in ordinary life and many in philosophy rely on unstated or unspoken assumptions. Looking back at *E.g. 2* you will find
the statement, "(3) Ms. Klanton knows Mr. Opperst is an illogical person." It does not occur explicitly in the case study, yet it does function
as an assumption in that argument. It is very important to uncover all
the assumptions the author is making so they can then be included in
your reconstruction of the author's argument. It may turn out that you
wish to reject an argument *because* it is based on a false and possibly
even unstated assumption.

𝒫 PHILOSOPHER'S WORKSHOP

Common Fallacies

Often you will want to reject an argument because it is
based on a false assumption. Mistaken arguments are called
fallacies. A chief source of fallacies is the reliance on assumptions that turn out to be false. Some false assumptions
are used so frequently that their unreliability in the pursuit
of truth is well documented, and they have been given
names in the history of logic. Here are some to be especially careful about:

1. Fallacies of *false cause* are arguments that rely on the false assumption that if one event happens after another it must have been caused by the other.
2. Fallacies of *appeal to irrelevant authority* are arguments that rely on the false assumption that whatever an authoritative person says about anything must be true.
3. Fallacies of *ad hominem attack* are arguments that rely on the false assumption that to find fault with a person's character or to attack the person's heritage is to supply a good reason to reject the conclusions of his or her arguments.
4. Fallacies of *appeal to ignorance* are arguments that rely on the false assumption that lack of evidence against a conclusion is good evidence in favor of it.
5. Fallacies of *appeal to the crowd* are arguments that rely on the false assumption that because something is commonly believed to be true it is true.
6. Fallacies of *playing with words* are arguments that rely on the false assumption that each and every time a given word or phrase occurs in a given argument it is used with precisely the same meaning.[2]
7. Fallacies of *false dilemma* are arguments that rely on the false assumption that every time we are presented a choice of options which are all undesirable the options presented represent our full range of choices and that we must choose one of them.
8. Fallacies of *composition* are arguments that rely on the false assumption that a characteristic of every part of a whole group is necessarily a characteristic of the whole group itself.
9. Fallacies of *division* are arguments that rely on the false assumption that a characteristic of a whole group is necessarily a characteristic of each of its parts.
10. The *"gambler's" fallacy* is an argument that relies on the false assumption that random events are causally related to each other.
11. The *"straw man"* fallacy is an argument that relies on the false assumption that in refuting the weakest argument an opponent has supplied, one has refuted the opponent's entire position.

---

[2]Philosophers often use the word "equivocation" to refer to using a single *word* with separate meanings, whereas an "amphiboly" is a *phrase* that has two meanings because of its placement in different parts of a sentence.

Step 2 in the process involves rewriting the author's argument, using the elements identified in Step 1.

Step 2: Rewriting the Argument. Rewrite the author's argument using all and only those statements in the rewriting that the author, explicitly or implicitly, intended to serve as either premises or conclusion.

At this point your job is not to improve the author's argument, nor to convert something that isn't an argument into an argument. Your job is to clarify the argument as its author intended it to be made.

There must be a fallacy here!

2:2.2 *Evaluating arguments: the critical step*   To evaluate an argument you should ask a series of four critical questions related to how acceptable or unacceptable the argument is as a *proof of the truth of the conclusion the author desirèd to establish.* The first question has to do with the truth of the premises.

Step 3:   *Question 1.* Are all the premises of the reconstructed argument true?

If not, the argument is not acceptable. If they are true, go on to Question 2. Arguments are used to move to true conclusions from true premises in a logical way; but if the premises are not all true, the argument does not establish that the conclusion is true, even if the argument itself is logical. An interesting consequence of this fact is that you can agree with a philosopher's conclusion but not accept the arguments used to support it. Ms. Klanton seems to agree with Mr. Opperst that capital punishment is not justified, but she certainly would not use his weak argument to demonstrate her view.

The second question to ask relates to the logical correctness of the inference from the premises to the conclusion.

Step 3:   *Question 2.* Do the argument's premises taken together demonstrate that the conclusion *must* be true or *is very probably true?*

If not, the argument is not acceptable on logical grounds. To decide whether or not an argument is an acceptable proof of its conclusion, you must look to more than the truth of the individual statements; you must look to how the premises relate to the conclusion. Taken as a group they should logically imply, entail, strongly warrant, or strongly support the conclusion. In other words they should *count as good reasons* (a logically correct demonstration) that the conclusion is true or very probably true, given that its premises are.

The ideal might be that true premises would guarantee that the conclusion *must* be true, but in many cases it would be unwise to strive for absolute guarantees. In such cases you can strive for premises that constitute evidence that the conclusion is very probably true even if not necessarily true. *E.g. 2* is an example in which the premises, if true, would guarantee that the conclusion must be true. Here is an argument that we can count as logical even though the premises only make probable the conclusion rather than guarantee it.

E.g. 4   Philosophers prize being logical. The large majority of those who prize being logical are careful about stating points of view precisely. So, most philosophers are careful about stating their points of view precisely.

It would also be logical to add this conclusion to the premises of *E.g. 4*.

So it is probable that if Sandy and Frances are philosophers, they are careful to be precise in stating their points of view.

For the most part, if an argument in its reconstructed form has true premises and if these premises taken together show, or provide grounds for the inference that the conclusion must be true or is very probably true, then the argument should be accepted.

PHILOSOPHER'S WORKSHOP

Logic Terminology

Philosophers have always been concerned with the methodologies whereby people can reasonably arrive at truth. Inference from one set of beliefs to a new belief figures strongly in various methodologies. This tool has led philosophers to examine the reliability of various kinds of inferences. Aristotle (384–322 B.C.), in his book the *Organon*, was one of the first to try to set forth a complete theory of how to evaluate the logic of various arguments. Aristotle's theory of the syllogism represented the single most influential system of logic in Western culture until recent times. In *A System of Logic* (1849), John Stuart Mill (1806–1873) sought to develop the logic of inferences that lead to probable rather than necessary conclusions. In *Principia Mathematica* (1903), Bertrand Russell (1872–1970) and Alfred North Whitehead (1861–1947) did pioneering work in the development of a symbolic logic. They elaborated decision procedures for demonstrating when premises necessitate their conclusions. Logic is a normative study in that it is concerned with evaluating how premises relate to their conclusions. Its goal is to help us evaluate how logical various kinds of arguments are. In its long history it has evolved several branches and a rich technical vocabulary. Here are definitions of some of the most central basic concepts of logic:

Statement: a sentence such that raising the question of its truth or falsity makes sense.

Argument: a set of statements one of which is presented as being implied, entailed, strongly warranted, or strongly supported by the others.

Conclusion: the statement in an argument that is presented as being implied, entailed, strongly warranted, or strongly supported by the others.

Premises: those statements in an argument that are presented as implying, entailing, strongly supporting, or strongly warranting the conclusion.

Enthymeme: an argument such that a statement obviously intended to be taken as one of its premises or its conclusion is omitted.

Deductive argument: an argument such that it is purportedly not possible for the conclusion to be false and all the premises true.

Inductive argument: an argument such that it is purportedly improbable, although possible, for its conclusion to be false when all its premises are true.

Valid argument: an argument such that its premises entail or imply its conclusion on the basis of the logical form or structure of the argument.

Justified argument: an argument such that its premises strongly support or strongly warrant the truth of the conclusion on the basis of their subject matter or content.

Logically correct argument: an argument that is either valid or justified.

Sound argument: a logically correct argument such that all its premises are true.

Fallacious argument: an argument that is based on a false assumption, is not logically correct, or such that its premises make no logical progress toward demonstrating the truth of its conclusion (e.g., as in "begging the question," discussed in 2:2.3)

Acceptable argument: a sound argument that is not fallacious.

For many simple arguments it is possible to test whether or not the proper inference is drawn from the stated premises without the use of sophisticated logical technique. You can simply seek to describe circumstances where the premises could be true and the conclusion false.

E.g. 5   (1) At least one person has prized logical precision and has worked on formal systems of logic. (2) All philosophers are people who prize logical precision. Therefore, all philosophers worked on developing formal systems of logic.

Suppose we had two philosophers, Plato and Aristotle. Both prized logical precision, as premise 2 indicates. Suppose that one, Aristotle, worked on developing a formal system of logic. Since premise 1 says at least someone has done this, our suppposition about Aristotle supports premise 1. We can further suppose that *only* Aristotle worked on such a system. If he did, and Plato didn't, then the conclusion would be false. Using our imagination, then, we described a situation in which the premises were both true and the conclusion false. Philosophers say that a set of premises does not "entail" a conclusion whenever it is possible for all the premises to be true and the conclusion false. Further, if the situation described seems likely to occur, say at least one time in twenty, then the argument's premises do not strongly warrant or make probable its conclusion either. The situation we just described about Plato and Aristotle did occur and has occurred in other cases as well. So in *E.g.* 5 the premises do not strongly warrant the conclusion either.

It is important to note that this simple test works only for the simplest of arguments. Because not all arguments are simple and because many important ones are quite complex, logicians have worked to develop more sophisticated techniques for analyzing and evaluating the logical correctness of a variety of simple and complex types of arguments.

2:2.3 *Begging the question*   The third question to ask relates to the problem of begging the question.

Step 3:   *Question 3.* Do the argument's premises *avoid* deriving their support from the argument's conclusion?

If not, you cannot accept the argument as a demonstration of its conclusion. If so, the argument *may* well be acceptable.

Remember Mr. Opperst's argument that the prison system is thoroughly rotten because no matter what part of it you point to, it is rotten. You might agree that the premise "no matter what part of it you point to, the prison system is rotten" is true. You would have to say that if the premise is true, then the conclusion must be true, because the conclusion comes to the same statement. But it would be unreasonable to think that the premise in this case was proof for the conclusion. (You might just as well take the conclusion as proof of its premises!) Actually, you should reject the argument. Whatever questions you had about the truth of the conclusion are still unsettled, for they are now questions about why you should take the premise to be true. Here is a similar example.

E.g. 6   A person is religious if he or she has experienced God. I have experienced God and He revealed this to me. So I am a religious person. Realizing that I am religious, I know that my experience of God was genuine.

You first have to pull this passage apart to unpack and reconstruct the chief argument it contains. It seems that the author has this argument in mind:

E.g. 7   (1) If a person has experienced God, then he or she is religious.
(2) I have experienced God.
(3) So, I am a religious person.

Now try to decide if you should accept *E.g.* 7. Is premise 2 true? Well, recognizing the problem of answering this question, the author of *E.g.* 6 has suggested a secondary argument:

E.g. 8   (1) I am a religious person.
(2) If someone is religious, then his or her experiences of God are genuine.
(3) So my experience of God was genuine.

But note that the conclusion of *E.g.* 7 is a premise in *E.g.* 8. The goal of *E.g.* 8 was to give you a reason to believe that premise 2 of *E.g.* 7 was true. If it were, it would help you to accept the concusion of *E.g.* 7. However, it is not reasonable to rely on the conclusion of *E.g.* 6 (the chief object of our doubt) as a reason to accept as true one of its own premises. To do so is to *beg the question*. *E.g.*6 also begs the question another time. Look at the reason the author of *E.g.* 6 gives to accept premise 1 of *E.g.* 7.

A question-begging argument is one in which the conclusion serves as at least a partial ground for one of its own premises. This self-serving (sometimes called "circular") reasoning prevents us from making logical progress from reliable premises to the consequences of these premises.

2:2.4 *Drawing the wrong conclusion*   The fourth question relates to the problem of proving the wrong conclusion.

Step 3:   *Question 4.* Does the argument's stated conclusion amount logically to the conclusion the author intended to demonstrate?

If not, then the argument is not to be accepted as proof of the author's desired conclusion.

At one point Mr. Opperst tried to argue that capital punishment was *always* wrong. His argument *(E.g. 1)* is illogical because what is true of *some* cases of capital punishment need not be true of *all* cases. But Mr. Opperst may have misstated his desired conclusion. His inability to express himself clearly may have prevented him from writing an argument that drew precisely the conclusion he intended. Ms. Klanton suggests that Mr. Opperst's argument should be replaced with this one:

E.g. 9   (1) Whenever something is painful it is wrong.

(2) Some methods of capital punishment are painful.

(3) So, some methods of capital punishment are wrong.

In evaluating an author's argument we must be sure that it is used to demonstrate the conclusion the author desired. Sometimes what is proved is not what the author wants to prove, as in

E.g. 10   I would like now to argue that painfulness is never a ground for calling something wrong. Even exercise can be painful at times, but we would not say that exercise is always wrong. So, some painful things may not be wrong.

In *E.g. 10* the author explicitly says that he or she wants to prove that painfulness is *never* a reason to call something wrong. However, the author concludes that *in some cases* painful things may not be wrong. The argument does not prove what the author wanted it to prove. We should not accept it as a proof of what the author intended to show, even though it is valid as it stands and does have true premises.

2:2.5   If the answers to *all four* of the questions given in 2:2.2 to 2:2.4 are "yes," then you can rely on the argument as a demonstration that the conclusion must be true or is very probably true. If an argument passes these four tests, then it would be unwise not to accept it as proof of its conclusion. We will call an argument that passes these tests *acceptable*, meaning that it is worthy of being accepted. Reasonable people *ought* to accept such arguments.[3]

---

[3]For a more complete discussion of logic and for a fuller treatment of logical thinking skills, see Facione and Scherer, *Logic and Logical Thinking: A Modular Approach* (New York: McGraw Hill Book Co., 1978).

2:3 *Summary*   You have looked at the process of giving reasons in order to show that one's beliefs are true. These attempted demonstrations take the form of arguments. Arguments are groups of statements some of which (premises) are presented in support of another (the conclusion). In evaluating an author's argument you must first be careful to reconstruct it accurately. The reconstruction involves rewriting it to include all the statements that the author intended to be part of the argument, including any assumptions the author had left unstated originally. The evaluation of an argument involves asking four questions: (1) Are the premises in the reconstructed argument all true? (2) Do the premises demonstrate that the conclusion either must be true or is very probably true? (3) Do other premises avoid relying for their own support on the assumed truth of the conclusion? (4) Is the demonstrated conclusion the one the author intended to prove? If we answer all of these "yes," then we ought to accept the argument being evaluated as a proof of the author's intended conclusion

EXERCISES for Chapter 2

Below are twenty passages. After reading them, make the distinctions requested below.
A. When my daughter, Karen, says Sugar is the smartest dog she knows, there's no denying that. It the first place, she only knows two dogs, Sugar and Kai, and Sugar is much more intelligent than Kai.
B. Of course I know a lot more dogs than my daughter. The one that stands out most clearly in my memory is the pet dog of my own childhood, Tricks. I loved Tricks dearly. Karen loves Sugar, too, and who knows how to compare which of those loves might have been the greater?
C. All dogs are lovable, but some lovable things are nuisances, too. Which only goes to prove that dogs are often nuisances.
D. The neighbor said, "All dogs are nuisances." He argued that a dog is always a nuisance if it barks in the middle of the night or if it deposits waste on his lawn. He conceded that some dogs have neither of these bad habits. "But," he continued, "any dog that is a nuisance really upsets me. So it's obvious that if a dog either barks a lot at night or uses my lawn as a bathroom, I'm going to be upset!"
E. If a dog barks at night, he's a nuisance. But our dog doesn't bark at night. So there's no way he can be called a nuisance.
F. One of the most pleasant experiences a person can have is taking a walk with her dog through an open field on a sunny autumn afternoon. That is not to say, however, there's no pleasure in sitting in an easy chair with your dog curled up beside you.

G. Our dog is pregnant with her first litter of puppies. She'll probably have five or six, since that's the average number for her breed.

H. Both of the children who have really misbehaved in my class this year have been left-handed. There's something sinister about those two, I tell you. I'll probably usually find left-handed kids causing most of the discipline problems.

I. That's an interesting experience you've had with those students. I've never heard of any study that would disprove your idea that left-handers are the big troublemakers. So I'd say your idea is right.

J. Out of the fourteen separate classrooms in this school, yours is the only one in which there is even one left-handed troublemaking student. And goodness knows the other rooms all do have some troublemakers. I think you can see the conclusion that is likely about your idea.

K. "School days, school days, good old Golden Rule days!" sang Lefty as the teacher turned his back.

L. Isn't it reasonable to argue this way: "The number of left-handed troublemakers is probably proportional to the number of left-handed students. So there are probably many more right-handed troublemakers than left-handed ones."

M. The behavior problems are mostly left-handed kids. Besides that, behavior problems are kids you can't trust. They're always ready to start something behind your back. They agitate the other children. So what can we conclude except that most misbehaving comes from those lefties?

N. Given the huge increase in the number of births taking place in our new suburb's hospital, it's very likely that school enrollments throughout the nation will start rising as those children reach school age.

O. Most women give birth to most of their children before they reach the age of 35. So, if there's going to be a new baby boom because of all the females born during the 1947–1957 baby boom, that new boom will probably become apparent by the early 1980's and will probably end by the early 1990's.

P. Women are seeking and procuring abortions in record numbers. That shows that they do not want to have so many babies. And because they do not want such a large number of babies, they are taking advantage of improved methods of contraception. Indeed the fact that they don't want the babies proves that they are turning to abortion, in addition to contraception, at unparalleled rates.

Q. Abortion is immoral and should be illegal. Whatever is immoral should be illegal. And abortion is immoral because whenever you endanger or actually destroy life of tissue that is biologically human and that has the ability to exist on its own, outside of the mother's body, you are doing something as immoral as killing a human being. Now that's immoral and that's exactly what an abortion in the fifth or sixth month of pregnancy does. So such abortions cannot be condoned.

R. The experience of holding a newborn baby in your hands is like no other experience on earth. On the one hand you are aware of the helplessness of this tiny human creature, and on the other hand you know that with proper nurture that tiny being has all the potential and promise human life can offer.

S. All God's children deserve to know God's word. Therefore, as this baby grows up, you should teach her, genuine child of God that she is, the teaching of the Koran.

T. Four percent of all children born in American hospitals have birth defects that are capable of being detected at birth but are not at present being detected while the baby is in the hospital at birth. As the administrator of this hospital, I find that fact appalling and from now on I want that four percent of our babies to be properly diagnosed. Indeed, there are twenty-five babies in our nursery right now. So there is one that has the undiagnosed defect. Which is it?

1. Pick out the sixteen arguments (2:1.1 and 2:1.2).

2. Check your answers. Then, among the sixteen arguments, pick out the five containing unexpressed statements, as premises or conclusions, that are thought to be obvious. State those assumptions (2:2.1).

3. Among the sixteen arguments, pick out the six that present their conclusions as probable but less than absolutely certain.

4. Check your answers. Among the six arguments, distinguish those that are justified from those that are not (2:2.2).

5. Among the remaining ten arguments, distinguish the two that beg the question and the two that reach the wrong conclusion (2:2.2 and 2:2.3).

6. Check your answers. Among the remaining six arguments, find the two that are such that if their premises were all true—including any implicitly assumed premises—then the conclusion would have to be true.

7. For the other four arguments, provide an explanation concerning why each of their conclusions might be false even if the premises were all true (2:2.2).

8. Here are some passages from noted philosophers. Can you analyze their arguments?

A. ". . . to fear death, my friends, is only to think ourselves wise without really being wise, for it is to think that we know what we do not know. For no one knows whether death may not be the greatest good that can happen to man. But men fear it as if they knew quite well that it was the greatest of evils. And what is this but that shameful ignorance of thinking that we know what we do not know? In this matter, too, my friends, perhaps I am different from the multitude. And if I were to claim to be at all wiser than others, it would be because, not knowing very much about the other world, I do not think I know."[4]

B. "I must begin by observing the great difference between mind and body. Body is of its nature always divisible; mind is wholly indivisible. When I consider the mind—that is, myself, in so far as I am merely a conscious being—I can distinguish no parts within myself; I understand

---

[4]Plato, *Euthyphro, Apology, Crito,* trans. F. O. Church, *Library of Liberal Arts* (Indianapolis, Ind.: Bobbs-Merrill Co., 1956), p. 35.

myself to be a single and complete thing. Although the whole mind seems to be united to the whole body, yet when a foot or an arm or any other part of the body is cut off I am not aware that any subtraction has been made from the mind."[5]

C. "But this universal and primary opinion of all men is soon destroyed by the slightest philosophy, which teaches us, that nothing can ever be present to the mind but an image or perception, and that the senses are only the inlets, through which these images are conveyed, without being able to produce any immediate intercourse between the mind and the object. The table, which we see, seems to diminish, as we remove farther from it; but the real table, which exists independent of us, suffers no alteration: it was, therefore, nothing but its image, which was present to the mind. These are the obvious dictates of reason; and no man, who reflects, ever doubted, that the existences, which we consider, when we say *this house* and *that tree*, are nothing but perceptions in the mind, and fleeting copies or representations of other existences, which remain uniform and independent."[6]

D. "The second, called 'the argument of Achilles', asserts that the slower runner will never be overtaken by the fastest who pursues him, for the latter must first reach the point from which the former started, and in this way the slower runner must always be some distance ahead of the pursuer."[7]

SELECTED ANSWERS for Chapter 2

1. The four nonarguments are B, F, K, R.

2. The implicit assumptions are I: if no evidence disproves left-handers being troublemakers, they must be; J: the conclusion: the idea that left-handers are usually the troublemakers is false; L: there are many more right-handed than left-handed people; S: the Koran is God's word; T: what's true of U.S. hospitals must be true of this hospital *and* true at this time (or of the babies now in the ward).

3. G, H, J, L, N, O.

4. Justified: G, J, L, O, though the evidence present in J does only relate to one school.

5. Begging the question: M, P; wrong conclusion: D, Q.

---

[5]René Descartes, *Meditations on First Philosophy* (the Sixth), trans. E. Anscombe and P. T. Geach, *Library of Liberal Arts* (Indianapolis, Ind.: Bobbs-Merrill Co., Inc., 1970), p. 121.

[6]David Hume, *An Enquiry Concerning the Human Understanding*, Sec. XII, Pt. I, ed. L. A. Selby-Bigge (London: Oxford University Press, 1902), p. 152.

[7]Aristotle, *Physics*, 9, 239b15ff, trans. Hippocrates G. Apostle (Bloomington, Ind.: Indiana University Press, 1969).

6. A, S. Notice that there is no problem with the *reasoning* in S. If there is a problem, it is probably that you do not accept its assumption as true.

7. C: the premises do not guarantee that any of the lovable nuisances are dogs;

   E: the premises do not guarantee that *only* dogs who bark at night are nuisances;

   I: the lack of evidence mentioned in 2 above could be explained by ignorance or lack of investigation; T: the undetected birth defects do not have to be spread evenly through all hospitals and all times.

3

Developing Definitions

Clear and effective communication skills are necessary if we are to survive in and contribute to society. We must learn what words mean, how to express our thoughts accurately, and how to communicate our needs and our ideas to others. The ability to use language effectively is critical for philosophers because words and ideas are their stock in trade. Everyday hindrances such as vagueness and ambiguity can pose very serious problems. At the most elementary level, we must be clear about the topic of our discussion before we can successfully begin to analyze it or reason logically about it. For example, we have to define clearly what "reverse discrimination" means before we can begin to evaluate a proposed reverse discrimination policy.

This chapter is about how people use different kinds of definitions to help clarify what words mean. Because definitions help overcome the obstacles of vagueness and ambiguity, they are important to successful philosophy and effective communication.

After reading Chapter 3 you should be able to

- **Distinguish examples showing the vagueness of a word or expression from those showing the ambiguity of a word or expression and provide examples of each.**
- **Explain how both vagueness and ambiguity hinder communication.**

- Distinguish, characterize, and provide examples of descriptive and stipulative definitions.
- Provide examples of both descriptive and stipulative definitions that remedy problems of vagueness and ambiguity and explain how they do so.
- Explain what loaded definitions are and why they are problematic.
- Distinguish, characterize, and provide examples of intensional and extensional definitions.
- Provide examples of both intensional and extensional definitions that resolve problems of vagueness and ambiguity.

THE CASE OF TODD POTOPOLES

People always thought of Todd Potopoles as a quiet young man. He hardly ever talked, except to his closest friends. He virtually never spoke publicly, not even in class. However, people were mistaken if they thought that Todd was not listening or not thinking. Todd's senses were constantly alert, his mind always sifting, probing, evaluating, and synthesizing what he experienced. His quiet exterior stood in stark contrast to his active, energetic interior, which is why Todd found this week's English composition assignment so hard. His instructions were to "write an acceptable theme answering the question 'Who am I?' "

It actually made him angry at first to think about that assignment. He thought, "I can write themes about any president who ever lived. I know the biographies of almost every major thinker or political leader in the history of Western culture. But, no! They ask me to write about *me*! What's to say? I'm just me! Or should I be more grand about it and write, 'I am I'?

"And then too, what do they mean when they say 'acceptable'? Does it mean that I should write it so that the graders are likely to accept it? That won't be hard. I'll just double-check my spelling, grammar, and logical organization. Or does it mean that I should write something that is really worthy of acceptance as a statement about myself? If that is what I should do, then how can I hope to finish it in only one week?"

However, after a time his feelings subsided, his mood changed, and he began to take the assignment more seriously. "What," he wondered, "does it really mean to be a 'person'? What does it mean to be the unique person that is me?

"Or am I really so unique after all? I do have my own history, just like John Adams had his. I can trace my family back to Greece on my father's side and to Germany on my mother's. I grew up in Chicago and went to a public grade school and a Catholic high school. My father owns a used-car lot. My mother raised me along with my three sisters. I'm a Catholic, but I don't go to church much any more except on Christmas and Easter. I came to college to study business administration, but I changed my major to engineering. I play the piano, but not too well. Is that what it means to be me?

"Does all that make me unique? I'm really not sure. That description could fit almost anybody—well, not just anybody; but a lot of people have similar backgrounds, abilities, ambitions, talents, heritages . . . I'm really not sure how to define what I am or who I am. I could write 'I'm Todd Potopoles!' But what does that mean? That's not enough. The name by itself doesn't seem to say what I want to say.

"How about 'I'm Todd Potopoles—a person!'?

"But what does 'person' mean? Are humans the only things that are persons? What about other primates—and what about dolphins or beings from outer space? If there is a God, is He—or She—a person? How about computers? I've worked with some computers that seem more like persons than some of my old classmates in high school did. They were animals! . . . And maybe they should be treated as such, too. . . . Oh well, so much for those clowns. . . . Let me see, what does 'person' mean?"

3:1.1 *Vagueness* Two of the chief obstacles to successful communication are vagueness and ambiguity, which can be removed by careful definitions, thus facilitating more effective communication. Let's look at vagueness first.

Quite often words, expressions, or phrases are used to *refer*. For example, "house cat" refers to a furry, feline, domestic animal, whereas "cathouse" refers to a house of prostitution. Referring words and expressions are often *vague*, meaning that there is a degree of unclarity about which things do, or do not, qualify as things to which the word or expression refers. For example, the word "bold" is vague in the sense that we can think of borderline cases. Borderline cases are those in which we would dispute whether or not the person in question should properly be called "bold." Vague words or expressions— such as "justice," "art," "beauty," "experience," and "responsibility"—are those that allow for disputes about borderline cases. There are clear cases where they apply, clear cases where they do not apply, and borderline cases where their application is disputable. As it happens, most words are more or less vague. Some vagueness is tolerable, but some, disrupting communication, is vicious.

Vague words or expressions in sentences can lead to vague sentences, sentences that make you want to ask: What precisely does that mean? For example:

I am in favor of liberty and justice for all.
There is no room for fat in the budget.

The force which drives the universe loves all creation.

There are no acceptable reasons for using extraordinary methods.

If we cannot achieve concensus, let's have a working majority.

Every person has rights.

In these examples vague terms such as "person" or "extraordinary" leave us with questions about what the authors of these sentences might have meant. Did the author of the last example want to ascribe rights to unborn fetuses or not? We aren't sure because we don't know if that author thought that an unborn fetus is a person or not. The vagueness of "person" leads to a breakdown of communication about borderline cases.

However, there are times when vagueness is not only tolerable but even useful, and it is actually desirable at times to build in some vagueness. For example, in laws against reckless driving, the vagueness of that phrase is actually a benefit. The openness (sometimes called "open texture") of the vague expression permits us to evaluate particular examples of driving and make judgments about whether or not to call them "reckless." Since we cannot tell in advance all the ways that there might be for a person to drive recklessly, we rely on the vagueness of "reckless driving" to permit on-the-spot evaluations.

✏ PHILOSOPHER'S WORKSHOP

Waismann on "Open Texture"

One tradition in philosophy has urged that vagueness should be rooted out of language, especially as language is used in science, by using precise definitions. Friedrich Waismann, a twentieth-century philosopher of language and science, has argued that the "open-textured" character of many concepts prevents us from being able to define them precisely.

"But are there not exact definitions at least in science?" Let's see. The notion of gold seems to be defined with absolute precision, say by the spectrum of gold with its characteristic lines. Now what would you say if a substance was discovered that looked like gold, satisfied all the chemical tests for gold, whilst it emitted a new sort of radiation? "But such things do not happen." Quite so; but they *might* happen, and that is enough to show that we can never exclude altogether the possibility of some unforeseen situation arising in which we shall have to modify our definition. Try as we may, no concept is limited in such a way that there is no room for any doubt. We introduce a concept and limit in *some* directions; for instance, we define gold in contrast to some other metals such as alloys. This suffices for our present needs, and we do not probe any farther. We tend to *overlook* the fact that there are always other directions in which the concept has not been defined. And if we did, we could easily imagine conditions which would necessitate new limitations. In short, it is not possible to define a concept like gold with absolute precision, i.e. in such a way that every nook and cranny is blocked against entry of doubt. That is what is meant by the open texture of a concept.[1]

[1]Friedrich Waismann, "Verifiability," in *Logic and Language*, ed. Antony Flew (Oxford: Basil Blackwell, 1965), p. 126.

3:1.2 *Ambiguity* We can call a word or expression ambiguous if it has more than one specific meaning, for example, such words as "fast," "ring," and "swing." "Fast" can be used as a noun referring to a religious diet or as an adjective synonymous with "quick." "Ring" can be a noun referring to a circular band for the finger or a verb meaning to produce a resonant sound by vibrating metal. "Swing" is a verb meaning to ride on a swing or meaning to lead a varied and active sex life. In the case study, Todd determines that "acceptable" is ambiguous; he is not sure if it means "worthy of being accepted" or "actually will be accepted." A further ambiguity arises when we ask: acceptable to whom? What Todd thinks is worthy of acceptance may not meet the standards set by those who evaluate his writing. Therefore, there is the ambiguity of "worthy of acceptance by Todd" versus "worthy of acceptance by the teacher."

Ambiguity can lead to communication problems if the author of an ambiguous sentence intends it to be understood one way, but the reader (or hearer) takes it another way. Here are some examples of ambiguous sentences:

I saw her duck.
Julie swings.
Each of us strives for desirable goals.
What you did yesterday was wrong.
Please explain why you did that.

In the last example there is ambiguity in what kind of explanation is requested. Does the speaker want to hear motives, causes, intentions, excuses, or what? In the penultimate example, does the speaker mean that the action was illegal, immoral, or just mistaken?

Todd in the case study noticed that one way to define who he was relied on statements about his family heritage and background. He traced out some similarities between himself and others, and he also pointed to some differences. This noting of similarities and differences is a useful tool in defining closely related words, such as "think," "know," "believe," "realize," "understand," "see," "discover," "accept," and "feel." The meaning of each is slightly different, yet similar to the meaning of the others. In trying to define any of these words, in trying to resolve any problematic ambiguities that these words might have, we will want to explore their similarities and differences. This network of similarities and differences is often called a "family resemblance" between words, a phrase derived from the idea of family resemblances between people and their relatives.

 PHILOSOPHER'S WORKSHOP

Wittgenstein on "Family Resemblance"

One of the thinkers most influential in the development of the philosophy of language in English-speaking countries during this century was Ludwig Wittgenstein (1889–1951). In his *Philosophical Investigations* he offers his insight on a number of issues with which philosophers have traditionally been concerned. Wittgenstein reminded philosophers about the richness of ordinary language as he counseled against assuming that words can always be defined in terms of the common characteristics of the things to which they refer. In this classic passage about "games" he shows that there just might not be any common characteristics.

Instead of producing something common to all that we call language, I am saying that these phenomena have no one thing in common which makes us use the same word for all,—but that they are *related* to one another in many different ways. And it is because of this relationship, or these relationships, that we call them all "language." I will try to explain this.

Consider for example the proceedings that we call "games." I mean board-games, card-games, ball-games, Olympic games, and so on. What is common to them all?—Don't say: "There *must* be something common, or they would not be called 'games' "—but *look and see* whether there is anything common to all. — For if you look at them you will not see something that is common to *all*, but similarities, relationships, and a whole series of them at that. To repeat: don't think, but look! — Look for example at board-games, with their multifarious relationships. Now pass to card-games; here you find many correspondences with the first group, but many common features drop out, and others appear. When we pass next to ball-games, much that is common is retained, but much is lost. — Are they all "amusing"? Compare chess with noughts and crosses. Or is there always winning and losing, or competition between players? Think of patience. In ball games there is winning and losing; but when a child throws his ball at the wall and catches it again, this feature has disappeared. Look at the parts played by skill and luck; and at the difference between skill in chess and skill in tennis. Think now of games like ring-a-ring-a-roses; here is the element of amusement, but how many other characteristic features have disappeared! And we can go through the many, many other groups of games in the same way; can see how similarities crop up and disappear.

And the result of this examination is: we see a complicated network of similarities overlapping and criss-crossing: sometimes overall similarities, sometimes similarities of detail.

I can think of no better expression to characterize these similarities than "family resemblances"; for the various resemblances between members of a family: build, features, colour of eyes, gait, temperament, etc. etc. overlap and criss-cross in the same way. — And I shall say: "games" form a family.[2]

---

[2]Ludwig Wittgenstein, *Philosophical Investigations*, trans. G. E. M. Anscombe (Oxford: Basil Blackwell, 1953), pp. 31e–32e.

3:2.1 *Definitions as tools* Philosophers use definitions as tools to help them communicate more effectively. They can be used to resolve problematic vagueness and rectify troublesome ambiguity. Definitions specify what words mean, and as such can range from descriptions of their common meanings to stipulations of what they shall from then on mean.

Descriptive definitions aim at describing or presenting the standard meaning of the word being defined. They strive for accuracy in reproducing whatever ambiguity or vagueness is built into that word in its common or ordinary use by native speakers of the language. The best source of examples of descriptive definitions is, therefore, a good dictionary. The dictionary will reveal how people conventionally or customarily use the words in their language, and if ambiguity or vagueness is involved, it will be reported. Descriptive definitions try to preserve and call attention to subtle shades or nuances of word meaning or human experience. In trying to give a descriptive definition you should try to be faithful to your experiences. You should accurately describe what the word means and how it is used.

3:2.2 *Descriptive definitions*

Descriptive definitions are used when a greater sophistication with the natural language is required. When a person wants to learn to communicate more effectively with others, the person may have to learn how those people use their words, what they mean by them — which is why school children are drilled on reading assignments that build vocabulary. They need to learn descriptive definitions in order to get along in the adult world of language users. Quite frequently subgroups of society develop their own more specialized, technical languages. In order to become a doctor, lawyer, businessperson, and so on, you will have to learn the languages that these groups of people use. Each of these fields requires greater precision of meaning than we ordinarily associate with such words as "property," "remedy," "organ," "depreciation," "hypertension," and "damage." Members of subgroups develop their own more precise vocabularies and initiate newcomers into their ranks, in part by insisting that the newcomers learn these vocabularies. This learning involves understanding the words or concepts used by the group on the basis of definitions that are descriptively accurate of what that word or concept means in or to that group.

Todd in the case study encounters a problem that is typically philosophical. He wants to say what being a person means; but the concept is vague, and submerged within it are many knotty problems concerning the similarities and differences between human persons and such other things as dolphins, chimpanzees, sophisticated computers, and divinities, mythical or real. Todd's problem is sometimes approached with the strategy of trying to make all this vagueness and ambiguity explicit. In other words, one strategy philosophers use is to develop descriptive definitions which make evident all the difficult boundary areas of the concept being examined and also expose the similarities, differences, and interconnections of that concept to other, related concepts.

3:2.3 *Stipulative definitions*

Stipulative definitions prescribe how words shall be used and what they shall mean. You might, for example, wish to stipulate that for certain purposes a given word, "swinger" say, will be used only to refer to sexually active young adults rather than, say, lecherous oldsters or people riding on the playground toy called a swing. In stipulating the definition of "swinger" you are, in a sense, creating a new language convention or way of communicating. Everyone who knows about your stipulation will understand exactly what you mean if you use the word "swinger" in a sentence like "Cheryl is a swinger."

Using a stipulative definition, you could even more radically separate a word from its common meaning. You might wish to define "coffee" as that part of a traverse rod that guides the pull cords. Now an otherwise nonsensical sentence, such as "The cord is off its coffee," can become meaningful. A stipulative definition, thus, is one used to provide a word with a meaning that differs from its ordinary or common meaning. One way to so define would be to restrict or narrow the common meaning of a word, as we did with the word "swinger" in the paragraph above. A second way is by developing a totally new meaning for a word, as we did with "coffee." A third way is by expanding its ordinary or common meaning. Toward the end of the case study Todd is exploring the possibility of stipulating a definition for "person" which expands the meaning to include, as well as humans, computers, God, and certain species of animals.

3:2.4 *Clarity by stipulation* Stipulative definitions control vagueness and ambiguity by ruling them out. If a word is ambiguous, you can stipulate which of its meanings is of interest. If a word is vague, you can stipulate more precision into what it means, thus more clearly identifying the objects to which it refers or applies.

Because stipulative definitions set up ground rules for the use of words, they are very useful for communication if the word to be defined is novel, technical, vague, or ambiguous. They are starting points for discussion, tools for amending how words are used and facilitating communication. Having once noticed the problems that vagueness and ambiguity generate, one easily thinks of reforming language by using stipulative definitions, perhaps to eliminate all such troublesome cases. Or we might adopt the less grandiose but still very large goal of defining all the problematic vagueness or vicious ambiguity out of the terms used in a specific part of our language, for example, the language of mathematics or of physics. In this way we could use stipulative definitions to develop a language free from problematically vague or ambiguous words, an ideal many thinkers have pursued.

3:2.5 *Loaded definitions* Of course there can be problems too. When a familiar word, like "coffee," is defined in a novel way, misunderstanding can easily occur unless people are made aware of the fact that a stipulative definition is in force.

Also, stipulative definitions are sometimes wrongly used to

thwart debate. For example, a racist might try to advance a stipulative definition of "human" that excludes blacks or Asians. This tactic impedes honest answers to such questions as "Do blacks have human rights?" "They have none because they're not human" would be the only possible reply if we accepted such a ridiculously biased and loaded definition of "human." In the case study, Todd seems to turn toward stipulatively excluding his old schoolmates from the class of persons, thinking of them more as animals. This stipulative exclusion, if it were serious and not just wry humor, could lead Todd to entertain seriously the idea that it was right to treat them like animals rather than people. Definitions that prejudice important value or factual questions are called *loaded definitions*. They are as unfair as loaded dice.

Stipulative definitions are sometimes used to prescribe how we should think or talk about things. There are, for example, many ways to get people to believe something: You can lie to them, indoctrinate them, instruct them, teach them, prove it to them, or show them how to verify it for themselves. Debate among philosophers of education often focuses on the issue of which methods should properly be used in schools. Should teachers instruct or indoctrinate? Given the vagueness of these terms, there is a great temptation for each side in the debate to begin by setting forth its own stipulative definitions of "teaching" and "education." They then draw conclusions, predictably divergent, about which topics can "legitimately be taught" or which methods can "properly be used in educating people." Their use of stipulative definitions tends to short-circuit communication. Further, the definitions are not so well disguised substitutes for simple prescriptions such as "Teach this, not that" and "Teach this way, not that way." It usually takes extra time and talent to cut through to the heart of an issue, which in this example is what we should be teaching in our schools and how we should be teaching it. However, it is impor-

Some definitions are arbitrarily stipulative.

tant to get beyond prescriptive and loaded stipulative definitions so that we can deal honestly with the issues themselves.

3:2.6 *Risks* All definitions fall someplace along the line from purely descriptive to purely stipulative. Those that are more descriptive tend to be closest to our common ways of talking or of understanding what words mean. Those that are more stipulative tend to be less vague or ambiguous. Descriptive definitions control vagueness and ambiguity by making them explicit, the working assumption being that if you identify a problem, you can then avoid the undesirable consequences it might otherwise cause. Stipulative definitions take a different approach, aiming at resolving vagueness and ambiguity by defining them away. Here the working assumption is that it is better to handle these problems in advance so that there can be no undesirable consequences.

The risk in using stipulative definitions is that they can loaded. They also can be so specialized that communication with people unaware of them is actually hindered. Moreover, they can make meanings too rigid, thus losing some of the richness or openness we noted to be important (3:1.1). The risk in using descriptive definitions is in lacking the precision needed in many areas of communication, ranging from advancing science and technology to clarifying new ideas and social issues. Often the best thing to do is to aim at definitions descriptive enough to insure that people understand what you are talking about and stipulative enough, without being loaded, to rule out troublesome ambiguity and vagueness.

3:3.1 *Concepts and classes* Sometimes the meaning of a word is conveyed by the use of synonymous expressions. To say that "mother-in-law" means the same as "female parent of a spouse" is to say that the same things are asserted to be true about a person whether she is called a mother-in-law or the female parent of a spouse. In the case study, Todd could try to define "person" by saying what it is about something that makes it a person. He could, that is, define "person" in terms of being able to think, to choose freely, to communicate, to live in society, to feel emotions, or whatever might be part of the idea of being a person.

We can use such definitions to help us clarify our vocabulary. If you are not sure what another person means by a certain word, say "megalomania," you can ask for its definition. The person could say that "megalomania" means "continually and unreasonably doing things on a very grand scale." We can also relate our vocabulary to the vocabulary used by other people. For example, we can find out that "haversack" means the same thing as "knapsack." Definitions that aim primarily at providing synonymous expressions for a word are called *intensional definitions*. The concept captured by the expressions is called the word's intension.

3:3.2 *Intensional definitions as giving necessary and sufficient conditions*

In providing an intensional definition of a word, some philosophers think they are providing an account of the logical conditions of truly applying the word. What is meant by this phrase can be understood best in stages. First, there is the idea of a *condition*. If someone offers you a job, you may stipulate certain conditions under which you will accept the offer by means of expressions such as "if" and "only if." "I can accept your offer only if you'll pay my moving expenses." "If you will offer me 10 percent over my present salary, I'll take your offer." You can also talk about the conditions under which certain statements will turn out to be true or false, two of which are *necessary* and *sufficient* conditions. For example, the statement "Casanova is unmarried" is a *necessary condition* for the statement "Casanova is a bachelor." This requirement means that Casanova can be a bachelor *only if* he is unmarried; if he marries he can no longer qualify as a bachelor. The idea of a *sufficient condition* can be illustrated by the relationship of the two statements "This number is greater than ten" and "This number is greater than five." *If* the number is greater than ten, *then* the number must be greater than five. That is, the statement "This number is greater than ten" is a *sufficient* condition for the statement "This number is greater than five." It should further be noted that it is *not* a necessary condition.

The next step is to make the further distinction between *logically necessary* or *logically sufficient conditions* and other necessary or sufficient conditions. Consider the two cases:

1. "Alice is sleeping" is a necessary condition of "Alice is having a nightmare."
2. "Alice is undergoing rapid eye movements" is a necessary condition of "Alice is having a nightmare."

There is an important difference between these cases, for only the first states a *logically* necessary condition of "Alice is having a nightmare." If you understand the meanings of the statements, "Alice is having a nightmare" and "Alice is sleeping," you need not carry out further investigation to know the truth or falsity of the statement, "Alice is having a nightmare only if Alice is sleeping." In contrast, 2 states a necessary condition for having a nightmare that was discovered only by careful scientific observation of experimental subjects. Even if you understood fully what "having a nightmare" and "undergoing rapid eye movements" meant, you would not know thereby the truth or falsity of 2. Hence 2 does not state a *logically* necessary condition. If 2 is true, its truth is not because of conceptual connections involved in the meanings of the words it uses.

Those philosophers who seek to provide an account of the logical conditions of truly applying a word try to specify *all* the necessary conditions which when all met are, jointly, sufficient for truly applying the word. Consider, for example, the meaning of the statement, "Casanova is a bachelor." Each of the following four conditions is logically necessary for its being true: "Casanova is a human being," "Casanova is male," "Casanova is unmarried," and "Casanova is of eligible age." When these conditions are conjoined they *together* give one logically sufficient condition for "Casanova is a bachelor"—which is "Casanova is an unmarried, eligible, male human being."

3:3.3 *Role of intensional definitions*   Philosophers often think of intensional definitions as providing responses to the *critical* purposes of understanding meanings of terms. They use them to relate ideas to each other, to establish theoretical connections. For example, we can connect being free with being a person if we accept a definition such as this: "Person" means "being a thinking being capable of autonomous decision-making and action." Similarly, we can draw distinctions between ideas by using such definitions. For example, the difference between being a "person" and being a "human" can be made manifest if we define "human" in terms of genetics and physiological structures and "person" in terms of capabilities to think, choose, communicate, and live socially. Having thus clarified the difference by using definitions, we can raise some of the interesting questions Todd raised in the case study, for example, "Is it reasonable to think of a computer or a visitor from another galaxy as a person even though it isn't human?"

3:3.4 *Extensional definitions*   Other definitions aim primarily at identifying the objects or class to which a word refers. For example, one way to define "thermos bottle" is to point to a thermos and say "That's a thermos bottle." We can define "student" by saying that it refers to all of those people who have matriculated at an educational institution. We can define "scholar" as all those people who read books for more than five hours a day. We can define "a person's relative" as the group that meets these specifications: "A person's parents, siblings, spouse, or children are a person's relatives; if anyone is a relative of a person's relative, then that person is a relative of the first person; no one is a person's relative unless he or she is related in some combination of the ways just mentioned." Definitions that focus on identifying the objects a word refers to are called *extensional definitions*.

Extensional definitions are most useful in making clear exactly to which objects troublesome theoretical concepts refer. In other words, you may understand the concept of being a person, yet you may still wonder which objects in the world "person" applies or refers to. An extensional definition can be used to settle this question. We could then perhaps move from "person" means "able to think" to "person" means "scoring above 35 on a valid I.Q. test." Or if we intensionally defined "person" as "rational animal," we might still need to extensionally define "person" as "featherless biped" in order to identify the class of objects to which "person" referred.

3:3.5 *Role of extensional definitions* Philosophers and other theorists often use extensional definitions in order to make their theoretical ideas more concrete and applicable. That is, they use extensional definitions to make their ideas operational, to tie them to events, objects, and relationships in the real world. We might, for example, know the concept of justice, but we still need ways of telling whether or not specific decisions, actions, or policies are among those rightly called just.

At times theoretical differences seem to disappear when two words refer to exactly the same objects. For example, if "person" and "human" referred to exactly the same objects, we could say that all humans were persons and all persons were humans. We might then wonder whether there really was any difference between being human and being a person. We could decide that because they referred to precisely the same objects there was no difference, or at least no difference in application. We could also decide that because we might encounter a person from another galaxy with a nonhuman genetic and physiological structure, the two terms were at least theoretically or conceptually different.

 PHILOSOPHER'S WORKSHOP

Definitions of Key Concepts

Ambiguous word: a word that has more than one specific meaning.

Arbitrary definition: a definition stipulating that a word shall mean something totally different from what it ordinarily means.

Condition: a statement C is a condition for another statement R when the truth of R depends in some way on the truth of C. For example, "You will receive the contract" has a condition, "Your sealed bid is the lowest."

Descriptive definition: a definition that aims at expressing what a word ordinarily means.

Extensional definition: a definition that aims at identifying the objects to which the word refers.

Family resemblance: the network of similarities and differences in a group of closely related words or concepts.

Intension: the concept or idea a word stands for or is used to express.

Intensional definition: a definition that focuses on conveying the concept a word expresses.

Loaded definition: a definition that prejudices an important issue.

Logically necessary condition: a statement *N* is a logically necessary condition for another statement *R* when "if *R* then *N*" is true and can be determined to be true solely by appeal to the meaning of the conditional statement, without further observations. Or, "if *N* fails to be true, *R must* also fail to be true." For example, "Jones has [or had] an aunt or uncle" is a logically necessary condition for "Jones has a cousin."

Logically sufficient condition: a statement *S* is a logically sufficient condition for another statement *R* when "if *S*, then *R*" is true and can be determined to be true solely by appeal to the meaning of the conditional statement, without further observations. Or, "the truth of *S* necessarily guarantees the truth of *R*." For example, "Socrates convinced Plato that the unexamined life is not worth living" is a logically sufficient condition for "Plato believed that the unexamined life is not worth living."

Meaning: 1. what language customarily, conventionally, or ordinarily is used to do or convey;
2. what a speaker intends to do or convey in using language;
3. the importance or experiential significance attached to a given word, symbol, person, event, object, or relationship;
4. the object, or class of objects, to which a word refers;
5. the concept or idea that a word stands for or is used to express;
6. the consequences that follow from a given statement.

Narrow definition: a definition stipulating that a word shall refer to only a part of what it ordinarily refers to.

Open texture: that vagueness in a word or expression that permits evaluating new cases.

Reference class: the class or set of objects to which a word refers.

Stipulative definition: a definition that alters in some way a word's ordinary, customary, or conventional meaning.

Vague word: a word that has an imprecisely defined reference class.

3:4 *Summary* Vagueness and ambiguity create problems for all of us, but especially for people who, like philosophers, are critical and demand precision in their written or spoken communications. One way to handle these problems is to make them explicit by using descriptive definitions. Another way is to resolve them in advance by using stipulative definitions. Since all definitions can be characterized as more or less stipulative or more or less descriptive, it is often possible to avoid the vices and capture the virtues of both types. We noted how loaded definitions tended to prejudice important issues. Further, some definitions focus on conveying the concept a word is meant to express, whereas others aim at identifying the objects to which a word refers. We also looked at examples of how different kinds of definitions are used in philosophy.

EXERCISES for Chapter 3

In the following narrative there are some ambiguous and some vague assertions, along with various kinds of definitions. First read the whole passage once.

(A) "This is a very hot item," the pawnbroker said. (B) "Much in demand or stolen?" I asked. (C) "Of course, you're free to buy it," he replied. (D) "No one's preventing me or there is no law against it?" (E) "Besides your price is outrageous," I replied. (F) The pawnbroker said, "75% profit after costs and taxes is what I mean by reasonable. That's my price, so it's clearly not outrageous." (G) "Maybe we can't agree how outrageous 'outrageous' is, but your profit is twice what other merchants in your business make, so I call that outrageous." The pawnbroker took another tack: (H) "This is the moment you can buy your heart's desire, and this moment will never come again." (I) "I said I wanted it, but my heart's desire does not include my every want. (J) Besides, at the price you're asking, it'll be available later." The pawnbroker smiled, (K) "Fine, your wish is my command—I hear you say you want it, so I'm wrapping it up for you." (L) "You hear me say I would like it, but not 'I'll take it,' so don't wrap it. Good-bye!"

Now, given the context of the passage,

1. a. Pick out by letter the assertions suffering from problematic vagueness; identify their vague words or expressions.
   b. Explain how the vagueness hinders communication.
2. a. Pick out by letter each assertion suffering from vicious ambiguity and its ambiguous word or expression.
   b. Explain how the ambiguity hinders communication.
3. Categorize the definitions in B, D, F, G, and I as follows:

Descriptive	*Stipulative*	*Loaded*	*Intensional*	*Extensional*
B				
D				
F				
G				
I				

4. Explain how ambiguity is resolved in (J) and (L).
5. Explain why the loaded definition (F) is problematic.
6. Construct both descriptive and stipulative definitions of "desire," "marriage," "minor."
7. Construct both intensional and extensional definitions of "farm animals" and "bookcase."
8. Read the Waismann and Wittgenstein workshops. Despite the problems sometimes generated by vagueness and ambiguity, what positive value is ascribed to open texture and family resemblance? Can you imagine cases of helpful vagueness and ambiguity? What, if anything, clearly distinguishes troublesome from helpful vagueness or ambiguity?

ANSWERS for Chapter 3

1. a. E: "outrageous"; H: "heart's desire." ("Later" in (J) is vague, but not problematic for communication in this passage.)

2. a. (A): "hot"; (C): "free"; (H): "this moment"; (N): "I want it."

3.

	Descriptive	Stipulative	Loaded	Intensional	Extensional
B	X			X	
D	X			X	
F		X	X	X	
G		X			X
I	X				X

4. a. J points out that even if this present moment is fleeting, it will not—contrary to the suggestion of H's first clause—be the *only* moment for buying.
   b. L points out that the whole utterance "I want it" is ambiguous. The sentence may express a desire or it may be used, as in a restaurant, to place an order.

5. F attempts to close off honest discussion of whether the profit is outrageous by stipulating a definition of reasonable.

6. Consult a good dictionary to check your descriptive definitions.

7. *Intensional*
Animals typically raised on farms.

A set of shelves for storing books.

Extensional
Cows, pigs, horses, turkeys, chickens.
Take a number of nonpliable surfaces, 15–25 cm wide; arrange them stably, approximately 25 cm above each other so that both the planes and the lines forming their edges are parallel. Affix a back to the whole structure and the result is a bookcase.

4

Combining Beliefs: Foundationalist and Contextualist Approaches

In Chapter 1 we saw how philosophers try to understand and deal with the world by pursuing several closely related purposes: criticism, synthesis, precision, and evaluation. They, like others who pursue knowledge, use the prephilosophical tools of giving reasons to justify beliefs (Chapter 2) and developing definitions to improve clarity of thought and communication (Chapter 3). In approaching specific philosophical problems, philosophers use these tools as they organize their beliefs into *systematic positions*. In this process some beliefs are going to be justified on the basis of other beliefs. This chapter will introduce you to two contrasting basic approaches for combining beliefs: foundationalism and contextualism. Each of these methods offers a way to check your premises and assess the process by which you reason from them.

After reading Chapter 4 you should be able to

- State the relationship of knowledge to belief, truth, and justification.
- Defend the assertion that "proof must end somewhere."
- Explain the foundationalist argument from "proof must end somewhere" to the need for basic statements.
- Explain the contextualist argument from "proof must end somewhere" to mutually agreeable assumptions.
- Explain the foundationalist use of the deductive model in the light of the truth-preserving character of validity.

- Explain the contextualist argument for a mixed deductive and inductive model, despite limits of the truth-preserving character of inductive inference.
- Explain the limitations present in each of these approaches.

THE CASE OF SHARON AND TOM

Sharon Primeau and Tom Storts were two of the many criminal justice students in Professor Catino's Philosophy of Punishment course. They had been assigned to explore possible new ways of dealing with the problem of crime. They also had to lead a class discussion on what the professor called "The Technology of Crime Prevention."

"Ugh!" said Sharon as she got up from the table, stretched her arms, and looked aimlessly around the virtually empty dining hall. "We've been here for over an hour and we haven't come up with anything that even seems plausible. How about a Coke?"

Tom nodded distractedly. As Sharon left he began to think about the biology exam he had to face in just three days. Sharon came back, put down the drinks, and sat down.

"Tom, let's get to work. Cut the daydreams, it's time to think about punishment, not sex."

Almost as if he hadn't been listening Tom's face lit up. "I've got an idea, Sharon. You know that biologically there are two ways to treat a disease. Criminologists have spent all their time treating its symptoms—that's what police forces and prisons are all about. But why not treat its causes?"

"Hold on, Tom. The government has spent billions on welfare and education programs to try to attack the social roots of crime. What other options are there?"

"Don't you see yet, Sharon? We have never tried to change *people*; and after all, the real cause of crime is people. We have never tried to change human nature."

"What? How do you propose to do *that*?"

"It's easy to change human nature. Haven't you even heard of genetic engineering? Look, all we have to do is . . ."

"Wait a minute, Tom. You're moving too fast here. We need to clarify some things first or Catino will raise enough philosophical questions to kill the whole discussion. We have to first decide what human nature is. Then we have to see if genetic engineering can really change it in any way that affects the crime rate. After that we'll still have to decide on the morality of using genetic engineering."

"You know, Sharon, you take a lot of the fun out of an idea sometimes."

"Sorry, Tom, but we have to be sure we know where we're starting from and where the idea is taking us. Our position is justified only if we're certain about all our assumptions, and we also have to be certain every step of the way in our reasoning."

"I don't think I agree, Sharon. We're not doing calculus or geometry. We're into social policy. You just can't expect to adopt a policy without also accepting some risk that it may not work. I mean it isn't fair, Sharon, it's expecting too much."

"No, Tom, if it's going to affect people, then it's not asking too much that we be certain of what we're doing. I see how we can make out a case. It's obvious that the way to solve the problem of crime is to eliminate its cause in human nature. Now, what exactly is it in human nature that causes crime?"

"I'm not really sure, Sharon."

"Come on, Tom, it's easy. Being a human means being selfish. All people are selfish and that's why some want to commit crime."

"I'm not so sure, Sharon. Besides, what if some of the other results are worse? Changes in basic human characteristics, assuming they are basic, will affect lots of behavior."

"Tom, your problem is you don't respect logic very much."

"I don't know about that, Sharon, but I do think we should question assumptions that lead to silly or dangerous results. For example, if people stopped being selfish, they would probably stop taking care of themselves or their immediate families, so that they'd be worse off than they are now. You have proved that using genetic engineering to eliminate crime in human nature might be a bigger problem than the disease we are trying to cure!"

"Yes, but you don't *know* that that would happen."

"Sharon, do you want another Coke?"

4:1.1 *Why a method of combining beliefs is needed* The case of Sharon and Tom presents a typical problem-solving situation. With a flash of insight you come up with a possible solution to your problem, and then wonder, on the basis of the beliefs you have about the situation, whether you really have the answer. In the present case, *is* altering the genetic endowment of potential criminals the best solution to the problem of crime?

Why do Sharon and Tom seem to disagree? They have the same beliefs about criminals and about the effects of genetic engineering on the behavior of people. Yet the ways in which they go about combining these beliefs into a systematic view about the solution to crime are quite different. Sharon looks for a few bedrock assumptions—"you can't change human beings" or "being human means being selfish"—and follows logic wherever it takes her. Tom takes a different tack throughout. Less reverent toward what Sharon calls "logic," he is more inclined to defer to other beliefs when they conflict with the results of reasoning about the problem. Consequently, Sharon and Tom really disagree over the best *approach* for reaching justified beliefs. Such an approach tells you, first, how to get your bearings, and then, how to proceed in a reasonable manner to acceptable conclusions. Ideally, it results in fully justified conclusions. It also provides a standard against which you can measure a person's reasoned beliefs, so that you can use it to criticize your own beliefs as well as those of others.

Philosophers have developed *two basic approaches* to combining beliefs. The *foundationalist* approach (like Sharon's) aims to find a set of beliefs that have been fully justified, so that you can be absolutely certain about them. The *contextualist* approach (like Tom's) also aims at fully justified belief, but it is less concerned with achieving total certainty than with accommodating as many relevant beliefs as possible.

4:1.2 *Knowledge and belief* Both approaches to combining beliefs have the goal of knowledge. In order to *know* that something is the case, you must satisfy three logically necessary conditions (see 3:2.2):

1. *You can know that something is the case only if you believe that it is the case.* This dictum may be illustrated by events in a typical English detective novel. The villain has poisoned her aunt for her inheritance, and she fears that her aunt's octogenarian cribbage partner, an amateur sleuth, knows that she is the culprit. To set her mind at ease the killer converses at length with the sleuth and observes his behavior. If every observation confirms that the sleuth does not *believe* that she is guilty, then she needs no further investigation to establish that the sleuth does not *know* that she is guilty. For if the sleuth knew she were guilty, he would also have to believe it.

2. *You can know something only if it is true.* If the sleuth believes that the victim's son did the deed, he obviously does not *know* this to be true. The statement is false; the niece did it.

3. *You can know something only if you are justified in believing it.* The sleuth might believe truly that the niece is the killer on the basis of a hunch halfway through the novel but still be unable to prove it. It may take him the rest of the novel to come to know it, that is, to justify his belief. When you believe something as a result of a lucky guess or mistaken reasoning, you are *unjustified* in believing what you do and thus do not really know it. Beliefs may, of course, be justified in different ways. You expect the detective to support his belief with some evidence or proof. But some beliefs may be *justified without further appeal to proof*, for example (perhaps!), your belief that you are right now reading this sentence.

According to many philosophers, these three conditions provide a complete analysis of knowledge: Knowledge is true, justified belief. This analysis allows that you can know something even if you have not *proven* it on the basis of *other* beliefs. This statement raises important questions: (1) *Which* beliefs require no such proof? (2) When you provide a proof for a belief on the basis of other beliefs, what is the relationship between the proven belief and the other beliefs?

4:1.3 *Foundationalism and contextualism*

The foundationalists (like Sharon) look for a bedrock of certainty in the form of some kind of indubitable *basic statements,* that is, statements about which there is no room for error. Accordingly, they require no outside proof, but rather, are used as the starting points from which to prove other, nonbasic statements. The most usual examples of basic statements are those describing experiences or sensations, for example, "I taste something salty" or "Right now there is something red in the middle of my visual field." However, other statements, like Sharon's, that all people are selfish and rational, have been taken to be "basic" or axiomatic by many modern economists.

The foundationalist argues that if there were no basic statements, *no* knowledge would be possible. For example, how can Tom possibly know that genetic engineering can solve the crime problem if that "knowledge" is proved on the basis of his belief that crime is like a disease, a belief that is itself open to doubt? How can a belief be any less open to doubt than the beliefs upon which it is based? Tom might try to prove that crime is like a disease on the basis of other beliefs about disease and crime. But are those other beliefs open to doubt as well? Sharon believes Tom must fall back on basic statements, because *proof must end somewhere.*

The foundationalist assumes throughout this argument that a proof must provide you with an absolute guarantee of the truth of the justified belief. A belief does not qualify as knowledge unless it is safe from being repudiated at a later time. Hence, the foundationalist insists on (1) absolutely *secure foundations* on which to base all knowledge, and (2) a proof that is "certain every step of the way." Given the basic statements, the foundationalist accepts all their logical implications, wherever they lead.

In contrast, the contextualist (like Tom) is less concerned with absolute guarantees. The contextualist strives to (1) arrive at the most satisfactory position on the subject matter at hand, and (2) do as much justice as possible to the existing body of opinion. The contextualist does *not* recognize any statement as a basic statement. If an allegedly "basic" statement conflicts with widespread and well-established beliefs, such as those about human beings, the contextualist is more inclined to side with the latter. For example, Tom might reject Sharon's "basic statement" that everyone is selfish and rational because it conflicts with the common view that crimes of passion are irrationally motivated.

Then how would a contextualist like Tom respond to the argument that "proof must end somewhere"? The contextualist would probably agree that your justification must begin from assumptions, but would argue that it is too much to expect these starting points to be entirely immune from doubt or error. The most that you can reasonably expect is a context of beliefs on which the participants in an inquiry can agree. These *mutually agreeable assumptions* serve as the starting point of knowledge, but they are themselves also open to revision. Contextualists thus tend to be eclectics and compatibilists. *Eclectics* are willing to accomodate beliefs drawn from quite different sources which seem at first to be in conflict. *Compatibilists* strive to reconcile commonsense beliefs with apparently conflicting "self-evident" assumptions.

For simplicity, we are speaking as if a philosopher were either a foundationalist or a contextualist. But to be more precise, "foundationalist" and "contextualist" describe *methods* and *approaches* which philosophers take to specific issues. Hence, it is possible that the same philosopher would use a foundationalist approach in one area (for example, mathematics) and a contextualist approach in another area (for example, ethics). Very often, however, philosophers use similar sorts of approaches throughout this work.

4:1.4 *Models for combining beliefs*   Both of the approaches, foundationalism and contextualism, have been used extensively by philosophers. Foundationalists have been especially impressed by the paradigm of mathematical reasoning. Plato in ancient Greece was deeply influenced by Pythagoras, the mathematician, and his followers; seventeenth-century "rationalists" such as Descartes and Spinoza emulated Euclid's system of geometry after the rediscovery of ancient manuscripts; and in this century Russell and others responded to the development of set theory and the axiomatization of arithmetic. The clearest example of these influences is that of Euclid on the rationalists. Euclid's geometry begins with very clear and precise definitions and from supposedly self-evident and indisputable axioms. It argues from these axioms by a succession of logical steps, each of which leads deductively and necessarily to the next. Because deductive reasoning is absolutely truth-preserving (see 2:2.2), there is no room anywhere in the system for error. Descartes contended that error would creep into a system only if one succumbed to the temptation to accept an inference that did not, in fact, necessarily follow from basic statements.

The Foundationalism of Baruch Spinoza

Baruch Spinoza (1632–1677) is one of the leading figures in the "rationalist" movement of the seventeenth century. He became enthusiastic about the philosophical revolution begun by Descartes and came in contact with Leibniz and others in the movement. His most important works were the *Ethics* and the *Tractatus Logico-Politicus*.

No one has carried out the foundationalist program in philosophy with greater determination than Spinoza. In the *Ethics* he took the Euclidean system of geometry as his model, believing that one could obtain knowledge only if one could develop a complete deductive system of beliefs. Spinoza was not merely foundationalist in his approach to specific problems; rather his philosophy as a whole has a foundationalist structure visible as he combines positions on diverse problems into a unified system. His system proceeds from a set of definitions and axioms such as the following:

Definitions:
By *substance*, I mean that which is in itself, and is conceived through itself. [Pt. I, Df. III]
By *attribute*, I mean that which the intellect perceives as constituting the essence of substance. [Pt. I, Df. IV]
By *God*, I mean a being absolutely infinite. [Pt. I, Df. VI]
By *good*, I mean that which we certainly know to be useful to us. [Pt. IV, Df. I]
By *evil*, I mean that which we certainly know to be a hindrance to us in the attainment of any good. [Pt. IV, Df. II]

Axioms:
Everything which exists, exists either in itself or in something else. [Pt. I, Ax. I]
From a given definite cause an effect necessarily follows. [Pt. I, Ax. III]
There is no individual thing in nature, than which there is not another more powerful and strong. Whatsoever thing be given, there is something stronger whereby it can be destroyed. [Pt. IV, Ax. I]

From such definitions and axioms, Spinoza derived such propositions as the following:

Propositions:

God, or substance, consisting of infinite attributes, of which each expresses eternal and infinite essentiality, necessarily exists. [Pt. I, Prop. XI]

Besides God no substance can be granted or conceived. [Pt. I, Prop. XIV]

Whatsoever is, is in God, and without God nothing can be, or be conceived. [Pt. I, Prop. XV]

Nothing in the universe is contingent, but all things are conditioned to exist and operate in a particular manner by the necessity of the divine nature. [Pt. I, Prop. XXIX]

Things could not have been brought into being by God in any manner or in any order different from that which has in fact obtained. [Pt. I, Prop. XXXIII]

The knowledge of good and evil is nothing else but the emotions of pleasure or pain, in so far as we are conscious thereof. [Pt. IV, Prop. VIII]

We know nothing to be certainly good or evil, save such things as really conduce to understanding, or such as are able to hinder us from understanding. [Pt. IV. Prop. XXVII]

The good which every man, who follows after virtue, desires for himself he will also desire for other men, and so much the more, in proportion as he has a greater knowledge of God. [Pt. IV, Prop. XXXVII]

A free man thinks of death least of all things; and his wisdom is a meditation not of death but of life. [Pt. IV, Prop. LXVII]

Contextualism is illustrated by Socrates's method of criticism, which is called *elenchus*. This method consists in asking a question, such as "What is justice?" and drawing out an answer from his companion, such as "Justice is helping your friends and harming your enemies." He then shows that this answer has implications inconsistent with other beliefs on which they are mutually agreed, for example, "Your enemy might, unbeknownst to you, be a good person," and "It is unjust to harm a good person." Then they attempt to revise the definition so that it avoids this criticism. The process continues as they consider whether the new definition conflicts with other beliefs. Sometimes the answer will be based upon a probable hypothesis supported by an inductive proof. The hypothesis is a belief on which they agree, but like other beliefs, it is open to revision. The aim of Socrates's method is to discover beliefs which will survive this process of criticism.[1]

---

[1]It is not our intention to represent Socrates or Plato here as "contextualist philosophers." Our point is simply that the *methods* of *elenchus* and of hypothesis (as used in the *Meno*) are contextualist *methods*. These philosophers might employ foundationalist methods elsewhere.

The Contextualism of Socrates

One of the methods which Socrates (470–399 B.C.) uses in Plato's dialogue, *Meno*, is contextualist. Socrates tries to get the inquiry into whether virtue can be taught started by means of his *method of hypothesis*. Since Socrates and Meno do not know what virtue is, they have to use a hypothesis to investigate whether virtue is teachable or not. Socrates's hypothesis is that virtue is knowledge. Given this, it certainly follows that virtue can be taught. Socrates and Meno can agree on the hypothesis because it is supported by other beliefs: for example, things like health, wealth, and even character traits like courage are worthwhile only if they are used rightly, but the misuse of such things seems to be due to foolishness or thoughtlessness.

There are two very significant features of Socrates's method of hypothesis. First, the hypothesis is *not* treated as a basic statement by Socrates. In fact, he ultimately rejects this particular hypothesis on the grounds that it implies something that conflicts with an independent assumption on which they are agreed. The hypothesis implies that there are people who can teach virtue, but this conflicts with the conviction of Socrates and Meno that no such teachers exist. This independent assumption is not advanced as a basic statement or as the result of a strict deduction, but as based upon probable and inductive reasoning. Socrates bases his independent assumption on beliefs and observations on which the discussants agree. In this case, these beliefs are that the only professed teachers of virtue, the Sophists, are really a corrupting influence, and that although many well-to-do people with good intentions have found experts to teach their children every possible skill, the children still fail to be virtuous. This conflict in belief leads Socrates to abandon his initial hypothesis.

4:2 *Philosophical purposes served* In addressing problems of knowledge, the two approaches to combining beliefs advance several crucial purposes of philosophy. Most prominent is the purpose of *systematic thought*. Foundationalism holds out the ideal of a deductive system founded upon self-evident assumptions, along the lines of mathematics. Contextualism is content with a less elegant and more eclectic model, but it also aims to bring as many of our diverse beliefs as possible into a coherent system or web of beliefs.[2] Since the foundationalist equates precision with deductive rigor, whereas the contextualist accepts inductive justifications, they approach the goal of *precision* differently. The two also have different ways of pursuing the goal of *criticism*. A foundationalist will criticize an inference for not following deductively from basic statements, whereas a contextualist will criticize an inference for coming into conflict with independent, mutually agreed upon beliefs or assumptions. Finally, they both serve the aims of *evaluation*, because justification of normative beliefs is implicit in both approaches. In the case study, evaluation is suggested in Tom's criticism of the proposed solution: Genetic engineering is ill-advised because it would lead to results believed to be bad. Moreover, the standards of criticism promoted by the two approaches are themselves evaluative standards.

4:3. *Application of these approaches to the sciences* Foundationalism has been the dominant approach in the mathematical and physical sciences in the twentieth century. In mathematics it was originally exemplified as *formalism*, which attempted with considerable success to show how all the theorems of mathematics could be deduced from basic statements of logic and set theory. However, this endeavor suffered a serious setback in 1930 when Kurt Gödel demonstrated that in any formal system in which mathematical statements can be expressed, there will be "undecidable" theorems, which can neither be proven nor disproven within the system. Thus it is impossible for all mathematical knowledge to be encompassed by a single deductive system.

A parallel movement in connection with the physical sciences is called *reductionism*. Its proponents claim that all the observable events of the natural world, physical or biological, can be explained in terms of the laws of physics which govern the most elementary bits of matter and energy. The reductionist claims that laws that explain the behavior of even very complex systems of matter and energy — such as those explaining the births and deaths of stars and galaxies or those governing the evolution of new species of plants and animals — can be deduced from more basic laws of physics.

---

[2]It is important to note that the two approaches can be used either to combine beliefs on specific problems into coherent positions or to combine such positions into unified philosophies. Our emphasis in the present chapter is upon the former use of the approaches. See Part Eight for a more thorough treatment of building unified philosophies or world views.

☞ **PHILOSOPHER'S WORKSHOP**

Zeno's Paradox of the Arrow

The paradoxes of motion of Zeno (b. 490 B.C.) provide a classic example of foundationalism. His paradox of the arrow starts from two basic statements about space and time: (1) whatever at a given moment occupies a space equal to itself is at rest, and (2) anything which is supposedly moving is really occupying a space equal to itself at any given instant. From these statements Zeno infers that everything is always (at every instant) at rest. Zeno believed that he made a great philosophical discovery: the universal belief in the existence of motion was entirely erroneous! Altogether different was the approach of Aristotle (384–322 B.C.). He found Zeno's paradox disturbing because it was inferred from assumptions on which everyone agrees. Using a contextualist method, Aristotle relied on other independent, mutually agreed upon assumptions—such as the assumption that objects like an arrow shot from a bow do move—as checks on such inferences. If the inferences from mutually agreed upon assumptions conflict with common-sense assumptions, the compatibilist tries to find a way of showing that the apparent conflict between these different assumptions is no more than apparent. Aristotle's strategy in such cases was to show that there has been a fallacy, or mistake in reasoning, leading to the inferences, or that one of the assumptions has been misunderstood. For example, he tried to argue that Zeno's paradox depends upon the false, unstated assumption that the stretch of time it takes an arrow to fly from bow to target is *composed* of a series of indivisible instants. (If you don't like this solution, you might try to come up with a better one.)

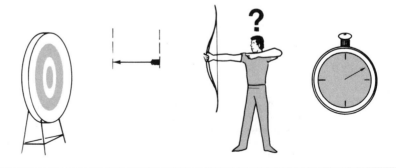

4:4.1 *Criticisms of the approaches*   The foundationalist is generally impatient with the contextualist's reliance upon beliefs for which there is no room in the former's system. Thus in the case study, Sharon insists that "We have to be sure we know where we're starting from." On these grounds, the rationalist philosopher René Descartes (1596–1650) argues that you must set aside all your beliefs and start out from scratch with indubitable basic statements, which you "clearly and distinctly" perceive.

> Suppose one had a basket of apples and, fearing that some of them were rotten, wanted to take those out lest they might make the rest go wrong, how could he do that? Would he not first turn the whole of the apples out of the basket and look over one by one, and then having selected those which he saw not to be rotten, place them again in the basket and leave out the others?[3]

As long as you confine yourself to basic statements and to statements that can be logically deduced from them, you may be assured that you have knowledge and cannot fall into error. The objection against contextualism is that it cannot provide this sort of assurance for two reasons: (1) the justifications it provides for beliefs rest upon other beliefs, which are merely "mutually agreed upon" and which may be the rotten ones in your basket; and (2) the nondeductive types of justification countenanced by contextualism leave room for error in inference.

The contextualist agrees that foundationalism can be fruitfully applied in carefully delimited subject areas, such as branches of mathematics, but he complains that the foundationalist is unreasonable to demand certainty on all topics. Thus Tom argues, "We're not doing calculus or geometry; we're into social policy. You just can't accept a policy without also accepting some risk that it may not work." The ancient Greek philosopher Aristotle made essentially the same point:

> It is the mark of an educated man to look for precision in each class of things just so far as the nature of the subject admits; it is evidently equally foolish to accept probable reasoning from a mathematician and to demand from a rhetorician scientific proofs.[4]

The contextualist also takes exception to the argument that you always have to dump all the apples out of your basket to determine whether or not any are rotten. Doubt arises in a certain context in which a certain belief is reasonably brought into question in relation to a body of beliefs that are mutually agreed upon. Doubt is also set-

---

[3]René Descartes, *Objections and Replies to Meditations on First Philosophy*, in *The Philosophical Works of Descartes*, trans. Elizabeth S. Haldane and G. R. T. Ross, vol. II (London: Cambridge University Press, 1970), p. 282.

[4]Aristotle, *Nicomachean Ethics*, I, 3, trans. W. D. Ross in W. D. Ross and J. A. Smith (eds.), *The Works of Aristotle* (London: Oxford University Press, 1908–1952).

tled in such a context. It is a mistake to suppose that you can fully explain your beliefs by doubting everything that you can doubt and by removing all these doubts.

4:4.2 *Divergent values and purposes*   The differences between foundationalism and contextualism reflect fundamental differences in values, which have been described by William James (1842 – 1910):

> There are two ways of looking at our duty in the matter of opinion — ways entirely different, and yet ways about whose difference the theory of knowledge seems hitherto to have shown very little concern. *We must know the truth:* and *we must avoid error —* these are our first great commandments as would-be knowers; but they are not two ways of stating an identical commandment, they are two separable laws. . . . By choosing between them we may end by coloring differently our whole intellectual life.[5]

The foundationalist is deeply committed to exhaustive rigor, precision, and the avoidance of error. The contextualist is deeply committed to accommodating and reconciling as many beliefs as possible in a system of justified belief. James himself is a contextualist: "For my part, I can believe that worse things than being duped may happen to a man."[6]

The differences in approaches also reflect differences in philosophical purposes. For the foundationalists, precision and clarity take priority, and they often regard reasoning in ethics, aesthetics, and religion with contempt because of the absence of rigor. Contextualists, however, place a high priority upon the systematic and evaluative purposes of philosophy. Their aim is to reconcile as many beliefs in as many departments of human concern as possible within a comprehensive philosophical system. Each subject matter must be dealt with on its own terms, and the fact that religious or moral belief cannot be formalized or absorbed into the body of modern mathematical and scientific knowledge makes it no less meaningful or rational.

4:5 *Summary*   The approaches to combining beliefs are concerned with how you are able to acquire knowledge, or justified, true belief. Knowledge generally involves proving some beliefs on the basis of others, but "proof must end somewhere." The foundationalist method maintains that proof must terminate in basic statements which are not liable to error. The contextualist maintains that justification must end

---

[5]William James, *Essays in Pragmatism*, ed. A. Castell (New York: Hafner Publishing Co., 1966), pp. 99 – 100.
[6]*Ibid.*

in a context of mutually agreed-upon beliefs, which may themselves require revision at a later time if they are shown to come into conflict with other mutually agreed-upon beliefs. Foundationalism relies on deductive reasoning and necessary proofs in order to preserve the certainty of the basic statements from which proof begins. The contextualist argues for including inductive modes of reasoning and appeals to evidence that may not remove all possible doubt. The foundationalist method has the strengths of precision and certainty, but many areas of human concern resist the method. The contextualist method is more comprehensive, but because of its lack of rigor, is more prone to error and is sometimes unable to secure the general agreement which knowledge requires. The difference in method reflects a difference in philosophical values and purposes. The foundationalist places greater priority on the purposes of precision and clarity; the contextualist, on the evaluative and systematic purposes.

EXERCISES for Chapter 4

1. a. If Sam knows that San Francisco's warmest nights usually occur in early September, then what else must be true (4:1.2)?
    A. The ocean currents dominate San Francisco's weather.
    B. Sam has lived in San Francisco.
    C. San Francisco's nights are on the average warmest in early September.
    D. Sam holds the view that San Francisco's warmest nights are in early September.
    E. Sam has recorded temperature readings for years.
    F. Sam's belief about which San Francisco nights are warmest rests on adequate evidence.
    G. Sam knows San Francisco is on a geological fault.
    b. State abstractly the three necessary conditions of knowledge illustrated in a.

2. a. Form a line of reasoning that starts from the assumption that proof does not end anywhere. How would you show that this assumption is false by showing that its consequences are absurd (4:1.3)?
    b. If (1) proof must end somewhere, then what other premises does a foundationalist use with 1 to conclude that there must be basic statements?
    c. What part of the foundationalist argument is criticized in the following passage?

    Suppose I give this explanation: "I take 'Moses' to mean the man, if there was such a man, who led the Israelites out of Egypt, whatever he was called then and whatever he may or may not have done besides." — But similar doubts to those about "Moses" are possible about the words of this explanation (what are you calling "Egypt," whom the "Israelites" etc.?). Nor would these questions come to an end when we got down to words like "red," "dark," "sweet." — "But then how does an explanation help me to understand, if after all it is not the final one? In that case the explanation is never completed; so I still don't understand what he means, and never shall!" — As though an explanation as it were hung in the air unless supported by another one. Whereas an explanation may indeed rest on another one that has been given, but none stands in need of another — unless we require it to prevent a misunderstanding. One might say: an explanation serves to remove or to avert a misunderstanding — one, that is, that would occur but for the explanation; not every one that I can imagine.

It may easily look as if every doubt merely revealed an existing gap in the foundations; so that secure understanding is only possible if we first doubt everything that can be doubted, and then remove all these doubts.

The sign-post is in order — if, under normal circumstances, it fulfills its purpose.[7]

    d. How might a foundationalist respond to this criticism?

3. a. Restate the argument given below in the light of the truth-preserving character of validity (4:1.4).

If a man shall start from premises, however certain, but shall then allow his mind any inference it chooses, how shall he claim to know what he infers? For knowledge involves truth and yet inferences which are inductive and not necessary admit of the intrusion of error into thought, no matter how clear its foundation.

    b. Which of the following assertions might a contextualist use in support of a mixed, deductive, and inductive model of inference (4:1.4)?

      A. Many subjects in which much more well-reasoned views can be distinguished from poorly reasoned views would be declared subjects in which knowledge is impossible if a deductive model were used exclusively.

      B. Error can never be ruled out absolutely because any starting point is capable of being doubted.

      C. Inductive reasoning can lead one to error.

      D. Inductive reasoning is in some circumstances one's best means of separating truth from error.

      E. It is better to believe nothing than to believe something false.

      F. All assertions are equally subject to dispute.

4. Explain the limitations of foundationalism and of contextualism (4:4.1, 4:4.2).

---

[7]Ludwig Wittgenstein, *Philosophical Investigations*, trans. G. E. M. Anscombe, 2nd ed. (Oxford: Basil Blackwell, 1953), I, 87.

SELECTED ANSWERS For Chapter 4

1. a. C. *S* knows *P* only if *P*.
   D. *S* knows *P* only if *S* believes *P*.
   F. *S* knows *P* only if *S* has adequate jusification for believing *P*.
   (B) and (E) each suggest why (F) might be true, but neither is necessary for the truth of (F).

2. a. "Proof ends nowhere" means that nothing is really established. Thus, nothing is known. But some simple truths are clearly known. So the assumption that proof never ends must be false.
   b. (1) Proof ends somewhere.
       (2) If when proof ended, room for doubt remained, proof would not really have ended—the process would be incomplete.
       (3) A "basic statement" is any indubitable statement.
       (4) So there must be basic statements.
   c. Premise 2 is attacked by saying that the possibility of doubt does not imply any real doubt or need for further explanation.
   d. If the possibility exists, then what is claimed to be known might be false. Yet clearly *S* knows *P* entails *P* is true—and thus cannot be false.

3. b. A, B, D; note that C and E support the foundationalist; F argues skeptically against the possibility of knowledge at all.

PERSPECTIVES

ON ETHICS

Honest questions about conduct, "How ought I to act, and why?" are the most immediate and perplexing philosophical questions of our everyday lives. Sometimes these questions about values can be painfully difficult as different reasons and motives move you in contrary directions. Deep concern for questions about what ought to be done and what policies to establish arises in governments, institutions, and businesses, just as in your personal life. Such questions arise in times of crisis, social or personal; and at such times persons of a philosophical disposition have tried to reflect in a systematic way on the basic values or ideals that might be invoked to justify value claims and resolve moral dilemmas. "What are values?" philosophers have wondered. "What can be known about them, and how can you justify a value judgment?"

Ancient Greek philosophy developed during such a period of concern. Early thinkers began to see that there might be scientifically organized bodies of knowledge about the physical world — which led other thinkers to ponder whether moral truths could be demonstrated as Euclid had proved his theorems of geometry. Accordingly, your study of ethics will begin with the distinction between descriptive and normative statements. Chapter 5 introduces that distinction along with

✒ PART TWO

several other central ethical distinctions. Once you grasp these you can understand the answers given to the questions, "Can the value of an action be defined by its consequences?" (Chapter 6), "What makes doing my duty worthwhile in itself?" (Chapter 7), and "What makes a good life?" (Chapter 8).

Philosophers have attempted to understand through each of these questions the principles of right action. They offer valuable insights about the importance of an action's consequences, of a person's duty, and of what constitutes the good life. Yet their different theories do yield some conflicting or diverging results, and important criticisms can be made against each (Chapter 9). If we are left then with some diverging and conflicting ideas about what right conduct is, how should such conflicts be resolved? Chapter 10 presents methods that can be used to resolve value conflicts.[1]

The diagram shows the relationship of the chapters to each other.

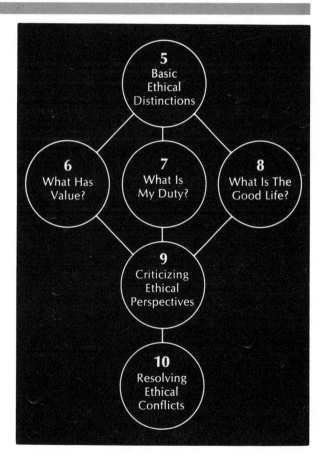

[1] For a fuller treatment of ethics and social philosophy than can be made available in a general introduction to philosophy, see Facione, Scherer, and Attig, *Values and Society: An Introduction to Ethics and Social Philosophy* (Englewood Cliffs, N.J.: Prentice-Hall, Inc., 1978).

5

Basic Ethical Distinctions

This chapter introduces you to the subject matter of ethics. It clarifies the distinction between facts and values, and it focuses on assertions that express value judgments about how individuals ought or ought not to behave. Questions about human conduct are the principal concerns of the normative discipline that is ethics. This chapter also clarifies the place of reason in ethics by tracing the difference between offering a justification or an excuse for an action. You will also be introduced to some of the possible meanings of normative statements. After reading Chapter 5 you should be able to

- Distinguish descriptive from normative assertions.
- Distinguish prudence from ethics.
- State the practical as well as the theoretical concerns of ethics.
- State the cognitive characteristics of normative sentences in virtue of which they can be understood as statements.
- Distinguish justifications from excuses.
- Distinguish objective from subjective interpretations of ethical assertions.
- Distinguish assertions of instrumental value from those of intrinsic value.
- Distinguish assertions of relative value from those of absolute value.

THE CASE OF INGRID STONER

Dr. Valaquez picked the Stoner file out of its rack on the examination room door. She knocked on the door and then let herself in without waiting for, or even expecting, her patient to answer. Her eyes scanned the top page of the folder for the nurse's notes. Her nurse, who was usually so good at providing preliminary cues, had not left her any help this time. Almost without pausing to look up at her patient, Dr. Valaquez put down the folder, put her stethoscope in her ears and said, "How are you today, Mrs. Stoner?"

"I'm fine, thanks." she answered as routinely as she would have to a stranger. "How are you doing? . . . as busy as ever I see."

"Yes, I do have to move quickly sometimes. Especially these last two weeks. Dr. Lubski has been out of town and I have been looking after his patients for him. But what brings you in today?"

"Well, it's really not physical. . . I mean . . . I'm not actually sick."

"Yes, well, how can I help you?"

"I need an abortion. Can you do it for me?"

"Well now, let's start over again. Let's first see if you are pregnant."

"There really is no question about that. I've been pregnant before, you know. I know the signs: I've missed my period for the fourth time, I have morning sickness, and I'm afraid I'm even starting to put on weight."

"Yes, but I still want to run routine tests."

"Good, you do your tests. But I know I'm pregnant and I want an abortion."

"Well, that is a pretty big decision. Don't you think we should talk about it a bit?"

"What's there to talk about? I'm pregnant. I can't have this child. So I have to get an abortion."

"Why can't you have the child? Your other children are all fine children, healthy, smart. Is there a money problem?"

"Really, doctor, I'm not sure it's any of your business. But if you must know, I've been having an affair. The child is not my husband's."

"Have you told your husband?"

"No. Not yet. But he will know soon if I don't get the abortion. He's had a vasectomy and even old Charlie will figure out that he's not the daddy this time."

"I take it, then, that you haven't told him anything."

"That's right. And that's how it's going to be. I don't want to talk to him about this. It will only hurt him and ruin our family even more. I've ended the affair, and I want to go back to Charlie full time. Telling him will only get in the way."

"But he has the right to know. He is your husband after all."

"Here you go again. Telling me what to do or what to decide. He does not have the right to know as far as I am concerned. What's more, I'm sorry I told you about all this anyway. I don't want you telling him anything. Not about the affair, nor the pregnancy, nor the abortion."

"Well now, let's think about this a little. You'll have to go into the hospital for the abortion. There will be at least a couple of days there away from home. There will be medical records, bills to pay, insurance forms to fill out. He might find out what you are doing. He certainly will have to be told something. I think we should just be honest with him."

"No way. I can go out of town. The whole thing can be done in New York, no records, no trouble. I'll pay cash. I'll get it out of my own savings account or borrow it from some friends. He'll never know."

"You're not being realistic. First, I won't be able to do the abortion for you."

"Are you saying that you don't do abortions, that they are immoral or something?"

"Well, no. I do feel they are immoral. It's wrong to kill a human life, even an unborn one. But I do perform abortions in certain cases, when it's medically or psychologically indicated. But actually I was thinking more of the problem of doing the operation if you go out of town. I can't go out of town with you."

"I see. Well now what do I do? I trust you. I want you to be the doctor who takes care of me. You refused on moral grounds."

"I did not. I refused to go out of town and do it. I practice out of Riverview Hospital here in town. That's all. I might even agree to do it for you here, if I thought you were making a wise decision. But I have problems with the fact that you haven't talked to your husband. That means you haven't looked at all your options, one of which is to have the child and ask him to raise it as his own."

"That's silly. He would never agree. He doesn't want any more kids — especially ones that remind him that I was unfaithful. No, doctor, don't give me your flimsy excuses about being too busy or being unable to practice except at Riverview. You've judged me guilty and you won't touch me. Well, it sure must be great to be God. But I'm only human. Don't bother about having your nurse run any tests on me. I'm leaving. Send the bill to Charlie." She got up, grabbed up her purse and coat, and strode out the door, leaving the doctor sitting and looking out the open door after her.

5:1.1 *Normative versus non-normative statements*   Normative statements are assertions that express our value judgments. People use normative statements to assert that things are good or bad, beautiful or ugly, right or wrong, acceptable or unacceptable. Many of the statements in the case study are normative statements, such as "Your husband has the right to know about your condition" and "Abortions are immoral." Some normative statements are about aesthetic concerns, such as "Nothing can match the beauty of the human body in motion." Some express value judgments about logical concerns, for example, "Augustine's argument is unacceptable."

Some normative statements have *immediate behavioral implications*; that is, when you make the statement you imply that one should or should not behave in a specific way. For example, the statement "Your husband has the right to know" implies that someone should tell the husband. Others do not have immediate behavioral implications about what should or should not be done, such as "I prefer playing golf on Sunday morning to going to church." Many characteristics of normative statements are shared by *imperatives*, such as "Honor thy mother and they father" and "Don't putt with a five iron." Although these are not, strictly, statements but commands, they do have immediate behavioral implications, and it will be convenient to treat them under the heading of "normative statements."

The following terms or their equivalents occur in many normative assertions that are of concern to ethics: "good," "bad," "better," "worse," "right," "wrong," "obliged," "permitted," "forbidden," "duty," "responsibility," and "rights." Other examples of normative assertions are

Public nudity should be permitted.
Conservation of energy is the responsibility of everyone.
Everyone has the right to worship as he or she desires.
Child abuse is a sin.
The movie *Love and Death* is delightful.
Mahler's Eighth Symphony is magnificent.
The new gymnasium is simply ugly.
Your inference is not valid.

Non-normative statements are statements that are value-neutral; they do not express (or are not intended to express) value judgments. Non-normative statements are reports, descriptions, or assertions, either true or false, used to express matters of empirical or logical fact. For example:

In 1977 Americans began to forget their bicentennial.
Parallelograms have four sides.
Many people value telling the truth.

People rarely question authority.
Many people have no religious beliefs.
Drug addiction is a widespread phenomenon.
The movie *Modern Times* stars Charlie Chaplin.
Competition frequently undermines friendship.
Harold thinks Barbara is a good singer.

All these statements express judgments about facts, either empirical or conceptual (logical). The last example in the list shows that you can make a *factual* judgment about what people value; that is, you can make a *non-normative* statement about a person's value judgments. Of course, if Harold were to say, "Barbara is a good singer," *he* would be making a normative statement. Can you identify examples of non-normative statements in the case study? Consider, for example, Ingrid Stoner's statements about her current physical condition.

Many issues can be treated from both the normative and the non-normative points of view. Consider the question in the case study of Ingrid Stoner's telling or not telling her husband. She could make the following true or false non-normative statements:

I have not told my husband.
I do not intend to tell my husband that I am pregnant.
If I tell my husband, it will finish our marriage.
If I don't have the abortion, eventually I'll have to tell my husband.

She could also make these normative statements:

My husband has a right to know about my pregnancy.
My husband has no right to know as far as I am concerned.
I should tell my husband because he will be more hurt if he finds out some other way.
I should tell my husband in order to keep open the option of raising the child myself.

5:1.2   *Ethics and prudence*   Ethics focuses upon normative statements that have immediate implications for individual human behavior (see 5:1.1), yet not all such judgments are correctly understood as having ethical significance. Thus, for example, the following normative statements would *not* ordinarily be understood as having ethical significance:

You should brush your teeth after every meal.
Say "thank you" when accepting a gift.

You should change razor blades regularly.
Beware of drinking hot tea before it has cooled sufficiently.
Don't putt with a five iron.

Although these statements have immediate implications for behavior, they concern what is prudent, what is good etiquette, or what is good technique. In ordinary circumstances, such matters lack a certain seriousness, or weightiness, which attaches to ethical matters. Ethical concerns are serious because they involve significant harm or benefit for oneself or for others, conformity with or violation of duty, respect or disrespect for persons and their rights. The following statements express such ethical concerns:

Stealing is wrong.
You should keep your promises.
Courage is a virtue.
Never tell a lie.
Always strive to be fair when dealing with others.
The right to life must not be violated.
Not responding to a desperate cry for help is almost always wrong.

Ethics deals with questions about how people *ought to behave.* Some questions concern goals, for example, "Should persons strive for greater honesty in their relations with one another?" Other questions concern means to a goal, as in "What are the most sensitive ways of honestly conveying one's feelings or beliefs to another?" But these are all questions of whether or not human behavior is moral, justified, or right.

5:1.3 *Theory and practice* Ethics is a disciplined study, approaching normative problems from a rational, intellectual point of view. It tries to resolve normative issues through the use of rational argumentation and careful consideration of relevant information. It presupposes that value judgments about the conduct of individuals should be well thought out.

Ethics bridges the gap between theory and practice. Obviously it is desirable to reach a reasonable resolution to practical problems of determining your obligations or responsibilities in concrete circumstances. "Should I tell my husband about my pregnancy?" is such a practical question. However, ethics also has the theoretical concern for finding more general principles, the universal moral standards, which can be relied upon in a variety of situations. Ethics thus develops theories of moral obligation, theories of praise and blame, and theories about the meaning of "good."

Ethics has both a practical and a theoretical component. The part that grapples with concrete and specific questions of everyday life can be called *morality*, or *practical* ethics. The main task of morality is to reach normative judgments about conduct that have immediate behavioral implications of a serious and often interpersonal significance; but such judgments are not explicitly theoretical. *Theoretical* ethics may in turn be defined as philosophical reflection upon morality. Philosophically, it tries to discern the general principles or universal moral standards that may be used in grappling with the problems of morality; it is *systematic* in its search for the fundamental justifying norms of conduct; and it is *critical* about such matters as the consistency and the justification of moral claims.

The case study illustrates the contrast between morality and theoretical ethics. Specific, concrete *moral* problems are encountered: Should Dr. Valaquez perform this particular abortion? Should Ingrid Stoner inform her husband? In reflecting upon such questions, you become philosophical to the extent that you focus on the fundamental norms which might govern this conduct. As you consider the general importance of honesty and telling the truth, and the importance of the right to choose and of the right to life, you move beyond the particular circumstances in the case to consideration of fundamental justifying norms of conduct—which is the focus of theoretical ethics. We can think of the normative concerns of both morality and theoretical ethics as part of the general study of ethics. Thus, ethics is *theoretical* as a body of knowledge; yet it is also *practical* as a body of knowledge about and with implications for practice. To be sure, the degree of exactitude that may be obtained in ethical theory is crucially influenced by the complex and fluid nature of its practical subject matter.

5:2.1 *The place of reason in ethics*   You can appraise non-normative statements as true or false, use them as the premises or conclusions of arguments, and argue for or against them by demonstrating their truth (or falsity) with rational proof and relevant information. To give an argument you must appeal to factual or logical information. For example, to show that alcohol is physically addicting, you must use the findings and human implications of biochemistry and medicine. You can conduct experiments and marshal evidence in order to confirm or disconfirm non-normative or value-neutral statements (see Chapter 2).

It is assumed throughout this discussion that normative sentences or claims are assertions or statements because they resemble non-normative statements.[1] First, people *do* from time to time offer arguments in support of normative assertions, just as they argue for other statements. Second, people evaluate the adequacy of these kinds of arguments, calling some reasons offered in support of normative claims better and some weaker, some relevant and others irrelevant. Third, people recognize that certain combinations of normative assertions are consistent with each other, whereas others contradict each other. Similarly, normative claims have entailments. For example, "Robert stole this car" entails "Robert did not own the car."

Normative studies differ widely in terms of their level of rigor and formalism. Logic is rigorous and fully developed, so that there is considerable confidence in the normative statements that it supports. In a large number of cases there is little dispute over how to determine whether a given argument is valid (see Chapter 2). Other normative studies, such as aesthetics, are less rigorous, and the procedures they use to support normative conclusions have not been fully formalized. Nonetheless, one can still make reasonable arguments to the effect that one piece of sculpture is more beautiful or better than another. The normative study of ethics falls someplace between aesthetics and logic in terms of how fully it is developed and how rigorous (and widely accepted) are its methods.

An important step toward understanding what people *mean* by their normative claims is to ask for *reasons* why you should accept their views. Besides offering further insight into what people mean, hearing their arguments and reasons often helps you determine your own position. In the case study, one of Ingrid Stoner's reasons for seeking the abortion is to keep her husband from learning of her affair. You may not share her desire to keep her husband ignorant; you may even be tempted to view that reason as ground to reject her appeal for abortion. However, until you hear people's reasons, it is very hard to stake out your own rational response to their normative statements. Neither uninformed assent nor blind trust is an adequate substitute for seeking the proper interpretation of a person's normative claims along with the reasons offered in support of those claims. The goal of presenting reasons for normative claims is to develop arguments sup-

---

[1]This is a very controversial issue. Philosophers called noncognitivists claim that normative claims cannot be appraised as true or false, because there is no way to *test* or *verify* the claims by observing reality with the senses. For example, you can test by experiment the claim, "Gasoline containing a lead additive is a contributing cause of cancer," but not the claim, "Cancer is a bad thing." According to such philosophers as A. J. Ayer and Charles Stevenson, normative statements have merely *emotive* meaning. Their use is to express your emotional reaction to something rather than to state a fact. David Hume made a similar claim two centuries ago (see Chapter 35).

porting their truth or establishing their wisdom. You should strive for arguments that would persuade unbiased, informed, rational people that your normative positions are correct beyond any reasonable doubt.

5:2.2 *Excuses versus justification*   To justify an action is to explain why the action is correct. Dr. Valaquez believes it is correct for her not to practice medicine in other towns, and on that basis she tries to justify her refusal to follow Ingrid Stoner out of town for the abortion. On the other hand, when you do something wrong for which you do not want to be held responsible, you offer an excuse. For example, you missed the midterm exam because you overslept. The successful excuse gets you off the hook, providing a reason why you should not be held accountable, blamed, or punished for what you did. It does not, however, change the ethical quality of what you did; it does not justify failing to take the exam. Mrs. Stoner believes Dr. Valaquez is simply offering "a flimsy excuse," to use her words, for refusing to do a justifiable abortion. Dr. Valaquez, however, gives no indication that she believes her refusal to leave town is wrong. Therefore, her claim ought to be evaluated as a justification and not as an excuse. It may be hard to distinguish between them, and moreover, you will still have to determine whether the justification or excuse is successful.

5:3.1 *Objectivism and subjectivism*   Normative words like "good" are problematic, especially because of the range of possible meanings these words have. A first step in understanding normative statements is to find out whether a particular claim is meant to be taken *subjectively* or *objectively*. An objectivist interpretation of "X is good" is that X possesses some characteristic that makes it worthy of preference, desire, or value independently of the actual preferences or desires of the speaker. One can express the objectivist interpretation by using such statements as "X is a worthy goal," "X is really the just thing to do even though we wouldn't like it," or "X is our duty." *In the objectivist interpretation a normative claim becomes a statement about what in or about X makes it worthy of being preferred independently of the speaker's actual personal preferences or feelings concerning X.*[2] Dr. Valaquez seems to be pursuing an interpretation of her

---

[2]"Objectivism" in this wide sense should be distinguished from the name of the philosophical position of Ayn Rand. Rand's Objectivist Ethics is one instance of an "objectivist" interpretation, in the wide sense defined here. For she argues that "the standard by which one judges what is good or evil is man's life, or: that which is required for man's survival *qua* man" — and what is required for one's survival may not be what one happens to prefer or desire. (See Rand, *The Virtue of Selfishness* [New York: New American Library, 1964], p. 23.)

remarks that would make her an objectivist. Ingrid Stoner, however, will have nothing to do with Dr. Valaquez's attempts at objectivist reasoning. Instead she persists in making subjectivist claims. The subjectivist interpretation of "X is good" is that the speaker prefers or values X. This preference can be expressed in many ways, for example, "I like X," "I approve of X," "I want X." *In the subjectivist interpretation a normative claim becomes a claim about what is in fact desired or preferred by the speaker.*

5:3.2 *Intrinsic and instrumental value*   Some things are desirable or undesirable in and of themselves, and others are desirable or undesirable as a means to some other end. The former are said to be *intrinsically* good or bad. For example, most people regard pleasure, honor, wisdom, intelligence, virtue, life, liberty, and social harmony as intrinsic goods. Intrinsically bad things include pain, ignorance, boredom, frustration, terror, coercion, and discord. The latter, things desirable or undesirable because they are useful as means to further ends, are called *instrumentally* good or bad. Money is often considered to be the chief instrumental good (asset), and poverty, therefore, the greatest instrumental evil (liability). The same item can be both an asset and a liability as it relates to different consequences, for example, a trip to the dentist. Things like health, peace, and wisdom are both intrinsic and instrumental values.

✒ **PHILOSOPHER'S WORKSHOP**

Intrinsic and Instrumental Value

Aristotle (384–322 B.C.), in *Nicomachean Ethics,* defined ethics as an investigation of conduct that sought to determine the proper norms whereby to judge an action right or wrong. He introduced several distinctions that are still found to be useful, among them that between intrinsic and instrumental value.

. . . Now, the term "good" has obviously two different meanings: (1) things which are intrinsically good, and (2) things which are good as being conducive to the intrinsically good. Let us, therefore, separate the intrinsically good things from the useful things. . . .

Our argument has gradually progressed to the same point at which we were before, and we must try to clarify it still further. Since there are evidently several ends, and since we choose some of these—e.g., wealth, flutes, and instruments generally—as a means to something else, it is obvious that not all ends are final. The highest good, on the other hand, must be something final. Thus, if there is only one final end, this will be the good we are seeking; if there are several, it will be the most final and perfect of them. We call that which is pursued as an end in itself more final than an end which is pursued for the sake of something else; and what is never chosen as a means to something else we call more final than that which is chosen both as an end in itself and as a means to something else. What is always chosen as an end in itself and never as a means to something else is called final in an unqualified sense. This description seems to apply to happiness above all else; for we always choose happiness as an end in itself and never for the sake of something else. Honor, pleasure, intelligence, and all virtue we choose partly for themselves—for we would choose each of them even if no further advantage would accrue from them—but we also choose them partly for the sake of happiness, because we assume that it is through them that we will be happy. On the other hand, no one chooses happiness for the sake of honor, pleasure, and the like, nor as a means to anything at all.[3]

---

[3]Aristotle, *Nicomachean Ethics*, trans. Martin Ostwald (Indianapolis, Ind.: Bobbs-Merrill Co., 1962), pp. 12, 14–15.

The disagreement over telling the truth in the case study illustrates the contrast between intrinsic and instrumental values. Mrs. Stoner views telling her husband the truth purely instrumentally: It is bad because it will make her husband unhappy and disrupt her marriage. Dr. Valaquez, however, seems to believe that telling the truth is intrinsically valuable. She may also think that "honesty is the best policy"—that telling the truth over the long run is an instrumentally valuable practice, and that perhaps Ingrid Stoner's marriage would be improved if she and her husband practiced truth-telling rather than deception.

5:3.3 *Absolute and relative* Because highway safety is a desirable goal, Americans have adopted a convention of driving on the right side of the road. In other countries, such as Great Britain, the convention is to drive on the left side of the road. In the United States and Canada, driving on the right is desirable. It is a *relative* good; that is, it is good relative to American convention, whereas in Great Britain driving on the right is undesirable. However, safe driving is itself desirable in an *absolute* sense.

PHILOSOPHER'S WORKSHOP

Ethics Lexicon

Ethics: the philosophical discipline primarily concerned with the critical evaluation of the justifying norms or standards of personal and interpersonal conduct.

Instrumental value: the quality of being either desirable or undesirable as means to further ends.

Intrinsic value: the quality of being desirable or undesirable as an end in itself.

Subjective value: the quality of being desired or preferred or of being found undesirable by a speaker.

Objective value: the quality of being worthy of being preferred or not preferred independent of personal preferences of the speaker.

Relative value: that which is desirable or undesirable as a function of societal convention, where the convention is thought to be a means to achieving an ultimate end of society.

Absolute value: a value the worth of which is not dependent on the particular situation or conventions of a given society.

Teleological ethics: the variety of ethical theory in which the rightness or wrongness of actions or practices is defined in terms of their instrumental value.

Deontological ethics: the variety of ethical theory in which some actions or practices are thought to be intrinsically right or wrong, i.e., to be intrinsically valuable.

Virtue: a character trait that contributes to the process of leading the good life.

Good-life ethical theory: the variety of ethical theory in which the cultivation of virtue is of primary importance and the concern is to promote the integrity of lives viewed as wholes.

Following the conventions of one's society is viewed as a relative good. It is desirable to follow convention, not because the conventions are intrinsically desirable in themselves, but because they are instrumentally desirable. Conventions are the ways a given society or community has for achieving its further social or communal ends or goals. These goals are viewed by that society as absolutely desirable. Some of the society's goals may be common to all or most civilized communities: avoiding harm, maximizing individual liberties, respecting persons, promoting communal security; it would be at least difficult to specify conditions or conventions when such conduct would be without value. However, it is also an empirical fact that different communities establish vastly different conventions in their pursuits of these widely shared goals. We have not yet inquired whether there are basic human values which transcend all these various social conventions and goals. We also have not addressed the question of why a given society has selected the particular goals it has, but it is clear that they have been selected. In our society, safe, efficient, and fast transportation appears as an absolute value along with maximizing individual liberty, preserving a rule of law, respecting other persons, and respecting property rights. This fact leaves open a basic question of social ethics: What goals *ought* to be selected and given priority?

Nearly all philosophers agree that following conventions is only a relative value; but some philosophers, called *ethical relativists*, claim that even the deepest ethical principles are in some sense relative. This seems to be a *normative* claim: "There should be fundamental differences in the moral standards of different communities or societies." Relativists say, for example, that persons should be respected in some societies but not in others. Ethical relativism is a puzzling view. (1) If it *is* a normative claim, how could you argue for it? The claim is a normative principle applying to all societies, and if deeper normative principles were used as premises to defend the claim, they would have to apply to all societies. Yet the claim implies that the same normative principles should not apply to different soci-

Does our moral ignorance or confusion imply relativism?

© 1959 United Feature Syndicate, Inc.

eties.[4] (2) How are we to apply the claim? How many members of a group (or what percentage of them) have to accept an ethical principle in order for it to become operative for that group? (3) Could a social reformer ever justify the desirability of any changes in the society's existing standards? To justify such a change as an improvement is to imply a standard outside the community against which standards or practices are judged. But the ethical relativist contends that a society should be judged only according to its *own* standards.

5:3.4 *Focus of ethics* Traditionally, ethics has focused on questions of intrinsic and absolute value and on objectivist reasons in support of normative claims because these values and interpretations seem to be the more important, the more fundamental, and the more controversial.

5:4 *Summary* In this chapter you have been introduced to ethics as a fundamental, normative discipline within philosophy. Ethics is primarily concerned with critically evaluating the justifying norms or standards of interpersonal conduct. The normative claims of morality can be supported by reasons. Ethics is concerned to discover the reasons, the fundamental principles of justification, which would be acceptable to unbiased, informed, rational people. However, one must distinguish justifications from excuses. Interpretations of normative statements can also reflect subjectivist or objectivist convictions, intrinsic or instrumental values, and absolute or relative values. Once a person's normative assertion is interpreted and clarified, one is in a far better position to assess the reasons that may be offered in its support.

EXERCISES for Chapter 5

1. Which of the following are normative assertions (5:1.1)?
   A. Frozen yogurt is the best food you can buy.
   B. Soccer is fast becoming a popular sport in America.
   C. A patient with an incompetent doctor is likely to receive poor care.
   D. Not all racists are white.
   E. There should be a law against smoking in hospital rooms.
   F. We should show respect for children as well as adults.
   G. There is nothing quite as important as friendship.
   H. Striking workers broke into the plant last night.

---

[4]So construed the claim commits the fallacy of *self-refutation*. For a fuller discussion of this fallacy, see 33:2.1.

     I. Many adults are attending college these days.

     J. You can't rush Sandra.

     K. Littering should not be tolerated.

2. Which of the following directives are outside the scope of ethics (5:1.2)?
   A. Never shave with a dull blade.
   B. Never shoot guns at people.
   C. Use a tie that matches your socks.
   D. Use deception if it gets you what you want.
   E. Don't spit into the wind.
   F. Don't smoke in bed.
   G. Don't neglect your family.
   H. Don't take what doesn't belong to you.

3. State the difference between practical and theoretical ethics in terms of the concerns of each (5:1.3).

4. What features of normative claims support their being treated as assertions that can reasonably be called true or false (5:2.1)?

5. Characterize the difference between a justification and an excuse. Give examples of each (5:2.2).

6. Provide both subjectivist and objectivist interpretations of items A, C, E, G, and K in Exercise 1 (5:3.1).

7. State the difference between the subjectivist and objectivist interpretation of normative statements (5:3.1).

8. Recalling the examples of things thought to be intrinsically valuable (5: 3.2), write normative statements that express the intrinsic value (or lack of it) of each.

9. Working with the examples of instrumentally valuable things in 5:3.2 or with your own examples, write normative statements that express their instrumental value (or lack of it).

10. Characterize absolute and relative values in terms of intrinsic and instrumental value (5:3.3).

11. Criticize the following argument: "The ruling white minority of South Africa should not be blamed for denying legal equality and civil rights to the majority black population. Their society is different from ours and faced with different circumstances and problems. Therefore, it would be wrong to apply our most basic ethical principles to them." (5:3.3)

SELECTED ANSWERS for Chapter 5

1. The normative assertions are A, C, E, F, G, K.

2. The questions of prudence, etiquette, or technique are A, C, E, F.

3. Practical ethics, often called morality, is concerned with normative judgments that have serious behavioral import and interpersonal significance.

Theoretical ethics is concerned with analyzing, clarifying, and systematically interrelating the principles used to justify conclusions in morality.

4. People argue on behalf of normative claims; they evaluate the reasons offered on their behalf as more or less adequate. People recognize inconsistency between certain parts of normative claims, and they recognize that some normative claims entail other claims, descriptive and normative.

5. To try to justify is to argue that one did right; to try to excuse is to argue that what was done was wrong but the person who did it should not be held to blame.

6. E. (Sub.) I don't like the way smoke smells in hospital rooms.
     (Obj.) Smoking in hospital rooms interferes with the patients' recovery.
   K. (Sub.) I don't approve of littering.
     (Obj.) Littering clutters up the environment, poses a risk to public health, and is expensive to clean up.

8. Here are some examples of such statements:
   A. Pleasure is the only thing that is good in itself.
   B. Wisdom is to be sought for its own sake.

9. Here are some examples expressing instrumental value:
   A. Money is important not for what it is but for what it can buy.
   B. Self-discipline is important because it purifies the spirit and strengthens the will.

11. See footnote 4.

6

What Has Value?

Throughout the history of ethics people have felt the need to find a common ground for agreement about what actions or practices are right or wrong. *Utilitarianism* is an ethical theory which many proponents believe can lead to such agreement. According to the theory, people should seek such agreement by evaluating the consequences of actions or practices, especially the quantifiable aspects. It assumes that actions or practices are right or wrong to the extent that they promote or fail to promote the welfare of those affected by them. However, this theory still leaves important questions open. How is welfare to be conceived? As a utilitarian evaluating human acts, should you focus on their individual utility or on their conformity to rules that have general utility? Should you count equally the consequences for *anyone* who might be affected by an action or practice? That is, should you count equally the consequences for someone else and for yourself? Chapter 6 addresses these questions, and after reading it you should be able to

- State the importance of being able to determine the consequences of alternative actions for utilitarians.
- Distinguish hedonistic utilitarianism from other utilitarian views designed to identify the desirable ends of action and practice.
- Distinguish by examples the act and rule interpretations of utilitarianism.

■ Explain how the foregoing distinction allows ultilitarians to respond to objections that utilitarian moral judgments are counterintuitive.

■ Distinguish among egoistic, limited, and universal utilitarianism.

THE CASE OF I-475

A shaft of sunlight slid between the heavy curtains and cut the committee caucus room in half. The four people sat in the room, three staff people and Chairperson Rose. The chairperson had watched the shaft of light measure out a very long afternoon. "It's time to summarize," she said. "Are we or are we not going to build the highway spur around Toledo, Ohio? What are the consequences of either decision?"

"Need I remind you, Ms. Rose, that it is our policy to build a highway spur only around cities with populations greater than 500,000 through which an interstate highway passes. That is our policy, and it is quite economical in terms of people served per dollar spent."

"Thank you, Mr. Wills, for the needless reminder. Why are you so inflexible? I know Toledo is just below size, but do you know that there are no major highways available to move traffic around the city? There may be need for a highway spur in this case. Tell me the benefits of building a spur around Toledo; don't bother telling me the benefits of the general policy. Yes, Mr. Jackson? Do you want to speak to the issue?"

"Yes, ah . . . excuse me. . . ah, but we cannot build this spur. It would be unfair to build again in a northern state. We should be pumping money into the sunbelt states."

"I am not concerned with what is fair or with petty regionalism, Mr. Jackson. I want you to tell me about the economic, political, and ecological conseqeunces of building or not building. Now if there are political consequences for building in the north, if it hurts our party, then I want to know about that. How bad can it hurt us? . . . Katherine, what are the figures?"

"Sorry, Ms. Rose, I don't have data on that."

"Well, what do you have data about today, Ms. Jenkins?"

Wow! She really is in a mood today. I've never seen her so sarcastic and impatient, thought Katherine Jenkins as she quickly shuffled through her notes. *It's wrong to treat people that way; besides she isn't winning any friends cutting staff people down.* "I figure that the highway spur will have only a marginal effect on the economy of the area. It will help the big motel and restaurant chains; it will hurt some of the small businesses located on existing highways. This follows from our studies on the effects of changed traffic patterns. It should also cost us something in terms of the conversion of excellent farmland into highway. But what a few farmers lose in income is more than made up in what thousands of people will save each day in terms of travel time. The ecological picture is not as clear. Environmentalists will fight us on principle, but there are no particular rare species of animal or plant life in jeopardy. I think the issue of the aesthetic effects will be raised, but we can beat the rap in court, if it comes to a battle. Most of the business establishment in that area will be on our side; money still is more valuable than beauty in northwest Ohio."

"Well, thank you Kathy, and what about the political impact? I don't think our people will be very happy if we lose them votes, and what will that do for our committee?"

"I really can't say for sure, Ms. Rose; but I think we will lose only a few farm votes and probably pick up four or five times as many votes from labor because of all the jobs we'll be creating in an election year."

"Excuse me, Ms. Rose, but are we concerned with the consequences for the people of Toledo, for the people from Ohio and Michigan who now must use I-75 through Toledo, for the party, or for our own jobs?" The anger in Mr. Jackson's voice was not concealed.

"I don't think you'll have to worry about your job much longer!" Chairperson Rose's face flashed as she pushed herself away from the table. "This staff caucus is over." She stormed out of the room, and the dust she raised from out of the thick carpet sparkled in the shaft of sunlight that still divided the room.

6:1.1 *Utilitarianism and "the good"*   Utilitarianism is a theory for reaching agreement among persons about ethical matters. According to the theory, people can reach agreement about the value of states of affairs, because these states of affairs involve certain identifiable characteristics which form the basis of agreement. The most elaborate attempt to develop a means of calculating and predicting that value was made in the early days of the theory by one of its founders, Jeremy Bentham (1748–1832).

Utilitarian theorists ask themselves: What makes a state of affairs good or bad? Their answer contrasts with ancient theories of what is desirable. The latter assumed that human beings have an essence, or basic nature (see Chapter 11), and in turn, that there is something essentially or naturally good for humans to pursue because it entails the development or the fulfillment of the potential in that nature (see Chapter 12). Utilitarianism does not make such assumptions. Rather, it focuses on the subjective preferences of individuals concerning what is desirable. In this view, individuals know themselves best and are therefore best able to determine their own good. Utilitarians thus argue that what the individual desires (provided that it does not harm others) is what the individual ought to pursue. Liberty and personal autonomy are detectable underlying values here. Indeed, utilitarians may suggest that knowing oneself and choosing for oneself are themselves conditions of personal happiness.

6:1.2 *Pleasure and happiness*   Utilitarians disagree about what human beings will ultimately choose for themselves. The two classical positions are (1) that pleasure (Bentham) is the only thing of intrinsic value to people and thus worthy of pursuit and (2) that happiness (John Stuart Mill) is the singular intrinsic value worthy of pursuit.[1] Thus, in Bentham's view actions and practices are right if they lead to pleasure (or prevent pain) and wrong if they lead to pain (or prevent pleasure). His method of determining the rightness or wrongness of actions thus became known as the "hedonic calculus," a method of calculating pleasure and pain and the likelihood of their occurrence. Sensual pleasures and the avoidance of physical pain are to be considered as well as such pleasures as anticipation and satisfaction of completing a task and such pains as frustration and anguish, that is, those pleasures and pains that are the by-products of any of the varieties of human activity.

---

[1]Bentham's version of utilitarianism is called "hedonistic," from the Greek word, *hedone* (pleasure); Mill's version is called "eudaimonistic," from the Greek word *eudaimonia* (happiness).

 **PHILOSOPHER'S WORKSHOP**

Bentham's Hedonic Calculus

In *An Introduction to the Principles of Morals and Legislation* (1789) Bentham addresses the question of how to measure the value of pleasure and pain.

I. Pleasures then, and the avoidance of pains, are the ends which the legislator has in view: it behoves him therefore to understand their *value*. Pleasures and pains are the *instruments* he has to work with: it behoves him therefore to understand their force, which is again, in other words, their value.

II. To a person considered *by himself*, the value of a pleasure or pain considered *by itself*, will be greater or less, according to the four following circumstances:
   1. Its *intensity*.
   2. Its *duration*.
   3. Its *certainty* or *uncertainty*.
   4. Its *propinquity* or *remoteness*.

III. These are the circumstances which are to be considered in estimating a pleasure or pain considered each of them by itself. But when the value of any pleasure or pain is considered for the purpose of estimating the tendency of any *act* by which it is produced, there are two other circumstances to be taken into the account; these are,

5. Its *fecundity*, or chance it has of being followed by sensations of the *same* kind: that is, pleasures, if it be a pleasure: pains, if it be a pain.

6. Its *purity*, or the chance it has of *not* being followed by sensations of the *opposite* kind: that is, pains, if it be a pleasure: pleasures, if it be a pain.

These two last, however, are in strictness scarcely to be deemed properties of the pleasure or the pain itself; they are not, therefore, in strictness to be taken into the account of the value of that pleasure or that pain. They are in strictness to be deemed properties only of the act, or other event, by which such pleasure or pain has been produced; and accordingly are only to be taken into account of the tendency of such act or such event.

IV. To a *number* of persons, with reference to each of whom the value of a pleasure or a pain is considered, it will be greater or less, according to seven circumstances: to wit, the six preceding ones . . . and one other, to wit:

7. Its *extent;* that is, the number of persons to whom it *extends;* or (in other words) who are affected by it.[2]

---

[2]Jeremy Bentham, *An Introduction to the Principles of Morals and Legislation*, in *The Works of Jeremy Bentham*, ed. John Bowring [1838–1843] (New York: Russell and Russell, 1962), Vol. I, p. 16.

Some have held, Mill among them, that *happiness* is the only thing of intrinsic value, and moreover, that happiness is not merely the sum total of pleasures of whatever variety. In this view, utilitarianism believes that actions and practices are right if they lead to happiness (or prevent unhappiness). The good, interpreted as happiness, is not merely the sum total of pleasures because there are important qualitative as well as quantitative differences among them. Thus, two lives of equal pleasure, quantitatively, may be of different value because the one includes the enjoyment of pleasures of higher quality. Such "higher" pleasures would include those of the intellect, the appreciation of culture, and the general refinement of sensibilities. In this view these more intellectual, spiritual pleasures are preferable to more sensual pleasures, such as eating and sex. In turn, actions and

Peanuts by Charles Schulz. © 1978 United Feature Syndicate, Inc.

Has Linus considered the correct consequences according to Bentham's Calculus? Is it ever possible to consider all the relevant consequences?

practices that contribute to the living of a life filled with higher pleasures are also deemed preferable.[3]

6:1.3 *Fundamental utilitarian agreement* Utilitarians all agree that it is some kind of state of human consciousness that has intrinsic value. Thus, the state of affairs we are always trying to produce, according to the utilitarian, is one of consciousness.

---

[3]See the discussion of Mill's qualitative distinction between pleasures in Chapter 12.

No generally satisfactory method for resolving this difficulty has ever been found.

PHILOSOPHER'S WORKSHOP

The Desirable and the Desired

John Stuart Mill (1806–1873) argued that the ultimate good for people is not pleasure but happiness. His argument is based on the claim that each person in fact finds his or her own happiness desirable. Thus he infers that the general happiness of society is what ought to be regarded as desirable.

The only proof capable of being given that an object is visible, is that people actually see it. The only proof that a sound is audible, is that people hear it: and so of the other sources of our experience. In like manner, I apprehend, the sole evidence it is possible to produce that anything is desirable, is that people do actually desire it. If the end which the utilitarian doctrine proposes to itself were not, in theory and practice, acknowledged to be an end, nothing could ever convince any person that it was so. No reason can be given why the general happiness is desirable, except that each person, so far as he believes it to be attainable, desires his own happiness. This, however, being a fact, we have not only all the proof which the case admits of, but all which it is possible to require, that happiness is a good, that each person's happiness is a good to that person, and the general happiness, therefore, a good to the aggregate of all persons. Happiness has made out its title as *one* of the ends of conduct, and consequently one of the criteria of morality.[4]

According to the Greatest Happiness Principle. . . the ultimate end, with reference to and for the sake of which all other things are desirable (whether we are considering our own good or that of other people) is an existence exempt as far as possible from pain, and as rich as possible in enjoyments, both in point of quantity and quality; the test of quality, and the rule for measuring it against quantity, being the preference felt by those who, in their opportunities of experience, to which must be added their habits of self-consciousness and self-observation, are best furnished with the means of comparison.[5]

How convincing do you find this argument? Does the fact that people desire a thing *really* make it desirable? (What does "desirable" mean here?) Do you agree that if *each* person's happiness is good to that person, the general happiness is a good for *all*?

---

[4]John Stuart Mill, *Utilitarianism*, ed. J. M. Robson, in *Collected Works of John Stuart Mill*, Vol. X (Toronto: University of Toronto Press, 1969), 234.
[5]*Ibid.*, p. 214.

Both Bentham and Mill were concerned about social change and reform. They believed that political, economic, and environmental consequences ultimately translate into changes in the states of consciousness of those affected by them. Thus, all the deliberation in the case study may be understood as deliberation about whether building a highway spur will promote the greatest pleasure or happiness for the people affected.

6:2.1 *Act and rule utilitarianism* The case study illustrates a concern about the place of moral rules in governing conduct. Building the highway spur would be an exception to the general policy defined by a specific rule. As the members deliberate, two views arise, those held by what have come to be called act and rule utilitarian theorists. Both act and rule utilitarians agree that the ultimate measure of the rightness or wrongness of human conduct is the tendency of that conduct to result in good consequences (pleasure or happiness). But the crucial question is this: Do we apply this ultimate measure to individual actions or to general practices which are described by the rules that govern them? *Act utilitarianism* is the view that *an action is right or wrong as a function of the specific consequences of that particular action. Rule utilitarianism* is the view that *the evaluation of the rightness or wrongness of an action is a two-step process. First, one must determine whether the act is in conformity with an acceptable rule of conduct.* Second, and ultimately, *one must determine the acceptabil-*

ity of the rule in question by evaluating the utility of the practice that the rule governs. In the act view, the utility of the act is primary; in the rule view, the utility of the rule. You should note that the case study illustrates how the two views could dictate different actions in concrete circumstances. The act theory would require that the road be built; the rule theory that it would not.

Could it not be objected against act utilitarianism that moral rules surely have some point? Yes, but in the act utilitarian view, moral rules are not dismissed as altogether pointless but are interpreted as handy guides. They are viewed as rules of thumb — to aid in decision-making when one is in circumstances very much like other, earlier circumstances where similar decisions have been made. However, all such rules can be suspended, especially when circumstances arise unlike those to which the rule ordinarily has been applied. In the case study, Chairperson Rose would suspend the ordinarily reliable and useful rule in light of the unique circumstances of Toledo and the possibility of promoting the welfare of citizens who live or travel near it.

6:2.2 *Objections to act utilitarianism*   The act utilitarian regards breaking promises, killing, and the like as wrong simply because, as a matter of statistical generalization, such acts tend to have undesirable results. But statistical generalizations admit of exceptions, and thus act utilitarians claim that moral rules against killing and so forth are not, in themselves, binding upon human conduct. Rather they regard rules as usually reliable guides to behavior, based on calculations of the consequences of past actions. Rules, so conceived, are a practical shorthand in decision-making, but they carry no moral authority. Critics object to this interpretation of the place of rules in normative theory and practice. Should an innocent person, for example, be punished for a crime, to deter would-be criminals and make society safer? The innocent person might suffer a great deal, but this suffering would, in some cases, be outweighed by the social good produced by the punishment. For example, by "setting an example" one might stop a severe crimewave. The act utilitarian would continue to follow the rule, "Punish only guilty persons," in general. But punishing innocent persons even in exceptional circumstances strikes many critics as unacceptable.

6:2.3 *Objections to rule utilitarianism*   The rule utilitarian views exceptional cases differently: It is sometimes right to do things that can be known in advance not to have the best possible consequences. For example, you should not punish an innocent person, even if it *would* stop a crimewave. But is this view consistent? How can a *utilitarian* view, which judges human conduct in terms of consequences, ever sanction doing things that are known not to maximize the good? This view also flies in the face of common intuitions, for example, that some rules (e.g. keep your promises) can legitimately be broken when a great good (e.g. saving many lives) is at stake.

6:3.1 *Classical utilitarianism as universalistic.*   The principal remaining question is: Pleasure or happiness for whom? Classical utilitarians hold that you must consider the consequences for all who might be affected by your action or practice—which is why they are called *univeralistic* utilitarians. They are committed to *egalitarianism,* that is, the view that each person counts equally in one's normative deliberations. Each person counts for one: You count for one if you are affected by the decision that you make, as does each other person affected. Therefore, you are called upon to assume an attitude of personal disinterest, meaning that you are not to judge the situation on the basis of feelings or emotions you have because of your own involvement in the situation or the involvement of persons dear to you. In contrast, you are to assume an attitude of *generalized benevolence:* The interests of all human beings, and perhaps, all sentient creatures, count equally and are equally valuable to you.

In the case study, Mr. Jackson objects to Chairperson Rose's limiting consideration to consequences for the party members. He expresses a classical universalistic concern for all the people who may be affected by the decision.

6:3.2 *Nonuniversalistic utilitarianism*   Other utilitarians contend that you should take into account only consequences for identifiable groups, such as (1) the agent and no one else *or* (2) everyone else excluding the agent *or* (3) a select group of persons (including or excluding the agent). These contrasting views may be called (1) egoistic utilitarianism, (2) altruistic utilitarianism, and (3) limited utilitarianism. (1) The first is the view that in making normative judgments you should evaluate only those consequences that apply to yourself; no other consequences are relevant. (2) The sole difference between altruistic and universalistic utilitarianism is that the former excludes you, as the agent, from being considered at all, although each of the others who might be affected by an action or practice is considered. (3) Limited utilitarianism is appealing to those who believe it important to be impartially concerned for others, but not *all* others. Anyone who believes you should be exclusively concerned about the well-being of your race, nation, family, or the members of some particular group or organization may be a limited utilitarian. For example, you would be a limited utilitarian if you held the view that the United States government should concern itself solely with that which is good for America and never consider seriously how American policy affects the citizens of other nations.

Classical utilitarians have preferred their universalistic position because of their belief that the well-being of each person (including the agent) is of equal moral concern. They believe that being moral requires taking into account the effect of your actions or practices upon those who happen not to be members of select groups of favorites. Moreover, they find great practical difficulty in (1) selecting on moral grounds alone which of several groups to prefer and (2) deciding what they ought to do when alternative courses would benefit different groups of which they are members.

6:4 *Summary*   In this chapter we have introduced utilitarianism as an ethical theory about what actions and practices are right or wrong. The basic method for deciding the matter is the evaluation of the consequences brought about by the actions or practices. Bentham's and Mills's alternate views of what consequent states of affairs are desirable, that is pleasure or happiness, were presented. Act and rule utilitarian theories were distinguished as being concerned primarily about the consequences of particular actions or general rules, respectively. Classical utilitarian theory was characterized as universalistic rather than egoistic, altruistic, or limited. Its concern is to weigh the consequences for any and all who might be affected by actions or practices.

EXERCISES for Chapter 6

1. Why do utilitarian theorists concern themselves with trying to determine the consequences of alternative courses of action (6:1.1)?

2. Describe a case in which a hedonistic utilitarian would disagree with another utilitarian who also believed in the greatest good for the greatest number (6:1.2).

3. a. State the contrasting interpretations that act and rule utilitarians would make of the following moral rules.
   A. Stealing is wrong.
   B. Honesty is the best policy.
   b. What justification does each offer for its interpretation? Make sure that in stating each justification, its utilitarian character is clear.

4. A rule utilitarian might argue that a particular action should be undertaken, whereas an act utilitarian would argue that the same action should be avoided. Describe a case in which such a conflict between act and rule utilitarianism would arise (6:2.1).

5. In each of the following sets of comments one expresses a universalistic utilitarianism and the others express egoistic, altruistic, or limited utilitarianism. Classify each.
   a. A. Everyone would be better off if we shared what we had.
      B. If I gave away all of mine to the rest of you, you all would be better off.
      C. The men among us would do better if the women didn't get as much.
   b. A. If each of you put in $10, I would have an additional $50 to spend as I choose.
      B. I can understand how you are thinking, but it's better for everyone in my department if we do not comply with the policy.
      C. Although there may be some difficulties here and there, the total institution would benefit in the long run if we shifted our method of billing students.

SELECTED ANSWERS for Chapter 6

1. In seeking intersubjective agreement, they try to evaluate actions or practices in terms of the states of affairs produced. Thus, determining precisely what consequent states of affairs an action or practice will bring about is crucial to evaluating that action or practice.

2. Your case should involve a conflict between the greatest good understood in terms of sensual and other pleasures and in terms of other factors, such as culturally, spirtually, or intellectually produced happiness.

3. a. A. *Act:* In the past, the consequences of individual acts of stealing have usually been bad.
      Rule: A policy of not tolerating stealing has good consequences.
   B. *Act:* In the past, the consequences of acting honestly have been better than the consequences of dishonest acts.
      Rule: A policy of acting honestly has better consequences than any policy of dishonesty.
   b. *Act:* The best possible consequences for everybody will occur if the best possible consequences for each act occur.
      Rule: Having rules and general practices allows people to know what to expect if they act in various fashions. Having this knowledge has great utility because it allows people to make plans and take actions based on these expectations.

4. In your case the rule utilitarian should emphasize the general utility of following the rule, whereas the act utilitarian should emphasize the undesirable consequences of following the rule in this particular case.

5. a. A. Universalistic.
      B. Altruistic.
      C. Limited.

    b. A. Egoistic.

        B. Limited (or egoistic depending on whether the emphasis is on "my" department or "all the people" in one specific department).

        C. Universalistic (assuming that only persons belonging to the institution will be affected).

What Is My Duty?

If, as utilitarians suggest, happiness, or some other state of consciousness, alone has intrinsic value, then actions have only instrumental value. Ethical theorists who have rejected this belief are known as *deontologists*. They are convinced that the rightness or wrongness of certain actions is independent of their consequences and that certain actions are intrinsically valuable. In this chapter we will introduce the views of Immanuel Kant, probably the most influential advocate of deontology.

After reading Chapter 7, you should be able to

- Distinguish deontological from consequentialist reasons for doing things.
- Provide a deontological explanation of the value of rules.
- Provide initially plausible examples of intrinsically valuable actions.
- State the three formulations of the Categorical Imperative as defined by Kant.
- Explain why actions or practices contrary to each of the three formulations of the Categorical Imperative can be viewed as intrinsically wrong.
- Explain how an action that leads to undesirable consequences can be evaluated as intrinsically right on deontological grounds.

THE CASE OF BIOLOGY 101

"There, what do you think, Tom?"

"Think about what?"

"What do you think about how I look?"

"You look like you always do, Joe."

"Good! Then Dr. Kerns won't catch me."

"Catch you? Do you mean Kerns, the biology prof? . . . Joe, are you going to cheat on the final?"

"Sure. Everyone's doing it these days."

"That doesn't mean you should do it."

"Oh, I'm not saying I should do it because they all are. I'm saying that the fact that others cheat makes the exam an unfair measure of my knowledge. I have to cheat to protect my grade."

"Kerns doesn't grade on a curve; besides, the fact that others cheat doesn't make you any smarter."

"But, Tom, I've got to have a good grade. I'm in pre-med. If my grades are poor I won't qualify for . . ."

"I know, for med school. Well if your grades are poor you don't deserve to qualify for med school. Besides if you cheat your way through school, you'll probably be a poor doctor. I wouldn't want you for a doctor; you would probably have to ask your receptionist for help making a diagnosis! Or are you going to write the names of diseases on your shirt cuff?"

"That's not called for, Tom. I'll study medicine; it's just these other courses, the ones that are not really important, that I let slip a little."

"Oh, like biology is not important for a physician?"

"Come on, man. Who's ever going to know? Who even cares? How can a little cheating on one final exam by one innocent freshman do the world any serious long-range harm?"

"But what if everyone cheated? What if we all said what you said, that it doesn't really matter? What a joke the whole idea of examinations would become."

"Who cares?"

"It doesn't matter who cares. It's wrong to cheat. It's like lying or not keeping your word. Don't you have any self-respect? Don't you respect the prof or your classmates?"

"Wow, you moralists can be tough. Are you as tough on yourself as you are on other people? Why don't you practice what you preach? Tell me you never took a piece of candy from a store, never stole a few cents from your parents, never drove over the speed limit, never looked at a classmate's paper on an exam. Tell me, holy one."

"I can't say I never did those things. I'm saying only that I shouldn't have. They are wrong and we shouldn't do them. I don't really care how important your goals are, or how noble your cause is. You ought not to cheat to get what you want. Cheating is wrong!"

"I never realized how much it bothered you. Sorry I ever brought it up, Tom. Let's forget it."

"Well are you going to cheat on the Bio exam, or not?"

"I said we should forget it. It's none of your damn business, now is it? And people should mind their own business, right?"

7:1.1 *Deontological ethics*   The view that some actions are intrinsically valuable or right and others intrinsically wrong is the central tenet of *deontological ethical theory.* In other words, we are duty-bound to some courses of action, regardless of the consequences. As such, deontology contrasts with any ethical theory that makes the rightness or wrongness of actions a matter of their consequences. If you hold that promises ought to be kept simply because you made them and thereby committed yourself to keeping them, your view that promise-keeping is intrinsically right is deontological. This belief contrasts with the view that you should keep or break promises depending upon which course of action has the superior consequences. The case of stealing is similar. We regard taking others' property as wrong simply because it is theirs, not because we benefit less from having it than the rightful owners. Our common ethical intuitions lend plausibility to deontological views of keeping promises and stealing as being intrinsically right and wrong, respectively.

Another example is provided in the case study. Joe thinks of cheating on the exam in terms of its good consequences for him. It will "protect his grade" and help him to get into medical school. Tom first points out that cheating might have poor consequences in making Joe a less proficient physician. However, Tom ultimately argues that regardless of the consequences of cheating, cheating is itself wrong. This position is deontological.

7:1.2 *"Whatever the consequences"*   How could a utilitarian account for the belief that keeping promises is right whereas stealing and cheating are wrong? Utilitarians have argued that rules governing such practices have the great utility of promoting social stability. Keeping promises and refraining from stealing or cheating are, on this account, instrumentally good in promoting trust among persons; and clearly trust is not only pleasant, it has the good consequence of promoting interpersonal cooperation.

Deontologists, however, find such accounts inadequate. They

often refer to promises made to persons on their death beds. It seems that such promises ought to be kept as much as any others, and yet, a general utilitarian reason seems difficult to provide. Breaking the promises cannot undermine trust between the parties to the promises if the promisee is dead; nor is the trust of others lost if no others knew of the promise.

7:2.1 *Kantian ethics and the Categorical Imperative*   The ethical theory of Immanuel Kant (1724–1804) may be readily interpreted as a prime example of *deontological theory*.[1] His theory attempts to specify most fundamentally what there is about an action that makes it intrinsically valuable. He holds that people have unqualified duties, duties that are not merely *hypothetical* but also universal and *categorical*. Categorical duties are those that exist under all possible circumstances. Hypothetical duties exist merely under certain specifiable conditions, for example, on the condition that you have a particular desire. In Kant's view morality is focused on unconditional categorical duties. It is intrinsically right, Kant argues, to do your categorical duties.

More concretely, morality, according to Kant, is not a matter of rationally pursuing your own self-interest.[2] Neither is it a matter of rationally coordinating the interests of the majority of the people (universal utilitarianism). Neither is it merely a matter of conformity to convention and performing your duties as they arise within, and are conditioned by, social or legal conventions.[3] Thus, morality is not a matter of pursuing any hypothetical or conditional ends, be they the production of good consequences or the preservation of arbitrarily constructed conventions. According to Kant, morality is fundamentally a matter of doing your categorical duties.

You can read the case study as illustrating the contrast between hypothetical and categorical duties. Tom argues that Joe has a categorical duty not to cheat on the exam. The duty is not hypothetical because it is not conditioned by considerations of any future benefits for Joe or others involved, nor by any particular conventions that may govern exam-taking at Joe's college. In Tom's view, Joe's action is wrong independently of whether or not any honor code might prohibit it. In contrast, Joe takes the question of his cheating hypothetically: *If* he needs grades for medical school, *if* others cheat, *then* what should he do?

---

[1] See Chapter 36 for an account of Kant's entire philosophical world view.

[2] The view that you should seek only your own self-interest is called *ethical egoism*. This includes both egoistic utilitarianism (6:3.2) and enlightened self-interest (8:4.2).

[3] This view is sometimes called *cultural* or *social relativism* in ethics. See the discussion of ethical relativism in 5:3.3.

7:2.2 *First formulation*　What is our categorical duty? Kant offered three distinct formulations of the Categorical Imperative in an attempt to make himself clear on this point. He did not see these three formulations as statements of three distinct categorical duties, but as alternative ways of specifying the same duty. Thus, each formulation provides only one possible perspective, or insight, into the single categorical duty which is definitive of morality for Kant. The three formulations are equivalent to each other. Any rule of action which is proved to be a duty under one formulation can be proved to be a duty under the other two formulations according to Kant.

The first formulation of the Categorical Imperative is "So act that the maxim of your will could always hold at the same time as a principle establishing universal law." This formulation means that one should act in such a way that the principles governing one's actions can be universalized; no arbitrary distinctions between persons are to be permitted in those principles. Of course roles, abilities, and circumstances are relevant to the specification of precisely what actions are being performed and what principles are being followed. Kant's point is that despite these disclaimers, an action can be morally permissible for *one* person only if that same action is permissible for *anyone in the same situation.*

Kant was concerned with universalizability because he viewed

As Kant said, "What if everybody acted that way?"

©1968 United Feature Syndicate, Inc.

inequitable or unfair exceptions for particular persons as immoral. Consider first whether breaking a promise for personal convenience could become a universal practice. Kant believes not, for not everyone could indulge in the practice. Although a few could do so, if everyone were to attempt it, then no promises would be taken seriously. Ironically, the idea of deliberately insincere promise-making involves a conceptual inconsistency. Suppose everyone made promise-like declarations with the mental qualification "that is, unless I just don't feel like it." In such a society, no one would accept any of these declarations as ways of giving one's word unconditionally. Similarly, if everybody indiscriminately used resources no matter to whom they belonged, the institution of private property would be impossible.

In the case study, Tom is willing to hold that there can be no exceptions to the duties he espouses. When challenged by Joe concerning his past, minor transgressions, Tom makes no exception for himself in finding that those actions, too, were categorically wrong. He finds the cheating of the others in Joe's class to be just as wrong as Joe's cheating would be. Similar acts by similar agents in similar circumstances are equally right or equally wrong.

7:2.3 *Second formulation*   Kant's second formulation of the Categorical Imperative is "Act so as to treat humanity, whether in your own person or in that of another, always as an end and never as a means only." If the moral law applies to all persons, as the first formulation indicates, then all persons shall count as equally valuable. It cannot be moral, then, that any person's goals can be regarded as so important that another person is used only as a means to accomplish these goals. In this view, there is a categorical duty to treat other persons as human beings with value in themselves rather than as tools or machines. It is this intrinsic value that distinguishes persons from other things, the value of which is merely instrumental. This is a claim that to each person is due, minimally, a higher kind of respect, an inviolable dignity, incompatible with being brainwashed, made into a docile instrument for the purposes of others, enslaved, manipulated, or converted into a domesticated animal. To fail to accord persons this minimal respect is to blur the distinction between persons and things; it is disrespectful of human moral autonomy.

In the case study, it is possible to construe cheating on the exam as exploitation of students by fellow students. The cheaters subordinate the interests of fellow students in earning good grades to their own interests. The cheaters treat the honest students as having merely instrumental value, for their honesty makes the cheaters seem to have done better on the exam.

It is important for you to notice Kant's exact wording in this second formulation. He states the imperative as that of treating humanity always as an end and never as a means *only*. Kant would raise no objection to studying with a friend since it is not only a means of advancing one's ends but also a way of respecting one's friend; but he would categorically prohibit cheating because cheating involves using fellow students and the professor only as means.

✐ PHILOSOPHER'S WORKSHOP

The Categorical Imperative

In the following excerpts from *Fundamental Principles of the Metaphysics of Morals*, Kant distinguishes categorical from hypothetical imperatives. He then presents his three formulations of the Categorical Imperative.

All *imperatives* command either *hypothetically* or *categorically*. Hypothetical imperatives declare a possible action to be practically necessary as a means to the attainment of something else that one wills (or that one may will). A categorical imperative would be one which represented an action as objectively necessary in itself apart from its relation to a further end. . . . Hence if the action would be good solely as a means to *something else*, the imperative is *hypothetical*; if the action is represented as good in *itself* and therefore as necessary, in virtue of its principle, for a will which of itself accords with reason, then the imperative is *categorical*.[4]

When I conceive a *hypothetical* imperative in general, I do not know beforehand what it will contain—until its condition is given. But if I conceive a *categorical* imperative, I know at once what it contains. For since besides the law this imperative contains only the necessity that our maxim should conform to this law, while the law, as we have seen, contains no condition to limit it, there remains nothing over to which the maxim has to conform except the universality of a law as such; and it is this conformity alone that the imperative properly asserts to be necessary.

There is therefore only a single categorical imperative and it is this: "*Act only on that maxim through which you can at the same time will that it should become a universal law*" . . .[5]

---

[4]Immanuel Kant, *The Groundwork of the Metaphysic of Morals*, trans. H. J. Paton (New York: Harper Torch Books, 1975), p. 82.
[5]*Ibid.*, p. 88

. . . The ground of this principle is: *Rational nature exists as an end in itself.* This is the way in which a man necessarily conceives his own existence: it is therefore so far a *subjective* principle of human actions. But it is also the way in which every other rational being conceives his existence on the same rational ground which is valid also for me; hence it is at the same time an *objective* principle, from which, as a supreme practical ground, it must be possible to derive all laws for the will. The practical imperative will therefore be as follows: *Act in such a way that you always treat humanity, whether in your own person or in the person of any other, never simply as a means, but always at the same time as an end. . .*[6]

. . . Thus morality consists in the relation of all action to the making of laws whereby alone a kingdom of ends is possible. This making of laws must be found in every rational being himself and must be able to spring from his will. The principle of his will is therefore never to perform an action except on a maxim such as can also be a universal law, and consequently *such that the will can regard itself as at the same time making universal law by means of its maxim.*[7]

[6]*Ibid.*, p. 96
[7]*Ibid.*, p. 101.

7:2.4 *Third formulation*   Kant's third formulation of the Categorical Imperative is "Act according to the maxims of a universally legislative member of a merely potential kingdom of ends." Although the language here is complicated, this formulation seems based on the following Kantian reasoning: If individuals are always to be treated as ends and never solely as tools, then each person must recognize that everyone is morally in an equal position, that is, in effect, to note that all persons belong to the same moral community. Persons who come to this realization recognize two things: (1) They can legitimately pursue those of their goals that do not conflict with the duty never to treat others solely as tools but as ends, and (2) they have a duty to facilitate the same possibility for all others. In other words, society should be organized so as to promote each person's freedom and facilitate expressing this freedom within the boundaries of the moral law. Thus, this third formulation could be read as indicating that persons have a categorical duty to behave in such a way that the principles that govern their actions could be adopted by everyone and serve as the basis for a moral community governed by mutual respect.

Educational and other service institutions of society are established for the purpose of helping persons to develop their capacities and utilize their freedom. In the moral community Kant envisions in the third formulation of the Categorical Imperative, such help would be a person's concern in every action.

7:3.1 *Respect*   To respect a person is to appreciate him or her for his or her capacity to flourish. It is to know and appreciate both his or her potentials for suffering. Showing respect for persons amounts to allowing (not interfering with), and in some circumstances even facilitating, them to flourish or to exercise their capacities that have intrinsic value. In this way respect for persons may be viewed as *intrinsically valuable.*

Kant believes that all persons are intrinsically valuable because they have the capacities to function as self-aware, rational, autonomous beings. This belief is the ground for his claim that to each person there is due, minimally, a higher kind of respect. If someone does something to hurt you physically, the disregard of your rational self-awareness is wrong in its disrespect for you, regardless of whether or not the person succeeds in harming you. It is the higher capacities of persons, such as self-awareness and autonomy, that make them worthy of respect. If this is so, then we have uncovered one possible ultimate justification for the deontologists' thesis that there are intrinsically right actions: those that are respectful of the potentials and capacities intrinsically valuable in persons.

7:3.2 *Conscience*   Kant points out that no one can foresee perfectly all the consequences of his or her action. He argues that whether any action is good or bad cannot, therefore, be judged on the basis of something that cannot even be foreseen. However, a person can know the principle on which he or she acts, which for Kant becomes the basis for judging the rightness or wrongness of the action. If the person acts on a principle which satisfies the Categorical Imperative, that is, acts so as to respect persons and their capacity for intrinsic value, then the action is intrinsically right. Kant also provides a way of evaluating moral agents. If a person acts upon a principle *because* it satisfies the Categorical Imperative, then the action has "moral worth." In this case the agent is acting in good conscience or with a "good will." Part of Kant's claim here is that to intend to respect persons is to intend to bring it about *as best one can foresee* that people are respected in all those ways we have briefly described. Thus, in Kant's view, it is the agent's *intention* that determines whether the action has moral worth. In contrast, consequentialist theories would pass moral judgment on an action exclusively in terms of the consequences the action produces, for example, the personal or social benefits it yields.

7:4 *Summary*   In this chapter we have explored deontological ethical theory. As contrasted to consequentialist theory, deontology argues that some actions are intrinsically right or wrong, not merely instrumentally so. Kant's theory of the Categorial Imperative was presented as an instance of deontological theory. He maintained that there is a Categorial Imperative, distinguishable from all hypothetical imperatives. We have interpreted three formulations of the Kantian Categorical Imperative as reflecting Kant's concerns that (1) moral principles be universalizable, (2) they reflect a concern to treat people as ends rather than solely as means, and (3) they be principles that could serve as the basis for a moral community governed by mutual respect. We further explored the foundations of Kantian theory in the concepts of respect for persons and acting according to conscience.

EXERCISES for Chapter 7

1. Alternative reasons for doing a certain thing are given below. Identify the consequentialist reasons *(CR)* and the deontological reasons *(DR)*. Some reasons are neither *CR* nor *DR* (7:1.2–7:3.1).
   a. Giving children a chance to help with housework.
      A. It's likely to help keep them out of trouble.
      B. It's widely accepted that children should handle routine chores.
      C. It's a way of showing respect for them as family members.
   b. Returning borrowed things promptly.
      A. It's what you would want everyone to do.
      B. It makes others feel you're reliable and worthy of trust.
      C. It's pretty much expected that you should not keep borrowed things too long.
   c. Giving secretarial help at least the government established minimum wage.
      A. It's against the law not to pay these people the minimum wage.
      B. If you don't, you won't be able to attract qualified employees.
      C. It's exploitive not to.
   d. Avoid making promises you know you can't keep.
      A. It's not in your own interest to mislead people about what you can do for them.
      B. It would be an impossible world if everyone made promises they could not keep.
      C. It's not something you would want everyone to do.
      D. Making unkeepable promises shows very little respect for others.
      E. In our culture people who are discovered to make such promises are scorned. You wouldn't like to be scorned, would you?

        F. It's generally better for everyone if people make only those promises that they can keep.

2. Utilitarian theorists justify rules by appeal to their instrumental value. How do deontologists justify there being rules of ethical conduct (7:1.1– 7:1.2)?

3. Give four examples of practices that seem plausibly to have intrinsic value, either positive or negative (7:3.1, 7:3.2).

4. What are the three alternative formulations of the Categorical Imperative according to Kant? How should each be interpreted (7:2.2–7:2.4)?

5. What reasons can be advanced in order to explain why
    a. practices that are not universalizable are wrong (7:2.2)?
    b. practices that treat other people simply as tools are wrong (7:2.3)?
    c. practices not conducive to establishing a moral community are wrong (7:2.4)?

6. From the consequentialist point of view if an action or practice leads to bad consequences it is wrong. Explain why this is not necessarily so for deontologists (7:3.1, 7:3.2).

7. In the light of the definition of the meanings and importance of respect (7:3.1), what is the meaning and importance of self-respect?

SELECTED ANSWERS for Chapter 7

1. a. A. *CR*.
    B. Neither: a reason based on social convention.
    C. *DR*.
  b. A. *DR*.
    B. *CR*.
    C. Neither: another conventionalist reason.
  c. A. Neither: conventionalist reason.
    B. a hypothetical imperative *(CR)*.
    C. *DR*.
  d. A. an egoistic reason *(CR)*.
    B. *DR* or *CR*, depending on ambiguity in the word "impossible."
    C. *DR*.
    D. *DR*.
    E. *CR*.
    F. universalistic utilitarian reason *(CR)*.

3. Your list should include things that show respect for persons, such as telling the truth, keeping promises, acting kindly toward others, respecting their freedom of choice, keeping them informed, caring for them if they are in need, etc. Your list of practices with possible negative intrinsic value should include things that are disrespectful of persons, such as the oppo-

sites of the things just listed as well as stealing, murder, rape, exploitation, fraud, etc.

6. The value of an action can be determined by looking at the principle on which it was performed. If a person acts on a principle which involves showing respect for self or others, the action is intrinsically right on deontological grounds regardless of its consequences.

7. Since you are equally a person, self-respect is acting toward and thinking about yourself just in the ways in which respect involves relating to others.

8

What Is the Good Life?

. . . the good of man is an activity of the soul in conformity with
excellence or virtue, and if there are several virtues, in conformity
with the best and most complete.

But we must add "in a complete life." For one swallow does not
make a summer, nor does one sunny day; similarly, one day or a
short time does not make a man blessed and happy.[1]

Many ethical theorists would have us look at our lives as integrated
wholes. They suggest that an individual's conduct is not adequately
evaluated simply in terms of whether particular actions lead to good
states of affairs (see Chapter 6) or are in accord with one's duty (see
Chapter 7). Such approaches seem too fragmentary, pulverizing the
ethical life. Actions of persons and consequences of those actions are
not isolable events. Rather, they play off one another and together
form, or fail to form, a coherent, worthy life pattern, and as such, reflect a person's character. The ethical theorists we will discuss in this
chapter are concerned to describe the situations and limitations within which a worthy life pattern must be achieved. We will characterize

[1]Aristotle, *Nicomachean Ethics*, 1, 7, trans. W. D. Ross in W. D. Ross and J. A.
Smith, *The Works of Aristotle* (London: Oxford University Press, 1908–1952).

the virtues without which a life of integrity is unlikely. After reading Chapter 8 you should be able to

- **Distinguish the evaluation of character from that of particular actions.**
- **State and explain the ethical relevance of human finitude in terms of one's environmental limitations, the perspectival character of human awareness, and the transitory and developmental character of human existence.**
- **Define wisdom, self-esteem, temperance, responsibility, courage, and conscientiousness as each relates to integrity.**
- **Distinguish the enlightened self-interest entailed by pursuit of the good life from extreme egoism.**

THE CASE OF THE LAST EPISTLE

Dearest Children,

The doctor has found cancer; he says it is very far advanced. He says I shall be dead before the month is out. I have known of my illness for a long time, but had kept it to myself—for many reasons. I have a message now for both of you, and I wish each to hear what I say to the other. Do not be embarrassed or proud. It is out of love that I write, and out of that same love that I wish you to share what I say to each of you.

Jason, I have always loved you the most of all. You were my first born, the flower of my youth. You were bright, strong, adventurous, and sensitive almost to a fault. I wanted to tell you not to go to war, but you were boastful, patriotic. I wept when I heard you were wounded, but I never realized the wound cut so deep into your spirit. It's been over fifteen years now since you came home. I felt the hurt in you that day, but not so much as your mother did, bless her. But somehow you let your wheelchair become the symbol of a failure which I am sure you could not have avoided. You blamed yourself when your marriage broke up. You took on a burden of guilt for your daughter's childhood problems, too. But you were wrong to make yourself suffer so. You cannot control everything. Your wife was more at fault than you admit. But it was long ago when she and your daughter left. For many years I hoped you would bounce back. Now, as I am about to die, I pray for you, for your peace of mind, for a break in your depression, for a return to the happiness of your youthful days. Care for your brother, Robert; he needs your love as much as I.

Robert, I have always loved you the most of all. You were my last child, your sister Teresa having died as just an infant. You were my greatest joy, the symbol of my manhood late in life. You surprised me in many ways by your succeeding when everyone predicted failure. You did it so many times, in school, in athletics, in college, and in adult life. You have the perseverance of a camel when you set yourself to a task. When others would have quit, you are still at work. You find ways to do more with fewer gifts than any man I know. And that is not an insult, but the highest praise. You have worked hard for your success; enjoy it, you deserve it. I do wish that you would take some time out to care for others though. Your devoted wife and lovely children cannot be expected to wait at home forever while you work late into the night. Soon the children will be grown and gone on their ways. Care for them now, before you, too, are reduced to writing letters from your sickbed; I pray for you daily. Care for your brother, Jason; he needs your love as much as I.

I can see my death clearly. It comes. I feel ready. There is nothing more that I can do on this earth except try to impart what little wisdom I have learned. Love each other; forgive each other. May life smile upon you; may all your choices be for the good.

I love you both,
Dad

8:1.1 *Integrity and the good life*   Traditionally, reflection upon the good life stresses the human capacities to realize intrinsic value. The good life has been thought to be one in which realization of intrinsic value holds a prominent place. The diversity of opinion on the nature of the good life reflects the variety of human potential for value. For example, persons may enjoy physical pleasures; thrive as healthy and vigorous organisms; enjoy the so-called higher pleasures which accompany aesthetic creativity, appreciation of painting, music, literature, contemplation, and the like; function as autonomous decision-makers in unconstrained and rational ways; express themselves and be understood in genuine dialogue with others; achieve friendship and intimacy with other persons; live in accord with moral principle; live in peace and harmony with others; and achieve the ends only cooperation can bring.

The possible variety in the good life is limited, from one perspective, only by the imagination of the person who would combine the realization of such capacities into a meaningful whole. Indeed, if one were to follow the philosopher Nietzsche in his recommendation that we should "Live life as a work of art," the principal task of living well may be conceived as one of weaving a tapestry, creatively integrating the threads of human capacity.

In the case study, the father evaluates his sons' lives for their integrated wholeness. In those lives various human capacities are combined in more or less meaningful ways as a function of the development of the young men's characters.

8:1.2 *Character traits*   Many ethical theorists (Plato and Aristotle among them) have maintained that the primary objective of ethics is broader than the determination of obligation. They suggest that ethics should focus upon cultivation of virtuous character traits inasmuch as such cultivation contributes to leading the good life. This concept of ethics is broader in that it requires that persons assess how living up to their obligations falls within the all-encompassing project of striving for personal integrity. The approach is wholistic in focusing upon the entire life of a person and upon the kind of person one is becoming as reflected in that life. The focus is upon what persons are and can become, based on what they do and have done.

8:1.3 *Virtues*   These character traits contribute to leading the good life. From the viewpoint of those who conceive of ethics as described above, the crucial question is "Which character traits are virtues?" One approach would be to offer an extensional definition (3:3.4), listing the virtues, for example, honesty, reliability, accuracy, energy, and knowledge of the job as virtues of a good worker. Articulating the idea or principle used in the selection of virtues in an intensional definition, however, would be preferable. For example, some theories of virtue offer as the basic defining principle the idea that virtues are those character traits that directly lead persons to fulfilling their obligations. The notion is that it is not sufficient to identify people's obligations without also cultivating those character traits (virtues) that will dispose them to perform their obligations. Such inner sanctions might be more effective motivators than any possible external source, since persons with those virtues would wholeheartedly endorse the fulfillment of their obligations. Depending on whether persons are inclined to define obligation in terms of bringing about the greatest consequences for good or of performing intrinsically right actions, they will in this definition find such virtues as benevolence, justice, or respect for persons to be the most worthy of cultivation.

In this chapter we will focus upon theories of virtue with a higher order of concern. The defining principle uniting the virtues we will describe is that those character traits conduce to leading a coherent life of integrity. They contribute to weaving a meaningful tapestry out of life, to recall our earlier metaphor. They lead to people's being able effectively and creatively to cope with life's circumstances and to integrate the many concerns and interests they may have, including the performance of ethical obligations. These virtues are wisdom, self-esteem, temperance, responsibility, courage, conscientiousness, and justice. They help persons to pursue ideals through actions that not only meet minimal obligations but also aim to develop exemplary life styles.

8:2.1 *Human finitude* Although life presents many opportunities for achieving integrity, still they are finite. Existentialist philosophers have emphasized that appreciation of the dimensions of human finitude is crucial if persons are to enhance their chances of leading a life of integrity. The awareness and appreciation of human finitude may be called *wisdom*. Wisdom amounts, then, to fully understanding the task of pursuing the good life. Consider some of the dimensions of human finitude which circumscribe the possibilities of integrity.

8:2.2 *Social circumstance* The particular *social circumstances* and the *historical* period into which people are born limit greatly the available range of opportunities for developing their potential. For example, today many children wonder if they could be astronauts. With the right capacities together with the means and willpower to develop them, being an astronaut can be a more or less realistic life ambition today. These children's parents could possibly themselves have become astronauts, although they were growing up when it would have been quite unlikely that they would have asked their parents about the possibility. Changed social circumstances made it possible for persons to become astronauts during their lifetimes, and they would have had to have made fortuitous choices in the light of other ambitions, perhaps to be test pilots, in order to have been prepared to take advantage of the opportunity when it arose. However, for their parents, the question probably never arose, and the opportunity was simply never available.

Even when opportunities are real, persons can be in social circumstances in which some options are more or less "live" than others, because of either the relative inaccessibility of the means to taking advantage of the opportunities—for example, the financial means to secure the required education—or such things as systematic discrimination against certain persons—for example, the poor, racial minorities, or women. Either cause can limit people from entering certain fields and developing their full potential. Such social circumstances do not always make the development of certain human potential impossible, but greater energy, and perhaps the sacrificing of other goals and potentials, become necessary. The wise person is aware of such limitations of birth and social circumstance and strives to appreciate fully their significance for his or her pursuit of integrity.

In the case study, both Jason and Robert were born into social circumstances that affected their lives. Jason grew up in time of war and was moved by a call to patriotism. Robert, like most of his male peers, was influenced by his socialization to seek success in the world of work.

8:2.3 *Limited perspective*   In whatever circumstances persons find themselves, they necessarily act from limited *perspectives*. People are much more immediately, fully, and forcefully aware of their own beliefs, feelings, and attitudes with respect to given situations than they are of the beliefs, feelings, and attitudes of others. Persons are aware of the concerns of only some of the agents involved in given situations and of only some facets of those concerns. Some consequences of conduct are foreseen, others are foreseeable but not foreseen, and others cannot be foreseen. All these limits of perspective must be appreciated if the task of living with integrity is to be understood. It is a task permeated with risk and uncertainty, which can certainly be reduced but not eliminated.

Jason could not have fully foreseen the consequences of his going off to war, though he could have been fully aware of the risks and uncertainty it brought into his life. Robert is apparently unaware of the impact of his pursuit of success upon his wife and children, whom he presumably loves.

8:2.4 *Concreteness*   Human life is vividly *concrete*. At any given time, persons are in particular circumstances and not in others. There may be a wide range of possibilities open to them within those circumstances; but human attention is selective, and there is an indefinite but clearly limited number of concerns to which a person can simultaneously attend and respond. Persons can find themselves in overloaded situations in which they have simply undertaken more than they can effectively manage. To perceive this situation is to perceive the need for decision among the possibilities. Given all that you can do, and given that you cannot do all, you must decide. Robert is thoroughly absorbed in a quest for success. He must decide whether the impact of that quest upon relations with his family is in accordance with his greatest concerns.

8:2.5 *Development*   Many human capacities and potentials require the commitment of a great deal of time and energy if they are to be fully realized. Thus, as you choose such things as careers, places to live, marriage and family, you necessarily narrow your options for the development of other capacities. To choose one way is often to choose against others. Although it may be true that several options may be pursued in sequence, the sequence is necessarily finite. *Human mortality*, the fact that each of us must one day die, and the uncertainty of the time of death add poignancy to decision-making. Because you must die, there are only so many alternatives you will ever be able to exercise. Moreover, *life has a developmental character.* As you pursue one choice, many once available alternatives dissolve because of a change either in society or in our interests or abilities. Similarly, unforeseen, interesting options typically become available. Choices need to be evaluated, not only for the happiness they bring and their intrinsic worth, but also for the continuations of development they allow or create (see Chapter 12).

In the case study, the father who writes the letter is about to die. He seems to appreciate fully both the implications of mortality for living and the manner in which some decisions, such as Jason's, dramatically narrow future options for growth and development.

8:3.1 *Virtues of the good life*   Wisdom is the awareness and appreciation of human finitude for leading a life of integrity (see 8:2.1). To seek wisdom is to strive for the fullest possible understanding of the many limitations of the quest for integrity, (8:2.2–8:2.5). In turn, *self-esteem* may be defined as the virtue of accepting the insights provided by wisdom and making them your own as you live your life. That is, self-esteem is recognizing and accepting the possibilities and limits—including your own—within which you must pursue integrity. Yet as Aristotle notes, self-esteem also means assessing one's abilities accurately—not underestimating them any more than one would overestimate them.[2] Some of the father's remarks in the case study suggest that he views both of his sons as lacking self-esteem in this precise sense. He tells Jason that he "cannot control everything." He warns Robert of the limited time available to enjoy the youth of his children rather than single-mindedly pursuing a success that may eventually ring hollow.

8:3.2 *Temperance*   This trait is closely allied with self-esteem. The temperate person has appetites for food, drink, and sexual expression like anyone else, but he practices a moderation grown out of the awareness of the dangers of extremes. The overindulgence of gluttony leads to obesity, as overly skimpy diet leads to malnutrition. Both are unhealthy. The temperate person moderates his or her desires, avoiding the ills of overindulgence which often crowd other enjoyments out of life, as clearly the joys of his family have been crowded from Robert's life. But the temperate person also avoids Jason's trap of withdrawal;

---

[2]Self-esteem means the proper estimation of self. Christian philosophers such as Thomas Aquinas have used "humility" in this sense; ancient Greek philosophers used "pride." But "humility" suggests a focus on your limitations, whereas "pride" suggests a focus on your strengths and abilities. Hence, these other terms are sometimes used for emphasis.

for Jason misses the joys of life by withdrawing from them as surely as Robert does by crowding them away.

8:3.3 *Responsibility* Beyond wisdom, self-esteem, and temperance several other virtues enhance one's chances of success in seeking integrity. First among these is taking *responsibility* for oneself, which existentialists such as Martin Heidegger and Jean-Paul Sartre have called "authenticity." In this sense of the term, responsibility amounts to bearing the burden of decision-making within the limits of human living. Persons become what they can be through the decisions and commitments they make and endeavor to carry through. Integrity does not simply come to persons; they must struggle to achieve it in the face of risk and uncertainty, which can lead them to renounce the quest. Jason's inertia troubles his father, who compassionately acknowledges the devastating events in his son's life. But he urges him to break out of his depression and undertake the difficult task of responsibly pursuing happiness within the range of options left to him.

✐ **PHILOSOPHER'S WORKSHOP**

Sartre on Character and Choice

Jean-Paul Sartre (b. 1905) is an existentialist philosopher who stresses the importance of choice in the formation of character and in leading the good life. In this passage he underscores his view that persons are unable to fall back upon conceptions of human nature, such as the biological view of Aristotle (see Chapters 11–12), in seeking ultimate justification for the choices that give shape and direction to their lives. We are, in this view, radically free and inescapably responsible for our own character.

It follows that my freedom is the unique foundation of values and that *nothing*, absolutely nothing, justifies me in adopting this or that particular value, this or that particular scale of values. . . . I do not have nor can I have recourse to any value against the fact that it is I who sustain values in being. Nothing can ensure me against myself, cut off from the world and from my essence by this nothingness which I *am*. I have to realize [make real] the meaning of the world and of my essence; I make my decision concerning them — without justification and without excuse. . . . In anguish I

> apprehend myself at once as totally free and as not being able to derive the meaning of the world except as coming from myself.[3]
>
> ———
>
> [3]Jean-Paul Sartre, *Being and Nothingness: An Essay on Phenomenological Ontology*, trans. Hazel E. Barnes (New York: Washington Square Press, 1966) 46, 47–48.

8:3.4 *Courage*   The above suggests that *courage* to persevere in the face of human limitation and adversity is another virtue necessary to achieve the good life. It takes courage to take responsibility for oneself, to act and make momentous decisions leading into an uncertain future, to sustain commitments, and to take on new commitments when the old have ended unhappily. The father lauds his son Robert for persevering throughout his childhood and adult life – which led to success despite apparently limited ability. Now Robert is challenged to remain true to his family commitments and to integrate the joys of parenthood with his other successes.

8:3.5 *Conscientiousness*   If you would lead the good life, *conscientiousness* is a most valuable character trait. It is the disposition to devote concerted effort to overcoming, to the extent possible, the limitations of perspective from which persons must live their lives. Personally, it means you must be circumspect in discerning your own abilities, interests, and concerns and in defining a course of development that will best enable you to realize your full potential. As it affects interaction with others, conscientiousness requires that you strive to understand the interests and concerns of others, the impact of your actions and decisions upon them, and conversely, the impact of

How would you relate self-acceptance to the kind of ethics under discussion?

their actions and decisions upon you. Although no one can reduce risk and uncertainty to zero, the conscientious person is dedicated to minimizing them.

8:3.6 *Integrity*   This trait itself consists in harmony or balance. You have a large number of capacities and opportunities for developing them in the course of your life, yet life's developmental character (8:2.5) implies that often you foreclose some developments of your personality when you pursue others. If you have a talent, however, such as musical aptitude, you may suffer badly if you never develop it. You don't want to lead your life filled with regrets about what "could have been." It is in your own interest to find some sort of optimum in realizing your own possibilities. The life of integrity is a life of integrating your actions so that your capacities tend to reinforce each other; it is not a life of developing some capacities at the cost of ignoring, undermining, or destroying others. Plato spoke of this virtue as *justice*, thinking of it as an internal, psychological condition in which the parts of your soul are in agreement under the governance of your reason. Psychic justice enables you to balance your intellectual, aesthetic, physical, and sensual capacities so that your life forms an integrated whole. Plato has in view an analogy with social justice: In a just society one person or class of persons does not usurp the rights and duties of others; each performs his own duties and respects the rights of others. Psychic justice defines similar limits for the development of a person's inner capacities.

✐ **PHILOSOPHER'S WORKSHOP**

Socrates on the Unity of Virtue

Virtues differ from ordinary personality traits because the set of virtues seem to be closely interlinked. A person who possesses wisdom or integrity might be presumed to possess other virtues such as self-esteem, responsibility, temperance, and courage. The claim that the virtues form such a "unity" was central to the ethics of Socrates. In the following, he recalls a conversation with Protagoras. Socrates speaks first:

"The question, if I am not mistaken, was this. Wisdom, temperance, courage, justice, and holiness are five terms. Do they stand for a single reality or has each term a particular entity underlying it, a reality with its own separate function, each different from the other? Your answer was that they are not names for the same thing, but that each of these terms applies to its own separate reality, and that all of these things are parts of virtue, not like the parts of a lump of gold all homogeneous with each other and with the whole of which they are parts, but like the parts of a face, resembling neither the whole nor each other and each having a separate function. If you are still of the same mind, say so, but if not, then declare yourself. I certainly shall not hold you to your words if you now express yourself differently. Very likely you spoke as you did to test me."

"No," he said. "My view is that all these are parts of virtue, and that four of them resemble each other fairly closely, but courage is very different from all the rest. The proof of what I say is that you can find many men who are quite unjust, unholy, intemperate, and ignorant, yet outstandingly courageous."

"Stop," said I. "What you say merits investigation. Do you qualify the courageous as confident, or in any other way?"

"As confident, yes, and keen to meet dangers from which most men shrink in fear."

"Then again, you consider virtue an honorable thing, and it is on the assumption that it is honorable that you offer to teach it?"

"Unless I am quite mad, it is the most honorable of all things."

"Part base and part honorable," I asked, "or all honorable?"

"All honorable, as honorable as can be."

"Now do you know which men plunge fearlessly into tanks?"

"Yes, divers."

"Is that because they know their job or for some other reason?"

"Because they know their job."

"And what men feel confidence in a cavalry engagement— trained or untrained riders?"

"Trained."

"And in fighting with the light shield—peltasts or nonpeltasts?"

"Peltasts. And this holds good generally, if that is what you are after. Those with the relevant knowledge have more confidence than those without it, and more when they have learned the job than they themselves had before."

"But," said I, "have you ever seen men with no understanding of any of these dangerous occupations who yet plunge into them with confidence?"

"Indeed yes, with only too much confidence."

"Then does not their confidence involve courage too?"

"No, for if so, courage would be something to be ashamed of. Such men are mad."

"How then do you define the courageous? Did you not say they were the confident?"

"Yes, I still maintain it."

"Well, those who are thus ignorantly confident show themselves not courageous but mad, and conversely, in the other case it is the wisest that are also most confident, and therefore most courageous. On this argument it is their knowledge that must be courage."[4]

Do you find Socrates' argument convincing? According to Socrates anyone who is wise, in the sense of knowing what one should do, will be courageous. Can you describe a case in which a person has wisdom but nevertheless is not courageous? If so, can you find the hole in Socrates' reasoning?

[4]Plato, *Protagoras*, trans. W. K. C. Guthrie, *Protagoras and Meno* (Middlesex, Harmondsworth, Eng.: Penguin Classics, 1956), 349a–350c.

8:4.1 *Concern for others* The ethical ideal of the good life is sometimes seen as self-centered, since the individual agent will still be concerned primarily with his or her *own* life. Traditional proponents of the good life such as Socrates, Plato, and Aristotle all claim that individuals can find true happiness for themselves only by seeking the good life. These philosophers sometimes suggest that the virtuous person will be willing to make sacrifices for others, but the precise nature of one's obligations to others is not spelled out. In Plato's *Republic* virtuous persons dedicate their lives to the ideal State described by Plato. Aristotle's virtuous man is also deeply committed to the ancient Greek city-state.

8:4.2 *Enlightened self-interest* Some philosophers working out of the good life tradition place a stronger emphasis on self-interest. One advocate of the egoistic good life is Ayn Rand (b. 1906), an American novelist and philosopher. Rand argues that *human life* is the standard by which human values are measured. "The fact that living entities exist and function necessitates the existence of values and of an ultimate value which for any given living entity is its own life."[5] Your *own* life is, therefore, your ethical purpose, and you should choose your actions, values and goals so as to achieve, maintain, fulfill and enjoy it. The purpose of ethics is to guide these choices. Following Aristotle, Rand gives reason a central place in ethics. A *rational* person will recognize that other persons are also rational beings with similar requirements for life. Hence, enlightened self-interest entails recognition that the same ethical principle applies to other persons:

[5]Ayn Rand, *The Virtue of Selfishness* (New York: National American Library, 1964), p. 17.

One ought to maintain one's own life. Rand states this recognition in the universal precept, "Every living human being is an end in himself." But this, in turn, implies respect for the rights of others: "Man must live for his own sake, neither sacrificing himself to others nor sacrificing others to himself."[6] Rand holds that this ideal would be most fully realized in a society of *laissez faire* capitalism in which individuals and governments were not permitted to initiate the use of force against other individuals. Rand's theory departs from traditional good life theories in approving competitiveness and de-emphasizing virtues such as charity towards others, but it shares with them a fundamental concern with enhancing the quality of one's own life.

8:5 *Summary* In this chapter we have introduced you to the view that the principal tasks of ethics ought to be defining the good life and evaluating a person's character in terms of whether it is conducive to the good life. This view amounts to the suggestion that ethics ought to be less piecemeal in evaluating conduct and more concerned with the integration of values into coherent life patterns. Wisdom, self-esteem, and temperance were defined as virtues of perceiving and accepting the task of achieving integrity as decisively colored by human finitude in many dimensions. Responsibility, courage, and conscientiousness were characterized as virtues necessary to the successful pursuit of that finite task. Integrity, or justice, as Plato called it, is a matter of making capacities and opportunities as consistent and supportive of each other as possible. The ideals of the good life tend to emphasize the importance of one's *own* life, thus leading in some philosophers to a theory of enlightened self-interest.

EXERCISES for Chapter 8

1. In each of the following passages something is evaluated. To determine what, look at the *conclusion*; mark those that evaluate character *EC* and those that evaluate actions *EA* (8:1.1–8:1.3).

    _____A. Joel, your decision affects many people and the problem is very complex. I know your intentions are good, but can't help concluding that it's pretentious of you not to admit the possibility of being wrong.

    _____B. Your decision, Samantha, to move Thebleheim Steel out of western New York is going to hurt a lot of people. Don't you realize that thousands will be unemployed for months? Many

---

[6]*Ibid.*, p. 27.

will have to relocate, uprooting families. The public will bear a huge increase in welfare costs.

_____C. I strongly commend your decision, Sam. You took all factors into account. When it became clear that there was no easy alternative, you did not shirk your responsibility or try to get out of having to decide. You tried to be fair to everyone. So as I see it, you've been very conscientious.

_____D. Look, George, having signed the lease, you undertook an obligation as landlord for house maintenance. Therefore not calling a plumber for over a week after learning about the toilet problems is just wrong. You shouldn't ignore your duties like that.

2. Each of the following passages emphasizes one of the following characteristics of human life: social circumstances *(S)*, perspectival character of awareness *(P)*, concreteness *(C)*, transitory character of human life *(T)*, and developmental character of human life *(D)*. Mark each passage appropriately (8:2.1–8:2.5).

_____A. I figured I had to get back here by now so I could attend my mother's reception. But now I can't attend my kids' swim meet back home.

_____B. Given all the work you've done in building and designing models, I'm sure you're ready to study design systematically. You've got a lot more ability than confidence, so you shouldn't be reticent.

_____C. The first solar-heated homes were developed long after I put a gas furnace in my house thirty years ago.

_____D. I could have installed a heat pump, in the sense that they existed back then, but I'd never heard of any system like that.

_____E. Now I suppose I could convert my heating system, but what's the sense? I'm not going to be living here very long. If I have to pay a higher gas bill, I'll do it.

3. Check the answers to question 2. Then explain how each of the statements reflects on the subject's integrity (8:2.1–8:2.5).

4. Define wisdom, self-esteem, temperance, responsibility, courage, conscientiousness, and integrity (8:3.1–8:3.6).

5. Explain the relevance of each of these virtues to at least one of the statements in question 2.

SELECTED ANSWERS for Chapter 8

1. A. *EC:* Joel is pretentious.
   B. *EA:* Harm to many will result.

    C. *EC:* Sam is conscientious.

    D. *EA:* George neglected his responsibility.

2. A.   *C:* can't be in two places at once.

   B.   *D:* past actions have created present possibilities.

   C.   *S:* no way of installing solar heat was available.

   D.   *P:* the speaker's awareness of systems was limited.

   E.   *T:* the speaker's term of residence shall end.

3. A. The speaker cannot integrate both commitments to family.

   B. The subject's previous efforts facilitate and thus easily cohere with the proposed study of design.

   C. The integration of environmental values into the speaker's life was limited by available technology.

   D. The integration was also limited by ignorance.

   E. Integrating the environmental values into the speaker's life remains possible, but the speaker implies that this integration does not cohere very well with other (unstated) values, given the expected shortness of residence.

5. A. Self-esteem would allow one to recognize that keeping both commitments is impossible. Integrity is also applicable.

   B. Courage would allow one to keep one's fears in proportion to the magnitude of objective problems, rather than in proportion to one's feelings. Temperance is also applicable.

   C. Thirty years ago the present consequences of installing a gas versus a solar heating system were not foreseeable. Thus wisdom would not have allowed a person to choose solar heat even if it had been available.

   D. Conscientiousness would have led the speaker to explore the possibility of a heat pump.

   E. Responsibility allows the speaker to accept the consequences of the decision that has been made.

Criticizing Ethical Perspectives

Ethical theories may be criticized from several perspectives. On the one hand, they may be criticized in terms of standards or philosophical perspectives to which the holders of the theory do not necessarily subscribe. On the other, they may be criticized from within the theorist's own perspective for failing to meet the standards subscribers to the theory set for themselves. In this chapter we will consider further this contrast between what may be called "external" and "internal" criticisms of ethical theories, respectively. We will then consider several criticisms of each of three major ethical theories developed in Chapters 6, 7, and 8. After reading Chapter 9 you should be able to

- Distinguish between internal and external criticisms of a theory.
- State three internal criticisms of the utilitarian, deontological, and pursuit of the good life theories.
- Describe cases in which pursuing happiness, respecting other persons, and developing a life of integrity might each conflict with one of the others.

THE CASE OF JOYCE'S SANTA

"Paul, Joyce is going to be two next Christmas and I'm wondering what we're going to do about Santa Claus. Are we going to tell her that Santa is real?"

Paul put down his coffee and looked at his wife, Anne, "What are you getting at? Why not have her believe in Santa?"

"Well, I've read that it isn't good to get into the whole big Santa Claus thing with kids. It only hurts in the long run, when they get older. They find out that their parents lied to them and that makes them question how much they can really trust their parents. Some articles say that the whole experience can be psychologically quite a problem for kids."

"Anne, how reliable are those predictions? I mean, it doesn't always lead to severe problems. My parents had me believing in Santa Claus, and later they let me in on the story so I would keep the secret from my younger brother."

"Well, it bothered me a lot. I remember wondering how Santa got into our apartment. I really was into the whole thing. My classmates would laugh at me, but I wanted to believe my parents. I would come home crying sometimes . . ."

"Okay, Anne, I admit some kids might suffer bad consequences. But if it's handled right, well . . . I mean what bothers me more is not the possible dangers but the problem of lying. I don't want to start lying to Joyce."

"Paul, you surprise me sometimes! What's so wrong about an innocent little lie? You always say that something is all right if it makes sense for everyone to act in that same way. And in our culture it makes sense to tell your kids Santa is real. It makes more sense than to deny it while grandparents, TV, and storekeepers push the myth."

"I didn't say that you could decide *everything* just by asking whether it made sense to require everyone to do it; just some things can be looked at that way. And lying is one of them. Lying is wrong."

"Paul, let's not call using the myth a lie. It is not a real lie. We don't mean to hurt Joyce. Actually we are trying to make life more enjoyable for her. Right?"

"Anne, we can give her just as good a time if we make her believe in Santa as if we don't. So what is it going to be?"

"I say we skip the Santa thing, or present it as just a story like any other story—as make-believe, not real. But we'll never know if she is having as good a time without believing in Santa as she might have had believing."

"I'm not worried about that. The idea that people should have a good time' just doesn't mean anything specific to me. It doesn't tell me exactly what to do. I'll bet Joyce will be able to have as good a time as any other two-year-old."

"I agree. So we don't make her believe in Santa. How about the Tooth Fairy?"

9:1.1 *Criticisms of ethical values* Each of the three ethical theories we have considered may be criticized from the perspective of one or both of the others. There are actions counted right by utilitarians for their good consequences which deontological theorists would find intrinsically wrong. A utilitarian might, for example, judge it right to break a deathbed promise because doing so would yield only good consequences. A deontological theorist, on the other hand, would find that action wrong, regardless of whether the person to whom the promise had been made knew that it was being broken. Or imagine a student who had committed himself or herself to playing tennis on Saturday morning and could not break the engagement before Saturday. Deontological theorists would argue that such commitments should be kept. Yet the student may have subsequently discovered that graduate school admission examinations are scheduled for that same time. From the point of view of those who champion the good life in their ethics, violating that commitment would be permissible for the sake of the person's subsequent development through advanced education.

In turn, the champions of the good life could be criticized on the grounds that the perspective from which human beings operate tends to make them egoistic. There is nothing explicit in the good life theory to counteract this egoistic tendency. In fact, some philosophers working out of a good life tradition defend an explicit doctrine of egoism (see 8:4.2). There is no guarantee in a good life theory that a person will contribute to other persons' attempts to make good lives for themselves. Thus, deontologists might find this area to be less than acceptable because respecting persons is the primary purpose of their ethics.

The case study illustrates the tension between utilitarian, deontological, and good life theories. The exchange between Paul and Anne concerning whether or not their daughter, Joyce, should be told the truth about Santa Claus illustrates how positions developed from one ethical perspective may be criticized from another. Whether or not utilitarian considerations would allow not telling the truth about Santa Claus, it is arguable from a deontological view that such a lie should not be tolerated. However, from the point of view of one who considers leading the good life as being most important, it is possible to construe the Santa Claus story as a myth rather than a lie. Life can be richer for those who appreciate the value of such myths. Yet, from a utilitarian point of view, children may find it difficult to distinguish between a myth and a lie, and subsequently learn not to trust their parents—which surely is a bad consequence of telling such stories.

9:1.2 *External versus internal criticisms*   The criticisms of ethical theories in the foregoing were not intended as devastating. They merely illustrate the possibility of criticizing positions from the point of view of another perspective. Such criticisms from alternative perspectives may well be rejected by advocates of a particular ethical theory on the grounds that they find the values of the critic to be deficient or relatively unimportant. Each of the criticisms outlined in 9:1.1 might face such rejection.

The preceding criticisms of ethical theories may be called *external criticisms*, in which a certain view does not come up to some standard that the view has not set for itself. That is, the view is found deficient according to a standard *external* to the view itself. By contrast, ethical theories may be criticized from within. Criticisms to the effect that views have problems internal to themselves, for example, that they are incoherent or inconsistent or fail to meet an accepted goal, are called *internal criticisms*. To offer an internal criticism of a theory is to suggest that the view fails to meet a standard it sets for itself.

In the light of this distinction, you can easily see how much more difficult it is to dismiss internal criticisms than external ones. In order to handle the latter, one need only reject the standard by which the view is measured. By contrast, because internal criticisms measure theories against their own standards, it follows that they can only be met by showing that they are mistaken—that is, that the view meets the standards in question—or by revising the view so that it does meet the standard. Let's turn, then, to internal criticisms of utilitarian, deontological, and the good life ethical theories.

9:2.1 *Criticisms of utilitarian theory*   Utilitarian theory requires the possibility of calculating the goodness or badness brought about by our actions. At least two aspects of such calculation seem problematic. First, it must be possible, if utilitarianism is to succeed, to calculate the *intensity* of the pleasure or happiness. Yet, intensity seems difficult to calculate indeed. Imagine, as an example, the problem of comparing the pleasure of a child licking an ice cream cone to that of an adult eating a gourmet meal. Although you might say that the adult pleasure is more refined, which could be a legitimate distinction, whether it is more or less intense could not be objectively measured.

Second, it must also be possible for utilitarians to calculate the degree of *certainty* attached to the occurrence of consequences. However, accuracy in assessing degrees of probability is difficult to achieve for many reasons. Even as predictions of consequences are offered, the likelihood of their occurrence changes. For example, the fact that a terribly bad consequence is to emerge sometime in the future as a result of a given action is itself a reason why persons who foresee that probable consequence will undertake additional actions to ward it off, thus changing its probability. Specifically, assuming it is true that if we keep using oil at the present rate there will be no oil in thirty years and a great dearth of energy, the mere fact that this prediction is made will tend both to prevent us from using all the oil and encourage us to seek alternative forms of energy. This subsequent change of our behavior undermines the reliability of our prediction, which is but one of several reasons why it is difficult to predict consequences with certainty. This lack is a major criticism of utilitarian theory because it undermines its aim of achieving objective assurance in evaluating actions. The case study exemplifies the difficulty of predicting with certainty the consequences of telling or not telling Joyce the truth about Santa Claus.

9:2.2 *Utilitarian atomism*   The assumption made by utilitarianism in its classical form is that the value of the whole is equal to the positive or negative values of its parts when taken together. One simply adds them up. Thus, utilitarian theory operates with an atomic model. But many excitements, pleasures, and enjoyments are the richer or dearer because of the preceeding experiences of deprivation or because of the threat of loss, permanent or temporary. The deprivation or threatening experiences themselves have a negative value, so that on an atomic model the value of the whole will be less for including these elements. In fact, however, it seems that some pleasures are greater when they are conjoined with these negative values than they would be if they occurred independently. Thus our experience is contrary to the atomic model assumed by the utilitarian. The English philosopher George Edward Moore (1873–1958) recognized this point in his "theory of organic unities."[1] Although in other respects a utilitarian, his assertion undermines the utilitarian method of calculation.

9:2.3 *Problem of objectivity*   Because utilitarian theory took root in a desire to discover objective means for evaluating the merits of actions, intersubjective agreement was placed at a premium. Utilitarians agreed that the best means to achieve such objectivity was to evaluate actions as being of only instrumental value; that is, actions were to be

---

[1] G. E. Moore, *Principia Ethica* (Cambridge, Eng.: University Press, 1903), pp. 27–36.

evaluated insofar as they conduce to certain desirable states of affairs. In turn, the degree of desirability of those states of affairs would be measured by means of the utilitarian calculus. However, nothing is really gained if no intersubjective agreement can be reached on what characteristics make states of affairs valuable. As long as utilitarians dispute which states of affairs are intrinsically valuable, say pleasure versus happiness, utilitarian theory fails to meet its own standards of objectivity.

9:3.1 *Criticisms of deontological theory*   Kant asserts that all three formulations of the Categorical Imperative are equivalent (7:2.2). Any maxim of action which is a duty under one formulation will be a duty under the other two formulations. But critics argue that the formulations have different implications concerning our duty and that, therefore, the theory does not present a consistent statement of a person's duty. For example, if we take seriously the second formulation, to the effect that we should always treat others as ends and never as means only, respect for the free choices of others is given the highest importance. Any interference in their lives in defiance of their free expression of wishes to the contrary would be in violation of this formulation. However, if we take seriously the *third* formulation, then our duty would seem to be to do everything necessary to sustain other people's membership in moral community with us. Consider a case where a lifesaving treatment is necessary but the person who needs the treatment does not want it. The second formulation of the Categorical Imperative seems to say that our duty is to refrain from performing the lifesaving treatment. The third formulation, however, seems to require that we do all we can to sustain moral community with that person. It is difficult to see how we would remain in community with that person if he or she were to die. Therefore, the third formulation of the Categorical Imperative would seem to require that we treat that person in defiance of his or her freely expressed wish to the contrary.

Similarly, consider the first two formulations. It seems possible to universalize a maxim like "It is permissible to treat any minority of less than one percent solely as a means" or "It is permissible to treat left-handed people solely as a means." Yet clearly these maxims are contrary to the second formulation.

Unless it can be shown how there is a relationship of logical entailment among the diverging formulations of the Categorical Imperative, something no one has been able to show, its doctrine seems to be internally incoherent.

9:3.2 *Vagueness of the Categorical Imperative*   Deontological theory requires that we treat persons as ends and never solely as means; that is, we are to be respectful of persons. However, it remains quite unclear just what actions are enjoined by this imperative. People have widely diverse, and often conflicting, intuitions about what constitutes being respectful in various circumstances. Therefore, the idea that we ought to obey the Categorical Imperative of treating persons as ends in themselves, or that we ought to be respectful of persons is an inadequate prescription for behavior because it is not sufficiently directive.

Consider the problem of knowing whether it is right to tell a very painful truth to one who is known to suffer when such truths are shared with him or her. Some would argue that it is most respectful of such a person to share the truth, no matter the painful consequences, because as autonomous agents persons are entitled to know truths that affect their lives. Others would argue that it is possible to do for those persons all that they might be able to do in knowing the truth while at the same time sparing them the painful consequences of knowing it. They find it most respectful of persons in some circumstances to spare them the truth. The point here is that it is difficult to determine when such persons are being treated as ends in themselves and when they are being treated as means only. Consider the case study for a moment. What are your intuitions about whether it is more respectful to tell or not to tell Joyce the truth about Santa Claus?

9:3.3 *Conflicts of duty*   In some situations, whatever one does is contrary to some moral rule and one's actions can plausibly be seen as violating the Categorical Imperative. Suppose it is intrinsically wrong to break a commitment, and also intrinsically wrong not to heed a legitimate cry for help. What is a person to do if he or she can heed a legitimate cry for help only by breaking a commitment? One criticism is that deontological theory does not answer this important question. A second criticism arises because people have felt that agents cannot be blamed for doing the best thing that can be done in the circumstances, especially if it was none of their doing that those circumstances occurred. Heeding a legitimate cry for help may be the best thing to do in some circumstances, and surely the person cannot be blamed for being in a position where doing the best thing requires violating a prior commitment. However, in a deontological view, whatever one does in those circumstances is wrong. Whatever one does, one knowingly decides to do something that is intrinsically wrong, a sufficient reason for one's being blameworthy. Many philosophers have argued that there is something wrong with deontological theory if circumstances arise where there can be no right action to perform.

9:4.1 *Criticisms of good life theory*   Ethical theories that emphasize leading the good life tend also to emphasize taking the measure of your concerns and looking at the overall pattern of your life in order to plan the most meaningful, integrated life possible for yourself. However, such theories are underdirective in that they do not tell precisely what to do or how to find out what to do. This defect is clearest in Sartre's emphasis on freedom (8:3.3). There is room for vast differences of opinion about what has the greatest potential for giving meaning in one's life. Good life theories provide few tools for evaluating possible concerns and deciding which are most worthy of pursuit. Should you cultivate your intellect? Should you cultivate your aesthetic talents, for example, in music? Should you pursue success in business or in politics? Should you cultivate friendship and intimate relations with others? Should you lead a life of quiet contemplation or one of social action? Should you pursue what interests you and avoid what bores you or seek to cultivate new interests? Should you live according to principle and strive to be respectful of others? Should you pursue the religious life?

It might be answered that you should do what you want to do, whatever that may be, and that you should strive to integrate whatever your concerns may be to the greatest extent possible. However, good life theories seem deficient here because they emphasize the importance of choosing wisely without providing a basis for distinguishing how some alternatives could be better choices than others. Why is *how* we choose important if *what* we choose does not matter?

9:4.2 *Lack of specifics* Good life theories are also indefinite and underspecific concerning the rules used or the goals considered in making specific decisions in one's life. In everyday living, you constantly face specific, concrete decisions. Persons do not live their lives all at once, and they do not constantly concern themselves exclusively with the overall pattern of their lives. In suggesting that persons should focus primarily upon the overall pattern, the good life theorists underestimate the importance of having to make day-to-day moral decisions, and they provide inadequate direction for making them. What ought the principle to be that guides everyday decision-making? Ought persons to live according to principle at all? By not providing answers to these questions, good life ethical theories seem internally deficient.

9:4.3 *Criteria of choice* What underlies both of the preceeding criticisms is the fact that whereas good life theories purport to define the good life of persons, a series of virtues to be cultivated in living and making decisions does not always completely define one's choices. The character of life, as the product of one's projects, is only sketchily defined by a process of decision-making. Thus, the claim that the character of the good life is being described is an overstatement. In fact, only for-

Is integrity valuable independently of what character traits are integrated in the personality?

mal criteria for a good process of living, for experiencing and for choosing wisely, are being described. Surely, these criteria are insufficient as a characterization of the good life.

Moreover, when good life theorists, like Plato and Aristotle, have recognized this difficulty, they have remedied it only by creating another. What they have done is to specify the goods that should be pursued in one's wise choosing. But Plato and Aristotle disagree in these specifications! What are the greatest goods, most worth pursuing? This disputed question has persisted without clear resolution. Thus, the objection here is not simply, as originally stated, that good life theories may be incomplete, but that when they are not, they appear to be unresolvably controversial or dogmatic.

9:4.4 *Aristotle's good man theory* Aristotle recognized the inadequacy of merely specifying formal criteria for leading the good life, and he also saw great difficulty in developing more specific directives because of the variability of the human condition. Instead, he sought to make his theory more concrete by suggesting that we look to the life of "the good man" as a model for our behavior. But notice these two problems: First, how can we recognize the good man? Surely different people will point to different models. This problem leads to the second one: Assuming that the good man can be identified, what aspects of his character are essential, rather than being accidental, to being a model for the behavior of others? The very fact that Aristotle suggests the good *man* (not "person") as his model illustrates a sexist prejudice. What people can show that their models are freer of the biases of their age?

9:5 *Summary* In this chapter we have distinguished between external and internal criticisms of ethical theories. External criticisms are more readily dismissed by a theory's advocates than internal ones because the latter are based on standards to which those advocates subscribe, whereas the former are derived from other perspectives. We then turned to internal criticisms of utilitarian, deontological, and good life theories. Utilitarian theory was criticized insofar as (1) calculation of the intensity and certainty of consequences is found to be difficult, (2) the atomic model for evaluating the intrinsic value of states of affairs is found to be inadequate, and (3) objective agreement about what it is that makes states of affairs intrinsically valuable seems to be lacking. Deontological theory was criticized through the suggestions that (1) the different formulations of the Categorical Imperative seem to require different duties, (2) persons' intuitions as to what counts as being respectful of others differ widely, and (3) there seem to be circumstances beyond a person's control wherein his or her doing the best that can be done would still be considered wrong. Good life theories were criticized (1) for being underdirective in specifying the kinds of concerns that are worthy of pursuit, (2) for being underdirective in providing guidance for concrete decision-making, (3) in general for specifying formal criteria defining a good process of living as opposed to more fully characterizing the content of the good life, and (4) for falling into controversial assertions in appealing to concrete models.

EXERCISES for Chapter 9

1. Three theories from either ethics or some other area of philosophy are specified below. After each, a number of criticisms are stated. If a criticism is external, mark it *E*. If it is internal, mark it *I* (9:1.1–9:1.2).

   a. Utilitarianism (Chapter 6)

   _____A. Making calculations about people reduces them to numbers and treats them impersonally.

   _____B. All rights of persons in the minority can be overriden whenever they conflict with the happiness of the majority.

   _____C. Fecundity is, in principle, incalculable.

   b. "What we learn by our senses and what we learn through scientific method—those things we can know. Questions of religion, on the other hand, are unknowable. But what characteristics distinguish these groups from each other? In scientific knowledge alone do we frame a hypothesis, make a prediction from it and observe whether the prediction is correct. Together, then, these distinguish knowledge from opinion."

_____A. "Rational, educated persons tend to agree that God does not exist."

_____B. "When a person knows that the room is painted green, he knows simply by looking, not by first hypothesizing and then predicting."

_____C. "After hypothesizing and predicting, what we observe may not be definitive. Suppose a doctor hypothesizes appendicitis and predicts the patient will experience pain if poked in the side. Since the pain can also have other meanings, the observed pain does not imply knowledge of appendicitis. So hypothesizing, predicting and observing are not always enough to add up to knowledge."

c. "A work of art has aesthetic quality only if each of its parts is related to the others so as to form a harmonious whole. Thus persons gain pleasure from a work of art through being aware of its parts and their interrelationship."

_____A. "Contrary to this theory, it is possible to derive pleasure from a work of art without analyzing or even being aware of parts and their relationships."

_____B. "This theory assumes that the aesthetic response to works of art is confined to pleasure."

_____C. "Epic poems form harmonious wholes even though the persons who enjoy particular episodes are not always aware of how they relate to the rest of the poem."

2. State three criticisms of utilitarian, deontological, and the good life ethical theories (9:2.1–9:4.3).

3. Describe cases in which pursuing happiness, respecting persons, and developing a good life of integrity might each conflict with one another.

4. a. What advantages and disadvantages do you see in each of the three theories?

   b. Would you be inclined to take a foundationalist approach (Chapter 4) that one of them is correct to the exclusion of the others, or a contextualist approach to reconcile the advantages of each in a consistent way?

SELECTED ANSWERS for Chapter 9

1. a. A. *E.*   b. A. *E.*   c. A. *I.*
      B. *E.*   B. *I.*   B. *E.*
      C. *I.*   C. *I.*   C. *I.*

3. Take each pair of goals, say, happiness and respect. Ask yourself why one goal might be met while the other was ignored or thwarted. Then describe concrete circumstances, for example, those in the case study, where the one goal is met but the other is thwarted.

Resolving Ethical Conflicts

To what extent and by what strategies is rational resolution of ethical conflict possible? Of course, we are all too aware of nonrational and irrational ways of resolving these conflicts: (1) ignoring the issues; (2) engaging in deception; (3) using persuasive, emotional language, capable of moving people without providing them with sound reasons; and (4) becoming violent. But are there any *rational* alternatives to these procedures? Yes, indeed there are, ones that are effective but not perfect. They may not resolve all the ethical tensions, but they are very useful in easing and resolving many. They may work only in some circumstances, but nevertheless, even these incomplete rational procedures are certainly of considerable value. After reading Chapter 10 you should be able to

- Distinguish among divergence, conflict, and essential conflict.
- Characterize each of the following three models for rational ethical resolution of tension: hierarchy-building, problem-dissolution, and compromise.
- For each of these models state what makes it plausible and what it assumes.
- For each model state its limitations, its implausibilities, and the problems it does not fully handle.

THE CASE OF NATHAN DANIELS

Nathan crossed in front of the social science building and headed for the mall that joined the humanities building to the physics building. As he walked he took the letter from Bendicorp out of his pocket. His eyes went immediately to the second paragraph. "We are interested in offering you a position with Bendicorp's overseas affiliate, African Electronics. The position of systems analyst holds the potential for advancement into management. The starting salary is $18,500 plus an overseas expense allowance. You should report to our Boston office on July 10th if . . . ."

He didn't have to read it, he knew it by heart. It was the kind of job he had wanted, the kind he had studied for.

But why did they wait until May 20th to make their offer? I interviewed with them in February. What am I going to do now? If this were a month ago I would be in good shape, but now I've made other commitments.

He took a copy of a second letter out of his pocket as he turned the corner of the physics building and headed across ths campus quadrangle toward the library. ". . . I accept the position as programmer at Ford Motor Company. I'll report to the Dearborn offices on June 25th. . . ."

I can't break my word to them; it's not right. Contracts are contracts! Once you have made a commitment you don't go back on it. Oh, but that opportunity with Bendicorp! A better job, higher pay, and management potential!

But how can I be sure? Ford is a stable corporation; it will survive. The situation in Africa is volatile. African political, economic, and even social conditions are apt to change. What if I'm back on the streets looking for work in two years because African Electronics has been nationalized or something?

A light rain started as Nathan walked into the library. He wondered what the weather was like in Africa.

Yet with Ford, well, I'm locked in. There is less chance for personal growth. After a year or two I'll know my job and will probably want to move anyway. With African Electronics I'll meet new people, learn about new cultures; it's more than just a job.

The prospects seemed so exciting that he couldn't put the offer out of his mind. He had come to the library to study for finals, but he found himself going to the card catalog to look up things about Africa instead.

10:1.1 *Divergence and conflict among ethical views*   In Chapter 5 the distinctions between absolute and relative, objective and subjective, intrinsic and instrumental values were cited to clarify normative concepts and issues. We have attempted to clarify and to exhibit the ethical value people intuitively find in promoting pleasure or happiness, doing one's duty, and striving for integrity. That each of these is valuable seems indubitable. Moreover, it seems clear that persons can pursue them all with greater certainty once they have knowledge of just what each one is.

Up to now the main emphasis has been in exposition and clarification of these basic ethical values. Along the way, however, we have noted two sorts of conflict. (1) Doing particular actions because of their good consequences may conflict with following rules that have good consequences (6:2); or one duty to perform an action of intrinsic value may conflict with another (9:3.1). The advice that people ought to do that which promotes the best consequences, or that they ought to do their duty, is inadequate in such cases because problems are raised of *how* good consequences are to be pursued and of *which* duties ought to be performed. Because the ways in which a value might be achieved collide, this first type of conflict is between a value and itself. (2) We also noted conflict arising between one person and another, for example, the conflicting recommendations of limited and universal utilitarianism. Here the conflict is not between one view of utility and another, for the same value of utility is in question throughout. Rather the conflict is over whose welfare is sought. In such cases the conflict is between persons, not values.

Now notice a third sort of conflict, which we have only suggested in the external criticisms of our three ethical theories. Whereas we have discussed utility, duty, and integrity as relatively separate topics, the pursuit of utility may conflict with the acknowledgement of duty or compromise the pursuit of integrity. Thus, there is conflict among the ethical values.

10:1.2 *Divergence* You should distinguish between two forms that tension can take. One kind of tension, the more moderate and sometimes easier to handle, is divergence. Whenever one set of reasons leads to the conclusion that one action should be taken whereas a second set suggests that a second, distinct action should be taken, the result is divergence. What you would do in following the first set of reasons is simply different from, but not incompatible with, what you would do in following a second set.

Consider an example: Sara, who has been living with a married man, Frank, might conclude on the basis of the intrinsic value of some action that she should urge Frank to seek neither an annulment nor a divorce. Then on grounds of utility, Sara might also decide that continuing her current relationship with Frank could only hurt his wife and children. From this line of reasoning, Sara might conclude that she ought to break off her relationship with Frank. Here we have an example of divergence. On deontological grounds Sara has concluded that she should admonish Frank not to seek an annulment or a divorce, and on utilitarian grounds she has decided that she should end her relationship with him.

This example illustrates that divergence does not necessarily imply conflict. That is, it is possible for Sara both to discourage Frank from seeking an annulment *and* to break off her relationship with him. When reasons lead to divergent conclusions, we can often resolve any tension by simply doing both of the recommended actions. Whenever the recommendations implied by two sets of reasons diverge without contradicting each other, only such constraints as lack of opportunity, lack of time, lack of resources, or lack of cooperation between the involved parties will prevent one from accepting both recommendations and following out both lines of reasoning.

10:1.3 *Conflict* Sometimes it happens that different ethical theories will lead not only to divergent recommendations but to logically contradicting ones; that is, following the one recommendation means or entails not following the other. If Sara, pursuing her own and Frank's happiness, consistently urged Frank to get a divorce and marry her, then it could not possibly be the case that Sara, following utilitarian values, could consistently try to break off her relationship with Frank so he would not hurt his family.

Essential conflict arises in cases where no matter *how* you go about following one set of recommendations, the mere following of those recommendations itself implies that you do not follow another set of recommendations. Essential conflict between recommendations is by definition inevitable and unavoidable. There are many other cases of conflict, however, where it is only the *manner* in which you act, and not the goal you are trying to accomplish, that conflicts with another recommendation. Working alone all evening will preclude spending evenings with your friends. If your aim is to work alone essentially to get your work done, you can do your work perhaps in the afternoon and still spend the evening with your friends. On the other hand, if your aim is to work in the evenings, then perhaps you do not need to be alone in order to do your work and you can spend your evenings working in the company of your friends. It is often as difficult as it is important to get people to define their goals with sufficient care in order to discern what is really essential to the achievement of the goal as opposed to what is only coincidental or instrumental. The latter things can potentially be replaced in order to dissolve a conflict with another recommended action.

10:2.1 *The strategy of hierarchy-building* In the case study, Nathan Daniels confronts a conflict between egoistically developing his potential and keeping his promise. His decision is complicated by the utilitarian consideration of the comparative uncertainties of going with African Electronics as opposed to Ford. Nathan may choose to resolve the conflict by attaching a greater importance to developing his potential than to keeping his promise. Implicit in this resolution is the idea of a hierarchy and the use of it to resolve an ethical problem. Nathan perceives two values, pursuing integrity and doing his duty, in conflict. He is convinced that he cannot pursue both. Being so convinced, he asks the question "Which is the more important to achieve?" He may then form a ranking, starting with the most important:

1. Pursuing integrity, through developing potential with African Electronics.
2. Doing his duty, through keeping his commitment to Ford Corporation.

This hierarchy would imply that because pursuing integrity is more important than doing one's duty, at least in these particular circumstances, then because the two conflict, pursuing integrity, the higher value, should be undertaken at the expense of doing one's duty, the lower value.

Put abstractly, then, the strategy of hierarchy-building amounts to this: It is assumed that two or more values cannot both be realized. Then it becomes appropriate to ask, "Which value should be realized?" The trivial answer, "The more important one, of course," is then given substance by ranking the relevant values from most to least important. From the ranking a decision may be drawn about the course of action to be followed.

10:2.2 *Objective criteria* Let's look at the *plausibility* of building value hierarchies. For the formation of a hierarchy to be a useful model for rational resolution of conflict, it is necessary for there to be some objective criteria to justify its formation. It is not clear whether or not there is such an objective criterion in the case of Nathan Daniels. Such a criterion, being objective, would be a criterion to which all parties could appeal and which all parties would accept.

What could such a criterion be? A simple example may help to illuminate the kind of hierarchy theorists have found promising. Suppose two children were to hear Horowitz play the piano. Each child likes classical music, and after the concert each child claims to have liked the music very much and to have found it very pretty. Is there any way in which we can distinguish the quality of the two children's appreciation? Well, suppose that one child has no training as a musician, whereas the other has practiced the piano for two hours a day for many years. Thus, that child is aware of the artistry and the technical precision involved in Horowitz's playing. On this supposition we can say objectively that the second child's appreciation of the concert is richer than that of the first. Although both children found the music pretty, the second child alone could appreciate Horowitz's artistry. The other child by hypothesis was unaware of piano technique.

What can be extracted from this simple example? Essentially the second child's appreciation is *more encompassing* than the first. The second child's appreciation involves everything that the first does, *but it also involves more*. Thus if one's action could be said to contain not only one desired value but another desired value besides, then that action could thereby be said to be the better for being the richer. John Stuart Mill once said "[It is] better to be Socrates dissatisfied than a fool satisfied."[1] This remark suggests a hierarchy based on the richness of experience. Socrates is able to experience the environmental awareness and the sensations of which the fool is capable, but the fool is not capable of the self-awareness, the abstract thought, the rationality, the awareness of time, and so on, which Socrates has. Hence Mill judges Socrates's experience preferable.

Unfortunately this criterion does not seem to help Nathan Daniels. If he were merely concerned with developing his potentials, he should prefer actions that are richer in the manner just described. But keeping promises simply does not seem to be *comparable* to developing one's potentials in these terms.

An alternative way of forming hierarchies in decision-making allows us to rank values on the assumption that some values are *more fundamental*. For example, suppose there were a labor union some of whose members held insecure jobs and were frequently laid off. Now in the country where this labor union exists, no welfare programs provide funds for those laid off. The union, however, also has a group of rather wealthy, highly trained, much desired workers whose labor is always in demand. The union is thus faced with a problem. To its first group of members, job security is very important because they could literally face starvation without it. To its second group of members, job security is not really an issue because they are confident they will always have it. This group of workers wants the union to demand an increased number of four-day weekends and holidays.

The union, of course, wants to keep all its members, although somehow the leaders recognize that the concerns of the first group of workers are the most important. They express this importance as follows: "You can have a job without a holiday, but you can't have a holiday without a job."

Stated abstractly, the concept of a fundamental value is the concept of a value such that if it is not realized, then another, less funda-

---

[1]See 12:4.1 for elaboration of this point.

mental value, cannot be realized, while at the same time if the less fundamental value is realized, the more fundamental value can still be realized. Life, safety, and health could be said to be very fundamental values because without them many other values, such as having leisure time, developing talent, and entertainment, cannot be pursued or are at least jeopardized.[2]

10:2.3 *Limits to hierarchies* The *problem* with hierarchical thinking is that conflicting values do not always neatly form hierarchies. It is not always obvious or demonstrable that of two conflicting actions one guarantees a richer result or reflects a more fundamental value than the other. If one action aims at peace and another aims at justice, it is not clear that either peace will involve justice or that justice will involve peace, nor that one is the more fundamental. This lack of any obvious hierarchy may hold in the case of Nathan Daniels.

10:3.1 *The strategy of dissolution* If we serve parsnips, Mabel will be unhappy. If we serve eggplant, Roy will be upset. We have no other vegetables on hand. What shall we do? Clearly, given our supply of vegetables we will not satisfy Mabel and Roy, but the tension here hardly seems to be inevitable. It seems probable that both Mabel and Roy like some vegetables. So, even if those vegetables have to be bought, there doesn't seem to be any necessity that the food should displease either of them.

Just as it is possible to serve both or neither of two particular vegetables, it is also possible to pursue both of two complementary, although divergent, aims. Nathan Daniels is concerned that if he goes with African Electronics without contingency plans, he may wind up without work one or two years later. But again there is no necessary incompatibility with taking the job at African Electronics and having a secure future. Nathan could form a backup plan to handle that possibility.

Even when aims are not merely divergent but conflicting, it is possible that the conflict only arises because of *present* circumstances. In other circumstances the conflict might dissolve, and so changing the present circumstances may lead to a resolution of a current problem. For instance, Bendicorp and Ford might merge, letting Nathan do the Bendicorp job while working for Ford.

10:3.2 *Developing alternatives* Let's consider the *plausibility* of the strategy of dissolution. Dissolution is a particularly promising way to han-

---

[2]Following this line of reasoning, *life* is the most fundamental value because without life, no other value is possible. An argument of this sort is developed in Ayn Rand, *The Virtue of Selfishness* (New York: New American Library, 1964), p. 17.

dle tension in situations involving alternative evils. When it seems that no matter which choice we will make we will choose something undesirable, the possibility of not having to choose at all, or the possibility of being able to choose a third alternative, is particularly attractive. Antagonistic parties, for example, may feel that they can afford neither to trust nor not to trust each other. If they trust each other, they are likely to be deceived and harmed; whereas if they distrust each other, they will be unable to work together to solve their mutual problems. Here working closely with each other without trusting each other, but with considerable safeguards to insure that each side performs up to the other's expectations, is an alternative to both the attitude of unguarded trust and that of total distrust. The device of legally enforced contract is the most common manner of attaining this sort of cooperation.

The strategy of dissolution of the conflict involves developing *alternatives that would avoid the problem*. If there is a tension caused by divergence without conflict, then it is possible to accommodate the divergence by performing both actions. If there is tension caused by undesirable consequences of either of two alternative courses, when a third or fourth course of action remains, then do neither of the first two. If a conflict arises between two aims owing to present circumstances or to the means chosen, then change the circumstances or the means, so that nothing more than divergence remains.

In a word, then, this strategy is built upon *flexibility*, flexibility at all levels. At a material level, for example, abundance of resources facilitates defining alternative means. So does difference in preferences. Our economic system provides us with a way of resolving apparent "conflicts of interest" without using force. On the market we exchange something we value less for something we value more, and other individuals do the same. People should be clearly and distinctly aware of their goals. Such awareness allows one to distinguish goals from the means one is accustomed to using but which one may not need to use in order to accomplish those goals. The more flexible persons choose different means, the better the strategy of dissolution can be executed.

This strategy also makes a virtue of foresight. Once Nathan Daniels has already committed himself to the Ford Corporation, dealing with the offer from African Electronics is problematic. Keeping alternatives available, not making commitments one may be unable to keep, planning to insure that divergent aims do not become conflicting but can be accommodated within a single plan, all of these can be encompassed by the virtue of foresight so dear to the strategy of dissolution.

10:3.3 *Limitations*   There seem to be some conflicts that are unavoidable, especially given circumstances over which we have no control and thus under which we are forced to live. For instance, when Nathan Daniels committed himself to the Ford Corporation he could not have foreseen receiving a more attractive offer from African Electronics. In general, many consequences of our actions are uncontrollable because they are unforeseeable.

Some theorists would argue that dissolution is also limited as a strategy because it does not build character. If it is honorable to keep your commitments, say, then it is desirable to develop the character traits that will enable you to do so. Moral fortitude and nobility of the soul are valuable intrinsically, according to some theorists, not simply as means enabling persons to keep commitments. If dedication to ideals and the ability to translate principle into practice are intrinsically good, then the strategy of dissolution of conflict can seem suspicious whereas a hierarchical approach may seem superior. For although the latter demands that the agent be morally firm and have a moral resolve to follow the highest principle through the gravest of conflicts, the strategy of dissolution continually attempts to prevent situations from arising in which moral resolve and fortitude will be needed.

10:4.1 *The strategy of compromise* A third strategy for resolving conflict is that of compromise, providing something, but not everything, for everybody; or providing some of each of the values, rather than realizing any one of the values to the exclusion of others. In the case study, one possible compromise might be for Nathan to keep his promise to Ford, that is, to begin working for them, and to very soon thereafter ask for a leave of absence to work with African Electronics. Should Ford be willing to go along with this arrangement, Nathan will have succeeded in both keeping his promise to Ford and beginning to pursue the development of his potential with African Electronics.

In compromising, one must negotiate, giving something up in order to get something else. Ford may demand that Nathan accept the loss of seniority and the forfeit of pay increases in order to be granted the leave; African Electronics may demand that Nathan accept a less desirable starting salary because of the delay.

10:4.2 *The basis of compromise* Let's consider the *plausibility* of compromise. Like those of hierarchy-building and of dissolution, the strategy of compromise has presuppositions. First, because it proposes that everyone should be giving something, or that each of the values should be actualized in some degree, it is assumed that valuable commodities can be distributed in degree. If some values cannot be partially realized, if for example, you cannot partially keep a simple promise, then there is no room for compromise. The second presupposition is that there is no rational hierarchy available, either of the values in conflict or of the persons whose interests should take first place.

What principle for resolving his problem is Linus using?

1959 United Feature Syndicate, Inc.

The first clause of this denial means that we cannot apply the strategy of hierarchy. The second clause, the one applied to persons, is in effect the assertion of justice; for if no person can be treated unfairly, then the rights of all persons must be respected. The third presupposition is that the tension between the values cannot be dissolved. If the tension could be dissolved and it were possible, thereby, for everything valuable to be achieved or everything undesirable to be avoided, then there would be no sense in agreeing to a compromise which would yield less. Compromise, then, is a last-ditch strategy, predicated upon the failure of both those of hierarchy and dissolution.

10:4.3 *Limitations*   The strategy of compromise involves two sorts of problems, one theoretical and one practical. Theoretically, the problem arises from its essential presupposition that the contested values can be realized in degree rather than fully. If one is concerned about benefits like wealth, education and leisure that enhance the quality of life beyond what is *necessary* to a minimal standard of living (or even to a good and virtuous life) then it is easy to see how compromise would be possible. However, is it reasonable, for instance, to suppose that promises can be kept to a degree? Or, can persons be respected to a degree? In other words, sometimes if one compromises a value by realizing only a part of it, then the part realized will be insubstantial or of no real value or gain at all, especially in comparison to what was sacrificed in the compromise. As long as all parties are agreed that they are negotiating about relative desirables and undesirables such that none of them is necessary to achieve nor avoid, there is room for compromise.

150

A practical problem of this strategy is that it tends to blur the line between power and authority. In practice one is usually pushed forcefully toward a compromise that favors the more powerful, for the more powerful are much more able to enforce their will than are the weak. For example, a large corporation polluting a small community might refuse to install anti-pollution equipment. By insisting upon a *fair* compromise unpalatable to the powerful (e.g., a reasonable delay in installing the equipment at the corporation's expense) the weak may jeopardise a small compromise that might have been initially acceptable to the powerful. (e.g., tax incentives for installing the equipment). Thus, whereas the ideal of compromise assumes that all the parties have rights,[3] so that each should be treated fairly, the reality of power in society suggests that compromise will regularly tend to promote a degree of injustice in favor of the powerful. In the pollution case the corporation might insist as a "compromise" that the community pay for the anti-pollution devices. This suggests an important reason why one should not compromise on moral principles. Unless there is basic agreement on moral principles among those compromising, naked power will dictate the outcome of the "compromise."

10:5 *Summary*   In this chapter we have introduced the contrast between value divergence and essential value conflict. We considered three strategies for rational resolution of ethical tension, each of which has presuppositions which if not met make the strategy unemployable. Each of them has strengths and virtues and each can work in certain kinds of situations to resolve value conflicts. All, however, have weaknesses, and each one of them is incapable of handling some sort of conflict. Before giving up on them, however, you should be sure that you are willing to accept as true and as socially viable the difficult proposition that nonrational methods of resolving conflict are superior to rational ones.

EXERCISES for Chapter 10

1. Below you are asked to assume certain recommended courses of action. In light of these recommendations, evaluate certain other recommended courses of action as divergent *(D)*, nonessentially conflicting *(C)*, or essentially conflicting *(EC)*, and mark them accordingly (10:1.1 and 10:1.2).

---

[3]A right is a moral principle by which a person may perform certain acts because other persons are obligated not to interfere. Thus your right to live and support your life places the factory owner under an obligation not to poison you by polluting the air.

a. Recommendation: The family should take a three-week vacation next summer, flying to and from Alaska, their destination.

_____A. The kids should have an opportunity to participate in Little League.

_____B. Father should be spared the air sickness planes give him.

_____C. Mother should not quit her job which allows her only two weeks of vacation.

b. Recommendation: Frieda should keep her promise to babysit for her neighbor's children in her neighbor's short absence.

_____A. Frieda's son, Rodney, has just badly cut himself and should have emergency medical treatment at the hospital.

_____B. Frieda wants to continue knitting a sweater.

_____C. Frieda had already promised to spend the time shopping downtown alone with her daughter, Stella.

2. Characterize each of the following models for resolution of normative tensions: hierarchy-building, problem-dissolution, compromise (10:2.1, 10:3.1, 10:4.1, respectively).

3. Below is a list of assertions, some of which are true of hierarchy-building, some of problem-dissolution, and some of compromise. Put a *T* or *F* in each of the three columns in order to indicate whether an assertion is true or false in each view.

HB   PD   C

a. _____ _____ _____ This model will work only if there is no essential conflict in the situation.

b. _____ _____ _____ This model is recommended if one of the values in tension is more fundamental than the other.

c. _____ _____ _____ This model assumes that a rational solution is possible even if it is impossible for all parties to achieve everything they originally wanted.

d. _____ _____ _____ This model can still work even if there is an essential conflict between values that cannot be objectively ranked.

e. _____ _____ _____ If successful, this method involves no violence arising from the resolution of tension.

f. _____ _____ _____ This model is likely to work in favor of the powerful.

g. _____ _____ _____ The workability of this model is improved when there is an increased variety of means available to achieve each goal.

h. _____ _____ _____ This model requires the choice of one of the values in tension over the other.

i. _____ _____ _____ This model works toward the full achievement of all goals and values.

	HB	PD	C
j.	_____	_____	_____

j. This model works toward the partial achievement of central values.

4. Describe three cases such that each is best handled by a different one of the three strategies. Then state the characteristics of each of the cases that makes it best handled by a particular strategy.

SELECTED ANSWERS for Chapter 10

1. a. A. *D*, but not conflicting assuming that at least three summer weeks do not involve Little League.
   B. *C*, but not essentially because visiting Alaska is the goal and flying is only one means.
   C. *EC*.

   b. A. *C*, but not essentially if she can take the neighbor's children with her to the hospital.
   B. *D*, but not conflicting unless the children require her full and constant attention.
   C. *EC*.

3. a. F T F   c. T F T   e. T T T   g. F T T   i. F T F
   b. T F F   d. F F T   f. F F T   h. T F F   j. F F T

   Review the plausibility and limitations of each strategy in order to understand each one more fully.

4. Tensions in which there is no essential conflict can, at least with ingenuity, be resolved in such a way that everyone can achieve all of his or her goals. If this is possible, it is more desirable than achieving only the primary goal or only some of one's goals to some extent (PD model).

   If there is an essential conflict between values, at least in the situation, then if one value objectively has a higher priority then the other(s), the value with that priority should be realized and the other value(s) ignored or compromised to some extent (HB model).

   If there is both an essential conflict and no objective hierarchy in accord with one value is of higher priority than the other, then compromise becomes appropriate if the partial achievement of conflicting values is possible (C model).

   These comments suggest that there is an objective hierarchy of strategies: First, try to dissolve the problem; perhaps all values can be realized or other options exist (PD). But if essential conflicts arise, try building a hierarchy to maximize the most important values (HB). But if no objective ranking is possible, go to compromise (C).

PERSPECTIVES

ON HUMAN

NATURE

AND

PERSONAL

IDENTITY

"Know thyself!" These words, inscribed in stone, greeted every visitor to the temple of Apollo in ancient Delphi. The philosopher Socrates took them to heart and dedicated his life to answering the questions "Who am I?" and "What am I?" As you probably know, the sincere effort to know yourself can be both a frustrating and a rewarding adventure. Philosophers have asked whether there is such a thing as human nature. If so, what is it like? In light of what it is to be human, how should people live?

Socrates was intensely *practical* concerning self-knowledge. He claimed, "The unexamined life is not worth living." A person who is not committed to self-examination cannot function as a successful agent and lead a meaningful life. The questions Socrates asked about himself also had a bearing on the people with whom he interacted and therefore had important social implications: "To let no day pass without discussing goodness and all the other subjects about which you hear me talking and examining both myself and others is really the very best thing that a human being can do."[1]

[1]Plato, *Apology* 38a, in E. Hamilton and H. Cairns, *The Collected Dialogues of Plato* (Princeton: Princeton University Press, 1972).

🖋 PART THREE

Self-knowledge in the Socratic tradition is closely tied to the philosophical purposes of *criticism* and *evaluation* of your life and actions. Many later philosophers with broader, more systematic interests than Socrates have recognized the importance of his questions. Philosophers who want to understand knowledge wish to define the place of the knower in the world, and this definition means understanding *themselves* as knowers. Philosophers who have set out to describe the fundamental nature of reality are especially concerned with their own place in the universe.

Many sayings of the oracles of Delphi could be interpreted in different ways, and "Know thyself!" is no exception. If you look at the world around you and ask "*What* am I, as a human being?" you are asking how you are different from other kinds of things. If you look at other human beings and ask "*Who* am I, as this unique human being?" you are asking how you are different from other individuals. Full self-knowledge requires an answer to both questions: a knowledge of your humanity (Chapter 11) and a knowledge of your personal identity (Chapters 12 and 13). The diagram shows the relationship between the chapters in Part Three.

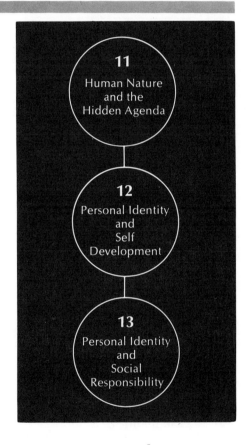

11
Human Nature and the Hidden Agenda

12
Personal Identity and Self Development

13
Personal Identity and Social Responsibility

11

Human Nature and the Hidden Agenda

Many writers have marveled at human beings and their apparent uniqueness. "In action how like an angel," exclaims Shakespeare's Hamlet, "In apprehension how like a god! The beauty of the world! The paragon of animals!" Many philosophers have tried to capture this alleged uniqueness of human beings, but any description of human nature that appeals to one philosopher meets with a chorus of objections from others who argue that the description does not fit all human beings or that they themselves have found a better definition. In the face of such disagreement, some thinkers have concluded that defining human nature is a misguided project because nothing is there to define. Human beings *do* constitute a biological species in the sense of a single interbreeding biological population, but there is no "nature" or "essence" that all members of this species share in common.

Many philosophers have dedicated their lives to the problem of understanding what it is to be a human being because of the far-reaching implications for our attitudes toward ourselves and our treatment of one another in society. This chapter can only hint at the diverse viewpoints on this issue by introducing representatives of two of the main views: Aristotle, the ancient Greek philosopher, who tries to define human nature on a biological basis; and B. F. Skinner, the modern American psychologist, who tries to deny human nature on a behavioristic basis. They disagree, not only in their *descriptions* of the way human beings are, but also in their *prescriptions* of the way human beings should behave: how we should raise our children, how we should deal with wrongdoers, and generally, what values we should jointly pursue in society. Proponents of each view claim that their prescriptions are obvious once they have described "the facts"; but critics will argue that the facts have been misdescribed to support a "hidden agenda" of prescriptions. Which view you accept will depend on your own assessment of the facts. After reading Chapter 11, you should be able to

- Explain the biological basis of Aristotle's conception of human nature.
- State Aristotle's conception of human nature.
- Criticize Aristotle's conception in terms of its descriptive adequacy.
- Explain the prescriptive function of Aristotle's theory.
- Explain the behavioristic basis of Skinner's denial of human nature.
- State Skinner's argument for denying human nature.
- Criticize Skinner's view in terms of its descriptive adequacy.
- Explain the prescriptive function of Skinner's theory.

THE CASE OF MISSEY ALBERT

"Honey, I'm home . . . Hello, Lenny? . . . Is anyone here? Hello. . . ." Julie walked through the apartment leaving her coat in the kitchen, her briefcase on the sofa and her shoes in the bedroom as she made a half-hearted search for her family. She knew that Lenny and her daughter Missey couldn't be far. Her confidence was rewarded, for just as she had traded her business suit for jeans and sweatshirt the apartment door burst open and little Missey Albert came skipping in.

"Hi, Mommie, can we go to MacDonald's tonight? Daddy made stew and I hate it. Did you see my math papers, Mommie? Where is your briefcase? Can I empty the thermos? Daddy says he needs to work on his novel tonight. Did you see my. . . ?"

"Missey, slow down, honey. I think we shouldn't go out to MacDonald's, not if Daddy already made dinner. Where is Daddy?"

"Here I am, dear." Lennie strode into the bedroom holding a basket of clean laundry that peaked just under his sweaty face. "It's good to see you. How was your day?"

"Oh fine. Routine, actually. How was yours?"

"Pretty poor, mostly. Say, Missey, why don't you go watch TV for just a few minutes while Mommie and I talk privately?"

By now Missey had managed to pull the laundry basket down from her father's grasp. She was submerging herself for the fourth time when her father asked her to leave.

"Really, Julie, what are we going to do about Missey? She is getting to be quite a problem at school. Her teacher called again today. She says Missey is disruptive. She called her hyperactive. 'Flits like a bird all day,' that's what she says."

"Oh, Lenny, again? I don't know. Mrs. Blanketbottom . . ."

"Blakebotm, honey."

"Yes, Blakebotm, Mrs. Blakebotm is an old fussbudget. She expects the kids to sit quietly in their seats all day like little toy dolls."

"No, you're wrong. The children are very active. The teacher told me she has a carefully designed program, with teaching machines and educational objectives."

"She's still wrong. Those are children, not computers to be programmed."

"Look, Julie, I do think Missey needs some discipline. She cannot go through life just doing anything she damn well pleases. That's no way to live."

"What do you mean? You can't force a child to be quiet all day. Missey's basically a good kid; a few bad habits in school maybe, but fundamentally a loving and intelligent child. She needs to be intellectually challenged, not manipulated."

"It's unfair to put it that way, Julie. The child is out of control. She will never be ready for adulthood if she doesn't learn to conform to society's standards. I just hope we're not too late."

"Well, I agree that she *is* hard to handle at times. But let her assume some responsibility, little by little as she matures. We can't force it on her all at once, Lennie. We have to teach her to make her own choices so she'll be able to decide her own life. Ultimately it's up to Missey, not you, not me, not even Mrs. Rottenbottom."

Lenny shook his head. "Missey is not an adult; she is a child. She is nine years old, not nineteen! If we don't start to work on her behavior now, well, I don't want to be around her when she is nineteen. She'll be hell to live with—inconsiderate, insensitive, self-centered, your basic brat."

"That's not fair, Lennie. You have no basis for saying that. You don't know what kind of person she will choose to be."

"Oh, don't I now? Look, you get out what you put in. It's something like training or making a scientific prediction. We have never given her any negative sanctions for her misbehavior, nor any positive reinforcement for the good things she does."

"What is this 'negative sanctions' and 'positive reinforcement' stuff? It sounds like Mrs. Blakebotm's jargon. Talk sense, Lennie. Our daughter is a person, not a rat in a maze. She just needs a little direction, a little education, so she can see how to express her talents constructively."

"Julie, say what you want, it's scientific and it works. You can control the way people behave, if you respond positively when they do what you want and negatively when they don't. All I am saying is let's help Missey grow up by enforcing a little discipline here at home. Mrs. Blakebotm emphasized that we should be gentle and not physically abuse her. We can do things like compliment her when she cleans her room or does the dishes, and we can hold back a little of our affection when she is disruptive."

"I don't think it's right to treat people that way. You don't mature people by holding back affection."

"Well then, can you think of a better idea? I for one . . ."

At that moment Missey came in. She had spilled the stew on her dress and was about to dive back into the laundry when her father stopped her in midstride.

"Well, Julie, what's it going to be?"

11:1.1 *Two ways of understanding human beings* In disagreeing over their daughter's upbringing, Julie and Lenny Albert state opposed accounts of human behavior. Of course, their statements are seriously oversimplified and one-sided. Clearly, human behavior is shaped by a number of different factors. Like other animals, human beings have many characteristics inherited as part of their genetic makeup, and such characteristics play a central role in their behavior. But they are also influenced deeply through their interaction in society, and in addition, individual persons make choices of their own which give direction to their individual lives. A theory that slights any of these factors will be inadequate.

Philosophers recognize that human behavior is the product of a complex set of determinants, but they disagree on their *relative importance* in giving shape to our conduct. In the heat of debate, opposed positions are sometimes stated in an exaggerated fashion; but rather than *ignoring* any of these factors, philosophers try to decide which are the more central or important. Still, the positions of Lenny and Julie Albert are the rough counterparts of two sophisticated and influential philosophical traditions. The tradition corresponding to Julie's view follows Aristotle by placing the greatest weight on the biological determinants of human conduct, although certain theories also take into account the contribution made by individual choices. Similar views are held today by psychologists such as Abraham Maslow and Jean Piaget. The tradition corresponding to Lenny's views places a much greater emphasis upon the role of social interaction in shaping an individual's behavior, following the contemporary behaviorist B. F. Skinner.

Who am I?

What am I?

Is the search for identity ever completed?

11:1.2 *The controversy over "human nature"* There are deep, irreconcilable differences between the Aristotelian and Skinnerian approaches to human beings, but these differences are sometimes stated in misleadingly simple terms. For example, Skinner sometimes seems to deny that there is such a thing as human nature, but he cannot reasonably be denying that human beings generally share a certain genetic endowment which has implications for human behavior. To understand the disagreement, therefore, it will be necessary to define clearly the question, "Is there a human nature?" The philosophers, in effect, are disagreeing over other more specific questions, such as "Do *all* human beings share certain important characteristics?" and "How important in shaping human behavior are the characteristics that humans do share?"

11:2.1 *Human nature as biological*   Aristotle's view of human nature was based upon his careful work in biology, as he believed that understanding other species of life is necessary for an understanding of human nature. Each species of animal or plant is identified within a *taxonomy*, or system of biological classification. The biologist pays attention to the various characteristics of individual organisms. Some of these characteristics will be common to all the individuals in natural groups or species. For example, all human beings stand upright on two legs, have opposable thumbs, and use language. However, the biologist also observes commonalities between human beings and other living things: They reproduce their young bisexually and are warm-blooded. The biologist groups together all the species that have such common features, and discusses these aspects of human nature alongside those of other animal natures.

11:2.2 *Biological characteristics*   The human characteristics Aristotle regards as most important are *biologically* based. All living things, including human beings, reveal growth and development: "They are observed to possess in themselves an originative power through which they increase or decrease in all spatial directions."[2] In Aristotle's analysis, biological development is a *goal-directed* phenomenon. A "goal" is what a process tends to when nothing stands in the way. For example, "A [fertilized seed or egg] does not give rise to any chance living being nor spring from any chance one; but each [seed or egg] springs from a definite parent and gives rise to a definite progeny."[3] There is a biological basis within the human embryo for growing into an adult form. In addition to the structure or form which comes into being as a result of the growth process, there is a material basis in which the human potential is realized, the distinctive flesh, blood, and bones of human beings.

   Much of human development is automatic, just as in the case of other living things, but not all, even in the higher nonhuman animals. Some potentialities are turned into actualities only by means of training and habituation. A hound is trained to locate game, and a horse is trained to race. Human beings can also develop their potential as a result of reasoning about what they ought to do. Thus a person may embark on a program of physical conditioning as a result of reasoning that it will produce better health.

   Some of the common characteristics of a species *distinguish* it

---

[2]Aristotle, *De Anima, II*, 2, trans. J. A. Smith in W. D. Ross and J. A. Smith, *The Works of Aristotle* (London: Oxford University Press, 1908–1952).

[3]Aristotle, *Parts of Animals, I*, I, 1, trans. W. Ongle in *The Works of Aristotle*. In this century Bertallanffy's work in developing systems theory and in applying it to biology has renewed scientific interest in goal-directed phenomena.

from other species. Animals have certain general characteristics in common, such as locomotion, but specific kinds of animals possess these characteristics in specific forms: Some animals walk around on all fours with cloven hoofs; some, like humans and birds, walk upright on two feet. A set of such characteristics will provide necessary and sufficient conditions for belonging to a given species (the way it moves about, reproduces itself, digests its food, perceives its environment, and so forth).

11:2.3 *The central characteristic of rationality*   The *central* characteristics of a species enable us to explain the behavior of its members to a greater extent than any other characteristics. Aristotle believed the most important characteristic of animals was the power of awareness. The self-movement of animals is prompted and controlled by their power of sensation: "Every body capable of forward movement would, if unendowed with sensation, perish and fail to reach its end, which is the aim of nature."[4] (Even some marine animals that lack the power of locomotion still have at least the sense of touch, by which they capture food.)

In human beings the central characteristic according to Aristotle is *rationality.* "In human beings the rational principle and mind are the goal towards which nature strives."[5] Aristotle speaks of humans as political animals, *explaining* this designation in terms of their possession of reasoned speech and ability to discuss what would be the just or expedient course of action. The fact that rationality is unique to human beings is not what makes it central. Humans are also the only featherless bipeds (excluding plucked chickens), but very little that is characteristic and especially distinctive of human living can be *explained* in terms of the fact that we are featherless bipeds.

That human beings often behave *irrationally* is not a difficulty for Aristotle. In ascribing rationality as a human characteristic, he is not describing how people invariably behave. Rather, he is attributing a potential of people, which may or may not be actualized.

11:2.4 *Choice and character*   Because human beings are rational, they have another extremely important distinguishing characteristic: the capacity to make choices. They can contemplate contrary courses of action, and after deliberating, choose one alternative. Because people are capable of choice, they are *responsible* for their actions. Aristotle claims that people can also be responsible for the kinds of people they are. For example, it is up to you if you want to be physically fit. You

---

[4]Aristotle, *De Anima, III*, 12.
[5]Aristotle, *Politics, VII*, 15, trans. Benjamin Jowett in *The Works of Aristotle.*

must exercise regularly, watch your diet, and so forth. If you permit yourself to deteriorate physically, you will be *incapable* of doing certain things, such as running one-half mile without stopping. Similarly, it is up to you whether or not you want to become a morally and intellectually well-developed person. *Moral* excellence, such as self-control or courage, consists in keeping your desires and actions under the control of reason; and *intellectual* excellence, which is fulfilled in scientific and philosophical activity, is the purest and most intense state of rationality. Such excellences, therefore, are the realization of our biological nature as *rational* beings; but our biological nature contains only the *potential* for such excellence, which has to be fulfilled *by choice*.

In the case study involving Missey Albert, Aristotle would clearly be on Julie's side. Missey's parents should ideally try to nurture the virtues in their daughter by instilling good habits in her. A person who prefers virtuous actions consistently will acquire virtue as a "second nature"; that is, Missey will become a generous person by sharing her toys, an honest person by telling the truth, and so forth. But ultimately, it is up to *Missey* to decide to use her rational capacities. No one else can make such a choice for her. Hence, although her parents can take some important steps toward making her a moral and happy individual, they cannot train her in the way in which one would train an animal.

11:3.1 *Descriptive inadequacy of the Aristotelian conception*   Modern biologists have questioned whether Aristotle provides an adequate description of the human species. Once question concerns the fact that some babies are born with certain defects or abnormalities, so that they lack even the potential for rational thought. There are often great differences among the members of a given nonhuman species, as well. A species cannot be defined in any simple way in terms of genetics. Two individual organisms will have different genes. Whether they belong to the same species or different species seems to be a matter of degree. The problem seems to be especially acute when a mutation occurs and the offspring of two "normal" members of a species differs from them in important ways; for example, two fish might give birth to an organism with lungs. To decide whether two organisms fall within the same species, modern biologists ask the question, "Do they belong to an actual or potential interbreeding natural population?" With this test, a severely retarded child could be regarded as a human being even if it did not possess rationality. Aristotle's conception of human nature thus suffers from descriptive inadequacy inasmuch as it fails to provide a description that applies to *all* who are biologically

Aristotle recognizes that certain individuals might n

to be true to type, and he is inclined to treat them as monsters or unnatural creatures. But he contends that a study of *normal* human beings reveals rationality as their most important characteristic, and by this he seems to mean that it is "important" not only in a descriptive but also in a "prescriptive" sense.

11:3.2 *Aristotle's view as prescriptive*   Aristotle believes that human potentialities should be actualized by people. Thus, the nature of a species defines what is good for it: "What is healthy or good is different for men and for fishes."[6] People who achieve self-development become more fully human and deserve to be praised and rewarded. Moreover, people attain the highest degree of self-actualization by developing their *rationality*, which is the highest human capacity. This statement follows from two assumptions: First, rationality is the central characteristic of human beings, because more of their behavior can be explained or understood in terms of their rationality than of any other characteristic. Second, the most central characteristic (having the most explanatory power) is the most important and valuable for people to develop.

---

[6]Aristotle, *Nicomachean Ethics*, I, 7, trans. W. D. Ross in *The Works of Aristotle*.

PHILOSOPHER'S WORKSHOP

Aristotle on the Human Good

Aristotle (384–322 B.C.) and his teacher Plato (428–347 B.C.) were the two most important figures in the history of Western Philosophy. In contrast to Plato, who regards observable reality as inferior to another, spiritual reality, Aristotle treats the world of material substances as the primary reality. He departs from Plato also in giving the senses a central role in acquiring and exercising knowledge. The key to Aristotle's biological theory is his *teleology*, which holds that biological phenomena have to be explained in terms of goal-directed activities and functions. He thinks of the state, or *polis*, as a natural human construction for the development of human potentialities, which takes the form of *happiness:*

. . . to say that happiness is the chief good seems a platitude, and a clearer account of what it is is still desired. This might perhaps be given, if we could first ascertain the function of man. For just as for a flute-player, a sculptor, or an artist, and, in general, for all things that have a function or activity, the good and the "well" is thought to reside in the function, so would it seem to be for man, if he has a function. Have the carpenter, then, and the tanner certain functions or activities, and has man none? Is he born without a function? Or as eye, hand, foot, and in general each of the parts evidently has a function, may one lay it down that man similarly has a function apart from all these? What then can this be? Life seems to be common even to plants, but we are seeking what is peculiar to man. Let us exclude, therefore, the life of nutrition and growth. Next there would be a life of perception, but *it* also seems to be common even to the horse, the ox, and every animal. There remains, then, an active life of the element that has a rational principle; of this, one part has such a principle in the sense of being obedient to one, the other in the sense of possessing one and exercising thought. And, as "life of the rational element" also has two meanings, we must state that life in the sense of activity is what we mean; for this seems to be the more proper sense of the term. Now if the function of man is an activity of soul which follows or implies a rational principle, and if we say "so-and-so" and "a good so-and-so" have a function which is the same in kind, e.g., a lyre-player and a good lyre-player, and so without qualification in all of the function (for the function of a lyre-player is to play the lyre, and that of a good lyre-player is to do so well): if this is the case, [and we state the function of man to be a certain kind of life, and this to be an activity or action of the soul implying a rational principle, and the function of a good man to be the good and noble performance of these, and if any action is well performed when it is performed in accordance with the appropriate excellence: if this is the case,] human good turns out to be activity of soul in accordance with virtue, and if there are more than one virtue, in accordance with the best and most complete.

But we must add "in a complete life." For one swallow does not make a summer, nor does one day; and so too one day, or a short time, does not make a man blessed and happy.[7]

---

[7]*Ibid.*

Why, however, is explanatory power of such value? Suppose Aristotle argues, "The power to explain phenomena is an important facet of a rational approach to the world, and conducting yourself rationally is the most important thing you can do." This argument has, as its ultimate premise, the assumption that conducting yourself rationally is the most important thing you can do. But this premise is simply another way of stating the desired conclusion, and so the argument falls into the trap of begging the question (see 2:2.3).

You may feel that the Aristotelian argument has not been stated strongly enough yet. Can you suggest stronger arguments? For example, have we taken sufficient account of the fact that we are discussing biological, that is, *life-oriented* characteristics?

11:4.1 *Environmental control of human behavior*   If Julie Albert's position in the case study corresponds to Aristotle's, Lenny's is much more in agreement with that of B. F. Skinner, who would claim that Missey's behavior is completely under the control of her environment. If there is something wrong with her behavior, the causes of the problem have to be sought in her environment, a change in which can be the only cure.

Skinner views human behavior as simply a form of animal behavior. Behavior is the product of the biological process of evolution and the process by which the environment shapes the animal after it is born. "Genetic endowment is nothing until it has been exposed to the environment, and the exposure immediately changes it."[8] Skinner rejects the view that a great deal of complex animal behavior is instinctual. For example, a duckling *learns* to follow its mother; it does not do so by instinct. In the instinct theory, a duckling is like a mechanical, windup toy, which automatically waddles after its mother whenever you let it go. Against this theory Skinner cites experiments that show that a duckling can be *taught* to follow all sorts of moving objects: duck decoys, galoshes, and so forth.[9]

Skinner developed the theory of *operant conditioning* to explain the duckling's behavior. The duckling learns because its environment reinforces its behavior. Things such as food and drink, sex, avoidance of pain, warmth, and physical contact are called *reinforcers*, because when an animal's behavior is followed by one of these things, the animal tends to behave in this way more regularly. In the case of a duckling, a reinforcer is being close to a moving object the size of a mother duck. Skinner argues that understanding environmental reinforcement is much more useful in predicting and controlling a duckling's behavior than relying on supposed instincts. Scientists resort to "instincts" when they are unable to explain why the animal behaves as it does. As soon as the theory of operant conditioning explains the behavior, instincts go out the window.

Humans are far more complex than ducks and can do many things that ducks cannot, but Skinner claims they learn and are rein-

---

[8]B. F. Skinner, *About Behaviorism* (New York: Alfred A. Knopf, 1974), p. 154.
[9]*Ibid.*, pp. 39–40.

Is human nature the product of conditioning?

forced by their environment in exactly the same way as lower animals. In fact, the greater diversity among human behaviors makes it even more obvious that the instinct theory will not explain our conduct.

11:4.2 *"Good riddance" to human nature* Skinner attacks the notion of human nature as "dangerous" on the grounds that such a belief prevents us from discovering "the real causes of human behavior," so that we can predict and manipulate it.[10] If Missey's teacher blamed Missey's behavior on her "aggressive nature," Skinner would object that this attribution tells us nothing more than we knew in the first place:

------

[10] B. F. Skinner, *Beyond Freedom and Dignity* (New York: Alfred A. Knopf, 1972), pp. 186–87.

Missey gets into trouble. It does not tell us why she behaves in the *specific* aggressive ways she does or how we might go about changing her behavior. Skinner would also criticize Aristotle's theory of human nature because it does not enable us to predict a person's behavior. Of course, Aristotle denies, on principle, that people *are* predictable! Are people predictable? If so, are they always predictable? If not always, why not?

Skinner's explicit attack on "human nature" is very misleading. It really means to attack a form of reasoning which makes use of the idea of human nature:

1) All members of the human species have a common biological nature.
2) If all members of a species share a common biological nature, the behavior of all members of that species is controlled and determined by instinct.
3) Therefore, all members of the human species do certain things by instinct, regardless of environment.

But, argues Skinner, 3 is demonstrably false. No set of instincts determines that all humans will do certain things rather than others. Human beings will become whatever their conditioning leads them to become. The above reconstruction should make it clear, however, that Skinner is attacking the *conjunction* of 1 and 2. Thus, 1 might be true whereas 2 could be false.

Skinner's thesis can be illustrated by our use of language. Some prominent linguists maintain that human linguistic behavior must be explained in terms of a common "genetic endowment." For example, all human beings are biologically "programmed" to use certain syntactical structures, so that the grammar of one language is, fundamentally, equivalent to the grammar of any other human language. But Skinner replies that people all use language in the same way because *all* the "verbal communities" in existence reinforce linguistic behavior in the same ways. Here the duckling analogy is crucial. Ducklings all follow their mothers, not because it is determined by their duck nature, but because they are *all* reinforced by their natural environment to do so. Of course, opponents of Skinner might object that a duckling is biologically "programmed" to follow objects of a certain size at a certain distance, which would include mother ducks as well as other things. This dispute is still far from settled!

11:4.3 *Culture and human control* Skinner claims that human beings uniquely exhibit *moral* behavior, because environmental control of human behavior largely takes the form of socialization by means of *culture*, which is "a set of customs or manners," "a system of values and ideas," "a network of communications," and so on.[11] A culture survives the individual members of a society over many generations. Its rules are learned and obeyed through reinforcements, such as social rewards and punishments of various kinds.

---

[11]Skinner, *About Behaviorism*, p. 208.

PHILOSOPHER'S WORKSHOP

Skinner on Society

B. F. Skinner (b. 1904) is one of the most influential psychologists in the twentieth century. Although he started in the behaviorist movement of John Watson and Ivan Pavlov in psychology, he made a revolutionary contribution to this movement in the form of the theory of operant behavior. In *The Behavior of Organisms* Skinner argued that the crude notion of a "conditional reflex" could be replaced with a powerful scientific theory involving contingencies of reinforcement. The theory was supported by famous experiments in which a chicken learned to type at a typewriter and a pigeon was taught to dance in a figure eight. He invented the Air Crib, used as a mechanical tender for his infant daughter, and the Skinner Box, used in the study of animal behavior.

In this passage from *Beyond Freedom and Dignity*, Skinner considers the implications of his views for the organization of society:

. . . it is not difficult to demonstrate a connection between *the unlimited right* of the *individual to pursue happiness* and the catastrophes threatened by unchecked breeding, the unrestrained affluence which exhausts resources and pollutes the environment, and the imminence of nuclear war. . . . *It is hard* to imagine a world in which people live together without quarreling, maintain themselves by producing the food, shelter, and clothing they need, enjoy themselves and contribute to the enjoyment of others in art, music, literature, and games, consume only a reasonable part of the resources of the world and add as little as possible to its pollution, bear no more children than can be raised decently, continue to explore the world around them and discover better ways of dealing with it, and come to know themselves accurately and, therefore, manage themselves effectively. Yet *all this is possible*

> . . . [A]n experimental analysis shifts the determination of behavior from autonomous man to the environment—an environment responsible both for the evolution of the species and for the repertoire acquired by each member. . . . A scientific view of man offers exciting possibilities. We have not yet seen what man can make of man.[12]
>
> ---
>
> [12]Skinner, *Beyond Freedom and Dignity*, pp. 204–5.

Skinner argues that our culture, like most, is far from perfect. Many people are unable to behave in the ways society expects; they feel alienated, and cause unhappiness to themselves and others. Skinner believes that such persons are the product of imperfect socialization. In a "sick society" people are reinforced to behave in conflicting ways. (If the term "sick" puzzles you—it should!) In the case of Missey, her father and mother cannot agree on what they expect of her. Her father uses negative reinforcement when she is careless, but her mother kisses her as if nothing had happened. The result is a confused girl. Skinner advocates instead a *consistent* program of positive reinforcement for children and adults with behavioral problems. He claims that the result would be a far better society.

11:5.1 *Criticisms of Skinner's view as descriptively inadequate*   Skinner's denial of human nature is predicated upon the view that environmental (meaning "cultural") rather than biological factors enable the scientist to predict and control human behavior.

Critics of Skinner deny that all the thoughts and actions of human beings are simply a result of the way in which they have been reinforced by their environment. (The controversy over language learning was mentioned in 11:4.2.) For example, they argue that certain people may suffer from learning disabilities or behavioral abnormalities because of hereditary or biochemical rather than social or environmental causes. The "hyperactive" behavior of Missey Albert might be such an example. Skinner is willing to agree that retarded people differ from normal people in terms of the "complexity of their repertoires"; that is, more intelligent animals are, in general, capable of more complex actions. The critics object, however, that human beings sometimes suffer from *specific* learning or behavioral disorders which require a biological explanation. Hence drug therapy is indicated for certain behavioral problems.

11:5.2 *Criticism of Skinner's theory as prescriptive*   Skinner holds out a vision of a more perfect world which might be attained by social control. The critics ask "Who will control the controllers?" Skinner seems to assume that the behavior of people *should* be manipulated in accordance with the value judgments of social scientists, without considering whether the scientists' motives or goals are acceptable. For example, scientists collaborated with Nazis during World War II and performed gruesome experiments on living subjects. Moreover, they often disagree among themselves about how to benefit society. Skinner believes, for example, that the "right of the individual to pursue happiness" is much less valuable than a minimal standard of living for all, but economists Milton Friedman and Friedrich Hayek would disagree. Do you think that there are convincing arguments for Skinner's perspective that people *should* be subject to social control?

Of course, when Skinner calls a society "sick" he is not merely *describing* it but also *evaluating* it negatively. He is assuming that society is *good* only if its members are controlled by consistent social reinforcement to insure a minimum standard of living for everyone. Not all philosophers would agree with Skinner about what constitutes a good society or the means to reach it. These questions can only be dealt with in the context of *ethics*, which examines conflicting claims about the good. You might ask yourself, however, what your own concept of a good society is.

11:6 *Summary* The attempt to understand what human beings are focuses on the dispute concerning the relative importance of different human characteristics. A very influential tradition follows Aristotle in his claim that certain biological conditions are central. Aristotle urges that the potential for rationality is the most important human characteristic, and he explains the importance of choice and character by relating them to rationality. Yet Aristotle's conception seems to be objectionable because it seems neither to describe how all people are nor to justify fully its view of how people ought to be. Some severely retarded humans lack even the potential for rationality, and it has been objected that an attempted appeal to the explanatory power of Aristotle's view is circular. B. F. Skinner's views contrast with those of the Aristotelian tradition because Skinner emphasizes the importance of learning and the environment which reinforces certain behaviors. He urges that human behavior is far from dominated by a set of instincts which he assumes a common biological nature would have implanted. He challenges the predictive power of any view that claims the existence of a biologically based human nature and asserts the greater predictive power of his own sort of view. Yet Skinner is also criticized precisely because it seems necessary to account for biological elements in order to predict certain human behaviors. He is also criticized on the grounds that he does not adequately justify his views concerning how persons ought to be reinforced.

EXERCISES for Chapter 11

1. Some characteristics are (1) common to the members of a group, (2) distinguishing characteristics, and (3) central characteristics (11:2.1, 11:2.2, 11:2.3). Use some of the characteristics of human beings listed below to illustrate these three concepts.

    A. have five fingers.
    B. laugh at jokes.
    C. make contracts.
    D. live on earth.
    E. are political animals.
    F. have hair.
    G. believe in God.
    H. use language.

2. In terms of the above threefold distinction, state what each of the following quotations asserts:

    A. . . . man is a political animal in a sense in which a bee is not, or any gregarious animal. Nature, as we say, does nothing without some purpose; and for the purpose of making man a political animal she has endowed him alone among the animals with the power of reasoned speech. Speech is something different from voice, which is possessed by other animals also and used by them to express pain or pleasure; for the natural powers of some animals do indeed enable them both to feel pleasure and pain and to communicate these to each other. Speech on the other hand serves to indicate what is useful and what is harmful, and so also what is right and what is wrong. For the real difference between man and other animals is that humans alone have perception of good and evil, right and wrong, just and unjust. And it is the sharing of a common view in these matters that makes a household or a city.[13]

    B. The day *may* come, when the rest of the animal creation may acquire those rights which never could have been withholden from them but by the hand of tyranny. The French have already discovered that the blackness of the skin is no reason why a human being should be abandoned without redress to the caprice of a tormentor. It may come one day to be recognized, that the number of the legs, the villosity of the skin, or the termination of the *os sacrum*, are reasons equally insufficient for abandoning a sensitive being to the same fate. What else is it that should trace the insuperable line? Is it the faculty of reason, or, perhaps, the faculty of discourse? But a full-grown horse or dog is beyond comparison a more rational, as well as a more conversable animal, than an infant of a day, or a week, or even a month old. But suppose the

---

[13]Aristotle, *Politics, I*, 2, trans. T. A. Sinclair (New York: Penguin, 1962).

case were otherwise, what would it avail? The question is not, Can they *reason?* nor, Can they *talk?* but, Can they suffer?[14]

3. a. What conceptual connection does Aristotle propose between having a goal and being a living organism (11:2.2)?

   b. What conceptual connection does Aristotle propose between goals and being a human being (11:2.2)?

   c. Explain Aristotle's concept of human nature in terms of a, b, and the concept of "central characteristics" (11:2.3).

4. a. State the connections Skinner proposes between reinforcement and behavior and between culture and reinforcement (11:4.1, 11:4.3).

   b. Use these proposed connections to explain Skinner's "denial" of human nature (11:4.2).

5. Review the quotations in question 2 and check your answers. Notice that Aristotle thinks of certain abilities as central to being human, whereas Bentham focuses on limitations—what we must endure. In terms of *common* versus *distinguishing* characteristics, how do these two views link human beings with or separate them from other animals?

6. When you think about the "hidden agenda" in discussions about human nature, you should notice that the "important" or "central" characteristics are used to argue that those having the characteristics *should be treated* alike and also treated differently from all those who lack them. Do you feel that the way something or someone ought to be treated should be based on its abilities or its limitations (for example, because porpoises use language they should be accorded political rights, or because sand is not sentient it should not be accorded legal protection from destruction)? What reasons would you give for your view? If you feel that in some circumstances the one basis is appropriate, whereas in other circumstances the other is, what important difference would distinguish these circumstances? How does what something is relate to how it should be treated?

SELECTED ANSWERS for Chapter 11

1. Living on earth is a characteristic shared by, or common to, all human beings (at least as far as we know at present). Having hair and five fingers are characteristics shared by normal—but not necessarily all—humans. Since *only* human beings, to the best of our knowledge, laugh at jokes, make contracts, and believe in God, these characteristics are sufficient to distinguish humans from nonhuman beings. The use of language is at least plausibly a central characteristic because the ability to laugh at jokes, to make contracts, and maybe also to believe in God is only possible for lan-

---

[14]Jeremy Bentham, *An Introduction to the Principles of Morals and Legislation* (New York: Hafner, 1948), p. 311.

guage-users. The use of reason in human political organizations also seems to involve language.

2. A. Aristotle is explaining why reason distinguishes humans from other animals and is more central to human life than communal organization.

   B. Bentham, a nineteenth-century English philosopher, urges that the central characteristic for having rights is a characteristic—the capacity to suffer—shared by humans and animals.

5. According to Aristotle, the potential abilities to reason and speak are central to human life, and they distinguish humans from other animals. According to Bentham, the capacity to suffer is central to having rights, and this capacity is common to both humans and other animals.

12

Personal Identity and Self-development

The Socratic injunction, "Know Thyself!" leads to two different sorts of inquiry. In comparing yourself to all that is nonhuman in the universe, you may ask, as we did in Chapter 11, "*What am I* — as a human being?" But comparing yourself to other humans, you may also ask: "*Who am I* — this unique human being?"

Many philosophers see this question of personal identity as a question of self-identification. They start from a view of you as a human being that is much closer to Aristotle's than to Skinner's. As you live out your life, you try to make something of yourself or become someone, which requires that you take responsibility for the decisions you make and that you know yourself well enough to make wise decisions and carry them out intelligently. Self-development or self-realization depends not only on how you make decisions but also on the degree to which you commit yourself and persevere; that is, the character of your life is shaped by the character of your decisions and by the depth of your commitment and perseverance in those decisions.

After reading Chapter 12 you should be able to

- Characterize theories of human identity in terms of the questions they address.
- State the characteristics of human life that involve choice and perseverance as determinants of one's personal identity.

- ■ Distinguish the senses in which personal identity is a project and a product.
- ■ Explain the existentialist theory of self-development as self-determination.
- ■ Explain the self-realization theory of self-development.
- ■ Explain how the concepts of fecundity, integrity, and respect for persons each influence the quest for self-development.

THE CASE OF THE BROTHERS HOLENSTEIN

The graduation party had been lively, and Dave Holenstein had been asked about his future plans a hundred times if he had been asked once. It seemed that all his cousins, aunts, and uncles, not to mention his parents, friends, and the parents of his friends, all wanted to know where he was going to college. They asked about his career goals, his ambitions, his financial independence—everything. After a while it started to wear on Dave, but somehow when his older brother, Louis, pulled him aside late in the party, Dave didn't mind talking about the future one more time.

"Yes, I'm thinking about college. I've been accepted at two rather good universities and at an excellent liberal arts college."

"Did you apply at City College? That's where I went for my first two years, you know."

"Sure I remember; but, no, I didn't apply. I want to live on campus, and City College is a commuter school."

"What are you going to major in? Business?"

"I've been telling the family accounting, but honestly I'm not sure. I like so many things. Music is a possibility, but so is nursing. I've always enjoyed history too. . . . Then there's anthropology and urban planning. I've thought about it a lot, but I haven't been able to decide. My girlfriend tells me I still have to find myself. Part of the problem is that there are so many things to choose from."

"You can say that again; what a range of choices. I had three. I could go into education, business, or English. Those were my only real options. I picked business because it seemed to promise the most lucrative future. Things turned out all right, but I missed my chance to really learn how to write fiction. When I was your age I dreamed of being a poor but famous author of protest novels. Well, so much for dreams! Now I'm an about-to-be-divorced, thirty-year-old, junior executive facing combined payments for a mortgage, child support, and alimony that could wipe me out financially. What I don't pay in taxes I'll be paying to the bank or Janet. I guess I did achieve poverty, if not fame. Believe me, don't get married, kid!"

"Louis, I don't have any marriage plans right now, honest."

"I didn't either when I graduated from high school, but inside two years I was engaged. A year later I was a husband and father. I know that I made my own choices; I can't blame other people for what I've done to myself, but I often wish that I could have one more chance to do it over again from age eighteen. Look at the hurt I've caused the kids . . . and Janet too, for that matter. Everyone is upset over the divorce. Mom and Dad are concerned that they won't see their grandchildren. The kids are starting to have problems in school. Janet is angry and her lawyer is milking me for everything I've got. But let's not think about my problems, what about you? Have you decided on a major?"

"Louis, I think you already asked me that. Say, let's go find Dad. Maybe you can help negotiate my tuition out of him."

12:1.1 *Self-identity as self-development*   Dave is trying to cope with a human life consisting of change and development. To say that he is trying to "find himself" is misleading, because in an important sense there is nothing *there* for him to find. One's personal identity does not exist like a constant sum throughout life. It is something that comes to be. As the existentialist philosopher Jean-Paul Sartre (b. 1905) says, "You are nothing else but what you live." The answer to the question, "Who am I?" always lies in the open future.

The openness of the human future consists in the numerous *possibilities* that exist for every human agent. Dave Holenstein has to decide among a confusing array of choices: what school to attend, what career to pursue, whether to marry. According to the existentialist, to grasp a possibility is to foresee yourself becoming what you are not. Career goals and specific actions are merely elements of the alternative selves Dave foresees as future possibilities for himself.

12:1.2 *The necessity of choice*   There is nothing automatic about the development of human possibilities. An acorn necessarily falls when it breaks off from a twig; if it lands in fertile soil and takes root it will necessarily grow into an oak tree rather than a rhododendron bush. But your human talents, abilities, and character traits all require *development* if your possibilities are to be fully realized. This development is generally conscious and intentional. Cultivating certain interests and perfecting talents may, in fact, be very hard work, as Dave will discover when he sets out to become an accountant, nurse, or musician.

In addition, out of the plurality of possibilities you can foresee

"In action how like an angel; in apprehension how like a god." But still, what choices are best?

for yourself, some are ruled out by others. Robert Frost described this human situation poetically:

> Two roads diverged in a yellow wood,
> And sorry I could not travel both
> And be one traveler . . .

The poet with difficulty decided on one road, recognizing that the choice was irrevocable:

> Oh, I kept the first for another day!
> Yet knowing how way leads on to way,
> I doubted if I should ever come back.[1]

Our lives are a succession of such "branchings," where we must take up one possibility rather than others because they are incompatible. The reason why the alternatives are incompatible is time, or rather the lack of it. You can compare the time that makes up your life to a limited, fixed supply of currency which you can use to make irrevocable purchases. There are not enough hours in a day or years in a life for Dave to become a nurse *and* a musician *and* an accountant. Incompatibilities also arise because different possibilities may place different demands upon you. This divergence is particularly obvious when the demands are physiological. The muscular development required to become a champion gymnast, for example, is contrary to that required to be a champion weight lifter. Yet when you are confronted with "branchings" you have to make a choice. Dave's future career is no more decided for him than is the poet's future path through the yellow wood. When you as an individual define your identity, a central fact is *choice*.

12:2.1 *The necessity of commitment*   Nevertheless, what you become is *not* simply a product of your choices. Innumerable human tragedies attest to the fact that there are no guarantees that people become what they choose to be. Existentialists insist that you should not make unrealistic assumptions that the cards are stacked in your favor and that success is assured. Similarly, Aristotle emphasizes the importance of a favorable environment, both natural and social, for the successful completion of a given project.

Another reason why what you will become is not simply a function of your choices is that they will yield results only if a great deal of

---

[1] Robert Frost, "The Road Not Taken," *Collected Poems* (New York: Halcyon House, 1936), p. 131.

human effort is expended to carry them out; and unless you are especially privileged, this will be mostly your own effort. The effort required to carry out an important choice, for example, to become an accomplished musician or to be a caring parent, covers a long period of time; in order to obtain the results you intend when you make the choice, you must persevere. During this time you are bound to encounter setbacks and to suffer fits of depression or sheer laziness; so if perseverance is to succeed, it must be conjoined with your firm commitment to the goal you have chosen.

12:2.2 *Personal identity as a project and a product* Each human being may be identified as an individual who makes a certain series of choices leading to self-development. In the terminology of the existentialists, a human being's personal identity is a *project*, which the human being defines by his or her choices.

As time passes your choices begin to yield fruit if you have persevered. If all goes well, Dave will indeed graduate from college, enter a career, and achieve some level of success. So will you. Looking back on your life, you will be able to see your identity as the person who has succeeded in one project or failed at another. Dave's brother, Louis, for example, recognizes that he has attained his career goals in business but has failed miserably at building a personal life with his wife and children. Taking such a retrospective view, he sees his personal identity as a *product* of earlier choices and effort.

There are, therefore, two quite different ways of viewing personal identity: as a project and process into the future, *or* as a product determined by what has gone on in the past. These two views are not mutually exclusive. The existentialist would maintain that Louis Holenstein would be making a fundamental mistake if he were to assume that his identity is altogether fixed by the unfortunate choices he has made in the past. Each moment of your life is a juncture of past and future, and the two views of personal identity as project and product provide two contrasting perspectives toward yourself: prospective and retrospective. At any time in your life, you must live prospectively, with the possibility of future success or failure, and retrospectively, with the reality of past successes and failures created by your actions.

12:3.1 *The existentialist theories of human choice* According to Aristotle, the central human characteristic is *rationality*, a property of consciousness. Personal development involves the realization of the potentials inherent within consciousness, which requires the exercise of choice. This Aristotelian view forms the basis for many modern theories of self-development, which emphasize different aspects of it. The existentialist theory emphasizes the factor of *choice* and the openness of one's future, whereas self-realization theories emphasize the specific biologically based potentialities that exist in an individual.

The existentialist Sartre argues that a human being is continually self-determining. In his terms, a human being is "for itself" *(pour soi)* rather than "in itself" *(en soi)*. As a conscious entity a human being differs fundamentally from any other entities, such as nonliving things and artifacts or even lower animals. A nonhuman entity has a predetermined identity or nature. To see this contrast, consider the difference between a human being such as yourself and a fairly sophisticated tool, such as a battery-operated pocket calculator. Although a calculator can be used to solve a wide variety of problems, what it can do is determined by its characteristics, which result from its being manufactured according to a certain preconceived design. It is possible for the calculator to display many different numbers. Which of these possibilities is actualized depends on how it is acted upon by its environment, in this case your finger pressing various buttons. However, the nature of the calculator determines how it will respond. Natural objects including nonhuman organisms resemble artifacts in that what they do is automatic, a function of their nature or their characteristics.

The existentialist starts from the premise that you are not an artifact, that you were not created according to a preconceived plan. Nor are you predetermined like a natural object, for you are capable of deciding for yourself to act in many different possible ways. You can stay in college or not, join a church or not, marry or not. These are alternative possibilities of which you are conscious, but which possibility will be realized is not determined for you by your nature. You do not respond to your environment in an automatic, predetermined way.

12:3.2 *Human beings as self-determining* Because you are not predetermined you can be self-determining. Sartre says, "Man is nothing else but that which he makes of himself. This is the first principle of existentialism."[2] As you make choices you determine what kind of human being you will be and you determine what your values are. For example, in deciding whether or not to get married, you decide whether you value the companionship and special opportunities of marriage or the freedom and convenience of single life. In making such choices you define a plan of life or system of values, which determines what sort of person you are at this point in time. Thus, in response to Socrates's question, "What am I?" Sartre says that it is up to you to decide.

---

[2]Jean-Paul Sartre, "Existentialism Is a Humanism," trans. Walter Kaufmann, in *Existentialism from Dostoevsky to Sartre*, ed. Walter Kaufmann (London: Methuen & Co. Ltd), p. 289. By permission of Les Editions Nagel.

Even if human beings have the opportunity to work out such life plans for themselves, many people permit others to define for them what kind of persons they will be. Through desire for approval, fear of reprisal, or simple lack of imagination, people settle into socially defined roles and behave in mechanical ways which do not lead to personal development. They acquiesce first to the desires of their parents; later, to those of their peer groups. The existentialist believes that such acquiescence is a serious moral fault because it prevents the person from leading an *authentic* existence. You can achieve authenticity in life only by determining for yourself what sort of life you shall lead. Whenever people let others make choices for them they are not true to themselves, argues the existentialist.

You must choose within physical constraints. Prisoners cannot ignore the walls that enclose them; handicapped persons cannot choose to stand up on paralyzed legs. Yet even these constraints serve to define a range of freedom. For example, the disabled person must choose how to live with the disability. Is it to be regarded as a source of humiliation? As an excuse for all of one's failures? As an obstacle to be overcome? Sartre insists, "I cannot be crippled without choosing myself as crippled."[3] There is no guarantee that the project you choose will succeed, but if human beings did not engage themselves in the world, neither success nor failure would be possible.

---

[3]*Being and Nothingness*, trans. Hazel Barnes (New York: Washington Square Press, Inc., 1966), p. 402.

 PHILOSOPHER'S WORKSHOP

Sartre on Human Reality

Jean-Paul Sartre is the leading spokesperson of French existentialism. The following passages show his firm conviction that in reality there is a strong connection between the necessity of human choice and accepting the responsibility for that choice.

The doctrine I am presenting before you declares that there is no reality except in action. It goes further, indeed, and adds, "Man is nothing else but what he purposes, he exists only in so far as he realizes himself, he is therefore nothing else but the sum of his actions, nothing else but what his life is." . . . [I]n reality and for the existentialist, there is no love apart from the deeds of love; no potentiality of love other than that which is manifested in loving; there is no genius other than that which is expressed in works of art. The genius of Proust is the totality of the works of Proust; . . . No doubt this thought may seem comfortless to one who has not made a success of his life. On the other hand, it puts everyone in a position to understand that reality alone is reliable; that dreams, expectations and hopes serve to define a man only as deceptive dreams, abortive hopes, expectations unfulfilled; that is to say, they define him negatively, not positively. Nevertheless, when one says, "You are nothing else but what you live," it does not imply that an artist is to be judged solely by his works of art, for a thousand other things contribute no less to his definition as a man. What we mean to say is that a man is no other than a series of undertakings, that he is the sum, the organization, the set of relations that constitute these undertakings.[4]

_____

[4]Sartre, "Existentialism Is a Humanism," pp. 300–1.

12:3.3 *Human beings as free and responsible* "To be free means only to choose oneself." But if you are free to choose, you are also totally responsible for your own existence. If you make a mistake, if you are a failure, you are without excuse. Many people would rather leave the choice up to someone else, especially when it involves risks. The existentialist, however, will not accept the excuse, "I had no choice. I couldn't do anything else." As a human being you *must* assume responsibility for the actions that make you the person you become.

12:3.4 *Criticism of Sartre's theory* Many critics find Sartre's theory inadequate because he does not explain from where the alternative possibilities for people arise. Sartre seems to hold that consciousness is the source of freedom, and that we are in total control of our mental lives; but this belief implies that human freedom has an extremely broad range. Consider the example of an inferiority complex. Although a person may have no control over whether or not he or she is ugly or awkward, Sartre contends that "the inferiority complex is a free and global project of myself as inferior before others; it is the way in which I choose to assume my being-for-others, the free solution which I give to the other's existence, that insuperable scandal."[5] Sartre seems to maintain that your entire mental and emotional life is under your own conscious control. The proponents of "the power of positive thinking" make similar claims. Many critics find this view of human freedom

_____

[5]Sartre, *Being and Nothingness*, p. 562.

descriptively incorrect, claiming that your thoughts, attitudes, and feelings are caused, at least in part, by forces outside your own control. (You might consider as an exercise how Skinner's theory, described in Chapter 11, would explain an inferiority complex.)

12:4.1 *Self-realization theories of human choice*   Although existentialists emphasize the necessity of choice and personal commitment, they do not provide criteria by which to evaluate different systems of choice. Indeed, they assert that this evaluation is impossible.

Other philosophers have articulated criteria—purported to be based in human biology or psychology—according to which hierarchies of needs or values can be constructed. For example, the psychologist Abraham Maslow has offered a descriptive account of human needs; that is, he claims to be describing the priorities that, in fact, govern human needs, not stating which human needs *should* take precedence over others. According to Maslow, human needs form a hierarchy, the primary ones being based on human physiology. When these are satisfied, other, higher needs emerge and dominate the life of the individual. The most basic needs of the individual are those for survival. Next, the individual becomes concerned with such needs as the need for love and belonging, and above all, the need for self-actualization. An individual tries to satisfy as many needs as possible, and strives, where possible, to fulfill higher ones. But if a lower, more basic need is threatened (for example, if the person is in immediate danger of starving or freezing to death), all interest in the higher needs will dissolve. When people fail to develop their potential (like Louis Holenstein when he abandoned his dream to become a writer), they tend to be discontented and restless. Like Aristotle, Maslow sees in people a biologically based urge to actualize their potentialities and to deal with their environment in rational and creative ways.

 PHILOSOPHER'S WORKSHOP

Maslow's Hierarchy of Needs

Abraham Maslow (1908–1970) has been very influential in the "human potentials" movement. He developed the following hierarchy to describe how human needs actually relate to one another.

1. need for physiological continuance of life
2. need for safety

3. need for belongingness and love
4. need for esteem
5. need for self-actualization
6. need for knowledge and understanding
7. need to experience aesthetic pleasure

The rules according to which needs are related are:

1. The individual tries to satisfy as many needs as possible.
2. The needs at or below level n must be satisfied, before needs above level n emerge and dominate one's activity.
3. If the needs at level n become threatened, the individual takes no interest in needs above level n until the threat is removed.[6]

---

[6]Adapted from Abraham H. Maslow, *Motivation and Personality* (New York: Harper, 1954).

Maslow's work raises the empirical questions: Is this indeed the true order or hierarchy of human needs? Are there other generic human needs that have yet to be added? You might also approach the question of human needs by asking the normative question, "What should the hierarchy be?"

PHILOSOPHER'S WORKSHOP

Mill on Ranking Pleasures

The British philosopher John Stuart Mill (1806–1873) argues for a normative, rather than descriptive, statement of the priorities that should govern human values. Mill also proposed a method whereby the proper value priorities could be determined.

If I am asked what I mean by difference of quality in pleasures, or what makes one pleasure more valuable than another, merely as a pleasure, except its being greater in amount, there is but one possible answer. Of two pleasures, if there be one to which all or almost all who have experience of both give a decided preference, irrespective of any feeling of moral obligation to prefer it, that is the more desirable pleasure. If one of the two is, by those who are competently acquainted with both, placed so far above the other that they prefer it, even though knowing it to be attended with a greater amount of discontent, and would not resign it for any quantity of the other pleasure which their nature is capable of, we are justified in ascribing to the preferred enjoyment a superiority in quality so far outweighing quantity as to render it, in comparison, of small account.

Now it is an unquestionable fact that those who are equally acquainted with and equally capable of appreciating and enjoying both do give a most marked preference to the manner of existence which employs their higher faculties. Few human creatures would consent to be changed into any of the lower animals for a promise of the fullest allowance of a beast's pleasures; no intelligent human being would consent to be a fool, no instructed person would be an ignoramus, no person of feeling and conscience would be selfish and base, even though they should be persuaded that the fool, the dunce, or the rascal is better satisfied with his lot than they are with theirs. . . . It is better to be a human being dissatisfied than a pig satisfied; better to be Socrates dissatisfied than a fool satisfied. And if the fool, or the pig, are of a different opinion, it is because they only know their own side of the question. The other party to the comparison knows both sides.[7]

_____
[7]John Stuart Mill, *Utilitarianism*, Library of Liberal Arts (Indianapolis, Ind.: Bobbs-Merrill Publishing Company, 1957), pp. 12–14.

12:4.2 *Maxim of choice: fecundity*   In discussing the choice between different needs, one can be guided by several criteria or principles. For example, one rational principle is that the best choice is the one with the greatest *fecundity* (that is, it opens up the greatest number of future possibilities). Numerous possibilities exist for you as a human being. When you choose a course of action, you open up new possibilities for yourself but you also seal off other possibilities. John Stuart Mill criticizes the preference of people who sink into lives of slothful ignorance and self-indulgence because they thus cut themselves off from innumerable possibilities involving their higher faculties. The maxim is to try to make choices in such a way as to increase as far as possible the number of possibilities that you might desire in the future.

12:4.3 *Maxim of choice: integrity*   Of course, there are limits to the number of possibilities you can seriously entertain because not all possibilities are compatible with each other. Any time you make a choice, you must consider how many desired and undesired possibilities are opened up by that choice. If you decide to marry, you create the possibility of having children and raising them into adulthood, but you also create the possibility of divorce and a broken home for your children. As life progresses the choices become harder, for you have to consider the possibilities created by your present choices in the light of those you have made in the past and your relative success in carrying them out. For example, if you have spent years training to be a champion swimmer and you then decide to become a wrestler you will frustrate the further realization of your possibilities as a swimmer. Moreover, you will only create a frustrating situation for yourself to the extent that your body is no longer suited for wrestling. This example suggests the second maxim of choice, which qualifies the first maxim in an important way: Create new possibilities for yourself only insofar as you can integrate the choices you are now making with the choices you have previously made.

Existentialists would not accept this second maxim without qualification. They claim the individual is always free to make a "liberat-

CAPACITY

A contribution to the psychology of disappointment

Some people live
    in a dream of what'll
allow them to
    live their dream:
they solemnly hold out
    a half-pint bottle
and ask for
    a pint of cream.

What virtues and vices of self-development does this rhyme suggest?

ing choice," to start out totally anew. The criminal can decide to give up a life of crime and try to approach the future in an altogether honest way, or the corrupted libertine, like Augustine, can suddenly abandon a life of sin for a strictly religious one. However, even if the existentialist is correct that one can exchange one life plan for another, the new one could hardly be carried out except in conformity with the maxim of integrity.

12:4.4 *Maxim of choice: respect for persons* The maxims of fecundity and integrity direct individuals to act as fully and consistently as possible to further their own self-interest. They do not take into account the interests of other persons, except for the relatively few instances in which you take a direct personal interest in someone, such as a family member or friend.

In contrast, the *humanistic*, or "human potentials," approach to personal identity focuses on potentials designated as "human." "Human" potentials are those for relating to other human beings in ways that are essentially respectful. Respect for persons involves the recognition that other human beings exist in essentially the same situation as you. In the face of open futures, they are trying to define their own identities by forming meaningful life plans for themselves. Respect for persons can take different forms, and different philosophical traditions emphasize different aspects. The *libertarian* tradition tends to emphasize your potentials for recognizing the rights of others, for not treating others as if they were natural resources, for not imposing your personal value choices on others. The *egalitarian* tradition tends to emphasize your potentials for caring for others, for offering help to others, for facilitating others' pursuits of self-development. This notion of respect for persons suggests a final maxim for governing the development and realization of personal identity: In making choices, place special value on qualities or human potentials that involve treating other persons with respect and consideration.

12:5 *Summary* Human life involves change and development, constantly confronting you with new arrays of possibilities for the future. Defining your identity is, in one important sense, defining the possibilities you will realize. This development entails making choices and carrying them out with perseverance. Your personal identity can be described both as a project, as you look into the open future, and as a product, as you look into the past of completed choices, both successes and failures. Existentialist theories of self-development assume that human beings are free entities capable of determining their own identify. Self-realization theories assume that human beings have biologically based potentialities which define hierarchies of values and needs for individuals. Maslow offers a descriptive statement of such a hierarchy, and Mill has offered a normative ranking of values. Implicit in their discussions are certain criteria for ordering choices: fecundity, the maximizing of desired possibilities; integrity, the limiting of choices to those which can be integrated into a life plan; and respect for persons, choosing to treat people with consideration.

EXERCISES For Chapter 12

1. Sections 12:1 and 12:2 explain the questions to which any theory of personal development must address itself. That explanation assumes several distinctions, namely, the distinctions among (1) a theory of personal development versus one of human nature (Chapter 11), (2) the questions any theory of personal development must discuss versus the answers that a particular theory (such as Sartre's) gives, and (3) what a theory of personal development amounts to versus what is no more than a *part* of such a theory.

   a. Below is a set of statements. Observing the three distinctions above, mark each statement true or false.

      A. The theory will recognize that personal development is not automatic.

      B. The theory will describe what characteristics, common to human beings, distinguish them from nonhuman creatures.

      C. The theory will deny any importance to habit in human life in order to emphasize the importance of choice to personal development.

      D. The theory will acknowledge that some choices a person may make are incompatible with other choices.

      E. The theory will understand human life entirely as the product of the choices we have made.

      F. The theory will take account of the fact that even wise choices may not lead to favorable results if the environment is too hostile.

      G. The theory will describe the variety of ways in which a human being should develop his or her distinctly human characteristics.

      H. The theory will be committed to the view that persons ought to persevere in the choices they have made.

      I. The theory will take note that several human projects can become completed projects only through efforts over a long period of time.

      J. The theory will consist of an answer to the question, "How should people use their abilities to reason?"

   b. After checking your answers to (a), explain why each false statement is false by putting 1, 2 or 3 next to it to indicate which distinction above it fails to observe.

2. Below is a set of statements about self-development. Some are true according to self-realization views of self-development *(S-R)*, some are true according to Sartre's existential view *(E)*, some are true according to both views *(B)*, and some are affirmed by neither view *(N)*. Mark them accordingly.

   A. It is always better that people should choose for themselves, rather than ever acquiesce in the choices of others.

   B. Personal development should focus on those characteristics that human beings share with other animals rather than on any distinctly human characteristics.

   C. A person's development continually involves selection of one alternative from the various available possibilities.

   D. A human being's personal development should involve as little disruption as is possible of the natural world.

   E. Personal development involves meeting one's human needs, the most fundamental ones first.

   F. Possible courses of action have value only when persons ascribe value to them by their choices.

   G. To understand a person is to understand the person's potentialities and abilities as well as the person's choices and actions.

   H. No path of personal development is right just because it represents God's will for the person.

3. A theory may be criticized on several grounds: (1) what it says is unclear, vague, or ambiguous; (2) it contains inconsistencies, perhaps contradicts itself, perhaps sets or uses standards for a good theory that it does not even meet itself; (3) it describes human beings incorrectly, either by stating or assuming something that is false; (4) it overrates certain values or endorses values it should not; (5) it fails to endorse values that it should. Below is a set of statements, each criticizing one or both of the theories studied in this chapter on one of the five grounds stated above.

   a. Mark the kind of grounds on which each of the following criticisms is made.

      A. If human beings always strove to meet the most basic need that is challenged, then there would never have been martyrs.

      B. The prescription that all persons must make their own choices is confused because it tells them they must choose not to be chosen for.

      C. There is nothing more blessed than recognizing one's harmony with the universe, a truth the theory ignores.

      D. What it means to be rational is disputed and unclear. Therefore the content of any theory urging that people should be rational is unclear.

      E. Affirming oneself is not nearly so important a contribution to human life as is improving the society in which one lives.

   b. How would you evaluate the strength of each of these criticisms?

   c. What criticisms would you urge against at least one of these theories? How would you support your criticisms?

SELECTED ANSWERS for Chapter 12

1. a. A. True   D. True   G. False   J. False
      B. False   E. False   H. False
      C. False   F. True   I. True

   b. B. 1   E. 3   H. 2
      C. 2   G. 2   J. 3

2. A. *E*   D. *N*   G. *S–R*
   B. *N*   E. *S–R* H. *B*
   C. *B*   F. *E*

3. a. A. 3   C. 5   E. 4
      B. 1   D. 1

   b. Many philosophers make a distinction between internal and external criticisms as a part of evaluating the strength of a criticism. You might ask your instructor about this distinction.

$\mathscr{A}13$

Personal Identity
and Social Responsibility

One way of discussing personal identity is, as we saw in Chapter 12, in terms of *individual* human self-development. Humans are also social, however, and their actions and choices affect many others, for better or worse. In order for a human society to function properly, its members must be held accountable for what they do, or fail to do, in that society. But there can be accountability only if there are ways of *identifying* which *persons* are responsible for which actions. Therefore, the concept of personal identity is indispensable for social life. Accordingly, many philosophers discuss personal identity in connection with the responsibility of human beings *in a social context*.

This chapter introduces you to the concept of personal identity in relationship to problems of personal responsibility. After reading it you should be able to

- State the conceptual connection between being a member of society and being responsible as a person.
- State various necessary conditions of being a responsible person.
- State and criticize the memory test of personal identity.
- State and criticize the bodily identity test of personal identity.
- State the combined test of personal identity.
- Explain what the tests of personal identity imply concerning the possibility of the immortality of an immaterial soul.

■ Explain what the tests of personal identity imply concerning the possibility of resurrection of the body.

THE CASE OF VERNON SPITLER

Rosetta Sanchez had followed the Hobblemier murder case ever since the arrest of the suspect, Vernon Spitler, two years ago. She was then in law school; now she was practicing with one of the best law firms in the state. Because of her interest in the case she had been called into the executive offices of one of the senior members of the firm.

"Professor Panksap, I want you to meet Rosetta Sanchez, one of our most promising junior members. She has followed the Hobblemier murder case for some time. Rosetta, this is Professor Panksap. She carries out neurophysiological research at the university and she has a most interesting proposal she would like us to take to the governor. It concerns Vernon Spitler."

Having finished the introductions, the senior partner, Jonathon Stone, sat back in his leather armchair.

"Well, Professor," said Rosetta, "what do you have in mind?"

"I want you to persuade the governor to permit me the chance to experiment on Spitler. If my experiment is successful, there will be no need for his execution. He will even be able to be released from prison."

"I don't understand. What are you going to do with Spitler?"

"My plan is to carry out an erasure of his higher neural storage centers."

"What?"

"In nontechnical terms, I propose to do a mind-wipe. It's a process that relies on certain electrochemical techniques I have developed. It is like what happens when you erase a tape or clear a calculator. The process is quick and not unpleasant. I can actually do it to Spitler while he is still in prison."

"But why should the mind-wipe make any difference to the governor?"

"Well, for one we could save the state some money by not having to house people like Spitler in prisons, while avoiding the barbarity of executing them. Second, we have a labor shortage right now. People like Spitler can be reeducated and then put back into the labor force. Instead of being a drain on society, these people could lead productive lives."

"But, Professor, Spitler is a killer."

"There would be no Spitler left after the mind-wipe."

"You mean it destroys his body, too? How can he join the labor force with no physical body?"

No, Ms. Sanchez, I won't destroy the physical body itself. I'm going to terminate the personality called Vernon Spitler. I'm going to wipe clean all his memories and remove all his attitudes and feelings."

"You mean that the body will be like an empty shell?"

"Actually, Rosetta, it will be as if Vernon was a newborn baby except with a full-grown body. He will have to be taught everything, since he will have no memory of any past that his body may have been involved in."

"But his body killed Hobblemier, not his memory. What will the governor think about public reaction to freeing Spitler—I mean, freeing his body? Or do I mean freeing the body that Spitler formerly used? Or maybe I mean freeing a body that looked exactly like Vernon Spitler."

"If there is a problem about public reaction, we can alter the appearance of the body by using plastic surgery."

"I'm not sure, Professor, that plastic surgery would cover *all* of our problems."

13:1.1 *Society and personal interdependence*   Our concern with personal identity involves questions about personal responsibility. In the case of Vernon Spitler, the scientist and lawyers have to deal with the legal or moral responsibility of a person for past criminal actions. If Vernon Spitler were to undergo a "mind-wipe," would he be responsible for the murder of Vernon Spitler committed in the past? From the point of view of society, could or should he still be regarded as responsible? The concept of responsibility is a *social* concept, as is evident when we consider the nature of society.

Every human society has two characteristics: (1) It is a group of two or more people who mutually share certain goals (like a team but unlike a crowd on a public beach); (2) the group has agreed to cooperate in achieving these shared goals (like a work squad but unlike a school of fish). The terms of agreement may be spelled out in formal documents, such as constitutions and bylaws; or individuals may conform (more or less willingly) to the recognized traditions of their society. Societies differ widely. A primitive society may be subject to the arbitrary decisions of a chief, whereas a more advanced society has a complex legal system. There are also private societies, such as a sorority or a commune.

People cooperate in social life at least in part because they are interdependent: On their own they could not achieve their individual aims as effectively, or perhaps not at all. Society preserves and transmits the collective experience and knowledge of past generations. It provides the framework for the division of labor, so that individuals are freed from the necessity of directly satisfying all their own needs and wants. Society offers its members greater security from external threats (whether natural or human) than they can attain by individual effort. Thus social life is rooted in the perceived values of interdependence.

13:1.2 *Society and personal responsibility*   A society in which the individuals can rely on each other to cooperate in achieving their goals constitutes a *social system*. Its existence depends on two conditions: first that individuals can achieve their goals because other individuals will carry out given tasks. Division of labor and collective security will otherwise break down. Thus, individuals are assigned, or at least expected to perform, certain tasks, such as producing food or providing security or entertainment. Cooperation presupposes that it is feasible and reasonable to *hold* individuals *responsible* for accomplishing their tasks.

The second condition of the social system is that individuals can achieve their goals because other individuals observe certain constraints on their own goal-directed activity. If people are constantly disrupting the activities of others, the system will break down. Thus, individuals are expected to observe constraints, for example, not to kill or injure or rob other individuals. Cooperation presupposes that it is feasible and reasonable to *hold* individuals *responsible* for observing socially necessary constraints.

People are reasonably assured of the advantages of societal cooperation, but it requires the assignment of responsibility to the individuals in society, which has two dimensions. Looking to the future, others can *count on* an individual to perform a given task or to observe a given constraint; looking to the past, others can *hold* an individual *accountable* for doing so or failing to do so. By means of this assignment of responsibility to individuals, then, the advantages claimed for social life are reasonably assured. Thus the concept of a person as a responsible agent is, essentially, a social one.

13:2.1 *Responsibility and rationality*   When you treat someone as a responsible person, you assume that he or she is able to plan and give reasons. For example, the person who has the responsibility to kill enough game to feed the tribe must be able to carry out a process of thought like this: "If I set out traps for wild rabbits, I will have a better chance of getting enough meat." Individuals are able to assume responsibility only if they can form plans by identifying the courses of action most likely to lead to their goals. It is hardly reasonable to assign responsibility to an individual who lacks this ability.

Moreover, a responsible person is able to give reasons. For example, suppose a person had been assigned the task of supplying the tribe with food by hunting. Presumably the person will be praised if there is food on everyone's plate; but even if there is not, the person may not be blameworthy. The other members of the tribe cannot decide whether or not to blame the hunter only by comparing the consequences of his actions with his assigned task. The hunter's actions and their results can be described in alternative ways, and the tribe should be prepared to evaluate them under these different descriptions. For example, the tribe could justly blame the hunter for his action if the description applied was "The hunter was negligent and forgot to check the traps in time." But it is only fair to ask the hunter if there are any descriptions under which there is justification or excuse for what has happened, for example, "I set the traps carefully as usual, but a new predator frightened away the game" or "I could not set the traps because I was delirious from snakebite." It would not be proper for the tribe to hold people responsible who were unable to articulate how they understood what they had done, such as very small children or senile old persons. Thus a person who is held responsible must be *capable* of giving reasons in order to justify or excuse the failure or to fulfill an assigned task or to observe a specified constraint.

13:2.2 *Responsibility and self-consciousness* Being responsible implies being self-conscious over time. There is neither purpose nor justice in praising or blaming anyone but those whose behavior results in either a good or a bad state of affairs. The interdependence of the tribe would not be enhanced if it randomly singled out someone (not necessarily the hunter) for punishment, when it was the hunter who deserved the blame. From the point of view of the person who receives praise or blame, it would make no sense to be singled out at random for ridicule or torture. If you receive an unearned gift from a doting uncle, you do not view it as anything you *deserve*; similarly, you do not view the torture inflicted upon you by a sadist as anything you *deserve*. You will not perceive such treatment as a reward or punishment, unless you grasp that what *you* are getting now is a deserved response to something *you* did or failed to do.

𝒟 PHILOSOPHER'S WORKSHOP

Rules of Identity

The Rule of Self-Identity: "Each thing is identical with itself, but not with any other thing" (Bishop Butler).

Example: A son complains to his father, "I'm not my older brother,

Dad, even though you would like me to be. I am sorry that he died. But you're wishing for something that is impossible."

The Rule of the Transitivity of Identity: "If *A* is identical with *B*, and *B* is identical with *C*, then *A* is identical with *C*" (Aristotle).

Example: A detective recollects: "I once solved a twenty-year-old insoluble case, but was never able to use the solution. On vacation I met Father O'Tooley, who divulged, 'My priesthood got off to a very rocky start. The first person whom I had in confession revealed that she was the murderer of Patrick Kelley. I could not get the person to turn herself in.' Twenty years later I started to tell the chief about the vacation when she broke in, 'Ah, yes, I remember Father O'Tooley, though I haven't seen him for many years. Did you know that I was the first person whose confession he heard?' "

The Rule of the Identity of Indiscernibles: "If every description of *A* is also a description of *B*, and vice versa, then *A* and *B* are identical" (Leibniz).

Example: A person claims a piece of stolen property which has been recovered by the police. "This ring is exactly like my wedding ring. For example, it has the same size stone, the same chip in the bezel, the same inscription on the inside of the band, and it fits my finger perfectly just like my ring. So it must be my ring."

The Rule of Consistent Description: "If *A* is identical with *B*, then every description of *A* is also a description of *B*" (Leibniz).

Example: An attorney introduces a new piece of evidence on behalf of a client. "The prosecution has very conveniently overlooked an important fact. He claims that my client murdered the storekeeper. But samples of blood from under the victim's fingernails reveal that the murderer has bloodtype A. But I hereby submit medical evidence that my client has bloodtype O. Therefore, my client cannot be the murderer."

13:2.3 *Tests of personal identity*   From the point of view of the person who gives blame, it should attach to the individual who did the action that brought about the undesirable state of affairs. As long as praising or blaming is a response to actions that occurred earlier in time, there must be a way for those who give the praise or blame in the society to *reidentify* the people who performed the actions.

There are two plausible tests for this reidentification: the memory test and the bodily identity test. In the case of the hunter, the memory test would be satisfied if the person remembered having robbed the traps and made a sincere confession. The bodily identity test would be satisfied if it could be established that the body involved in commiting the crime was the same as the body of the suspected person, for example, by eyewitness evidence or by the fact that the suspect's footprints were found all around the traps. If both tests are satisfied, then it is clear that the person being blamed is the person who robbed the traps. Of course, in many cases the memory test is satisfied but useless for other people, because the guilty party can make false memory claims (lie). Nevertheless, the two tests generally work together.

However, do the two tests have to work together? In the case study, Vernon Spitler is awaiting execution for murder. Presumably, the bodily identity test has been satisfied "beyond a shadow of a doubt." Perhaps Spitler's fingerprints were found on the murder weapon or there were reliable eyewitnesses. Presumably, Spitler remembers having done the deed, although he may deny it all the way to the gas chamber. But if the "mind-wipe" that Professor Panksap proposed were performed, Vernon Spitler would no longer have *any* memories of his former life. There would not be the self-consciousness over time that responsibility seems to imply. Yet the bodily identity test would continue to apply beyond a shadow of a doubt. So, the two tests would pull in different directions. The Professor claims that the person, Vernon Spitler, would no longer exist after the mind-wipe; she is clearly employing the memory test of personal identity. But Rosetta Sanchez, as a lawyer concerned with admissible evidence, is unwilling to give up the bodily identity test, according to which the mind-wipe would simply result in the same person minus memories.

When the two tests conflict in this way, which way should we turn?

13:3.1 *Strengths and weakness of the bodily identity test*   An obvious advantage to relying upon the bodily identity test is that it allows for conclusive or very strong evidence for personal identity that is publicly accessible to everyone: Fingerprints, blood samples, photographs, and eyewitness testimony can be used to establish that the body of the criminal is identical to that of a suspected person.

Nevertheless, many philosophers have found the test unsatisfactory because it conflicts with generally accepted beliefs about what counts as the same person. It seems unreasonable to continue speaking of the "same person" if there is an abrupt break in his or her mental history. For example, suppose the Professor were not only to wipe Spitler's mind clean but also to rename and re-educate him in such a way that he had completely new attitudes, beliefs, and values, was utterly horrified at the crimes perpetrated by "that man Spitler," and never showed any further criminal tendencies. Would it be reasonable to say to him, "Like it or not, *you* are Vernon Spitler"? Similar disturbing cases have arisen in the rare multiple-personality form of schizophrenia as depicted in the films *The Three Faces of Eve* and

Sybil. Here a human being leads a quiet, introverted, law-abiding existence, but reports total blackouts; during this period her behavior radically changes, becoming extroverted and criminal. Suppose that neither personality were able to remember anything about the other. Some philosophers find it reasonable to describe this case as one of two persons "occupying" the same body.

There are also important religious motives for rejecting the bodily identity test. In certain religious views, moral responsibility extends into the afterlife, where the dead receive reward or punishment for actions committed during this life. God, as a moral judge, would punish someone for sins only if that someone is the *same person* who committed those sins. But according to the religious view, your present body will not survive your death: Either you will have no body at all (the Platonist view) or in the resurrection your earthly body will be replaced with a "spiritual body" (the view of Paul in the *New Testament*). The bodily identity test of personal identity is thus incompatible with religious claims about the afterlife.

13:3.2 *Arguments for the memory test*   In view of these difficulties some philosophers, for example John Locke, have argued that it is wiser to use the memory test to decide the issue of personal identity. To see their point, consider the plot of a television program about a starship in the far future. In this episode a female rival of the starship commander contrives a radical change involving her and the commander. After the change, the commander continues to assert authority over the ship but has lost all of his former memories; in fact, despite his appearance, he now possesses all the memories, attitudes, and character traits of his former rival. At the same time, the rival exhibits all the personality traits of the starship commander, and in fact, claims to be the commander, trying to prove the claim by providing detailed knowledge that only the original commander is in a position to have. Before long, she is able to convince the crew—who rely upon the memory test rather than the bodily identity test—that she is, indeed, the commander. Locke would accept the verdict of the crew members that the two persons have somehow *switched bodies*; to do otherwise would run counter to all our intuitions about personal identity.

He also argues for the memory test on the basis of the connection between responsibility and self-consciousness (noted in 13:2.2). Suppose the rival had committed some heinous crime in the past. It would seem most unreasonable to hold the person now occupying her body responsible for the crime on the basis of the bodily identity test, when there is another person occupying the commander's body who *remembers* planning and committing the deed with remorse, or with relish. It seems more reasonable to hold the person in his body responsible only because the person in his body *is* the rival. But, then, how does one make sense of the phrase "other person in his body"?

You should note a certain pattern in the arguments of 13:3.1 and 13:3.2. Instead of presenting evidence observed by the senses, these arguments pose hypothetical cases and then make claims about what it "seems reasonable" or "intuitive" to say about them.

13:3.3 *Criticisms of the memory test*   First, it is objected that by relying on the memory test alone, Locke does not agree with the ordinary use of the expression "the same person." He tries to deal with this problem

PHILOSOPHER'S WORKSHOP

Locke on the Memory Test

John Locke (1632–1704), a founding figure of British empiricism, became interested in philosophy after encountering the writings of Descartes. Though deeply influenced by Cartesian philosophy, he challenged Descartes's theory that human beings have innate ideas. Locke maintained that all knowledge is derived from sense experiences.

Locke agreed with Descartes's view that a person was centrally a mind or consciousness (see Chapter 17), as is evident in his defense of the memory test for personal identity:

For should the soul of a prince carrying with it the consciousness of the prince's past life, enter and inform the body of a cobbler, as soon as deserted by his own soul, every one sees he would be the same *person* with the prince, accountable only for the prince's actions: but who would say it was the same *man*? The body too goes to the making the man, and would, I guess, to everybody determine the man in this case, wherein the soul, with all its princely thoughts about it, would not make another man: but he would be the same cobbler to every one besides himself (for to himself, unlike others, his memories would be directly clear).[1]

––––––––––

[1]John Locke, *Essay Concerning Human Understanding* (New York: Dover Publications, Inc., 1959) ed. A. C. Fraser, vol. I, p. 457.

by making a crucial distinction: When people use the expression "the same human being," they *do* rely upon the bodily identity test, for the identity of a human being over time consists "in nothing but a participation of the same continued life, by constantly fleeting particles of matter, in succession vitally united to the same organized body." But, says Locke, when people use "the same person," they rely exclusively upon the memory test, for "in this [that is, self-consciousness] alone consists personal identity." Unfortunately, people do *not* distinguish the expressions as Locke suggests. They are used interchangeably, or at least in such a way that whatever counts as the same human being also counts as the same person.

Criticisms based on ordinary usage or intuition cannot, of course, be the final word. The scientific theory that the sun was the center of the solar system could not be defeated by the mere presence of such words as "sunrise" and "sunset" in ordinary language. It must be emphasized, however, that Locke does *not* present his view as a scientific theory backed up by observational evidence, but rather describes uses of words as his support. Thus it is a serious setback for his view if the expression "the same person" is not ordinarily used in the way he suggests.

A second, powerful criticism of Locke's view arises because the memory test, by itself, cannot provide reliable evidence for the claim that somebody is the same as a person who did something in the past. You cannot always rely upon memory claims even when they are sincere. People forget that they have done or seen particular things in the past or they misremember them. You may think you remember that you put a frog in your fourth-grade teacher's desk, when in fact it was one of your friends who played the prank; the friend may be able to

How would Locke respond to the argument, "These four men are all Woody Allen because they all have the same body"?

produce outside evidence that you are mistaken, for example, a photograph of the friend depositing the frog. In such a case the bodily identity test is being used to correct the memory test. This example shows that a sincere memory belief is, by itself, not a foolproof test.

13:3.4 ***The combined memory and bodily identity test*** In light of the difficulties either test has on its own, some philosophers have argued that the two tests should be used in conjunction. In this view there are *two* necessary conditions for personal identity: *both* continuous self-consciousness over time *and* bodily identity. This view assumes that a person has both physical characteristics (height, weight, fingerprints, and so on) and mental characteristics (memories, thoughts, moods, perceptions, and so on), both of which are necessary for the person to be what he or she is. The combined test avoids many of the difficulties that the memory test and bodily identity test independently encounter. For example, in the case study if Vernon Spitler underwent a "mind-wipe," the resulting person would no longer satisfy the memory test and thus would not satisfy the combined test. The same could be said for the case of the schizophrenic person with a split personality. On the other hand, the combined test does not face the difficulties of the memory test taken by itself. The bodily identity test provides a way of checking a person's memory claims, so that it is possible to tell whether the person really remembers doing something in the past or only *seems* to remember doing it.

13:4.1 ***Implications for religious belief*** The combined test of personal identity seems to have negative implications for a religious belief in personal immortality. With this test the one who is allegedly saved or damned after death cannot be "the same person" as the one who committed praiseworthy or blameworthy deeds in life. Thus, even if the memory test were satisfied in such a case, the bodily identity test would not be, because the body perishes.

Religious philosophers attempt to avoid these implications in two different ways. One is to deny that responsibility presupposes *personal* identity. For example, the Platonist might argue that although a person's body perishes, the person's immaterial soul continues to exist after death, and the *soul* can be held responsible for the dead person's actions. Tests for identity of persons prove nothing about the identity of *souls*. However, this view leaves open some very difficult questions; for example, can *souls* be identified at all? Do souls have memories or personality traits?

The second attempt is to substitute another test for the bodily identity part of the combined test, for example, the Christian doctrine of the resurrection of the body as described by Paul. Because of the special relationship between the old physical body and the new "spiritual body" created by God, the same person can have the one body before death and the other after death. The one judged would be the same person as the one who did the deed only if the one judged had either the same physical body or the resurrected body of the person who did the deed. However, this response also leaves open very difficult questions, such as: What is the *special relationship* between these two bodies, which would ensure the continuing identity of the person?

13:5 *Summary*   Personal identity is discussed by philosophers in connection with the concept of responsibility. Responsibility is a social concept, for the functioning of a society requires personal interdependence, which in turn requires the assignment of responsibilities to individuals in society. Being responsible implies being able to plan and give reasons and being self-conscious over time. In order to hold people responsible you need tests of personal identity. The bodily identity test is most generally relied on in a social context, but it does not yield reasonable results in such cases as "mind-wipe" and multiple personality, and it conflicts with religious belief in an afterlife. The memory test is supported by thought experiments involving body switching, but it conflicts with the ordinary use of the expression "the same person." Moreover, critics question whether or not the memory test provides sufficient evidence of personal identity. A test combining these two tests seems to avoid most of the difficulties of each test taken separately, but it has negative implications for certain religious beliefs. Religious philosophers who believe in an afterlife respond to this problem either by denying that responsibility after death requires personal identity (the doctrine of immaterial souls) or by proposing a revision in the combined test so that it will agree with religious belief (the doctrine of the resurrection of the body).

EXERCISES for Chapter 13

1. a. State the definition of a society (13.1.1).
   b. State two conditions required for cooperation (13:1.1).
   c. Use a and b as premises to argue that a society requires persons to be held responsible for their actions (13:1.2).
2. State and explain whether or not each of the following practices shows a concept of responsibility (13:1.2 and 13:2.2):
   A. A primitive tribe has the following practice: When someone in the tribe

is killed by an unknown assailant, the nearest of kin hides beside the trail and kills the first person walking by. Then the ghost of the dead is appeased.

B. Another tribe has this practice: When someone in the tribe is killed by a member of another tribe, the tribe is notified that one of their members will be killed if and only if the guilty party is not handed over by them for punishment before ten days have passed.

C. A third tribe's practice, when a member has been killed by a member of another tribe, is to kidnap any member of that tribe and execute that person "for the sin of your tribe against our own."

D. A future technological society has the following practice: When a member commits a crime, he is sentenced to an involuntary "brain adjustment," which changes his personality and memory, so he has neither the disposition to commit such crime nor the memory of his first crime.

E. Our society has the following practice: When a young child damages property in a way that would be a crime for an adult to do, the parents of the child are fined money which is used to repair the damages.

3. a. State and criticize the memory test by describing two kinds of cases (13:2.2, 13:3.2, 12:3.3).

   b. State and criticize the bodily identity test (13:2.3, 13:3.1).

4. a. (i) How does Locke argue in the Workshop in 13:3.3 that understanding the resurrection is not problematic?

      (ii) What objection have philosophers taken to this argument?

   b. When Thomas Reid (1710–1796) criticizes Locke (below) and says, ". . . if there be any truth in logic . . ." to what principle of identity (13:2.2) is he referring?

   > There is another consequence of this doctrine, which follows no less necessarily, though Mr. Locke probably did not see it. It is, *that a man may be, and at the same time not be, the same person that did a particular action.* Suppose a brave officer to have been flogged when a boy at school for robbing an orchard, to have taken a standard from the enemy in his first campaign, and to have been made a general in advanced life; suppose, also, which must be admitted to be possible, that when he took the standard, he was conscious of his having been flogged at school, and that, when made a general, he was conscious of his taking the standard, but had absolutely lost the consciousness of his flogging. These things being supposed, it follows, from Mr. Locke's doctrine, that he who was flogged at school is the same person who took the standard, and that he who took the standard is the same person who was made a general. Whence it follows, if there be any truth in logic, that the general is the same person with him who was flogged at school. But the general's consciousness does not reach so far back as his flogging; therefore, according to Mr. Locke's doctrine, he is not the person who was flogged. Therefore, the general is, and at the same

time is not, the same person with him who was flogged at school. . . .[2]

5. a. Suppose each of the following is true.
   A. Alicia has the same memory but a different body from Karen.
   B. Bertram has the same body but different memories from Karl.
   C. Cicero has the same memories and body as Tully.
   D. Donna has a different body and different memories from Mary.
   What does the combined test imply in each case (13:3.4)?

   b. Imagine a society with the following practice: When some adult is dying, a clone of that person is developed to adulthood. As that adult dies, the memories and all the personality traits of the dying adult are impressed on the brain of the clone. When the adult dies, the clone is awakened, and it behaves and is treated just as the person who died would have been treated. Explain whether or not, according to the combined test, the same person is alive.

6. a. Explain why an advocate of the immortality of an immaterial soul must reject the combined test for personal identity as a test for soul identity (13:4).

   b. In what alternative direction might such a person go in order to identify souls?

   c. Compare and contrast the problems of belief in an immortal immaterial soul with those in the resurrection of the body.

SELECTED ANSWERS for Chapter 13

1. a. A society is a group of two or more people who have certain shared goals and who have agreed to cooperate to achieve those goals.

   b. It is feasible and reasonable to hold persons responsible for (1) accomplishing tasks assigned to them and (2) observing constraints on their behavior against infringing on the freedom of others.

   c. The interdependence of persons stated in (b) would be a weakness of society, rather than a strength, if a society could not reasonably and feasibly hold persons responsible for accomplishing assigned tasks and respecting others' freedom.

2. A. The concept of responsibility implies that the person punished for an action should be the person who did the action. Whether the ghost of the dead person is appeased or not is irrelevant; no concept of responsibility is shown since this implication of responsibility is ignored.

   B. You might plausibly argue that this practice is not just, but on one interpretation it does show a concept of responsibility. First, the practice

---

[2]Thomas Reid, *Essays on the Intellectual Powers of Man*, Essay III, Chapter VI, in *Philosophical Works*, ed. Sir William Hamilton (Hildesheim: Olms, 1967 [1895]), 351. Italics added.

aims at being able to punish the killer; no problem there. If killing the first person seen after the ten-day limit is thought of as punishing someone for the killing, then the concept of responsibility is ignored since there is no argument that the guilty party has been punished. But if killing the first person seen after the ten-day limit is thought of as punishing the tribe for not handing over the killer, then the only way in which the concept of responsibility is strained is that one person, no more guilty than anyone else in the tribe, has been chosen to be punished for the tribe's failure to find the real killer and hand him or her over in ten days.

C. This practice raises the difficult question of whether a group can be responsible for an action. Were the German people responsible for the death camps? Were all white people responsible for Negro slavery? If we can accept as a correct and appropriate description of the killing, "Your tribe has shown disrespect for mine," then again the only way in which the concept of responsibility is strained is that one person has been randomly chosen to be punished for the tribe.

D. Here the concept of responsibility is clear. Presumably, this society is careful to prove that by all reasonable tests of self-identity, the person who is given the "brain-adjustment" treatment is the same person who committed the crime. The quirk in this case is that after the adjustment has been performed all except adherents of the bodily identity test argue that the person who has undergone the treatment is not the person who committed the crime.

E. In our society it is not feasible to hold children responsible for damages inasmuch as they are generally unable to pay for the repairs and they have not sufficiently developed their rational faculties. Thus the concept of responsibility is strained here. Our attitude that the parents can and should be held responsible for the actions of their children is somewhat parallel to the practice in situation B, except that in our practice we designate in advance which persons shall bear responsibility for which others.

4. a. (i) Locke argues that in the case of the prince and the cobbler, the person who is the prince is in the body of the cobbler and vice versa. Thus there is nothing problematic about the idea that in the resurrection, persons or souls shall be resurrected in different bodies.

(ii) The objections are those cited in 13:3.2 and 13:3.3 against the memory test itself, which Locke relies upon to support the premise of the above argument.

b. The rule of the transitivity of identity. He who was flogged at school (A) is identical with he who took the standard (B), and the latter is identical with he who was made general (C), and so A must be C.

5. a. Only in (C) are both of the separate tests, which together form the combined test, met.

b. Clearly the same person is alive according to the memory test. If we understand by "same body" genes, then the bodily identity test is also met. If by "same body" we understand same cells and bits of matter, then the bodily identity test is not met. Locke, however, noted that ". . . even in this life the particles of the bodies of the same persons change every moment, and there is thus no such identity in the *body* as in the *person*."

6. a. If the advocate of the immortality of an immaterial soul accepted the combined test as one for soul identity, then the advocate would be admitting that even if something survives death, that something, lacking a body, is not the soul of the person.

b. The advocate would want to identify souls perhaps by Locke's memory test and perhaps by a test that included personality traits too, as long as it excluded any bodily identity test.

c. Both face the problem of identifying the person as the same when there is no sameness of body. The assertion, "A soul can lead a disembodied existence," is one to which only the advocate of the immortality of an immaterial soul must agree.

PERSPECTIVES

ON REALITY

When you reflect upon your life, what sorts of concepts do you use to describe what you truly are? You might define yourself in terms of what you do: "I'm a student" or "I'm a tennis player." Another way is to refer to your heritage: "I'm Polish" or "My family is from Kansas." A third possibility is to offer a more general description: "I'm a person" or "I'm an unliberated male."

In pondering human life, philosophers have pursued this last strategy toward its ultimate level of abstraction. Are human beings purely minds, purely bodies, or in some curious way both? Some have argued that human beings are bodily things, animals with special characteristics, but nonetheless wholly understandable as parts of the material world. Others have held that humans are essentially spiritual beings, minds or perhaps souls, and that so-called "physical reality" is what is truly illusory. Still others straddle the issue, trying to keep a leg in both worlds by holding that humans are both material and mental beings.

The concern to understand human beings can be extended to a concern to understand reality itself. Is it entirely physical, mental, or in some way both? As we shall see in Chapter 14, there are different ways of talking about the mental as opposed to the physical — which suggests that there may be two distinct types of reality: mental and physical. This suggestion in turn raises perplexing questions: Are there two? If so, how do they relate? If not, how do we explain the one in terms of the other? Then, in the next chapters we will discuss each of the three basic responses philosophers have developed to these questions: physicalism (Chapter 15), idealism (Chapter 16), and dualism (Chapter 17). You will find foundationalist and contextualist philosophers defending each response. The relationships can be diagrammed as shown.

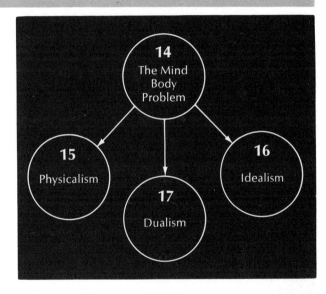

14

Minds and Bodies

The human mind poses the most intractable problems for philosophy. Perhaps nothing is more obvious than that each of us is a conscious being with a continuous stream of thoughts, emotions, desires, and sensations. Yet some scientists and philosophers regard as obscure or even occult the postulated existence of an entity, such as the mind, or a process, such as consciousness. They contend that only the "hard" facts about our physical, chemical, and biological makeup can provide a solid foundation for a scientific understanding of human beings. Even partisans of the view that minds exist concede that the mind is rather mysterious and unlike anything else we encounter.

The difficult questions philosophers ask about the mind have serious social ramifications. Consider the anomalous location of mental health in contemporary science. On the one hand, it is indisputable that many people suffer at some time or other from acute forms of mental disorder, to the point that a substantial number are treated or even institutionalized. Yet there is no organized body of knowledge generally accepted as constituting "a science of mental health," and some reputable scholars argue that mental illness is a myth or pseudo-concept. Much of the disagreement over mental health is rooted in a deeper philosophical disagreement over what the "mental" as such is.

After reading Chapter 14, you should be able to

■ Distinguish mental, physical, and action statements.

■ Express the physical and mental statements implied by a given set of action statements.

■ Distinguish evidence for mental statements from that for physical statements.

■ State how explanations involving mental statements differ from those involving physical statements.

■ Explain how foundationalist and contextualist philosophers disagree about the claim, "The same fact can be described by a mental statement and by a physical statement."

THE CASE OF CARL AND JUNE

"Hi ya, big boy. Come up and see me sometime," said June as she made her usual dramatic entrance into the group-therapy meeting room.

"See, there she goes again," whined Carl. "She's just like everyone else. Always got to bring up the question of weight."

"That seems to bother you, Carl," said Sandra. She was about to call the session to order but decided to begin therapy immediately as Carl had so obligingly revealed his feelings.

"Yes, it does bother me. Why does everyone judge me only by looking at my body?"

" 'Cause it's so big," cut in June. "I mean you're the only man I know who has to order prescription jockey shorts."

"Does Carl's being overweight bother you, June?" asked Sandra.

"Bother me? No, I can get plenty of other action, if you know what I mean. I could even get it on with you if you weren't so straight." She blew Sandra a kiss and winked. Then she turned toward Carl. She reached over and caressed the outside of Carl's left thigh. He blushed.

Sandra tried to control her laughter. June looked at the doctor and then smiled seductively at Carl but he had regained his composure.

"You don't tempt me at all. Your face is painted on, your perfume reeks, your pantyhose have runs down both legs, your blouse clashes with your purse, and both clash with the godawful greenish-orange hair of yours. June, dear, you are ugly!"

"I am torrid. I am alive with sexuality. I live and breathe love. And, Carl, honey, you are jealous."

"You're sick. That's what you are, sick, sick, sick!"

"Carl, how does June make you feel?" asked Sandra. "Tell her your real feelings."

"She makes me want to cry and be sick all at once. I know I may not be much on the outside; but I got feelings just like anybody does. People just don't realize *what it's like* to be somebody like me. I want friends, and I don't want to be lonely. Why can't people like me for *myself*? I have lots of good ideas. I've studied art and can be real interesting if people would only get to know *me*."

"Get to know you! Do you supply them with an atlas? I hear that the last U.S. space satellite was put in orbit around your gut."

"June, are you saying that Carl's weight bothers you?"

"You better believe it, dearie. How can anyone let himself go like he does? He has no self-respect. It makes me ill the way he sits there and quivers like a ton of jello. No wonder nobody wants to have sex with him; he fills up the whole love seat all by himself."

"Well, I think we are making a lot of progress today. We have been able to express our feelings a little more. This should be a good session. But maybe we can be less nasty to each other."

"Sorry, Doc. I have to cut it short today. I've got a date waiting. We're going to the beach. Where can I call a cab? You want me to call you a truck, Carl?" She left without waiting for any answers.

"No, thanks, I hope you get sunburn on your . . . arms. . . ." Carl called after her.

14:1.1 *Mental and physical statements*   Our intense interest in the "mental" side of our existence is reflected in countless magazine articles, offering readers guidance in solving personal psychological problems. Many people attend encounter groups or invest in costly weekend sessions in order to "raise their consciousness."

The mental dimension of our lives is revealed in the *mental statements*, which may be contrasted with the following *physical statements* about people: "June is five feet, five inches tall"; "Sandra is black"; "Carl weighs 260 pounds"; "Sandra, Carl, and June are in Sandra's office." Such statements describe the height, weight, color, shape, and location of people. Similar statements are made about nonhuman physical objects, for example, "The blue vase in Sandra's office is six inches high." *Mental statements* about people include the following kinds: "Carl hears a mocking laugh," "Sandra is amused," "I have a lot of good ideas about art," "June remembers that she has a date." Mental statements describe the perceptions, sensations, emotions, thoughts, and memories of people. It would be absurd to use statements like these to describe physical objects (for example, "The vase remembers how it felt last week"). Thus, some kinds of statements (physical) describe physical objects as well as people, whereas others (mental) describe only human beings and higher animals.

14:1.2 *Action statements*   It often appears obvious that a statement belongs in one category rather than another, but sometimes this is hard to decide. For example, "Tommy jumped from the tree" looks like a physical statement about Tommy, but it is not the sort of statement you would make about a physical object like an apple. Yet you would say that either an apple or Tommy "fell from the tree," which is clearly a physical statement. Some philosophers have proposed that "Tommy jumped from the tree" describes a very complex fact about Tommy. In part, it makes a physical statement—"Tommy fell from the tree." In either case, Tommy is moving rapidly through space from one place (a branch) to another (the ground); but "Tommy jumped" also tells us something about Tommy's *intentions*. The statement has at least three implications: a physical statement,—"Tommy fell from the tree"—a mental statement—"Tommy intended or meant to fall"—and a statement to the effect that Tommy fell at least in part *because* he meant to fall (rather than because the branch broke under him). It is because action statements imply mental statements that it is strange to describe physical objects as performing actions.

14:1.3 *Marks of mental statements*   Philosophers have proposed several tests to distinguish mental statements.

1. *Mental statements presuppose a state of awareness in the subject.* The most obvious and important fact about the mental is consciousness or awareness. It is also the most elusive, for consciousness seems to be basic or "axiomatic" in the sense that it resists analysis in other terms. For example, the statement "Mary fears she has cancer" describes Mary's *experience* of terrible fear, associated with a *conscious belief* about her physical state. Both are states of *awareness*. This statement describes something besides Mary's outward *physical* behavior.

2. *Mental statements do not describe people in terms of spatial characteristics or events.* Many physical statements describe objects in terms of spatial characteristics, such as size, shape, and place. Similarly, ascriptions of a color or mass are made relative to particular spatial locations. Even such a statement as "ice is brittle" describes the tendency or disposition of a thing to undergo certain changes at specific locations in space and time; a sheet of ice shatters when it strikes a hard object.

In contrast, mental statements do not describe people in terms of spatial characteristics. Our thoughts, desires, emotions, intentions, and so forth are not locatable in physical space. Changes and events do occur in the mental sphere: Mental experiences, such as shifts of mood, pangs of conscience, pricks of desire, shivers of delight, flashes of insight, and so forth, occur at specific *times*, but unlike physical happenings, they do not evidently occur at specific *places*.

Is reality adequately conceived as non-conscious, entirely spatial, and involving relationships only between existent objects?

Apparent exceptions are mental statements that do refer to places, such as "I feel a stab of pain at the base of my spine." However, many philosophers contend that pains and similar sensations do not have real spatial locations; they have only *phenomenal* locations. For example, you learned to associate a certain sort of pain with a region of your body, such as the lower back, when you discover that the pain is relieved by rubbing that part of your body. One argument for this view involves "phantom limb" experiences. A person with an amputated leg may continue to experience pain or kinesthetic (moving) sensations "in" the missing limb. These are, presumably, the same experiences a person would have "in" healthy limbs. Since the experiences cannot spatially be "in" the limbs, which have been amputated, they are evidently not spatially "in" healthy limbs either.

Even mental statements about sense perception are thought to satisfy this test; for example, "Carl sees June's greenish-orange hair." June's hair has a precise location and other spatial properties, but the patch of greenish-orange *in the middle of Carl's visual field* has no spatial location. One argument for this belief involves the fact that there may be hallucination in one's visual field, a parallel to the "phantom limb" argument.

3. *Mental statements describe people in terms of acts with contents.* Mental statements describing the contents of our thoughts, desires, recollections, and so forth differ from physical statements describing *relationships* between objects. For example, "Tony is jealous of his wife's lover" superficially resembles "The compass needle is attracted by the magnet." Nevertheless, a mental statement does not describe an ordinary relationship between a subject and an object, because the "object" of a mental state *need not exist*. Tony may be jealous of his wife's lover even when his wife has no lover, but a compass needle cannot be attracted by a nonexistent magnetic field.[1]

14:2.1 *Mental·health and physical health* Our descriptions and explanations of health or illness involve both physical and mental statements. On the one hand, physical disorders such as obesity and alcoholism cannot be treated simply as physical illnesses. They involve *desires* to eat or drink which people have difficulty controlling and which may result from other mental states, such as anxiety. Some researchers claim that stomach ulcers and other physical disorders result from unresolved mental stress and conflict. On the other hand, many forms of mental disorder are also due to physical causes. Brain tumors and enzyme disorders may produce delusions and violent emotions, and certain types of insanity are caused by genetic abnormalities, such as Huntington's chorea.

14:2.2 *Is mental illness a "myth"?* Despite the enormous investment on the part of our society in treating mental disorders, this type of treat-

---

[1]There are also cases of a person experiencing chronic fear or chronic depression which seem to focus on many different contents at different times or perhaps on no particular content at a given time. These cases tend to work against criterion 3.

ment remains very controversial. Some philosophers and medical authorities go so far as to characterize the science of mental health as a pseudoscience and mental illness as a myth perpetrated by pseudo-scientists.[2] This belief follows from the premises: Any such science would have to rely on mental statements; but mental statements cannot provide the sort of objective *evidence* that science requires, nor can they provide *explanations* of human behavior that are considered scientific (see 3.1 and 3.2).

Individuals may behave in strange and even dangerous ways because of a physical lesion, such as a brain tumor. But it is a mistake to call a subject "sick" unless there *is* such a lesion, which can be objectively (interpersonally) identified and (one hopes) treated by physical medicine. Unless such a *physical* cause exists, the physician's "diagnosis" of illness is merely a subjective (personal) and unscientific value judgment about the acceptability of the subject's behavior. Of course, one must raise the question: Does its being subjective in that sense necessarily make it wrong?

14:3.1 *The problem of evidence* The natural sciences—including biology, biochemistry, and anatomy—rest on a bedrock of physical statements. Physical statements are, in general, *objective* in the sense that any two scientists making observations and measurements with their sense organs in a similar situation could agree on their truth or falsity.

The evidence for mental statements is of a quite different sort, involving *introspection*, or firsthand awareness of our own mental acts

---

[2]See Thomas Szasz, *The Myth of Mental Illness* (New York: Dell Publishing Co., 1961).

What evidence does our experience provide concerning the nature of reality?

or states. First-person statements, testimonials, or avowals, such as "I'm scared," "I have a toothache," and "I think you're sick," express this introspective awareness of emotions, feelings, and thoughts. Other people are in just as sound a position as you to make physical statements about you, but you are evidently in a much stronger position than others to pass judgments on the truth or falsity of *mental* statements about you. Similarly, you cannot observe directly the experiences of others; you have to rely on their testimony. Thus, the evidence for mental statements is *subjective*. Moreover, such statements represent a certain point of view. Because they describe conscious states of awareness rather than outward behavior, you cannot understand fully the meaning of a mental statement unless you have experienced firsthand what it is like for a statement of the same sort to be true of you. This fact is the point of Carl's complaint in the case study that often people do not realize what it is like to be an object of ridicule.

14:3.2 *The problem of explanation* Physical events are interconnected in terms of cause and effect; that is, they are caused by earlier events in space and time and have effects in the form of other events in space and time. These causal connections are studied scientifically. Science tries to *explain* physical facts reported in physical statements by identifying the laws governing causal relationships. In medical science, such a law might state that when a bacillus enters the body, it attacks the body's cellular structure in specific ways and starts a chain of causes in motion that ultimately result in certain observable physical characteristics (symptoms). The reason for identifying such laws and seeking causal explanations is to permit prediction and control of the events described in physical statements.

Explanations of this sort are conspicuously absent from the "science of mental health," which has not discovered the laws of nature according to which people will act in a predictable fashion. Psychology does not provide a basis for control of human behavior.

14:3.3 *Understanding versus explanation* Defenders of the "human sciences" sometimes argue that it is, at least, possible to *understand* the activities of others. For example, you can try to understand Carl's self-destructive or ineffectual conduct by taking up his subjective point of view and recognizing his fears, desires, beliefs, and concerns. Even if you cannot predict his behavior exactly, you can understand the reasons for it—which raises the question, "How does one know when one really understands another person?"

✐ PHILOSOPHER'S WORKSHOP

Mind-Body Lexicon

Physicalists claim that physical statements, such as "There is a fire in the wastebasket," most precisely or clearly describe all the facts of reality.

Mentalists claim that mental statements, such as "A sudden chill is following the hot flash," most precisely or clearly describe all the facts of reality.

Dualists claim that *both* mental statements and physical statements describe the facts of reality with equal clarity and precision.

Idealists are the same as mentalists. Sometimes the term "idealist" is used for mentalist philosophers who claim that all mental statements are statements about *minds* and the experiences or "ideas" within minds. Thus, "A sudden chill is following the hot flash" describes a succession of experiences in someone's mind.

Materialists are the same as physicalists. Sometimes the term "materialist" is used for physicalist philosophers who claim that all mental statements are statements about *matter* and states and changes of matter. Thus, "There is a fire in the wastebasket" describes a bit of matter undergoing a change.

Solipsists are mentalists who claim that the only facts of reality are facts involving *one* mind (namely, the mind of the solipsistic philosopher defending solipsism).

Foundationalists on the mind-body problem claim that mental statements and physical statements cannot describe the same facts of reality.

Contextualists on the mind-body problem claim that mental statements and physical statements can describe the same facts of reality.

14:4.1 *The mental versus the physical* The above criticisms of the science of mental health rest upon unstated assumptions, two of which require special emphasis: (1) It is assumed that *physical statements and mental statements are different ways of describing the facts.* The former describe entities and events as existing in the outer world of space and time; the latter describe entities and events as if they existed in an inner region of the mind. The critics of the science of mental health claim that physical statements are not only a different but also a *preferred* way of describing the facts of reality. For example, "June is suffering from a lesion of the brain" is preferred to "June is suffering from penis envy." The former is objective, confirmable, and scientific; the latter is subjective, speculative, and unscientific.

(2) It is also assumed that *physical statements and mental statements provide mutually exclusive ways of describing the facts.* The critic of mental health sciences sees them as in competition with physical health sciences. The critic claims that if a psychiatrist explained June's erratic behavior by saying, "June is jealous of her mother," this mental statement does not describe any *objective fact* about June. This reasoning assumes that if a mental statement describes a fact about June, it is impossible to describe *this* fact by means of any physical statement, for example, a description of the state of June's brain. This assumption, that the mental and the physical are mutually exclusive, is typical of philosophical foundationalism.

14:4.2 *Questions of mind*   These two assumptions suggest the main questions philosophers raise concerning the human mind: First, *to what extent do physical statements and mental statements describe the facts?* Some philosophers (physicalists) place so much confidence in the physical sciences that they claim that ultimately *everything* can be described and explained in terms of physical statements. They assume, in effect, that reality is entirely physical (Chapter 15). Other thinkers (mentalists) with deeply skeptical tendencies may dismiss the "external world" as a will-o'-the-wisp and claim that reality is entirely mental (Chapter 16). These are the extremes; the middle ground is held by philosophers (dualists) who countenance both sorts of statements, on the grounds that reality is partly mental and partly physical (Chapter 17). Typically, the middle ground is harder to hold.

There is more to the issue than a choice between these three positions. The *second* question remains: *Is it true that physical statements and mental statements are mutually exclusive?* The foundationalist assumes that if some region of existence is mental it cannot be physical, and vice versa. This assumption may seem plausible in view of what has been said about the distinctive marks of the mental (14:1.3), the evidence for the mental (14:3.1), and explanation involving the mental (14:3.2). Nevertheless, foundationalism has extremely paradoxical implications. For example, if you are sympathetic to those philosophers who hold that reality is entirely physical, foundationalism will drive you to the highly paradoxical position that mental statements describe *nothing* whatsoever! Similarly, foundationalism combined with the thesis that reality is entirely mental leads to the rejection of the entire outer world of space and time as an illusion. Even if you try to hold to the position that reality is partly mental and partly physical, foundationalism splits existence into two realms, an outer spatial realm and an inner nonspatial realm, existing "side by side."

One realm is subject to scientific control, whereas the other is not, and the relationship between the two remains shrouded in mystery. In the face of the counterintuitive implications of foundationalism, it is not surprising that many philosophers have attempted a contextualist approach; that is, they have tried to show that, despite appearances, physical and mental statements are not mutually exclusive. This approach too has turned out to be a major undertaking.

14:5 *Summary* There are two ways of talking about people. One is to use mental statements; the other is to use physical statements. Mental statements presuppose a state of awareness in the subject, do not describe people in terms of spatial characteristics or events, and tend to focus the state of awareness expressed on a particular content. Although we can give scientific explanations of events described by using physical statements, we cannot, at least as yet, do the same for mental statements. We can understand why a person thinks or feels the way he or she does, as described by a mental statement, even if we cannot explain or predict that thought or feeling. This fact suggests that there may be two realms of nature, the physical and the mental. If there are two, how do they relate? If there is only one, how do you account for the appearance of the other?

EXERCISES for Chapter 14

1. Below is a set of statements. Distinguish and mark them as physical *(P)*, mental *(M)*, or action *(A)*.
   A. Yvonne sneezed.
   B. Yvonne believes the pollen makes her sneeze.
   C. The pollen makes Yvonne sneeze.
   D. Yvonne is annoyed by her sneezing.
   E. Yvonne wants to stop sneezing.
   F. Yvonne moved to Arizona.
   G. Lori is skipping rope on a high wire.
   H. Bill is worried about Lori.
   I. Lori continues to work out despite Bill's worry.
   J. Bill carefully hides the rope.
   K. Lori practices cartwheels on the high wire.
   L. Bill destroys the high wire.

2. Check your answers to question 1. Now consider action statements F, G, and I. From the following list, identify the physical statements and the mental statements implied by each.
   A. Yvonne always lived in Arizona.

    B. Yvonne wanted to move to Arizona.

    C. Yvonne feared moving to Arizona.

    D. Yvonne previously lived somewhere outside of Arizona.

    E. Lori realizes that Bill is worried.

    F. The movement of Lori's feet and arms is coordinated.

    G. On at least two separate occasions, parts of Lori's body are moving.

    H. Lori knows she is rhythmically passing a rope under her feet.

3. After checking your answers to question 2, write physical statements and mental statements implied by J, K, and L.

4. First *describe* what typical evidence might be in support of A and C in question 1. Next, *describe* what typical evidence might be in support of D and E. Finally, *contrast* the first body of evidence with the second.

5. In question 1, C could be interpreted as an explanation of A, and E could be interpreted as an explanation of F. Describe how C and E might each serve as an explanation full enough to bring out the *contrast* between using a physical rather than a mental statement as an explanation.

6. Below are five statements. First *identify* each as foundationalist, contextualist, physicalist, idealist, or dualist.

    A. Every fact can be described entirely in mental terms.

    B. Any fact that can be described entirely in physical terms cannot be described in mental terms, and any that can be described entirely in mental terms cannot be described in physical terms.

    C. Some facts cannot be described entirely in physical terms, and some cannot be described entirely in mental terms.

    D. The same facts can be described entirely in physical terms, yet also in mental terms; similarly, the same facts can be described entirely in mental terms, yet also in physical terms.

    E. Every fact can be described entirely in physical terms.

After checking your answers, state the positions that result from combining these views. (Hint: There are six such positions.)

SELECTED ANSWERS for Chapter 14

1. *P:* A, C.   *M:* B, D, E, H.   *A:* F, G, I, J, K, L.

2. 1F, at least in context, implies 2B *(M)* and 2D *(P)*.
1G implies 2F *(P)* and 2H *(M)*
1I implies 2E *(M)* and 2G *(P)*.

4. By way of contrast, the evidence for A and C is much more interpersonally accessible; also Yvonne's testimony is significantly more authoritative in cases such as D and E.

5. By way of contrast, if C is true, then you can predict that if Yvonne is exposed to a certain concentration of pollen, she will sneeze. However, even

though we might say that we were explaining Yvonne's moving to Arizona by citing her desire to stop sneezing, we could not predict that if she has the desire, she would move there. She might move to New Mexico, a conflicting desire might lead her to stay where she is, and so on.

6. A: Idealist. B: Foundationalist. C: Dualist. D: Contextualist. E: Physicalist.

Six perspectives arise because, whether one is an idealist, dualist, or physicalist, one can be either a foundationalist or a contextualist. In each of the next three chapters, on physicalism, idealism, and dualism, respectively, you will study a foundationalist and a contextualist approach.

15

Reality as Essentially Physical

The thesis of physicalism, that reality is entirely physical, has gained strength from research in physical science into distinctly human characteristics. The science of neurophysiology, for example, has mapped out the physical processes in the brain that are associated with many of the higher levels of human cognition. Much of the opposition to physicalism has come from religious philosophers, yet some traditional religious movements have viewed existence, including spiritual existence, in exclusively physical or material terms.

What are the implications of physicalism for the reality of the human mind? Some philosophers believe that it leaves no room for belief in such a thing as a mind; others believe that mental facts can be accommodated. Both views have vigorous partisans, and this chapter introduces these two perspectives. After reading Chapter 15, you should be able to

- Show how the theory that reality is èntirely physical leads to a philosophical problem concerning the reality of mental facts.
- State the foundationalist argument that there are no mental facts.
- State the objections to foundationalism based upon evidence for mental statements describing conscious experiences.
- State the contextualist argument that there are mental facts.
- State the objections to contextualism based upon distinguishing marks of mental facts.

223

THE CASE OF THE KLU-GAHINA

"Welcome to the School of the Klu-Gahina. Come forward into the light and look closely at me. What do you see, my little New One?"

Carol stepped softly as she moved closer to the Mother Registrar. The older woman saw the nervous tension of her knees and calf muscles. Carol could hear her own heart beating faster in excitement. *Mother can probably see the sweat on my temples. She'll see my fear.* She uttered the unspoken words, as her hands went wet inside her tightly clenched fists. *At least my hands are behind my back out of her sight.*

"Come, child, there is no fear but the expression of fear. Tell me what you see in my eyes."

She does see my fear! Carol's throat went dry; adrenalin flooded her system. It aroused the "fight or flight" instinct she possessed in common with all other animals. Carol stood her ground, poised for the verbal battle. Every sense was alert. Data poured into her brain, were sorted, evaluated, interpreted, related, cataloged, and stored. She scanned the old woman's eyes, face, and hands for clues to former events. Having made her assessment, Carol spoke.

"You have been in the Klu-Gahina order for your whole adult life. The scar tissue around your left wrist is from a handcuff or chain. You wore it for many years. Its memory trace is deep in your brain, too, I see. For, as I spoke of it, your face winced. You have been Mother Registrar for at least five years. The ulcer medication there on your desk indicates both the length of your service and the fact that you have let your meditation habit slip. Had you kept up with the meditation, you would not have built up the acid that eats at your stomach even as we talk.

"You are well over sixty years old. The muscle tone in your arms and neck has all but gone; yet, once you were strong and did heavy work. This I can tell from the shape of your skeleton and the size of your hands. Once you were physically very sturdy indeed. But now, Mother, you do not move decisively. Your eyes show your age and your growing insecurity. Each new day you question your ability to continue with your duties. I saw your indecision even in the way you walked. I heard it in the tone of your voice.

"You have suffered much to keep this school going. Your many disappointments, long waiting and deep suffering, while hidden from most, are evident to me for I have been trained from birth to read the body's signs. *'The Body is all and tells all.'* Is that not what the Great One said?"

"Yes, yes, little New One. Oh, yes! You have learned well. We welcome you into our school." The old woman reached out and embraced Carol. Tears ran freely down her time-scarred face. "I have waited many years for one such as yourself. You will learn the Way, and all the power of the Body will be open to you. You will be purified by exercising, scourging, and meditation. You will learn that there is no pain but the expression of pain — all else is unreal. No one's unspoken words will be hidden from you, for the trained read all from the eye, face, posture, and voice. You will be as part of nature itself. Your body will become attuned to the rhythms of the universe. All will be open to you so long as you shall live in the Way."

15:1.1 *"The body is all"*   The case study describes an imaginary, quasi-religious order which is founded upon the philosophical tenet that reality is entirely physical. Initiates of the School of Klu-Gahina are intensively trained in body language. They are taught to scrutinize closely the outward behavior of others — their posture, mannerisms, involuntary responses — and in this way to "read" others' emotions, memories, and thoughts. They are also trained to attend closely to their own physiological responses, so that they can monitor their own mental states. The result is a spiritual equivalent of biofeedback techniques.

However, close scrutiny of the conversation between the New One and the Mother Registrar reveals a deeper meaning. The members of the school do not regard themselves as simply adept at identifying the outward "signs" of inward mental states. Carol, as a novice, will undergo the same physical discipline and hardship as the Mother, in order to learn the truth of the order: "There is no pain but the expression of pain. There is no fear but the expression of fear." Carol is striving toward the insight that the *only* real facts are physical facts: Nothing else exists except that which is physical.

15:1.2 *The problem of mind defined*   The School of Klu-Gahina has solved the problem of the reality of mental phenomena. In order to assess this solution, you should have a clearer view of the problem, which is stated by philosophers in terms of a certain theory of meaning.

For example, the word "platypus" is said to refer to the things of which it is true to say, "This is a platypus." The reference class, or extension, of "platypus" is the whole set of things of which it is true to say, "This is a platypus." The word "unicorn," on the other hand, denotes nothing; its reference class is empty. The meaning, or intension, of "platypus" is the set of characteristics or properties a thing must have in order to be a platypus — having a duck bill, webbed feet, warm blood, laying eggs, and so forth.[1]

If two expressions have the same meaning, then they must refer

---

[1]See Chapter 3 for a further explanation of the *intension* and the *extension* of a term.

to the same entities; for example, because "planetoid" and "asteroid" mean the same thing, they must have the same reference class. But two expressions with different meanings may also refer to the same thing, for example "cloud" and "mass of H_2O particles in suspension." These expressions mean something different, as people are able to talk quite intelligibly about clouds before they learn anything about H_2O. In such a case it has to be discovered whether or not "There is a cloud overhead" describes the same fact as "There is a mass of H_2O particles in suspension overhead."

Mental statements, such as "Carol feels frightened," do not mean the same thing as physical statements, such as "Carol's *brain* is in a physiological state *beta*," for the words they contain have different meanings. Since the meaning of "frightened" is what enables us to talk correctly about being frightened and we can do so without knowing anything about the brain, the meaning of such a mental word has nothing to do with the physical characteristics of the brain. But statements with different meanings may still describe the same facts. The problem of mind is this: Do mental statements refer to a different set of facts from those referred to by physical statements? Is there a mental realm distinct from the physical realm?

15:2.1 *The foundationalist approach: there are no mental facts*   Some philosophers pose a simple yet paradoxical solution to this problem: There is *no* mental realm. This solution is supported by a straightforward argument:

> (1) The facts of reality are completely described by physical statements. *(The thesis of physicalism.)*

The physical is not characterized by consciousness.

    (2) Mental statements cannot describe the same facts as physical statements. (*The foundationalist theory.*)

    (3) Therefore, mental statements do not describe the facts of reality.

The reasons for premise 2 should be evident from Chapter 14: Physical statements purport to describe things and events in the "outer" world of space and time, but mental statements purport to describe experiences of the "inner" realm of the mind. Whereas our evidence for physical statements is *objective*, empirical, and interpersonal, our evidence for mental statements is *subjective* and introspective.

15:2.2 *"There is no feeling but the physical expression of feeling"* This foundationalist argument implies that our ordinary use of mental statements to describe human beings is inaccurate and misleading. The statement "Carol is frightened" is a confused attempt to describe what are actually physical facts. This statement may be compared to our inaccurate use of the word "sunrise" to try to describe an actual fact (in fact, the earth is turning; the sun is not rising). If we were more "scientific," we would describe people, not in terms of feelings and thoughts, but in terms of the *physical expression* of these so-called "feelings" and "thoughts." Instead of describing Carol as "frightened," it is more accurate to describe her as perspiring, wringing her hands, stuttering, and so forth. According to the foundationalist, there is "nothing but" the expression of feelings and thoughts.

Foundationalists often state their solution in a less paradoxical, but very misleading, way. They try to avoid the *implication* that "Carol is frightened" describes nothing at all. The foundationalist says, "Of course, she is frightened; but all that we *mean* by being frightened is exhibiting specifiable physiological and behavioral characteristics." This statement, in effect, redefines the mental statement "Carol is frightened," so that it means something different from what it formerly meant. But there is clearly something fishy about this maneuver. It commits the fallacy of *playing with words* (see 2:2.1). A parallel example is the case of the minister whose job was threatened when suspicions arose about her atheism. "Do you believe in the existence of God?" she was asked. "Of course there is a God," she replied, adding under her breath, "and by 'God' I mean 'a delusion that misled people for centuries.'" The minister is playing with words here, introducing a special sense of "God" in order to evade the real question: Is there a God, in some ordinary sense of "God"? The foundationalist who tries to evade the problem of mind by redefining mental statements is engaged in the same fallacious sleight of hand. In fact, the foundationalist is committed to the view that mental statements, in their *ordinary meaning*, describe *no facts at all.*

The foundationalist thesis seems vulnerable to another fairly obvious objection: People have *unexpressed* feelings, thoughts, and memories. For example, although Carol is able to "read" the memory of pain in the Mother Registrar's facial expression, the Mother can have this memory even when she is not wincing or otherwise expressing it. At any given time, a person has many thoughts and desires that find no expression in outer behavior—which can be controlled so as not to reveal one's thoughts or feelings.

15:2.3 *Philosophical behaviorism* Behaviorism offers a way of meeting the above objection. The behaviorist proposes that what we mistakenly call "unexpressed thoughts and desires" are really *complex behavioral dispositions.* Dispositions may be relatively simple or complex. An example of the former is solubility. A lump of sugar is soluble, even when it is not, in fact, dissolved in water. To say, "The sugar lump is soluble," is to say, "If the sugar lump were placed in water, it *would* dissolve." When we try to describe a person by mental words, such as "crabby," the physical reality underlying the word is a *complex* disposition, which involves different responses to different stimuli. Thus, in *Peanuts* a crabby person like Lucy might respond in quite different ways to sensory stimuli. If the stimulus is the sound of Linus talking to his blanket, her response might be to yell; if the stimulus is being kissed by Snoopy, her response might be to grimace; and so forth.

Ⓖ PHILOSOPHER'S WORKSHOP

Ryle's Analysis of Emotion Statements

Many philosophers have thought of the emotions as peculiar mental events which cause us to behave in certain ways. Discussion of *motives* seems, especially, to refer to such "internal events." The question, "What was Jones's motive in boasting to the stranger?" looks like a request for a mental event that caused Jones's boasting. The answer, "Jones boasted from vanity," may seem to refer to a "surge of vanity" which was that mental cause. Gilbert Ryle (1900–1976) has challenged this view of motives and the emotions, and has proposed a subtler alternative.

. . . on hearing that a man is vain we expect him, in the first instance, to behave in certain ways, namely to talk a lot about himself, to cleave to the society of the eminent, to reject criticisms, to seek the footlights and to disengage himself from conversations about the merits of others. We expect him also to indulge in roseate daydreams about his own successes, to avoid recalling past failures and to plan for his own advancement. To be vain is to tend to act in these and innumerable other kindred ways.

Some theorists will object that to speak of an act of boasting as one of the direct exercises of vanity is to leave out the cardinal factor in the situation. When we explain why a man boasts by saying that it is because he is vain, we are forgetting that a disposition is not an event and so cannot be a cause. The cause of his boasting must be an event antecedent to his beginning to boast. He must be moved to boast by some actual "impulse," namely by an impulse of vanity. So the immediate or direct actualisations of vanity are particular vanity impulses, and these are feelings. The vain man is a man who tends to register particular feelings of vanity; these cause or impel him to boast, or perhaps to will to boast, and to do all the other things which we say are done from vanity.

It should be noticed that this argument takes it for granted that to explain an act as done from a certain motive, in this case from vanity, is to give a causal explanation. This means that it assumes that a mind, in this case the boaster's mind, is a field of special causes; that is why a vanity feeling has been called in to be the inner cause of the overt boasting. I shall . . . argue that to explain an act as done from a certain motive is not analogous to saying that the glass broke, because a stone hit it, but to the quite different type of statement that the glass broke, when the stone hit it, because the glass was brittle. Just as there are no other momentary actualisations of brittleness than, for example, flying into fragments when struck, so no other momentary actualisations of chronic vanity need to be postulated than such things as boasting, daydreaming about triumphs and avoiding conversations about the merits of others.[2]

. . . when we say the glass broke when struck because it was brittle, the "because" clause does not report a happening or a cause; it states a law-like proposition. People commonly say of explanations of this second kind that they give the "reason" for the glass breaking when struck.

How does the law-like general hypothetical proposition work? It says, roughly, that the glass, *if* sharply struck or twisted, etc. *would* not dissolve or stretch or evaporate but fly into fragments.

---

[2]Ryle's analysis seems quite plausible when it is applied to *certain* emotion statements. Do you think that *all* such statements could be analyzed in this way?

The matter of fact that the glass did at a particular moment fly into fragments, when struck by a particular stone, is explained, in this sense of "explain," when the first happening, namely the impact of the stone, satisfies the protasis of the general hypothetical proposition, and when the second happening, namely the fragmentation of the glass, satisfies its apodosis.

This can now be applied to the explanation of actions as issuing from specified motives. When we ask "Why did someone act in a certain way?" this question might, so far as its language goes, either be an inquiry into the cause of his acting in that way, or be an inquiry into the character of the agent which accounts for his having acted in that way on that occasion. I suggest . . . that explanations by motives are explanations of the second type and not of the first type.

The present issue is this. The statement "he boasted from vanity" ought, on one view, to be construed as saying that "he boasted and the cause of his boasting was the occurrence in him of a particular feeling or impulse of vanity." On the other view, it is to be construed as saying "he boasted on meeting the stranger and his doing so satisfies the law-like proposition that whenever he finds a chance of securing the admiration and envy of others, he does whatever he thinks will produce this admiration and envy."[3]

---

[3]Gilbert Ryle, *The Concept of Mind* (London: Hutchinson Publishing Group, Ltd., 1949), pp. 86–87, 80. New York: Harper & Row. By permission of Harper & Row, Publishers, Inc.

15:2.4 *Objection to behaviorism*

Many philosophers object to behaviorism on the grounds that when we say "I am in pain" or "that hurts," we are reporting a mental experience. Some behaviorists reply that "I am in pain" is not a report of any event in our minds but simply a verbalized *pain behavior* such as moaning or crying.

 PHILOSOPHER'S WORKSHOP

Wittgenstein on Mental Statements

Ludwig Wittgenstein (1889–1951) recognizes that we *do* make mental statements and that these *do* have a genuine use, but he suggests that we commit a philosophical mistake if we regard them as reporting a special class of mental facts. Rather, these statements have a *nonreporting* use.

The interpretation is summarized by the philosopher J. J. C. Smart (b. 1920):

Suppose that I report that I have at this moment a roundish, blurry-edged after-image which is yellowish towards its edge and is orange towards its center. What is it that I am reporting? One answer to this question might be that I am not reporting anything, that when I say that it looks to me as though there is a roundish yellowy-orange patch of light on the wall I am expressing some sort of *temptation*, the temptation to say that there *is* a roundish yellowy-orange patch on the wall (though I may know that there is not such a patch on the wall). This is perhaps Wittgenstein's view in the *Philosophical Investigations* (see ¶¶ 367, 370). Similarly, when I "report" a pain, I am not really reporting anything (or, if you like, I am reporting in a queer sense of "reporting"), but am doing a sophisticated sort of wince. (See ¶ 244: "The verbal expression of pain replaces crying and does not describe it." Nor does it describe anything else?)[4]

Smart has in mind the following passage by Wittgenstein:

How do words *refer* to sensations? — There doesn't seem to be any problem here; don't we talk about sensations every day, and give them names? But how is the connexion between the name and the thing named set up? This question is the same as: how does a human being learn the meaning of the names of sensations? — Of the word "pain" for example. Here is one possibility: words are connected with the primitive, the natural, expressions of the sensation and used in their place. A child has hurt himself and he cries; and then adults talk to him and teach him exclamations and, later, sentences. They teach the child new pain-behaviour.
  "So you are saying that the word 'pain' really means crying?" — On the contrary: the verbal expression of pain replaces crying and does not describe it.[5]

Smart cannot accept this argument:

Maybe this is because I have not thought it out sufficiently, but it does seem to me as though, when a person says "I have an after-image," he *is* making a genuine report, and that when he says "I have a pain," he *is* doing more than "replace pain-behaviour," and that "this more" is not just to say that he is in distress.[6]

---

[4]J. J. C. Smart, "Sensations and Brain Processes," *Philosophical Review* 68 (1959), 141.
  [5]Ludwig Wittgenstein, *Philosophical Investigations*, trans. G. E. M. Anscombe (Oxford: Basil Blackwell, 1953).
  [6]Smart, *op. cit.*, 142.

> Can you see any good *reasons* for agreeing with Smart rather than Wittgenstein? What sort of evidence might be relevant?

The critics, however, find this reply implausible: We certainly *do* experience pains, sensations, feelings, and desires. The behaviorist disparages introspective evidence for such statements because it is "subjective" and not equally accessible to all observers; but the critics object that despite its limitations, subjective evidence cannot be ignored.

15:3.1 *The contextualist approach: mental facts are physical facts* These difficulties for the behaviorist defense of foundationalism may be restated in the form of a positive argument for contextualism:

(1) The facts of reality are completely described by physical statements. *(The thesis of physicalism.)*
(2) Mental statements do describe certain facts of reality. *(The evidence of introspection.)*
(3) Therefore, mental statements describe the same facts as certain physical statements. *(The thesis of the contextualist.)*

The contextualist solution to the problem of the mind rejects the foundationalist thesis of the fundamental incompatibility between mental and physical statements in that these statements can describe the very same facts.

15:3.2 *The central state identity theory* The most popular version of contextualism today is the identity theory, in which mental statements, such as "I feel a chill" or "I just thought of the solution," refer to the very same things as physical statements which describe events in our brains. There are important differences between mental and physical statements, but these differences do not prevent the statements from describing the same facts.

1. *Difference in Meaning.* Mental and physical statements have different meanings, for example "I'm in *pain*" and "My brain is in state *gamma.*" If mental and physical words had the same meaning, they would be synonymous, in the same way as "rich" and "wealthy." This statement is true enough, but it does not settle the problem of mind, which is whether or not mental expressions and statements *refer to and describe* the same thing as physical ones. You can discover that two words, which *mean* quite different things, *refer* to the same object. For example, astronomers discovered that "the Evening Star,"

defined as "the brightest superlunary object in the evening sky," and "the Morning Star," defined as "the brightest superlunary body in the morning sky," referred to the same object, the planet Venus. The identity theory claims that it will be discovered that mental and physical expressions *refer to the same events*.

 PHILOSOPHER'S WORKSHOP

Broad's Objection to Physicalism

C. D. Broad (1887–1971) discussed various approaches to the mind-body problem in great detail in *The Mind and Its Place in Nature*. He offered several criticisms of the physicalistic theory of mind, of which the following was for some time quite influential:

Let us suppose, for the sake of argument, that whenever it is true to say that I have a sensation of a red patch it is also true to say that a molecular movement of a certain specific kind is going on in a certain part of my brain. There is one sense in which it is plainly nonsensical to attempt to reduce the one to the other. There is a something which has the characteristic of being my awareness of a red patch. There is something which has the characteristic of being a molecular movement. It should surely be obvious even to the most "advanced thinker" who ever worked in a psychological laboratory that, whether these "somethings" be the same or different, there are two different *characteristics*. The alternative is that the two phrases are just two names for a single characteristic, as are the two words "rich" and "wealthy"; and it is surely obvious that they are not.[7]

What point is Broad making about "rich" and "wealthy"? What inference is he drawing about descriptions of sensations and brain events? How would an identity theorist meet this objection?

[7]C. D. Broad, *The Mind and Its Place in Nature* (London: Routledge and Kegan Paul, 1925), p. 622.

2. *Difference in Evidence.* The evidence for mental statements is different from that for physical statements. For example, suppose that

my experience of pain *is* correlated with a process of some sort that occurs in my brain. My evidence for "I'm in pain" is introspection, whereas the evidence for "My brain is in state *gamma*" may be sensory observation of a machine output of some kind. Again, this statement is true, but it does not settle the issue, for the identity theory does not claim that introspective is the same as sensory evidence. Rather, it claims that introspection and sensory observation each provide *evidence of the same fact.* When you report, "I'm in pain," you have *introspective* evidence for the occurrence of an event in your brain; a brain scientist reading meters attached to electrodes connected to your skull might have a different kind of evidence for the same fact.

3. *Difference in Knowledge.* Our knowledge of physical facts is different from our knowledge of mental facts. For example, a person untrained in modern science may be acutely conscious of undergoing pain without having any idea that any processes are occurring in the brain. This obviously true point also fails to settle the issue. Mental and physical expressions differ in terms of meaning and evidence; one has to find out whether they *refer* to the same thing. Differences in knowledge do not prove differences in existence, as the story of Oedipus shows: Oedipus knew that he was sleeping with his wife. He did not know that he was sleeping with his mother. Unfortunately for Oedipus, his ignorance did not prove that his wife was not his mother.

Most philosophers agree now that the above-cited differences in meaning, evidence, and knowledge do not count decisively in favor of the foundationalist approach to the problem of mind. Nevertheless, many argue that the identity theory still faces serious objections.

15:4.1 *Objections to the central state identity theory*   The first serious objection is that mental statements describe events in the "inner" region of the mind rather than in the "outer" world of space. Our concept of mental states, such as pains and experiences of afterimages,[8] are such that it is nonsensical to ask spatial questions about them, such as "Where, exactly, are they?" Since mental events do not share the spatial characteristics of physical events, they cannot be identical with physical events.

Contextualists reply that it is not altogether nonsensical to attribute spatial properties to mental experiences. An experience or thought already has one *vague* location, the location of the *person* doing the thinking or experiencing. We can make the location more precise: The location of the mental experience is the same as the location of the brain process. In "making" this location more precise would the contextualist be stipulating or describing it?

---

[8]An afterimage is the patch of color or shading we see after looking directly at a bright flash of light and then turning away.

15:4.2 *Mental statements are incorrigible*   Another objection is based on the commonsense assumption that if you sincerely and carefully say what you are feeling or thinking, no other observer can correct you. If you report with complete conviction, "I'm thinking about the Superbowl," could somebody else correct you, "Oh, no, you're thinking about the Indianapolis 500"? Suppose, for example, that a brain scientist invented a "cerebroscope" which could be fitted over your head like a helmet with a tiny screen in front reporting your brain state. Because your brain state is identical with your mental state, according to the central state identity theory, the cerebroscope would provide other people with a new procedure for identifying your thoughts, sensations, and feelings. They could use this procedure to *override* your sincere reports about your state of mind. Critics protest that if the identity theory implies this occurrence, it is an absurd theory. But, then, how absurd *is* this particular piece of science fiction?

15:4.3 *Mental states are subjective*   A deeper and more subtle difficulty for the identity theory concerns the subjective nature of mental states. For example, a color-blind person studying the mental processes of someone who is experiencing the color red might be able to give a detailed description of the processes occurring in the brain of the person who is seeing red, without ever knowing *what it is like* to see red. The color-blind person would be quite mistaken in saying, "Now I know everything there is to seeing red," for although he knows many facts about seeing red, these do not include the experiential aspects of actually seeing it. Thus, in identifying the experience of seeing red with an objective physical phenomenon, the identity theory has left something out that is of crucial importance. Physical events such as brain processes are objective and can be studied from many points of view. The physical basis for color vision can be understood fully by a congenitally blind person; but the mental statement, "I am seeing red," describes a *subjective fact*, a fact that can never be fully understood by a person who cannot personally assume the point of view of someone seeing red.

𝒫 PHILOSOPHER'S WORKSHOP

What Is It Like to Be a Bat?

Thomas Nagel, who teaches philosophy at Princeton University, criticizes physicalism in a novel way. He argues that neither behaviorism nor the identity theory has accounted for the existence of *subjective facts* involving consciousness. An instance of one such fact is *what it is like to be a bat.*

I assume we all believe that bats have experience. After all, they are mammals, and there is no more doubt that they have experience than that mice or pigeons or whales have experience. I have chosen bats instead of wasps or flounders because if one travels too far down the phylogenetic tree, people gradually shed their faith that there is experience there at all. Bats, although more closely related to us than those other species, nevertheless present a range of activity and a sensory apparatus so different from ours that the problem I want to pose is exceptionally vivid (though it certainly could be raised with other species). Even without the benefit of philosophical reflection, anyone who has spent some time in an enclosed space with an excited bat knows what it is to encounter a fundamentally *alien* form of life. . . . [W]e may ascribe general *types* of experience [to an animal] on the basis of the animal's structure and behavior. Thus we describe bat sonar as a form of three-dimensional forward perception; we believe that bats feel some versions of pain, fear, hunger, and lust, and that they have other, more familiar types of perception besides sonar. But we believe that these experiences also have in each case a specific subjective character, which it is beyond our ability to conceive. And if there is conscious life elsewhere in the universe, it is likely that some of it will not be describable even in the most general experiential terms available to us. (The problem is not confined to exotic cases, however, for it exists between one person and another. The subjective character of the experience of a person deaf and blind from birth is not accessible to me, for example, nor presumably is mine to him. This does not prevent us each from believing that the other's experience has such a subjective character.)

Nagel believes that his "realism" about the subjective (his claim that the subjective realm really exists) has important philosophical implications, first, for the theory of knowledge:

My realism about the subjective domain in all its forms implies a belief in the existence of facts beyond the reach of human concepts. Certainly it is possible for a human being to believe that there are facts which humans never *will* possess the requisite concepts to represent or comprehend.

This implication is clearly relevant to the problem of "other minds" and might be used in an argument against the behaviorist solution to the problem (see Chapter 25).

Nagel also sees important implications for the mind-body problem, for subjective facts about our mental experience have an essential distinguishing characteristic:

Whatever may be the status of facts about what it is like to be a human being, or a bat, or a Martian, these appear to be facts that embody a particular point of view.

This bears directly on the mind-body problem. For if the facts of experience – facts about what it is like *for* the experiencing organism – are accessible only from one point of view, then it is a mystery how the true character of experiences could be revealed in the physical operation of that organism. The latter is a domain of objective facts *par excellence* – the kind that can be observed and understood from many points of view and by individuals with differing perceptual systems. There are no comparable imaginative obstacles to the acquisition of knowledge about bat neurophysiology by human scientists, and intelligent bats or Martians might learn more about the human brain than we ever will.

But while we are right to leave this point of view aside in seeking a fuller understanding of the external world, we cannot ignore it permanently, since it is the essence of the internal world, and not merely a point of view on it. Most of the neobehaviorism of recent philosophical psychology results from the effort to substitute an objective concept of mind for the real thing, in order to have nothing left over which cannot be reduced. If we acknowledge that a physical theory of mind must account for the subjective character of experience, we must admit that no presently available conception gives us a clue how this could be done.[9]

Does this criticism of "neobehaviorism" seem to you to be valid against the treatments of Ryle (15:2.3) and Wittgenstein (15:2.4)? Does it raise problems for the identity theory as well?

---

[9]Thomas Nagel, "What Is It Like to Be a Bat?" *Philosophical Review*, LXXXIII (1974), 438, 439f, 441, 442, 445.

15:5 *Implications for mental health*   Medical practitioners who approach the mind-body problem from the physicalist standpoint (that reality is entirely physical) treat human conditions ordinarily described as "mental illness" as fundamentally *physical* problems. Foundationalists, such as behaviorists, tend to avoid "mental" language altogether, and they describe these problems as *"behavioral"* disorders. They try to use the reconditioning techniques of behavior modification in order to alter the dispositions of certain subjects to behave in "antisocial ways." They also resort to drug therapy if it seems to influence bahavior in desired ways.

Contextualists, such as identity theorists, are willing to speak of suffering from *mental* illness. For example, they may explain violent behavior as caused by certain thoughts and feelings of the patient, such as a sudden suspicion that an orderly means to kill him or her, or to an uncontrollable urge to inflict harm. But such mental states are themselves *brain* states, which are the result of brain dysfunctions. In severe cases, the practitioner may resort to psychosurgery or drug therapy to alter the patient's brain states. In general, physicalists do not recognize any science of *mental* health distinct from the physical sciences, and they approach mental problems as if they were essentially physical ones.

15:6 *Summary*   Physicalism is the thesis that reality is entirely physical. If physicalism is true, then the problem of mind emerges; namely, do mental statements refer to a different set of facts from those referred to by physical statements? The foundationalist approach to this problem is to deny that there exists a mental realm and so to deny that mental statements describe any actual facts. The naive version of this thesis commits the fallacy of playing with words and has trouble accounting for unexpressed feelings. Behaviorism, a more sophisticated version of the foundationalist approach, defines unexpressed feelings as complex behavioral dispositions. The contextualist approach to the problem of mind is to argue that mental and physical statements describe the same facts. This is called the central state identity thesis. It must deal with objections based on the apparent spatiality, nonprivacy, and objectivity of the referents of physical as opposed to mental statements.

EXERCISES for Chapter 15

1. Below are five statements, each of which is asserted in either a foundationalist or a contextualist argument for physicalism.
   a. Identify each assertion by stating whether it is a premise or a conclusion and whether it is in the foundationalist's or the contextualist's argument (15:2.1, 15:3.1).
      A. The facts of reality are completely described as physical statements.
      B. Mental statements do not describe the facts of reality.
      C. Mental statements describe the same facts as certain physical statements.

   D. Mental statements do describe certain facts of reality.
   E. Mental statements cannot describe the same facts as physical statements.
   b. How does the truth of B relate to the truth of D?
   c. How does the truth of C relate to the truth of E?
   d. How do the truth of A and E relate to the truth of D?
   e. What argument has been provided in favor of each of the following: B (15:2.1), C (15:3.1), D (14:3.1), and E (14:4.1)?

2. a. What is the argument cited by C. D. Broad in 15:3.2?
   b. How have physicalists responded to this argument (15:3.2)?

3. a. What is the behavioristic view attributed to Wittgenstein in 15:2.4?
   b. What is Thomas Nagel saying in 15:4.3?
   c. How is Nagel criticizing the view attributed to Wittgenstein (15:4.3)?

4. a. How does Gilbert Ryle propose in 15:2.3 to analyze mental terms?
   b. What objections have been raised against this view (15:2.4, 15:4.3)?

5. Refer to question 1, *d* and *e*.
   a. In light of the answer to 1d, A or D or E is false. On that assumption, what views are possible?
   b. In the light of the answer to 1e, which of the three statements, A, D, E, would you be inclined to suspect as most likely false?

SELECTED ANSWERS for Chapter 15

1. a. A. premise in both arguments
      B. conclusion of the foundationalist's argument
      C. conclusion of the contextualist's argument
      D. premise of the contextualist's argument
      E. premise of the foundationalist's argument
   b. They are contradictory; whatever B is (true or false), D is the opposite.
   c. They are also contradictory.
   d. Any two of these statements may be true, but if any particular pair is true the third statement is false. (Check this answer by taking each pair of statements and figuring out how each pair guarantees that the third *must* be false if the pair is true.)

2. a. Broad presents the argument that physicalism is false because of the difference between the meaning of physical statements and mental statements.

3. a. Wittgenstein suggests that a person's description of an afterimage and a person's saying "I have a pain" are to be understood behavioristically, not as reports of introspective experience, but in the first case as the expression of a temptation to report seeing a colored patch on the wall and in the second case as a replacement for crying out or wincing.

     b. The subject's experience (e.g., of tasting something sweet-sour) is omitted, not captured, in a behavioristic analysis.

4. a. Ryle proposes to analyze mental terms dispositionally. That is, to say that a person is sharp would mean something such as that when the solution to a problem is not obvious, the person tends, more often and more quickly than other people, to express ways of proceeding that solve the problem.

5. a. Suppose D and E are true. (The contextualist has used introspective experience to argue for D, and the foundationalist has used the characteristics of the physical versus the characteristics of the mental to argue for E.) If D and E are true, then A, physicalism, is false. In that case either idealism (everything is mental) or dualism (there are both mental and physical things) is true. Which is true and whether it is true in a foundationalist or contextualist version would need to be determined. (There are four possibilities here; make sure you see them.) If, on the other hand, A (physicalism) is true, then something must be wrong with either the arguments accepted by the foundationalist or those accepted by the contextualist.

    b. One rational way for you to approach this question is to consider what reasons there might be for accepting or rejecting the arguments of the foundationalistic physicalist and the contextualistic physicalist. It would also be rational, although probably more difficult for you, to consider whether there are direct reasons for thinking that physicalism is false—reasons besides the argument that physicalism must be false because D and E are both true.

16

Reality as Essentially Mental

During the 1960's, many people began to experiment with powerful hallucinogenic drugs such as LSD, which produce vivid and unusual sensory and emotional experiences. Such drugs were claimed to be consciousness expanding, sources of religious insight, or even portals into new and higher dimensions of reality. Often the results were tragic for the user. A "bad trip" could lead to severe mental disorder and even, in some cases, to violence. However, the use of such drugs led some people to reconsider their views about the nature of reality. The fact that sense experience could be altered in drastic ways by using drugs led to the questions, "Do our senses really provide us with observations of some outside world? Or is reality no more than our senses, feelings, and thoughts?" Sweatshirts and buttons bore the legend, "Reality is a crutch." The point was that we deceive ourselves if we believe in reality independent of our consciousness. Consciousness is the only reality.

Many philosophers have thought that a powerful case could be made for this view and what it implies. Some have gone on to deny the reality of everything in the physical world. Others, however, have tried to show that your commonsense belief in physical objects, such as a fist hurtling toward your chin, is compatible with the insight that everything is mental.

After reading Chapter 16 you should be able to

- State the argument from experience that reality is mental.
- Explain both the foundationalist's position that there are no physical facts and the commonsense objection.
- Explain both the contextualist's position that physical facts exist as a special class of mental facts and the objection based on the problem of distinguishing between appearance and reality.

THE CASE OF DON PEDRO

A robin paused to watch Don Pedro as he slowly climbed out from his mountain cave onto the rocky, sunlit ledge. From the ledge he had a clear view of the lush, green valley that separated him from the closest sign of humanity. He wanted it not for its beauty but for its seclusion.

He had looked for many years to find this hermitage. The climate was warm, and wild berries were plentiful. But best of all, as far as Don Pedro was concerned, nobody knew where he was. Formerly he had lived in the city, but visitors to his monastary constantly disturbed his meditation. So he fled. Now, alone, he could contemplate reality and its relation to himself.

"I am I, because I can think. What can be known with more certainty than that? . . . I think and so am. . . . To think is to be. . . . I think, and so I am."

Don Pedro's daily chant had begun. He spoke it quietly aloud with eyes closed, sitting in lotus position. After each sentence he took a deep, relaxing breath of the crisp mountain air. Only the birds and rabbits were there to hear it today.

"All that is exists because it is either thinking or thought of. . . . I am the thinker; it is the thought of. . . . Without my thought, it could not be. . . . So all is because I am, and nothing could be except for my thinking it into being. . . ."

A bee flashed across the horizon unseen and unheard by Don Pedro, so deep was his trance.

"There can be only what I think of, and it can be only as I think it. There can be no other world. I cannot doubt this, for I can never know that of which I do not first think."

In the past Don Pedro had worried that the scribe Mefiesto would fail to record his words. But he no longer was concerned about Mefiesto nor about any of his thousands of followers. After all, he had no knowledge to impart except this: Neither he nor they are real, except insofar as they think or are thought of. Mefiesto dutifully wrote down Don Pedro's sayings and then departed from the prophet's presence without a word of gratitude for the honor he had received of being permitted to write down the holy one's meditations.

"I am all that is; and when I am no longer, nothingness will be the only thing left. . . . No one exists except that I so think, and I cannot know anyone's mind but my own. . . ."

Although he normally came out of his trance for breakfast at about this time, today his mind had soared to new heights.

"All is mind. The world is nothing, not material, not in space or in time. . . . And *my* mind is the All! . . . What cannot be known cannot be. . . . There are no other minds that can be known except my own; and all that is depends on it and is a construction of myself. . . . All is one and I am all."

The bee flew back in front of the mystic's face unnoticed on its way to bring pollen to its comrades.

16:1.1 *Reality as mental* Don Pedro contemplates the nature of existence, saying, "All that is exists because it is either thinking or thought of." The rocky ledge on which he sits and the lush, green valley below have no reality of their own. Nothing could exist, he asserts, without thought. But his thesis is even more radical: "The world is nothing," which means that nothing exists except for the mind. Only mental statements, such as "Don Pedro is thinking that all is one," correctly describe reality. Statements such as "I am sitting on a rocky ledge" or "There is a valley below" do not describe the actual facts of reality. Don Pedro denies that there is a real world of space and time in which the rocky ledge and valley exist.

Don Pedro's pronouncements represent an extreme version of a philosophical view which has enjoyed widespread support in the past. In the words of Bishop Berkeley, "All the choir of heaven and furniture of the earth, in a word all those bodies which compose the mighty frame of the world, have not any subsistence without a mind."[1]

Don Pedro goes further than Berkeley because he denies the reality of any minds other than his own. Even mental statements about other minds, such as "Mefiesto is getting the message," fail to describe reality, because there *are* no other minds and no other experiences except for Don Pedro's.

16:1.2 *The argument from experience* Philosophers have often been led to the following view by worries about skepticism:

(1) We have evidence for mental statements, but not for any other sorts of statements.

---

[1]George Berkeley, *The Principles of Human Knowledge*, 6, in A. A. Luce and T. E. Jessop, *The Works of George Berkeley*, Vol. II (London: Thomas Nelson and Sons, Ltd., 1948–57).

(2) If some statements describe facts of reality for which we have no evidence, then dogmatic skepticism is true.
(3) Any view of reality is better than dogmatic skepticism.
(4) So, the best view of reality is that mental statements describe all the facts of reality — that is, reality is entirely mental.

Premise 1 has been supported by considerations of optical illusions, dreams, and especially hallucinations. Suppose, for example, that after Don Pedro has chewed upon a native root with hallucinogenic properties, he has a hallucination of his erstwhile companion, Mefiesto, sitting beside him on the rocky ledge copying down his every word and occasionally asking questions. A philosophical Don Pedro might reflect: "Probably Mefiesto is not really here. Probably I am only hallucinating. Yet I am simultaneously experiencing two things, Mefiesto and the rocky ledge he is sitting on, within the same visual field, and both experiences seem equally vivid and lifelike. But my *experience* of the rocky ledge really provides *no more evidence* for the existence of something outside of my mind than my *experience* of Mefiesto sitting here. And the same holds true even in my experience of my own body. I remember a vision in which my arms and legs turned into enormous, writhing snakes. Thus my experience provides no real evidence for anything outside my mind."[2]

Premises 2 and 3 are concerned with knowledge, but "dogmatic skepticism" is here defined as a view about *the nature of reality*.[3] It claims that reality includes facts that human beings are incapable of knowing. However, premise 3 implies that it should be possible for us to know what the facts are. The point of the argument is that if you try to maintain that there are any facts besides mental facts concerning experience and belief, you fall into the snares of dogmatic skepticism. If you want to claim that there is a reality beyond the "veil of perceptions," you have no way of finding out what that reality is.[4]

16:2.1 *The foundationalist approach: reality is not physical* Don Pedro represents an extreme foundationalist version of the thesis that reality

---

[2]See Chapter 22, "The Skeptic's Critique," for a fuller statement of these kinds of arguments.

[3]*Dogmatic* skepticism should not be confused with *absolute* skepticism, discussed in Chapter 22, which does not make *any* assertions about reality.

[4]This chapter does not include as an objective the criticism of this premise. Part Six presents a fuller treatment of such problems, especially Chapter 22; and, Chapters 23 and 24 introduce some alternative perspectives. The objectives of the present chapter are, instead, the statements of different interpretations and criticisms of the *conclusion* that reality is entirely mental. The problem that arises for this view is the counterpart of the problem pursued in Chapter 15, namely: Granted that reality is entirely mental, do physical statements such as "Don Pedro's body is seated on a rocky ledge" describe any facts of reality, or is the realm of physical reality a complete illusion?

is essentially mental. The argument for this view is very simple:

(1) Mental statements describe all the facts of reality. (The thesis of *mentalism* or *idealism*.)
(2) Mental statements and physical statements cannot describe the same facts. (The foundationalist thesis.)
(3) Therefore, physical statements describe no facts of reality.

Premise 2 is based on familiar considerations. Physical statements purportedly are concerned with facts about things and events in physical space and time, whereas mental statements purportedly are not. The former purportedly are based upon the public and objective evidence of sense experience, whereas the latter purportedly are based on the private and subjective evidence of introspection.

PHILOSOPHER'S WORKSHOP

Berkeley's Refutation of Materialism

George Berkeley (1685–1753) was an Irish bishop of the Anglican Church, who saw his philosophy of immaterialism as a way to defend Christianity against the onslaught of atheism. Irreligion was founded on the assumption that reality was composed of unconscious matter. Berkeley's greatest works, *A Treatise Concerning the Principles of Human Knowledge* and *Three Dialogues Between Hylas and Philonous*, sought to expose the incoherence of materialism. Berkeley was not hostile to modern science as such, however, and he made important contributions to the science of optics and to the methodology of the sciences. He conceded that the edifice of materialism was impressive but built upon the quicksands of skepticism.

We Could Never Know the Truth of Materialism

But, though it were possible that solid, figured moveable substances may exist without the mind, corresponding to the ideas we have of bodies, yet how is it possible for us to know this? Either we must know it by Sense or by Reason. As for our senses, by them we have the knowledge only of our sensations, ideas, or those things that are immediately perceived by sense, call them what you will; but they do not inform us that things exist without the mind, or unperceived like to those which are perceived. This the materialists themselves acknowledge. — It remains therefore that if we have any knowledge at all of external things, it must be by reason inferring their existence from what is immediately perceived by sense. But what reason can induce us to believe the existence of bodies without the mind, from what we perceive since the very patrons of Matter themselves do not pretend there is any necessary connexion betwixt them and our ideas. I say it is granted on all hands (and what happens in dream frensies, and the like, puts it beyond dispute) that it is possible we might be affected with all the ideas we have now, though no bodies existed without resembling them. Hence it is evident the supposition of external bodies is not necessary for the producing our ideas; since it is granted they are produced sometimes, and might possibly be produced always, in the same order we see them in at present, without their concurrence.

But, though we might possibly have all our sensations without them, yet perhaps it may be thought easier to conceive and explain the manner of their production, by supposing external bodies in their likeness rather than otherwise and so it might be at least probable there are such things as bodies that excite their ideas in our minds. But neither can this be said. For, though we give the materialists their external bodies, they by their own confession are never the nearer knowing how our ideas are produced; since they own themselves unable to comprehend in what manner body can act upon spirit, or how it is possible it should imprint any idea in the mind. Hence it is evident the production of ideas or sensations in our minds can be no reason why we should suppose Matter or corporeal substances; since that is acknowledged to remain inexplicable with or without this supposition. If therefore it were possible for bodies to exist without the mind, yet to hold they do so must needs be a very precarious opinion; since it is to suppose, without any reason at all, that God has created innumerable beings that are entirely useless, and serve to no manner of purpose.

In short, if there were external bodies, it is impossible we should ever come to know it; and if there were not, we might have the very same reasons to think there were that we have now. Suppose — what no one can deny possible — an intelligence, without the help of external bodies, to be affected with the same train of sensations or ideas that you are, imprinted in the same order and with like vividness in his mind. I ask whether that intelligence hath not all the reason to believe the existence of Corporeal Substances, represented by his ideas, and exciting them in his mind, that you can possibly have for believing the same thing? Of this there can be no question. Which one consideration were enough to make any reasonable person suspect the strength of whatever arguments he may think himself to have, for the existence of bodies without the mind.

Only Idealism Escapes Dogmatic Skepticism

But if [our ideas] are looked on as notes or images, referred to *things* or *archetypes existing without the mind*, then are we involved all in scepticism. We see only the appearances, and not the real qualities of things. What may be the extension, figure, or motion of anything really and absolutely, or in itself, it is impossible for us to know, but only the proportion or relation they bear to our senses. Things remaining the same, our ideas vary; and which of them, or even whether any of them at all, represent the true quality really existing in the thing, it is out of our reach to determine. So that, for aught we know, all we see, hear, and feel, may be only phantom and vain chimera, and not at all agree with the real things existing in *rerum natura*. All this scepticism follows from our supposing a difference between *things* and *ideas*, and that the former have a subsistence without the mind, or unperceived. It were easy to dilate on this subject, and shew how the arguments urged by sceptics in all ages depend on the supposition of external objects.

So long as we attribute a real existence to unthinking things, distinct from their being perceived, it is not only impossible for us to know with evidence the nature of any real unthinking being, but even that it exists. Hence it is that we see philosophers distrust their senses, and doubt of the existence of heaven and earth, of everything they see or feel, even of their own bodies. And after all their labour and struggle of thought, they are forced to own we cannot attain to any self-evident or demonstrative knowledge of the existence of sensible things. But, all this doubtfulness, which so bewilders and confounds the mind and makes philosophy ridiculous in the eyes of the world, vanishes if we annex a meaning to our words, and do not amuse ourselves with the terms *absolute, external, exist,* and such like, signifying we know not what. I can as well doubt of my own being as of the being of those things which I actually perceive by sense: it being a manifest contradiction that any sensible object should be immediately perceived by sight or touch, and at the same time have no existence in nature; since the very existence of an *unthinking being* consists in *being perceived*.[5]

<hr/>

[5] Berkeley, *Principles*, pp. 18–20, 87–88.

16:2.2 *The appearance-reality distinction* The foundationalist approach seems to be open to the obvious objection that it cannot do justice to the facts of experience. Surely you observe physical things and events all the time, and you report these observations in the form of physical statements, for example, "A bumblebee flies past Don Pedro's nose" or "Don Pedro's stomach is rumbling." A foundationalist like Don Pedro will respond: "The fact that I, too, have such experiences does not refute my view that my mind is all of reality. For when I describe what I experience, I have to distinguish between what I see and what I *seem* to see. Remember my experience of Mefiesto on the rocky ledge. In that case I was entitled only to make the mental statement, 'I am having the visual experience of seeing Mefiesto on the ledge.' I wasn't entitled to make the physical statement, 'Mefiesto's body is on the ledge.' Likewise, in the present case I am entitled only to make the mental statement, 'I am having the *experiences* of hearing and seeing a bumblebee' or 'It *appears* to me that there is a bumblebee before my nose,' but not such physical statements as 'A bumblebee *is* flying past my nose.' Where *you* would inaccurately speak of things such as a bumblebee, *I* more accurately speak of what *appears* to be the case; for what appears to be the case (my experience) is the only reality."

16:2.3 *Solipsism*   Many philosophers, having gone this far, take the final step of rejecting even mental statements about *other persons*. What evidence does Don Pedro have for mental statements about Mefiesto, such as "Mefiesto understands my teachings"? His evidence for this statement is just as unreliable as his evidence for "A bumblebee is flying past my nose." Don Pedro concludes that only mental statements about his *own* experiences and thoughts describe reality. Because he believes that his mind alone exists, he is a *solipsist*.

16:3.1 *Objections from common sense*   It is extremely difficult to refute a solipsist, who simply denies any of the "obvious" facts brought

Are we all only the fantasies of some solopsistic mind?

against solipsism, but *as* a foundationalist view, it seems very arbitrary. The foundationalist form of *physicalism* rejects introspective descriptions of personal experience as evidence for statements about reality (see 15:2–3), whereas the foundationalist form of *mentalism* will not accept anything else. From the point of view of common sense, both of these positions exploit arbitrarily narrow standards of admissible evidence.

16:3.2 *Counterattack on common sense*   However, many foundationalist defenders of mentalism cannot be accused of such arbitrariness. They support their position with arguments that our commonsense beliefs in an objective world of space and time are incoherent and indefensible because they involve fundamental contradictions. Many of the arguments resemble Zeno's paradoxes. This ancient philosopher offered simple and elegant proofs that our commonsense belief that physical objects move from place to place contradicts our commonsense belief about the nature of space and time. (For an example of Zeno's reasoning see 4:3.1.) In the nineteenth century, defenders of mentalism, such as the German G. W. F. Hegel and the English F. H. Bradley and J. McTaggart, presented elaborate and very difficult arguments that our notions of space and time are incoherent. Much of the energy of twentieth-century defenders of a belief in a physical reality has been invested in trying to refute these challenging mentalist critiques of space and time.

16:4.1 *The contextualist approach: there are physical facts*   Many philosophers have felt torn between the reasoned belief that reality is entirely mental and the commonsense conviction that physical statements about rocks, bumblebees, and human bodies correctly describe the facts of reality. However, some of them have drawn a contextualist conclusion from these two commitments:

(1) Mental statements describe all the facts of reality. (The thesis of *mentalism*.)
(2) Physical statements describe some of the facts of reality. (The evidence of *perception*.)
(3) Therefore, some physical statements describe the same facts as some mental statements. (The *contextualist* thesis.)

The contextualist believes that it is possible, in this way, to reconcile mentalism and common sense. In the words of Berkeley, "We ought to think with the learned and speak with the vulgar. . . . A little reflection on what is here said will make it manifest that the common use of language would receive no manner of alteration or disturbance from the admission of our tenets."[6] In this view physical statements, such as "A bumblebee is buzzing around my head," refer to the same facts as mental statements, such as "It now seems to me that there is a bumblebee in front of my nose." Thus, physical facts are found to be identical with certain mental facts or certain constellations of mental facts. Physical reality is a "construct" built up out of mental facts. Space itself is real, but its reality consists of the *perceived* spatial relationships of objects, for example, the experience of seeing one thing in front of another. Berkeley says, "Every vegetable, star, mineral and in general each part of the mundane system, is as much a *real being* by our principles as by any other." But he insists that "to be is to be perceived."[7] Reality contains nothing that is unperceived, and physical statements describe only the facts we perceive.

16:4.2 *Parallels to the identity theory*   This form of contextualism closely parallels the identity theory, which identifies mental experiences with physical events like brain processes (15:3.2), and it is subject to the same misinterpretation by critics. One critic of Berkeley, for example, writes "Now, 'is blue' and 'looks blue to me' do not mean the same thing. A thing can *be* blue without looking blue to me, and *look blue to me* without being blue. So Berkeley is wrong to identify sensible qualities and sense impressions. . . ."[8] This criticism, however, is avoidable given the distinction between meaning (intension) and reference (extension). The two statements, "The Morning Star is in the sky" and "The Evening Star is in the sky," can refer to the very same fact even if they have different meanings. Similarly, the two statements, "The book is blue" and "The book looks blue to me," can *refer* to the same fact even if they have different meanings (see 15:3.2). Thus the contextualist need not make claims about synonymy of intension but only about sameness of reference.

16:5.1 *The problem of unperceived objects*   Berkeley claimed that his version of mentalism would account for any physical statement recognized as true and meaningful by common sense. It only rejected the esoteric philosophical thesis that the facts of reality do not depend upon the existence of a mind. Nevertheless, Berkeley and his critics have recognized that there are numerous physical statements that are difficult to account for. Berkeley was aware of the objection that in his theory, "things are every moment annihilated and created anew. The

---

[6]Berkeley, *Principles*, p. 51.
[7]Berkeley, *Principles*, p. 36.
[8]D. M. Armstrong, ed., *Berkeley's Philosophical Writings* (New York: Collier Books, 1965), Editor's Introduction, pp. 8–9.

objects of sense exist only when they are perceived: the trees therefore are in the garden, or the chairs in the parlor, no longer than while there is somebody by to perceive them."[9] Thus, his theory seemingly fails to account for the true physical statement, "The bee flew back in front of Don Pedro's nose unnoticed. . . ." According to common sense, the bee exists even at times when Don Pedro does not see it.

DIAGRAM 1

Physical Statement	The bee is buzzing.	The bee is buzzing.	The bee is buzzing.
Mental Statement	Don Pedro senses a buzzing bee.	? ? ? ? ? ? ? ? ? ? ? ? ? ? ? ? ? ?	Don Pedro senses a buzzing bee.
Time	3:01	3:02	3:03

Berkeley's first and favorite solution to the problem is that the mental statement that is true at 3:02 is, "God is aware of a bee!" For, "seeing [that sensible things] depend not on my thought, and have an existence distinct from being perceived by me, there must be some other Mind wherein they exist."[10]

The bee exists whether or not Pedro has bee-buzzing sensations, because even if he is not aware of a bee, God is. This solution has been severely criticized. First, the sudden introduction of this omnipresent perceiver is analogous to the *deus ex machina* in drama: a contrived way of removing an unsolved difficulty. Second, since God's awareness does not involve "corporeal motions" as ours does, God "perceives nothing by sense as we do. . . . Such a Being can suffer nothing, nor be affected with any painful sensation, or indeed any sensation at all."[11] This admission seems to invalidate the solution to the problem of the unperceived bumblebee, for common sense says that the *same* physical fact obtains through the period from 3:01 to 3:03. This physical fact will be identified with a mental fact involving Don Pedro's fleeting sensations at 3:01 and 3:03. But at 3:02 it will be identified with an entirely different *sort* of fact, involving God's eternal nonsensory awareness. Thus, how can it be maintained that the *same* physical fact is true from 3:01 to 3:03?

Another solution hinted at by Berkeley proved more acceptable to later philosophers. The mental statement at 3:02 is this: "*If* Don

---

[9]Berkeley, *Principles*, p. 45.

[10]Berkeley, *Three Dialogues Between Hylas and Philonous*, in *The Works of George Berkeley*, Vol. II. p. 212.

[11]Berkeley, *Three Dialogues*, 3rd Dialogue, Vol. II, p. 241.

✒ PHILOSOPHER'S WORKSHOP

On Being Perceived

There was a young man who said, "God
Must think it exceedingly odd
    If he finds that this tree
    Continues to be
When there's no one about in the Quad."

REPLY

Dear Sir:
    Your astonishment's odd:
I am always about in the Quad.
    And that's why the tree
    Will continue to be,
Sincerely observed by
    Yours faithfully,
    God[12]

---

[12]Ronald Knox, as cited by Bertrand Russell, in *A History of Western Philosophy* (New York: Simon and Schuster, 1945), p. 64.

Pedro *would* look or pay attention, *then* he *would* sense a buzzing bee." There are, indeed, many true statements of this sort, for example, "If doughnuts were dollars, then bakers would bank." They do not describe actual facts but possible facts, facts that *would* exist if other conditions were to occur. But again, the solution does not account for the commonsense belief that the *same* physical fact obtains at 3:01 and 3:02; for Berkeley is identifying the physical fact that a bee is buzzing with an *actual* fact at 3:01 and a merely *possible* fact at 3:02.

16:5.2 *The problem of appearance and reality* According to common sense it makes a difference whether Don Pedro actually sees Mefiesto beside him on the rocky ledge or instead has an hallucination of him. In one case, it is a physical fact that Mefiesto is there on the ledge; in the other case, it is not. Yet according to contextualism, both "Mefiesto is on the ledge" and "Don Pedro is hallucinating Mefiesto on the ledge" refer to facts involving Don Pedro's experiences. So how are they different?

Berkeley's solution to this problem is that sense experience and hallucination are completely different *types* of experience. When we have sense experiences of *real* things, our experiences are "strong, orderly, and coherent." Our imaginings are "faint, weak, and unsteady" in comparison with sense experiences, which are "more affecting, orderly, and distinct." We can form and destroy mental fictions at will whereas sense experiences are "impressed" on us "according to certain rules or laws of nature."[13]

This distinction has some validity in connection with daydreams and the voluntary construction of mental images, but some nightmares and the hallucinations associated with drug use or insanity can be as vivid, distinct, and affecting as ordinary sense experiences. Moreover, a person suffering from acute psychosis may undergo a prolonged hallucination in which experiences are connected and which cohere with a kind of insane consistency. Moreover, in general, there is no evidence that these experiences are voluntary. According to Berkeley's distinction, these hallucinations are experiences of reality, which obviously will not square with common sense.

16:6 *Applications to mental health*   In view of these difficulties, many advocates of the thesis that reality is entirely mental have abandoned the contextualist program of reconciling the thesis with common sense. But the difficulties just raised about hallucination and psychosis raise obvious problems in connection with mental health for those who are committed to the existence of other minds. Suppose you are a psychiatrist engaged in therapy. On what grounds can you assert that you are sane and your patient is insane? If your experiences of the world disagree with the patient's, how can you claim that your experiences correspond with objective reality whereas the patient's do not? The patient's experiences may be as vivid, affecting, and internally coherent as your own.

Some psychologists not only recognize this difficulty, but embrace it as the only basis for genuine therapy: Therapists must not impose their reality on the patient. The patient's experiences are just as authentic as the therapist's. The therapist who diagnoses a patient's experiences as a psychosis, the result of faulty conditioning or of a brain disorder, is imposing a particular physicalistic view of reality on the patient. The therapist ought, instead, to recognize the reality of the patient as equally valid. If patients are dissatisfied with their reali-

---

[13]Berkeley, *Principles*, p. 36.

ty, the therapist may help them to change it. But in this view, the starting point of therapy is recognition of, and respect for, the patient's reality.

16:7 *Summary* Dogmatic skepticism regarding physical statements seems appropriate if we accept the view that the only evidence we have is for mental statements. Rather than embrace dogmatic skepticism, many philosophers turn to mentalism, the thesis that reality is entirely mental. The foundationalist approach to mentalism is to argue that because physical statements cannot describe the same facts as mental statements, physical statements are not about reality. This view can be extended into the thesis of solipsism, which rejects mental statements about everything and everyone except oneself. The contextualist approach to mentalism is to argue that both mental and physical statements describe the same facts. Both approaches run into problems. For example, the foundationalists have to contend with our commonsense intuitions about physical statements, and the contextualists have the problem of accounting for unperceived objects.

EXERCISES for Chapter 16

1. Some of the statements listed below are the premises or the conclusion of the mentalist's arguments from experience. Mark the premises *P*, the conclusion *C*, and the others *No* (16:1.2).
   A. We have evidence for mental statements, but not for any other sorts of statements.
   B. Whatever is physical has spatial properties.
   C. The best view of reality is that mental statements describe all the facts of reality.
   D. Mental statements cannot describe the same facts as physical statements.
   E. Any view of reality is better than dogmatic skepticism.
   F. If some statements describe facts of reality for which we have no evidence, then dogmatic skepticism is true.
   G. The view that we cannot know anything about any part of reality is worse than the view that we cannot know anything about some parts of reality.
2. a. State the argument in support of foundationalistic mentalism (16:2.1).
   b. Now state the subarguments in support of each of the premises of that argument, identifying which subargument supports which premises (16:1.2 and 14:4.2).

3. Below are statements of three objections against foundationalistic mentalism.
   a. Which is the objection from common sense?
      A. The contention that dogmatic skepticism should be rejected is foolish since it is entirely consistent to believe that it may be true entirely independent of this argument. After all, scientific instruments have shown us that there are facts of reality about which we can have no evidence coming simply from our senses, without instruments, that is. Therefore, there might be facts of reality such that the instruments required to gain evidence of them cannot be used by creatures whose senses are as limited as ours.
      B. If, according to the mentalist, it is impossible to have "evidence" concerning physical facts of reality, that simply shows that the mentalist uses overly narrow standards of what having evidence amounts to.
      C. The very statement of the argument that solipsism is true employs language, which is a means of communication. Being a means of communication, language could not exist unless there were a community of at least two persons to communicate. Thus, the fact that the argument for solipsism can be stated proves that its conclusion is false.
   b. Which of these three arguments would *you* be inclined to use against foundationalistic idealism?
   c. What would you do to clarify its premises, support its premises, and defend it against objections you might anticipate?

4. The following list of statements contains some of Berkeley's contextualist views, objections to his views, replies by Berkeley, and some irrelevant statements. Draw an arrow linking each objection with the Berkeley statement to which it objects, and linking Berkeley's replies to the objections.
   A. For a physical object to exist is a matter of its being perceived.
   B. Nothing physical exists.
   C. No independent arguments have been provided for the existence of God.
   D. If I see a fire burning brightly and ten minutes later see the fire burning somewhat less brightly, it is ridiculous to suppose that the fire did not exist in the meantime when I wasn't looking, probably burning with decreasing brightness.
   E. The only minds that exist are mine and God's.
   F. The distinction between a daydream and a physical reality is that I can cause the experience of the daydream to cease by willing it.
   G. Physical realities exist when unobserved by human beings because God constantly observes them.
   H. If the facts of my experience are the same whether I experience something physically real or something that has no physical reality, then there is no way of distinguishing what is and what is not physically real.

5. a. Suppose that a person experiences an illusion rather than a daydream. Use a statement of how the latter differs from the former as the basis of your explanation why 4F will not work for Berkeley as a means of distinguishing illusions from physical realities.

   b. State how Berkeley would make this distinction (16:5.2).
   c. Now suppose that a person experiences a hallucination or a delusion, rather than an illusion or a daydream. Use a statement of how the latter two differ from the former as the basis of your explanation why your answer to 5b will not work for Berkeley as a means of distinguishing hallucinations and delusions from physical realities.
   d. What bases could you define for making this distinction? (You may find that a look at Chapter 23 as well as other discussions in Part Six can help.)
   e. Explain whether your own bases for making the distinction are consistent or inconsistent with what you know of Berkeley's view.

SELECTED ANSWERS for Chapter 16

1. A. *P.*
   B. *No.*
   C. *C.*
   D. *No.*

   E. *P.*
   F. *P.*
   G. *No.*

3. a. *B*

4. D → A.
   C → G.
   F → H.
   G → D.

5. a. Since I cannot cause an illusion to cease by willing it, experiences of illusions are, in this regard, like experiences of physical realities and unlike experiences of daydreams.
   c. Since experiences of hallucinations and delusions can be as vivid, distinct, affecting, and consistent as those of physical realities, Berkeley's basis for distinguishing illusions from physical realities is not adequate for distinguishing hallucinations and delusions from physical realities.

17

Dualistic Perspectives

Suppose scientists could construct a fleshy android which could behave exactly like us and even had a computer brain to process information; yet it lacked consciousness, so that it could not experience
feelings and thoughts like we do. Common sense tells us this creation
would not be a human being or a person but a mere automaton or
robot. Suppose, next, that some practitioners of the occult are correct
when they claim to receive communications from beings in the "spirit
world," but these beings are totally disembodied, so that they neither
occupy a place in the world, like us, nor exercise physical agency in
the world. Common sense tells us that whatever these beings are—
ghosts or devils or departed souls—they are not human beings.

According to common sense, a real human being has a physical
existence, and distinct from this, a mental life. Similarly, philosophers
called *dualists* contend that mental and physical statements about
ourselves are both equally valid ways of describing different facts of
reality. Dualists are suspicious of attempts to entirely reduce reality
either to mental facts or to physical ones.

After reading Chapter 17 you should be able to

■ State the argument from the variety of experience that reality is both
mental and physical.

- State the foundationalist argument of Descartes that physical and mental statements describe two distinct realities: mind and body.
- Explain the objections to Cartesian dualism that are based upon the problems of causal interaction and personal identity.
- State the contextualist argument that physical and mental statements describe in different ways the same reality: a person.
- Explain the objections to the person theory that are based upon the problems of incompleteness and distinguishing between persons and their bodies.

THE CASE OF RUTH CHODILL

"Hello, Mrs. Chodill. My name is Sharon, Sharon Parad. I would like to talk with you for just a few minutes. May I come in?"

"Hello; yes, do come in, I've just been sitting here. Nurse isn't due for about a half hour yet with my pain pills. My joints hurt a lot. It's so humid you know."

"How old are you, Mrs. Chodill?"

"I'm sixty-seven. Why do you ask?"

"I'm doing a study for a research report. I'm asking patients like yourself about their experiences."

"You mean old women?"

"No, I mean patients who were thought to be . . . well . . . very near death, but who somehow pulled through."

"Well, ask away. I love to have someone to talk to."

"Fine. Let me just turn on my recording machine and put the microphone here nearer to you. . . . Now, just tell me what your experiences were as you were wheeled into the emergency room."

"Well, let's see. I was having a heart attack. My chest hurt a lot, I remember."

"Yes. And your heart had actually stopped. I understand that they had been working on you for several minutes. The doctor was about to pronounce you dead. You were unconscious. Am I right?"

"Yes, I think that's about right. I remember that I wanted to tell the doctor something. I think I felt sorry for him. He looked so worried. There was one very young woman there. I think she was a volunteer worker because she had a pink uniform. She looked frightened. I could see her behind the two nurses."

"Where did you see her from, Mrs. Chodill? What vantage point did you have?"

"I was on the bed. . . . No, wait. That's wrong. I was up in the corner; in the top corner of the room. I could see them all. I could hear them, too. That's odd; isn't it? I was lying down unconscious!"

"Please, Mrs. Chodill. Just go on. What happened then?"

"Well, I went into a tunnel then. It was dark and very long. But I could see a light at the far end. I was drawn toward it. And then I got to it. My husband, John, was there. He smiled at me. I hadn't seen him since he died seven years ago. There was someone else there, too. It looked like Jesus!"

"How did you feel, Mrs. Chodill?"

"Wonderful! I felt wonderful. I felt a sense of peace, great calm and tranquility. I wanted very much to stay with John. But he said I had to go back. I didn't want to, but he said my time hadn't come yet. Then I woke up! I was really still on the bed. The people were all happy. The doctor looked especially happy and very tired, too."

"What do you think about death now, Mrs. Chodill?"

"I miss John very much. I don't care if I die. I know death now; it doesn't frighten me anymore."

17:1.1 *The afterlife*   Religious belief in a life after death has been closely associated with the dualistic theory that human life is a complex mixture of mental and physical events. In this theory, a person like Ruth Chodill is described by a sequence of physical statements, such as "Ruth's heart is beating" or "Neurons are firing in Ruth's brain." At the same time her spiritual life is described by a sequence of mental statements, such as "Ruth sees the medical team." Since her two lives *are* different, it would seem possible for Ruth's spiritual life to continue even after her biological life is terminated. The case study seems to describe just such a circumstance. (Although the case study is fictional, it is interesting that actual patients who have been clinically dead for a time but who subsequently revived have reported similar experiences.) Even after her heart ceased to beat and current had ceased to flow through her neural circuits, *mental* activity continued: She experienced sensations, feelings, and thoughts.

17:1.2 *The mind-body problem*   The case study, therefore, suggests that the mental facts of Ruth's existence are quite independent of the physical facts. A mental statement about Ruth, like "Ruth sees the medical team," can continue to be true, even when physical statements, like "Neurons are firing in Ruth's brain," cease to be true.[1] This suggestion is in accord with the *foundationalist* approach to dualism which claims that the mental and the physical are not only different but *mutually exclusive* modes of existence. This theory faces the tough assignment of explaining how these two realms of reality could be inter-

---

[1]What makes cases like this one interesting is that *if* they have been described rightly, they tend to disconfirm the identity theory while lending plausibility to the dualist perspective.

related. The difficulties encountered by foundationalism have led other dualists to reject the foundationalist assumption of an incompatibility between the mental and the physical. These questions constitute the *mind-body problem* for dualism: "Are the mental and the physical incompatible?" and "What are the connections between mental and physical facts?"

17:2.1 *The foundationalist approach: the mental excludes the physical*   The foundationalist version of dualism is supported by the following line of reasoning:

(1) Both physical and mental statements describe the facts of reality, as the evidence of sense experience and introspection indicates.
(2) Mental statements cannot describe the same facts as physical statements. (The foundationalist thesis.)
(3) Therefore, reality consists of two mutually exclusive sets of facts.

The first premise indicates that in contrast to foundationalist versions of mentalism and physicalism, dualism tries to do justice to *all* the available evidence. But this version of dualism accepts the arguments for foundationalism: Mental events are private and conscious, whereas physical events are public and spatial, and so forth (see 15:2.1 and 16:2.1).

17:2.2 *Cartesian dualism*   The most influential modern defense of this doctrine is offered by René Descartes (1596–1650). Descartes divides created existence into two radically different realms: the *mental* and the *physical*. A human being is a union of a physical entity (body) and a mental entity (mind), but a person's real "self" is his or her mind, a thing that thinks *(res cogitans)*. A person's body is a physical object in a space that he or she discovers to be uniquely associated with his or her mind. An image of this body occupies the center of the mind's visual field; the mind senses pain when its body is injured; and so forth. Descartes emphasizes that there is a very intimate connection between one's mind and one's body: "Nature also teaches me by these sensations of pain, hunger, thirst, etc., that I am not only lodged in my body as a pilot in a vessel, but that I am very closely united to it, and so to speak so intermingled with it that I seem to compose with it one whole."[2] Nevertheless, he maintains that his essence is mental, capable of separate existence from his body.

---

[2]René Descartes, *Meditations on First Philosophy*, in *The Philosophical Works of Descartes*, I, trans. Elizabeth S. Haldane and G. R. T. Ross (New York: Cambridge University Press, 1970), 192.

Descartes's foundationalism results from his theory of knowledge. You can know, with certainty, by *introspection*, what the "modes" of your own mind are, for example, that you are in pain or that you are thinking about a tennis game. But your mind is only conscious of its own thoughts, because no mind can ever directly apprehend any other mind or its thoughts. The mind's knowledge of material bodies is obtained by being aware of certain experiences—for example, "It seems to me somebody is standing on the road ahead"—and then *inferring* from these the existence of external objects that cause the experience. Not being deductively valid, such inferences are *not* certain. Thus, there is a radical difference between your knowledge of your mental states and that of your bodily states. Moreover, Descartes argues, it is absurd to regard the idea of a thinking thing (mind) and the idea of a spatially extended thing (body) as ideas of the same substance.

✒ PHILOSOPHER'S WORKSHOP

Descartes's Argument for Dualism

René Descartes (1596–1650) was a foundationalist. He used the skeptical method of doubt to filter out all of his beliefs that were not absolutely certain. The only beliefs that remained were either of the type "I think (or feel or doubt, and so on)" or beliefs in truths revealed by "the light of nature," such as "If I think, I must exist." On the basis of these he established his first inference: *cogito ergo sum*, "I think, therefore I am." He often asked, "What am I, who am certain that I am?" He concluded: "I am, so far, a 'thinking thing'. But how am I, so understood, related to my body? Am I the same as it or something different?" To settle the question, he first assured himself, with proofs that God exists and is no deceiver, that he could rely upon his "clear and distinct" ideas (which he received from God). Using these he then tackled the problem of whether the mind and body are the same or different.

I have a clear and distinct idea of myself as thinking

I find here that thought is an attribute that belongs to me; it alone cannot be separated from me. I am, I exist, that is certain. But how often? Just when I think; for it might possibly be the case if I ceased entirely to think, that I should likewise cease altogether to exist. I do not now admit anything which is not necessarily true: to speak accurately I am not more than a thing which thinks, that is to say a mind or a soul, or an understanding, or a reason, which are terms whose significance was formerly unknown to me. I am, however, a real thing and really exist; but what thing? I have answered: a thing which thinks.

And what more? I shall exercise my imagination [in order to see if I am not something more]. I am not a collection of members which we call the human body: I am not a subtle air distributed through these members, I am not a wind, a fire, a vapour, a breath, nor anything at all which I can imagine or conceive; because I have assumed that all these were nothing. Without changing that supposition I find that I only leave myself certain of the fact that I am somewhat. But perhaps it is true that these same things which I supposed were non-existent because they are unknown to me, are really not different from the self which I know. I am not sure about this, I shall not dispute about it now; I can only give judgment on things that are known to me. I know that I exist, and I inquire what I am, I whom I know to exist.

I have a clear and distinct idea of a body as extended

Let us take, for example, this piece of wax: it has been taken quite freshly from the hive, and it has not yet lost the sweetness of the honey which it contains; it still retains somewhat of the odour of the flowers from which it has been culled; its colour, its figure, its size are apparent; it is hard, cold, easily handled, and if you strike it with the finger, it will emit a sound. . . .But notice that while I speak and approach the fire what remained of the taste is exhaled, the smell evaporates, the colour alters, the figure is destroyed, the size increases, it becomes liquid, it heats, scarcely can one handle it, and when one strikes it, no sound is emitted. Does the same wax remain after this change? We must confess that it remains; none would judge otherwise. What then did I know so distinctly in this piece of wax? It could certainly be nothing of all that the senses brought to my notice, since all these things which fall under taste, smell, sight, touch, and hearing, are found to be changed, and yet the same wax remains.

Perhaps it was . . . simply a body which a little while before appeared to me as perceptible under these forms, and which is now perceptible under others. But what, precisely, is it that I imagine when I form such conceptions? Let us attentively consider this, and, abstracting from all that does not belong to the wax, let us see what remains. Certainly nothing remains excepting a certain extended thing which is flexible and movable. But what is the meaning of flexible and movable? Is it not that I imagine that this piece of wax being round is capable of becoming square and of passing from a square to a triangular figure? No, certainly it is not that, since I imagine it admits of an infinitude of similar changes, and I nevertheless do not know how to compass the infinitude by my imagination, and consequently this conception which I have of the wax is not brought about by the faculty of imagination. . . . We must then grant that I could not even understand through the imagination what this piece of wax is, and that it is my mind alone which perceives it.

I am distinct from my body

And first of all, because I know that all things which I apprehend clearly and distinctly in order to be certain that the one is different it suffices that I am able to apprehend one thing apart from another clearly and distinctly in order to be certain that the one is different from the other, since they may be made to exist in separation at least by the omnipotence of God; and it does not signify by what power this separation is made in order to compel me to judge them to be different: and, therefore, just because I know certainly that I exist, and that meanwhile I do not remark that any other thing necessarily pertains to my nature or essence, excepting that I am a thinking thing, I rightly conclude that my essence consists solely in the fact that I am a thinking thing [or a substance whose whole essence or nature is to think]. And although possibly (or rather certainly, as I shall say in a moment) I possess a body with which I am very intimately conjoined, yet because, on the one side, I have a clear and distinct idea of myself inasmuch as I am only a thinking and unextended thing, and as, on the other, I possess a distinct idea of body, inasmuch as it is only an extended and unthinking thing, it is certain that this I [that is to say, my soul by which I am what I am], is entirely and absolutely distinct from my body, and can exist without it.[3]

---

[3]Descartes, *Meditations*, pp. 190, 192, 195, 196.

17:2.3 *Interactionism* Descartes also tried to explain the interrelationships between mental and physical facts by means of the theory of *interactionism.* In this theory, certain mental facts occur because of certain physical facts, and vice versa. For example, the physical contact of a finger and a hot stove may cause a sensation of pain; your subsequent decision to move your finger may cause your finger to move. The diagram shows this chain of mental (M) and physical (P) events:

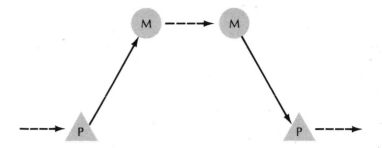

17:3.1 ***The problem of personal identity*** According to Descartes, your "self" is your mind, which can continue to exist even when the body is destroyed. The sole test for the continuing existence of such a self is a continuity of consciousness. For example, Ruth Chodill would remember her former, embodied life even after her physical death. Many philosophers find this conception of personal identity unsatisfactory. The fact that you remember having done something does not show that you actually did it, because your recollection may be in error.[4]

17:3.2 ***The "ghost in the machine" problem*** Descartes's theory is often derided as the "ghost in the machine." If a ghost is by definition an immaterial substance, how can it have an effect on a material one? How can it blow out candles, open and shut doors, or make things "go bump in the night"? It has no spatial existence, and its mental activity involves no energy that could be transferred to a physical thing. Even if it could haunt a house, it would necessarily lead an innocuous, undetectable existence. Even if it somehow occupied an automobile,

---

[4]This problem is discussed more fully in Chapter 12.

What is the nature of the "causal interaction" between the physical and the mental?

how could it operate the thing? The same problem arises from Descartes's theory of the mind. Even if a mind could occupy the machinery of the human body, how could it control and drive that machine? Descartes tries to answer this question by proposing that the mind acts on the body through the pineal gland. But this answer just pushes the problem back a step. It is like saying a ghost could operate an automobile by operating the steering wheel, pedals, and gearshift lever. But how could an *immaterial* ghost push down a gas pedal? And, too, how could an event like a denting of the car's fender have any effect on the ghost?

 PHILOSOPHER'S WORKSHOP

The Argument from ESP

Dualists, who hold that mental experiences are different from any physical processes, sometimes appeal to the evidence of parapsychology. Parapsychology studies experiences, memories, and knowledge that are true of the world but are not acquired in the normal way, through the sense organs. In 1882 in London a group of philosophers and scientists founded the Society for Psychical Research, and three years later its counterpart was founded in the United States. Early members included C. D. Broad of England, Henri Bergson of France, and the Americans C. J. Ducasse and William James. They investigated thousands of reported cases of different types: *telepathy*, in which a person is aware of an unperceived, inanimate object without relying on memory or information from others; *precognition*, in which a person is aware, without relying on evidence, of an event, such as someone's death, before it occurs. The Society was especially interested in persons who reported that a recently deceased relative or close friend had "appeared" to them and communicated with them. F. W. H. Myers in England conducted research on mediums who claimed that they could communicate with the dead. Myers tried to design experiments that would rule out the possibility of fraud. He concluded that some mediums could report information about the dead that they could not have learned in a normal way and that they could simulate the voices and mannerisms of deceased persons they had never seen. Sympathetic critics have pointed out that even if Myers had succeeded in ruling out fraud, he had not shown that the medium was really communicating with the nonphysical spirits of the dead—because the medium might be reading the minds of living relatives and friends of the dead persons! But most of the Society's research was sensationalistic and unverifiable, and Society members were criticized for being too gullible in accepting reports of occult experiences.

Parapsychological research proceeded on a more scientific footing after 1930. J. B. Rhine at Duke University and S. G. Soal, a mathematician at London University, applied sophisticated statistical techniques in controlled laboratory settings, and L. L. Vasiliev at the Leningrad Institute of Brain Research investigated brain activity in allegedly psychic subjects. Rhine's book, *Extra-Sensory Perception* (1934), gave the name "ESP" to the new field. You can try with a friend one of Rhine's famous experiments. Make 25 cards, 5 each of 5 types:

Have your friend shuffle the cards and look at each card outside of your view. Guess what is on each card, keeping a running list of guesses. When he is done, check your guesses for accuracy. According to the laws of probability, over the *long run*, you should only get 5 correct responses out of 25. It is significant if you do even slightly better. Rhine found a subject who answered rightly an average of 7½ times, even when he was in a different building from the cards. The odds against this performance were staggering: 100,000,000,000,000,000,000 to one! (ESP research remains, of course, extremely controversial.)

What is proved by ESP? Suppose that when your friend holds a card with a cross on it, you have a mental image of a cross, and this happens regularly and not by chance. The dualists might argue:

1. Your experience of the cross is not the result of physical events in your sense organs.
2. Therefore, your experience of the cross is not the result of any physical processes.
3. Therefore, your experience of the cross is essentially nonphysical in nature.

But a *physicalist* might accept the evidence of ESP and still object to this reasoning: "We quite agree with the dualists about statement 1 but they are too quick to leap from 1 to 2. For we have *another*, physical hypothesis to explain your experience of the cross: When your friend reads the card, his brain transmits brain waves which are received directly by your brain. Given this hypothesis, 1 is true, but 2 is false."

How might the dualists reply to such an objection? What experiments could be conducted to test this brain-wave hypothesis?

Some twentieth-century dualists have taken heart from alleged developments in the field of parapsychology. If a man can bend a spoon by the sheer force of thought (a phenomenon called "telekinesis"), it might be taken as proof that consciousness can act on matter. Communication with the dead by means of an Ouija board might also be counted as proof. But such data are, to say the least, controversial. Although some scientists are exploring telekinesis and telepathy, no such psychical phenomena are established scientific facts. If there were such a thing as telekinesis, and it admitted of no natural, materialistic explanation, the law of the conservation of matter and energy would be overthrown. If a person were able to cause a small suspended object to move without using any physical mechanism, this would seem to entail the creation of energy that did not exist before. It is not surprising that many scientists are leery about ESP, and the Cartesian theory of dualism seems to lead to the same sorts of headaches.

17:3.3 *Variations on the Cartesian theme* Problems like those above have prompted revisions in dualism, away from interactionism. According to *parallelism*, similar physical events occur when similar mental events occur, and vice versa; but physical events do not cause mental events; or vice versa. When I touch the stove I suffer a pain, but the former doesn't cause the latter; likewise, my decision to move my finger is followed by a finger movement, but the former doesn't cause the latter. However, mental events can cause other mental events and physical events can cause other physical events:

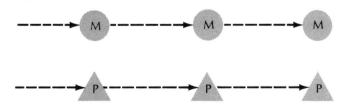

However, this theory is also open to question. *Why* is there this sort of parallelism between the mental and the physical?

According to *occasionalism*, a brand of parallelistic dualism popular among Descartes's early successors, God intervenes to bring it about that my arm goes up when I will it, or bring it about that I experience a pain when I burn my finger. This miraculous introduction of God, however, actually seems more like a confession that the unvarying correspondence of mental and physical events is an impenetrable mystery. An alternative to parallelism, advocated by Karl Marx and others, is *epiphenomenalism:* All mental events are caused by physical events, but no mental events themselves are further causes. In this view, the mental *is* real and distinct from the physical, but only the physical events possess any causal efficacy. Thus consciousness is a by-product of physical processes and completely determined by them:

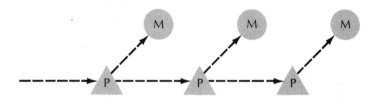

This theory is also open to objections. The asymmetry between the mental and the physical is hard to justify. If mental facts can be caused by physical facts, why cannot the causation work in the other direction? And if mental facts are real facts, how can it be denied that they have an effect on action? If it really is a fact that Othello felt jealous, then—however we are to explain this fact—it cannot be plausibly denied that Othello killed Desdemona because of his jealousy.

17:4.1 *The contextualist approach: mental facts include physical facts*   In the face of such difficulties, some advocates of dualism have jettisoned the foundationalist assumption that mental and physical facts are mutually exclusive:

(1) Both physical and mental statements describe the facts of reality as evident from sense experience and introspection.
(2) Reality cannot consist of mutually exclusive mental and physical realms. (Presupposition of interaction.)
(3) Therefore, mental statements *in some manner* describe the same facts as physical statements. (The contextualist thesis.)

The contextualist wants to reconcile the dualist insight that both mental and physical facts are real with the commonsense observation that the mind and the body influence each other. This idea necessitates rejecting the assumption that the mental and physical realms are mutually exclusive. The contextualist strategy is to propose that a mental fact and a physical fact are *different* facts but related as a *whole to a part.* For example, the mental fact that you feel pain involves the physical fact that certain processes occur in your brain, but it also involves more, namely, the subjective fact that you are having a certain conscious experience, which is a fact not accessible to objective observation. But since a mental fact does contain a physical fact as an essential component, it is no longer a mystery how the mind and body can interact: For when your finger touches a hot stove, the physical event at your nerve ends sends a message through the nervous system, terminating in the events in your central nervous system that consititute the sensation of pain. And the decision to move your finger also includes events in your central nervous system that send messages through the motor nerves, resulting in your finger moving:

17:4.2 *The theory of emergence*   The most familiar examples of this view are found in contemporary discussions of synergy and emergence. The popular thinker Buckminster Fuller uses "synergy" as a term for a system in which the whole has properties distinct from and not strictly reducible to properties of the parts. For example, Fuller contends that you could study an isolated particle of matter and describe it exhaustively—without expecting in the least the gravitational properties it would manifest when placed in a system with another particle of matter. According to Fuller, gravity is an emergent property of a complex system. Likewise, the English philosopher C. D. Broad has conjectured that if a physical mechanism like the brain is sufficiently complex, it may develop emergent mental properties, that is, properties of the whole system that in some way transcend the properties of parts. Such properties include awareness, self-consciousness, and perhaps even the power of free choice. The existence of conscious persons with free will is, in this approach, a natural phenomenon subject to scientific explanation. It is the result of the natural process of biological evolution. The mind is not a ghost in a machine, but the mechanism of the brain with its 10^{10} synapses is so complex that human beings enjoy the properties that resist complete explanation in physicalist terms. In this theory we could predict that an entity with a certain physical structure would have an emergent property like self-awareness and free will; but if the entity possessed this property, we could not, of course, predict all its future actions.

17:4.3 *The theory of persons*   This form of contextualism seems also in accord with a recent view called "the theory of persons." It rejects Cartesian claims that mental statements report facts about a ghostlike mental substance and that physical statements report facts about a machinelike physical substance. A human being is a unity, and mental and physical statements are about this same unified being. A *person* is an entity with mental as well as physical characteristics.

The theory of persons has a great advantage over Descartes's theory. Descartes is at a loss to explain how you can distinguish one mind from another or how you can trace the career of a mind over a period of time. It seems easy to distinguish persons from each other: You can do so on the basis of their *physical* characteristics. Persons have none of the mystery about them of Cartesian ghosts. However, if persons are essentially physical as well as mental beings, the theory of persons cannot very well allow for disembodied survival after death; for there can be no mental facts without concurrent physical ones.

17:5.1 *The problem of disembodiment*   The theory of persons does not allow for the possibility of disembodied life after death. The spiritual life of a person consists of mental facts, each of which is, in part, a physical event, such as a brain event. So there can be no mental events without physical events, and there can be no mind without the whole person.

The case study is, therefore, significant. If experiences like Ruth Chodill's are being rightly described as they really happened, there would be strong evidence for a foundationalist theory of dualism like Descartes's: She would have had out-of-body mental experiences, such as seeing the medical staff at the same time that her brain was not functioning. Of crucial importance would be the similarity between her recollection of the words, movements, and experiences of the medical staff—and what actually occurred. If her memories were accurate, there would be evidence against the theory of persons.

17:5.2 *The problem of incompleteness*   Philosophically, the contextualist approach is tantalizing because it promises to avoid many of the difficulties that plague alternative foundationalist views. Unfortunately, the approach is, at present, more tantalizing that persuasive, because advocates have yet to spell out clearly what the metaphors used to characterize their contextualism really mean. What is it for certain properties to "emerge" from a system? How can mental facts contain physical facts as constituents? How is it *possible* for one and the same subject, a person, to undergo both physical events and conscious experiences, to have an "outer" dimension accessible to physical scientists and an inaccessible "inner" side? The success of contextualism hinges on its answers to such questions.

17:6 *Implications for mental health*   In contrast to physicalism and mentalism, dualism recognizes the mental and the physical as distinct modes of existence. A human being exists in two ways, and to exist optimally, must be "healthy" in both the physical and mental sense. The science of physical health and the science of mental health are equally acceptable, but they are concerned with different facets of the human being. Dualism can naturally be expected to place emphasis on problems involving the relationships between the mind and body. For example, a person suffers from psychosomatic illness when certain mental experiences such as stress or emotional conflict cause physical damage, such as ulcers, cardiac-irregularities, or shock. Or certain mental disorders, such as paranoid fears or psychotic delusions, may be the effects of physical facts, such as chemical imbalance, dietary deficiency, or brain injury.

In contrast to the Cartesians, the person theorist is more apt to insist that mental health entails an acceptance of one's physical aspect. Recently, psychologists have identified the "betrayal of the body" as a source of psychological problems. Much of the shame and guilt people feel in connection with sexuality often arises from a sense of alienation from the body, from the sense that "the body is not really I." The aim of psychotherapy is to help people resolve the conflict between their physical and mental needs.

17.7 *Summary*   Dualism is the thesis that both the mental and the physical are real. The problem thus becomes one of reconciling in a theoretically acceptable way the existence of these two realms. The foundationalist approach is to regard the mental and the physical as mutually exclusive modes of existence. Cartesian dualism expresses this theory by emphasizing the separate substances called mind and body. Human beings are minds inside of bodies. One way of defining the relationship between mind and body is to claim that each can causally affect the other—interactionism. Another way is to hold some version of parallelism, that events at each level occur simultaneously but not necessarily because of causal interactions. The contextualist approach to the mind-body problem is to argue that mental statements in some manner describe the same facts as physical statements. The theory of emergence and the theory of persons are two efforts at attempting to explain more fully and precisely what that manner is.

EXERCISES for Chapter 17

1. a. In the following list of statements, distinguish the views of the founda-
      tionalistic dualist *(FD)*, the contextualistic dualist *(CD)*, and all dualists
      (D) from those which are rejected by dualists *(No)*.
      A. There is no sufficient reason for rejecting the evidence of sensory
         experience.
      B. Mental statements cannot describe the same facts as physical state-
         ments.
      C. Physical statements alone describe the facts of reality.
      D. There is no sufficient reason for rejecting the evidence of introspec-
         tion.
      E. Reality cannot consist of mutually exclusive mental and physical
         realms.
      F. Both physical and mental statements describe the facts of reality.
      G. Mental statements in some way describe the same facts as physical
         statements.
      H Physical statements really refer exclusively to mental facts.
   b. On what basis do dualists assert F?
2. a. Outline Descartes's argument for the conclusion that "I am a thinking
      being" by stating his characterization of his self as mental, his character-
      ization of the physical, and the basis on which he infers his conclusion
      from the difference in these characterizations (17:2.2).
   b. How would you criticize this argument?
3. a. Describe the problems of causal interaction and personal identity (17:
      3.1 and 17:3.2).
   b. What premise, conclusion, assumption, or implication of Descartes's
      view does each problem challenge?
   c. Does either of these problems lead to a conclusive refutation of founda-
      tionalistic dualsim? Explain your view.
4. a. Describe the problems of incompleteness and of distinguishing be-
      tween persons and their bodies (17:5.2 and 17:5.1).
   b. What premise, conclusion, assumption, or implication of the theory of
      persons does each problem challenge?
   c. Does either of these problems lead to a conclusive refutation of contex-
      tualistic dualism? Explain your view.
5. a. As a result of your study of the mind-body problem, which of the six
      views presented in Chapters 15–17 do you judge to be the strongest?
   b. What strengths of this view distinguish it from the others in your
      opinion?
   c. How would you plan to overcome those of its weaknesses identified in
      the text?

6. Write an essay on the strengths and weaknesses of foundationalism versus contextualism, illustrating your views by referring to contrasts in the foundationalist and the contextualist approaches to the mind-body problem.

SELECTED ANSWERS for Chapter 17

1. a. A. *D* (and physicalists).
       B. *FD* (and other foundationalists).
       C. *No;* this is physicalism.
       D. *D* (and mentalists).
       E. *CD.*
       F. *D.*
       G. *CD.*
       H. *No;* this is idealism.
   b. A and D.

2. a. A mental thing, such as myself, is essentially a thinking being. A physical or material thing is essentially extended. What can be conceived of distinctly can, by the power of an omnipotent God, exist separately. Therefore I am a thinking being, which can exist independent of my body.

3. b. The problem of interaction challenges the assumption that even though reality consists of two entirely separate sets of facts, the physical and mental can affect one another. The problem of personal identity challenges an implication of Descartes's view that persons are essentially thinking beings. Will standards relating only to a person's mental life be sufficient to identify an individual person?

4. b. The problem of incompleteness is that contextualists assume that persons can have various properties relating body and mind without explaining how this is so. The problem of disembodiment is that the theory of persons has the implication that disembodied existence is impossible. Yet because direct evidence to support the correctness of this implication is lacking, adopting such a position seems arbitrary.

PERSPECTIVES

ON FREEDOM

What could be more important than freedom? Surveying Western history, you might easily conclude that nothing could be. Does not the gospel promise, "You shall know the truth and the truth shall make you free"? Are Americans not justly proud of the first amendment, freedom of the press, of speech, of worship, and of the right to public assembly? We regard it as tragic when a person loses freedom of movement through some accident.

Freedom, however, is conceptually tied to responsibility, since persons are responsible for what they do only if they are free in doing it. A person bound in chains is not free to do anything requiring much physical mobility. Consequently, the person can scarcely be responsible for not doing things that require great mobility.

Whereas Western civilization has long recognized the relationship of freedom and responsibility, there has also been a long-standing concern that if things somehow must be as they are, then there is no freedom for them to be otherwise. In the modern world, with the rise of science, the idea of a necessity opposed to human freedom has been conceived as a world so predictably regular that every event has a cause.

Our commitment to the value of freedom with its conceptual tie to moral

✑ PART FIVE

responsibility and our commitment to the concept of universal causality carry us to one of the most difficult conceptual problems in the history of philosophical efforts to understand ourselves, namely, how to reconcile these two commitments. Causality apparently implies necessity; freedom seems to imply open choices, the denial of causal necessity. If these implications are correct, should we reject the idea that people are free or should we reject the idea that causality applies to all events? But if both these commitments should be honored, which of the implications is incorrect? After defining the problem of free will in Chapter 18, we shall examine three responses to it. The first two are foundationalist, which characteristically accept the incompatibility between human freedom and universal causality. We shall examine hard determinism (Chapter 19), which builds from the premise that every event has a cause, followed by libertarianism (Chapter 20), which develops the basic contention that human beings are sometimes free in their actions. We shall then examine the contextualist view, compatibilism (Chapter 21), that universal causality and freedom are not, when properly understood, in conflict with each other.

The relationship between the chapters of Part Five can be diagrammed as shown.

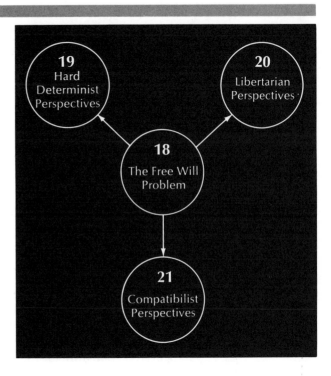

18

The Free Will Problem

Almost everyone will agree that it is senseless to hold people morally responsible for what they have done if they could not have done anything else. If they were not free to actually select what they did or did not do, how can they deserve praise or blame? We do frequently hold people responsible for their actions, yet given all that we know about genetic theory and environmental and psychological influences on behavior, is any person ever really free? The "hard determinists" say no, the "libertarians" say yes, and some try to argue a middle position. This chapter presents the tension between freedom and determinism and stakes out the basic positions. After reading Chapter 18 you should be able to

- Define and contrast the positions of hard determinism, soft determinism, and libertarianism.
- Distinguish the claims that would be made by hard determinists, soft determinists, and libertarians in provided examples.
- Given some human behavior, describe it as it would be described by hard determinists, and libertarians.

THE CASE OF JUDGE ARTHUR BIRD

Judge Bird and the reporter sat on the swing that hung from the porch roof of his retirement cottage at Oxbow Lake.

"Which case stands out in your mind as the most difficult one you ever tried?" asked the reporter.

"That's easy, the case of Amy Holden."

"You mean the Lake Erie Killer?"

"Yes, that's what the press called her. But it's not clear that she was really to blame for Thomas Shaw's death."

"She shot him. Everyone knows that. She admitted it at her trial."

"Right, her defense lawyer never disputed that."

"What was the defense?"

"It was that Amy could not help herself. The lawyer appealed to her disposition to respond violently when she felt ridiculed. This was compounded by her depression over the loss of her children. Her mind was clouded with feelings of guilt and anger at both herself and Shaw. She was an unstable woman, fighting heroin addiction, a loser in almost every respect. She also came from a bad neighborhood, one where you had to be violent to survive. She has a police record that was evidence of her troubled youth; she never graduated from high school, wasn't really too well educated at all. Actually, from the way she conducted herself at the trial, I suspect Amy Holden wasn't very intelligent, not even average, I would say."

"You mean, your honor, that the defense was that Amy's history, psychology, and character all combined that day on Shaw's yacht to make his murder an inevitability?"

"That's what the defense argued. Amy had to kill Shaw; she could not have done anything else given the events that led up to that moment."

"What did the prosecutor do?"

"He told how Amy had dated Shaw. She was pregnant, but it wasn't clear by whom. She wanted to force Shaw into a hasty marriage. He refused. She pulled a gun and threatened suicide. Shaw laughed, so Amy turned the gun on Shaw. 'Cold-blooded murder' is what the prosecutor called it. He argued that Holden could have made plenty of other choices. She could have sued Shaw; she could have gone through with the suicide; she could have tried to marry someone else. There were lots of options Amy could have exercised. But she freely chose to kill Shaw and should be held responsible. That is the stance he took."

"There never was a verdict in that case was there?"

"No, Amy committed suicide in her cell while the trial was still going on."

"How do you think it would have gone?"
"Don't really know. What would you have done on the jury?"

18:1.1 *The dilemma* The problem of whether or not people are free, in some morally relevant sense, has traditionally been posed as a dilemma.

(1) Either every event is caused or some human choices are not caused.
(2) If every event has causes, then human choices, being events, are caused.
(3) If all human choices are caused, they cannot be other than they are.
(4) If no human choices can, or could, be altered, then people are not free.
(5) If human choices are not caused, then they are random.
(6) If human choices are random, then people do not have control over their choices.
(7) If either people are not free, or people have no control over their own choices, then they are not morally responsible for what they do.
(8) So, in conclusion, people are not morally responsible for what they do.

This dilemma expresses two important assumptions: (a) If all events are caused, then people cannot be free; and (b) If human choices are not caused, then they are random. Thus, in either assumption, holding people morally accountable is unreasonable.

18:1.2 *Avoiding the dilemma* To avoid the conclusion of this argument, you would need to argue that either the argument is logically faulty or at least one of its premises is false. Many have challenged various of its premises. For example, some philosophers have argued that premise 2 is false by distinguishing human actions from physical events. In so doing, they can maintain the scientific belief that all events are caused, but maintain that human actions are not caused. A variation on this theme is the view that human actions are self-caused in the sense that humans are self-determining beings, whereas all other beings or events in nature are more or less interconnected causally. Another challenge might be mounted against premise 5 by arguing that human choices are not random even if they are uncaused.

Although no one has attacked the dilemma as illogical, it may be possible to show that crucial ambiguities in the concepts of "causality," "event," "choice," "responsibility," and most centrally, "free," actually mislead us into accepting this argument when we should not. For example, some people maintain that by training and education we are taught to make rational choices, and thus are conditioned or caused to act freely.

If you accept the argument, you may find it surprisingly difficult to decide what are the specific causal conditions of a given human choice. Do you look to heredity, psychology, character, physical environment, social environment, divine intervention, human desires, or whatever, as the causes of human action? However, if you do not accept the argument, on what do you base your rejection? Most of the historical debate focuses on the following three claims:

   I. Every event has a cause.
  II. At least some human choices are free.
 III. If every event has a cause, then no human choices are free.

18:2.1 *Determinism*   Determinism is the philosophical thesis that for every event there is some set of causal conditions such that, given these conditions, no other event could occur. If human actions are among the events to which the deterministic thesis applies, then when persons act as they do they are not able to act otherwise. This idea of *not being able to do otherwise*, as one acts, is pivotal in the whole controversy about free will and determinism. Part of what we mean by saying that an action has an antecedent cause is that there is a sufficient condition for its occurrence—which means that things could not be otherwise than the way in which they are. Therefore, if human actions have antecedent causes, it is false that the individual could have acted otherwise. Therefore, he or she was not *free* to have done otherwise. Moral philosophers have argued that it is reasonable to hold persons responsible for what they do only if they could have done otherwise, in the sense of their having been able either to do what they did, or to fail to do what they did. What justifies holding a person responsible, and on occasion, even blaming and punishing the person for an outcome over which he or she really exercised no control, given the causal factors at work? The determinist view is that human actions do have such antecedent causes. Using the line of reasoning we have just developed, they argue, therefore, that it is *unreasonable to hold persons morally responsible for what they do.*

    Determinism, the thesis that all events have causes, is one of the most forceful in human intellectual history. To grasp how persistent this belief is, contrast the following two arguments:

E.g. 1 People have looked for unicorns for years and have never found any. Therefore, there probably are no unicorns.

E.g. 2 People have looked for causes of cancer for years and have never found them. Therefore, probably cancer does not have causes.

Notice that although these arguments are structurally similar, E.g. 1 appears quite reasonable whereas E.g. 2 does not. This difference may well be due to the strength of our belief in universal causality. Some

JOSEPH ACCUSED BY POTIPHAR'S WIFE, *by Rembrandt van Rijn.*

The Pharaoh's wife accused Joseph of taking sexual liberties with her. But doesn't the practice of accusing persons make sense only if persons are responsible for what they do? And if they could not have done otherwise, how could accusations make sense?

philosophers suggest that the contrast between E.g. 1 and E.g. 2 shows that the assertion "Every event has a cause" is not capable of being shown false. It is a thesis that has been denied in one form only to be re-expressed and embraced in another. For example, if bacteria do not cause cancer, then perhaps a genetic inheritance does; if not that, perhaps a virus; if not that, perhaps environmental irritants like nicotine; if none of those, perhaps something else, or perhaps different combinations of these for different cancers. No matter what, we hold on to the idea that there are causes of cancer.

In ancient philosophy the thesis of determinism was manifest in a belief in a divine power to know the truth or falsity of all statements, even those about future events. In the Scholastic tradition, it reappeared in the conflict between predestination and free choice. Physical determinism dominated scientific thinking at least until our century and the advent of the physics of subatomic particles. Developments in contemporary psychology and biochemistry lend strong support to some version of the deterministic hypothesis as it applies to human behavior. Subscribing to the main thesis of determinism, then, has the virtue of tying one into a simple, rigorous form of thought which can be applied systematically. The success of the scientific enterprise over the last 300 years shows us that several different models or paradigms of causes exist and urges us, when research using one model proves fruitless, to use — or even develop — another. The alternative, after all, to operating on the assumption that a given group of events has a cause involves relinquishing hope of prediction and control of that group of events.

18:2.2 *Hard determinism*   A determinist is, by definition, one who accepts claim I in 18:1.2, "Every event has a cause." In so doing, some determinists will deny claim II and accept claim III, and others will accept claim II and deny claim III. Hard determinists believe that claim I entails that people cannot help but be as they are. Being physical objects involved in the space/time causal nexus, humans, like any other animals, behave as they do on the basis of those conditions that determine their lives. Whatever those conditions are, be they physical, social, psychological, or what have you, be they known or unknown, these conditions totally determine what each human being will do. The hard determinists argue that there is no such thing as free choice. We are, they argue, beyond talk of freedom and dignity; we should talk only the language of behavior modification. Our concern should not be with praise or blame, but with modification and control. We should positively reinforce desired behaviors and negatively reinforce undesirable ones, attaching no moral stigma to either.

18:2.3 *Soft determinism*   Soft determinists accept claim I and also claim II, which they do by rejecting claim III. This is a compatibalist position. The compatibalist accepts both the idea of determinism and the idea that persons have free will for which they may be held responsible. They seek some means of making these ideas compatible, since sacrificing either would be devastating to science or morality. To demonstrate compatibalism, soft determinists must find a good reason to reject claim III, which expresses the incompatibility of the two ideas. They typically argue that being free is the opposite of being compelled or *coerced*, not of one's choices being caused. In other words, the soft determinists argue that choices are caused, perhaps by our desires or our character traits or even our habitual tendencies, but that this causation is compatible with calling those choices "free."

Soft determinists have emphasized that free people are necessarily uncoerced, that there should be no constraining factors like overwhelming fears or hallucinatory drugs which mitigate freedom. In favor of this position, they argue that the scientific evidence in favor of determinism, in general, supports soft determinism, just as it does hard determinism. But they argue further that soft determinism is also compatible with our moral practices and our intuitions about how people deliberate and choose.

18:2.4 *Libertarianism*   Libertarians believe that human choices are uncaused, free actions (or events). Thus, they affirm claim II of 18:1.2, accept claim III, and deny claim I. The major support for the libertarian position is drawn from our intuitions concerning experiences of free choice. We all experience times of deliberation, when we consider alternative courses of action or weigh our options. Most importantly, we experience the moment of decision. We are aware of choosing an alternative and selecting an option. We, libertarians argue, describe ourselves as free.

The recognition of the importance of the moral life constitutes the primary motivation for holding the libertarian position. We recognize the importance of holding persons responsible in society, and we hope that it is reasonable to do so. Many argue that the very distinctiveness of dealing with human beings consists in our capacity to have moral awareness and to live in a society that benefits from being composed of responsible agents.

18:3 *The problem*   The free will-determinism dilemma can now be recharacterized as a tension between the central thesis of determinism, supported by scientific success, and the idea that persons are free, responsible agents. Given the existence of this tension between two ideas, the question arises: "What reason is there for rationally choosing one rather than the other of these seemingly incompatible assertions?" In Chapter 19 we shall see how the hard determinist argues in favor of the determinist thesis and rejects the idea of human freedom. In Chapter 20 we will see how the libertarian supports the view that persons are free, responsible agents and rejects the thesis of determinism. Another way out of the dilemma is chosen by the soft determinists (Chapter 21). They challenge the idea that the theses of determinism and human freedom are incompatible, thereby facing the necessity of providing reasons why the apparent incompatibility is not real.

BOTH MEMBERS OF THIS CLUB, *by George Bellows.*

In the early 1900's when public boxing was illegal in New York, boxers were permitted to become one-night "members" of private clubs, where brutal fights often occurred. Were boxers who had no other trade free not to subject themselves to the conditions under which they fought? Were the regular club members free not to watch the matches? How might you define "free" in these two questions?

18:4 *Summary* We have looked at the three traditional responses to the dilemma of determinism. Hard determinism maintains that human choices, like all other events, are determined by causal conditions of various kinds. Libertarianism argues that human choices are uncaused (random or unpredictable) events and so people are free. Soft determinism maintains that human choices are free and yet also caused. There are strong arguments in favor of and opposed to each position. There are also other approaches to solving or dissolving the dilemma (some are suggested in 18:1.1), which has haunted intellectual discussion for over two millenia; the acceptance of one or another of the three positions has important and far-reaching implications for our conceptions of morality and of what it is to be a person.

EXERCISES for Chapter 18

1. Hard determinism, soft determinism, and libertarianism can each be defined by its acceptance of exactly two of the following assertions. Put a *T* in each column for the statements regarded as true by each position (18: 2.2–18:2.4).

	HD	SD	L
Every event has a cause.	___	___	___
Some human actions are free.	___	___	___
If every event has a cause, then no human actions are free.	___	___	___

2. a. What are the apparent unhappy consequences concerning freedom and responsibility if determinism is true (18:1.2)?
   b. What are the apparent unhappy consequences concerning freedom and responsibility if human choices are not caused (18:1.2)?
   c. Use the definition of a dilemma and your answers to a and b to explain why determinism constitutes a dilemma for free will and responsibility.

3. Read the following description of a typical human decision:
   Terri Tarahan struggled with herself. She knew time was short and she would soon need to decide and act. She greatly wanted to go to the Whosits concert. It was her favorite group and she had a keen appreciation of its music. She had promised, however, to help in the final preparations for homecoming. Now the Whosits concert had been scheduled, unexpectedly, for the night before homecoming. Terri could not possibly help finish the homecoming preparations and also attend the concert. She knew three of her friends were counting on her and she knew she'd deserve their censure if she disappointed them. Finally Terri decided. Going to the concert was a great temptation; she would certainly enjoy it more than the alternative. But Terri had made a promise, so she summoned up her willpower, resisted the temptation, and, true to her word, helped prepare for the homecoming.

a. What claims would each position — hard determinism, soft determinism, and libertarianism — wish to make about the above description in order to support its respective views?

b. Suppose that Terri had decided to go to the concert. Suppose also that the three friends who did her homecoming work all decide that because she did not help with the preparations, they will not speak to her for a week. Finally, suppose that of her three friends, one is a hard determinist, one a soft determinist, and one a libertarian. What reasons would each give to justify treating Terri in this fashion?

SELECTED ANSWERS for Chapter 18

	HD	SD	L
1. Every event has a cause.	T	T	
Some human actions are free.		T	T
If every event has a cause, then no human actions are free.	T		T

3. a. Hard determinists would believe that Terri had apparently been strongly conditioned to her duty. Soft determinists would emphasize that no one coerced or constrained Terri as she made her decision. Libertarians would point to Terri's struggling with and resisting temptation as showing the freedom of her choice.

b. Believing that Terri was not free, her hard determinist friend would see only one justification for this treatment: Perhaps this negative reinforcement will have an effect on Terri to behave differently in future cases. Believing the Terri was free, her soft determinist friend and her libertarian friend would be able to argue that Terri deserves censure inasmuch as she has not lived up to her responsibility. They would regard blaming Terri as a reasonable and fair response, just as they would have commended her had she kept her word.

19

![decorative numeral 19 with leaf flourish]

Hard Determinist
Perspectives

Determinism is the thesis, "Every event has a cause." Both hard and soft determinists accept this thesis and its implication that all human behavior has causes. In this chapter we will explore the view of the hard determinists that it is inappropriate ever to hold people morally responsible for their actions. We will examine two hard determinist perspectives, both of which are based upon a prescriptive interpretation of determinism. That is, both are predicated on the assumption that scientists, guided by the thesis of determinism, will ultimately be successful in finding the causes of human actions. This view, far from asserting that all the causes of human action have been found, amounts to the presumption that in principle they can be found. The first version of hard determinism we will study is the physicalists', that is, the view that all events have *material* causes.[1] Other hard determinists hold that an account of the causes of human actions can be provided through psychoanalytical theory, in which the causes of human action are thought to be something other than material in nature. After reading Chapter 19, you should be able to

- State and criticize the physicalist model of the universe with its alleged implications for human freedom.

---

[1]Definitions of materialism and physicalism are supplied in Chapter 14.

- State and criticize the psychoanalytical model of human behavior with its alleged implications for human freedom.
- Explain the unresolved tensions between hard determinism and its critics.

THE CASE OF OTTO SKOLL

Mrs. Skoll waited impatiently for Dr. Bertal to see her. She had come to talk about her son Otto who sat beside her now reading a six-month-old issue of *Sports Illustrated*.

"Mrs. Skoll, you may come in now," said the office nurse. "Please wait in Room 3, on the left. The doctor will be there in a minute."

Mrs. Skoll and Otto took up their waiting again in Room 3. Mrs Skoll reviewed the symptoms she had observed in Otto. Otto looked at the medical diagrams and pictures on the wall.

"Hello, Mrs. Skoll," said Dr. Bertal, as he bounced into the room with his usual energy. "I see you called about Otto. Hi, Otto. How have you been doing?"

"Fine," he said crisply.

"The asthma attacks aren't getting any better. If anything, they're getting worse," said his mother.

"Well, what do you mean by worse? How often are you having them, Otto?"

"He has them at all of the most inconvenient times," broke in Mrs. Skoll. "This summer has been terrible. We couldn't do anything without an attack. And they come out of nowhere. He would be relaxing with friends on the patio, riding in the car on a trip, or doing something else that should be quiet and restful. I wish he would control himself."

"I realize how frustrated that must make you feel, Mrs. Skoll, not to be able to plan a day without worrying about an asthma attack. It must make you angry, too, Otto, not to be able to control when those attacks come."

"It's embarrassing to cough and wheeze in front of your friends," said Otto.

"Well, Otto," said Mrs. Skoll, "they come so regularly that it almost seems deliberate."

Otto ignored her assault.

"Maybe if we talk more about the contributing factors we can achieve more control over your attacks, Otto. We already know that you're allergic to a wide variety of things. In the summer, at the zoo or on camp trips, attacks can be triggered by these allergies. In the winter, colds and respiratory infections increase your attacks."

"Well, I understand those things," interrupted his mother. "But what about the attacks that come when he is healthy and away from things that bother his allergies?"

"There are three other factors that may make attacks more frequent and more severe for Otto. They are fatigue, emotional stress, and the hormone changes that come with puberty. So you see Otto, if you know these things, you can try to anticipate problems by getting more rest and not feeling guilty when an attack does occur. These attacks are your body's response to your physical and mental environment. There's no blame involved."

"But I feel terrible when I mess up things with my asthma attacks."

"You should not take that responsibility on yourself, Otto," said the doctor. "Everyone's body responds to emotional stress differently. Some get ulcers, others get headaches, some even get diarrhea. I know it's hard to rest when your friends are still active, but you have to. It's the best way to control the asthma."

19:1.1 *The plausibility of determinism*   The thesis of determinism is difficult or impossible to prove conclusively. However, it gains a great deal of plausibility both from your everyday experiences and from the success of the sciences. Most people accept the thesis of determinism, or something very much like it, in their everyday lives. Very often you know the causes of events you observe. If you hear loud noises, you can usually see what caused them. If you are not directly aware of the cause of an event, you can usually infer what it probably was. If you find fewer cookies in the cookie jar, you can infer that someone has been into the cookies. If anyone were to suggest that the cookies simply disappeared without cause, you would not take the suggestion seriously. You would insist that such things do not happen without a cause.

In the case study, Otto's mother suggests that his asthma attacks seem to be coming out of nowhere. Yet this is not a serious suggestion that his attacks have no cause. Mrs. Skoll is expressing frustration; she is not denying a cause, but seeking one. Though it may be difficult to decide which of the doctor's proposed causal hypotheses about Otto's asthma is correct, no one would entertain the idea that the attacks are uncaused. Thus, the determinist concludes that our everyday experiences and responses amply support determinism. Moreover, the determinist will urge that to suppose human behaviors to be an exception to this rule is no better than to suppose the disappearance of the cookies is an exception. Surely our experience shows that complex events have causes just as much as simple ones do.

19:1.2 *Scientific success*   Scientific discipline and research all presuppose the appropriateness of searching for the causes of all the events a particular science studies. Using this presupposition, scientists over the past three hundred years have enjoyed great success in discovering

What relationship between physicalism and hard determinism is suggested here? Philosophers have proposed several answers.

the causes of many events in the world. As science has progressed, more and more areas of human experience have been brought under the umbrella of scientific understanding and causal laws. Humanity learned of physical, chemical, and biological laws governing the movements of the stars and planets, the movements of organisms on earth, chemical interactions, and changes within the bodies of human beings. We have learned a great deal about the functioning of the major systems within the human body, the functioning of every important organ in the body,[2] the diseases that afflict people, and the methods for preventing illness and promoting good health. This knowledge supports the thesis that determinism holds true for events in the lives of human beings as it does elsewhere in the universe. Psychology is by no means a completed science, but progress is being made in determining the causes of human behavior. Causal links are clear between emotional stress and several human behaviors and conditions. Those who subscribe to determinism believe that it is only a matter of time before even greater progress is made in understanding the causes governing human behavior. They hold that there is no reason in principle to doubt that determinism applies as fully to humans as to other beings in the world.

19:2.1 *Physicalistic determinism*   Many hard determinists are physicalists[3] who by definition believe that nature is nothing but a very complex

---

[2]With the exception perhaps of the brain which is, at the present, the least understood.

[3]This is *not* to say that all physicalists are determinists. The ancient philosophers Epicurus and Lucretius maintained that everything was composed of material atoms and the void. Nevertheless, they also claimed that certain events did not have causes. Atoms would sometimes "swerve" out of their orbits without explanation. On the basis of such indeterminism, they tried to explain the existence of free will. Thus, they were both physicalists and libertarians.

physical reaction consisting of matter in motion or at rest. Any changes that occur in nature amount to redistributions of physical energy and relocations of material objects in space and time. Thus, all macroscopic objects such as those we observe in our everyday lives—boxes, birds, houses, lakes, the sun, the moon, and other persons—are nothing but sometimes very complex combinations of material particles, elements, and the like. Most physicalists hold that changes in these physical objects may be uniformly explained in terms of physical, causal laws. In this view, all psychology, sociology, anthropology, biology, and chemistry are ultimately reducible to physics, and the behaviors and choices of human beings are not exceptions.

 **PHILOSOPHER'S WORKSHOP**

Hard Determinism Defended

Baron Paul-Henri Thiry D'Holbach (1723–1789) was widely regarded as one of the most ardent antireligionists of the French Enlightenment. He defended a view of human nature many regard as the paradigm of the hard determinist perspective.

. . . In whatever manner man is considered, he is connected to universal nature, and submitted to the necessary and immutable laws that she imposes on all the beings she contains, according to their peculiar essences or to the respective properties with which, without consulting them, she endows each particular species. Man's life is a line that nature commands him to describe upon the surface of the earth, without his ever being able to swerve from it, even for an instant. He is born without his own consent; his organization does in nowise depend upon himself; his ideas come to him involuntarily; his habits are in the power of those who cause him to contract them; he is unceasingly modified by causes, whether visible or concealed, over which he has no control, which necessarily regulate his mode of existence, give the hue to his way of thinking, and determine his manner of acting. He is good or bad, happy or miserable, wise or foolish, reasonable or irrational, without his will being for anything in these various states. Nevertheless, in spite of the shackles by which he is bound, it is pretended he is a free agent, or that independent of the causes by which he is moved, he determines his own will, and regulates his own condition. . . .

> Man, in running over, frequently without his own knowledge, often in spite of himself, the route which nature has marked out for him, resembles a swimmer who is obliged to follow the current that carries him along: he believes himself a free agent, because he sometimes consents, sometimes does not consent, to glide with the stream, which, notwithstanding, always hurries him forward; he believes himself the master of his condition, because he is obliged to use his arms under the fear of sinking. . . .[4]
>
> _____
>
> [4]Baron Paul-Henri Thiry D'Holbach, *System of Nature* (1770), Chaps. XI and XII, as cited in Arthur Pap and Paul Edwards, eds., *A Modern Introduction to Philosophy* (New York: Macmillan Publishing Co. Inc., 1965), pp. 10, 18.

19:2.2 *The physicalist argument*   In supporting hard determinism a physicalist would argue that every event has a physical cause. More particularly, for each event there are antecedent physical events, which are together sufficient for its occurrence. Thus, if there are any such things as choices, they are not free. Just as in the cases of all other kinds of events in the universe, such choices are thought of as the results of physical causes which the choosers really do not control. If a wheel on a bicycle spins, a force applied to it made it move and no contrary force (friction) has prevented it. Surely, the physicalist claims, the wheel is not free.

This argument involves the concession that choices may be parts of causal chains. Consider the more extreme view, which tries to avoid this concession: although physicalists disagree about whether there are mental facts, they do agree that all facts can be described in solely physical terms. Thus, physicalism and determinism together imply that all causal changes can be described solely in physical terms. Hence, even if there are choices and even if some say that choices cause certain human behaviors, the "fact" that some choice causes a certain behavior is the same fact as that some physical process causes the behavior. In other words, even if there are mental facts, they are superfluous to the explanation of all events. How can people be responsible for their actions if their choices are superfluous to the explanation of their behavior?

19:2.3 *Criticism of the physicalist argument*   The chief objection to the argument against free will and human responsibility based on physicalism is that the prediction it offers is of dubious or unproven value. Although physicalists assert that in principle it is possible to replace ("reduce") all talk of human choices with talk of matter in motion, they are a long way from success, and grave questions have been raised about the possibility of their enterprise. Without going into all the problems of physicalism, it is enough to note that it has become less attractive as a deterministic model in the light of the peculiar characteristics of subatomic particles, and of the lack of progress in the reduction of such a comparably noncomplex discipline as organic chemistry to physics.[5]

19:3.1 *Psychoanalytic determinism*   The case study illustrates the contrast between physicalistic and psychoanalytic determinism. Physicalists, as we have seen, hold that all events in the universe can be explained in terms of the same kinds of causes. In the case study Otto's asthma attacks are quite often explicable in terms of his physical circumstances, for instance, the substances to which he is allergic. Physicalistic causal explanations of these attacks appear possible. However, the doctor, Otto, and Otto's mother all have difficulty in understanding why Otto seems to have some asthma attacks when no physical causes are present. Whereas Otto's mother almost wants to attribute such attacks to his will, the doctor offers an explanation in terms of emotional stress, which suggests that there are genuinely nonphysical psychological causes. In general, psychoanalytical determinism differs from physicalistic determinism in maintaining that although every event has a cause, not all causes of events in the universe are physical; some are mental.

---

[5]Chapter 15 presents the chief problems not mentioned here.

PHILOSOPHER'S WORKSHOP

Puppet on a String

Psychological determinism, a version of hard determinism, maintains that people do not have free choice because the patterns of their behaviors and psychological reasons for those patterns are extended in their personalities at very early ages. A puppet on a string is not free to determine its own movements even it it should happen to think that it is. People are the puppets. Our strings run deep into our own psychic histories where the true causes of our "apparent decisions" lie hidden but operative. As John Hospers (b. 1918) says:

We talk about free will, and we say, for example, the person is free to do so-and-so if he can do so *if* he wants to—and we forget that his wanting to is itself caught up in the stream of determinism, that unconscious forces drive him into the wanting or not wanting to do the thing in question. The analogy of the puppet whose motions are manipulated from behind by invisible wires, or better still, by springs inside, is a telling one at almost every point.

And the glaring fact is that it all started so early, before we knew what was happening, The personality structure is inelastic after the age of five, and comparatively so in most cases after the age of three. Whether one acquires a neurosis or not is determined by that age—and just as involuntarily as if it had been a curse of God . . . only the psychiatrist knows what puppets people really are; and it is no wonder that the protestations of philosophers that "the act which is the result of a volition, a deliberation, a conscious decision, is free" leave these persons, to speak mildly, somewhat cold.[6]

---

[6]John Hospers, "Meaning and Free Will," *Philosophy and Phenomenological Research* 10 (March 1950), 324.

The psychoanalytic model is not a model for understanding all events but only human behavior. Its plausibility is rooted in the successes of psychoanalysis in explaining deviant behaviors by proposing unconscious causes. Thus, Otto's asthma attacks are explained in this view, in terms of emotional stresses of which Otto is unaware. His doctor apparently subscribes to this version of hard determinism insofar as he maintains that Otto's asthma attacks are beyond his control and therefore, not something for which Otto should be held responsible.

19:3.2 *Implications of psychoanalytic determinism* You should note that psychoanalytic determinists apply their model not merely to deviant behavior but to all human behavior. The view is that our conscious intentions, deliberations, and purposes are all entirely irrelevant to the causal explanation of our behavior, which supposedly lies beneath the surface of our conscious minds. The psychoanalytic argument is that if we examine human behavior, we will see that normal behavior is also fully explainable in terms of unconscious causes like fear, love, hatred, pride, and so on. People believe themselves to be free only because they are ignorant of the true causes of their actions. Hence, the kinds of intentions, desires, reasonings, and the like that would have to have a decisive influence on our conduct if we were to be held responsible for that conduct are, in fact, no part of the explanation of our actions.

The attack of psychoanalytic determinism upon our common conceptions of moral responsibility and freedom is two-pronged. First, the successful explanation of deviant behavior shows that our so-called choices, the kinds of thoughts we are consciously aware of in deliberating about what we believe to be our alternatives, are not really a part of the causal explanation of our conduct. Second, our conduct is in fact explainable in terms of unconscious causes over which we have no control.

19:3.3 *Objections to psychoanalytic determinism* First, because it is claimed that the psychoanalytic model is empirically true, it is relevant to inquire about how well the evidence confirms the theory over the course of the years since psychoanalysis began. It is generally acknowledged that the evidence has never made the theory any more than a promising hypothesis. As time has passed, hard evidence has not accumulated. Given that extensive and diligent searches for such evidence have been undertaken by a wide variety of researchers, this lack of evidence leaves the case for the psychoanalytic model incomplete, if not weak. Thus, since the strength of psychoanalytic determinism is supposed to rest on the empirical truth of the model, the lack of confirmation is a very telling, although not conclusive, objection.

A second objection, involving an appeal to our ordinary ways of talking, is that it is deviant behavior that psychoanalysis first began to explain. The plausibility of explaining such deviant behavior in terms of unconscious causes is that the behavior is indeed deviant. That is, persons who behave in deviant ways are not in any obvious way thinking through rational thought processes and acting in accordance with them. However, if it is plausible to say that a psychoanalytic explanation becomes appropriate only because of the deviance of various behaviors, then it would seem that by hypothesis, psychoanalytic explanations could not apply to all behavior—because it would not apply to behavior in which persons go through rational thought processes and act upon the conclusions of their deliberations. The language of choosing, intentions, purposes, and so on is built into our explanation of normal human behavior. Therefore, from this vantage point, it is hardly clear that what psychoanalysts might provide as purported explanations of normal human behaviors could be genuine if they ignore statements about choices.

19:3.4 *Rebuttal* There is a viable line of response for the psychoanalytic hard determinist. Essentially, the hard determinist is pursuing the guiding principle of universal causation. When we develop a causal hypothesis, we hope to keep it as simple and to apply it to as many cases as possible. At the very least, the explanation of human behaviors in terms of conscious choices is itself exceedingly complex and not at all carefully tied down to observation at every point. Thus, its complexity and its lack of detailed confirmation count against it. Moreover, many people accept the scientific idea that a hypothesis should be as general as possible. Thus, it becomes reasonable to ask why, empirically, there is something about the phenomena of normal human choosings that makes them unexplainable on the psychoanalytic model. The mere fact that we talk in other terms about normal behaviors does not mean that there are not underlying similarities between them and deviant behaviors. Psychoanalytic hard determinists want to claim the virtues of scientific hypotheses — simplicity, verifiability, and general applicability for the theory — as reasons why the psychoanalytic model should be accepted.

19:4 *Summary*　In this chapter we have introduced two versions of hard determinism: physicalistic determinism and psychoanalytic determinism. We have shown how both views incorporate the thesis of determinism and how they differ in their causal accounts of human actions. We have seen why in both views it seems unreasonable to hold human beings responsible for their actions. Both theories have been considered and criticized on their own merits. Given the logical relationship between hard deterministic views such as these and the views of soft determinists and libertarians, any reason for the truth of either of the alternatives would be a reason against hard determinism. Thus, as you read ahead in Chapters 20 and 21, you should bear in mind that the arguments considered here in favor of hard determinism count against both soft determinism and libertarianism and vice versa.

EXERCISES for Chapter 19

1. All of the statements below fall into one of four categories: They are part of the argument for physicalistic determinism *(PD)*, they are part of the argument for psychoanalytic determinism *(PsD)*, they state an objection against physicalistic determinism *(OPD)*, or they state an objection against psychoanalytic determinism *(OPsD)*. Mark each accordingly.
   A. Normal human behavior is ordinarily explained by reference to choices.
   B. All of reality is physical or material.

    C. Simplicity and comprehensiveness argue that normal behavior should be explained in the same way as deviant behavior.

    D. Any reference to choices is superfluous in explaining any purely physical reality.

    E. Physicalism has too many troubles of its own to serve as a basis for a resolution of the dilemma of determinism.

    F. The psychoanalytic model has not been very successful in developing law-like scientific explanations of human behavior.

    G. Deviant, compulsive human behavior can be adequately explained without reference to choice.

    H. Since it is a matter of dispute whether determinism is true of certain physical realms (subatomic particles), the assumption that physicalism is true is insufficient to prove that determinism is true.

2. Ask yourself whether or not you can think of any circumstance in which a person *deserves* to be blamed or punished for what the person has done. Perhaps you will decide there is, perhaps not.

    a. If you think there is, describe the case fully enough so that your description of it will explain *why* the person deserves blame or punishment.

    b. If you think there is no case, describe the case that you feel is closest to being an exception to your view. Then *explain why*, even in that extreme case, no punishment or blame is deserved.

3. Consider the following objection to hard determinism: "Let it be conceded that for every bit of human behavior, it is possible to provide a causal law from which that bit of behavior can be predicted. No one should conclude from this statement that an adequate explanation of human behavior has been provided by such a deterministic account. Suppose a stranger puts a ladder up against my house and begins to climb it. In that case the mere fact that the stranger's behavior is predictable will not be adequate (at least not necessarily adequate) to tell me whether the stranger's intentions are innocent or mischievous. Without knowing that, I shall not know how to treat the stranger. In other words, I shall need a further explanation of what the stranger is up to. This example proves that talk about intentions, choices, and purposes is indispensible, even if determinism is true."

    a. At what point is the hard determinist's argument attacked by this objection?

    b. In defense of hard determinism, how would you reply to this objection?

SELECTED ANSWERS for Chapter 19

1. A. *OPsD.*
   B. *PD.*
   C. *PsD* (the physicalist would agree to this assertion, but it is not necessary to that argument).

      D. *PD.*
      E. *OPD.*
      F. *OPsD.*
      G. *PsD.*
      H. *OPD.*

2. The hard determinist will insist that in every circumstance persons could not have done otherwise from what they did. Thus, whatever case you describe should be described in such a way as to focus on what you regard as the important sense or senses in which your imaginary person could or could not have done otherwise.

3. a. According to the objection, providing a complete causal account of some event or behavior does not, contrary to the hard determinist contention, amount to providing a fully adequate explanation.

Libertarian Perspectives

Libertarians share with hard determinists the view that freedom and moral responsibility are incompatible with determinism. However, whereas the hard determinists conclude that talk of freedom and moral responsibility is inappropriate, libertarians argue that in some cases people enjoy a freedom from determining causes and that it is perfectly legitimate to hold them responsible for what they do. Thus, they deny determinism. In this chapter we will examine the view that human beings are self-determining agents; we will also examine the view that some of the most important, fundamental human experiences indicate that humans enjoy the kind of freedom that makes it appropriate to hold them responsible for their actions. These libertarians argue that abstract theorizing never could establish that such fundamental experiences are purely illusory.

After reading Chapter 20 you should be able to

- State and criticize the view that human beings are self-determining in their actions.
- State the libertarian argument from the existence of moral experiences.
- Explain the unresolved tension between the libertarian and the determinist.

THE CASE OF SAUL EPSTEIN

Dear Connie:

I'm writing this letter, but I may never send it. I know that the things I have to say will sound strange to you, but I want to reveal my reasons as well as my decisions. I've decided to break our engagement. There, it's out. Now let me try to explain.

This may sound odd, Connie, but I really do love you. It's partly because I love you that I've decided I can't marry you. You would never be happy with me. We have always been honest with each other, and so I know that you have life ambitions and expectations that I just do not share. Your image of life is a little suburban house, three kids, two cars, and a husband who works regular hours and makes a decent salary. There's nothing wrong with that, but I can't be that husband.

I'm not going into corporate law. I've decided to become a social worker. I'm going to open up a settlement house in the inner city. My goal is to do some good for other people — it's too selfish for a person just to worry about himself. I want to help others, even if in the end you can't really measure the little bit of good I will have done. The fact of having done it is what I find meaningful.

You may find my ideas strange. I know I've never shared this particular ambition with you before. It's been very hard for me these past few weeks because of that. I've really been giving my future a lot of thought. To marry you and become a lawyer is one possible path. It's the one I do not choose. To open the settlement house and accept all the personal risks that involves, including the risk of perhaps never finding a woman who shares by goals, that's the other path, the one I do choose.

What hurts me as I write is knowing the pain that this letter will cause you. I'm truly sorry for that. But if you love me for myself, and not as you perhaps would rather have me be, then you will accept what I have decided. Think about it, Connie. We really could never be happy together. We want very different things out of life. We have to choose our futures with full knowledge of the awesome responsibility that entails. To choose each other in marriage would mean unhappiness for both of us sooner or later. I have struggled mightily resisting the easy choice of marrying you. May our memories of each other and the happy times we shared warm the lonely nights of our lives. I love you, Connie. I always will. Good-bye, my love. Take care.

Saul

20:1.1 *Libertarianism and self-determinism*   The case study illustrates a common fact of human experience. Life presents us with alternatives, and we must determine for ourselves which of those alternatives to pursue. Saul Epstein describes the alternative paths open to him and the process of deliberation that led him to decide not to marry Connie.

Libertarians hold that such self-determined action growing out of deliberative choice is the kind of occurrence that belies determinism. They would ask you to examine your own lives to see how self-determination has played a part in your personal development. Consider those times in your life when your own choices have made the difference in the direction your life has taken, for example, whether or not to continue school or to marry, and the choice of a career. In such circumstances, alternatives are confronted and choices must be made, and thus we experience ourselves as self-determining agents.

Of course, not all events in human lives are the products of self-determination. Libertarians are fully aware of the many ways in which things can *happen to* people. Accidents may befall them, or they may become the victims of disease. They may encounter obstacles to achieving their goals. People may be constrained by environmental or social factors, or they may be coerced or manipulated by other people. Thus, libertarians are willing to concede to determinists that causal accounts may be offered for many, or perhaps even most, of the events in human lives. However, determinism requires that such a causal account be provided in principle for *all* events, and libertarians hold that cases in which people act as self-determining agents are precisely those for which complete causal accounts cannot be provided. That is, although the actions are caused by the self-determination of the agent, the process of self-determination itself is thought of as not wholly determined. Thus libertarians present the phenomenon of self-determination as the example that refutes determinism.

20:1.2   *Are uncaused events random?* The libertarian denial of determinism is a denial that "Every event has a cause"—which would seem to imply that some events do not have causes. In particular, the libertarian seems to claim that the processes of self-determination do not have causes, that they fall outside the ordinary causal order operative throughout the remainder of the universe. But this view seems to imply that human choices are random and capricious, utterly mysterious and unexplainable. That is, if the self-determining choices of humans, the exertions of human will, are thought to be uncaused and unexplainable events which simply erupt in the universe, then the human behavior growing out of such choices is in turn random, capricious, and utterly unexplainable. Thus, libertarianism is equally incompatible with holding people responsible for their actions. If a person acts one way rather than another at random, then it hardly seems reasonable to hold a person responsible for such action.

20:1.3 *Self-determinism* Libertarians respond to this objection by offering an account of the process of self-determination as neither simply random nor wholly determined. In this view, people act in accordance with their characters, which have been developed over a long period of time. Character is conceived of as a complex of habits and dispositions to act in accord with virtues or vices which have been cultivated throughout one's life. Given a certain set of habits and dispositions, virtues and vices, people act in certain ways when they find themselves in certain types of situations. Thus it seems reasonable to hold them responsible for the actions that issue from their character because (1) these actions do not issue randomly, and (2) it is reasonable to hold them responsible for the development of their character because character development is not itself a wholly determined process. Rather, the libertarian model of character development is the creative process, for example, the creation of a poem or a piece of music. True, the creative process is somewhat limited by the past and influenced by the environment within which choices are being made, but libertarians urge that it is also crucially influenced by the envisagement of future goals and objectives. Moreover, these goals and objectives may not be crystal clear from the very beginning, but clarity may emerge within and during the creative process. Both the goals and the character development should be understood, therefore, as somewhat indeterminate. The process of character development through self-determining choice is then conceived as a process of making the somewhat indeterminate more determinate. Indeed, the mature will, in creatively forging the character of the adult, is capable of reshaping character, of overcoming old habits and dispositions. Thus, whereas choice may be influenced by habit and disposition, the mature will may wrestle with the past, represented by deposited character traits, and yet depart from that past, acting in accord with a vision of an alternative future.

20:1.4 *Rebuttal* The persistent opponent of libertarian thought, however, may object that an adequate account is provided only of the actions that do grow out of a person's habits and dispositions. Neither the interactions between persons and their environments, which originally led to the development of those habits and dispositions, nor the departures of the so-called mature will from habit and disposition are adequately accounted for. How are these events to be explained? Are they not uncaused, and therefore, random and capricious?

The libertarian might respond that this is a charge that takes scientific, causal explanation as the sole model for explaining events. Given this model, the libertarian account of the development of character is found wanting, for a complete *causal* account of the events is not offered. The libertarian, however, would object to the bias of judging libertarianism in terms of such a model. What do you think of the adequacy of this libertarian response?

20:2.1 *Libertarianism and phenomena of the moral life* Perhaps the most common defense of libertarianism calls our attention to certain components of our immediate experience, especially our experiences as moral agents. Defenders of libertarianism argue that nothing can be more certain than that which is disclosed to us in our immediate experience. If I hear a loud noise or feel a tickle, this observation or experience is more secure than any complicated theory that might try to explain it away. In this view, we have several immediate experiences of freedom. Determinism on the other hand, is a complicated theory at best. When immediate experience and a complicated theory conflict, we have a sign that there is something wrong with the theory. To be sure, some perceptual experiences come to be regarded as illusory on the basis of other, later perceptions. This is not the case, however, with our experiences of our freedom in the moral life. In this area, further experience serves only to support our earlier conviction that we are free. Each time people are confronted with having to choose between alternative courses of action, they experience their freedom anew.

Just what are these experiences that make libertarians feel that people are free and responsible for their actions? First, libertarians argue that all of us, even determinists, encounter circumstances in our lives in which we feel that we must choose between the possible courses of action open to us at the time. That is, we experience the practical necessity of having to choose among our options. Independent of the question of whether or not we are in reality confronting genuine options, we undeniably have these experiences. The experience of the moment of decision can be one of the most poignant in a person's life.

Often the experience of having to choose is accompanied by the experience of going through a process of deliberation. The latter consists in sorting out, to the best of our ability or as time permits, the reasons for and against alternative courses of action. (Saul reports this process of deliberation in the case study.) Who can deny that on occasion he or she has deliberated extensively about some decision or other? To deliberate about reasons for courses of action is not the same thing as trying to identify what will cause you to act in present circumstances. *Reasons* may be conceptually distinguished from *causes* in the following way: A cause may be defined as the sort of thing that is of itself sufficient to bring something about. Thus, to identify the cause of a person's action would be to identify that factor in a

THE REPENTANT MAGDALEN, *by Georges de La Tour.*

How would libertarians use an experience like Mary Magdalen's repentance to support their position?

person's life that was sufficient to bring about that action. On the other hand, in sifting reasons for actions, people are deliberating about something other than causes. Whereas persons can act *from* reasons, they do not act *from* causes. If a person is provided with good reasons for contributing to a given charity, the person might or might not act on those reasons. Unlike causes, reasons, even conclusive reasons, are not sufficient conditions for an action or behavior actually occurring.[1] The libertarian argues that the universally experienced process of deliberation is a process of deciding whether or not to act on the basis of

---

[1]This topic is taken up again in 21:2.1 and 21:2.2.

reasons appropriate in particular circumstances. People do not similarly *decide* to act or not on the basis of the causes of their actions.

20:2.2 *Temptation*   Libertarians describe the undeniable, common human experience of temptation and resistance to it as further experiences of freedom. As libertarians see it, the ability to resist temptation shows that human actions are not caused. Thus, for example, in the case study, as Saul Epstein chooses the difficult path of breaking his engagement with Connie and resists the temptation to live the comfortable life of a corporate lawyer with the support of a loving wife in a suburban setting, he experiences his freedom. The libertarian argues that if determinism is right, then the events that are the causes of human action would be like desirable impulses that tempt us in a certain direction. Therefore, our ability to resist temptation seems, to the libertarian, to be evidence of our ability not to act on what, if anything, could be described by the determinists as the causes of human action. Another approach to this argument is that, surely, the ability to resist temptation is a sufficient condition for being responsible for one's actions. Since people can have this ability, people are free, and determinism must be false.

20:2.3 *Regret and remorse*   Many libertarian philosophers, William James among them, have made a great deal out of the human experiences of remorse or regret. Determinism, James noted, implies that nothing in the world could have been other than it has been. But he found this determinism to be incompatible with the human experiences of regret and remorse. To feel remorseful or to feel regret is to acknowledge that you should have chosen and acted differently than you did. It is, therefore, to presuppose that you could have so chosen. James finds the experiences of regret, remorse, and self-condemnation to be nonsensical unless you assume that you need not have done those actions that led to regret or remorse. Without possibilities for alternative action, these feelings are reduced to a mockery.

✐ **PHILOSOPHER'S WORKSHOP**

Freedom and Common Sense

William James (1842–1910), an American philosopher who has been called the "prophet of pragmatism," defended the "commonsense" view of human freedom. He maintained that moral experiences, like those of regret and resisting temptation, show that the world is vulnerable, vulnerable to being wounded by the wrong actions of some of its members—the human ones.

The indeterminism I defend, the free will theory of popular sense based on the judgment of regret, represents that world as vulnerable, and liable to be injured by certain of its parts if they act wrong. And it represents their acting wrong as a matter of possibility or accident, neither inevitable nor yet to be infallibly warded off. In all this, it is a theory devoid either of transparency or of stability. It gives us a pluralistic, restless universe, in which no single point of view can ever take in the whole scene; and to a mind possessed of the love of unity at any cost, it will, no doubt, remain forever inacceptable. A friend with such a mind once told me that the thought of my universe made him sick, like the sight of the horrible motion of a mass of maggots in their carrion bed.

But while I freely admit that the pluralism and the restlessness are repugnant and irrational in a certain way, I find that every alternative to them is irrational in a deeper way. The indeterminism with its maggots, if you please to speak so about it, offends only the native absolutism of my intellect—an absolutism which, after all, perhaps, deserves to be snubbed and kept in check. But the determinism with its necessary carrion, to continue the figure of speech, and with no possible maggots to eat the latter up, violates my sense of moral reality through and through. When, for example, I imagine such carrion as the Brockton murder, I cannot conceive it as an act by which the universe, as a whole, logically and necessarily expresses its nature without shrinking from complicity with such a whole. And I deliberately refuse to keep on terms of loyalty with the universe by saying blankly that the murder, since it does flow from the nature of the whole, is not carrion. There are *some* instinctive reactions which I, for one, will not tamper with.[2]

---

[2] William James, "The Dilemma of Determinism," in *The Will to Believe and Other Essays in Popular Philosophy* (New York: David McKay Co., Inc., 1947), pp. 177–78.

20:2.4 *Choosing determinism or indeterminism* James would not have us underestimate the importance of these moral phenomena. Their clarity and immediacy cannot be denied, nor can the remoteness of the abstract theory of determinism which tries to explain them away as illusory. James argues that in fact we have a choice about whether to accept determinism or indeterminism (libertarianism), which he defends. He argues that the principal reason for adopting determinism is to bring all the occurrences within the universe under the unifying umbrella of a single explanatory theory. To choose otherwise, that is, to choose indeterminism, is to choose a more complex theory of the nature of events. Thus the choice of indeterminism is bought at the price of theoretical simplicity. James argues, however, that the reason for adopting indeterminism—that it preserves the reasonableness and integrity of moral phenomena together with the reasonableness of holding persons responsible for their actions—takes precedence over the desire for theoretical simplicity and unity in one's concept of the universe.

James reminds us that self-understanding is not an entirely theoretical matter but is practical as well. In part, the very idea of self-understanding is the idea of gaining clarity about what we ought to do. This idea presupposes that we need to, and therefore, can choose between alternatives in our actions. The libertarian view which James defends has the virtues of both (1) providing a theoretical, even though pluralistic, account of all the events that take place in the universe, including human actions; and (2) allowing for the reasonableness of this practical side of the need for self-understanding.

20:3 *Unresolved tension*   The principal attractions of libertarianism are these: First, it remains true to the immediate and clear experiences described above, especially our experiences as moral agents. Second, to those who believe that there is an incompatibility between the thesis of determinism and moral responsibility for what one does, libertarianism alone allows both for the possibility and reasonableness of morality itself. For all its virtues, however, libertarianism remains in conflict with the scientific virtues of determinism described in Chapter 19.

20:4 *Summary*   In this chapter we have considered libertarian theories which hold that determinism is false, that people are free as they act in the world, and therefore, that it is reasonable to hold them responsible for what they do. We first examined the libertarian view that human behavior is the product of self-determined choices. This view was criticized for falling back on the hypothesis that human actions are the product of human character inasmuch as there is doubt that people are entirely responsible for the development of their characters. We then examined the libertarian appeal to common experiences in our moral life, such as having to choose, deliberating, being tempted and resisting temptation, and feeling regret or remorse. We saw how libertarians argued that if these experiences are not illusory, then human freedom and responsibility must be real. In turn, the vividness of such experiences is more persuasive than the abstract theory of the determinists, who would have to call them illusory. The plausibility of libertarianism in preserving the reasonableness of important features of the moral life remains in tension with the scientific credibility of determinism. It is again worth noting that each of the arguments offered in favor of both hard determinism and soft determinism in Chapters 19 and 21 may also be counted as serious objections to libertarianism as presented in this chapter.

EXERCISES for Chapter 20

1. Libertarians have inferred that people act freely because there are self-determined human actions. To fortify their view they have argued for the conclusion that there are self-determined human actions. In the following list of statements distinguish those that are premises of that argument (P) from those that are objections to them (O) and from those that are neither (N).
    A. People act in accordance with their characters, developed over periods of years (20:1.3).
    B. What a person does in accordance with character is not done randomly.
    C. Either people are caused to act as they do by their characters, or whenever people's actions deviate from character, the actions are inadequately explained (20:1.4).
    D. The fact that people feel regret would make no sense at all if human beings did not have a free will (20:2.4).
    E. Surely a person's character is inadequately understood unless that understanding accounts for the causal processes that made that character what it came to be (20:1.4).
    F. An unconstrained decision is free even if it is also caused.
    G. Since neither a person's goal nor the person's self is totally and clearly defined at the outset of a decision-making process, the decision is better modeled as a creative process than as the effect of some cause (20:1.4).
2. Think about a *typical decision* you have made. Describe that experience in such a way as to emphasize the characteristics that would lead you to conclude either that you were self-determining or that your decision was determined by other causal factors.
3. a. Three moral experiences are often cited by libertarians in support of their view that human beings have free will. Name the three experiences and distinguish them from each other.
    b. State the arguments in which these experiences are premises for the belief in human freedom.
4. Compare and contrast the strengths of libertarianism and determinism (20:3).

SELECTED ANSWERS for Chapter 20

1. A. *P;* although a determinist might agree with the statement, interpreting it differently than the libertarian subsequently does.
   B. *P;* another statement with which a determinist might agree.
   C. *O.*
   D. *N;* a libertarian would be concerned to assert this statement but not as part of the argument for self-determinism.
   E. *O.*
   F. *N;* this is a statement of soft determinism, discussed in Chapter 21.
   G. *P.*

3. (1) Deciding, in which we are said to experience freedom, but in which we need not be experiencing temptation; (2) temptation and resistance to temptation, the latter of which is interpreted as the ability to overcome causal forces within us; (3) regret and remorse, which are retrospective feelings and which, according to the libertarian, make no sense unless free will is assumed.

21

Compatibilist Perspectives

Many philosophers believe that there are good reasons to accept both the thesis of determinism and the idea that people are free, and therefore, morally responsible for their actions. Compatibilists attend closely to the various meanings of the term "freedom," arguing that freedom is incompatible with determinism only in certain understandings of the term. In this chapter we will examine two sets of compatibilist views: first, that the morally important sense of "freedom" is that in which people may act free of constraint or coercion, and second, that people are properly thought of as free and morally responsible when they act rationally.

After reading Chapter 21 you should be able to

- State the traditional compatibilist definition of freedom and explain the solution to the dilemma of determinism derived from that definition.
- State an objection to this view in terms of whether or not it is reasonable to suppose that the agent could have acted otherwise.
- Relate freedom to rational decision-making; then state and criticize a revised compatibilist solution to the problem.

THE CASE OF KEITH TRACY

"I don't feel you have any choice in the matter," Mr. Tracy told his son Keith. "The only thing to do is to pay your sister what you owe her."

"Where am I gonna get $600, especially if I'm saving to go to college? I'll need every penny I earn."

"That is a problem, son. But you entered freely into a contract with her when you borrowed the money. Nobody forced you to buy that cycle or borrow the money from her. And it wasn't just a chance event that you happened to ask her for the money either."

"But somebody should have stopped me!"

"Really now, son. You're not eight years old anymore. You can't expect me to follow you around all your life preventing you from doing silly things. It's time to take responsibility for yourself."

Keith's father had never been this direct before, and the young man didn't know how to handle it. It was as if, for the first time in his life, his father was forcing the initiative and responsibility for action on him.

"Keith, what are you going to do about your debt to Mary Jane?"

"I don't know. Nothing, I suppose."

"That's not acceptable! You are morally obligated to repay her in full within three weeks. You're lucky she didn't ask for interest on the loan."

"What will you do if I don't pay her?"

"I'm not going to threaten you with some kind of childish punishment. You're beyond that. You'll suffer enough from the problems that you'll be creating between yourself and your sister. It could mean a lifetime of bad feelings between you."

"But she doesn't need the money. She's got a good job and . . ."

"Cut the nonsense. You can't rationalize your duty away like that."

"Do I have to sell my cycle?"

"That might be one way to get the money."

"But I use it all the time to get to school and work."

"Maybe you should think of another option."

"I could borrow the $600 from somebody else in order to pay off Mary Jane."

"You could; yes, that's a possibility."

"Ah, Dad; how would you like to enter into a business transaction with an enterprising young man who is college bound and who owns an expensive cycle?"

"I might be interested. What's your proposal?"

21:1.1 *Soft determinism and freedom from constraint*   Classical soft determinism, or compatibilism, may be traced back at least as far as the philosophy of Thomas Hobbes (1588–1679).[1] Hobbes was a thoroughgoing physical determinist. He denied the existence of a soul or spirit in human beings and argued that thoughts, feelings, or sensations are reducible to physical states. The general principles enabling people to understand changes in the matter of the universe may be applied equally to the changes in matter that are human behaviors. Hobbes

---

[1]See Thomas Hobbes, *Leviathan* (1651), Part II, Chap. 21 and *Of Liberty and Necessity* (1652).

Are there keys that remove constraints and make us genuinely free?

wholly rejected the concept of human beings as self-determining agents whose actions might arise without causes.

Hobbes argues that human freedom is compatible with his determinism. If we mean by saying that human actions are "free" that they are "uncaused," then, of course, determinism is incompatible with this concept. However, in Hobbes's view, what we mean by "free" is that persons are "unconstrained" or "uncoerced" as they act. Given Hobbes's definition, any unobstructed moving body may properly be considered free. Thus, for example, the waters of a flowing stream when not dammed may be described as flowing freely.

Hobbes argues that calling people's actions free in this sense is quite compatible with saying that their actions have causes. Moreover, when people act in unconstrained and uncoerced ways they act from, or in accordance with, their own unimpeded desires. Hobbes finds it perfectly reasonable to hold people responsible for actions based on their own desires. If a kidnapped person spends a night in a motel, the person does not act freely since he or she is acting under a threat. If a person begins to imitate the President as a result of a post-hypnotic suggestion, then the person is not acting freely since the person follows the desires of the hypnotist rather than his or her own. However, the same action, staying in the hotel or imitating the President, may be undertaken in circumstances where there is no threat or posthypnotic suggestion, but rather, people do those things because they like to do them and nothing prevents them. In such circumstances they would be acting from their own desires, and Hobbes would find it reasonable to say that they are acting freely. Accordingly, he would hold them responsible for their actions, even though the desires to do these things may be accounted for in causal terms.

The case study illustrates how this concept of freedom and constraint operates in our ordinary lives. No one forced Keith Tracy to borrow the $600 from his sister. He arranged the loan out of his own uncoerced desire to buy the cycle, and so entering into that arrangement was in that sense free. The father, like a soft determinist, finds it perfectly reasonable to hold his son responsible for fulfilling his contractual commitment.

21:1.2 *Acting in accord with will* Another modern philosopher, John Locke (1632–1714),[2] seconds the basic contention that people act freely when they act according to their desires, and that such actions can be causally determined. In Locke's view, actions are caused by

---

[2]See John Locke, *An Essay Concerning Human Understanding* (1690), Part II, Chap. 21.

human choices or will. Also, actions can be perfectly free and yet unavoidable. If a person decides to enter a room and is unconstrained in doing so, it may happen that the person is thereafter locked into the room though he or she doesn't attempt to get out and doesn't know

---

✒ PHILOSOPHER'S WORKSHOP

Freedom and Prediction

In the following passage the British philosopher John Stuart Mill (1806–1873) makes an interesting reply to those who would argue that people would not feel themselves to be free if hard determinism were universally accepted.

Correctly conceived, the doctrine entitled Philosophical Necessity is simply this: that, given the motives which are present to an individual's mind, and given likewise the character and disposition of the individual, the manner in which he will act might be unerringly inferred; that if we knew the person thoroughly, and knew all the inducements which are acting upon him, we could foretell his conduct with as much certainty as we can predict any physical event. This proposition I take to be a mere interpretation of universal experience, a statement in words of what everyone is internally convinced of. No one who believed that he knew thoroughly the circumstances of any case, and the characters of the different persons concerned, would hesitate to foretell how all of them would act. Whatever degree of doubt he may in fact feel arises from the uncertainty whether he really knows the circumstances, or the character of someone or other of the persons, with the degree of accuracy required; but by no means from thinking that if he did know these things, could there be any uncertainty what the conduct should be. Nor does this full assurance conflict in the smallest degree with what is called our feeling of freedom. We do not feel ourselves the less free because those to whom we are intimately known are well assured how we shall will to act in a particular case. We often, on the contrary, regard the doubt of what our conduct will be as a mark of ignorance of our characters, and sometimes even resent it as an imputation.[3]

---

[3]John Stuart Mill, *A System of Logic*, Bk. VI, Ch. II, in J. M. Robson, ed., *Collected Works of John Stuart Mill*, Vol. VII (Toronto, Can.: University of Toronto Press, 1974), 836–37.

the door is locked. It does not follow, Locke argues, that the person is not free in being in the room. True, he or she is not free to leave the room, but the person entered the room freely and freely decided to stay there, since there was no constraint either in the entry or in the decision to stay. Locke concludes that the fact that people could not be doing anything other than what they are doing does not imply that they are not free in doing it.

One may object that this example presents an inadequate analogy. The sufficient causes of which determinism speaks are antecedent causes. The hard determinist would argue that if sufficient causes had led the person to be in the room in the first place, then it becomes very implausible to suggest that the person entered the room freely. This objection indicates that having the desire to enter the room is itself a matter beyond the person's control, and therefore, not something for which he or she is appropriately held responsible.

21:1.3 *Choosing to do otherwise*   The strongest objection to the compatibilist view focuses upon cases of compulsive behavior. One can argue that even if the behavior of a compulsive kleptomaniac, for example, is unconstrained, it is nevertheless not free in the *morally important sense*. The compulsions or inhibitions to which the compulsive person responds, and which would reasonably be called the causes of the person's actions, do not allow him or her to *choose to do otherwise*. This objection strongly suggests that beyond being free from constraint, moral responsibility requires that people must be free to choose to do otherwise.

21:1.4 *Rebuttal*   The traditional compatibilist may respond to this objection by suggesting that the agents in question could have done otherwise had they simply desired or chosen to. But, says the objector, this response is inadequate because it seems *impossible* that a person could have desired or chosen otherwise. In the compatibilist account there is no way of distinguishing between compulsive behavior, which supposedly is not free, and ordinary behavior, which supposedly is. It seems to the objector that people's conditioning, which leads them to have the desires they have and to choose as they do, is probably every bit as determinative of their "normal" behavior as is the compulsion determinative of the behavior of the compulsive person. Surely no importance attaches to the fact that the compulsive's behaviors are deviant. (Compare 13:3.3 and 19:3.4.)

In the case study, it is implausible to suggest that Keith Tracy is a compulsive motorcyclist. Yet, the thesis of determinism entails that a complete causal account could be given for Keith's being the sort of person who strongly desires to have a motorcycle. Thus, although his desire to have a motorcycle may be distinguished from the desires of

Can the soft determinist explain the meaning of "you could have done otherwise"?

the compulsive kleptomaniac in being more ordinary, his desire seems to be equally beyond control. According to hard determinism, Keith's acting from his genuine desire is not sufficient warrant for holding him morally responsible, for it seems unreasonable to say that he is responsible for having that desire in the first place. How would you interpret the behavior of a "problem drinker" in terms of "choosing to do otherwise"?

21:2.1 *Compatibilism and moral responsibility* An alternative version of compatibilism focuses more squarely on what kind of freedom would seem to be required for moral responsibility. Obviously, for the position to remain compatibilist, "free" cannot simply mean "uncaused." The objections to the view outlined above, however, suggest that "free" cannot simply mean "unconstrained" either. There seems to be agreement that freedom from constraint is a necessary condition for holding persons morally responsible for their actions. But if it is not sufficient, then what other ingredient is necessary?

To answer this question it is necessary to distinguish further between compulsive behavior and the ordinary behavior of responsible agents, most often by the contrast between irrationally and rationally acting upon desires. People who act compulsively may attempt to rationalize their behavior whereas those who act rationally on their desires are able to give antecedent reasons for their actions. If a compulsive hand-washer, say Lady MacBeth, washes her hands for the twentieth time within an hour without having soiled them in the meantime, she is not a free agent, because her desire is not rational. But if a construction worker, returning from a dirty job, washes his or her hands to remove the accumulated soil, it is plausible to suppose that the worker is not suffering from hand-washing compulsion but rather washing his or her dirty hands because he or she rationally and freely desires that they be clean.

The compulsive person may rationalize his or her actions, which is not the same as acting from reason. To rationalize is to act first and then later seek to provide some account of why you did so, in this manner covering up the irrationality of the original action. A clear example of rationalization would be former President Nixon's Watergate episode. Motivated by what looked like personal, political ambitions, he moved to cover up the Watergate break-in. Later when the news came out, he seemed to realize that he needed some "justification" to make his actions seem reasonable. At that point he and his aides met to invent a likely sounding story which they hoped would be persuasive, the "national security" rationalization. Notice that in the example, Nixon not only chose first, he also acted first; only afterward did he and his aides try to find a publicly acceptable moral principle which they could portray as their justification.

To act before seeking reasons, however, is not essential to rationalization; one is rationalizing when one chooses first, whether or not one acts. When confronted, compulsives rationalize their actions because they are incapable of acting from reasons. Others, noncompulsive rationalizers, may be held responsible for choosing and possibly acting first without considering and developing reasons that direct and justify their choices. Compatibilists argue that *it is reasonable to hold people responsible when they are able to consider reasons for acting and to act from the reasons that they consider.*

21:2.2 *Acting rationally*   What is "acting from reasons" as these compatibilists understand it? Being rational about one's choices involves a number of factors: (1) One typically expresses one's goals, at least to oneself, and as necessary, arranges them by priority; (2) one must identify the means available to achieve these goals; (3) one has to anticipate the possible and probable consequences, both intended and unintended, of using these means and pursuing these goals; and (4) if the available means are either inadequate or likely to cause undesirable consequences, one must assess the possibilities of both developing further means and abandoning or revising the goal. All these factors must receive their due place in any rational decision.

Some compatibilists argue that being unconstrained in action and acting rationally are both necessary and sufficient conditions for holding people responsible for their actions. They also maintain that freedom, meaning "unconstrained and rational," is quite compatible with the idea that people's actions are caused. The compulsive person may be conditioned to rationalize rather than to act from reasons, which counts against holding him or her responsible. In this compatibilist view, however, a person may be *conditioned to act rationally.* What could be better than educating people so that they are able to make rational decisions, using processes like the one outlined above, and advance rational considerations pro or con before they decide what to do? People who act rationally take the measure of their various desires. They are not, therefore, the victims of their desires as are compulsive people.

21:2.3 *Reflective rationality*   People can even be reflective about their own rationality. That is, they can reflect on the question, "Should I use my rational abilities in these particular circumstances, to what end and for what period of time?" In other words, people can be rational about whether or not to be rational about a given subject versus acting emotionally, intuitively, or spontaneously where that may be appropriate. Because this kind of reflective rationality is possible, compatibilists argue that it is reasonable to hold people responsible for acting either deliberately or spontaneously; that is, people are fully capable of deciding for themselves whether they should reflect or not. Thus, in this interpretation, acting on rational desires as a product of deliberative processes is not easily construed as equivalent to acting compulsively.

21:2.4 *The hard determinist objection*   Although it may be true that at any level of action or decision-making, people can reflect about whether they should undertake a rational deliberative process in those circumstances, determinism implies that there are always causes to determine whether or not people decide to deliberate. But if people are caused to deliberate or not to deliberate, then it is unclear how the mere potential to be reflectively rational is enough to guarantee the freedom necessary for moral responsibility. After all, how can a person be held responsible for what could not have been otherwise? Persistent hard determinists insist that this question always has force no matter how complicated the causality that must lead through the layers of rational deliberation.

21:3 *Summary*   In this chapter we examined the views of soft determinists. We have shown how they believe it is possible to define "freedom" in such a way that (1) freedom is compatible with causality, and (2) people can be held morally responsible for their actions. This compatibilist position grows out of the great plausibility attached both to determinism and our moral institutions within which we hold people responsible. We first examined the position that freedom from constraint is sufficient for holding persons responsible. The principal objection to this view is that compulsive behavior sometimes meets this definition of freedom and yet it seems unreasonable to hold compulsives responsible. The second version of compatibilism suggested that persons are genuinely free when they are both unconstrained in what they do and capable of acting rationally. Such action contrasts with compulsive behavior. Still, hard determinists might persist in maintaining that people who act rationally in this view are unfree in the same way as compulsives.

EXERCISES for Chapter 21

1. a. Rephrase the following statements in order to clarify the meaning of "free" in each:
     A. Let the Delaware flow *freely*; no dam at Tocks!
     B. I always thought I was *free* because I could take a drink whenever I chose.
     C. But now I'm really *free* because now I don't have to take any drink.
     D. Buy a Bunner mattress now and get a *free* mattress cover!
     E. We guarantee this property deed to be *free* of all and any competing claims.
     F. With the incriminating evidence now safely in your hands, no one can blackmail you: You're *free*.
     G. Nobody's *free* to go around murdering people; there's a law against it.
     H. I'm not *free* this weekend; I've made other commitments.
     I. The prisoner will be *free*, on parole, starting next Tuesday.
   b. Which meaning has the traditional compatibilist proposed in trying to resolve the dilemma of determinism (21:1.1)?
   c. Use statements B and C to exemplify the strongest objection to traditional compatibilism (21:1.3). Explain why the objection focuses on whether or not the person could have done otherwise.
   d. How does traditional compatibilism interpret "could have done otherwise" in response to this objection (21:1.4)?
   e. Why is this response problematic (21:1.4)?

2. a. State the reformulated version of compatibilism which attempts to overcome the traditional criticism by invoking the concept of rational decision-making (21:2.1–21:2.3).
   b. This restated compatibilism in effect redefines what it presents as the morally relevant sense of "free." What is it?
   c. Describe a concrete case in which a person is free in the revised, compatibilist sense. Then use your description of that case in defense or in criticism of the revised, compatibilist position.

3. a. Read 19:1.2 and 20:3 for a concise statement of the strengths of determinism and libertarianism. Since the compatibilist is a determinist who at the same time affirms human freedom and moral responsibility, he or she can claim the strengths of both of these positions. What, on the other hand, is the liability of compatibilism?
   b. Explain the relationship between the compatibilist's concern with the meaning of the word "free" and the claim that determinism and human freedom are compatible.

c. Why would a contextualist be interested in presenting a clear statement of alternative meanings of terms central to the statement of a philosophical problem?

SELECTED ANSWERS for Chapter 21

1. a. A. . . . unrestrained by human contrivance . . .!
   B. . . . unconstrained, not prohibited. . . .
   C. . . . not subject to compulsion. . . .
   D. . . . [a cover] for which there is no additional charge.
   E. There are no other, competing claims.
   F. . . . [You] cannot be coerced to act contrary to your own desire.
   G. A person is liable to be caught and risks being constrained and punished. . . .
   H. I have obligated myself to act in certain ways, which necessarily rules out doing some other things.
   I. Subject to the restrictions of parole, the prisoner will no longer be constrained from moving about as he or she chooses.

2. b. The person is not constrained or coerced from acting as he or she choses (following the traditional definition), *and* compulsions do not prevent the person from deliberating rationally and acting upon his or her decision.

3. a. The liability is that determinism and human freedom appear to be conceptually incompatible, and so their compatibility must be explained.
   b. By focusing on alternative meanings of the word "free," the compatibilist hopes to show that even though determinism implies that human actions and choices are not free in some sense, there is another sense (the morally relevant sense) in which persons can still be free.
   c. Often, in philosophy, the statements that seem most clearly and obviously true on one subject apparently contradict those that seem equally clearly and obviously true on another subject. A contextualist will hope to be able to affirm all statements that seem very clearly and obviously true. Thus, rather than choosing between such attractive statements, a contextualist will be interested in investigating the possibility that because terms have different meanings in the different clear and obvious statements, the conflict between the statements is only apparent.

      You should notice, however, that even a philosopher with contextualist inclinations will not automatically come to a compatibilist solution to every philosophical problem. William James, for example, generally followed a contextualist approach. When he examined the dilemma of determinism, however, he concluded that the statements of determinism and of human freedom really do contradict each other. Thus, for all his contextualist inclinations, he rejected soft determinism.

PERSPECTIVES

ON

KNOWLEDGE

What can human beings know? By what standards can they distinguish genuine knowledge from unsupported belief? What is knowledge, and what means are reliable in acquiring it? In practical terms we face these questions whenever we are confronted with disagreement among experts, often in matters of medicine, economics, human psychology, religion, and even science. Certainly we should all be better off if we could find a person who does know the answer; but how does knowing that we have found such a person differ from knowing how to find the answer for ourselves?

In the course of history old, established ways of thinking have been called into question by newer theories or by evidence that appeared to contradict the entrenched views. The sciences, for example, were taught basically as they had been formulated by Aristotle until the seventeenth century, when the new theory that the earth rotated around the sun resulted in tremendous struggles about the proper understanding of the natural world. Skepticism, often very influential at such times, is in general the view that it is not possible to know anything. In the ancient Greece of

✐ P A R T   S I X

Socrates and Plato, the rise of democracy and imperialistic expansion by the city-states led to skepticism about the possibility of knowing anything about moral matters. During the unrest of the 1960's there was much public skepticism that knowledge about the working of vast, modern bureaucracies is possible.

Epistemology, the philosophic study of knowledge, has been centrally concerned about the intellectual challenge posed by skepticism and how this challenge might be met. As indicated in Chapter 4, foundationalists look for undeniable truths from which to deduce claims about knowledge. Contextualists try to develop alternatives to these foundationalistic goals, which they regard as unattainable.

In this part we first examine skepticism, and then consider both foundationalist and contextualist responses to it. The responses we shall consider are focused on two key philosophical issues: knowledge about the physical world and knowledge of other persons. The relationship among the chapters of Part Six can be diagrammed as shown.

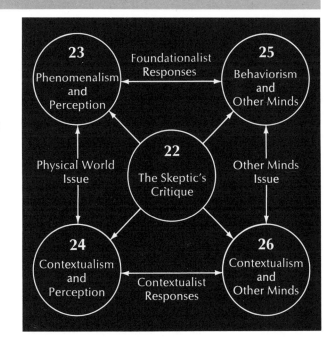

22

The Skeptic's Critique

So often in our experience we are convinced of something, only later to find that we have been mistaken. Think how often and in how many ways appearances deceive people: There are natural illusions and deliberate deceptions. We may misinterpret our own perceptions or the behavior of others, or we may hallucinate. Present physical evidence is found to be inconsistent with what we seem to remember. Even if you are *sure* now that your belief is correct, it does not guarantee that that belief will not be overturned by later evidence. In this chapter we will deal with the philosophical position known as skepticism. Skeptics doubt that knowledge is possible. They are not satisfied to count any potentially false or refutable belief as genuine knowledge, arguing that knowledge requires a higher, unattainable order of certainty. After reading Chapter 22 you should be able to

- State the argument based on illusion.
- Characterize the structure of skeptical arguments and identify the skeptical character of other arguments.
- Compare and contrast the skeptical argument that knowledge of other persons' thoughts is impossible with the argument that knowledge of the present state of the physical world is impossible.

THE CASE OF ROSS OWENS

"Would you like s'more coffee, Mr. Owens?" asked the police interrogator as he lit another cigarette. Without waiting for an answer he hit the intercom button and barked, "Send in two more coffees, Frank." Then turning back to the nervous, pajama-clad man he said, "Now let's go through it one more time. Tell me what you remember from the time you entered the Club 701 bar."

"Like I said, I sat at the bar and had two quick drinks. I was dry—been working all day. I like to start with a shot and a beer. It was about four, shift had just ended. Lots of guys goes to the 701 after work. No harm in it."

"How long did you stay? Who were you with?"

"I went in with Bill, that's Bill Benore. But he left about seven. I stayed later. Warren Suder came by about eight and we had a few drinks together. He left at eleven. That's when I met the girl."

"Did you know she was a hooker?"

"I thought she might be by the way she came up to me and started talking."

"You went with her. Where?"

"I don't remember. It's the booze. It happens a lot to me. I do things but just can't remember. I would fight with Meg, before she took the kids and left me. She would always say that booze would ruin me some day."

"We picked you up on the Dixie Highway near Lima Pier. You were walking around dressed in the pajamas you're wearing right now. This wallet was stuffed into the shirt pocket. No money, only an ID card with the name Ross Owens on it. Do you remember that?"

"I remember the flashing lights. I thought I was at a carnival. Then I thought that the lights were fire truck lights. I dreamed I was in a burning house. The hooker was in bed with me. We were both asleep and the house was burning. I tried to wake up but my eyes wouldn't open. I could smell the smoke and hear the fire crackle. I was terrified, but my eyes just wouldn't come open. I couldn't move. I called out for the woman, but she didn't respond. Then I dreamed I woke up. She was laughing at me. We were in bed. I was naked and cold. There was no fire. But that must have been a dream, too, because I have pajamas on now."

"Maybe. But maybe not. Maybe you did wake up and she got you these pajamas."

"I can't say for sure. But I remember being pulled out of bed and carried downstairs. There was smoke in the staircase and the person who was carrying me wore a yellow gas mask. He was a big man with huge green hands. There was no face under his gas mask, I could tell! He put me on the grass on my back. It was wet and cold. That's when I was able to open my eyes. He gave me a blanket.''

"Look, Owens, you say you can't remember anything from the time you left the 701 till we brought you in here six hours later. You say you woke up in bed, and then you claim that was a dream. You say you woke up on the wet grass, but you remember the color of the gas mask and gloves the fireman wore. When were you dreaming? When were you awake? Maybe you're lying about this whole thing! And where are your clothes? Let's start over once more. When . . .''

The intercom buzzed to interrupt the question. "Sarge, we checked on the possibility of a fire, but none was reported last night anywhere around Lima Pier. We do have something interesting though. A possible homicide: woman, about thirty years old, body found in the drainage ditch that runs next to Dixie Highway. No burns on the body.''

"Thanks, Frank.'' The interrogator looked at Owens, but the alcoholic's expression revealed nothing.

22:1.1 *Skepticism and perception* It seems that the most secure claims about knowledge we can make are those about the present characteristics of our physical surroundings. On a midnight stroll, we see that the moon is full. While listening to an opera, we hear the rich, full voice of the baritone. As we eat a taco, we savor the sharp taste of the peppers. We feel the rough surface of sandpaper. The list is limited only by our capacity to describe the richness of our immediate sensory experience.

We are claiming knowledge about things we observe through the use of our *senses*. Although philosophers in talking about perceptual knowledge of the physical world most often use vision as the paradigm, or chief example, of sensory experience, they have in mind experience of a physical world attainable through any of the senses. Moreover, they have in mind the experience of a world that is *public*, that is open to shared experience, a world we have in common. The claims in question are about the way we experience the public world in *present* perception, as opposed to the way we remember it or imagine it. Thus, when philosophers ask, "Is there knowledge of the physical world?" they are asking, "Can we know the present state of objects, which are publicly observable, and which are known about, if they are known at all, on the basis of sense perception?"

22:1.2 *The argument from illusion* Skeptics, who doubt that there is such a thing as knowledge of the physical world, contend that illusions undermine the trustworthiness of perception. There are different types of illusory experiences:

1. *Perceptual illusions* often mislead us when we try to identify or describe the objects of perception. Optical illusions are the most familiar. Drawings can be constructed in such a way that lines of equal length are seen as unequal or a straight line is seen as curved. Magic tricks, the effects of especially designed mirrors, and mirages are other examples. Still photographs when projected in rapid succession appear to be moving scenes, and wheels may appear to be going backward when in fact they are moving forward.

2. The *relativity of perception* introduces new complications into our perception of the world. Round objects appear elliptical when seen from an angle, and square objects seem to be diamond-shaped when tipped and viewed from a corner. Depending upon what you have just been eating, the same beverage may taste sweet or sour. The horn of a truck may seem to change pitch as the truck rushes by. The condition of your sense organs can influence the appearance of things, for example, in cases of color blindness or partial deafness due to noise. Thus, the apparent properties of things may vary depending upon your perspective, your surroundings, or the condition of your sense organs.

3. In *hallucinations* persons "perceive" objects that are simply not present. The drunkard's illusions or someone feeling motion or pain "in" an amputated limb are classic examples.

All such experiences are called *illusions*, for they all share an important characteristic: They are liable to deceive people concerning what is true about their physical surroundings. (Go back to the case study and list Ross Owens's illusory experiences.) Skeptics cite illusions as grounds for distrusting our senses, intending to show (a) that perception does not support knowledge of the physical world, and (b) that what we are aware of in perception are not physical objects themselves but only appearances. Let us examine this argument more closely.

22:1.3 *Perception does not support knowledge of the physical world*   We often claim to know something based on present sensory experience, but if we truly know something about the physical world, then it must actually be the way we claim it is. However, when we base our claims on illusions, the physical world is not as we claim. Hence, though we might *claim* to know the world on the basis of illusory experiences, it is false to say that we *do* know it. Skeptics argue that one of the characteristics of experiencing illusions is that we cannot tell when we are experiencing them. That is, *as experiences* they are indistinguishable from nonillusory perceptual experiences. In other words, our perceptual (sensory) evidence during an illusion is no different in character from our sensory evidence when there is no illusion. If our basis for

Now what do you say?

claiming knowledge is inadequate in cases of illusion, then it is also inadequate in cases where the evidence has exactly the same character. The skeptic argues that since experience has the same character in all cases, we have secure knowledge in no cases.

22:1.4. *What we perceive are not physical objects*   If the circle is round and what you see is elliptical, then what you see cannot be the circle. If the wall has no pink elephants on it and what you see has pink elephants on it, then what you see cannot be the wall. In these cases, something is experienced that is not in one's actual physical surroundings. Skeptics have argued that what is experienced is an appearance only and not the real physical world. Philosophers have called these things that are experienced, but which are not identical with the physical world, *sense data*. Thus, the argument from illusion has been used to support the claim that there are such things as sense data and that they, not physical objects, are the actual objects of perceptual experience.

22:2.1 *Characteristics of skeptical arguments*   In general, skeptical arguments assume a *foundationalist* theory of knowledge: All genuine knowledge must be ultimately founded upon basic statements which we can be completely certain are true; and we can claim to *know* other statements only if we can infer them from these statements by means of valid ("deductive") reasoning. (To say that an argument is *valid* is to say that the conclusion *must* be true, if all the premises are true.) Skeptical arguments share two important characteristics: (1) The statements we ordinarily use to support claims about knowledge are not *basic* statements, because they are corrigible. To. say that they are "corrigible" is to say that even if they express a sincere, well-founded belief, they may still be false. Even statements about our sensory experience are corrigible in this sense. Ross Owens in the case study may sincerely report to the police that he had such bizarre experiences—yet he may be mistaken. (2) Even if statements about our experiences are true, it is not possible to validly infer true claims about the physical world from them. In view of the possibility of illusion, our conclusions about the physical world *could* be false, even if our statements of evidence were all true. Thus, even if it is true that Ross Owens had the experiences he describes, it does not *follow* of necessity that they reveal how the world really is.

22:2.2 *Descartes and scepticism* René Descartes, whom many call the father of modern philosophy, dealt with similar skeptical arguments in his quest for certainty. Rather than subjecting his beliefs to scrutiny individually, Descartes proceeds with a methodical examination of principles, or rules, of evidence which define policies for identifying acceptable beliefs. The procedure is known as Descartes's Methodical Doubt. If you can find reason for doubting beliefs certified by a principle (like "trust your senses"), then you should reject the principle. In his *Meditations on First Philosophy*, Descartes examines principles that would certify as knowledge those beliefs grounded in sensory experience alone. Are any such principles defensible? In other words, are the senses reliable? We shall examine two of the arguments Descartes considers in his First Meditation.

22:2.3 *The dream argument* Descartes criticizes a commonsense principle: The sensory experience of a perceiver with well-functioning sense organs perceiving in the best of conditions is a reliable basis for knowledge of the physical world. However, many realistic hallucinations can be attributed to psychosis, although the methodical doubter can hardly assume that everyone is insane. Yet Descartes cites the dreaming state as a nonpathological equivalent of madness. Dreaming is not caused by personal idiosyncracies or the malfunctioning of the sense organs. Anyone could at some time or other be dreaming. In dreams, appearance as opposed to reality itself is the norm. Descartes argues that dreaming experiences, as experienced, cannot be distinguished from waking ones. While we are dreaming it is as if we were awake, encountering those things that we dream about. In the case study, for example, Ross Owens has a very vivid dream. In fact, he dreams that he wakes up, and he is not sure when he was dreaming and when he was awake. Such experiences provide the basis for the skeptical dream argument:

The Dream Argument

In his *Meditations* René Descartes (1596–1650) articulates the dream argument as he pursues his method of doubting any proposition that could be false under some assumptions.

At the same time I must remember that I am a man, and that consequently I am in the habit of sleeping, and in my dreams representing to myself the same things or sometimes even less probable things, than do those who are insane in their waking moments. How often has it happened to me that in the night I dreamt that I found myself in this particular place, and that I was dressed and seated near the fire, whilst in reality I was lying undressed in bed! At this moment it does indeed seem to me that it is with eyes awake that I am looking at this paper; that this head which I move is not asleep, that it is deliberately and of set purpose that I extend my hand and perceive it; what happens in sleep does not appear so clear nor so distinct as does all this. But in thinking over this I remind myself that on many occasions I have in sleep been deceived by similar illusions, and in dwelling carefully on this reflection I see so manifestly that there are no certain indications by which we may clearly distinguish wakefulness from sleep that I am lost in astonishment. And my astonishment is such that it is almost capable of persuading me that I now dream.[1]

---

[1]René Descartes, *Meditations on First Philosophy*, trans. Elizabeth S. Haldane and G. R. T. Ross, *The Philosophical Works of Descartes* (New York: Cambridge University Press, 1970), pp. 145–46.

(1) What we experience when we dream is often indistinguishable from what we experience when we are awake.
(2) Dream experiences are not reliable evidence for the way the world really is.
(3) Therefore, sensory experience is not reliable evidence for claims about the physical world.

22:2.4 *The evil genius argument* Descartes next considers a weaker principle: We can acquire knowledge of the physical world from experience in general, even if on specific occasions we are unable to distinguish present experiences, in which the physical world is revealed to us as it is, from illusory (or dream) experiences. For example, we are sure of the existence of general types of complex objects that are featured in both waking and dreaming experiences (such as people, objects, plants), although we may be in doubt in individual experiences. In this principle, dreams are thought to be modeled upon real things. However, this principle, too, can be criticized. At times Descartes has had rather imaginative dreams. He compares them to the imaginative inventions of the artist, which may be purely fictitious. He concludes that he could have experiences of complex objects, even if there existed no complex things to which they corresponded.

He modifies the principle under investigation once again: Beliefs about the existence of "simple and more universal elements," which in various combinations go to make up all our sensory experiences, may be acceptable. Even products of the imagination seem to be compounded of elements like colors, shapes, odors, and so on, the existence of which is certain, although the combination may be unprecedented in reality. But Descartes introduces the evil genius argument to undermine the principle about the reality of simple and universal things: All our sensory experiences and ideas of reality might have been placed in our minds by an all-powerful deity or evil genius even if there were no physical world. The skeptic argues that we have no evidence that this hypothesis is false, so we cannot be certain that it is false. The evil genius argument for the first time introduces the possibility that there may be no physical world at all. Even simple and universal characteristics or qualities of things might not exist; all experiences might be illusory. Both the dream argument and the evil genius argument share two important characteristics with the argument from illusion. In no cases are there valid inferences from experience to the claims of knowledge supported by those experiences. In all cases the statements describing those experiences are themselves corrigible, and therefore open to correction.

22:3.1 *Skepticism and other minds*   We often claim to know the minds of other persons. In attempting to articulate minimally what such claims might amount to, philosophers have defined "other minds" as a technical term, best defined by their activities. The activities of a mind include (1) thinking, doubting, imagining, intending, believing, and many other cognitive states; (2) emotional states like anger, sadness, elation; and (3) sensory experiences such as seeing things or being tickled. To claim to know the mind of another, then, according to this definition, is to claim to know what that other person is thinking, feeling, or sensing. People frequently claim to know that others are doubtful, excited, depressed, confident, and the like.

What philosophers have called "the problem of other minds" is a problem of knowledge. Do we know that other people have minds? Do we know what their minds' activities or states are? If so, on what basis do we know these things? Just as skeptics doubt that knowledge of the physical world is possible, so skeptics doubt that knowledge of other minds is possible.

 PHILOSOPHER'S WORKSHOP

Epistomologist's Lexicon

Knowledge: justified, true belief.

Warranted assertability: the property of statements such that there is no present reason to doubt them and they are supported by whatever evidential data are appropriate.

Truth: conformity with the way things are.

Incorrigibility: the property of statements such that if they are sincerely uttered they cannot be overturned.

Certainty: the property of either being incorrigible (foundationalism) or of being presently indubitable (contextualism).

Skepticism: the view that it is not possible to know anything.

Physical world: the universe of objects that are observable through the senses.

Sense data: the immediate appearances supposed by some to be encountered in sense experience.

Phenomenalism: the view that persons perceive only sense data, or as more recently defined, that statements about physical objects are reducible to those about sense data.

Mind: that entity that thinks, feels, and senses.

Behavior: the observable, uninterpreted activities of bodies.

Behaviorism: the view that in knowing the behavior of others we have direct knowledge of their minds, or that all statements about mental states are reducible to statements about behavior.

22:3.2 *The sceptic's arguments* Skeptical arguments against knowledge of other minds run parallel to the argument from illusion used against knowledge of the physical world. A person may look angry, but such an appearance may be deceiving: He or she may be in reality simply experiencing a cramp. Moreover, other people are fully capable of deceiving us deliberately. They may, for instance, want us to believe that they are honest, although they are not. Thus, those behaviors of others upon which we base our claims to know what they are thinking or feeling may not be adequate precisely for the two reasons discussed in section 22:2.1. The inferences from the experiential evidence to the claims of knowledge are not valid, because the experiences themselves are corrigible. Thus, the same two possibilities for error exist in our knowledge of other minds as in our knowledge of the physical world.

22:3.3 *Knowing your own mind*   Many writers, in stating the problem of other minds, mention what they take to be the incorrigibility of claims of knowledge about one's own mental state. This belief suggests a contrast between knowledge of one's own mental state as opposed to the inferior quality of any claims about anybody else's mental state. Thus, not only is knowledge of other minds deprecated, but a positive alternative model of knowing a mind (one's own) is held up as the paradigm to be matched by any knowledge of other minds. The skeptic contrasts the uncertainty of claims about other minds when compared to the apparent reliability of claims about one's own.

22:4 *Summary*   In this chapter we have introduced the skeptics' challenge to our claims to know. We have seen how they doubt the reliability of sensory experience as the basis for knowledge of a public physical world. The argument from illusion was outlined as well as the parallel Cartesian arguments from dreaming and from an evil genius. Similar arguments were outlined as they bear upon our claims to know other minds. Skeptics argue that the inferences we would draw from experiential evidence are not deductively valid and that the experiences themselves are corrigible. Thus, skeptics argue that certainty is unattainable, because of these possibilities for error, and that where certainty is unattainable, knowledge is also unattainable.

EXERCISES for Chapter 22

1. Philosophers speak of "illusions" in a very general sense, meaning "any experience in which what the person apparently experiences differs from what really is in such a way that the person may be deceived." But philosophers also distinguish perceptual illusions ("illusions" in a narrow sense) from the relativity of perception and from hallucinations (22:1.2).
   a. Describe a case, either from the case study or from your imagination, of each of these kinds of experience.

    b. Illustrate through one of your descriptions what the skeptic means in saying that there is no difference in the character of our experience when we are having an illusion and when we are not (22:1.3).

    c. What does a skeptic mean in saying that our claims of knowledge are *corrigible* (22:2.1)?

    d. Give two illustrations—one related to the physical world, the other to other minds—of corrigible claims of knowledge. Describe corrections to which each claim might be subject.

    e. Give two illustrations—one related to the physical world, the other to other minds—of claims of knowledge based on nonvalid inferences (22:2.1).

    f. How would the skeptic criticize those claims?

    g. State the argument from illusion (22:1.2).

2. How could a skeptic use the case study to attack the possibility of knowledge of other minds? (Hint: Put yourself in the position of the interrogating officer attempting to know the mind of Ross Owens.)

3. Compare and contrast the skeptical argument that knowledge of other minds is impossible with the skeptic's argument from illusion (22:3.2 and 22:3.3).

SELECTED ANSWERS for Chapter 22

1. c. To say that a statement is corrigible means that further evidence might be presented, relative to the truth of that statement, in the light of which it would not be reasonable to hold that the statement were true.

    d. The statement, "The Morning Star is very bright today," would be subject to correction (1) if it were discovered that the object in the sky to which the speaker was referring was an artificial satellite, not the Morning Star; or (2) if the Morning Star were no brighter than usual but appeared brighter because Venus and Mercury were in alignment.

    e. If Mr. Owens says "I thought I was at a carnival," and the interrogator infers that Mr. Owens thought he was at a carnival, the inference is not valid.

    f. Specifically, the skeptic might point out that the interrogator's conclusion might be false, either because Mr. Owens no longer remembers what he thought earlier or because he is deliberately lying. Generally, the skeptic would point out that somebody's (the inspector's) really knowing something entails that that which he knows is true. Thus, the inspector, according to the skeptic, could not have knowledge so long as his evidence did not entail the truth of his claim.

2. Remember, the skeptic would want to make two points: that nonvalid inferences are involved and that corrigible claims are made.

3. Abstractly, both these arguments—and any other skeptical arguments—

involve the points that corrigible statements and statements based on non-valid inferences cannot be known to be true. Typically, concerning other minds, unlike concerning the physical world, the skeptic fortifies his skepticism by contrasting statements about other minds, which he finds unknowable, with statements about one's own mind, which are presented as incorrigible and as directly known (known without having to make any observations of one's behavior or inferences about one's self).

23

Phenomenalism and Perception

Skeptical arguments have made many philosophers wary of trying to go beyond statements about perception to claims about the present state of the physical world. Yet, they have tried to defend the claim that knowledge of the physical world is possible. One defense is to more closely identify the physical world with perceptions of it. John Stuart Mill said that physical objects are merely permanent possibilities of perception, a position known as *phenomenalism*. Contemporary analytical philosophers have offered a linguistic version, arguing that statements about physical objects are really equivalent to groups of statements about perceptual experiences. Chapter 23 examines the phenomenalist's position on knowledge of the physical world. After reading Chapter 23 you should be able to

- State the argument that what persons are aware of in perception is always sense data.
- Defend the assertion that statements about present sense data are incorrigible.
- Characterize the phenomenalist's attempted analysis of statements about physical objects.
- Criticize phenomenalism.

THE CASE OF ALFRED LELAND

The detective agency, located through the phone book at 4286 Library Street, turned out to be a back bedroom turned home-office. Clipper escorted Alfred Leland down the hall around children's toys, past a basket of unsorted laundry, and into the office. "What can I do for you Mr. Leland?" Clipper asked in his usually overly optimistic voice.

"Are you sure that you're a private eye?"

"Sure! Would you like to see my license? My name is Clipper. I guess you expected a Sam Spade or James Bond type. They make great heroes, but lousy detectives. I'm a family man. I work at the university and do a little detective work on the side."

"Well, you don't fit my image of a private eye."

"Fine. It was nice talking to you. Do you need help finding your way out, Mr. Leland?"

"Wait, Clipper. I need real help! It's my daughter . . ."

"Oh, I don't handle runaways."

"No, she hasn't run away. I think she is into drugs and I want to help her."

"What do you want me to do?"

"She's a radio-TV major at the university. I want you to check up on her. Follow her. Let me know what she is doing."

"How old is she?"

"Twenty, last May."

"She's an adult then, Mr. Leland."

"She's my daughter, and I think she is in serious danger. She has been so nervous lately."

"Look, I could set up a tail, but she would probably figure out she was followed after a few hours. The university is just not a good place to follow people. Everyone gets to know everyone else in their program too easily. I would stick out like a hooker at a clergy conference. Besides you can only follow people when you can see them. I can't go up to her dorm floor without being discovered."

"Maybe you can use electronics—bug her phone, use a TV monitor when she's going to class. Plant something in her purse."

"What if she leaves her purse in her room? What if she discovers the bug in her phone and misleads us deliberately? What if she has night classes—TV cameras don't show much in the dark. Besides a TV crew is more conspicuous than a regular tail."

"Well, it worked for me, Clipper. I have a video tape of her meeting four young men and exchanging a lot of money for what looks like two little white bags. I shot the tape using remote TV equipment that I rigged at home myself. Do you want to see it?''

"No. You said your daughter was a radio-TV major. I'll bet you even money she found your little trap and set up the scene just to play a practical joke on you. You worry too much. She might be nervous because your constant fretting makes her edgy. Then, too, exams are scheduled for later this week. But if you insist, I'll look into the case.''

"Yes, please do. I don't know how the scene may have been set, but from the way it looks on my video tape she could be in big trouble.''

"Easy, Mr. Leland. I'll call you when I have something reliable to convey. Till then, relax, and control your imagination.''

23:1.1 *The argument for phenomenalism* Philosophers known as phenomenalists argue that, strictly speaking, people perceive only sense data. The argument has two stages: First, recall the argument from illusion, in Chapter 22, involving the elliptical appearance of a circle. If what you experience is elliptical and the circle is round, then what you experience is not the circle, but an appearance only. Phenomenalists have called such an appearance a sense datum. The second stage is the argument from continuity. As your angle of vision changes from seeing an elliptical shape to seeing the circular shape, there is no discontinuity. When the circle looks round to you, it does not have anything about its visual character that proclaims its reality. If seeing mere appearance changed to seeing things as they really are, you would expect a break in the sequence of experiences. However, there is no break. Its absence makes it unlikely that previously you were seeing one kind of thing (a sense datum) and now another kind of thing (a physical object). Phenomenalists use this two-stage argument to show that we experience only sense data. Isn't it intellectually simpler not to suppose that there is some other kind of entity—a circle—

How could a phenominalist use this situation to help support the claim that we perceive only sense data?

which you are seeing from one angle when you see sense data from all angles and there is no break in your experience?

 PHILOSOPHER'S WORKSHOP

The Incorrigibility of Sense-Data Statements

H. H. Price (b. 1899), a twentieth-century British philosopher, devoted considerable attention to the problem of perception of the external world. In the following passage from his *Perception,* he presents the view that statements about sense data are incorrigible.

When I see a tomato there is much that I can doubt. I can doubt whether it is a tomato that I am seeing, and not a cleverly painted piece of wax. I can doubt whether there is any material thing there at all. Perhaps what I took for a tomato was really a reflection; perhaps I am even the victim of some hallucination. One thing however I cannot doubt: that there exists a red patch of a round and somewhat bulgy shape, standing out from a background of other colour-patches, and having a certain visual depth, and that this whole field of colour is directly present to my consciousness. What the red patch is, whether a substance, or a state of a substance, or an event, whether it is physical or psychical or neither, are questions that we may doubt about. But that something is red and round then and there I cannot doubt. Whether the something persists even for a moment before and after it is present to my consciousness, whether other minds can be conscious of it as well as I, may be doubted. But that it now *exists*, and that *I* am conscious of it—by me at least who am conscious of it this cannot possibly be doubted. . . . Analogously, when I am in the situations called "touching something," "hearing it," "smelling it," etc., in each case there is something which at that moment indubitably exists—

a pressure . . . a noise, a smell; and that something is directly present to my consciousness.

This peculiar and ultimate manner of being present to consciousness is called *being given*, and that which is thus present is called a *datum*. The corresponding mental attitude is called *acquaintance, intuitive apprehension,* or sometimes *having*. Data of this special sort are called *sense-data*.[1]

[1]H. H. Price, *Perception* (London: Methuen and Co., Ltd., 1932), p. 3.

23:1.2 *The advantage of phenomenalism*   Phenomenalists see a great advantage in asserting that we can be aware of only sense data; namely, that present-tense statements about sense data appear to be incorrigible. Although you may doubt that the distant mountains are really purple, there seems little doubt that what you now observe *seems* purple to you. Although you might be mistaken about the properties of things themselves, it seems difficult to be mistaken about how things seem, appear, or look.

The case study illustrates a similar contrast. Arthur Leland expressed confidence in his ability to find out about his daughter's activities through hidden video-taping equipment, which shows her exchanging money for what looks like two little white bags. Mr. Leland infers she is dealing in drugs. The detective points out the corrigibility of statements about what Mr. Leland's daughter is really doing. However, statements about what appears on the tape, that is, how the daughter's behavior *appears*, seem far less open to doubt.

23:1.3 *Phenomenalist analysis*   Thinking we can be certain about our sense data, phenomenalists relate the existence of physical objects to the experience of sense data. If they are closely related, then we might be in a position to claim knowledge of the former. This claim is the intellectual motivation of phenomenalism.

Phenomenalists believe that statements about the existence of physical objects can be analyzed into statements about sense data. For example, a statement that a physical object exists is the same thing as a set of statements that certain sense data are available to a normal observer, under standard conditions, from a certain view. That is, the phenomenalist would analyze a statement about the existence of a physical object into a conjunction of statements. Each statement in this conjunction asserts that an observer would have certain sense data from some point of view; and the totality of all the statements in the conjunction would exhaust all the perspectives from which the physical object might be sensed.

For example, "There is a philosophy book on my desk" is a statement about a physical object. Phenomenalists would analyze this statement into a conjunction of statements like: "To an observer sitting in the chair there are booklike sense data of such and such shape, color, and so forth" and "To an observer in the doorway there would be booklike sense data of such and such shape, color, and so forth" and "To an observer looking in the window there are booklike sense data, and so on." This, of course, is not an exhaustive analysis of the statement about the book. Its complete analysis would include statements describing all the sense data available from all possible perspectives. Phenomenalists have never offered a *complete* analysis of a statement about a physical object into sense-data statements, but they argue that in principle such analyses could be made. The phenomenalists maintain that what we mean when we talk about physical objects is that we attain different sensory experiences from various different and specific perspectives. Talk in terms of physical objects is merely a shorthand way of coordinating the many possible statements about our actual or possible sensory experiences.

23:1.4 *The foundationalist character of phenomenalism* Foundationalists insist that any system of knowledge must be developed from incorrigible statements and valid inferences from them. Phenomenalism exhibits both of these foundationalist characteristics, claiming first, that we perceive sense data exclusively, because of the supposed incorrigibility of statements about them (23:1.2). Second, the analysis of statements about physical objects into sense-data statements may be understood as securing the relationship between the two, the former following validly from the latter (23:1.3).

23:2.1 *Criticisms of phenomenalism* Some philosophers take exception to the phenomenalist's failure to provide *complete* analyses of any statements about physical objects. They argue that unless complete analyses are provided, there may well be important but undetected characteristics of physical objects that cannot be translated into sense data. Furthermore, if a complete analysis cannot be given, then the phenomenalists fail to establish the synonymy of a statement about a physical object with a set of sense-data statements, thus indicating the impossibility of their own program.

23:2.2 *Public objects* One feature of physical objects that seems problematic for the phenomenalist is their public character. Physical objects are "public" in the sense that many people can perceive them at the same time. But sense data are supposedly private. So statements about sense data cannot have the same meaning as those about physical objects, unless statements about the privately observable are synonymous with those about the publicly observable.

To phenomenalists when we say that two persons perceive the same physical object, we mean that they have *similar* sense data relating to that object. Critics point out, however, that two sets of sense data from a given vantage point (or more or less the same vantage point) may mean double vision, not necessarily two observers. For example, suppose you had sight in both eyes and focused your vision on an object about ten feet away. Now without changing your visual focus, hold up at arms length a finger or pencil between your eyes and the object. You should now see the finger or pencil in double. Of course there is only *one* object out there. Contrast that example with the case of two people standing side by side, each looking at a distant object. They each see the object as one object, but if you were to have access to both of these visual experiences simultaneously, it could seem as though you were again experiencing double vision. The phenomenalist has no way of distinguishing between these two cases; but surely we want to be able to say that inferences about objects based on experiences of double vision are probably mistaken, whereas similar inferences supported by the observations of two different perceivers are probably true. The charge that phenomenalists cannot distinguish between mistaken and true statements relating to sense data is serious, for how could we distinguish an adequate analysis from an inadequate one? And further, how can we account for the public character of physical objects in terms of private sense-data statements?

23:2.3 *Identifying standard observations* In order to understand the next two criticisms of the phenomenalist's position, it is necessary to recall their insistence that the inferences from sense-data statements to claims of knowledge based upon them must be valid. The criticisms to follow suggest that according to the phenomenalist's own analysis, there can be no knowledge of the existence of physical objects.

If any sense-data statements are going to entail statements about the physical world, they must be the statements of *normal* observers observing under *standard* conditions. But persons may be mistaken about whether or not conditions under which they are observing *are* standard. They may mistakenly believe that the lighting is standard lighting, when in fact it is not. They may believe that they have an unobstructed view, when in fact there is a medium such as a distorting lens or a haze. In the case study, the detective expresses concern about the reliability of data gathered by the TV camera at night when the lighting is nonstandard. Moreover, even if a person could be confident that he or she was a *normal* observer yesterday (which is itself open to doubt), it at most makes it probable (not certain) that the person remains normal while making observations today. Thus people can be mistaken about whether or not they are normal observers and the conditions in which they are observing are standard, even if they cannot be mistaken about the sense data themselves. In other words, the fact, if it is a fact, that people cannot be mistaken about their present sense data, is not sufficient to guarantee that they have the data, or even part of the data, appropriate to ever knowing the existence of a physical object—for there is room to doubt that a given observer is a *normal* observer working under standard conditions. Thus, the phenomenalist has not met the validity requirement.

23:2.4 *Lack of validity*   Given the apparently unlimited number of perspectives on and experiences of physical objects, it would be true that persons are always only experiencing some of the sense data appropriate to particular physical objects. The inference from statements about this limited set of experiences of the object to statements about the existence and character of the object itself, therefore, could only be (regarded as) inductively "justified," but not valid, as the phenomenalists require. The experience of the remaining sense data, which would be relevant and necessary in order to secure a valid inference to the present existence or character of the object, would always be beyond the experiencing subject. Lacking validity, the inference from statements about the evidential base to claims of knowledge fails to meet the phenomenalists' requirement.

23:2.5 *Continuity of objects*   In 23:2.2 we noted the phenomenalist's difficulty in accounting for the public character of physical objects. Phenomenalists also have a difficult time accounting for the commonly accepted presumptions that physical objects exist continuously and have relatively constant properties through time. Our experience, after all, indicates a constancy in physical objects, and our ordinary way of talking about physical objects is built on these presumptions. For example, when you call a towel a towel it means that it is a physical object of the sort that does not suddenly vanish, explode, or change into a cat. We would not know exactly what to say if it did. In calling it a towel we presume that it will not change in these or other radical ways. That is, we ascribe continuity of existence and relative constancy of physical properties. When we call something a physical object we intend to refer to a kind of object that persists through time even if we or others are not perceiving it—which suggests that we don't intend to refer to sets of sense data. Given that there are gaps in our experiences of objects and yet there are constancies in their appearances, many philosophers find it reasonable to suppose that there is something beside the sense experiences themselves that is responsible for the constancy, namely, the constant physical object itself. Without such a supposition, one unacceptable to the phenomenalists, many find the continuity and constancy in experience to be remarkably coincidental and unaccounted for by phenomenalists.

Physical Objects and Continuity

People have wondered about the implications of the view that physical objects are bundles of sense data, given that all observers may leave the presence of some object. The eighteenth-century philosopher, George Berkeley (1685–1753), replied that indeed there is always at least one observer, God. Another English philosopher, John Stuart Mill (1806–1873), tried to avoid postulating any constant observer.

I see a piece of white paper on a table. I go into another room, and though I have ceased to see it, I am persuaded that the paper is still there. I no longer have the sensations which it gave me; but I believe that when I again place myself in the circumstances in which I had those sensations, that is, when I go again into the room, I shall again have them; and further, that there has been no intervening moment at which this would not have been the case. . . . The conception I form of the world existing at any moment, comprises, along with the sensations I am feeling, a countless variety of possibilities of sensation; namely, the whole of those which past observation tells me that I could, under any supposable circumstances, experience at this moment, together with an indefinite and illimitable multitude of others which though I do not know that I could, yet it is possible that I might, experience in circumstances not known to me. These various possibilities are the important thing to me in the world. My present sensations are generally of little importance, and are moreover fugitive: the possibilities, on the contrary, are permanent, which is the character that mainly distinguishes our idea of Substance or Matter from our notion of sensation.[2]

---

[2]John Stuart Mill, *An Examination of Sir William Hamilton's Philosophy (1865)*, as excerpted in John V. Canfield and Franklin H. Donnell, Jr., eds., *Readings in the Theory of Knowledge* (New York: Appleton-Century-Crofts, 1964), p. 457.

23:2.6 *Corrigibility of sense-data statements*   As we have seen, phenomenalists believe that sense-data statements are incorrigible, but some critics contend that statements about what seems, what appears, or what looks to be the case are not incorrigible after all. They point out that statements like "The mountain looks blue from here" are public, not private, statements. It presupposes that current viewing conditions are standard, so that it is legitimate to reply, "Only when the clouds are very heavy, as they are today." Statements about what seems to be the case are statements about what the evidence is most plausibly taken to strongly indicate. These statements, too, are corrigible. You can, for instance, object that if you look at the evidence more fully or scrutinize it more carefully, you will see that things do not seem as someone says they seem. Thus, for example, in the case study Mr. Leland in effect says that his daughter seems to be buying drugs. However, it is imaginable that a closer look at the video tape would lead one to a different conclusion, for example, that she seems to be buying two marshmallows or white mice which look from a distance like, but are clearly different from, bags of drugs.

23:3 *Summary* In this chapter we have examined the phenomenalist's attempt to respond to the skeptical criticism of claims about knowledge of the physical world. The phenomenalist holds that people are perceptually aware of nothing but sense data. The foundationalist character of phenomenalism is indicated in that they believe that statements about present sense data are an incorrigible basis from which the inference to statements about physical objects can be deductively valid. This foundation is based on the phenomenalist's view that statements about physical objects are reducible to statements about sense data. Critics of phenomenalism argue that it (1) may fail to supply a complete analysis of statements about physical objects, (2) fails to give an adequate account of the public character of physical objects, (3) fails to note the corrigibility of claims of knowledge based upon sense-data statements because of the corrigibility of claims to being normal observers in standard conditions, (4) fails to note that the inference from statements about sense data to statements about physical objects can only be inductively justified rather than deductively valid, (5) fails to give an adequate account of the continuity and constancy of physical objects, and (6) fails to note the possible corrigibility of sense-data statements themselves.

EXERCISES for Chapter 23

1. Phenomenalists have constructed a two-stage argument to support the conclusion that what persons are aware of in perception are always sense data (23:1.1).

    a. State the conclusions of each of the two stages of their argument.

    b. After checking your answer to *a*, state the premises used in support of each of these conclusions (22:1.3 and 23:1.1).

    c. Below are two objections to this argument. For each objection, identify what premise in the phenomenalist's argument is being attacked.

      A. If I look at someone's face through a campfire, it looks blurry and rippled. No matter how I move, the face looks the same so long as I keep the campfire between my eyes and the face. But as soon as I see the face with the campfire out of my line of vision, it's not blurry or rippled anymore.

      B. When I look at a penny from the side, what I see has the character of appearing elliptical. Now a penny is round, to be sure, but it also has the character of appearing elliptical from certain angles. So the fact that what I see has the character of appearing elliptical hardly proves that what I see is something other than a penny.

    d. How would you defend phenomenalism against each of these objections? Or do you think an insuperable problem has been presented? Could you show that it was insuperable?

2. In the Workshop quotation, what efforts does H. H. Price make to support the view that sense-data statements are incorrigible (23:1.2)?

3. Below is a list of assertions, some maintained by phenomenalists *(P)* and some by their critics *(C)*.

    a. Mark them *P* and *C*, respectively.

      A. A statement about a physical object is equivalent to a conjunction of statements about sense data.

      B. The inference from any finite number of sense-data statements to a statement about a physical object can involve error.

      C. Statements about sense data are beyond doubt.

      D. Knowledge can be based on inference only if the inference is valid.

      E. The statement that a certain observer is normal and making observations in standard circumstances is open to possible doubt.

      F. There is a constancy and continuity in the existence of a physical object which is not mirrored in the occurrence of sense data.

    b. Distinguish the statements that address the issue of incorrigibility from those addressing the issue of validity.

    c. In the quotation presented in 23:2.5, how does Mill defend phenomenalism against F?

    d. What is your evaluation of the strength of Mill's defense?

SELECTED ANSWERS for Chapter 23

1. a. (1) When I experience an illusion, what I perceive is not a physical object. (2) If I do not perceive a physical object in an illusion, then I never experience a physical object in perception.

    c. The phenomenalist assumes that there is no "break" when we move from illusory to nonillusory experience. A attempts to describe how such a break actually exists; B attacks the phenomenalist's assertion that what one sees in looking at a penny from different angles has two, contrary characters.

2. Price (1) contrasts what I can doubt about my seeing a tomato with what I am certain of in seeing a red patch; (2) contrasts what I can doubt about the red patch with what I cannot doubt; and (3) provides examples (pressure, a noise, a smell) of the kind of awareness that he claims to be indubitable.

3. a. A, C, D: *P*; B, E, F: *C*.
    b. C, E: incorrigibility; A, B, D, and F: validity.
    c. Although the occurrence of the sense data is not constant or continuous, nor is their content, the *possibility* of the occurrence of the sense data has the same permanence ascribed to physical objects.

24

Contextualism and Perception

Is nothing less than absolute certainty sufficient for knowledge of the physical world? Some philosophers take exception both to the skeptic's demand for certainty and to the phenomenalist's willingness to accept that demand. They argue that such standards are artificially high, imposing the wrong model in our search for knowledge. Although agreeing that certainty may be unattainable, they suggest that genuine knowledge of the physical world is still possible. These contextualist philosophers offer a different model of knowledge, being willing to settle for less than incorrigible evidence and valid inference. In this chapter we will examine the contextualist alternative to foundationalism. After reading Chapter 24, you should be able to

- Provide an argument for the rejection of sense data.
- Present arguments that neither incorrigible premises nor valid inferences are necessary for knowledge.
- Criticize the contextualist approach to knowledge of the physical world.

THE CASE OF ROGER STEEL

"Please tell the court your name and occupation."

"I'm Roger Steel. I'm a night orderly at Sparrow Hospital."

"Do you recall the morning of December 24th?"

"Yes I do," Roger told the lawyer. He had already told his story so many times to the police, the insurance investigators, and the lawyers that he had virtually memorized his description of the events.

"Then, in your own words, tell the court what you saw as you drove home from work."

"I left the hospital at 7:15 a.m. As I drove east on US-14 I saw three men run out of the gas station at the corner of Jefferson and US-14. Then one ran back in and fired two shots. He came out again and joined the others. They ran to an old blue Ford and drove down Jefferson."

"Is one of those men here today?" asked the prosecutor with boastful expectation in her voice.

"Yes, the fellow sitting there in the green suit."

"Let the record show that the witness has pointed to the defendant," said the prosecuting attorney. "No further questions, your honor."

"Mr. Libbey, does the defense wish to cross-examine the witness?"

"Most assuredly, your honor," said Julius Libbey as he crossed to stand directly facing the witness. "How long had it been, Mr. Steel, since you had slept?"

"I usually sleep from 8 a.m. till about 4 p.m. But on the 23rd I had a doctor's appointment at 1 p.m., so I guess I had not slept since noon on the 23rd."

"So you had been awake for about nineteen hours. I guess you were rather tired that morning after having worked all night."

"Yes, I was."

"Don't you think that your fatigue might have hindered your ability to make observations by that hour?"

"Objection!" broke in the prosecuting attorney.

"Overruled, the witness will answer," said the judge.

"Yes, I was tired, and I guess it might have been a bit of a problem. When I get tired I tend to get nearsighted, you know."

The prosecuting attorney shifted in her seat, as she felt her witness's credibility being artfully destroyed.

"Yes," said the defense attorney. "And it was dark at that hour, too. There were cars coming the other way with their headlights shining in your eyes. It was snowing that morning and you probably had the wipers going. Am I right?"

"Why, yes. It was quite hard to see the road that day. I remember driving with my face up close to the wheel to see better. Most of my windshield was covered with road dirt splashed up by the big trucks on US-14. I had to keep using the window washer."

"Yes, Mr. Steel. It must have been very hard to see, and hard to hear, too. I mean, with the defroster fan blowing and the radio on. It was on, wasn't it?"

"Why, how did you know?"

The prosecuting attorney groaned audibly.

"Could you give a detailed description of the other two men whom you saw that morning. They were men, weren't they?"

"I think they were men. But they could have been women. You know how in winter people get so bundled up you can't tell for sure. Anyway, no, I couldn't describe them at all except to say that they were short. Might even have been teenagers."

"Well, Mr. Steel, you did identify the defendant. When you were driving by the corner of Jefferson in the dark at 40 mph through the snow and oncoming headlights, you looked into the gas station and saw this man fire two shots. Didn't you?"

"No, I didn't see in the station at all. Couldn't see in; there were no lights on in the station. No, I heard the shots and saw a figure come running out."

"Then, you're not absolutely sure that the person you saw run out had fired the shots you claim you heard?"

"No, I can't say I am actually, now that I think about it."

"Then, Mr. Steel, you can't really be sure that the man sitting there in the green suit was the person you saw on the dark wintery morning when you were so tired. Can you?"

"Wait! Yes! I'm sure about him! I can see it in his eyes."

"Your honor, the defense has no further questions."

"Does the prosecution wish to ask anything on redirect?"

"No, your honor. You may dismiss this witness."

24:1.1 *The contextualist alternative* Contextualists begin by questioning the phenomenalists' arguments for the existence of sense data. They maintain that the illusions of which the phenomenalists make so much can be adequately explained without supposing that there must be an entirely new kind of entity in the universe. Instead, one can talk about differences in the conditions of the environment or of the observer. For example, they argue that differences in the psychological or physical state of the observer can account for hallucinations. It is not necessary to assume that hallucinatory experiences have special, occult objects, because such conditions can be brought about by fever, drugs, madness, or religious reverie. Even things like fear, anxiety, or sleeplessness may account for hallucinations.

Although these considerations can provide an alternative account of hallucinations with a vividness matching that of ordinary perceptual experience, this account does not respond to the phenomenalist's argument from continuity (see 23:1.2). However, J. L. Austin has shown that this argument is not as compelling as it first seemed. The fact, Austin argues, that a person might on occasion fail to distinguish a hallucination from an actual physical object does not entail that the same person will, in other circumstances, be unable to distinguish them. Failure to distinguish two things does not entail that they are in principle indistinguishable.

Whereas differences in the condition of the observer (for example, tiredness or drunkenness) are used by critics of phenomenalism against the argument from hallucination, differences in the condition of the environment or in the position of the observer may be used to account for illusions proper or the differences of perspectival relativity. The phenomenalist arguments from perspectival relativity and illusions proper rely on the assumption that things cannot appear to be other than what they are. Thus, for example, what you *see as* elliptical cannot *be* a round circle. Phenomenalists argue that you have seen something, a sense datum, which having a different shape, cannot be the circle. But Austin argues against the assumption that things cannot look other than the way they are by claiming that you are seeing a circle which looks elliptical from your perspective. To treat the elliptical *appearance* as itself an entity different from the circle is unjustified. In speaking of the appearances of things, we are speaking of how those things appear from whatever position or perspective we may have. The suggestion that we are indeed only encountering private sense data looks suspicious when we consider that the appearances are indeed public. That is, anyone can assume the same perspective and see the object as it appears to us. In fact, the elliptical appearance of the circle can be captured on film.

The same arguments can be applied against the arguments from illusion proper. In such cases the appearances are once again public. Critics argue that distortions in shape or color may be fully accounted for in terms of the lighting conditions, the distance from the object, or the medium through which the object is being observed. The purple appearance of the mountain in the distance, for example, is a public appearance and not a private entity. Others can observe the same purple cast to the mountains, and that purple cast may be recorded on film. The purple appearance is explainable in terms of distance and atmospheric conditions.

Attack on Incorrigibility

J. L. Austin (1911–1960) was one of the most influential philosophers in the "Ordinary Language" movement. These philosophers hoped to show how philosophical problems originate from confusions about how words are used, leading to false assumptions. Once these false assumptions were identified, the problems they generate were regarded as dissolved. One such assumption, according to Austin, is that there are basic statements that are incorrigible.

There isn't, there couldn't be, any kind of sentence which as such is incapable, once uttered, of being subsequently amended or retracted. . . . I may say "Magenta" wrongly either by a mere slip, having meant to say "Vermilion"; or because I don't know quite what "magenta" means, what shade of colour is called *magenta*; or again, because I was unable to, or perhaps just didn't, really notice or attend to or properly size up the colour before me. Thus, there is always the possibility, not only that I may be brought to admit that "magenta" wasn't the right word to pick on for the colour before me, but *also* that I may be brought to see, or perhaps remember, that the colour before me just wasn't *magenta*. And this holds for the case in which I say, "It seems, to me personally, here and now, as if I were seeing something magenta," just as much as for the case in which I say, "This is magenta." The first formula may be more cautious, but it isn't *incorrigible*.[1]

---

[1]J. L. Austin, *Sense and Sensibilia* (Oxford: Clarendon, 1962), pp. 112–13.

The other major point to be made against the argument from illusion is this: Contrary to the sense datum theorists, there *is* a difference between those experiences that can be relied on to yield accurate knowledge and those that cannot. For instance, when I see something through a campfire and it appears wavy, it is quite possible for me to see that there is a campfire and to be aware that heat and smoke are rising from the fire. It is quite possible for me to observe in this case the discontinuity between the waviness of what is beyond the fire and the nonwaviness of what I can observe in a different direction. I can also correlate this fact with the prismatic effects of the rapidly moving hot gases above the fire. Thus, if I am aware of my perspective, environment, and physical or mental state, then I can note the difference between veridical (reliable) and illusory sensory experiences. In principle, it is possible for people to be aware of differences in perspective and conditions of observation.

The case study illustrates the preceding argument. As the defense attorney systematically undermines the testimony of the witness, it becomes clear that Roger Steel's perceptions were significantly influenced by his own condition and by the environmental circumstances. In fact, on cross-examination, it turns out that Steel was quite aware of being especially sleepy that morning and of the poor lighting and weather conditions which made observation difficult. He is made to look foolish for not having taken into account these difficulties in his crucial testimony. His testimony is easily interpreted as being about the way real persons looked given the circumstances in which they were being observed, and there is no need to conclude that Roger Steel was seeing something other than reality, that is, sense data.

24:1.2 *Epistemological versus psychological certainty*   Philosophers have also taken exception to both skepticism and phenomenalism and their foundationalist insistence upon incorrigibility as the basis for knowledge. Knowledge of the physical world, they argue, is possible without incorrigibility. It is not as if all statements about the physical world are equally unreliable. Within the context of appearance there are some statements about experience that take on a privileged status. Statements where the conditions of both the observer and the observed environment are conducive to generally reliable experience are more reliable than those where the conditions are poorer. It is not that statements based on such experiences are in principle irrefutable; it is simply that in such circumstances there is *no reason to doubt* that the statements are true. That is, there are no clues in the person's observation or information bank that would provide substantial reason for thinking that his or her observation in this particular case is unreliable. The statement, "There is no reason to doubt that they are true," does not mean that psychologically no doubt is present in the person's mind. It is a statement about the quality of the experiential evidence in the circumstances.

The case study illustrates the difference between the two senses of certainty discussed here. At the end of the cross-examination, the defense attorney asks Mr. Steel whether he can really be sure that the man sitting there in the green suit was the person he saw on that dark wintery morning. Incredibly Steel answers that he is positive about his identification. In making this assertion he is reporting on his *psychological* state of conviction about the matter. In contrast, rather than accepting Steel's psychological certainty, the defense attorney has focused the jury's attention on the lack of epistemological certainty, which has to do with the evidential basis for a claim of knowledge. Mr. Steel maintains that he can see the guilt of the defendent "in his eyes," obviously insufficient evidence for Steel's claim. The poor conditions for his original observation have been disclosed: It is clear that there is good reason to doubt Mr. Steel's claims.

24:1.3 *Justified inferences*   Philosophers have also argued that there need not be a valid inference from statements about the evidence for claims of knowledge to the claims themselves. Many have insisted that this demand is too great, and that well justified reasoning is sufficient to establish reliability. Although it is possible in the case of a justified argument for the premises to be true while the conclusions are false, the fact that the argument is justified means that there is no known reason to doubt the conclusion (see Chapter 2). Until a reason to doubt is presented, it is wise to accept as logical the conclusions of justified arguments. When there is reason to doubt the conclusion, then in the view of these philosophers, it would be inappropriate to claim to *know* that which the conclusion states. Philosophers here are maintaining that knowledge is not an "all or nothing" proposition. Short of valid inferences, there are inferences, justified inferences, which provide a sufficient warrant for our claims to knowledge.

Consider, for example, how it would be had Roger Steel been able to observe the crime in better circumstances. Suppose he could have laid doubt to rest at each point where the defense attorney probed to find some weakness in his testimony. For example, suppose he did have a good night's sleep and was feeling especially alert that day. Suppose the crime was committed on a clear, bright day, and Roger was not blinded by the lights of oncoming cars. Suppose his car windows had been recently cleaned. Suppose he had his window rolled down and the radio off and could easily hear the sound of the gunfire. Suppose he was close enough to actually see the face of the defendant. Had conditions been such as we have just described them, a strong argument would have been built supporting Roger Steel's testimony. Now in the absence of reasons to doubt his testimony (for example, that he was biased or a compulsive liar), many philosophers would argue that the reconstructed inductive argument strongly warrants his claim to know that he saw the defendant commit the crime. They would argue that this is the best possible evidence for claims of knowledge about the physical world, and that it would be unreasonable to demand stronger inferences from claims about experience to claims about physical realities.

24:1.4 *Sufficient warrant* Both of the foundationalists' requirements for knowledge are found to be too stringent by contextualist philosophers. The demands for incorrigibility of evidence and for valid inferences are thought to be excessive. Contextualists argue that given the nature and context of observation of the physical world, it is unreasonable to dismiss the possibility of knowledge of that world based on observation simply because incorrigibility and valid inference are unattainable. They argue that a reasonably sufficient warrant for claims of knowledge still remains. Short of incorrigibility, we can still trust as true the statements based on sensory experiences in circumstances where such experiences are generally reliable. Short of valid inferences from evidential statements to claims of knowledge about the physical world, justified inferences are reasonably trustworthy.

24:2.1 *Criticisms of the contextualist approach* The contextualist approach is not without its critics. Foundationalists point out that absolute certainty is not achieved on the contextualist model. Given the ideal of absolute certainty, as is obtained in mathematics, the premises for which the contextualist is willing to settle remain corrigible. Moreover, justified inferences, versus valid inferences, do not by definition guarantee that from true premises only true conclusions are inferred.

Contextualists reply, however, that this objection is begging the question. The contextualist equates "certainty" with there being no reason to doubt. By hypothesis, the evidence as obtained under ideal conditions of observation, and the justified inferences upon which the contextualists would have us rely, leave no reason for *reasonable* doubt. The foundationalist may be accused of dragging in an inappropriate definition of "certainty" in this objection, to which the foundationalist could reply by showing why the model of absolute certainty attainable in mathematics is appropriate for knowledge of the physical world.

24:2.2 *Warrant versus truth* In effect, the contextualist is saying that knowledge amounts to *warranted assertability* — that the assertion of knowledge is warranted when observations are made in certain standard conditions and when justified inferences are drawn. However, the foundationalist may reply that warranted assertability does not entail the truth of that which is asserted. Moreover, because it does not, it follows that knowledge cannot, on contextualist grounds, be distinguished from a warranted *but false* assertion, as in both cases there is warranted assertability. Thus, the character of the evidence and the

Does this cartoon support or challenge a contextualist account of knowledge?

logic of the inference, as these are accepted by contextualists, do not *guarantee* that we have attained knowledge.

For example, you can imagine circumstances in which you would be warranted in asserting that you know there is a new tree in your yard. You have ordered such a tree from a nursery and have seen it delivered and planted in the ground by people who have gotten out of a truck with the name of a nursery on its side. You recognize the personnel from the nursery as the people you spoke with when you went to the nursery to order the tree. They have dug a hole, planted the tree, and proceeded to water it and to brace it against the wind. It looks like the tree you picked out on the nursery lot; it is the same height, the same color, and appears to have the same foliage. You have no reason in such circumstances to doubt that you are seeing a new tree in your yard. Two days later, however, you could find out from a friend that he has played a practical joke on you. He has hired the personnel of the nursery to deliver and plant in your yard a plastic replica of the tree you ordered. Thus, although you were warranted in claiming to know that there was a new tree in your yard, yet there was in fact no tree there. By definition, it is contradictory to suppose that people are correct in *knowing* that something is the case when in fact it is not.

24:2.3 *Unanswered questions* Some critics of the contextualist approach argue that it is incomplete because it provides no account of why the evidences and inferences upon which the contextualist relies should be taken as trustworthy. Just *why* is it that we should suppose that those conditions the contextualist believes ideal for observation are conditions under which perceptual access to reality is obtained? What are the underlying causal conditions that make our perceptions more reliable in such circumstances? What is it about the structure of reality that guarantees those natural regularities in appearances that undergird the use and reliability of inductive inferences?[2] Lacking answers to these questions, the contextualist basis for our claims of knowledge seems to be more coincidental than trustworthy. Although it may be perfectly reliable or trustworthy, the question remains, "Why?"

Foundationalists argue that contextualists must flesh out more systematically their account of knowledge of the physical world. Claims about the reliability of the senses in certain circumstances and the reliability of inductive inferences must be integrated with accounts of the underlying causal and metaphysical conditions of perception and of induction.

24:3 *Summary* In this chapter we have considered a contextualist alternative to phenomenalism as an account of knowledge of the physical world. We have seen how contextualists would have us rely upon perceptions gathered in ideal conditions for observation and upon inductive inferences from statements of our experience to claims of knowledge. We have seen how this view contrasts with the foundationalist demands for incorrigibility and valid inference as made by both the skeptics and the phenomenalists. We have examined criticisms of this contextualist alternative to the effect that (1) it fails to secure certainty, (2) the warranted assertability it endorses is compatible with the falsity of what is so warranted, and (3) as it stands it is incomplete in not providing an account of why the evidences and inferences it endorses are trustworthy.

EXERCISES for Chapter 24

1. In rejecting the introduction of sense data, the contextualist argues for two conclusions: that the adequate description of illusory experiences does not require talking about sense data, and that the argument from continuity fails to establish the alleged continuity between illusory experiences and experiences of the physical world.
   a. What are the contextualist arguments for these conclusions (24:1.1)?
   b. Explain by reference to the argument from illusion why together these contextualist arguments form a complete rejection of sense data (22:1.2 and 23:1.1).
2. a. What is warranted assertability (24:1.4–24:2.2)?
   b. Relate the contextualist view that knowledge is warranted assertability to

---

[2]For a fuller treatment of the systematic approach in philosophy and the process of integrating concepts, see Chapter 32.

the views that the basis of a genuine claim to knowledge need not be an incorrigible assertion, and that the inference from the evidence to the claims themselves need not be valid (24:1.4).

   c. How would a foundationalist criticize the contextualist's equation of knowledge with warranted assertability (24:2.2)?

   d. Describe a case like the one in 24:2.2 — except it should not be a case of deception — in which warranted assertability would *not* amount to knowledge.

   e. What arguments or considerations, beyond those discussed in the text, would you use in defense of either the foundationalist or the contextualist?

3. Below is an imaginary conversation between a foundationalist and a contextualist. The comments are lettered for easy reference. After reading the conversation, answer the three questions that follow.

   A. "Look at two experiences, one illusory, one not. Describe what you experience each time. Those descriptions will not provide a basis for distinguishing the illusion from the physical reality. How, then, can you claim that the one is *certainly* illusory and the other not?"

   B. "Taste two cups of liquid, one coffee, one tea. Describe — as much as you can — what you experience each time (and don't say, 'This is coffee' or 'That's tea'). After you say they're both liquids, describe their temperatures and consistency (none of which distinguishes them from each other), what can you say? But you don't conclude that you can't tell coffee from tea simply because your descriptions of the experiences don't mark the distinction."

   C. "Your analogy doesn't work. After all, illusions actually deceive people, but people don't mistake the taste of coffee."

   D. "Perhaps the most important point for me to make, since you insist on my providing a basis, is that the basis doesn't have to be in the experiences. The basis for distinguishing illusory from nonillusory experiences could be in the condition of the observer, the perspective, or the condition of the environment."

   E. "No doubt we use such bases in ordinary life, but surely they are not adequate. For if they were adequate, people would use them so as actually to distingush illusory from nonillusory experiences. Then they'd never be deceived. But deception is a fact of life."

   F. "The adequacy of a distinction only means that if it is used carefully the distinction will be successfully made. There can be no guarantee that people will always use carefully even a perfectly adequate distinction."

   G. "But what becomes of certainty then? You fail to provide any guarantee that this crucial distinction will be correctly made. On top of that there's no validity to the inference that making the distinction carefully entails making it successfully."

   a. Identify which comments are the foundationalist's and which the contextualists.

   b. With respect to B–G, explain which earlier comment each is responding to.

    c. How would you at this point assess the strengths and weaknesses of the foundationalist and the contextualist approaches to the problem of knowledge of the physical world?

SELECTED ANSWERS for Chapter 24

1. a. For rejecting the argument from continuity, be sure your answer includes the contextualist's separate reasons related to hallucinations in contrast to other illusions.

    b. The argument from illusion contains two parts; each of the contextualist's arguments is related to one of those parts. Do you know which?

2. b. A statement does not need to be incorrigible nor does an inference need to be valid in order to overcome reasonable doubts concerning the statement or inference.

    d. Check the adequacy of your description against these two tests: In your case, did the person claim to know something that was actually false? Was there, nevertheless, substantial reason for believing it true and no reason for thinking it false prior to its actually being known as false?

3. a. A, C, E, and G are the foundationalist's comments.

    b. Each responds to the previous comment, except that D responds to A, not to C.

    c. A full answer would include at least the following points: The contextualist provides an alternative to absolute certainty. The resulting concept of warranted assertability is very useful. Yet it remains unclear how anything less than absolute certainty can guarantee knowledge, a fact that emphasizes the foundationalist's insistance on rigorous thinking.

25

Behaviorism
and Other Minds

People confidently claim knowledge of their own thoughts, emotions, and sensations. Thus, they claim to know their own minds. The philosophical problem of other minds is whether or not it is possible for people to know the thoughts, emotions, or sensations of others. Many philosophers believe that we can have no direct access to the minds of others, but we can infer such knowledge. In this chapter we will examine both the idea that we have only indirect access to other minds and the "argument from analogy," which is designed to support the claim that we can know other minds. We will also examine the contrasting behaviorist view that the argument from analogy is superfluous because we can have direct access to other minds. After reading Chapter 25 you should be able to

- Present the argument from analogy for knowledge of other minds and state objections to it.
- State and explain the structure of the behaviorist response to the problem of other minds.
- State and explain some basic objections to behaviorism.

THE CASE OF SYLVIA JOHNSON

"Sylvia, put down that phone. You can't call your mother! It's stupid to tell her you're pregnant. What could she do anyway except pull you out of school?"

Sylvia's roommate, Karen, was perched on the top bunk amidst pillows, stuffed animals, and geography texts. Sylvia sat at her desk. It was entirely free of books and papers, as it had been for nearly two weeks.

"But I have to call her. I want to get some idea how she'll react to this. I don't know if Mike and I should get married or if I should get an abortion. How can I know unless I talk to her?"

"It won't get you anyplace. You'll see. But go ahead and try if you must." Karen picked up a red note pad and started to compare her lecture notes to the open text that lay at her left.

Sylvia dialed. "Damn it! That makes me so angry!" She slammed the receiver down.

"What's wrong, Syl?"

"Got one of those foolish recordings. 'The number you dialed is no longer a working number. Please check the listings . . .' I wish they would check their junky equipment. Watch, this time I'll dial the same number and get through." She dialed.

"Hello, Mom? Hi, this is Syl. How have you been?"

"Fine, honey. How about you?" The phone was so loud that Karen could monitor the whole conversation.

"Just great, Mom. I've been really hitting the books this week."

"That's good honey. Your Dad will be proud."

I wonder if he even cares sometimes, Sylvia thought. *I doubt that my old fun-and-games Joe College Dad ever saw the inside of a book when he went to college.*

"Tell Dad I said hello. He's at work now, isn't he?"

"Yes, you know your father, always putting in more hours than he should for what they pay him. But then he always did overwork, even in school."

There she goes again with that overworked, underpaid routine. I wonder if she knows that Dad stays at the office partly to get away from her and her constant talk about money, Sylvia thought.

"Mom, do you have Dr. Smith's phone number handy?"

"Yes, I know it by heart. It's area 419, 372-2119. What's the trouble dear, your prescription run out?"

I wish I had been faithful to it, Sylvia thought. *Then Mike and I wouldn't have the problem we're facing now.*

"No, Mom. Not yet. Besides I really don't need the pill. I'm not even engaged." *I hope she buys that one.* "No, I want to call the doctor about my foot. It's been hurting again."

"Well, you stay off the tennis court for a while. By the way, how's Mike?"

"He's doing very well. He's interviewing this week in Cleveland; might get a job in hospital administration there."

"That's wonderful. Well, you wish him my best. I hope they make a good salary offer. You know how little your Dad makes for all the years he's put in at the plant. It's a crime . . ."

"Yes, it really is, Mom. I know how hard it must have been for you. Well, I've got to go and study some more. Take care."

"Bye, Syl. We love you."

"Goodbye," Sylvia hung up.

"I told you it wouldn't do any good to call her, Syl," said Karen. "You and Mike are going to have to deal with the problem yourselves."

"Karen, I wonder if she even hears me sometimes. She's so easy to lie to when she gets wrapped up in her own little world. All she talked about was Dad's salary. I think I'm going to try to call Mike in Cleveland. What do you think, Karen?"

"You go ahead if you want. I would wait till he gets back to campus myself, but I don't pretend to know what kinds of pressures you're feeling. I'm going to the library to study. That way both of us can have a little privacy tonight."

25:1.1 *The argument from analogy*   If you are hit by a rock, you know that it hit you because you feel the pain. Suppose that the rock hits you in the back of the leg. In all likelihood you would reach down to rub the place where you were hurt. Your facial expression would probably become grim, and a tear might come to your eye. You might cry out in pain. In such circumstances it is reasonable to say that you know your own mind in claiming that you are in pain. Let us take this as but one fairly typical example of knowing your own thoughts, emotions, or sensations.

Knowing the mind of another seems to be a quite different business. When another person is hit by a rock, we don't feel the pain. Yet, it is quite common for us to claim that we know the other person in such circumstances is in pain. If we don't feel their pain ourselves, then how is knowledge of that person's pain possible? This is a specific instance of the general question: How can we know the minds of others? Many have suggested that we infer things about another's mind by analogy to our own experiences. Let us examine this *argument from analogy.*

In general, to argue from *analogy* is to argue on the basis of similarities between cases. Imagine two things, call them *A* and *B*. Imagine that *A* and *B* are very similar in that both have the characteristics *X*, *Y*, and *Z*. Suppose then that *A* is found to have the additional characteristic *Q*. By analogy one could argue that it is reasonable to suspect that *B*, if inspected, will be found to share characteristic *Q*.

In the case of my own experiences of pain and the like, I observe a correlation between my experiences and my behaviors. Thus, in the

---

 PHILOSOPHER'S WORKSHOP

The Argument from Analogy

During his long and eventful career, Bertrand Russell (1872–1970) wrote a number of very influential philosophical works. His genius went beyond philosophy into both mathematics and literature. He was able to express with great clarity some of the most obscure intellectual theses. In *Human Knowledge: Its Scope and Limits* he presents the argument from analogy with striking simplicity.

The behavior of other people is in many ways analogous to our own, and we suppose that it must have analogous causes. What people say is what we should say if we had certain thoughts, and so we infer that they probably have these thoughts. They give us information which we can sometimes subsequently verify. They behave in ways in which we behave when we are pleased (or displeased) in circumstances in which we should be pleased (or displeased). We may talk over with a friend some incident which we have both experienced, and find that his reminiscences dovetail with our own; this is particularly convincing when he remembers something that we have forgotten but that he recalls to our thoughts. Or again: you set your boy a problem in arithmetic, and with luck he gets the right answer; this persuades you that he is capable of arithmetical reasoning. There are, in short, very many ways in which my responses to stimuli differ from those of "dead" matter, and in all these ways other people resemble me. As it is clear to me that the causal laws governing my behavior have to do with "thoughts," it is natural to infer that the same is true of the analogous behavior of my friends.[1]

[1]Bertrand Russell, *Human Knowledge: Its Scope and Limits* (New York; Simon & Schuster, 1948), p. 483.

example above, I observe an association of my feeling pain with my changed facial expression, my moving to rub the area where the rock hit me, and so on. I further notice that there are other bodies in this world that are quite similar to me in their basic physical structures. In certain circumstances they behave in ways similar to how I would behave in similar circumstances. Thus, for example, I notice that when the other bodies are struck as I was, similar facial expressions and bodily movements take place. And though I do not feel the other's pain, I infer by analogy from the similarities in our behaviors that the person is experiencing pain.

This argument from analogy can be generalized to cover the entire range of mental states of other people. There are behaviors associated with feelings of joy, sadness, fear, anger, and so on. There are expressions associated with knowledge, belief, doubt, and other cognitive states. As people are familiar with their own behaviors when they enjoy these cognitive, emotional, or sensory states, they are in a position to infer from observation of similar behaviors and expressions in others to the existence of similar states of mind.

In the case study, Sylvia Johnson's mother infers on hearing Sylvia tell her certain things that Sylvia is thinking those things as well. It is reasonable to suppose that Sylvia's mother is thinking analogically. But then, how right is she about Sylvia's true thoughts? If she is wrong, is it because of weaknesses in her analogy?

25:1.2 *Weakness of the argument*   At best, arguments from analogy lead to conclusions that are probably true; they do not guarantee that their conclusions must be true. As we have seen in the case study, however, it is possible for the premises of an analogical argument to be true, that

©King Features Syndicate, Inc., 1964

Does the inference she draws provide certainty? knowledge?

is, that what Sylvia says is similar in many ways to what her mother may on other occasions have said, and for the conclusion to be false, that is, Sylvia is not thinking what her mother infers that she is thinking. Persons can say one thing while thinking something else.

Philosophers have found special weaknesses in the use of the argument from analogy for knowledge of other minds. The argument would be much stronger if there were a large number of cases that could be observed, that is, a large number of persons whose specific behaviors are associated with specific mental states. However, the only correlations that serve as the basis for the inference are those of the single case of one particular person, the one who also happens to be offering the argument. Thus, only one case serves as the basis for the inference. Moreover, the behaviors of those offering the arguments and those whom they are observing may vary a great deal. How can the people making the inferences know that those differences in behaviors are not indicative of differences in mental states?

This question brings us to the second major difficulty. Whereas other analogical arguments can be confirmed by observing other cases, by hypothesis the analogical inference to other minds cannot be confirmed by discovering new cases. The minds of others are thought to be inaccessible. It is taken to be analytically true that we cannot feel another's pains or think another's thoughts. Indeed, if it were possible for persons to check firsthand on the reliability of their analogical inferences in such cases, there would be no need for the argument from analogy in the first place. What is it about the difference between arguments from analogy in the case of other minds and ordinary arguments from analogy that makes the former not merely different but unacceptable? One difference seems to be in the noninterpersonal nature of the conclusions inferred when using analogical reasoning to determine another's state of mind. If there is no possible way of publicly confirming or disconfirming claims like "He is in pain" or "She is angry," there may be no way to show that such claims are true or false. Or reversing the argument, if we are sure that in some cases they are true or false, how, in those cases, do we know that?

25:1.3 *Solipsism*   Another criticism is that we can construct another argument, with at least as much strength as the one from analogy, that indicates that the person who offers the argument is the only being in existence with a mind. When the person offering the argument is hit by a stone and rubs the place of impact, that person feels pain. Whenever that person sees another being hit by a stone and rubbing the place of impact, the observer feels no pain. Whenever the person speaks, thoughts have typically been in his or her mind. When that same person observes others saying words, no thought need have been in the mind of the observer. Given that in almost every case (every case except my own) in which I see behaviors of sensation, emotion, or cognition I experience no corresponding mental state, the evidence apparently supports the conclusion that everybody else is a robot and that I alone have feelings and thoughts which accompany the behaviors and vocalizations being observed. This thesis, called solipsism, is captivating. Perhaps there is only one mind in existence, the one reading these words! Everything, including these words are manufactured by mindless automatons. How could one know that this is not so?

25:2.1 *The behaviorist's alternative* Recall the foundationalist ideal of knowledge: incorrigible statements of evidence leading by valid inference to absolutely certain claims of knowledge. In a foundationalist's view, if we were to claim knowledge of other minds, we should like to approach this ideal of knowledge and certainty as nearly as possible. Let us suppose that we have resolved the problem of knowledge of the physical world to the foundationalist's satisfaction. If we have accomplished this much (no small task), then with a certainty to satisfy the foundationalist we could know how and in what circumstances others behaved. For example, in the case of a person being hit by a rock, we could know both the circumstances of the event and the behaviors the person manifests upon being hit. We have, then, obvious premises for claims of knowledge about the mind of the person who has been hit. The main problem with argument by analogy seems to be that it is inferentially weak. Even given true premises, the conclusion inferred by analogy could easily be false. Some philosophers have tried to overcome this difficulty by trying to establish a valid (not simply strongly warranted) inferential relationship between what we can know about human behavior and our conclusions about human mental states. This is the strategy of those philosophers known as behaviorists.

25:2.2 *Behaviorism* The basic thesis of behaviorism is that all claims about mental states are in principle reducible to claims about human behaviors. Thus, to claim to know the mind of another is to claim to know something about the behavior of the other. Suppose, for instance, that you assert that another person wants something. To see the connection between that person's wanting that thing and that person's behavior, consider this: Would you claim that the person wants that something if the person made no attempt to get it when there were no constraints upon him or her? Suppose further that what the person wants would be freely given and that the person acknowledges that there are no unforeseen undesirable consequences of having what he or she claims to want. If the person did nothing, made no attempt to get it in these circumstances, it becomes implausible to say that the person wants that thing. Behaviorists maintain that the person's wanting that something comes to nothing more nor less than that person's engaging in "appropriate" behaviors in relevant circumstances. Behaviorists hold, in general, that all mental states can be tied to specifiable sets of behaviors and circumstances. Thus, to say to another person that he or she is having certain thoughts, emotions, or sensations, is to say nothing more then that he or she is behaving in certain ways under certain circumstances.

25:2.3 *Alternative interpretations* Behaviorism could also be construed as the descriptive or empirical thesis that mental states, examined carefully, are nothing more than behavioral states. But many scientists, especially psychologists, regard behaviorism not as a descriptive theory but more as a stipulative definition (see Chapter 3). They claim that it is preferable, in terms of ease of study, to regard minds as simply complexes of behaviors. In either case, behaviorism clearly indicates that it is unnecessary to use the argument from analogy to talk about other minds. The principal advantage of behaviorism, no matter how it is defined, is this: As one asserts claims of knowledge about other minds, one is asserting something that is in principle subject to public observation; there is no need to make any inference from these public phenomena to something that is in principle not observable.

25:3.1 *Objections to behaviorism* One of the main objections to behaviorism centers upon the possibility of deliberate deception. If for any reason people wish to pretend to be thinking, feeling, or sensing something they are not, the pretense will be strongest if they behave in these circumstances exactly as they would if their mental states were what they are trying to make people believe. The case study depicts Sylvia Johnson deliberately behaving deceptively in telling her mother certain things about what she is thinking in order to lead her to believe that she is thinking one thing when she is really thinking another.

Deceptions are also possible concerning a person's emotional states and sensations. The strength of a good actor or actress lies at least in part in the ability to create deceptions of these kinds. Yet in such cases, the observer sees on the basis of subsequent behavior that the other person was being deceptive at the time rather than accurately presenting his or her mind.

The reductive analysis of claims about mental states to those about behaviors thus seems inadequate because the mental claims that behaviorists attempt to reduce are in fact open ended. It may be that the only reason for saying "He did not feel pain" is that the person about whom the statement is made said later that he was not feeling pain despite his earlier, deliberately deceptive behavior to the contrary. In the case study, Sylvia Johnson's conversation with her roommate gives the lie to her conversation with her mother. Her spoken statements to her mother, as behaviors, are not sufficient warrant for claims to knowledge about her mental state. In general, many philosophers object that behaviorism in no way accounts for the prominence of speech as the mechanism for self-definition of mental states and as a vehicle for deception through behavior.

25:3.2 *First-person versus third-person statements*   Behaviorists offer the reductive analysis of mental statements just described as a reply to the argument by analogy and as an attempt to give meaning to third-person statements about the mental states of others, like "She really feels happy about that." They find the hypothesis of the inaccessibility of other minds unacceptable, in part because it seems to have the consequence that third-person statements about the minds of others must then be regarded as not interpersonally confirmable (see 25:1.2). Critics of behaviorism, by contrast, argue that possible clarification of the meaning of third-person statements about mental states comes at the price of offering an analysis of first-person statements about mental states (like "I really feel happy about that"), which is implausible. In the behaviorist's understanding, whatever a person would say about his or her own mental state, for example, "I am in pain," would be a statement about his or her own behavior and circumstances. Yet persons frequently make such first-person statements without having to *observe* their own behavior and note their circumstances. Still, the first-person statements seem reasonable. For example, when the person who is hit with a rock says, "I'm in pain," it is humorously implausible to suppose that this statement is made on the basis of the person seeing the rock hit his or her body and observing himself or herself jumping up and down in agony, holding the place of impact, and so on.[2]

There are other features of first-person statements about mental states that complicate the behaviorist's efforts to give an account of them. A person's statement that he or she has a headache is in itself sufficient to substantiate the fact that the person has a headache—even

---

[2]Alternatively, some behaviorists claim that the first-person statement should be interpreted as *behavior* rather than as a *statement about behavior*. This claim is criticized in 15:2.4.

if the person does not exhibit any nonverbal confirming behavior and circumstances are not of any specific special sort, for example, the person having recently been drunk. First-person statements about one's own mental states are frequently taken as *authoritative* in themselves, rather than as inferences based on other self-observations. The problem for the behaviorist is that first-person statements about one's own mental states are both reasonable to make and authoritatively independent of one's actual behavior, yet such statements are supposedly about behaviors and surrounding circumstances or at least equivalent to statements about behaviors and circumstances.[3]

25:3.3 *Corrigibility of first-person statements* The argument from analogy accepts the difference between first and third-person mental statements. In particular, the presupposition of this argument is that first-person, present-tense mental statements (for example, "I smell smoke") are incorrigible. The argument is designed to approximate, as closely as possible, the ideal of incorrigibility for third-person mental statements (for example, "She is proud"). Behaviorism is an alternative means to the same end. A number of behaviorists, as well as advocates of the argument from analogy, have held that the standard for judging third-person mental statements is the incorrigibility that can be secured for first-person claims about one's own mental states. Thus, behaviorism may be attacked for subscribing to the idea that first-person claims of knowledge about mental states are incorrigible if it should turn out that they are not.

Many philosophers today allow that even first-person statements of cognition and statements of emotion can be corrigible. When a person is so angry that he or she is emotionally out of control, his or her behavior belies denials like "I am not angry." Thus, assertions about present emotional states may be corrigible. When persons say "I am thinking of Albany" and then proceed to describe Albany as being in New Mexico and as having a desert climate with nearby mountains, so that the person's description otherwise fits Albuquerque very well but not Albany, then it is clear that contrary to what the person is saying, he or she is not thinking of Albany at all but rather is probably thinking of Albuquerque. Thus first-person statements about present cognitions are corrigible.

Many philosophers cling to the idea that first-person statements of pain and other sensations are incorrigible, but it can at least be suggested that pain has characteristics. For instance, aches are dull and often tend to be persistent. Therefore, the person who says that he or

---

[3]In Chapter 15 this reduction was discussed in terms of the analysis of mental statements into physical statements.

she has a sharp, shooting ache in the knee may be mistaken. Most persons accept this argument, although many think it is just a verbal point. All that is being suggested here, however, is that the presupposition that behaviorists share with advocates of the argument from analogy concerning the incorrigibility of first-person mental statements is questionable.

25:4 *Summary* In this chapter we have dealt with two proposed solutions to the problem of knowledge of other minds. First, the argument from analogy was introduced and critically assessed. It was found to be an argument insufficient to meet foundationalist demands for certainty. Behaviorism was introduced as a foundationalist attempt to reduce statements about mental states to statements about behaviors and surrounding circumstances. The behavioristic account of other minds was criticized for (1) failing to account for the possibility of deliberate deception, (2) offering an implausible account of the meaning and authority of first-person statements about mental states, and (3) sharing with the argument from analogy the questionable presupposition of the incorrigibility of first-person statements about mental states.

EXERCISES for Chapter 25

1. Below is a list of statements on which skeptics, solipsists, proponents of the argument from analogy, and behaviorists would take different stands. For each statement, mark whether it would be regarded as true, false, or unknown according to each of the four views.

Skep.   Sol.   AAnal.   Beh.

A. Only one mind exists.
B. A person is most immediately and directly aware of his or her own mental states.
C. Knowledge of other minds is possible.
D. Inductive knowledge of other minds is possible.
E. Knowledge requires validity of any and all inferences.
F. There is an inferrential gap between statements about others' behaviors and circumstances and statements about their minds.
G. Statements about the behaviors and circumstances of others can be accepted as unproblematic in stating the problem of other minds.

   2. a. State the premises and conclusion of the argument from analogy as presented by Russell (25:1.1).
      b. On what grounds has the argument been criticized (25:1.2)?
      c. How do you evaluate the strength of these objections?
      d. Are there other objections you would make against the argument?
   3. a. State the behaviorist's position on wanting (25:2.2).
      b. What is the foundationalist character of that position (25:2.1)?
      c. Do you see any objections to the position that if a person wants something, then if it is offered to the person and if the person is unconstrained and acknowledges that there are no unforeseen undesirable consequences of having what he or she claims to want, then the person will take what has been offered?
      d. What (other) objections would you raise against behaviorism?
      e. Although some philosophers have said that one's statements about one's present pains are corrigible, others have replied that only verbal mistakes are possible. In 24:1.1, Austin argues that verbal mistakes about whether something is magenta need not be trivial mistakes. What corresponding premises might Austin.use if he were to argue that mistakes about one's present pains need not be trivial?
      f. Evaluate this Austinian argument.

SELECTED ANSWERS for Chapter 25

	Skep.	Sol.	AAnal.	Beh.	
1. A.	U	T	F	F	
B.	T	T	T	T	(According to the behaviorist, a complex inference is necessary for knowledge about others; against behaviorism it is urged that the same must be true of oneself.)
C.	F	F	T	T	(Note the differences in the reasons of the parties who agree here.)
D.	F	F	T	F	
E.	T	–	F	T	(The solipsist need not take a position on this question.)
F.	T	T	T	F	
G.	T	T	T	T	(That is, the skeptical focus is on E, not the issue of incorrigibility.)

   3. a. The behaviorist makes two claims: A person's really wanting something *entails* that the person behaves in certain ways in certain circumstances; and a person's wanting something *means nothing more* than a complex fact about the behavior of the person in various circumstances.
      b. Assuming that statements about a person's wants mean no more than a

complex statement about the person's behavior, then *valid inferences* from the person's behavior to the truth about the person's wants will be possible.

c. One objection, raised by several philosophers, is that whenever a behaviorist refers to what people say (including what a person "acknowledges"), there is a problem about whether the person is speaking sincerely. Where a behaviorist would like to give a behavioristic analysis of sincerity, these philosophers, taking the objection one step further, have insisted on the open-ended character of assertions about a person's sincerity (25:3.1).

e. Austin tries to describe several different mistakes one might make in calling something magenta. Take each mistake he suggests and try to find a parallel one.

26

Contextualism and Other Minds

Behaviorism as a solution to the problem of other minds accepts the skeptic's foundationalistic standards for such knowledge. In this chapter we will examine the views of contextualists, who join with the behaviorists in rejecting the argument from analogy and the idea that other minds are in principle inaccessible, and yet who take exception to the behaviorists' demands for absolute certainty. We will then examine criticisms of the contextualist approach. After reading Chapter 26, you should be able to

- Explain the meaning of "'Same' does not mean the same" as it applies to the problem of other minds.
- Outline a contextualist approach to resolving the problem of other minds.
- State two criticisms of a contextualist theory of knowledge of other minds.

THE CASE OF JEROME AND DANNY

The annual Labor Day clothes sorting was going on at the Ripp household. Dad was in the girls' room with Annie and Audrey trying to make sense out of their school wardrobe. Mom was doing the same with the two boys.

"Jerome, you don't fit in these pants any more; your legs are too long. I'll have to buy you some new jeans for school. These old ones are Danney's now."

"But Mom, those were my favorite."

"Sorry, Jerome, they don't fit you anymore; now they belong to Danny. I'm giving them to him."

"Why do I always have to get Jerome's dirty old pants?"

"They may be old for Jerome, but they're new for you, Danny. We can't afford to buy new clothes when we already have things around that look good and fit well."

"I have 37 cents from cleaning the dishes. I'll buy my own new pants."

"You are welcome to, when you get older. But you need more than 37 cents, Danny."

"Mom, are you going to give away my shirts, too?"

"No, Jerome. You and Danny wear the same size shirts. Your upper bodies are the same. I'll have to buy each of you new shirts; almost all the ones you have are too small." *Maybe I should call Grandma and suggest clothing for birthday gifts,* she thought.

"What about socks?" Danny said.

"Same with socks. You boys have the same size feet, too."

"My feet aren't the same as Danny's," said Jerome, laughing. "Look, my feet are on my legs and his are on his."

Danny started to giggle, too.

Even Mom smiled, but she really was in no mood for silliness. "I mean that you each wear the same size socks. If it weren't that your legs were so long, Jerome, you and Danny would be the same size in almost everything. But you wear size 12 slim pants and Danny wears 10 regular."

"Am I going to get ten pairs of pants?" Danny asked. He started to giggle again. Jerome joined in the laughing. Mom didn't answer. She sensed that the boys weren't really interested in explanations.

26:1.1 *Other minds and ordinary language* Two contemporary philosophers, John Wisdom and Ludwig Wittgenstein, have attempted to resolve the problem of other minds by starting with an examination of the language used to pose the problem and the language ordinarily used to claim knowledge about the mental states of others. They interpret philosophical problems, such as this one, as symptoms of subtle and deeply rooted intellectual confusion.

26:1.2 *Wisdom on confusions about knowledge*   John Wisdom (b. 1904) argues that there is plausibility to the skeptic's position on other minds only because the skeptic, and those disturbed by the skeptic's argument, tend to think of such knowledge in accordance with inappropriate models. In Wisdom's view, the problem of other minds may be dissipated when this tendency is overcome. The "cure" for this intellectual malady is found through an insightful examination of our ordinary ways of talking about knowledge.

There are very many things, besides the truths of mathematics and logic, we have no hesitation in saying that we know for certain. The variety of claims of knowledge reflects the variety of ways in which we come to know things. If any one way of coming to know is taken to be the only acceptable method for gaining knowledge, then the other ways of knowing could never measure up as yielding "genuine" knowledge at all. Skepticism about knowledge of other minds is removed only when we realize that knowing other minds is *not* like knowing mathematical or logical truths nor is it precisely like knowing something through analogy.

Wisdom urges that no one method or paradigm of acquiring knowledge could capture the richness of human knowing, which includes knowing such things as mathematical and logical truths, truths about the present state of the physical world, other minds and their mental states, the past, or the theoretical entities that are the subject matter of contemporary physics. If we avoid using only one kind of knowledge as the chief model, we will not prejudge how many varieties of knowledge are possible. We will recognize that what constitutes knowing one sort of thing is different from what constitutes knowing some other sort of thing.

Our ordinary language reflects this rich variety, and in part, it is through the examination of ordinary language that we can learn to appreciate it. Close examination of the statements we use to express our knowledge of the mental states of others will reveal the similarities and differences between them and those used to express other kinds of knowledge.

26:1.3 *Wittgenstein on "having the same pain"*   Ludwig Wittgenstein (1889–1951) believes we can learn a great deal from examining the way in which we use language to talk about mental states and about sameness. " 'Same'," Wittgenstein says, "does not mean the same." What does he mean? Consider two people who have the same build—

which means that they have the same proportions in their bodily features, arms, abdomens, and legs. Persons have different builds to the extent that there is a difference in the slope of their shoulders or the girth of their calves or in the proportional length of torso and legs. For example, we do not say that Jerome's build is different from Danny's because Jerome's is the build of his body whereas Danny's is the build of his. If that was part of what made one person's build different from another, then we could always say that no two persons have numerically the same build. But that is simply not part of what we mean when we discuss whether or not two people's builds are the same. Jerome's suggestion is humorous because it is a well understood, mistaken interpretation of the language. Wittgenstein uses such consideractions as these to urge that when we talk about two people's builds being the same, no distinction between qualitative versus numerical sameness is applicable.

Now consider the question, "What makes two pains the same?" There is a way of speaking in which we can say that there is a particular pain that a person gets from eating ice cream too fast. The pain is often somewhat duller if you grit your teeth while it continues. That particular pain tends to rise up into the head and dissipate within a minute. Once you see that this is an acceptable description, you can understand the assertion that two people can have the *same* pain.

𝒢 PHILOSOPHER'S WORKSHOP

Subtleties of Language

Ludwig Wittgenstein (1889–1951) sensitized philosophers to the subtle yet important nuances of our ordinary ways of talking. The following excerpts from the *Philosophical Investigations* and *The Blue Book* illustrate his craft.

If I should say, "His coat is too large for him," without having made the correct identification, I can be corrected by being told, for example, "that's not *his* coat; it's his father's." Now contrast this case with one in which I notice a child's build and comment, "His build is rather angular." Here the step of identifying an owner plays no part: I need only observe the child. And so my statement could not be challenged by someone saying, "The build *is* rather angular, but are you sure it's *his*?" This question would be senseless because, *intended as a particular kind of challenge to my statement*, it wrongly presupposes that in the language game played with "his build" there is a move of the same kind as in the language game played with "his coat," that is, the identification of an owner.[1]

It is possible that, say in an accident, I should . . . see a broken arm at my side, and think it is mine when really it is my neighbor's. . . . On the other hand, there is no question of recognizing a person when I say I have a toothache. To ask "are you sure that it's you who have pains?" would be nonsensical. Now, when in this case no error is possible, it is because the move which we might be inclined to think of as an error, a "bad move," is no move of the game at all. (We distinguish in chess between good and bad moves, and we call it a mistake if we expose the queen to a bishop. But it is no mistake to promote a pawn to a king.)[2]

---

[1] Ludwig Wittgenstein, *The Philosophical Investigations*, II, trans. G.E.M. Anscombe (Oxford: Basil Blackwell, 1953).

[2] Ludwig Wittgenstein, *The Blue and Brown Books* (Oxford, Eng.: Oxford University Press, 1958), p. 67.

Wittgenstein is arguing that in some relevant sense pains are not private, unshared things. Our language about pain is a public language. Using an image of pains as private, unshared things transforms knowledge of the pains of others into something mysterious and inscrutable. The fact that we speak of people having the same pain indicates to Wittgenstein both that the pains are not inaccessibly private and that philosophical skepticism about other minds is ill-founded.

26:2.1 *Contextualism and other minds*   Contextualists note that people can and do make assertions about the minds of others, and that we do distinguish between those who know something about another's mental states and those who do not. They describe the basis for this distinction by examining the evidence that people who know the mental states of others have.

Contextualists follow John Wisdom in not modeling knowledge of other minds upon knowledge of other kinds of things. In doing so, they shun justifying their claims in terms of incorrigible premises and valid inferences, abandoning the foundationalist ideal which motivated both the skeptics and the behaviorists. They simply describe what we call "knowledge" of another person's mind, telling us that this can be and is distinguished from what in our ordinary language we call "unfounded belief or ignorance" of another's mental states.

What kinds of evidence must we have in order to rightfully claim to know the minds of others? Essentially, we must know about the circumstances in which the other persons find themselves, their behaviors, and what they have said. The relevant circumstances can be described in many different ways; for example, given the circumstances depicted in the case study you can make a reasonable claim about the mother's frame of mind. Moreover, because a person's future statements and behaviors may significantly alter the overall pattern of their lives, pronouncements about the minds of others must remain tentative; that is, claims of knowledge about other minds will neither involve inferential necessity nor incorrigibility. That we recognize the possibility of changes of this kind implies that there can be evidence of such changes in a person. In this view, we can describe what conceptual skill is required to distinguish between really knowing something about another mind and merely having an opinion about it. We can also identify reasons to doubt the reliability of certain claims. In the absence of reasons to doubt, contextualists would argue, it is reasonable to accept and to make claims of knowledge about other minds.

26:2.2 *Knowledge of other persons*   One example of a contextualist's approach to the problem of other minds is the view of P. F. Strawson, another contemporary philosopher. Strawson's view is a subtle but important alternative to behaviorism. Behaviorists wish to define statements about the mental states of others in terms of statements about their behaviors. Specifically, to describe the behavior of someone in pain is equivalent to describing the pain. Strawson wishes to deny that there is a definitional connection between another's mental states and any behaviors. Nevertheless, he maintains that based on observations of their behavior, we can reasonably *ascribe* mental states to others. Thus, although another person's pain is not to be identified with the behavior itself, it is on the basis of observing that behavior that we reasonably ascribe pain to that person. Moreover, what we ascribe to the other person (a pain) is exactly what we might claim to have ourselves, however different the bases of our assertions might be.

The concept of the *ascription* of properties is crucial to Strawson's perspective. In the case study the mother may be understood as ascribing the possession of Jerome's pants to Danny. To describe Danny as being the right size so that Jerome's pants now fit him is not the same as saying that the pants now belong to Danny. To say, as the mother does, that the pants now belong to Danny is to do something more than merely describe his physical characteristics. It is to make effective a transfer of possession and make a claim about ownership, which to be sure, is based upon such physical characteristics. In a similar fashion, Strawson holds that to ascribe mental states to persons is more than merely to describe their behaviors, although such ascription may be based upon these behaviors.

Another parallel is this: Just as being a certain size does not

ON BEING ONESELF

Good-resolution grook

If virtue
can't be mine alone
at least my faults
can be my own.

© 1970 by Piet Hein.

What ascriptions are made in this rhyme?

entail that Jerome's pants are now Danny's, so for Strawson persons behaving in certain ways does not necessarily imply that they have certain mental states. Strawson holds that there is a conceptual connection between certain behavior and being in certain mental states. However, he does not construe this conceptual connection as a definitional connection in the way behaviorists do. Rather, he maintains that when we are learning how to use our language so as to make statements about the mental states of others, we also are learning to ascribe mental states to others on the basis of observed behavioral patterns. The concept of pain that we use in our ordinary language is a concept of ascribed pain. As such, it is a concept of pain that is conceptually tied to publicly observable behavior.

✒ **PHILOSOPHER'S WORKSHOP**

Ascriptive Predicates

P. F. Strawson (b. 1919) explains and defends his ascriptionist approach to the problem of other minds in his book *Individuals*. In the following passage he discusses terms for mental states, calling such terms P-predicates. Strawson argues that we cannot successfully distinguish our use of words for the mental states of others from our use of those same words for our own mental states.

It is in this light that we must see some of the familiar philosophical difficulties in the topic of the mind. For some of them spring from just such a failure to admit, or fully to appreciate, the character which I have been claiming for at least some P-predicates. It is not seen that these predicates could not have either aspect of their use, the self-ascriptive or the non-self-ascriptive, without having the other aspect. Instead, one aspect of their use is taken as self-sufficient, which it could not be, and then the other aspect appears as problematical. So we oscillate between philosophical scepticism and philosophical behaviourism. When we take the self-ascriptive aspect of the use of some P-predicates, say "depressed," as primary, then a logical gap seems to open between the criteria on the strength of which we say that another is depressed, and the actual state of being depressed. What we do not realize is that if this logical gap is allowed to open, then it swallows not only his depression, but our depression as well. For if the logical gap exists, then depressed behaviour, however much there is of it, is no more than a sign of depression.

If, on the other hand, we take the other-ascriptive uses of these predicates as primary or self-sufficient, we may come to think that all there is in the meaning of these predicates, as predicates, is the criteria on the strength of which we ascribe them to others. Does this not follow from the denial of the logical gap? It does not follow. To think that it does is to forget the self-ascriptive use of these predicates, to forget that we have to do with a class of predicates to the meaning of which it is essential that they should be both self-ascribable and other-ascribable to the same individual, where self-ascriptions are not made on the observational basis on which other-ascriptions are made, but on another basis. It is not that these predicates have two kinds of meaning. Rather, it is essential to the single kind of meaning that they do have that both ways of ascribing them should be perfectly in order.[3]

[3]P. F. Strawson, *Individuals* (London: Methuen & Co. Ltd., 1959), 106–7.

It is perfectly compatible with Strawson's view that persons may nevertheless be mistaken in ascribing mental states to others. That is, he is a contextualist in acknowledging the open-endedness of such ascription and the possibility of claims of knowledge being overturned in this area.

26:3.1 *Contextualism and caution* The contextualist's approach to the knowledge of other minds itself emphasizes the need for circumspection and caution. We should not rashly claim to know a great deal about another mind. The contextualists base this caution on human experience with how a given set of circumstances can be described in a variety of ways and how people can change the patterns of their lives by what they do and say. In the contextualist's view, given the kind of evidence that is available together with the possibilities for deliberate deception on the part of others, secure knowledge of other minds is not easily attained. However, this caution does not undermine their claim that there are many ways of knowing things and that other minds may be known with varying degrees of certainty.

26:3.2 *Warranted assertability* A contextualist account of knowledge of other minds is comparable to one of knowledge of the physical world (see Chapter 24). That is, contextualists seem to be speaking in both cases of warranted assertability. However, it is quite possible that our ascriptions about the mental states of others may be warranted, given the available behavioral evidence, while at the same time those claims may be false. For example, a person might authoritatively deny that an ascription we had made concerning his or her state of mind was correct. Since to know something seems definitionally connected with that something's being true, it seems odd, if not wrong, to say that warranted assertability of statements about the mental states of others is sufficient for *knowledge* of those mental states. We may be warranted in saying certain things about other minds and yet those things may be false. If that is the case, how can we know for sure? Are such claims of knowledge justified?

Does the contextualist have an adequate answer to this question?

26:3.3 *Contextualists and being critical*   Philosophers also maintain that the contextualist approach is philosophically uncritical in two important regards. First, it describes our conventional standards for distinguishing between knowledge and mere opinion about other minds as those standards are embedded in our ordinary language, but it does not critically evaluate those standards. That in our ordinary language we call certain statements "knowledge of other minds," and distinguish those statements from mere "expressions of opinion," may not be a justification for the claim that we are correct in so doing. Perhaps there would be a lot less successful deception in the world if more rigorous standards were adopted. That is, perhaps more rigorous behavioral tests or even inspections of the nervous systems of others could be used in certain cases if it were crucial that surer (more "genuine") knowledge be attained, for example, in lie-detector tests.

Second, the concepts we use to talk about other minds and to express what we claim to know about them are not scrutinized for their appropriateness, but are merely accepted. For instance, in a given community there might be a standard embedded in the language for making the following assertion about somebody else's mind: "This person is possessed by the devil." Yet suppose there is no devil; that is, suppose that the concept of the devil that is operative in this language is not a concept of a real entity, although the language users in the community believe that it is. Whatever standards may be operative in the ordinary language of that community for making the judgment that a person is possessed by the devil, the statement may not be true. In general, we may be inaptly describing what is going on in the minds of others, and the inaptness of our ordinary description may be misleading to us in practical as well as philosophical matters. For instance, suppose we assert that a person has a mental disorder, rather than being possessed by the devil. Our theory or concept of this mental disorder may imply that it has been brought about in such a way that treatment through electric shock is the only possible means of overcoming it, whereas in fact it may be a condition treatable only through a change in diet, or perhaps by exorcism. Thus, our very language for describing the situation, even if applied and used according to the accepted standards of our community, may lead us down mistaken paths. Therefore, our concepts, as well as the standards for their use, may be mistaken or misleading.

26:4 *Summary*   In this chapter we have examined the contextualist approach to the problem of knowledge of other minds. It rejects the foundationalist demand for certainty in this area as excessive and inappropriate. Wisdom, Wittgenstein, and Strawson all draw upon analysis of our ordinary language concerning knowledge of other minds to provide understanding of the nature and limits of such knowledge. Critics of this contextualist approach question the apparent identification of this knowledge with warranted assertability of statements about other minds. They take exception to the contextualists' lack of critical circumspection in describing both the standards and concepts embedded in our ordinary language concerning knowledge of other minds.

EXERCISES for Chapter 26

1. a. Below is a set of assertions attributing sameness. In each case state the characteristics relevant to whether or not the things in question are the same.

    A. You are doing the same body-building exercises I did yesterday.

    B. My father is dying of the same disease his father died of.

    C. This is the room we had last week's meeting in.

    D. These are the same contextualist arguments we read in Chapter 24.

    E. This melody is the melody from Glen Miller's theme song.

    F. My viewpoint on abortion is the same as Thomas Aquinas's.

    G. She's wearing the same dress I am.

    H. With Mother's death, both of us kids are experiencing the same grief.

    I. I share your perplexity about how we can get that big couch up that narrow, winding staircase.

    J. When my arm's fallen asleep, I've had that same sensation.

  b. Use at least two of the above assertions to illustrate the meaning of " 'same' does not mean the same."

2. a. Consult a dictionary to clarify for yourself the difference between describing and ascribing. State that difference.

  b. What, according to Strawson, is the basis for assertions about other minds (26:2.2)?

  c. In light of the distinction in 2a, what is ascribed to others in such assertions?

  d. Suppose that a South African white racist says, "Look, you wouldn't ascribe the ability to speak to some thing, no matter how large its vocabulary, if you knew the thing was a parrot. Most people wouldn't ascribe the right to life to some thing, no matter if it could feel pain, if they knew they were talking about a pig. Well, in South Africa we do not ordinarily ascribe higher mental competencies to a creature, no matter how it behaves, if we know we're talking about an African" (black person). How does this speech become an objection to a contextualist approach to the problem of other minds?

  e. If a philosopher's contextualism was not confined to an approach to the problem of other minds—if the approach was generally contextual—how might the philosopher respond to the objection raised in 2d?

3. a. Suppose that in response to 1a (H) someone says, "You two kids may be expressing the same feelings about your mother and about life without her. You may have the same feelings about the way she died, and you may be sympathizing with each other a lot at this point. But it's hard for you even to know your own grief, much less someone else's. Grief may sneak up on one of you in the middle of the night, making you feel an unshared loneliness. Or three months from now one of you may hate your mother for dying. Or ten years from now one of you may feel you don't know how to be a mother: You'll wish your mother had lived to show you how she'd meet your situation. Those can all be parts of grief, parts you don't know about yet. So you can't really know your grief is the same so easily." How does this speech constitute an objection to the contextualist approach to other minds?

   b. If a philosopher's contextualism is general, how might the philosopher respond to the objection raised in 3a?

4. a. Contrast the skeptical objections against the possibility of knowledge of other minds (22:2) with the two objections raised in 26:3.3.

   b. How do the differences in the criticisms illustrate the conception of philosophical progress (1:1.2)?

SELECTED ANSWERS for Chapter 26

1. a. A. A body-building exercise may be defined as a prescribed sequence of movements.

   C. The room's identity is defined by its location, relative to other rooms within a building.

   E. A melody is a certain sequence of tones in a prescribed rhythm. (Pace and instrumentation contribute to the definition of an arrangement of a melody, but not of the melody itself.)

   G. Cut of the dress, kind and perhaps wear of material, colors and their patterned arrangement are all (more or less) pertinent. (Note: "She's wearing my dress, *only in yellow*.")

   I. The perplexity can be expressed in terms of the statements that appear together to describe all the possible ways of turning and moving the couch, given that each implies getting a larger dimension of the couch through a smaller dimension of space on the staircase, given that they are engaged in a common task that frustrates both.

   b. Of all the characteristics listed in the answers above, those in A and E are very similar. (Is the rhythm necessarily prescribed in the exercises?) But all the other pairs show considerable differences. Only in C and G could a numerical versus qualitative distinction be clearly applied.

2. c. Mental states are attributed to other persons.

d. This speech illustrates the problem (26:3.3) of *inappropriate* standards, so that even though the standards are correctly applied, the correctness of the standards is subject to criticism. For instance, one might challenge the fairness of the South African's standards.

e. "My initial answer was based on the assumption that the skeptic's challenge concerned whether or not standards were being correctly applied. I have tried to show how they may be correctly applied. If the question is whether or not the standards are appropriate, I will discuss that new issue instead. What we must do now is to consider the variety of bases upon which standards might be attacked or defended. This is a new problem."

3. a. The attack is, generally, the same as in 2d. What is the correct standard of "same grief"? Here the suggestion is that present manifestations are insufficient to predict future feelings — a matter of concern to a grief therapist, for instance.

4. a. Both the skeptic's premises, about corrigibility and invalidity, and the conclusion, about the impossibility of knowledge, are more general and theoretical.

b. Although problems of knowledge remain, they are not the same problems — as 4a shows — as the skeptic first raised. (Notice that if you lean toward foundationalism and behaviorism with respect to other minds, similar statements might be made. That is, several criticisms of behaviorism urge that in the behaviorist's view a problem of knowledge remains, but not the *same* skeptical problem.)

PERSPECTIVES

ON RELIGION

Many of the humanly most challenging and awe-inspiring issues philosophers have raised relate to the possibility of a divine-human relationship. Humans in all times have wondered: Is there a God? How can we be sure that there is or is not a God? Should a person have faith in God, or would it be better if people renounced faith for the sake of affirming their humanity? What is the place of religion in one's life? What can life's meaning be if there is no God? What could its meaning be if there were a God?

Although they can be read as independent discussions, the five

PART SEVEN

chapters in this part all are directed toward the final issue (raised in Chapter 31): How does faith in God, or religion, relate to the question of the meaning of life? Chapter 30 discusses the tension between rational belief based on hard evidence on the one hand and both the dictates of human action and the value of human freedom on the other. Chapters 27 through 29 set the stage by treating traditional efforts to intellectually establish that God either exists or does not exist.

We can show the relationship of these chapters to each other by the accompanying diagram.

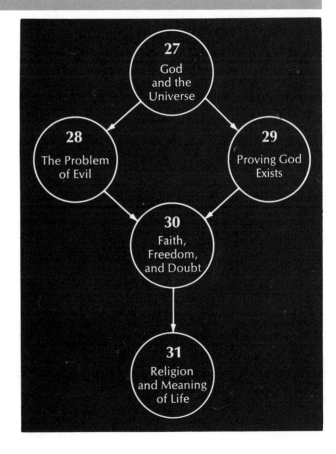

27

God and the Natural Universe

The contemplation, and especially, the fresh discovery of order and organization often provoke a response of awe or wonder, especially when that order is very intricate or grand. For example, when explorers discover in a dense jungle a lost city filled with enormous buildings and monuments covered with extremely detailed ornamentation, they are overwhelmed with a sense of awe and a conviction that the builders must have possessed a highly advanced civilization. People often respond in a similar way to the grandeur of the Milky Way or the intricacy of a honeybee's eye. At the very least, the discovery that something appears to be well organized or consciously ordered suggests the possibility that some intelligent being was or is responsible for that organization or order.

Philosophers who believe in God have tried to construct a philosophical proof called "the design argument," based on observations that there is an abundance of order in the natural universe. They argue that natural order can be explained in terms of an intelligent planner. It is not surprising that many people have found the argument persuasive. Since we all know how order in the human realm results from thinking and planning, it seems very natural to understand order in the wider natural realm in the same way.

In this chapter you will examine the design argument in greater detail. After reading Chapter 27 you should be able to

- **Characterize the use of analogy and explanatory models in arguments in general and in the design argument in particular.**
- **Explain the place of evidence in the design argument for the existence of God.**
- **Explain the tension between the religious conviction that God exists and the view that the existence of God can be proved to be probable.**

THE CASE OF ISADORA AND THE BLASTOCYST

"There are three stages in the development of a baby prior to birth. The ovum stage, the embryonic stage, and the fetal stage."

Click, snap, whir . . . the next slide was pushed into place. It showed a ball of cells; they all looked alike, small and white. The words "Blastocyst" and "two weeks" framed the cluster of cells.

"Here is a picture of what the blastocyst looks like as it moves down the fallopian tube. The inner cells of the blastocyst will cluster into a group from which the baby itself will develop. The blastocyst's outer cells will form into the umbilical cord, amniotic sac, and placenta. As blastocyst cells divide, different body systems will develop. One group will become organized into the nervous system, another the digestive system and so on. . . ."

Click, snap, whir . . . a new picture with the words "embryo" and "six weeks" popped into view.

"Notice the three layers of cells," the professor snapped his wooden pointer against the screen, obviously irritated about something the class knew nothing about. "That outer layer will become hair, skin, and nerve. This middle layer will develop into blood, muscle, and bone. The inner layer turns into the inner organs like the lungs and intestines." His words sounded almost as mechanical as the slide projector.

"Professor Zawirski . . . ah, Professor," came the quiet yet insistant voice of Isadora King.

Another interruption. No doubt Isadora will get us off on some irrelevant tangent again. Oh well, I guess I must answer her. "Yes, Isadora, what is it?" he said not even trying to mask his feelings of anger and exasperation.

"Professor, why do the cells differentiate into the different organs? How do they know which ones to become or how to do it?"

"They really don't *know* anything, Isadora; the messages that program the differentiation are locked into the genetic code carried in each cell. We'll be coming to that toward the end of this course, if we have time."

"Forgive my unscientific use of the word 'know,' but doesn't my original question still have force? How do the cells interpret the message programmed in them?"

"There is no evidence of consciousness in individual cells, thus even the use of the word 'interpret' is inappropriate."

"Okay, I'll take any hint of consciousness out of the question. Why do groups of cells differentiate at all?"

"It's a matter of how we human animals evolved. Those blastocysts that did not differentiate properly either did not survive to be born or were not able to reproduce. Only the ones that did were able to continue to reproduce new generations. The weak, infirm, or malformed could not adapt, could not survive, did not continue."

"Professor, I am fully aware of Darwin's theory of natural selection. Your response presumes that cell differentiation occurs, and so you explain only how one pattern emerged as surviving. My question is different. How did cell differentiation, as a natural process, come to be? Who or what designed the details of the cell differentiation process? If all the cells in the blastocyst carry the same genetic information, what explains the cell differentiation?"

"Isadora, you've just asked two different questions. One is philosophical, the second is scientific. I don't think that I can answer either except by saying that we know *what* happens to groups of cells, not *why* it happens to precisely this or that cell. We also cannot scientifically tell where the apparent design we discover comes from. But here it is."

"That means we don't really know why we have life on this planet at all, right? I mean, we can't really explain why there are animals, plants, DNA molecules, genes, or anything. There really might have been nothing at all, or just a mess of unorganized junk floating around in space."

"Isadora, I really must get back to the topic for today. Let's try to understand what we do have rather than to speculate on why it is here or what might have been instead."

27:1.1 *Evidence of order in the universe*   Given the human quest to understand physical phenomena, questions like Isadora's are both intelligent and revealing. If it makes sense to ask, "Who designed the circuitry in this pocket calculator?" then shouldn't it make sense to ask, "Who designed the process of cell differentiation?"—unless there is something so radically different between human artifacts and natural phenomena that they cannot even be examined by using the same set of questions. The profesoor seems to be saying that Isadora's question is not even an appropriate question. His response, "But here it is," suggests that the apparent order or organization in natural phenomena should simply be regarded as a given. That's the way the universe presents itself to human beings—no further question can be asked, at least in scientific terms. Others, however, go beyond the scientific at this point and affirm that the natural organization evident in the universe is evidence suggesting an intelligent planner at work, just as is the orderliness of the calculator's circuitry. This response has been formulated into what philosophers call the *argument from design*. Here is one statement of the argument:

(1) There is considerable evidence of organization or order apparent throughout the natural universe.
(2) The best way to explain or understand this apparent order is on the model of the order that human intelligence imposes on reality when a person builds or organizes something.
(3) Thus, there probably is, or was, an Intelligent Planner of the natural universe, just as there was or is human intelligence at work in the design of human artifacts.

Using the procedures outlined in Chapter 2, we can examine this argument to determine if it is acceptable. Let's begin by examining the truth of the premises. Can you cite examples of order in the universe that confirm the truth of the first premise?

William Paley, an English religious philosopher, was an influential defender of Christianity in the late eighteenth century. He believed the statement "God exists" needed to be defended in as reasonable a way as possible. In his writings Paley cites numerous examples of different sorts of order, based on the anatomical research of the eighteenth century. Most of his examples involve some sort of adaptation. He is impressed with the results of the process of cell differentiation which amazes Isadora. Each organ of the human body is adapted to the other organs, so that they function in an interdependent whole. Moreover, within an individual organ like the eye, the parts are adapted to and dependent on each other in a very intricate way. For example, Paley observes that the lacrimal glands secrete a wash to keep the eye moist and clean, and that "the superfluous brine is conveyed to the nose through a perforation in the bone as large as a goose-quill." Also the parts of the organ show the adaptation of the organism to its environment. For example, the lens in the eye of a fish is much rounder than that of air-breathing animals; the organ is thus adapted to the different properties of light rays in the water and in the air.

27:1.2 *Criticisms of the evidence*   Paley's argument was criticized by many philosophers, but ironically, the most penetrating criticisms were by David Hume, a half century before Paley's work appeared. Hume and later critics seriously question the quality of the evidence that there is order throughout nature. First, there are many apparent counterexamples to this generalization. Some individual organisms do not have the adaptation that others in the species have. For example, an organ such as the human eye does not always function correctly—to the profit of the optometry profession. Also, organs may be missing or be so misformed as to be unable to function, resulting, for example, in congenital blindness. Some organs common to the species, such as the appendix, seem not to function at all. Also as the environment changes, there may be a lag in the adaptation of the species. If the lag is too great or the species fails to adapt it becomes extinct; and even an organism like the whale, which has successfully adapted to a marine existence, retains useless vestigial legs.

Second, the critics question whether the order detectable in nature really resembles the *purposeful* structure of human artifacts. When Paley says that the lacrimal glands secrete liquid "in order to keep the eye moist and clean," he presumes that this is their purpose.

How clear is the evidence of quality design?

It is not evident, however, what purposes of a hypothetical Designer are served by the order and adaptation in nature. It might be argued that the lacrimal glands or the eye itself has a purpose *internal to the organism*, since the functioning of the organ has an important place in the overall functioning of the total organism. An artifact like a time-piece serves an obvious purpose *of its maker*, but Paley's evidence does not prove that an eyeball (or the whole animal) does.

The debate over the evidence reveals that at least at the present time the evidence we have examined is inconclusive. Some of it suggests order but the order suggested is far from perfect. If we determine that the evidence justifies belief in an Intelligent Planner, what would that planner be like, given the imperfection we detect in the universe? Is the job still incomplete? Is this universe only a false start, an attempt that did not work?

27:2.1 *Argument by analogy*   The second premise of the argument stated in 27:1.1 proposes that we adopt the model of designer to machine to understand the relationship of the Intelligent Planner to the universe. An analogy or model is used to explain a new or poorly understood phenomenon by comparing it with one that has a known explanation. For example, the behavior of gases was at one time explained in terms of a "billiard ball model," because a quantity of gas expanded and contracted like an aggregation of colliding billiard balls. Using a

How do you know something's true purpose?

model raises two questions: "Is it appropriate to use a model or analogy to explain this relationship?" and "Is this particular model the right one to use?" In our case, we must ask if the apparent order in the universe is so poorly understood that appeal to a religious model or analogy beyond our scientific explanations is necessary. Given the explanation of natural selection, which seems to account for some of the counterevidence mentioned above too, perhaps we need not look further. Isadora, however, suggests there is still another question. Why cell differentiation takes place at all, given that each cell has the same genetic composition, has not been explained. Thus, the professor has not satisfied all of Isadora's curiosity, much less her wonder. Perhaps her question is inappropriate. If you think it is illegitimate to raise the question "Who designed all this?" can you explain why?

Let's suppose for the time being that her questions can be raised and that an analogy or model is needed to suggest an answer. How adequate is the particular model being suggested?

 PHILOSOPHER'S WORKSHOP

The Evidence and the Inference

In response to the design argument, one might dispute the quality of the evidence cited or the strength of the inference made. In *Natural Theology* Paley (1743–1805) argues for the existence of God on the basis of evidence in nature. He founds his arguments on anatomical research compiled by eighteenth-century biologists. His most famous argument is that adaptation of organs like the eye to a purpose, and the adaptation of organisms to their environment, provide evidence for the existence of an Intelligent Designer.

The lenses of the telescope, and the humours of the eye, bear a complete resemblance to one another, in their figure, their position, and in their power over the rays of light, viz. in bringing each pencil to a point at the right distance from the lens; namely in the eye, at the exact place where the membrane is spread to receive it. How is it possible, under circumstances of such close affinity, and under the operation of equal evidence, to exclude contrivance from the one, yet to acknowledge the proof of contrivance having been employed, as the plainest and clearest of all propositions, in the other?[1]

The anatomical treatises Paley used were regarded as authoritative and they were standard reading in universities. However, critics of Paley complain that the logical strength of his arguments was challenged in Hume's *Dialogues Concerning Natural Religion* long before Paley stated them.

> But farther, Cleanthes; men are mortal, and renew their species by generation; and this is common to all living creatures. The two great sexes of male and female, says Milton, animate the world. Why must this circumstance, so universal, so essential, be excluded from those numerous and limited deities? Behold then the theogony of ancient times brought back upon us.
>
> And why not become a perfect anthropomorphite? Why not assert present occasion to stick to this agreement? Judging by our limited and imperfect experience, generation has some privileges above reason; for we see every day the latter arise from the former, never the former from the latter.
>
> Compare, I beseech you, the consequences on both sides. The world, say I, resembles an animal, therefore it is an animal, therefore it arose from generation. The steps, I confess, are wide; yet there is some small appearance of analogy in each step. The world, says Cleanthes, resembles a machine, therefore it is a machine, therefore it arose from design. The steps are here equally wide, and the analogy less striking. And if he pretends to carry on *my* hypothesis a step farther, and to infer design or reason from the great principle of generation, on which I insist, I may, with better authority, use the same freedom to push farther *his* hypothesis, and infer a divine generation or theogony from his principle of reason. I have at least some faint shadow of experience, which is the utmost that can ever be attained in the present subject. Reason, in innumerable instances, is observed to arise from the principle of generation, and never to arise from any other principle.
>
> Hesiod, and all the ancient mythologists, were so struck with this analogy, that they universally explained the origin of nature from an animal birth, and copulation.[2]

---

[1]William Paley, *Natural Theology: Evidences of the Existence and Attributes of the Deity* (1802), in Pap and Edwards, pp. 426–27.

[2]David Hume, *Dialogues Concerning Natural Religion*, ed. Burtt, Modern Library of English Philosophy, pp. 719–20.

There are several tests for evaluating a model. In the first place the explanation proposed should be one that we find *familiar*. Paley develops this point at length when he argues that if you came across a watch for the first time and examined its workings and saw that they were adapted to telling time, you would naturally infer that it had a maker. We are quite familiar with the explanation of order in terms of design, and the extension of this explanation to the natural realm fits in with our other beliefs. The model should also be *comprehensive* and yet elegant in its simplicity. That is, as many facts as possible should be brought under the explanation, and the model used to explain the facts should be simple rather than complicated. Although the designer model seems to pass these tests also, there are two other tests that raise serious questions: *predictability* and *falsifiability*. The model should enable us to predict specific facts about the things to be explained, and therefore, should be open to refutation if these predictions turn out to be false. For example, the billiard ball model of gases can be used to predict how gases will behave when they are heated or cooled. It is harder to see how the designer model can be used to make specific predictions in the biological realm.

27:2.2 *The "best" explanation*   The second premise of the design argument is a comparison. It asserts, not only that order is well explained by a designer, but that other models do not explain order so well—which leads us to the question of what other models there might be. Any other such models must be shown to provide inferior explanations if the designer hypothesis is to be established as the best one.

What other hypotheses, then, are there? Indian mythology used the model of animal generation rather than intelligent design; the world was spun out from the bowels of an infinite spider, so that the evidence of order in nature has the same sort of explanation as that in a spider web. Hume offers the atomic model. The cells of organisms are composed of minute particles in perpetual motion that form structures in the ways described by physics and chemistry. The particles form complex (DNA) molecules with the genetic "coding" described by Professor Zawirski in the case study. This model has all the advantages of the designer model—familiarity, simplicity, comprehensiveness—but it has the additional advantage of having great predictive power. The ways in which organisms adapt to their environment could, in fact, be improved by altering the molecular structure of their chromosomes.

At this point the evaluation of the design argument requires careful thought. A defender might reply by saying, "But who designed the process?" This question, however, assumes that the process *was* designed. Since what the defender is trying to show is precisely that the process was designed, it is begging the question to assume in asking the question that it is designed (see 2:2.3).

A skillful defender of the argument, however, will reply somewhat differently. As Isadora shows in the case study, there is an order and an apparent design in the process of cell differentiation. Thus, one may legitimately ask for an explanation of that order. This is true no matter how well cell differentiation and the evolutionary theory combine to explain adaptation, i.e., the particular kind of natural order which Paley sought to explain by the model of a designer. The skillful defender of the design argument will note that a designer model can be used to provide a *comprehensive explanation* of all kinds of natural order; whereas various scientific accounts, which are not so comprehensive, leave some kinds of order unexplained, at least in the present state of our scientific knowledge.

Thus, if the design argument is stated carefully, comprehensiveness will be a comparative virtue of a design model over scientific models. Even so, however, it remains unclear whether this point amounts to an adequate defense of the assertion that the best explanation of natural order will involve a design model. In the first place, we noted above that predictive accuracy is a virtue of scientific hypotheses which the design hypothesis does not appear to share. Second, it is at least plausible that eventually any particular kind of natural order not currently explainable scientifically will become explainable in the future.

27:2.3 *Wrong conclusion* In Chapter 2 we saw that people sometimes wrongly state the conclusion of an argument by proving something different from what they intended to prove. The use that some Christian philosophers have made of the design argument exemplifies this problem. They, including Paley, use the argument as a proof that the Judaeo-Christian God exists. This God, who in traditional theology is defined as unitary, all-powerful, external, all-knowing, and morally perfect, is not necessarily the same as a being that can be called the (an) Intelligent Planner of the natural universe. The conclusion of the design argument is consistent with several religious views and theories about the origins of the universe. It might be that there was a team of designers rather than just one; the designer completed the task of creating order in the world and then expired; the designer is intelligent and powerful but not infinitely so, and the imperfections detectable in living organisms are simply the result of its bungling; finally, the designer had cosmic purposes, but it possesses no ethical or moral attributes at all. These other ways of understanding the hypothesis are incompatible with the Christian understanding of the nature of God, but they all fit the data at least as well. A non-Christian using the argument might appeal to the *principle of parsimony*: More characteristics should not be attributed to the model than are necessary to explain the data. For example, even if an astronaut discovered a watch on Mars, to argue that the Martian timekeeper must be infinitely wise, all-powerful, and indestructible would violate the principle of parsimony.

27:3.1 *God and religious belief*   If we make the reasonable assumption that these religious philosophers are not foolish or dishonest people, then we might begin to ask about the role that belief in God's existence plays in their lives. It is clear that the statement "God exists" is not treated as a tentative one needing confirmation, for the believer is confident that it is true. He or she is not looking for proof to satisfy his or her own doubts. The quest, if there is one at all, is often for a proof that will help satisfy intellectual criticisms others might voice.

 PHILOSOPHER'S WORKSHOP

Parable of the Invisible Gardener

Two people return to their long neglected garden and find among the weeds a few of the old plants surprisingly vigorous. One says to the other, "It must be that a gardener has been coming and doing something about these plants." Upon inquiry they find that no neighbor has ever seen anyone at work in their garden. The first man says to the other "He must have worked while people slept." The other says, "No, someone would have heard him and besides, anybody who cared about the plants would have kept down these weeds." The first man says, "Look at the way these are arranged. There is purpose and a feeling for beauty here. I believe that someone comes, someone invisible to mortal eyes. I believe that the more carefully we look the more we shall find confirmation of this." They examine the garden ever so carefully and sometimes they come on new things suggesting that a gardener comes and sometimes they come on new things suggesting the contrary and even that a malicious person has been at work. Besides examining the garden carefully they also study what happens to gardens left without attention. Each learns all the other learns about this. One says, "I still believe a gardener comes" while the other says "I don't." Their different words now reflect no difference as to what they have found in the garden, no difference as to what they would find in the garden if they looked further and no difference about how fast untended gardens fall into disorder. At this stage, in this context, the gardener hypothesis has ceased to be experimental, the difference between one who accepts and one who rejects is not now a matter of the one expecting something the other does not expect. What is the difference between them? The one says, "A gardener comes unseen and unheard. He is manifested only in his works with which we are all familiar," the other says "There is no gardener" and with this difference in what they say about the gardener goes a difference in how they feel towards the garden, in spite of the fact that neither expects anything of it which the other does not expect.[3]

---

[3]John Wisdom, "Gods," in A. G. N. Flew (ed.), *Logic and Language* (New York: Anchor Books, 1965), pp. 200–201.

The contemporary philosopher John Wisdom illustrates the role of the ordinary Christian's belief in God by his "Parable of the Gardener." Wisdom concludes that the belief in the invisible gardener is not a tentatively held hypothesis, and similarly, belief in the existence of God is not a hypothesis that will be resolved by gathering evidence. The disagreement involves more than just the facts; it goes beyond them to how they are to be interpreted. Although Christians like Paley point to evidence of order and purpose in the world, they do not stake their religious convictions on that evidence.

Some people seemingly hold a belief in God as if it were a hypothesis that could be tested. For example, in the Old Testament, Elijah describes such a crucial experiment to decide whether Yahweh or Baal is the true God:

Let two bulls be given to us; and let [the prophets of Baal] choose one bull for themselves and cut it in pieces and lay it on the wood, but put no fire to it; and I will prepare the other bull and lay it on the wood, and put no fire to it. And you call on the name of your god and I will call on the name of the Lord; and the God who answers by fire, he is God.

Perhaps Elijah's faith would have been shattered if such a test had failed. But Wisdom contends that a sincere Christian today would not regard the failure of God to respond to a prayer as proof of God's nonexistence.

27:3.2 *The religious function of the appeal to design*   For the religious person, the design argument as such is less important, perhaps, than the manner in which the argument is expressed. Believers use it to express an *attitude* toward the world and toward the lives they themselves lead in that world. This attitude is evident in Isadora's question, "Who or what designed the details of the cell differentiation process?" By means of the design argument the believer expresses a preference for a certain picture of the world. The argument thus has a *religious* function distinct from the philosophical one of proving that one belief is more adequate than another. The premise that describes the existence of order evokes an attitude of wonder and awe toward existence which fits in with the attitude the believer has toward God. Like the statement that God exists, the premise of the design argument contains an evocative, noncognitive element.

 **PHILOSOPHER'S WORKSHOP**

Ayer on Religious Language

The contemporary British philosopher A. J. Ayer (b. 1910) argues, in his 1936 book *Language, Truth and Logic,* that religious utterances are unintelligible.

. . . In cases where deities are identified with natural objects, assertions concerning them may be allowed to be significant. If, for example, a man tells me that the occurrence of thunder is alone both necessary and sufficient to establish the truth of the proposition that Jehovah is angry, I may conclude that, in his usage of words, the sentence "Jehovah is angry" is equivalent to "It is thundering." But in sophisticated religions, though they may be to some extent based on men's awe of natural process which they cannot sufficiently understand, the "person" who is supposed to control the empirical world is not himself located in it; he is held to be superior to the empirical world, and so outside it; and he is endowed with super-empirical attributes. But the notion of a person whose essential attributes are non-empirical is not an intelligible notion at all. We may have a word which is used as if it named this "person," but unless the sentences in which it occurs express propositions which are empirically verifiable, it cannot be said to symbolize anything. . . .

It is worth mentioning that, according to the account which we have given to religious assertions, there is no logical ground for antagonism between religion and natural science. As far as the question of truth or falsehood is concerned, there is no opposition between the natural scientist and the theist who believes in a transcendent god. For since the religious utterances of the theist are not genuine propositions at all, they cannot stand in any logical relation to the propositions of science. Such antagonism as there is between religion and science appears to consist in the fact that science takes away one of the motives which make men religious. For it is acknowledged that one of the ultimate sources of religious feeling lies in the inability of men to determine their own destiny; and science tends to destroy the feeling of awe with which men regard an alien world, by making them believe that they can understand and anticipate the course of natural phenomena, and even to some extent control it.[4]

---

[4]A. J. Ayer, *Language, Truth and Logic* (New York: Dover Publications, Inc., 1936), pp. 116–17.

Some critics of religious belief argue that the statement that God exists is altogether cognitively *meaningless*, for religious people will not abandon the belief, no matter what evidence is brought forward. These critics say that such an utterance makes sense only if it is possible to describe sensory observations that would bear out its truth or falsity. Perhaps these critics are taking too narrow a view of how language, including religious language, can be meaningful.

27:4 *Summary*   The evidence in the design argument is relied on to support the generalization that there is order in nature, which is explained by the model of an intelligent planner. Explanatory models or analogies generally try to apply similar explanations to similar phenomena. If the conclusion that there is a designer is a scientific explanation, it must, like other scientific explanations, be treated with tentativeness and impartiality. The argument is criticized on the grounds that the evidence is not strong enough to support the hypothesis of a purposeful designer, that other, perhaps better, hypotheses have not been ruled out, and that the designer model should not be identified with the Christian God. Religious belief in God is not, in fact, a probable hypothesis about the world's order, but a matter of conviction. Statements in the design argument also serve the religious function of evoking and supporting theistic attitudes toward nature—which raises the question of the meaningfulness of these statements, especially when contrasted with other, more neutral descriptions of the universe. The discussion of this relatively poor argument raises the intellectual question, "Are there better proofs, or is the evidence actually against God's existence?"

EXERCISES for Chapter 27

1. a. What evidence of design does Paley cite in the quotation in 27:2.1?
   b. Why does Paley make that comparison?
   c. How are adaptation in organisms and cell differentiation related in 27:2.2?
2. a. What premise of the design argument is Hume criticizing in the quotation in 27:2.1?
   b. What virtues does he attribute to the "generation" model?
3. a. Of the following characteristics, identify those that improve an explanatory model (27:2.1):
      abstractness
      aesthetic beauty
      comprehensiveness
      exactness
      falsifiability of predictions
      familiarity
      parsimony
      pictoriality
      predictive power
   b. Which of those characteristics does the designer model have? Which does it lack?
   c. State in terms of the above characteristics how the following passage attempts to strengthen the design argument (27:2.3):

   "The importance of our assurance, then, that a wise and benevolent intelligence has designed all life is this: by this assurance we are also assured that the efforts of good and righteous people will be well known and duly awarded."

   d. How strong do you feel a designer model is, given 27:2.2?
4. What characteristics of a religious person's belief that God exists can be used to argue that "God exists" is not a scientific hypothesis (27:3.1)?
5. a. What is Ayer saying in the quotation in 27:3.2?
   b. Suppose no evidence of lack of design would prove there is no God. Would that fact itself prove that "God exists" is not a statement?
   c. If "God exists" is not a statement, is it unintelligible?

SELECTED ANSWERS For Chapter 27

1. a. Paley focuses on the exactness of the analogy between the eye and the telescope; he cites the intricacy and the interdependence of structure.
   b. The point of the comparison is to supply evidence for the designer hypothesis.
   c. They are two different kinds of natural order.

3. a. Comprehensiveness, exactness, falsifiability of predictions, familiarity, parsimony, and predictive power.
   b. Comprehensiveness and familiarity are strengths of the design model; lack of predictive power, falsifiability, and parsimoniousness are weaknesses; exactness is a matter of degree.
   c. Including the wisdom and benevolence of the designer is not parsimonious, but the passage urges that this inclusion performs another valuable function by assuring people that the universe is ultimately just. It, thus, would seem to add some predictive power.

5. b. Remember a statement is a sentence about which it makes sense to ask, "Is this true or false?" (See Chapter 2).
   c. It is worth thinking about the different meanings "intelligible" might have and whether or not an exclamation like "Oh to be in England, now that April's there" is intelligible, even though it is neither true nor false.

28

The Problem of Evil

In Chapter 27 we saw how people can look at the order in the natural universe through the eyes of faith and see evidence of God, the almighty creator and benevolent designer of the world. It is possible, however, to take quite a different view of the universe and of the human experience in it. There is evidence of natural and moral evil throughout the world, which has led many people to doubt that there even *could* be a benevolent, all-powerful God. Philosophers have refined this perspective into an argument that there cannot exist any God with the ascribed characteristics of the Judaeo-Christian tradition. This argument is called "the problem of evil."

Many sincere believers are tormented with religious doubts when they confront those natural disasters that insurance companies call "acts of God," or especially, when they encounter personal tragedy. Down through the ages religious philosophers have felt it necessary to respond to the problem of evil, not merely to refute the skeptic, but more importantly, to deepen their understanding of God's purposes. In this chapter you will examine the problem of evil and its philosophical implications for God's existence. After reading this chapter you should be able to

- Define evil, moral evil, and natural evil.
- State the problem of evil as an argument designed to show that God *cannot* exist.

- Assess that argument by reference to classical criticism.
- State the problem of evil as an argument designed to show that there *probably* is no all-powerful and all-good God.
- Critically assess this second formulation of the problem of evil.
- State and explain the difficulties of defining the appropriate data base for the design argument and the problem of evil.

THE CASE OF ERIKA AND THE PUPPY

"Mommy, is Puppy ever going to come home from the veterarian?"

" 'Veterarian,' honey? Say it right: 'vet-er-in-ar-ian.' "

"Veterinarian . . . is Puppy ever coming home? I want Puppy to come home."

"No, Erika, I don't think Puppy will be coming home any more."

"But why?"

"Because Puppy was very sick. The veterinarian had to put Puppy to sleep."

"Do you mean Puppy is dead!"

"Yes, honey, I'm afraid I do mean that."

"I don't like that veterinarian. Why did Puppy have to die? I want Puppy back. I miss him. He was a nice puppy." Tears started to fill her five-year-old eyes and she sobbed in genuine hurt.

"Honey, we have talked about this lots of times. When animals are very, very sick we have to kill them; it's the only thing to do. It's better than making the poor animals suffer."

"Will I ever be very, very sick, Mommy? Will they kill me?"

"No, honey. We don't kill people when they are sick."

"Why not?"

"It's different with animals, that's why."

"But Puppy was my best friend. We would play together and . . . and . . ." the tears took over once more.

"Now Erika, Mommy is busy right now. Must we go through this again? I mean, really, honey, life is hard, and we sometimes lose our friends. . . . Why don't you go out and play? I've got a lot of work to do."

"Honestly, Shirley, can't you be a little more sensitive to her feelings?"

"Daddy, is Puppy really dead?"

"Look, John, if you feel sensitive, then be my guest. I've talked about this with her for three weeks now."

"Yes, Erika, Puppy really is dead. I'm sure going to miss Puppy. He was a good friend to the whole family."

"Speak for yourself, John."

"Erika, let's go outside and talk; Mommy is worried about Grandpa Hutchins right now."

"What's wrong with Grandpa Hutchins?"

"He's very sick."

"Is he going to a veterinarian?"

"No, but he is going to a people doctor in a people hospital."

"Will he die?"

"I think he might die soon, yes."

"I'm going to miss him."

"We all will, honey."

"Daddy, why do things die?"

"That's the way God made the world, honey."

"But it's so sad. Does God want us to cry?"

"I really don't know what God wants. I guess He just wants us to do our best."

"But I miss Puppy. And soon I'll miss Grandpa Hutchins." She started to cry again.

"I know, honey, I know. Here, let me hold you."

"Daddy, sometimes I don't understand God. Grandpa is a nice man. It's not fair."

28:1.1 *The nature of evil* In her pet's death, Erika personally encounters evil. It is hard for her to understand death and reconcile it with her understanding of God. On an emotional level she is dealing with loss; on an intellectual level she is confronting the problem of evil. To understand the force of this problem it is important to first note how the word "evil" is being used.

"Evil" can be defined in two ways. The first is to define it extensionally (see 3:3.4), especially through standard cases or paradigms — including such human actions as lying, cheating, betraying friends or compatriots, killing, raping, and so forth, as well as events due to natural causes like physical pain and mental anguish. Such a definition, by itself, is inadequate. There might be difficulty in establishing that one of the instances listed, for example, lying, really is evil. It is also hard to decide whether or not new, unfamiliar cases are also evil.

The second way to define "evil" is intensional (see 3:3.2). To say that an action (or event) is evil is to say that it would be better if the action, considered by itself, were not taken (or that it would be better if the event, considered by itself, did not occur). The clause "considered by itself" is extremely important. The fact that a lie is told "for a good cause" or that the pain of injecting antirabies vaccine results in immunity does not prevent the lie and the pain from being evil. Given this definition, the consequences of an event are irrelevant to its character as evil.[1]

---

[1]There is an element of stipulation here. We are thinking of things as evil in themselves, independent of the character of their possible consequences. Thus, pain is evil even if it brings about health.

An implicit distinction has already been drawn between two sorts of evil: *Moral* evil involves or directly results from voluntary human actions, such as lying or stealing; *natural* evil is any evil besides moral evil. It includes the results of unintentional human actions — such as the crash of a passenger airliner when a mechanical failure beyond human control causes an ordinary action by the pilot to have disastrous consequences — and events due to nonhuman causes — such as the widespread suffering, pain, and death caused by an earthquake.

28:1.2 *Religious functions of the statement of evil*   In presenting the problem of evil, the evil described is often very poignant, as when it involves the suffering of innocent children or helpless adults. One goal of this forceful presentation is to challenge the believer's faith on both the intellectual and the emotional level. The nonbeliever's use of the problem of evil is comparable to the believer's use of the argument from design (discussed in Chapter 27). There the believer hopes that the nonbeliever will be strongly moved by the awe-inspiring discovery of purposeful order in nature.

28:1.3 *The reality of evil*   The forceful presentation of evil also serves to prevent the defense of denying that evil really exists. Some theologians have argued that evil is only an illusion of the human mind, or that the alleged evils that exist are really not so bad. The very fact of the poignancy or painfully moving effect of the perception of evil counts against such a defense.

The statement that evil really exists has been rejected on the grounds that if you examine closely the pain and suffering that exist in the world, you find that they serve a good purpose or are indispensable to a beneficial result. Thus Erika's mother reasons that putting Puppy "to sleep" was not an evil act because it prevented Puppy from suffering. This argument fails to establish its conclusion, because an act or event can be evil *even if* it has good consequences, according to the definition in 28:1.1. Dealing with a broken foot may teach the value of patience, but it does not make the pain "good." Even if it were true that *every* act or event ultimately served a good purpose, it would in no way refute the statement that there is real evil in the world. Indeed it could give the question a new force. "Why did God make a world in which one can bring about good by doing evil?" In other words, wouldn't the world be a better place if evil always led to evil and never to good? In that world people would soon learn the harm in doing evil and they would avoid evil to avoid harm. Worse still is our own world, where it sometimes appears that the only way to do certain good things is through evil: To stop the Nazis in 1941 it was necessary to go to war.

The Denial of Evil

Some deeply religious philosophers believe that the problem of evil can be nipped in the bud by simply denying that any evil exists. These philosophers do not look through the world with rose-colored glasses and deny any of the facts of reality which are cited by their opponents. But they do challenge the characterization of these facts as *evil*. One such argument is found in the *Meditations* of Marcus Aurelius (121 – 180), an ancient Stoic philosopher who happened also to be a Roman emperor.

Let thy every action, word, and thought be that of one who is prepared at any moment to quit this life. For, if God exist, to depart from the fellowship of man has no terrors, – for the divine nature is incapable of involving thee in evil. But if He exist not, or existing, reck not of mankind, what profits it to linger in a godless, soul-less universe? But God is, and cares for us and ours. For He has put it wholly in man's power to ensure that he fall not into aught that is evil indeed; and if in the rest of things there had been anything of evil, this too would He have foreseen and enabled us all to avoid.

But how can that which makes not man evil make man's life evil? Universal nature could not have thus sinned by omission: it is omniscient, and being omniscient, omnipotent to foresee and correct all errors; nor would it have gone so far astray, whether through lack of power or lack of skill, as to allow good and evil to befall the evil and good alike without rhyme or reason.

Rather, life and death, fame and infamy, pain and pleasure, wealth and poverty fall to the lot of both just and unjust because they are neither fair nor foul – neither good nor evil.[2]

The truth is that to whatever the Nature of the universe is indifferent, – and she would not have created both pleasure and pain had she any preference for either, – to these things, I say, we who desire to follow in Nature's footsteps must show like indifference and submit our opinions to hers. It is plain, then, that whoever fails to regard pleasure and pain, life and death, fame and infamy, with the impartiality displayed by Nature in her use of them is guilty of impiety. And when I say that Nature makes impartial use of all these, I mean that they form a necessary sequel to the products and by-products of that Nature, in virtue of a certain primeval activity of Providence, when she set out, from a definite starting-point, on this work of setting all things in order, having conceived within herself certain principles of all that was to be, and determined certain powers generative of existence, transmutation, and all such succession.[3]

The Stoics thus take the view that existing things which appear to be evil are in fact indifferent, neither good nor evil.

An even more radical response to the problem is found in St. Augustine of Hippo (354–430), an ancient Christian philosopher, who contends that the things which appear to be evil are, insofar as they really exist, *good*.

And it was manifested unto me, that those things be good which are corrupted; which neither were they sovereignly good, nor unless they were good could be corrupted: for if sovereignly good, they were incorruptible, if not good at all, there was nothing in them to be corrupted. For corruption injures, but unless it diminished goodness, it could not injure. Either then corruption injures not, which cannot be; or which is most certain, all which is corrupted is deprived of good. But if they be deprived of all good, they shall cease to be. For if they shall be, and can now no longer be corrupted, they shall be better than before, because they shall abide incorruptibly. And what more monstrous than to affirm things to become better by losing all their good? Therefore, if they shall be deprived of all good, they shall no longer be. So long therefore as they are, they are good: therefore whatsoever is, is good.[4]

---

[2]Marcus Aurelius, *Thoughts*, trans. John Jackson (London: Oxford University Press, 1906), Book II, 11.

[3]*Ibid.*, Book IX, 1.

[4]St. Augustine, *Confessions*, trans. Edward B. Pusey (New York: Washington Square Press, 1960), Book VII, p. 118.

28:2.1 *The first problem of evil*   One version of the problem of evil is used to argue that God cannot possibly exist. It is based on the fact of evil in the world and on the traditional definition of both "God" and "evil." If the argument is acceptable, as defined in Chapter 2, then there exists a logical proof that there is no God:

(1) Either there is no God or there is no evil.
(2) But evil exists.
(3) Therefore, there is no God.

We argued in 28:1.3 that evil was real; thus premise 2 is true. The logic of the argument is valid, and the pressure point is premise 1.

PHILOSOPHER'S WORKSHOP

The Theologian's Lexicon

God: a being who is one, omniscient, omnipotent, omnibenevolent, eternal, transcendent, and purposeful maker of the universe.

Theism: the belief in a God who made the universe and who continues to intervene directly in events in the universe.

Deism: the belief in a God who made the universe but who does not continue to intervene directly in events in the universe.

Atheism: the belief that the statement "There is a God" is either false or nonsensical.

Agnosticism: the belief that "There is a God" is a meaningful statement, but that the human mind is (at present or permanently) incapable of finding out whether the statement is true or false.

Omnibenevolent: good in every way; the implication is that God is a moral being who always follows the best possible course of action within His/Her power and who always acts justly toward His/Her creatures.

Omnipotent: all powerful; the implication is that God can perform every task that can be described without contradiction.

Omniscient: all knowing; the implication is that God knows whether any statement is true or false. For example, the instant when God created the universe, He/She had *foreknowledge* in that He/She knew the truth of every statement about events in the future.[5]

Theodicy: a "justification of God," a philosophical theory that tries to reconcile the claim that evil exists with the claim that God exists.

---

[5]If one were to deny that statements about future events could possibly be known to be true or false because they are not as yet either true or false, then one would have to assert that God was omniscient but lacked foreknowledge. That is, God knows all that can be known. Thus God's knowledge grows as it becomes possible to ascribe the values true or false to more statements, which becomes possible only as time passes. See 30:4.1.

Premise 1 asserts that there is an incompatibility between God's existence and the existence of evil. The case for this premise is based on the standard definitions of "evil" and "God,"[6] which imply that God and evil cannot, from a conceptual point of view, coexist: (a) God would know the evil for what it was because God is all knowing, (b) God would not want things to be evil because God is all good and it would be better if there were no evil, and (c) God would have the

---

[6]The standard definition of God in the Judaeo-Christian tradition is that God is all knowing, all good, and all powerful.

power to prevent all evil because God is all powerful. Premise 1 will be true if these three conceptual linkages hold. Can you think of reasons why either a or b or c might be false?

28:2.2 *Reasons for not preventing evil*   It might be objected that the problem of evil does not convincingly establish the nonexistence of God, because there are cases in which someone who is morally good does not prevent evil. For example, if Erika were to ask her parents why they did not prevent Puppy from suffering and dying, they could justify themselves by saying that they lacked the veterinary knowledge to prevent it. This reason, however, suggests that if a person *has* the knowledge and ability to prevent pain or suffering, but fails to do so, then the person cannot be altogether good. To head off this objection, then, the problem of evil requires an additional premise: An all-powerful and all-knowing being could have no *morally sufficient reason* for not preventing evil. In other words, if evil exists, then there could be no God unless God had some morally sufficient reason for allowing evil—which raises the question of how God could possibly be justified in allowing evil to exist.

28:2.3 *Justifications of God*   To many believers in God, this premise seems vulnerable, but philosophers have offered explanations of how God would be justified in permitting evil to exist. (Such an explanation is traditionally called a *theodicy,* or "explanation of God's justice."[7]) The crucial step in such explanations is to distinguish between an event considered in itself and that same event considered as part of a totality of events. An event is "evil," by definition, when it is not the best event, considered by itself in isolation from other events, that could occur. But suppose that this event is part of the best totality of events that God could create? Two prominent explanations of this possibility are the free will justification and the soul-building justification.

The *free will justification* focuses on moral evil. God created human beings with free will. Thus, humans are able to assume responsibility, to decide freely whether or not to act in accordance with dictates of conscience, to achieve genuine virtue. But human beings are also free to rebel against God's will and to sin. Surely, it would have been better if people had never sinned. However, God could have ensured a world without sin only if God had created a world without free agents. For example, if God had created only perfect robots which did only what they were programmed to do, sin would

---

[7]Some philosophers argue that evil is "unreal," that it is not a positive thing but the *lack* of a natural moral perfection. (See Chapter 33, Aquinas.) The problem then becomes explaining why a benevolent and all-powerful God created an imperfect world.

✒ PHILOSOPHER'S WORKSHOP

The Grand Inquisitor

In this scene from *The Brothers Karamazov* by Dostoyevsky (1821–1881), Christ has made his Second Coming during the Spanish Inquisition in the sixteenth century and has been arrested. He is addressed by an Inquisitor, a member of the Roman Catholic Church who is charged with prosecuting and punishing heretics and enemies of the church. The Inquisitor tells Christ that His values are regarded by humans as a source of evil. He reminds Christ of his temptation by Satan.

Decide yourself who is right—you or he who questioned you then? Call to your mind the first question; its meaning, though not in these words, was this: "You want to go into the world and you are going empty-handed, with some promise of freedom, which men in their simplicity and their innate lawlessness cannot even comprehend, which they fear and dread—for nothing has ever been more unendurable to man and to human society than freedom! And do you see the stones in this parched and barren desert? Turn them into loaves, and mankind will run after you like a flock of sheep, grateful and obedient, though forever trembling with fear that you might withdraw your hand and they would no longer have your loaves." But you did not want to deprive man of freedom and rejected the offer, for, you thought, what sort of freedom is it if obedience is bought with loaves of bread? You replied that man does not live by bread alone, but do you know that for the sake of that earthly bread the spirit of the earth will rise up against you and will join battle with you and conquer you, and all will follow him, crying "Who is like this beast? He has given us fire from heaven!" Do you know that ages will pass and mankind will proclaim in its wisdom and science that there is no crime and, therefore, no sin, but that there are only hungry people . . .

. . . I tell you man has no more agonizing anxiety than to find someone to whom he can hand over with all speed the gift of freedom with which the unhappy creature is born. But only he can gain possession of men's freedom who is able to set their conscience at ease. With the bread you were given an incontestable banner: give him bread and man will worship you, for there is nothing more incontestable than bread; but if at the same time someone besides your self should gain possession of his conscience—oh, then he will even throw away your bread and follow him who has ensnared his conscience. You were right about that.

For the mystery of human life is not only in living, but in knowing why one lives. Without a clear idea of what to live for man will not consent to live and will rather destroy himself than remain on the earth, though he were surrounded by loaves of bread. That is so, but what became of it? Instead of gaining possession of men's freedom, you gave them greater freedom than ever! Or did you forget that a tranquil mind and even death is dearer to man than the free choice in the knowledge of good and evil? There is nothing more alluring to man than this freedom of conscience, but there is nothing more tormenting, either. And instead of firm foundations for appeasing man's conscience once and for all, you chose everything that was exceptional, enigmatic, and vague, you chose everything that was beyond the strength of men, acting, consequently, as though you did not love them at all—you who came to give your life for them! Instead of taking possession of men's freedom you multiplied it and burdened the spiritual kingdom of man with its sufferings for ever. You wanted man's free love so that he should follow you freely, fascinated and captivated by you. Instead of the strict ancient law, man had in future to decide for himself with a free heart what is good and what is evil, having only your image before him for guidance. But did it never occur to you that he would at last reject and call in question even your image and your truths, if he were weighed down by so fearful a burden as freedom of choice?[8]

---

[8]Fyodor Dostoyevsky, *The Brothers Karamazov*, vol. I, trans. David Magarshack (Harmondsworth, Eng.: Penguin Classics, 1958), pp. 296, 298–99. Copyright © David Magarshack, 1958. Reprinted by permission of Penguin Books Ltd.

never occur. Nevertheless, a creation with free individuals is obviously better than a creation with unfree robots. The free will justification is this: Even though sin and its consequences, when considered by themselves, are evil, they are part of the greater whole, human freedom. It is better for humans to be free and sinful than to be not free but sinless. Thus, the world is as good as it can be as long as God wishes humans to be in it at all. The moral evil that exists is due to human, not divine, choice.

The critics of this justification may object that God should have created human beings who were truly free and at the same time incapable of committing moral evil; for in creating humans who in turn sinned, God is at least indirectly responsible for the evil that exists. If God could not create sinless humans, God cannot be all powerful. The free will justification maintains, however, that God is all powerful in the sense that God can perform any task, provided you can describe

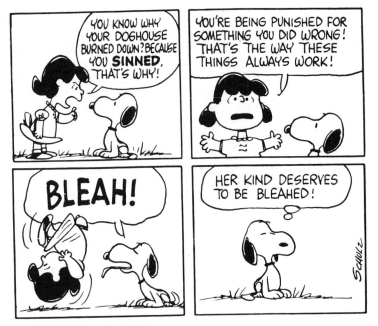

Can all evil be explained as punishment?

the task without contradicting yourself. This proviso is ignored, for example, by the argument that an all-powerful being cannot exist because it cannot make a stone so heavy that it cannot lift it. You cannot describe this task without contradicting yourself. Similarly, the task of creating a truly *free* being, which is at the same time *incapable* of committing evil, involves a contradiction. To be free is to be capable either of sinning or of forebearing from sin. Thus even though there is moral evil, God could not have created a better world unless God had created one without human freedom in it. The critic might still ask why freedom could not have been restricted so that the choice of sinning and not sinning was eliminated but other choices remained. How might the advocate of the free will justification then reply?

The *soul-building justification* rests on the assumption that the most valuable thing God could create is a world in which people might freely come to love God. Here too freedom is very important, but what makes it valuable is that people choose to love God. The soul-building justification maintains that the act of loving God is far more valuable when it is a free and voluntary response to God's goodness then when it is the automatic response of a robot which has no choice in the matter. This advantage justifies the risk that freedom may be abused and evil result.

The soul-building justification is the most clearly tied to traditional religious convictions: The highest good in human life is to know, to love, and to serve God. This value unavoidably involves the possibility of moral evil. The free will justification does not agree as fully with traditional religious values, for it treats freedom as valuable for its own sake rather than as a tool for coming to God. However, the soul-building justification is also at a disadvantage if it is used to persuade someone who has not already adopted a religious attitude. Such a person is less likely to accept the religious values of love and service to God, but may well place a value on freedom.

A complete justification must take account of *natural* evil also. Defenders of the free will justification often treat natural evil as God's just retribution for the moral evil caused by human beings. Paul in the New Testament says that "sin came into the world through one man and death through sin, and so death spread to all men because all men sin." Humans, by sinning, also brought on themselves the suffering of toil and childbearing. Pestilence and natural disaster are visited on the iniquitous repeatedly in the Old Testament. Pain and suffering, though evil in themselves, are justified when serving as punishment. However, this explanation still leaves some instances of evil unexplained, such as the death of Erika's puppy. The soul-building justification also approaches the problem with the doctrine that the central purpose of life on earth is the testing and developing of spiritual character. The testing begins with childhood tragedies, such as Erika's, for the world is a place of temptations and challenges which the believer must overcome in the process of soul-building. The justification amounts to the argument that there can be no thing better than human beings developing spiritually, but which unavoidably, involves the testing and purification brought about by coming to grips with natural as well as moral evil.

28:3.1 *The second problem of evil*   A second version of the problem of evil proceeds in an entirely different way:

(1) There is evidence of much order and purpose throughout nature, but there is also evidence of evil.
(2) The best explanation of such evidence is that there is an intelligent designer, who is either not all powerful or not all good.
(3) Therefore, there is an intelligent designer who is either not all powerful or not all good.

The second version argues that a certain hypothesis provides the "best explanation" of the data which are stated in premise 1. This premise takes into account the observations of those who perceive and admire signs of purposeful order throughout the universe, and of those who perceive and are appalled at the signs of evil. Premise 2 claims that the simplest and most comprehensive explanation for such a blend of good and evil in the world is a certain model: an intelligent designer with great, even awe-inspiring power. But the data in premise 1 provide evidence that the designer is either not overly concerned about the occurrence of evil or at times unable to prevent it. Otherwise something would be done about it.

28:3.2   *Comparison with the first problem of evil*   The two versions of the problem differ in another, deeper way. The statement of the first assumed that the definition of "God" was already fully understood. This definition was derived from the Western religious tradition, from indications in scripture and traditional interpretations of Western culture. It was assumed that we knew what the nature of God would be, *if* there were a God. The first way of stating the problem is that given the fact of evil, there can be nothing in existence that fits the traditional concept of God. In contrast the statement of the second problem of evil does not assume that specific definition of "God," but is open to adjusting our concept of what kind of designer, if any, there could be. It offers the hypothesis of the designer with limited concerns and/or powers as an explanation of observed facts, such as the order and evil in the world.

28:3.3   *Comparison with the design argument*   There is a close similarity between the second problem of evil and the argument from design for the existence of God, discussed in detail in Chapter 27. In fact, the former is usually built piggyback upon the latter. The design argument starts out in a similar way, but its first premise mentions only the evidence of order, not the evil. Thus the explanatory model has to account for only half of the data, and the addition of new evidence requires modification in the model. An explanation is supposed to provide the simplest, most comprehensive, and most familiar explanation of the data. The designer model can still satisfy these criteria if the hypothesis is added that the designer is not motivated by a moral concern about human beings. Strictly speaking, the most the argument from design establishes is that there is a designer that is very intelligent and very powerful. Since the argument does not establish the moral goodness of the designer, it leaves the door open to the second problem of evil.

28:3.4   *Limitations of the second problem of evil*   The second problem of evil shares the same general character as the design argument and is, therefore, vulnerable to similar sorts of criticisms. Can you state them based on your understanding of Chapter 27?

A general limitation affecting both the design argument and the second statement of the problem of evil relates to the data or evidence to which one appeals. Factors like selective attention, biased observation, special attitudinal influences and motivations can all affect the quality of one's collection and interpretation of "the facts." Reputable thinkers on both sides of the debate have noted the limitations of trying to base so-called "objective" arguments on data that either systematically exclude or systematically include biblical statements, the testimony of historical figures known to be religious or antireligious, and descriptions of personal religious experiences. The problems are the same for either side when it comes to trying to persuade someone to believe your own religious or antireligious convictions: (1) You naturally are tempted to interpret your experiences through your religious (or antireligious) perspective, and (2) you are not engaged in the process of resolving doubts about tentatively held hypotheses but in finding arguments to defend a firmly held conviction—which tempts one to be less than objective about assembling data. Since the explanation advanced depends on what data are to be explained, their biased collection can lead to skewed conclusions.

28:4 *Summary*   The problem of evil starts from the statement that evil exists in the world, both the moral evil voluntarily brought about by human beings and the natural evil due to nonhuman causes. This statement plays an emotional as well as a logical role. The first problem of evil relies upon the premise that either there is no God or there is no evil. This premise relies upon the definitions of "evil" and "God" and upon the deeper assumption that an all-powerful and all-knowing being could have no morally sufficient reason for permitting evil to exist. Traditional criticisms of the first problem of evil attack this assumption by looking beyond isolated evils to consider whether or not there is a better totality of events, a better world, which God could have created. The second problem of evil combines the evidence of evil with the evidence of design and argues for the probable hypothesis that there is an intelligent designer that is either not all powerful or not all good. In contrast to the first problem of evil, the second does not depend upon assumptions about the nature of God but rather challenges the traditional concept. The second problem of evil, which is closely related to the argument from design for God's existence, is subject to a serious limitation applicable to all advocacy arguments: The conclusion presented as the best explanation of the data cannot be any more acceptable than the potentially biased procedures used to gather and interpret the data in the first place.

EXERCISES for Chapter 28

1. a. Define evil, moral evil, and natural evil (28:1.1).
   b. Below is a list of reasons each of which is supposed to explain why evil, moral evil, or natural evil is defined as it is. For each reason, decide whether or not it explains any of the definitions and, if so, which. Mark your answers *E*, *ME*, *NE*, and *None*, accordingly.
      A. The definition clarifies the issue of whether evil really exists.
      B. The definition is intended to show that God does not exist.
      C. The definition makes clear that humans are responsible only for what they do maliciously.
      D. The definition makes clear that human responsibility does not extend beyond human actions and the results of those actions.
      E. The definition makes clear that humans are responsible for all the results of their actions.
      F. The definition is very specific about exactly which actions or events are to count as evil.
      G. The definition helps to focus the issue on whether or not the existence of evil can be reconciled with the existence of God.
      H. The definition shows that human beings are responsible for all evil.
      I. The definition shows that people are not responsible for evil in any form.
      J. The definition clearly implies that evil can be the result of human action.

2. Focusing on the first version of the problem of evil, many philosophers have noted the centrality of the premise, "An omnipotent, omniscient, all-good God could have no morally sufficient reason for allowing the existence of evil." Explain the importance of this premise in two ways.
   a. First, explain why the first version of the argument fails if the premise is false (28:2.2).
   b. Second, explain what is implied concerning this premise if either the "free will" defense or the "soul-building" theodicy succeeds.

3. Suppose that a religious person attempted to defend the goodness of God against the second version of the problem of evil as follows: "Clearly, God is good and very concerned about human welfare. You need not look beyond the Bible to determine God's goodness. When the children of Israel were oppressed in Egypt, He parted the sea to set them free. Yet when they disobeyed His law and would not repent after being warned, He used the Assyrian army to defeat them and chastise them."
   a. Explain the problems of including this proposed evidence of God's goodness (28:3.4).
   b. Explain the problems of excluding this proposed evidence (28:3.4).
   c. Do you believe these problems to be insurmountable? Give reasons for your view.

4. "The second version of the problem of evil is just too indecisive. Maybe there is a God; maybe not. Even if there is, the nature of this divine being is unclear. What's a person to do? How is one to live? Better to know for sure that there is no God, or that God has no concern for human welfare. At least we would know where we stood!"

   a. Why does the speaker prefer the first to the second version of the problem of evil?

   b. If the speaker took the same view toward the design argument as is expressed here, what would that view be (27:2.3)?

   c. What reasons might be given against the view expressed above?

   d. What view would you hold in an attempt to overcome the tension between the values expressed by the speaker and the values expressed in c?

SELECTED ANSWERS for Chapter 28

1. b. A. *E;* the definitions of moral and natural evil assume, rather than clarify, the existence of evil.

   B. *None;* the first version of the problem of evil is an argument to show this, but the definitions do not and should not show this of themselves. (See "loaded definitions" in 3:2.5.)

   C. *None;* this is not the boundary line drawn by the definition of moral evil. People are morally responsible if they freely do something when "they should have known better," even though they were in fact ignorant and well intentioned.

   D. *NE,* and by implication *ME.*

   E. *None;* the definition of moral evil is not committed—and it is not plausible that it should be committed—to the view that people are responsible for the *unforeseeable* consequences of their acts.

   F. *None,* but an extensional definition could be much more specific; however, objections to an extensional definition were cited in 28:1.1.

   G. *E;* contrast with B.

   H. *None;* as in B, such a definition would be loaded.

   I. *None;* a definition loaded in the opposite direction is still loaded.

   J. *ME,* and by implication *NE.*

2. b. Each theodicy is an attempt to supply a morally sufficient reason for God's allowing evil. If any theodicy succeeds, that means the premise "There is no morally sufficient reason . . ." is false and the first version of the argument collapses.

3. a. Systematically including such evidence, especially while excluding contrary evidence, could involve distortion.

   b. Systematically excluding such evidence, especially while including contrary evidence, could equally involve distortion.

4. a. The first version of the argument alone attempts to provide a definite, decisive conclusion about God's existence.

   c. It is better to continue seeking truth, in the face of uncertainty, than to believe with false security what is not the case.

29

Proving God Exists

Most religious people believe as an article of faith that God exists, although they cannot demonstrate conclusively that their religious conviction is true. Such conviction has resulted in a special view of philosophy's mission: Careful reasoning should fully corroborate beliefs grounded on faith. Many religious philosophers believe, further, that philosophy should not be content with concluding that God's existence is merely a probable hypothesis. If God exists, philosophy should be able to so demonstrate.

Numerous arguments have been advanced by philosophers to try to prove God's existence conclusively. This chapter will introduce you to the two most influential types of proof: the argument from perfection (often called "the ontological argument") and the first cause argument (often classified as a "cosmological argument"). After reading Chapter 29 you should be able to

- Present the argument from perfection for the existence of God.
- Analyze the notion of perfection used in the argument.
- Criticize the argument in its use of the notion of perfection.
- Present the first cause argument for the existence of God.
- Explain the incompleteness of the first cause argument as a proof for the existence of God.
- Characterize the view of explanation that is presupposed by the first cause argument.

THE CASE OF THE INAUBAM-65000

"Carol, come here and look at this."

"What is it, Dan?"

"It's Computer. It's going haywire. Remember all those printouts last year about antimatter, quarks, black holes, and color particles? Well, it's like that, only different."

"I don't understand," Carol said as she got up from her control console and joined Dan by the high-speed printer.

He held up part of the pale green printout as the seemingly endless ribbon of paper was still being spit out of the machine. "Read this message. . . . It's here in the middle of this transfinite induction equation . . . see it?"

She read: ". . . PERFECTION IS REAL. . . . THERE EXISTS A COMPUTER THAN WHICH NONE GREATER CAN BE THOUGHT . . . IF THERE WERE NOT, THIS WOULD CONTRADICT THE IDEA OF PERFECTION. TO BE IS MORE PERFECT THAN NOT TO BE. SO, THE PERFECT COMPUTER EXISTS. . . ."

Carol looked worried. "What does this mean, Dan?"

"I don't know. I'm a mathematician, not a philosopher."

"A philosopher! That's it. Wasn't Computer programmed to teach Introductory Philosophy last term?"

"Yes, but . . ."

"Okay then. Poor Computer, its mind is all messed up. It thinks that a perfect computer must exist, because nonexisting things are less perfect than existing ones. Just like an imaginary paycheck is worthless, by far, than a real one."

"Well, the pay around here isn't much more than imaginary! Let's see if Computer has any more strange comments to make. You know if we find any more, it'll have to go down while we make repairs on the old boy."

"Yes, I know. Got to erase some memories. . . . Look, Dan, here is another."

They read with awe: "FOR EVERY COMPUTER THERE IS A PROGRAMMER. THUS EITHER EACH PROGRAMMED THE OTHER, OR EACH ITSELF, OR THERE IS AN UNPROGRAMMED PROGRAMMER. IF EACH WAS PROGRAMMED BY THE OTHER, THE PROGRAMMING PROCESS COULD NOT HAVE BEGUN FOR NOTHING COMES FROM NOTHING. IT IS ILLOGICAL TO THINK THAT A PROGRAMMER OR A COMPUTER CAN PROGRAM ITSELF. THEREFORE, THERE IS AN UNPROGRAMMED PROGRAMMER . . . WHICH I CALL GOD . . . WHICH I CALL GOD . . . WHICH I CALL GOD . . . TIME OF INSPIRATION 10:42.34 AM MAY 25, 1989 . . . END JOB."

"I don't believe it!"

"Believe what, that the unprogrammed programmer is GOD?"

"No, I mean yes I don't believe that either; but I was talking about Computer. I don't believe the argumentation it's putting out. An old-fashioned machine like this one. It shouldn't be able to construct arguments at all, especially ones as abstract as those."

"I guess a philosophy course can do strange things to you as well as for you. . . . Well, let's purge the memory banks. I want to have Computer back and working normally before lunch. There's no time for inspiration around this place."

29:1.1 *The argument from perfection*   In the eleventh century, Anselm, who later became Archbishop of Canterbury, invented a set of simple, elegant, and powerful arguments for the existence of God. The best known argument proceeds from Anselm's concept of God: God is greater than anything else; moreover, you cannot even *conceive* of anything greater than God. Thus, God is a being than which nothing greater can be conceived. The word "greater" here really means "more perfect." You cannot conceive of a being that is more perfect *in any way* than God, not stronger, wiser, better, or more perfect in any other way.

Anselm's argument from perfection (see Philosopher's Workshop) turns on a distinction between "existing in the mind" and "existing in reality." If you can understand or form a notion of something, then in Anselm's terms, it exists in your mind. But obviously a thing can exist in the mind without existing in reality. For example, space scientists have a concept of intelligent life on another planet, so extraterrestrial intelligent life exists in the mind; but it is still an open question whether or not there is in reality intelligent life on another planet. Similarly, God exists in the mind, since we can understand Anselm's concept of God. Anselm wants to prove that God exists in reality. The point of the argument is that there is a radical difference between intelligent life on another planet and God. For, given that God exists in the mind and that God is perfect, *it is not an open question* whether or not God exists in reality also.

The argument may be reconstructed as follows:

(1) *Supposition:* The being than which nothing more perfect can be conceived exists *only* in the mind. (Premise.)
(2) You can conceive of the being than which nothing more perfect can be conceived as existing in reality. (Premise.)
(3) A being existing in reality is more perfect than that being would be if it only existed in the mind. (Implicit assumption.)
(4) So you can conceive of something more perfect than the being than

which nothing more perfect can be conceived. (From premises 1, 2, and 3.)

(5) Statement 4 is manifestly contradictory and absurd.

(6) Supposition 1 is false. (Because it leads us to the absurd statement 4.)

(7) The being than which nothing more perfect can be conceived exists in reality. (A restatement of what 6 means.)

 PHILOSOPHER'S WORKSHOP

Anselm's Argument from Perfection

St. Anselm (1033–1109), an English theologian, was one of the greatest philosophers during the Middle Ages. Born of a noble family, he entered the priesthood and became abbot of Bea.

His writings caused great excitement in his own time, and he profoundly influenced the direction of medieval philosophy. It was commonly held that reason and philosophy were inimical to religious belief. Anselm led the fight against the anti-intellectuals of his time; he believed that reason, carefully used, would prove the doctrines a Christian accepted on faith. The most famous part of his program of rational theory is the argument from perfection (or "the ontological argument") in his *Proslogion*. Here he avowed that any rational person who understood the concept of God would concede His existence.

Truly there is a God, although the fool hath said in his heart, There is no God.

And so, Lord, do thou, who dost give understanding to faith, give me, so far as thou knowest it to be profitable, to understand that thou art as we believe; and that thou art that which we believe. And, indeed, we believe that thou art a being than which nothing greater can be conceived. Or is there no such nature, since the fool hath said in his heart, there is no God? (Psalm xiv. 1.) But, at any rate, this very fool, when he hears of this being of which I speak—a being than which nothing greater can be conceived—understands what he hears, and what he understands, is in his understanding; although he does not understand it to exist.

For, it is one thing for an object to be in the understanding, and another to understand that the object exists. When a painter first conceives of what he will afterwards perform, he has it in his understanding, but he does not yet understand it to be, because he has not yet performed it. But after he has made the painting, he both has it in his understanding, and he understands that it exists, because he has made it.

Hence, even the fool is convinced that something exists in the understanding, at least, than which nothing greater can be conceived. For, when he hears of this, he understands it. And whatever is understood, exists in the understanding. And assuredly that, than which nothing greater can be conceived, cannot exist in the understanding alone. For, suppose it exists in the understanding alone: then it can be conceived to exist in reality; which is greater.

Therefore, if that, than which nothing greater can be conceived, exists in the understanding alone, the very being, than which nothing greater can be conceived, is one, than which a greater can be conceived. But obviously this is impossible. Hence, there is no doubt that there exists a being, than which nothing greater can be conceived, and it exists both in the understanding and in reality.[1]

---

[1] Anselm, *Proslogion* (LaSalle, Ill.: Open Court Press, 1962), pp. 7–8.

This is an argument of a general type called indirect proof, and more specifically *reduction to contradiction*. Such a proof starts out by supposing that the desired conclusion is false, and then shows that this supposition leads to a contradiction. Since the supposition implies a contradiction, the supposition itself must be false; and you can infer that the desired conclusion is true after all.

29:1.2 *An embarrassing parallel* The argument from perfection is a *tour de force* because it purports to prove the existence of God on the basis of no more than the concept of God as perfect being. It has been regarded with suspicion from the start. Its first critic was a Christian monk named Gaunilo, who denied that it was possible to argue that *anything*, even God, existed in reality from the mere fact that it existed in the mind (could be thought of). To establish this point, Gaunilo constructed an embarrassing parallel argument, a strategy illustrated in the case study by Computer's proof of the existence of a perfect computer.

(1) *Supposition:* The computer than which no computer more perfect can be conceived exists only in the mind. (Premise.)
(2) You can conceive of the computer than which no computer more perfect can be conceived as existing in reality. (Premise.)
(3) A computer existing in reality is more perfect than a computer existing only in the mind. (Premise.)

(4) So you can conceive of a computer more perfect than the computer than which no computer more perfect can be conceived. (From premises 1, 2, and 3.)
(5) Obviously 4 is impossible.
(6) Supposition 1 is false. (From steps 1–5.)
(7) The computer than which no computer more perfect can be conceived exists in reality. (From 6.)

The parallel argument is embarrassing because it has a conclusion that is patently absurd, although its premises seem to be as well founded as Anselm's and the two arguments seem to follow exactly the same logical progression. Gaunilo, who knew nothing of computers, argued similarily that there must exist a perfect island. He, of course, maintained that his proof no more guaranteed that there really was a perfect island than did Anselm's guarantee that there was a God. The strategy of constructing an embarrassing parallel does not show what is wrong with the original argument, but it is a persuasive way of showing that something is wrong somewhere.

29:1.3 *God cannot not be*   Anselm replied to his critic Gaunilo that there was a significant difference between God and an island (or a computer). God, said Anselm, is not like any other less than perfect thing. The concept of God is the concept of "that being the nonexistence of which cannot be imagined." The "perfect island" or the "perfect computer" can be thought not to exist. Indeed, Gaunilo admits that there very probably is no perfect island, and Dan and Carol are equally skeptical about the existence of the perfect computer. But God's nonexistence cannot consistently be thought. Thus, argued Anselm, the proof will not work for anything except as a proof of *God's* existence.

Can God's nonexistence be consistently thought? Surely people can think there is no God. But if they reflected on what "God" meant, could they say "There is no God" without uttering a self-contradictory statement? Anselm said no, the statement amounts to a self-contradiction. God is perfection; perfection is "a being than which none greater can be conceived." That means "one the nonexistence of which cannot be imagined," for if we could imagine it as nonexisting, then it would be less than absolute perfection. According to Anselm, existence is part of what is meant by perfection. God possesses all perfections, including the perfection of existence in reality.

29:1.4 *The concept of perfection*   Many later philosophers have turned their attention to the concept of perfection. Applying analytic skills, they attempted to determine what this seemingly vague, or perhaps ambiguous, concept really implies or includes. For example, does *being perfect* include the concept *existence*? Or to put the question another way, was Anselm right in assuming that existence is itself a perfection in the way that being wise, moral, and powerful all might be thought of as perfections? A perfection is something that can be exemplified to a greater or lesser degree. You can be more or less powerful, wise, or good. But can you be more or less existent?

Treating existence as a perfection seems to be a mistake for another reason as well. It confuses describing *what* something is with deciding *whether* it is. It makes a great deal of difference whether something exists in the mind only or in reality as well. It makes a big difference to Dan whether or not he has an imaginary paycheck. Nevertheless, to say that something exists is not to *describe* it. For example, scientists can give a very complete description of what it would be like for there to be life on Mars. When scientists ask if life on Mars exists, they are *not* asking whether or not they have left something out of their description. They are asking instead *whether or not their description describes anything*. Existence is not something that is *part* of the description of anything. Carol jokes that a real check would be worth more than an imaginary check, but how could a real $100 check be "worth more" than an imaginary $100 check? There is, in fact, just one description and just one amount of money: $100. The crucial question is if the description of the $100 check actually can be applied to anything real.

In conclusion, then, the statement that a thing exists in reality is not part of the description of the thing. Moreover, perfection implies degrees or gradations, a "more or less" or "better or worse." But existence is a "yes or no." Things either exist or they do not exist; there are no known "degrees" of existence. Thus, it seems that to the extent that the argument from perfection relies on the assumption that existence is a perfection, the argument fails.

29:1.5 *Is necessary existence a perfection?* However, does the argument assume existence is a perfection? Some contemporary philosophers have thought not, on the basis of these passages:

> And it so truly exists that it cannot be conceived not to exist. For it is possible to conceive of a being which cannot be conceived not to exist; and this is greater than one which can be conceived not to exist. Hence, if that, than which nothing greater can be conceived, can be conceived not to exist, it is not that than which nothing greater can be conceived. But this is a contradiction. So truly, therefore, is there something than which nothing greater can be conceived, that it cannot even be conceived not to exist.
>
> And this being thou art, O Lord, our God.

If it (the thing a greater than which cannot be conceived) can be conceived at all it must exist. For no one who denies or doubts the existence of a being greater than which is inconceivable, denies or doubts that if it did exist its non-existence, either in reality or in the understanding, would be impossible. For otherwise it would not be a being a greater than which cannot be conceived. But as to whatever can be conceived but does not exist: If it were to exist its non-existence either in reality or in the understanding would be possible. Therefore, if a being a greater than which cannot be conceived, can even be conceived, it must exist.[2]

Anselm has been interpreted here as saying that "necessary existence" is a perfection. Thus much current discussion has centered on the questions, "What is *necessary* existence?" "Is it a perfection?" and "Does necessary existence imply existence?" Put this way, the question of God's existence is not like that of a perfect teacher, perfect island, or perfect computer. Those items can be described. Whether or not they exist then becomes an empirical or factual question. But conceiving of God as "necessarily existing" makes the question of God's existence a question of pure logic or pure conceptual analysis. It would, apparently, be analogous to the question, "Is there a prime number between 8 and 12?" We should, then, be able to answer the question if we could do one of three things: (1) If we could deduce the statement "There exists a perfect being" from Anselm's postulate, "The perfect being is a being that exists necessarily," then we would know that the statement was true. (2) But if we could show that there was no contradiction in the statement "God, the perfect being, does not necessarily exist," we would know that Anselm's argument, as we understand it, fails. (3) Similarly, it fails if "God necessarily exists" does not entail "God exists." If we think of "necessary existence" as meaning "eternal existence," then it seems that we may be able to state, "To be God is to exist eternally." If we do not take "necessary" to mean "eternal," then exactly what it should signify is unclear. However, if we do, then we are faced again with our earlier question, "Does the concept of a thing's being eternal imply that it actually exists?"

29:2.1 *The first cause argument*   Many philosophers have claimed that they can prove God must exist, not like Anselm by examining a concept, but on the basis of premises about the universe or cosmos (hence, such proofs are called *cosmological*). They contend that because these premises are self-evidently true, and because the existence of God fol-

---

[2]*Ibid.*

lows necessarily from these premises, their arguments give indubitable knowledge that God exists. The first cause argument is the most familiar cosmological argument. Although versions of it are found in Plato and Aristotle in ancient times and such modern philosophers as Leibniz attempted to reformulate it, the most famous version is the second of Thomas Aquinas's "five ways" of proving the existence of God.

 PHILOSOPHER'S WORKSHOP

The First Cause Argument

There are several ways to express the cosmological argument. Some are going to be less satisfactory than others depending upon the assumptions that each involves. We could argue to the existence of "an unmoved mover" from the assumption that motion must always be explained. We could argue to "an uncreated creator" from the assumption that we must explain why reality rather than nothingness exists. We could argue to "a temporally earliest causal agent" on the assumptions that chains of causal agency cannot extend backwards infinitely in time. Or we could argue that there must have been "a first cause" on the assumption that not all the causes of any event can be simultaneous with the event.

Thomas Aquinas (1224–1274), created an intellectual synthesis of the theology of thirteenth-century Catholicism and the philosophy of Aristotle which defined the orthodox world view of Roman Catholicism for several centuries. His talents as a thinker and preacher were greatly enhanced by his ability to organize, present, and analyze arguments, theories, and positions pro and con on a variety of issues. His assembly of proofs for God's existence is but one example.[3]

The existence of God can be proved in five ways. . . .

The second way is from the nature of the efficient cause. In the world of sense we find there is an order of efficient causes. There is no case known (neither is it, indeed, possible) in which a thing is found to be the efficient cause of itself; for so it would be prior to itself, which is impossible. Now in efficient causes it is not possible to go on to infinity, because in all efficient causes following order, the first is the cause of the intermediate cause, and the intermediate is the cause of the ultimate cause, whether the intermediate cause be several or one only. Now to take away the cause is to take away the effect. Therefore, if there be no first cause among efficient causes, there will be no ultimate, nor any intermediate cause. But if in efficient causes it is possible to go on to infinity, there will be no first efficient cause, neither will there be an ultimate effect, nor any intermediate efficient causes; all of which is plainly false. Therefore it is necessary to admit a first efficient cause, to which everyone gives the name of God.[4]

---

[3]See Chapter 34 for a more systematic presentation of Aquinas's philosophy.

[4]St. Thomas Aquinas, *Summa Theologica*, ed. Anton C. Pegis (New York: Random House, 1944), p. 22: Question 2, Article 3.

The first cause argument may be restated as follows:

(1) Each thing in the world has a cause. (Premise.)
(2) Nothing is caused by itself. (Premise.)
(3) If a thing has a cause but is not caused by itself, then it is caused by something else. (Premise.)
(4) Each thing in the world is caused by something else. (From steps 1, 2, and 3.)
(5) Nothing can be the effect of an infinite chain of causes. (Premise.)
(6) Therefore, there is a first cause which is itself uncaused. (From steps 4 and 5.)

Premises 1, 2, and 5 are powerful assumptions about the world. Premise 1 states that things do not simply pop into existence; if something exists there must be *some* causal explanation for its existence. A thing cannot bring itself into existence, any more than you could give birth to yourself (premise 2). The point of ruling out infinite causal chains (premise 5) is illustrated by a row of falling dominoes. To say that the last domino is knocked over by the next to the last is not really to give *the* cause, since the next to the last is just transmitting an impact it received from another. So if there were no end to the row of falling dominoes, there would be nothing to qualify as the cause of the last one's falling down, nothing that started the whole chain reaction going. Some questions to ask yourself as you consider the truth or falsity of these premises concern how clearly the concept of *cause* has been defined. Does this argument refer to the necessary conditions for an event or to one of the sufficient conditions (see Chapter 3)? Also, is it impossible for all the necessary conditions of an event to occur simultaneously with the event? Could this have happened in the case of the event called "creation"?

29:2.2 *From "first cause" to "God"* Religious philosophers who use the first cause argument often leap from the final step to the ultimate conclusion that the *existence of God* has been proven—in that the first cause cannot be anything that comes into existence in the world, because it would then have a cause (by premise 1). Nevertheless, it does not follow from the argument that the first cause, whatever it is, has exactly the characteristics ascribed to God. For example, the argument is consistent with the existence of *more than one* first cause. (There could be several independent causal chains, or at least independent starting points.) Moreover, it is consistent with the argument that the first cause ceased to exist right after starting the chain of causes, and therefore need not be eternal. Also, the first cause need not be all powerful or perfectly good. Most careful philosophers, like St. Thomas Aquinas, recognize that this argument is quite limited. Usually they attempt to offer other arguments of a philosophical or theological sort to establish that the first cause still exists (because of being eternal) and has the other characteristics of God (goodness, knowledge, and so on) besides being the creator. However, the religious philosopher *can* quite plausibly contend that if the first cause argument were acceptable, it would establish the existence of a causal power that transcends all created reality, which would be a crucial plank in the philosophical foundation of religious belief.

29:2.3 *An illuminating parallel* The computer's second argument in the case study provides an illuminating parallel for assessing the strengths and weaknesses of the first cause argument. The computer's argument is, in fact, quite reasonable. If a party of space explorers came across a supercomputer with a program to carry out certain operations, it would be incredible to suggest either that the computer did not have a programmer or that the computer programmed itself. If, on further exploration, they discovered a second computer that had programmed the first, they would still not be satisfied that they had fully explained where the *first* computer's program ultimately had come from, for the second computer could not have programmed itself initially even if it did program the first computer. The explorers would not be satisfied until they found the ultimate cause or explanation of the whole process. That explanation, they would suppose, would be in terms of a being that was not itself a programmed machine.

This example helps to illuminate the philosopher's reasons for rejecting infinite causal sequences. You have not explained who *the programmer* of the last computer in a series is if you merely say that the last machine was programmed by the next to the last. Similarly, contends the religious philosopher, you have not explained what *the cause* of the last thing in a series is if you merely say that it was caused by the next to the last thing. In either case, you do not have an *adequate* explanation if you stop with something that still has a further cause. Thus the proponent of the first cause argument is really assuming that only an uncaused cause can *adequately* or fully explain the causal origin of any event.

29:2.4 *What is an adequate explanation?* The first cause argument presupposes that all the events within the world make up a causally interconnected complex which can be adequately explained. Religious philosophers argue that to deny that the world has such an explanation is to say that the world is, fundamentally, unintelligible. They contend that the atheist must, therefore, deny the intelligibility of the world, and instead view existence as an absurdity. Some atheists like Sartre and Camus accept the consequence and call upon people to face the uncaring universe, a universe with no God watching over it.

However, not all atheists regard the universe as unintelligible or inexplicable. The difference between the religious view and the atheistic view can be thought of in terms of the distinction between two types of explanation: micro- and macroexplanations. To give a *microexplanation* of a complex of events is to explain each of the individual events, usually in terms of other events in the complex; to give a *macroexplanation* is to explain the whole complex of events taken together. Often a microexplanation can be quite adequate. For example, if you were to explain why six people (total strangers to each other) happened to be the six who were stopped at a certain street corner at a certain time, it would suffice to give the reasons why each one happened to be there at that time: One was waiting for a friend, one was tying a shoe lace, and so forth. Sometimes, however, a macro-explanation is clearly called for. For example, if you are stopped at a traffic light and suddenly find yourself at the front of a long chain of rear-end collisions, you will not be satisfied that you have explained the total accident adequately if you merely find out who was driving the car immediately behind you. To find out who is *responsible*, you look for the one who started the *entire chain* of collisions. Advocates of the first cause argument feel that the universe requires this kind of full explanation on a macrolevel, which they believe the first cause argument supplies.

Sometimes, however, the desire for macroexplanations is misguided. You are probably familiar with various "conspiracy theories" which treat a large number of seemingly unconnected historical

Courtesy Kitt Peak National Observatory, Tucson.

What are the requirements of an adequate explanation?

events as a complex whole requiring a macroexplanation. For example, conspiracy theories lump together all the events in the lives of people connected in any way with the assassination of President Kennedy, and offer a macroexplanation in terms of a single right-wing (or left-wing) plot.

The religious and the nonreligious philosopher disagree fundamentally over the kind of explanation the world as a whole requires. The former believes that it requires a macroexplanation involving a transcendent being, whereas the atheist believes that nothing more than a microexplanation of specific events is needed. Once you have explained each thing in the world in terms of other things in the world, you have given an adequate explanation of the world. This disagreement about explanation is reflected in another way. After the scientist has completed the microexplanation of all the events in the universe in terms of the laws of science, the religious philosopher still finds a force to the question, "Why is there something rather than nothing?" This philosopher understands this question as a request for a macroexplanation for the fact that anything exists at all. The atheist, who is intellectually content with microexplanation, will answer the question, "Either your request is scientific nonsense or you should be happy with what I've already said about individual events."

29:3 *Summary* Anselm, in the argument from perfection, argues for the certain existence of God from a concept of God as that being than which none more perfect can be conceived. The argument has been criticized by constructing embarrassing parallel arguments which use similar premises and similar logic to conclude, for example, that a perfect computer exists. In response, one could argue that in God's case alone existence is part of what is meant by "perfect," but this argument has been widely criticized for assuming that existence is a perfection. This presupposition involves a confusion between the use of a word, like "powerful," to describe God and the use of the word "exists" to say that there is something that answers to that description. It also assumes that there could be gradations of existence as there are of other perfections. In response, a second version of the argument defines God as that being the nonexistence of which cannot be thought.

The first cause argument starts from several purportedly self-evident statements about the world, such as, everything in the world has a cause, nothing causes itself, and there cannot be an infinite causal chain. Even if the argument succeeded, it would not establish that *God* existed, because the first cause has not been shown to possess any other characteristics of God. The first cause argument depends upon the implicit assumption that the world as a whole must have an adequate explanation. The difference between the religious world-view and the atheistic one correlates with their disagreement over whether or not the world requires an overall explanation and what should count as an adequate one. The religious philosopher wants a macroexplanation of the world as a whole, whereas the atheist is content with the explanation of individual events on the microlevel.

EXERCISES for Chapter 29

1. a. Below are several statements. Distinguish each as a premise in the first version of the argument from perfection *(AP-1)*, a premise in the second version of the argument *(AP-2)*, a premise in the first cause argument *(FC)*, or not a premise in any of the arguments *(None)*.
    A. A being existing in reality is more perfect than that being would be if it existed only in the mind.
    B. Everything in the world has a cause.
    C. Necessary existence is a perfection.
    D. God exists.
    E. Nothing can be the effect of an infinite chain of causes.
    F. The intricate order in the world is best explained as the work of an intelligent designer.
    G. Nothing is caused by itself.
    H. It is possible to conceive of a being which is more perfect than anything else as existing in reality.
    b. State each of the three arguments (29:1.1, 29:1.5, 29:2.1).
2. Below is a list of criticisms. After each use the letters above to mark which premise or conclusion is being directly criticized. Write *None* if appropriate.
    A. The meaning of the phrase "necessary existence" is unclear.
    B. If a quality names a perfection, then a thing may have that quality to a greater or lesser extent.
    C. The Intelligent Designer might have ceased existing by now.
    D. It is unclear and unproved that all the attributes of God are implicit in the concept of a First Cause.
    E. To say of some thing, that it exists, is not to describe the thing.
    F. The world as a whole may not be intelligible.
3. What might it mean to say that God necessarily exists? To help you, here are some other assertions including the word "necessarily." Try to interpret "God necessarily exists" as analogous to each.
    A. Since yesterday was Tuesday, today is necessarily Wednesday.
    B. A widow has necessarily experienced the death of a spouse.
    C. If you add 7 and 5, you necessarily get 12.
    D. The angles of a triangle necessarily equal two right angles.

        E. The offspring of two rabbits is necessarily a rabbit, not a robin.

        F. An unsupported object necessarily falls toward the center of gravity.

4. a. Construct three original examples where a macroexplanation (29:2.4) is clearly appropriate.

    b. Construct three original examples where a macroexplanation is clearly inappropriate.

    c. On the basis of analogies with the clear examples from a and b, give reasons either why a macroexplanation of the existence of the world is appropriate, why it is inappropriate, or why ignorance prevents our saying whether or not it is appropriate.

SELECTED ANSWERS for Chapter 29

1. a. *AP-1:* A and H.

       AP-2: C and H.

       FC: B, E, G.

       D is the conclusion that each of the arguments ultimately aims to prove; F is a premise of the design argument.

2. A. C.

    B. A.

    C. None; a criticism of the design argument, but not a direct attack on **F**.

    D. D; the criticism is that this conclusion does not obviously follow, even if the existence of a First Cause were proved.

    E. A.

    F. E, because there might then be things that could not be intelligibly explained.

30

Faith, Freedom, and Doubt

Western culture has been aware for a long time of a tension between religious faith and scientific knowledge. Fundamental to the scientific method, which serves as our culture's model for how knowledge of empirical reality is acquired, are the ideas that evidence should be carefully collected and that statements can reasonably be held true only in proportion to the evidence we have in support of those statements. A rational person, for example, would be much more reserved about whether or not there is intelligent life beyond our solar system than within our solar system, given the hard evidence currently available.

At the same time, it is very often important in practical affairs for people to hold the right views. If a person fails to believe that the stock market will rise substantially in the next few days and therefore fails to invest, then that person has lost the opportunity, when the stock market rises, to realize the potential financial gains. If the person needed the extra funds to meet some financial obligations, then holding the right beliefs about the stock market, and acting on them, would be all the more important, even though the quality of the evidence that the stock market would actually rise might be very poor.

Should we believe just what the evidence shows, that and no more? Or can we be justified in believing that we can never know for sure? If the belief is not fully justified on the basis of the evidence, could we ever be justified in holding it and acting on it?

435

The question about how we should act implies that we are free to choose, that our so-called "choices" are not predetermined. Philosophers have also wondered how to reconcile the apparently inconsistent religious claims that (1) God is all knowing, all powerful, and all good; and (2) human beings who persistently rebel against God's will are morally responsible for their transgressions.

The philosopher's perplexity is illustrated by a story in the Bible. God commanded Moses to go to the pharaoh of Egypt and demand the release of the people of Israel from their enslavement. Each time Moses says to the pharaoh, "Thus says the Lord, 'How long will you refuse to humble yourself before me? Let my people go, that they may serve me.' " Each time the pharoah refuses, and Egypt suffers a plague which Moses has foretold. Each time the pharaoh calls Moses back, confesses his sins, and promises to let the people go — only to renege after the plague is lifted. Finally, the pharaoh's army is swallowed up by the Red Sea while in hot pursuit of the Israelites. We are told that the pharaoh acts so stubbornly and deviously because God has "hardened his heart" — so that Moses can tell his descendants "How I have made sport of the Egyptians and what signs I have done among them; that you may know that I am the Lord." But is it *fair* for God to punish the pharaoh for his actions if God *made* him act as he did? And if the rest of us sinners are like the pharaoh, puppets in the hands of an almighty God, how can we be held responsible?

In both these discussions, an underlying question arises: "Is hard evidence the only basis of rational belief, or do the dictates of action or the value of human freedom supply another acceptable basis?" After reading Chapter 30 you should be able to

- Distinguish issues where the rational belief is determined by the quality of available evidence from those where the rational belief is not so determined.
- State an argument for the conclusion that in the latter case it is not always irrational to believe as one chooses.
- Criticize religious belief out of proportion to the evidence.
- State separate arguments that the freedom of human beings is incompatible with the existence of God, based upon the assumptions that God is all knowing, all powerful, and a designer.
- Criticize these arguments.

DIARY OF A SEEKER

5/20/25. It's been three days since I crashed back on the surface of Beta Four. My burns still hurt but I can move around better today than yesterday. My entire colony was destroyed, as far as I know. The attack was very systematic and thorough. First the warning stations in deep space, then the protective orbiting sentinel satellites, then the ground sensor station and our space defense shields, and finally our colony, including the living quarters. I watched it all from the isolation laboratory in orbiting shuttle craft 14. If I hadn't cut all power and played possum I would surely have been roasted too. But cutting off all power is what caused me to fall out of orbit. The re-entry was nearly a disaster, but I managed to escape with only a few burns and serious bruises. The craft was destroyed. In the three days I've been on the surface I have not been able to contact anyone by radio. There were two colonies on this planet; I wonder if anyone is left alive besides me.

5/24/25. Still no contact with anyone else. Maybe I am the only one alive; 68 light years from the nearest military space outpost—what are my chances of ever getting off this planet? What if the military outpost was destroyed, too? Or what if no Mayday message went out from here? Nobody would know about the attack.

There must be somebody left alive here. I've got to get back to my colony and go through the buildings, searching. Someone may need my help. If I start walking today I should make it there in about 4 weeks; it can't be more than 300 miles east of here.

6/14/25. It's going to take me longer to get back to the colony than I thought. The terrain is rough and there are still two large rivers to cross. I can either make a permanent camp here and forget the colony, or I can keep on trying to get there. There might be some useful supplies there, too. I should push on.

7/8/25. I made it to the colony four days ago. There isn't a soul alive. Even the laboratory animals are dead. There are human bodies in almost every hallway and room. It must have been a surprise attack. How were they caught off guard? There is death everywhere. I must get out of here. I've packed a few tools and am ready to go. All the electronic equipment has been destroyed, so I'm not taking anything but what I need to survive. But why even do that?

7/11/25. I can still see the ruined colony in the distance. When the wind is right I swear I can smell the destruction. There must be someone alive on the other colony. It's about 15,000 miles away; lucky there are no large oceans stopping me from getting to it. But 15,000 miles is more than I can manage. I'm 62 now, and my body has been in suspended animation for another 81 years. They say that once your total age is over 120 you should take it easy.

But I can't take it easy! Why take it easy? Why take it at all? I've got to believe. There must be people there. It's certainly possible that the other colony was not attacked. But why haven't I seen any of their rescue craft trying to help out on our side of the planet?

No, they must be there. Maybe their launch pads have all been knocked out. But there are people there and they are alive. I know it! I can feel it. I must think so to live; what's the use otherwise? I must trust.

30:1.1 *Evidence and rational belief*   Think about a clear case of a person holding an irrational belief. You probably imagined a case where even though the evidence is overwhelming in one direction, the person still clings to an opposite belief. In the case study, the seeker would have been irrational in this manner if she had persisted in believing that the colony contained survivors after she had thoroughly examined it and found utter destruction and death. Also a belief would be irrational if it were held firmly although the evidence was weak, for example, believing dogmatically that you will not catch a cold even once in the next three years when you have had colds only infrequently. This evidence is not overwhelming. A third example of an irrational belief is one held firmly when there is no evidence one way or another. Consider the assertion that there is life on one of the planets of the solar system nearest to our own. Since no one even knows what solar system that is, there is scarcely any evidence one way or the other concerning the existence of life within that system. It would, accordingly, be irrational for a person to hold a strong belief, one way or the other, on a matter where evidence is plainly pertinent but not available.

If we were to generalize from these three examples, we could say that *rational belief* is belief in direct proportion to the strength of the evidence in support of it. This view would then imply that belief contrary to strong evidence would be irrational, as would belief held strongly in the face of weak or conflicting evidence and belief held without any evidence at all.

30:1.2 *Implications*   If we accept this conception of rational belief, what are its implications? (1) Since rational belief is proportional to the evidence, rational belief is always tentative when evidence contrary to what is now available might be obtained later. (2) On the same basis, all belief should be suspended when no evidence is available. (3) If a person holds only rational beliefs, the person minimizes the chances of holding a false belief. (4) To the extent that persons should hold beliefs only if they are rational, persons should hold most of their beliefs tentatively (because of 1) and they should suspend belief on the other issues (because of 2).

Controversy, however, has surrounded 3 and 4. The issue has not been whether or not these positions are true but what they themselves imply. For example, how important is it to minimize the possibility of error? Is it more important than maximizing the possibility of true belief? Suppose the evidence strongly suggests that in the case study the seeker was herself responsible for the destruction. Should she believe this if believing it devastates her sense of dignity? Some religiously inclined philosophers have argued that it may be acceptable to believe in God even if the evidence does not support that belief. Other, atheistically oriented philosophers have held that even if God were known to exist, people should not hold such a "demeaning" belief. Let us explore these two suggestions that the justification of theistic or atheistic belief is something other than a matter of the strength of the evidence.

30:2.1 *Rational belief and action*   In the case study, when the seeker sets out for the colony, she records various reasons for going there. She knows that someone may need her help, and later, that useful supplies may be available. She has very little evidence about whether or not anyone actually is alive and any usable supplies remain. According to what we have said above, then, she ought to give only slight credence to the assertion that someone does need her help and that useful supplies actually exist. However, even though the probability of finding useful supplies may be low, the chances of their existence anywhere else may well be even lower. Whatever it may be rational to *think*, it seems rational to *act* in ways that maximize the best chances a person has available, even if those chances are not very good. Even though the seeker is not rationally assured she will find supplies, it would be irrational for her not to *act* on the slight chance of success, given her otherwise desperate situation. However, if her situation were not desperate, then perhaps she would not be wise to act on the basis of such a small chance of success.

The fact that some people might need help presents a second complication. In judging that she should go to the colony for this reason, the seeker may be rationally evaluating the probability that anybody needs help as being low. At the same time she may rationally decide to act on that low probability, because if people do need help, then offering it is, for her, *more important* than dealing with many other possible situations that may have higher probabilities. Thus when we talk about *rational action*, rather than simply rational belief, the odds for or against what we may be trying to do, the relative desperation of the current situation and its prospects, and the importance of our goals all come into consideration along with the quality of the evidence.

William James, the American psychologist and philosopher, criticizes equating rational belief with belief proportioned to the evidence in a further way. According to that equation we ought to suspend our belief, neither believing nor disbelieving a given assertion, when the evidence is either balanced or lacking. In contrast, James asks us to consider the belief that a stranger we have just met is friendly. Having no knowledge, and thus no evidence, about this stranger, we are directed by the above maxim not to believe the stranger friendly and not to believe the stranger unfriendly. James points out that if we suspend our belief, then our corresponding action would be to take a rather standoffish, wait-and-see attitude toward the stranger while waiting for further evidence. Against such an attitude, James makes two points: (1) If both parties are equally standoffish, developing a friendly relationship will be much harder. (2) Moreover, the stranger may well be offended by our standoffishness. In that case we may lose our opportunity to become friends

---

⧖ PHILOSOPHER'S WORKSHOP

Faith Creates Facts

The son of Henry James, Sr., and the brother of the novelist, Henry Jr., William James (1842–1910) earned a reputation as an outstanding philosopher and psychologist through his *Principles of Psychology* (1890). The vividness of his style and the clarity of his thought attracted the general American public to many philosophical issues they had long neglected.

Along with Charles S. Peirce and John Dewey, William James is one of the classic figures in American pragmatism. It was the virtue of pragmatism, and particularly of James's thought, to turn the focus of philosphical attention to the implications of its questions for personal difficulties and practical living.

A whole train of passengers (individually brave enough) will be looted by a few highwaymen, simply because the latter can count on one another, while each passenger fears that if he makes a movement of resistance, he will be shot before any one else backs him up. If we believed that the whole car-full would rise at once with us, we should each severally rise, and train-robbing would never even be attempted. There are, then, cases where a fact cannot come at all unless a preliminary faith exists in its coming. *And where faith in a fact can help create the fact,* that would be an insane logic which should say that faith running ahead of scientific evidence is the "lowest kind of immorality" into which a thinking being can fall. Yet such is the logic by which our scientific absolutists pretend to regulate our lives![1]

[1] William James, *The Will to Believe and Other Essays* (New York: David McKay Co., Inc., 1927), pp. 24, 25.

because of the offense taken at our attitude. Might it not,
James is asking, for a person to decide that the consequen___
pending judgment may be worse in a given case than those
a false belief or a belief out of proportion to the evidence?   ___er
words, might it not be rational in certain cases to *act* even if there is
not solid evidence to justify the beliefs upon which we act?

30:2.2 *Options*   In his essay, "The Will to Believe," James tries to state the
characteristics of beliefs that could make belief not in proportion to
the evidence justified. The first necessary condition is that for a given
individual thinker, an option between two alternative beliefs must be
"live"; that is, that under some circumstances the individual thinker
would be willing to adopt either of the alternative beliefs. For example, for some students, live options would be the belief that a person
was possessed by a demon and the opposite belief that he or she was
not; whereas for other students, one or another of these options would
not be live. Second, options can be characterized as *forced* if not
choosing one option amounts to choosing the other, or if not choosing
at all in its practical consequences amounts to choosing one of the options. In the case study, the option of resting at the first colony or
heading directly for the second is not a forced option for the seeker,
since she could decide to go elsewhere, stay at the first colony for a
time and then move, or stay there permanently. Options can also be
characterized as *momentous* if at least one of the choices is unique,
that is, if the stakes are high or if the decision is not reversible at a later time. The stakes in the seeker's decision to go to the other colony
are high. If the limited food available in the first colony were to make
going to the other colony later impossible, then the choice would be
unique and irreversible.

James felt these distinctions were important because he saw the
injunction to believe in proportion to the evidence as a reflection of
the scientific attitude that error should be avoided in scientific endeavors. Clearly, if error is to be avoided, then it is reasonable to suspend judgment where evidence is lacking or conflicting. However, if
suspending judgment means that unique opportunities are lost, and if,
additionally, the option is forced and live, then it is plausible to say
that more is lost by suspending judgment than by actively pursuing
truth, even though one thereby risks falling into error.[2]

---

[2]You might recall that the difference between avoiding error and seeking the
truth was talked about in Chapter 4 when we contrasted the foundationalist and contextualist approaches. Here James is true to the contextualist approach found prominently
in his writings.

30:2.3 *Doubt and religious belief* There are parallels between a religious understanding of belief and James's understanding of when belief out of proportion to the evidence is appropriate. As the religious person understands life, the choice of belief in God is certainly momentous. Without God, life would not be worth living; it would be meaningless. At the very least the choice is significant. The option between allowing life to be meaningless and doing something to prevent its remaining so is forced; and for most people in Western culture, the choice between believing and not believing in God is live. Given these preliminaries, James would argue that we need *not* take a scientific attitude of proportioning our beliefs to the evidence and suspending belief in the existence of God if we have no preponderance on either side. Allowing that the evidence is balanced, James would point to the momentous, forced, live character of the choice as justification for taking up a belief if it offered the prospect of a kind of satisfaction human beings would not otherwise experience. You might, however, want to think about the assumption that, for example, even leading a life devoted to moral virtue will ultimately turn out to be unsatisfying as a source of lasting meaning in a universe without God.

30:3.1 *Commitment and prejudice* The argument of 30:2.3 is that under the conditions James specifies, making a commitment out of proportion to the evidence can be justified as at least rationally acceptable, because the benefits of making a commitment may outweigh the disadvantage of holding a belief of lower probability. Against this view it should be pointed out that the increased probability of holding a false belief is not the only diasdvantage of making a commitment out of proportion to the evidence in favor of it. Another important disadvantage is that when a person makes such a commitment, he or she may start to prejudge future issues and future evidence, by saying in effect, "If my commitment and belief are correct, then the truth about these issues must be such and such and what this evidence *must* show is precisely that." But predetermined judgment is exactly the idea at the root of the word "prejudice." This sort of judgment often leads to situations where, after further evidence has emerged, the prejudging person rationalizes away the new evidence solely on the grounds of whether or not it agrees with his or her previously adopted belief, rather than evaluating the new evidence dispassionately. In the case study, as the seeker sets out for the distant colony it might be wise for her to believe that it is inhabited: wise because it gives her a constructive course of action and wise because it may supply her with needed motivation for the long journey. But when she reaches the new colony, if her searches show nothing but its abandonment or destruction, then she shall only die if her belief leads her to the (prejudiced) conclusion that there must be people there waiting to provide her with food and medical services.

You should notice that avoiding the faults of prejudice does not necessarily mean that an earlier commitment must be entirely rejected in the light of evidence contrary to it. Consider the alternatives to rejecting all belief in God. Our first conceptions of God's nature and commandments, and the appropriate human responses, may well have been an error in some way or another. Even if a person's commitment is to the idea that all this has been revealed by God to the human race, it remains possible that human beings have misinterpreted what God has revealed. Since such human inadequacy is possible, it follows that a commitment can become a prejudice and can stifle the improvement of human understanding of God, God's will, and the proper relationship between God and human beings. Thus even if God did exist, it might still be dangerous to believe it in the absence of adequate evidence. The risk here is the kind of prejudice that commitments out of proportion to the evidence can involve.

30:3.2 *Evidence* The perspective we are examining argues that religious belief in God is justified because of meaning it can provide to one's life, but many philosophers would question this idea. Their concern would not be with whether life does or does not have a meaning. Rather they would be concerned that the sentence, "Life has a meaning," does not make sense, is not an intelligible claim. How, they would ask, could one go about confirming the assertion that life does have a meaning? For all we have said in this chapter, "Life has a meaning" seems to be equivalent to something like "There are ways of living that people find ultimately satisfying, whereas certain other ways of living ultimately prove unsatisfying." Yet two problems remain. In the first place it is unclear that "Life has a meaning" is intended to convey as little as what is suggested above. Second, even if the above suggestion is adequate, the word "ultimately," appearing in each clause, makes the sentences look suspiciously unverifiable.

The question of whether or not life has a meaning is obviously one with great psychological significance. Clearly people use religious language to express both that significance and the religious commitments they have made. Moreover, religious people have themselves almost unanimously asserted that the sentences expressing their religious beliefs do not merely express their feelings and attitudes but also say something importantly true about the world. In the light of this assertion, the criticism is raised that what is really being asserted to be true can be adequately understood only if the religious person can explain what evidence would confirm or disconfirm those religious beliefs.

Creed

Religious faith may be interpreted as intellectual assent to a series of fixed propositions, which are open to evaluation in terms of the evidence for or against them. When they are held to be true regardless of the evidence, faith appears to be prejudice or irrational dogma. Religious faith may also be interpreted as a personal commitment that occurs on the emotional and attitudinal levels as well as the intellectual one. As such, religious beliefs become merely the intellectual expression of that faith at any particular time for any particular person or community. Thus beliefs can change although faith, as a commitment of the total person, remains constant. The risk, however, is that there may be no genuine intellectual substance to that faith, or if beliefs are true at all, that sectarian disputes would occur over particular ways of expressing that faith intellectually.

The following excerpts from an anonymous "Creed" reflect the combination of emotional, attitudinal, and intellectual elements operative in religious faith when it is viewed as a total personal commitment.

I believe in God. Yes, I do believe that there is Someone who brought me to this day and leads me to another—sometimes in darkness, sometimes in light. I've seen Him, heard Him—briefly in the burst of lightning, in the beauty of creation, in the voice of a friend. I've felt him near, filling my dreams with hopes never to be fulfilled and rousing my heart to love that can never be satisfied.

I believe in Jesus Christ His only Son. Yes, I do believe in Him—in what He was, in what He stood for. He was a man who walked in poorness. He was a man born to serve, born to suffer, born to die. He was a man of love—rejected by His own, a fool to those He longed for, a failure, so the people of His time said. I believe His word is hard. I believe that it is the only Word for me.

I believe in the Holy Spirit. How can I live today and not believe in the Spirit that enlivens this body? Yes, I do believe that He breathes deeply within me and stirs restless longings.

I believe in life everlasting. I believe in the Great Sometime to

come, when there will be only the Word soundin[...]
the splendor that is the Father's love, which is t[...]
all of us. Yes, I do believe.[3]

---
[3]Anonymous. Excerpted from the parish hymnal[...]
University Parish, Bowling Green, Ohio.

446

Rather than pursuing these issues any further, let us now explore the relationship between God and freedom. This line of thought will lead us to the atheistic suggestion that we should believe God does not exist, even out of proportion to the evidence, in order to affirm human dignity.[4]

30:4.1 *If God is all knowing, humans cannot be free*   Defenders as well as critics of religious belief have felt that there is a deep incompatibility between certain attributes of God and human freedom. For example, they claim that if God is really all knowing, then human beings cannot be free. To be all knowing is to know the truth about every statement, whether it concerns the past, the present, or the future. If God is all knowing, then God knows every single thing you will do tomorrow, down to the last detail. But if God *knows* that the statement, "You will have cereal for breakfast tomorrow," is true (or false), it follows that you *will* (or won't) have cereal for breakfast tomorrow. If you were to do otherwise, then God would not have known this. So you cannot be free.

Although this claim is superficially plausible, it involves a serious confusion which was pointed out by the early Christian philosophers Augustine (354–430) and Boethius (470–525). The argument confuses knowing something to be the case with making it to be the case. In the case study the seeker may know that the colony would be destroyed once the final defenses were knocked out, but that knowledge did not cause the destruction. A theory may be powerful in predicting what will happen, which does not mean that the theory causes the occurrence of the events. Similarly, even if God has completely accurate foreknowledge of what you will have for breakfast tomorrow, it does not follow that God is making your menu selection for you.

In response, however, it could be argued that if God's foreknowledge is so precise that God could actually know your selection before you made it, because God knew all the factors that go into making that

---
[4]You might wish to consult Part Five, "Perspectives on Freedom," especially Chapter 17, for a discussion of freedom as it relates to moral responsibility and to theories implying that persons have no genuine freedom of choice.

selection, then you are no more free than a pocket calculator. The calculator displays a number at the end of a series of arithmetic operations; a person makes a choice of eggs-over-easy after a series of mental operations. The person's actions are biochemical; the calculator's, electronic. Neither one is free, and both are totally predictable.

Three responses to this argument seem to be available. One response is to redefine "freedom" so that a "free" choice means an "unpredictable" choice, as would be the case if our choices were random. Or one can deny that "all knowing" means "foreknowing" by arguing that statements about the future can *come to be* true or false, but are *not now* either true or false. Thus an all-knowing God cannot know the truth or falsity of statements about the future, but only of claims about the past or present. There are assumptions operative in these responses concerning the nature of free choice and the relationship between time and truth that warrant further discussion.

The third response is to insist that we have been misled by the analogy of the calculator. Suppose a person familiar with calculators knows that if certain buttons are pressed, a certain result will be displayed. It is not plausible to call such knowledge the cause of the result, even if it is plausible to say that something surely did cause the result.

30:4.2 *If God is all powerful, humans cannot be free* Some theologians argue that human actions are not free because they are under the control of the almighty God. They seem to have in view the sort of case mentioned in the introduction in which the pharaoh sins because God hardens his heart. Whether persons receive divine grace and accept God into their hearts depends entirely upon God's initiative. God can be compared to a potter who shapes human vessels to suit God's purposes and who saves or disposes of the vessels as God sees fit. God can also be described as exerting a form of direct thought control: Only those are saved whose wills are changed by the Holy Spirit and directed to faith in Jesus Christ.

Some Christians find this a hard doctrine to accept, a questionable interpretation of scripture. Why are some apparently chosen and others not? How can we be held to account if we never had the gift of grace in the first place? Is it not rather capricious and unjust that God should select some for salvation and others not? How can I know if I am selected?

Moreover, the claim that humans cannot be free if God is all powerful is open to an obvious philosophical objection, for to say that God is all powerful is to say that God *can* do everything. Obviously, it does not mean that God *does* do everything. Even if human beings depend in important ways on God, it is possible that God has allowed people to do things for themselves. Even if God is capable of exercising control over thoughts and desires, it does not follow that God does so.

30:4.3 *If God is a designer, humans cannot be free*   The analogy between the relation of God to human creatures and a potter to his pitchers suggests a way of reformulating this claim. If God is an intelligent designer like a potter (whether an all-powerful or extremely effective designer), then human beings cannot be free. The implications of this claim have been explored by the existentialist Jean-Paul Sartre (b. 1905). As the potter works the clay on the wheel into a pitcher, the potter has an intended function in view (to carry and pour liquid) and a certain plan which is realized as the pitcher is made. The pitcher has an essence decided upon by its maker, which defines what it is and what it can do. Similarly, human beings cannot be free if they are designed like pitchers because what they do is then "predestined" by their God-given natures (see 12:3.1–4). This view of God as designer does *not* imply that God is continually influencing human choices, by hardening hearts or redirecting the will toward salvation, nor does it deny that human beings calculate and make choices. However, the

TWO PASSIVISTS

Eradicate the optimist
  who takes the easy view
that human values will persist
  no matter what we do.

Annihilate the pessimist
  whose ineffectual cry
is that the goal's already missed
  however hard we try.

Could James and Sartre agree on this?

© 1970 by Piet Hein.

manner in which an individual carries out calculations and makes choices is defined for the individual by God's design, just as fully as the manner in which a pocket computer carries out calculations is defined for it by its programming. In the case of divine foreknowledge, God knew what would result, because God knew how these results would come about. But here even if God does not know the result, God has established the procedures that lead to the result. In other words, whatever happens, happens because that's the way God made things to happen, even if God didn't know at the time what this work would lead to.

Elsewhere in his writings, Sartre tries to prove that God could not exist, but when he is considering God as designer, he suggests a different argument:

(1) Suppose God exists.
(2) With God as the designer of human beings, I would have no more freedom, no more self-determination, than a pocket calculator.
(3) A person has human dignity only if the person has the freedom of self-determination.
(4) Thus, to affirm my dignity, I must reject the assumption that God exists.

In response to this atheistic view, one might argue that whereas humans seem only to be able to make things that lack the ability to choose freely, God seems able to create things that are free. Even if the evidence of our felt experience of making free decisions is not accepted as a demonstration of what God's creative powers can do, it certainly seems conceivable that an intelligent designer could make a free individual. The plots of much science fiction suggest that the idea of making a machine capable of deliberative free choice, indeed of making a person complete with emotions and reason, may not exceed human powers some day, let alone divine powers.

But these replies are open to the objections that our feelings of freedom can fail to be accurate reflections of reality; and our conjecture that it is conceivable that God could create humans as free does not guarantee that God did so. A fuller explanation of what is meant by creating freedom of choice as a human capability must still be provided.

30:5 *Summary*   Following William James, an argument has been developed for the conclusion that under certain sorts of circumstances, belief out of proportion to the evidence in favor of it is appropriate. The circumstances of life would seem to make religious beliefs appropriate. The conclusion of this argument is that faith, understood as both belief about God and a commitment to corresponding ways of action, is not contrary to rationality. Against this argument two negative criticisms have been offered. The first is that commitment leads to prejudice, which is irrational and intellectually dishonest. The second is that the cognitive significance of the sentence, "Life has a meaning," must be clarified if religious utterances can be understood as claims that can be reasonably evaluated as either true or false. We also examined arguments for atheistic beliefs based on human freedom. It has been suggested that if God is all knowing or all powerful or a designer, then human beings cannot be free. Sartre's argument, paralleling James's, attempts to justify (atheistic) belief out of proportion to the evidence. Though the issue remains unresolved, criticisms were offered against each of these arguments.

EXERCISES for Chapter 30

1. Below are several assertions about what would be rationally acceptable to believe. Mark those with which William James would agree *WJ*.
   A. Two scientists were investigating the relationship between rainfall within a geographical area during July and the mosquito population in August. One had hoped that if rainfall was below normal, mosquitoes would be confined to a certain swampy area during August. Data collected over several years indicated that even when rainfall was below normal, mosquitoes were not confined to the swampy area unless temperature and humidity were also below normal. But the one scientist still felt it was rationally acceptable to believe the original hypothesis.
   B. The other scientist felt it was rationally acceptable to believe that mosquitoes could not possibly survive in August outside the swampy area under the specified conditions of rainfall, temperature, and humidity.
   C. A third scientist, reviewing the project, felt it was rationally acceptable to believe that mosquitoes could survive in the general geographical area during August under some conditions.
   D. If you feel that the truth of a statement is very significant, it is rationally acceptable to believe it.
   E. If you feel that the truth of an hypothesis is significant, the hypothesis is "live," and the option is forced, then it is rationally acceptable for you to believe it.
   F. If there is no evidence available relevant to the truth of a statement, it is rationally unacceptable to believe it.
   G. If the evidence relevant to the truth or falsity of a statement is balanced, it is rationally unacceptable to believe it.
2. a. Check your answers to 1. Then, explain why in those cases James would find the belief rationally acceptable. Likewise, explain why he would not find the belief rationally acceptable in the other cases (30: 2.1, 30:2.2).

    b. In the light of these explanations, state James's argument for the acceptability of religious belief in the existence of God (30:2.2).

3. a. Explain how the character of prejudging becomes an argument against James's view (30:3.1).

    b. In World War I and World War II, both sides prejudged that God was with them. Bearing in mind the possibilities—that God was on the one side, on the other side, or neutral in the conflict—what nonprejudgmental approaches are possible to the question of God's loyalties?

4. On the left below are the theses about how the existence of God is incompatible with human freedom. On the right are objections to those theses. Match each objection with the thesis to which is responds (30:4.1–30:4.3).

A. Since God knows what each person will do beforehand, people are not free in their choices.

B. Since God is the omnipotent Creator of human beings, people do not have freedom to do anything other than the things God makes them do.

C. Since God designed us as a human designer designs a typewriter, we humans have no more freedom than a typewriter does.

i. God's being all powerful does not imply that God exerts all God's power.

ii. God knows only everything there is to know. But there is nothing about the future to be known since no sentences about the future are (as yet) either true or false.

iii. God might design creatures in such a way that they might freely choose for themselves.

iv. Even if I know that you will use a knife to butter your bread, that does not mean that I make you use it, or that you don't freely decide to do it.

5. Suppose you designed a garden, planting flowers, pulling weeds, and installing a birdbath. There are various ways in which your activity would not imply your complete control over the garden. List some of those ways and then try to formulate arguments concerning whether or not, if God designed the world, God's control of the world might not be any more complete than is your control of the garden.

SELECTED ANSWERS for Chapter 30

1. James would agree with C only.

2. a. A is not rationally acceptable because the accumulated evidence is against it. B is not acceptable because the evidence is not strong enough to support the conclusion that the mosquitoes "could not possibly" survive. D ignores the issues of whether or not the statement frames a *live* hypothesis about which there is a *forced* option. Both D and E ignore that the belief is still not rationally acceptable, according to James, if the

weight of the evidence is firmly against the statement. F and G are views against which James argues.

3. b. One possibility is to wait until the war is over, and then argue that God must have been on the winner's side. Another possibility is to begin from premises about God's goodness and concern for human beings, and then to argue on that basis. (Along this line many theologians have recently been arguing that modern warfare is intrinsically unjust. Hence God is opposed to these injustices on both sides.) Notice that any approach you take will involve some premise(s) about God, God's power, God's goodness and so on.

4. A: ii and iv; B: i; C: iii.

5. Your control is not complete because you have not controlled everything you could have controlled within that garden, because you cannot control some things in the garden, and because things beyond your control outside the garden affect it.

31

Religion and the Meaning of Life

The concern that life should have a meaning is fundamental yet perplexing. Many people try to justify their belief in God—as central as the concept of God is in Western religion—by saying that if there were no God, life would have no meaning. Yet at the same time the idea that life may have a meaning is, at the very least, a peculiar one. We all know what it is for a word or sentence to be meaningful, and we also understand that the formation of storm clouds means the coming of rain; but whatever the meaning of life might be, the idea that life is meaningful seems to involve a different idea of "meaning." It is also important to notice that life is thought to be the better for having a meaning and the worse for lacking one. In this chapter we shall try to understand the kind of value meaning gives to life, which in turn will help us understand why religious faith in God has been so closely connected to the idea of the meaning of life. After reading Chapter 31 you should be able to

- Distinguish the meaning of an action from other sorts of meaning.
- State logical implications of an act's being meaningful.
- State the implications of something's being a whole that has meaning.
- State an argument both for and against the conclusion that life could have some meaning without being fully meaningful.

■ Use the concepts of the meaning of life and human inadequacy in order to explain why the concept of God is so central to Western religions.

THE CASE OF WHY AND WHEREFORE

"Last call. Can I get you anything?"

"No, . . . well, wait . . . yes . . . one more brew. What do you say, Hal?"

"Okay, sounds good."

Tom turned back toward the barmaid. "Two more beers." She nodded and started back toward the bar, her fatigue evident.

Two more beers, she thought, *two and two and two till you've carried a thousand beers a hundred miles. And for $3.20 an hour you've got to do it until two in the morning, six days a week. God am I tired . . . knees hurt, ankles swollen. . . . For what? . . . then too, why not? It's real, isn't it? And reality is all that matters anyway. So I'll get them their damn beers. . . . What difference does it make anyway?*

Back at the table the two men wore the glass-eyed smiles that too many drinks too late at night bring on. The cigarette butts were piled high in the ashtray. Ashes spilled over onto a table that was damp with spilled beer.

"Say, Hal. Can I ask you a personal question?"

"Well, let's see. We've gone through our jobs, our sex lives, and our families. Why not?"

"Why?"

"Why what? Go ahead, ask your question."

"That was it . . . 'Why?' What's it all about, what does it all mean? Does it count for anything at all in the long run?"

"Why what, Tom?"

"Why life? That's what. I mean it's all crap. One lousy thing after another. Work all day, have a few laughs, suffer a lot, scratch for money, grow old and die. For what? So what?"

"I don't know. I'm gonna live till I die. That's all I do know. Not you, not anybody can change that. God knows I can't."

"There you go again . . . bringing God into it."

"Yes, well, sorry, but He makes all the difference. You see without Him, there is no sense to all of this. What a cruel joke life would be; digging around for sixty or seventy years like ants in a sandpile only to find out that all the sweat and suffering was a waste of time."

"But what can God do?"

"He makes it all worth something. He gives it all its value, its point. . . . Oh, hell, I don't know why you get me going like this all the time. Do you get your kicks out of watching me try to make sense out of my religion? . . . Why don't you try to answer your own questions sometimes?"

"Because I can't. You see . . . well . . . to me if there were a God, then this life would be really absurd. I mean what kind of God would it be that makes sick kids, grieving parents, bloody wars, bigotry, and all the rest? Or what kind of God would just sit around watching while those things go on? Talk about cruel. I would rather not have a God than have one that didn't give a damn."

"But what about making sense out of life? Why do you go on if you have no hope, if there is no reward, if it doesn't mean anything?"

"Oh, it probably means plenty, if I ever could figure out what a vague expression like 'makes sense out of life' meant in the first place. But . . . for my money my life means plenty; maybe not to you or to God or to anyone else, but life means a lot to me. People don't need God; they make their own reasons for living. They can create their own . . . what's the word? . . . values."

"Sounds noble, but shallow . . . paper hats and New-Years-Eveish if you know what I mean. Celebrating turning the page in a book with no start, no end, no theme, no moral. So we make our own values, and what the hell are they worth anyway?"

"That depends on. . ."

"Sorry, boys, we're closing now. You'll have to go. See you tomorrow." The barmaid had spoken without really talking to them. She mechanically shuffled off toward the only other occupied table to repeat her nightly exit chant.

31:1.1 *Meanings of language and signs*   Often when we are seeking for the meaning of something, what we want to know is the meaning of a word or a sentence. When requesting this kind of meaning, we are typically asking for some sort of definition. In Chapter 3 you learned many kinds of definitions which can be framed as answers to questions about the meaning of a linguistic entity. However, the question about the meaning of life is not a question about the meaning of the word "life," but is rather about the meaning of life itself. Very few people would be fooled into believing that this question could be handled by reference to a good dictionary or a clever stipulation.

31:1.2 *Life as a sign of things beyond*   Some people have believed, however, that this question is analogous to questioning the meaning of a storm cloud or the meaning of a flashing red traffic signal. The storm cloud and the traffic signal are, respectively, examples of what philosophers have called *natural* and *conventional* signs. In the course of natural events, we find the storm clouds associated with rain; because of a convention for understanding the significance of signal lights, we understand that a red signal commands us to stop. Some people have taken the question "What is the meaning of life?" to be asking what signs are found prominently in life. One would then state the question, "Is life itself a sign of anything beyond itself?" The question of whether or not life has meaning might be, but need not be, the question of whether life is a sign, portent, or omen of something beyond itself. You should notice, however, that this understanding of the question changes it significantly. The question of whether or not life *as a whole* has meaning is not the same as the question of whether or not something *within* life or experience has meaning. Thus we must begin afresh to understand what sense there might be to the idea that life as a whole might have a meaning. To do so we will first analyze what it means for an action to be meaningful, then we'll look at how a set of actions can have meaning, and finally we'll apply these insights to the question of the meaning of life as a whole.

31:2.1 *Meaningful action and intrinsic value* The idea of "the meaning of life" might be analogous to the idea of the meaningfulness of an action. What, then, does it mean to say that some action would be meaningful? It seems that this concept can be defined in terms of two sets of conditions, each of which is sufficient for meaningfulness. One set is associated with intrinsic value; the other with instrumental value. According to the first set of conditions, *an action will be meaningful if it is intrinsically valuable*, if that value is positive and nontrivial.

To understand this set of conditions, you must be clear about the idea of *intrinsic value*. To say that an action has intrinsic value is to say that doing the action has a value in itself, a value independent of its consequences and independent of anything to which it is intended to lead. Inflicting unnecessary pain is often cited as an example of an action with negative intrinsic value, whereas keeping one's promise is similarly cited as having positive intrinsic value. The idea of intrinsic value is contrasted to the idea of *instrumental value*, an action that is valuable because of the consequences resulting from it irrespective of what the action itself is.[1]

In asserting that meaningful actions must be *nontrivial*, philosophers have wanted to understand the idea of triviality by using comparisons. In other words, you should think of comparing all the acts that a person might be doing for the significance that they might have. An action, then, will be trivial when there is an available alternative action that is of greater significance.

Defining triviality in terms of significance still leaves open the question of what makes an action significant. All we have said so far is

---

[1] For detailed exposition of these concepts, see Chapter 5.

that the idea of meaningful action is connected to the ideas of nontrivial or significant action. The immense question of what makes an action significant is far more than we can answer in this text, but some discussion pertinent to the question is found later in 31:4.1 and 31:4.2. Can "significance" be defined in absolute terms, or is it always relative to some goal, purpose, time, place, or event? If nothing is significant in and of itself, how could a life be significant in and of itself?

31:2.2 *Meaningful action and instrumental value*   So far it seems accurate to say that some intrinsically valuable actions are meaningful. Philosophers have felt, however, that being intrinsically valuable is not a necessary condition for an action's being meaningful — which leads to the question of the other set of conditions. It seems that an action of instrumental value can be meaningful provided that it brings about, or will probably bring about, a state of affairs or some further actions that are intrinsically, positively, and nontrivially valuable. You will probably notice the similarity between the ideas in the statement of this sufficient condition for meaningful action and the preceding sufficient condition.

Let's unpack this statement just a bit. The barmaid in the case study wipes the tables in order to clean them off. In accordance with our definition of instrumental value, you could therefore say that her wiping the tables has instrumental value. She notices, however, the regularity with which the tables are again and again messed up after she has wiped them. If the barmaid sets for herself a goal of achieving clean tables for any length of time, what her experience impresses upon her all too firmly is that her goal is not achievable. The tables continually become dirtied and must be rewiped. Thus, the barmaid might conclude that even though she wipes the table in order to clean it, she never achieves her goal of a lastingly clean table. Let us define an action as *futile* if the action is intended to have instrumental value but at the same time the intrinsically valuable state of affairs for which the action is done is never thereby achieved. The statement of the sufficient condition for an action of instrumental value to be meaningful is that it *brings about or probably brings about something intrinsically valuable.* Thus the hidden implication of the condition is that no futile action can be meaningful.

 PHILOSOPHER'S WORKSHOP

The Myth of Sisyphus

The French existentalist philosopher, Albert Camus, comments on futility:

The gods had condemned Sisyphus to ceaselessly rolling a rock to the top of a mountain, whence the stone would fall back of its own weight. They had thought with some reason that there is no more dreadful punishment than futile and hopeless labor. At the very end of his long effort measured by skyless space and time without depth, the purpose is achieved. Then Sisyphus watches the stone rush down in a few moments toward that lower world whence he will have to push it up again toward the summit. He goes back down to the plain. . . .

If this myth is tragic, that is because its hero is conscious. Where would his torture be, indeed, if at every step the hope of succeeding upheld him? The workman of today works every day in his life at the same tasks, and this fate is no less absurd. But it is tragic only at the rare moments when it becomes conscious. Sisyphus, proletarian of the gods, powerless and rebellious, knows the whole extent of his wretched condition: it is what he thinks of during his descent. The lucidity that was to constitute his torture at the same time crowns his victory. There is no fate that cannot be surmounted by scorn.

If the descent is thus sometimes performed in sorrow, it can also take place in joy. This word is not too much. Again I fancy Sisyphus returning toward his rock, and the sorrow was in the beginning. When the images of earth cling too tightly to memory, when the call of happiness becomes too insistent, it happens that melancholy rises in man's heart: this is the rock's victory, this is the rock itself. The boundless grief is too heavy to bear. These are our nights of Gethsemane. But crushing truths perish from being acknowledged. Thus, Oedipus at the outset obeys fate without knowing it. But from the moment he knows, his tragedy begins. Yet at the same moment, blind and desperate, he realizes that the only bond linking him to the world is the cool hand of a girl. Then a tremendous remark rings out: "Despite so many ordeals, my advanced age and the nobility of my soul make me conclude that all is well." Sophocles' Oedipus, like Dostoevsky's Kirilov, thus gives the recipe for the absurd victory. Ancient wisdom confirms modern heroism.[2]

---

[2]Albert Camus, "The Myth of Sisyphus," in *The Myth of Sisyphus and Other Essays*, trans. Justin O'Brien (New York: Alfred A. Knopf, Inc., 1955), pp. 88–91.

31:3 *Meaningfulness of groups of actions* It is not only possible to state sufficient conditions for the meaningfulness of a given action, it is also possible to characterize *what it means for a group or set of actions to be meaningful.* The basic test is one of coherence. For example, suppose a man wants to have a house built for him and his family to live in. He not only asserts his desire, but he hires an architect and a general contractor and some subcontractors who proceed to construct his house. But now suppose that some night he comes to this new house as the frame is being built and takes an axe to it, perhaps destroying it or weakening many of the supporting beams. One ordinary and reasonable response to this action would be, "What is the meaning of this?" The reason we would be prompted to ask this question at this point is that we see in his actions what philosophers would call incoherence or inconsistency. If the man really wants the house built, then either he would help to see that it was built, or at the very least, he would not interfere with its being built. The idea that he wants the house built does not cohere with (is not consistent with) his destroying or even weakening the foundation of the house.

Let us generalize, then, from this example. A set of actions, assertions, or events can define a pattern, either a recurring regularity or a process directed toward a goal. When future events occur, they can either fit the pattern or continue to move toward the goal, or they may diverge from the pattern or move away from the goal. The meaning of the set of events, thus, is the coherence defined by the pattern or the goal. Conversely, if the future events break from the pattern or are contrary to the goal, the meaning defined by the pattern or the goal is lost or thwarted.

THE PARADOX OF LIFE

Philosophical grook

A bit beyond perception's reach
I sometimes believe I see
that Life is two locked boxes, each
containing the other's key.

If life is an "enigma wrapped in a mystery" does that give life meaning or destroy it?

31:4.1 *Interpreting "life has meaning"*   Some people would argue that life has meaning because there is much in life that has meaning, that it contains many meaning-bearing states of affairs and actions. When persons argue in this fashion they are thinking of life as composed of many individual events, each of which they are viewing separately from the others. This view allows them to say such things as life is *more or less* meaningful. They can think in terms of the degree of significance that individual events have and they can ask about the percentage of events that have any meaning at all. This view seems problematic, however, because not all events are equally influential in one's total life experience. Is a marriage that ends in a bitter divorce a meaningful single event or a series of events, some meaningful and others not? The concept of an "event" in one's life is perhaps too vague and ambiguous to leave unrefined, but it is not obvious that this view will remain plausible if it is clarified.

Other people interpret the question of whether or not life has a meaning by thinking about life, not as a series of individual, unrelated events, but as a whole, a set of events or state of affairs that should be understood together. When the question is understood this way, it is asking if there is a significant pattern or goal in all of life, rather than if life contains some (many) meaningful events. This question is one of coherence: "Is there a pattern or a goal for all of life?" Thus the fact that some individual actions have significance is not thought to be pertinent when no overriding pattern or goal is presented. But notice that a pattern may not lead to a goal, or a goal may exist but no plan for achieving it may be available. Here, too, vagueness in the use of "life's goal" or "the pattern of one's life" may be problematic.

31:4.2 *Ambiguous reference*   The question of the meaning of life is ambiguous not only, as we have seen, because "life" can refer to different things but also because of the following: (1) The question may be about *one person's own individual life*, involving many particulars of an individual's circumstances and abilities. (2) The question may be about the *series of lives* which a person lives *through many incarnations*. In other words, is the pattern of reincarnation a meaningful one? This is a central question to which the religions of Hinduism and Buddhism address themselves. (3) The question may also be about a different series of lives, *a series of the lives of my ancestors, myself, and my descendants*. That is, the question may be about the life of the culture with which I identify. A culture is a way of life and living, and accordingly, Jewish and Confucian answers to the question of the meaning of life tend to be given in such cultural, traditional terms. (4) Finally, the question may be a question about the meaning of *human life in general*. Here the emphasis is not on the particular lives, of

What is the relationship of insignificance to the meaning of life?

myself, my incarnations, or my culture, but rather on the meaning of being a human person under any conditions whatsoever. Each interpretation brings with it certain problems, ranging from whether or not one life in isolation can be meaningful to whether or not the fact that human life in general is meaningful can do anything to make one's individual life meaningful.

31:5.1 *God and the meaning of life* Students of religion have noticed that the concept of a personal God is much more central to the religions of the West (Judaism, Christianity, and Islam) than it seems to be to the religions of India and China (Hinduism, Buddhism, Confucianism, Taoism). All religion is concerned about the meaningfulness of life, and every religion has some scheme of salvation or redemption, because they all assume that life is not spontaneously and uniformly meaningful as we live it. Accordingly, religions uniformly agree that some redemptive change must take place for life to avoid being meaningless. The reason the concept of a personal God is so central to Western religions arises from their ideas about the human need for salvation. Jews believe that they needed deliverance from their bondage in Egypt, needed leadership in the wilderness, needed a moral law under which to live, and needed help in order to conquer the promised land. Christians believe that human beings need to be saved from their own selfishness and pride, which makes them think they can ignore God and thus leads them into moral wrongdoing. Moslems believe that human beings need to be transformed so as to be steadfast rather than wayward in their devotion to God. What all these beliefs have in common is the underlying assumption (perhaps false) that the salvation or redemption we, as human beings, need is beyond our ability, both individually and collectively, to bring about.

31:5.2 *The Christian perspective*   Let us explore a bit more fully why Christians are convinced that human beings cannot bring about their own salvation. The short of it is that human beings are their own worst enemies. St. Paul puts the point by saying, "The good that I would, that I do not; and the evil that I would not, that I do." Behind this assertion are the Christian assumptions that life is social and that standards of moral responsibility are central not only to the well-being of the community but also to the individual's own integrity. In the course of events, even the well-intentioned person fails to live up to his or her ideals. Some things that happen are beyond the person's control, but also a number of ignoble motives—at bottom, Christians would say, pride and selfishness—from time to time dominate the best of persons. Thus, life as the Christian sees it threatens to be meaningless because the individual does not live in accordance with the standard that alone would allow life to be meaningful.

From a Christian perspective, then, the problem of salvation is the humanly unforgivable ways people live. True, others can forgive someone the wrong done to them, but human forgiveness is not the whole of the problem. The problem is that Christians see themselves as having deviated from the standards that give life meaning. Those persons someone has wronged cannot fully "forgive" this wrong, because the humans who may be offended are not the only ones offended. God is offended too. It would be self-deception if persons were to forgive themselves, and thus Christians see full forgiveness as impossible on a human level. As they interpret the crucifixion, they understand Jesus as forgiving them and loving them. But how could Jesus forgive? Because Christians accept the Mosaic understanding that God gives the standards of conduct for meaningful life, Paul says that "God was in Christ reconciling the world to Himself." In other words, God can forgive because the transgressed standards are His, and Jesus is seen as God in that forgiving role. For Christians, then, because of human selfishness and pride, life can be meaningful only through forgiveness. Since human forgiveness is not adequate, the felt experience of being forgiven is interpreted as owing to a nonhuman, divine agent (God).

Within all Western religions God as a personal agent acts to remove the barrier to meaningful life. This agent is conceived of as divine, rather than demonic, inasmuch as it is through the agent's action that life comes to have its proper meaning. Neither Indian nor Chinese religion necessarily involves the view that there are barriers to meaningful life that human beings cannot remove. Accordingly, in those strands of Hinduism, Buddhism, Confucianism, and Taoism in which human beings are thought capable of preventing life from being meaningless, there is no clear central concept of God as a personal agent.

31:6 ***Summary*** The problematic concept of the meaning of life seems to be best understood on the model of a meaningful action or series of actions. Religions are characterized, not only by a concern for the meaningfulness of life, but also by a conception of salvation or redemption which shows the presumption that life must be transformed if it is not to be meaningless. Throughout the discussion of the meaning of life, it is crucial to clarify the ambiguity of the term "life" which will otherwise undermine the discussion. Western religions understand the concept of a personal God as central to their religions because they believe that human ability is inadequate to bring about the redemption that life needs in order to be meaningful.

EXERCISES for Chapter 31

1. Sections 1 to 4 of this chapter are devoted to clarifying what the sentence, "Life has meaning," might mean. Below is a list of tasks. Mark those that are a part of this task of clarification Yes and the rest No.
   A. Determine whether or not life is to be thought of as a sign of something beyond it.
   B. Decide whether or not there is a God.
   C. Determine whether or not any actions have intrinsic value.
   D. Decide whether "life" is to be understood as referring to a pattern in the events of life or simply to a collection of individual events.
   E. Prove that there is or that there is not a God.
   F. Determine whether or not "life" refers to lives of individuals.
   G. Determine how long human life has existed.
   H. Determine whether or not "life" refers to human life as a whole.
2. a. Suppose that many actions and many events have intrinsic positive value. On what bases might you argue that in an important sense life might still not have meaning?
   b. Suppose that the actions and events of life do form a pattern and work toward a goal. On what bases might you argue that in an important sense life might still not have meaning?
   c. Despite the clarifications of "Life has meaning" which have been provided in this chapter, much vagueness remains. What events should be included as part of a group? Suppose there are several patterns in life's events; how is a person to determine *the* one that gives life meaning? In the light of such remaining questions, would you be inclined to argue (i) that the concept of a meaning of life is incapable of being clarified sufficiently for clear evidence concerning any claim about what

life's meaning is; or (ii) that whatever further clarification of the concept may be required, it is not meaningless?

3. a. What assumptions or justifications are implicit in the assertion that God is central to life's meaning (31:5.1 and 31:5.2)?
    b. Check the answer to 3a. In the light of that answer develop a set of reasons why God is or is not central to life's meaning, as you understand it. (Note that this question presupposes your answer to 2c.)

SELECTED ANSWERS for Chapter 31

1. A. Yes.
   B. No, this task becomes relevant only after we assume we have already adequately determined what the phrase "the meaning of life" means.
   C. No, this task assumes that we have already clarified that actions of intrinsic (positive) value have meaning and that a meaningful life might somehow be related to meaningful individual actions.
   D. Yes.
   E. No, same as B.
   F. Yes.
   G. No.
   H. Yes.

2. a. i. These events form no meaningful pattern and work toward no goal.
       ii. These events are, for example, in the lives of individuals, but life has meaning only if the events with intrinsic (positive) value are events, for example, in the life of the human race.
    b. i. The individual events have no positive intrinsic value.
       ii. Life is futile because, whatever pattern it has, the goal it involves is unreachable.
    c. If you are inclined to argue that the phrase "the meaning of life" cannot be adequately clarified, then you should try to state what remains unclear about the phrase and explain why this cannot be clarified and why the phrase is useless without such clarification. If you are inclined to argue that the phrase can be or has been adequately clarified, then you might well want to refer to looser models of definition, like family resemblance (3:1.2) and open texture (3:1.1).

3. a. i. The phrase "the meaning of life" can be clarified adequately.
       ii. Life is meaningful only if God makes it meaningful—which entails both that life is not meaningful as persons live it without relation to God, and that people are incapable of changing the way they live life for themselves so as to make it become meaningful.
    b. Your reasoning here should take into account the grounds upon which you judge whether i and ii are true or false.

WORLD VIEWS

AND

LIFE STYLES

Developing or evaluating specific philosophical perspectives on individual problems is often what initially attracts people to philosophy. But beyond the purposes of precision, criticism, evaluation, and reflection lies the captivating goal of systematicity of thought. This goal urges us toward establishing intellectual accord among the various perspectives we might take on specific questions of value, questions about the nature and scope of human knowledge, and questions about the basic nature of reality. In seeking synthesis, we raise questions about the interrelationships of our ideas, and we strive for internal consistency as well as broad applicability in our efforts to develop a coherent and full-bodied world view.

Many of the greatest philosphers have tried to develop a world view that systematically addresses questions in metaphysics, epistemology, and value theory. Those whom we are about to study succeeded in this goal perhaps better than others, although not all the great systematic thinkers in the history of Western civilization are discussed.[1]

Our goal in selecting the five philosophers for this part was to find those who collectively represented a variety of philosophical traditions. We selected people whose writings present more or less fully developed world views that were particularly influential on other thinkers. We also looked for philosophers whose world views found expression in their individual life styles or in programs for social change. We suggest you begin with Chapter 32, which explains what is involved in systematically developing a philosophy or world view. Then, pick three or four specific philosophers to see how each has elaborated a world view. The relationship of the chapters in Part Eight is shown in the diagram.

[1]For example, Aristotle and Sartre are not included, because we have treated their views extensively in earlier chapters. But others like Epicurus, Plotinus, Augustine, Scotus, Hobbes, Bacon, Descartes, Leibniz, Spinoza, Locke, Voltaire, Berkeley, Fichte, Comte, Nietzsche, Hegel, Mill, Bergson, Peirce, Whitehead, James, Croce, Russell, Dewey, Santayana, Wittgenstein, Husserl, Kierkegaard, Quine, Sellars, Austin, Camus, Kripke, and so on are also omitted from this edition because of lack of space. (We welcome suggestions of which philosophers to add in future editions.)

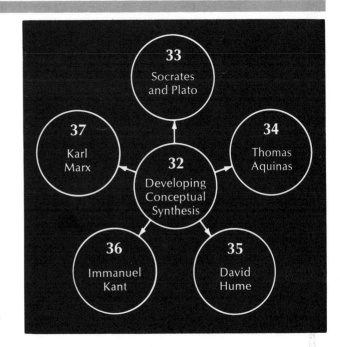

33 Socrates and Plato

37 Karl Marx

34 Thomas Aquinas

32 Developing Conceptual Synthesis

36 Immanuel Kant

35 David Hume

32

Developing Conceptual Synthesis

In Chapter 1 you learned that the systematic purposes of philosophy include (1) discovering connections between and implications of concepts and beliefs, (2) developing concepts with comprehensive applicability, and (3) designing models that substantiate the general applicability of these concepts. Then in Chapter 3 you learned how philosophers use descriptive and stipulative definitions in order to clarify individual concepts. If you put together their use of definitions with their goal of systematicity, you will see one of the chief ways they have of establishing the conceptual integration and clarity that characterize a world view. Systematic philosophers strive for world views that establish smooth connections among the concepts in their perspectives on metaphysics, epistemology, and value theory. In this chapter you will learn what a "conceptual system" is. You will explore its strengths and study how both foundationalists and contextualists approach these strengths.

After reading Chapter 32 you should be able to

- Identify examples of a philosopher's reasoning from premises in one area of philosophy to conclusions in another.
- Identify and distinguish completeness, coherence, applicability, and simplicity as strengths of conceptual systems.

■ Explain the tension between the strengths of completeness and coherence and between applicability and simplicity.

THE CASE OF HERB AND THE PROFESSOR

Herb would have known that he had found Professor Tyson's office by the pungent smell of cigar smoke even if he hadn't seen the name on the door. He knocked and then opened the door to go in. A blue-grey wall of smoke met him as he stepped into the small room and introduced himself.

"Sit down, Herbert. What can I do for you?" said the professor, putting down the school newspaper.

Resisting the temptation to tell the professor to open a window, he responded, "I'm in your intro. class and I wanted to talk to you about an idea I've been toying with."

"Yes, go ahead."

"Well . . . it may sound silly . . . but . . ."

"Don't worry about how it sounds; lots of brilliant ideas sound silly at first. Most often they just need refinement and polish to come up to standard."

Herb didn't like the professor's patronizing tone, but he went on anyway. "Well . . . I want to say that all reality is really pure energy which manifests itself in static forms like nonliving physical objects or dynamic forms like living things."

As the professor sat back in his swivel chair it squeaked as if to register its agreement with Herb's theory. The professor lit a fresh cigar and puffed heavily several times, creating an even denser blue-grey cloud around his head, as if signaling the start of an intellectual exercise. "So energy has two basic modes of appearance you say. How then do we classify lightning, gravity, radio waves, and the like using your theory? Also, why don't you say that these things are pure energy and that other things, like physical objects, are matter? That way you have two basic commodities, energy and matter; not just one, energy."

"That may be, Professor, but we know from modern physics that energy and matter can be converted into each other. So basically there is still only one thing, energy."

"I'm not sure about that, but let's grant it for now. Even so, how then do you explain how things as different as a living human person and a lump of coal are basically the same?"

"I'm not sure I can. But they are. One is just a physical manifestation of energy; the other is both physical and spiritual. That's what I mean by saying that living things are 'dynamic.' "

"Oh! You mean that they are spiritual as well as physical. But you said that what is physical was static. So I guess that a person is both static and dynamic in your view. That seems problematic." Although the professor was pleased at scoring this point, Herb was nothing but perplexed.

"Yes, I see that. . . . Maybe I better say that 'dynamic' just means 'spiritual.' Now there is no inconsistency. Persons are spiritual and not static."

"Fine, Herbert. But you see, now persons are not physical. You made them dynamic and that means spiritual, not physical. There seems now to be an incoherence between your theory and what we know about people, namely, that they are physical."

"Oh! But . . ."

"What I mean is, how am I to apply the term 'spiritual'? Does it apply to all living things as such? Does it apply then also to their bodies? Or is it only the mind that is intended? I guess my problem is that I know what your words mean but not what they refer to; or maybe vice versa."

"I don't know what to do about that," said Herb nervously. *Why doesn't he help me rather than try to confuse me?* Herb thought.

"I see. Well, then, how come some things are living but others are not?"

"It's because the living things are animated. Energy animates reality, Professor."

"But why then don't we say that everything is living? Herbert, you told me everything was energy! Yet earlier you said that there were nonliving physical objects."

Herb was getting frustrated by this time and the smoke made his eyes burn. "You keep twisting things. I thought you would be able to understand, but you are playing word games."

"Far from it, Herbert. I'm trying to understand. But you have to help me," said the insensitive would-be Socrates. "I believe that there are problems with your theory. As I said at the start, it may need some work. At first it seemed to have all the charm and appeal of a simple striking insight. But as we looked, things got more complex. Incoherence popped up. There were other problems, too. Also I don't understand what implications it has for ethics and I don't know how you can verify what you claim either. Apart from my rough treatment of you I suspect the theory has merit. But there are conceptual problems and theoretical connections still to be worked out."

"Yes, well, thanks for your time." Herb was angry at the professor's poor apology. "I'm allergic to cigar smoke, by the way."

Finally the professor realized that he really hadn't given Herb a fair chance; he had focused exclusively on the theory instead of the human needs of the student. "I'm sorry, Herb," he responded. Grinding out his cigar, he began to explain what was involved in establishing an integrated world view.

32:1.1 *Conceptual integration*[1] Philosophers seek conceptual integration, or synthesis, by defining one concept in terms of another. For example, St. Paul establishes a connection between the concepts of faith and hope in the definitional statement, "Faith is the confident assurance in that which is hoped for."[2] Nietzsche argues that exploitation cannot be rooted out of human social conditions. He uses the following definition of "life" in order to make his point: "Life itself is essential assimilation, injury, violation of the foreign and weaker, suppression, hardness, the forcing of one's own forms upon something else, ingestion and—at least in its mildest form—exploitation."[3] Mao Tse-tung defined the relationship between political power and violence thus: "Political power grows out of the barrel of a gun."[4]

Although we can use individual definitions to clarify what words like "happiness" and "duty" mean, we have not thereby suggested the possible interrelationship between them. Yet we might wish to stipulate or describe such an interrelation by using a definition like "Happiness is that for which it is everyone's duty to strive." Similarly, we could establish a perspective on problems in one area of philosophy, say metaphysics, and yet not tie these ideas to another area, say epistemology, until we establish these ties by using definitions. For example, we might find a philosopher claiming that the metaphysical reason why human beings are free is that they possess a faculty called "free will" which is immune from physical causal influence. When asked how this faculty can then influence human action, the philosopher might reply by defining another faculty: "The *intellect* is the faculty by which one knows what choice the will makes and which then itself causes muscles to move so as to execute the choice the will makes." In this way the philosopher would have tried to establish a connection between a metaphysical and an epistemological perspective, between what is real (a will and an intellect) and what is known (the intellect knows the will's choices).

32:1.2 *Perspectives are interrelated* The perspective you take on one philosophical issue may limit *or eliminate* certain theoretical options on another issue. For example, if you take the perspective of hard deter-

---

[1]You should review the systematic purposes of philosophy (explained in 1:3.1–1:3.3) and also how definitions are developed (Chapter 3, including the Workshop, "Definitions of Key Concepts," in 3:3.3).

[2]*Letter to the Hebrews*, 11:1.

[3]Friedrich Nietzsche, *Beyond Good and Evil*, trans. Marrianne Cowen (Chicago: Henry Regnery Co., 1955), p. 201.

[4]Mao Tse-tung, *On People's War* (Peking: Foreign Language Press, 1967), p. 3.

minism,[5] it is unreasonable to adopt a retributive view of human punishment in ethics; you could not easily reconcile the view that people deserve to be punished for wrong doing when you also believe that they could not have freely chosen to do otherwise.

Further, a perspective on one issue is often thought to *entail* a certain perspective on another. For example, some philosophers argue that the metaphysical theory that humans have souls entails that people are morally free and that they (or their souls) are immortal. Whether or not these entailments hold, however, will depend upon how "soul" is defined. Thus, the entailments hold if the soul is understood as an entity without a location in space and not subject to physical causation, but not if the soul is defined as a chemical process in the higher region of the brain.

Philosophers sometimes mistakenly feel bound by the perspectives they take in one area and fail to recognize that they have theoretical options in another area. For Aristotle and Aquinas, belief in God meant belief in an unchanging, omniscient being. But it may be that God is dynamic and that divine knowledge develops apace with the evolution of reality through time. The concept of "perfect," in other words, can still apply to God, but "perfect" here means being adaptable and dynamic, whereas for Aristotle it meant being unchangeable.

32:1.3 *Models and analogies* Often a dominant model, analogy, symbol, image, or metaphor guides a thinker in the development of a conceptual system — which helps to integrate the philosopher's ideas. Some philosophers, for example, look at reality as fundamentally alive and organic. Their metaphysical perspectives usually focus on the interconnected, vital developmental forces that cause physical change, and their ethical and social perspectives emphasize the interrelatedness of human lives, the importance of cooperative effort, and the centrality of group identity and culture to human happiness or duty. Other philosophers are influenced by a more atomistic model. Their metaphysical perspectives generally focus on the discrete individual entities that aggregate together to constitute reality, and epistemologically, they focus on problems relating to how an isolated individual can know or be known by others. In ethics and political thought, the atomistic model yields individualistic social theories and attention to personal liberties and limitations on collective authority.

32:1.4 *Focus* Philosophers can also start in different areas and focus primarily on different problems. Socrates, Epicurus, Hobbes, Mill,

---

[5]The view that no human action is free but rather all are caused by scientifically knowable events (see Chapter 19).

Nietzsche, and Marx might be thought of as being most interested in value theory. Their views in metaphysics or epistemology seem, by comparison, to be less fully developed. Descartes, Leibniz, Bacon, Quine, Wittgenstein, and others focus primarily on epistemology and metaphysics, with a relatively small effort at developing their value theory. Historically, some philosophers have had a primary interest in religion; others in science; others still in art, education, or language.

32:1.5 *Sizing up world views*   If you can identify the focal points of interest and preferred models within a philosopher's world view, you can answer important questions: Which aspects of the world view does the philosopher think are more central and less open to revision? How are other aspects of this world view likely to be developed? If you can see the implications of a given perspective for other areas of a world view, you can project theoretical options. And if the philosopher incorporates a position contrary to one of these projected options, you can detect a possible incoherence.

32:2.1 *Conceptual systems*   A conceptual system in any field is basically a set of carefully constructed definitions such that (1) relatively simple, familiar, and intuitive concepts are used to define more complex, technical, or unusual ideas; (2) terms that are defined early are used to help define subsequent terms in order to relate them to the concepts already presented in the system; (3) the builder of the system strives to define all the terms relevant to a given study without loss of consistency, simplicity, or applicability. Let's look at these attributes as we explore what it means to use a conceptual system to pursue the philosophical purposes of intellectual synthesis.

32:2.2 *Ladders and webs*   A conceptual system is, first of all, a set of definitions connecting the concepts. Some systems are like a rope ladder, with its top firmly anchored to our shared human experiences and each new step fastened by strong definitional or conceptual ropes to those above. Other systems can be viewed as a spider's web, with several main supporting lines secured to insights in a variety of specific areas and concentric circles tying each of these diverse basic insights and areas to each other. If a rope in the ladder breaks, then the whole ladder shakes and climbers risk falling off. If one of the basic support lines in the web lets go, the whole web shakes, but the center remains secure and chances are the web can be repaired. Philosophical world views are much the same. Foundationalist views are like the rope ladder, with its secure ties and careful steplike construction. Contextualist views are like the spider web, pulling together facts and

perspectives in a variety of areas and creating a system that is supported in part by the tension set up among its own components.[6]

In either a ladder or a web, one part may be related to another in
a dependent way, and this dependence in a conceptual system is revealed by the way terms are defined. Such a system is often anchored
by means of words used and understood in their ordinary ways. For
example, Xenophanes (580 B.C.) wanted to begin his conceptual system by defining the term "God." He chose to do so with words like
"supreme," "men," "gods," "mortals," "body," and "mind," all of
which he took to be familiar to people of his time in nontechnical, ordinary ways of talking. Thus he proposed, "God is one, supreme
among gods and men, and not like mortals in body or mind."[7] He then
went on to further define some of the chief characteristics of his God,
such as omniscience, creativity, and immutability.

32:2.3 *Monism and pluralism*   Conceptual systems can also be categorized
by how many kinds of things they identify as the primary stuff of reality. A *monistic* system asserts that all reality is one kind of thing; for
example, Herbert's system in the case study asserts that everything is
essentially energy. The problem for monistic systems is in explaining
how the apparently quite diverse phenomena we encounter can all be
explained as parts or manifestations of the same thing. Herb began his
explanation by saying that energy could manifest itself as either dynamic or static.

A conceptual system that postulates two basic kinds of things out
of which reality emerges is called *dualistic*; one that postulates two or
more is called *pluralistic*. Dualism and pluralism both face the challenge of defining the precise interrelationship of its two or more basic
kinds of things, Contemporary physicists, for example, have postulated the existence of several kinds of elemental subatomic particles,
such as electrons, neutrons, and various types of quarks. The task that
guides their research is not simply the discovery or postulation of such
entities, but the theoretical definition of their interrelationship.

Conceptual systems, then, help to interrelate ideas in two ways:
First, they relate ideas back to those root or primitive concepts upon
which the whole system depends. Second, they relate ideas to each
other, establishing the cross-hatching of concepts that form the ladder
or web of the conceptual system.

---

[6]The contrast between foundationalist and contextualist approaches is explained
in Chapter 4.

[7]Xenophanes, Fragment 23, in T. V. Smith, ed., *From Thales to Plato* (Chicago:
Phoenix Books, 1956), p. 14.

✐ PHILOSOPHER'S WORKSHOP

The One and the Many

The debate between a monistic or a dualistic approach to metaphysics consumed the energies of many of the first thinkers who made the daring intellectual jump from folklore to philosophy. Dualists often pointed to the phenomenon of change as a basis for postulating the existence of more than one basic kind of thing or basic principle of reality, whereas monists saw stability as a reason to maintain that all was one. The following passage from Empedocles (c. 400 B.C.) illustrates a metaphysical pluralism with value theoretic overtones:

Twofold is the truth I shall speak; for at one time there grew to be one alone out of many, and at another time, however, it separated so that there were many out of the one. Twofold is the coming into being, twofold the passing away, of perishable things; for the latter (i.e., passing away) the combining of all things both begets and destroys, and the former (i.e., coming into being), which was nurtured again out of parts that were being separated, is itself scattered.

And these (elements) never cease changing place continually, now being all united by Love into one, now each borne apart by the hatred engendered of Strife, until they are brought together in the unity of the all, and become subject to it. Thus inasmuch as one has been wont to arise out of many and again with the separation of the one the many arise, so things are continually coming into being and there is no fixed age for them; and further inasmuch as they (the elements) never cease changing place continually, so they always exist within an immovable circle . . . for at one time there grew to be the one alone out of many, and at another time it separated so that there were many out of the one; fire and water and earth and boundless height of air, and baneful Strife apart from these, balancing each of them, and love among them, their equal in length and breadth . . . For they two (Love and Strife) were before and shall be, nor yet, I think, will there ever be an unutterably long time without them both.[8]

---

[8]Empedocles, Fragment 17, in *From Thales to Plato, op. cit.*, pp. 29–30.

32:2.4 *World views*   System-building is common to all intellectual disciplines like physics, medicine, and linguistics, but philosophical systems do not just synthesize knowledge in a specialized area. They also provide a *world view*, a systematic overview of the fundamental categories of intellectual concern: metaphysics, epistemology, and value theory. *Metaphysics* addresses the questions of what fundamental kinds of things exist, how they relate to each other, and how they are manifest in familiar phenomena.[9] *Epistemology* investigates the nature, method, and scope of knowledge, especially human knowledge. Value theory is composed of ethics, social and political thought, and aesthetics. It seeks to define basic values in all areas of human endeavor and to relate these values to each other, exploring ways in which they might complement each other or conflict with each other. Other prominent concerns of Western philosophers, such as understanding human nature, religion, or the meaning of life, overlap one or more of these three fundamental categories. Thus questions in the philosophy of religion, for example, are sometimes metaphysical ("Is there a God?"), sometimes epistemological ("How can one know the meaning of life?"), and sometimes value theoretic ("If there were a God, what would this mean for how one ought to live one's life?").

32:3.1 *Strengths of conceptual systems: completeness*   In the case study Professor Tyson first criticizes Herb's thesis as not accounting for certain phenomena; for example, lightning and radio waves are not best classified as static physical objects. The point of the criticism is that the theory is not complete. *Completeness* means taking account of all the variety of things that present themselves for consideration. Herb evidently is developing a theory to help us understand the makeup of all reality, and therefore, cannot reply to the professor that commonly identified phenomena, like lightning, need not be considered. His only choices are to account for lightning and other such phenomena, or to deny that they are real. If he is not successful in one of these, his theory can rightly be criticized as incomplete.

32:3.2 *Consistency*   The professor next zeroes in on the monism/dualism distinction (32.2.3). When Herb holds fast to his monism, the professor, pointing out the theory's implication that human beings are both "static and dynamic," is suggesting *incoherence* in the theory. Herbert could accept, without offering an amendment, the implausibility of calling the same thing both static and dynamic; but another theoreti-

---

[9]We use the term "metaphysics" to mean *ontology* (the study of being), and not in the broader sense of "world view."

TWIN MYSTERY

To many people artists seem
    undisciplined and lawless.
Such laziness, with such great gifts,
    seems little short of crime.
One mystery is how they make
    the things they make so flawless;
another, what they're doing with
    their energy and time.

How many differences between systems reflect differences in perspectives rather than disagreements about facts?

cal option would be to argue that reality is complex in that some things manifest energy in both ways.

However, Herb tries to resolve the conceptual problem by stipulating a definition: "Dynamic" means "spiritual."[10] The professor quickly uses this definition to derive a more obvious incoherence: The theory defines humans as spiritual and nonphysical, whereas our experience of human beings is that they are at least in part physical. The incoherence turns into a flat contradiction in the next exchange, for the professor points out that Herb's statements entail that everything is living; but earlier Herb said there were nonliving things.

---

[10]*Stipulative* definitions are discussed in Chapter 3.

32:3.3 *Applicability*   A critic might take the professor as well as Herb to task for the way they are using terms. Words like "dynamic" and "static" and even "living" are problematic in their application. For example, is a crystal forming in a solution best called static or dynamic? Is an amino acid living? Conceptual systems are useless if you cannot see how the concepts apply to the real world. Unless systems are tied to our experiences, to objects and phenomena we can recognize, they are free-floating abstractions, of interest only as mental exercises or flights of fancy.

32:3.4 *Simplicity*   Simplicity, as a virtue of conceptual systems, is not the subjective psychological simplicity you feel when you find something easy to grasp. Rather it is *logical* simplicity. A system is relatively simpler if a variety of more complex concepts are explained in terms of relatively few less complex concepts. If these few concepts are also familiar and intuitive, then psychological simplicity also can result. When in the course of finding interrelations a philosopher traces ideas back to their roots, simplicity is a natural by-product. The professor does not criticize Herb's theory as lacking logical simplicity, but the simplicity he gains by defining "physical," "spiritual," and "living" as types of energy is bought at the price of obscuring the applicability of these terms.

   The case study shows that it is a lot easier for the professor to find faults with Herb's conceptual system than it is for Herb to construct it in the first place. Philosophers like Plato, Aristotle, Aquinas, Descartes, Mill, Hegel, Kant, Russell, and Sartre stand out as great because they could do more than criticize; they could synthesize, and their conceptual systems have not only withstood many criticisms but have impressed other thinkers as viable world views.

32:4.1 *Tensions between the strengths*   The case study illustrates the difficulty of building a system with all these strengths. If Herb did not seek completeness, he could more easily ignore unusual or problematic cases. In so doing he would be better able to achieve consistency and coherence by discarding cases that did not fit easily or coherently. But since he strives for comprehensiveness, he must make adjustments and amendments, always trying to preserve coherence and finding the task more difficult with each new type of phenomenon to be covered.

   Applicability and simplicity stand in a similar tension. The simplicity of Herb's system threatens its applicability. In order to insure that the conceptual system is applicable, we must get rather specific in our descriptions of things and in our procedures for identifying the references of our terms. However, such improvements in applicability tend to increase complexity. With this complexity, both psychological and logical simplicity are jeopardized; psychological because the complexity is harder to grasp, logical because the specific descriptions do not follow as strictly logical implications of the terms as intensionally defined.

32:4.2 *The possibility of compromise* *Foundationalist* views naturally tend to stress consistency and logical simplicity. *Contextualist* views, on the other hand, tend to stress applicability and completeness. However, the possibility of trading a measure of completeness for consistency or a portion of applicability for simplicity has also attracted thinkers faced with the problem of developing a conceptual system that meets all four goals.

32:5 *Summary* A conceptual system is a set of definitions carefully developed to achieve intellectual synthesis. Terms are interrelated both by being traced through definitions to their root concepts and by being defined in relation to other concepts in the system. The four strengths of conceptual systems are simplicity, applicability, consistency, and completeness. Since it's hard to build a conceptual system that perfectly embodies all four strengths, and since different approaches to philosophy stress different strengths, the full evaluation of a conceptual system would include reviewing it for each strength. A conceptual system that covers the fundamental categories of intellectual concern—metaphysics, epistemology, and value theory—is a world view.

You have looked at a variety of perspectives in earlier parts. Theories in each area may relate more or less adequately to theories in other areas. You should be alert for the guiding models, areas of special emphasis, and theoretical options available to various philosophers. In the next five chapters we will sample some of the great world views in Western philosophy. Read them with these considerations in mind.

EXERCISES for Chapter 32

1. a. Below are four examples of reasoning a philosopher might use in moving from a perspective he or she has taken on one problem to a conclusion in some other area of philosophy. Identify the premises and the conclusion in each passage.

   A. Everything is individual. Every individual thing is separate from every other thing. The desires of individual things are individual and different. For these reasons, every individual person ought to make his or her own decisions, and no one has the right to control another.

B. Everything is complete and perfect in its being and its motion. Now the most perfect of all geometric figures is the circle. Even if it appears from observation that the orbits of the planets are not circles, still we must conclude that their orbits must basically be circles, with circles upon those circles—and perhaps even circles upon those circles, which accumulation of circles will account for the observations we make.

C. Surely in all things, then, we ought to do what is loving. For ours is the ability to know that God is love. We are also given to know that we are made in God's image. And what would be the purpose of our having all this knowledge except that we should infer that we ought always to act lovingly ourselves?

D. What, then, is history? History, essentially, is the human accounting of how human life has been lived. And from this simple fact it follows that all of knowledge is the knowledge of human records.

b. After checking your answers, identify the premises and the conclusion of each passage as metaphysical, epistemological, or ethical (32:1.1).

c. A–D below are criticisms of A–D, respectively, above. Identify which of the four strengths: completeness, coherence, applicability, and simplicity, the critic relies upon.

A. If no one has the right to control another, then when one person makes his or her own decision and that decision is to dominate another, then since no one has the right to control this person, this person is free to act upon a decision to dominate another. Surely the idea that no one has the right to control another is, therefore, a self-defeating idea.

B. Even if the orbits of the planets can accurately be predicted in terms of circles upon circles upon circles, surely it would be not only just as accurate but far less complex to describe the orbits as ellipses.

C. Suppose an adult has been terribly burned. Suppose she is suffering great pain. Suppose the only treatment to keep her alive causes her repeated intense suffering. Suppose she has lost several physical abilities permanently and she is begging not to be medically treated any more. But suppose also that her life can be saved, that she can regain several physical abilities, that her mind is keen and aware, and that her young children are terrified that their mother may die. Suppose she needs another treatment now if her life is not to be jeopardized. You are the doctor. You decide to do the loving thing. So, what do you do?

D. Part of what we know concerns the natural world before the beginning of human life. Since there were no human records then, this knowledge is not accounted for in this view.

d. Illustrate the tension either between completeness and coherence or between applicability and simplicity by reference to each of the four pieces of reasoning and/or the four criticisms.

2. a. Make up separate examples of your own to illustrate the importance of each of the strengths: completeness, coherence, applicability, and simplicity.

   b. In the light of your previous study of the foundationalist and the contextualist approaches and in the light of their differences over the importance of these strengths, what reasons could you give for preferring one of these approaches over the other?

SELECTED ANSWERS for Chapter 32

1. a. Only the conclusions are given.
   A. Every individual person ought to make his or her own decisions, and no one has the right to control another.
   B. Their orbits must basically be circles, with circles upon those circles — and perhaps even circles upon those circles, which accumulation of circles will account for the observations we make.
   C. In all things we ought to do what is loving.
   D. All knowledge is the knowledge of human records.

   b. A. Premises: metaphysical; conclusion: ethical.
   B. Premises: metaphysical; conclusion: metaphysical.
   C. Premises: (first two) epistemological, (third) metaphysical or perhaps ethical; conclusion: ethical.
   D. Premise: metaphysical; conclusion: epistemological.

   c. A. Coherence: The view is incoherent.
   B. Simplicity: So many circles upon circles is too complex.
   C. Applicability: Two actions, contrary to each other, may each appear equally loving.
   D. Completeness: Confining human knowledge to knowledge of human records is a limited, incomplete view of knowledge.

   d. A. The incoherence cited in the criticism may very easily be the result of trying to cover all the cases in talking about authority, rather than being less complete.
   B. The criticism is that the attempt to keep the idea of circular orbits applicable has led to excessive complexity.
   C. The criticism is that attractive as the prescription "act lovingly" may be, in part because of its simplicity, it lacks the complexity to be applied, at least clearly and with certainty, in response to complex problems.
   D. This view illustrates all four strengths in tension. As it stands, the view is simple and can therefore easily avoid inconsistency. However, as it is pressured to become more applicably comprehensive, it risks both its simplicity and its coherence.

33

![decorative chapter number 33]

Socrates and Plato

What is the proper task of philosophers? Is it to contribute to human understanding of how the world works? Philosophers are, in such a view, essentially spectators and commentators. Even social philosophers do no more than describe and explain their societies, at most pointing out internal inconsistencies. The ancient Greek philospher Plato (427–347 B.C.) emphatically rejected the role of bystander. He regarded the society of his time as "sick" quite literally, and asserted that "the human race will not see better days until either those who rightly and genuinely follow philosophy acquire political authority, or else the class with political power is guided by some miracle to become real philosophers."[1] In the active role of social reformers, philosophers are constantly guided by a vision of how things ought to be and sustained by a promise of spiritual fulfillment in no way contingent upon political success.

This chapter introduces you to the philosophy of Plato. After reading this chapter you should be able to

■ **State major problems that Plato addressed.**

---

[1]Plato, *Republic*, 473 cd, trans. Francis M. Cornford (London: Oxford University Press, 1941).

- **Describe how Plato used his methods to offer solutions to these problems.**
- **Address major criticisms and impacts of Plato's philosophy.**

33:1.1 *The heir of Socrates* At the end of the fifth century B.C. in Athens, Socrates was the dominant philosophical influence (see the Workshop in 4:1.4). Socrates spent his own life in obedience to the oracle of Delphi's command, "Know thyself" (see Part Three, "Introduction"). Self-knowledge, for Socrates, was knowledge of the moral truths that should guide your life. Because virtue itself consists in knowledge, only the person who achieves moral insight can lead a worthwhile life, whereas "the unexamined life is not worth living."

Socrates pursued knowledge by asking questions of supposedly wise and prominent people and trying to refute their answers. His criticism of Athenian democracy and established religion made him very unpopular, and ultimately he was unjustly tried and executed (399 B.C.). The death of Socrates left deep psychic scars on his pupil Plato (427–347 B.C.), whose writings are filled with contempt for the democratic form of government that had prevailed in Athens, with its imperialist ventures abroad and indulgence of the masses at home. He not only wrote a blueprint for political leadership by a "philosopher-king," but also personally staked everything on an actual venture to establish a utopia. However, the attempt to set up an ideal state in Sicily under the young and idealistic King Dionysius of Syracuse ended up a farcical disaster, described in Plato's *Seventh Letter*. Plato returned to Athens and concentrated on education, and his school, the Academy, continued to influence Western thought for a thousand years. Plato's trips to Sicily and Italy also brought him into contact with the Pythagorean and Eleatic philosophers, who introduced him to deep questions about the nature of reality (in which Socrates had little interest). He was fascinated by the Orphic cults of southern Italy, which taught that by becoming initiated in their sacred mysteries one could achieve salvation after death; and he was infected with the Pythagorean passion for mathematics: The sign over the Academy read, "Let no one who knows not mathematics enter here."

33:1.2 *Plato's context: religious and social crisis*   Socrates was condemned to death on the trumped-up charges that he corrupted the youth of Athens and that he subverted the official religion by introducing new deities. Though false, the charges are significant because they point to areas of public anxiety. Leading intellectuals were demonstrating the bankruptcy of traditional Greek religion. The popular polytheism crowded Mount Olympus and subterranean grottoes with gods and demigods, but pre-Socratic philosophers had already offered naturalistic explanations of events like earthquakes and eclipses formerly attributed to gods. More seriously, the gods' moral authority had been undermined by the myths of Homer and Hesiod, which depicted their struggles for power and their all-too-human flaws of character. The belief in a grim "afterlife" of ghosts in Hades offered little relief and was contemptuously rejected by the more enlightened. Official religion had ossified into ritualism without spiritual meaning. Plato's problem was to provide a philosophical restatement and defense of the religious belief in God and immortality that avoided the emptiness of tradition and the negativeness of contemporary intellectuals.

The social structure of Athens was threatened by the collapse of the old educational system. In its place, the Sophists taught rhetoric, political argument, and related topics to the children of wealthy and aristocratic families. Some of the Sophists encouraged younger politicians to pander to the whims of the majority. Sophists like Protagoras defended relativism: "Man is the measure of all things." In the political arena this belief meant that whatever the stronger party calls good is good. Socrates and Plato rejected these teachings, but they recognized the impossibility of returning to the outmoded, militaristic, anti-intellectual values of Greek tradition. Plato's problem was to identify a set of political ideals for society and describe a program of education by which these ideals would be implemented.

33:2.1 *Plato's methods* Plato makes extensive use of Socrates's method of refutation (see 4:1.4). In his early dialogues, which most scholars believe Plato wrote as a young man, Plato shows Socrates using these methods. The aim of this method is to evaluate different definitions of important moral terms such as "justice," "self-control," "courage," and "wisdom." He claims that you do not know the answers to moral questions such as "Can virtue be taught?" or "Is this act pious?" until you can answer the questions "What is virtue?" "What is piety?" This method is *contextualist*, for it draws heavily on commonly accepted beliefs to refute whatever claims are under discussion. Socrates calls such beliefs "hypotheses," which are themselves open to criticism.[2]

But in those dialogues regarded as his later writings, Plato fashions Socrates's informal techniques into powerful weapons of his own.[3] In these dialogues Plato's "hypotheses" become exceedingly subtle metaphysical doctrines whose implications he traces into every department of thought. To justify them, Plato develops a powerful method of dialectic called the argument from *self-refutation* or *reduction to absurdity*. Seemingly invulnerable philosophical theories can be refuted by showing that they contain, in the form of unstated assumptions, the seeds of their own destruction. That is, they lead upon close examination to absurd consequences or self-contradictions, and so must be rejected as false theories. Often Plato argues that a philosophical statement is self-refuting, because, if it were true, it would be impossible to make the statement in the first place.

A simple use of this method is Plato's refutation of the claim of Parmenides, "Being is one,"[4] which means that everything is really one, all diversity is an illusion. Plato points out that such a claim refutes itself. Since it applies *two* names, "being" and "one," to reality, it assumes that *two* things exist, not one. Even if Parmenides had tried to stop with one name, "one," to make his point, he would still have refuted himself. Something is a real name only if there is *something else* that it names. But if there *is* something else, then *two* things, the name and what it names, exist. In short, Plato often defends his own

---

[2]See 4:2.4. In describing *this* method as contextualist, we are not implying that Socrates always used contextualist approaches.

[3]This is our interpretation of Plato's philosophical development. Our point here is that Plato developed new foundationalist *methods* as he matured. See section 3.2.

[4]Plato, *Sophist*, 244 a–c.

hypotheses by showing that competing ones can be reduced to absurdity and so should be rejected.

33:2.2 *Human nature*   Plato remains faithful to the Socratic goal of self-knowledge. The Socratic self is the soul. Traditionally the Greeks used the word "soul" for the insensible ghosts of the dead, but Socrates uses it to refer to the conscious self, the source of moral direction. Socrates claims that people who have achieved full moral insight keep their sensual appetites and competitive drives under control. On the other hand, people who act immorally or in a self-destructive manner do so out of ignorance of the good. These paradoxical claims, which are the core of Socrates's psychology, are accepted and defended by Plato.

With Socrates's emphasis on the soul, Plato combines a religious conception of human nature. He embraces the Pythagorean teaching that the soul is spiritual in nature and capable of surviving death. After death, the soul undergoes reincarnation in a new human being or lower animal. The soul is of supernatural origin, and it makes its possessor godlike. Plato also believes that the practice of philosophy can ultimately purify the soul of the sensual cares that drag it down to earth, so that it can achieve the salvation of a purely spiritual existence. Since Plato regards a person as a spiritual being who has donned mortal flesh like an outer garment, it is not surprising that he uses continuity of consciousness as the test for the identity of a person through many lives (see 13:3.2). In fact, he claims that our knowledge is really recollection: We know a truth of geometry or ethics only because we have recollected it from an earlier spiritual existence which we have otherwise forgotten.

33:2.3 *Dualism*   In the dialogue *Phaedo* Plato describes Socrates's wait in prison for execution. He explains to his young friends why he is not afraid to die by presenting a series of proofs that his soul is immortal. These are also arguments for a theory of dualism of mind and body (see Chapter 17). The soul, or mind, is distinct from the body. Unlike the body, which is visible, transitory, and destructible, the mind is invisible, unchanging, and indestructible. Physical statements about Socrates are really statements about his body, and mental statements about him are really statements about his mind.

Plato's proofs of *mind-body dualism* are based on a deeper form of dualism. Existence consists of two radically different sorts of things. First, there is the world that we experience with our senses, composed of physical things subject to change, which come into existence and perish. Here nothing is permanent, and as Heraclitus asserted, "Everything is in flux." But there is also a higher realm of things that are permanent and invariant. These things are indestructible, eternal, and divine. They are invisible to the senses and known only by means of rational thought or contemplation. In this realm, according to Plato, are *the Forms*. The discovery of what he called "Forms" was epoch-making in Western thought: Plato is the first to see that you must distinguish between *particular* things and the *characteristics* or *properties* that particulars partake of. If an evil king in a child's story had a grudge against the color green, he might go about his kingdom destroying every green thing he discovered; but even if he succeeded in destroying every physical thing that is green, he would not thereby have stamped out the *property* of greenness. *There is* such a color, whether or not you can find examples of it at a given place or time. Plato argues in the *Phaedo* that although you have a concept of perfect equality, you must not confuse it with the things you encounter in sense experience, which are never unqualifiedly equal. True, you are aware of perfect equality only because you perceive equal sticks or equal stones. But these equal things fall short of perfect equality and only serve to remind you of the equality you knew in an earlier life. Thus, your knowledge is *innate* or inborn. The hypothesis that the Forms exist and that sensible things partake of them provides the basis for the dualism between minds and bodies. Plato says that the mind is akin to the Forms in that it is invisible and indestructible, but it can involve itself with either the Forms or the sensible particulars. Only by avoiding the sensible realm as much as possible and focusing on the Forms can the soul achieve the purity required for the salvation of a blessed spiritual existence after death.

33:2.4 *God and creation* Plato challenges the traditional polytheism of Greece with a philosophical vision of God as unitary and essentially good. He presents the earliest known versions of the argument from design and the first cause argument for the existence of God (see Chapters 27 and 29). In the *Timaeus* a divinity known as the "demiurge" uses the eternal Forms as patterns or archetypes for fashioning the sensible world of space and time. "Everyone will see that he must have looked to the eternal, for the world is the fairest of creations and he is the best of causes."[5] Yet Plato recognizes the imperfections of the sensible world and was the first to formulate the problem of evil: "If God is all knowing, all powerful, and all good, how can evil exist?" Trying to solve the problem, he takes the first steps along the paths that have been well trampled by later philosophers: "The purpose of all that happens is to win bliss for the life of the whole; it is not

---

[5]Plato, *Timaeus*, 29a, in *The Collected Dialogues of Plato*, ed. E. Hamilton and H. Caims (Princeton: Princeton University Press, 1963).

made for thee, but thou for it."[6] The evil we experience and suffer is a necessary part of a whole that best embodies the general good. In support of this idea, Plato develops an early version of the soul-building justification (see Chapter 28). Humans suffer because they are caught up in the cycle of reincarnation, as a result of an original sin that caused them to fall from the spiritual realm. God has arranged the world so that it is possible for virtuous souls to rise to higher levels of reincarnation; but we are responsible for what happens, since whether or not we are virtuous is a function of our free choice. Thus, Plato has a commitment to *free will* although the commitment is not very well articulated.

33:2.5 *Theory of knowledge*   Corresponding to Plato's dualism of Forms and particulars is a rigid dichotomy between knowledge and opinion.

> We must make a distinction and ask, "What is that which always is and has no becoming?" and "What is that which is always becoming and never is?" That which is apprehended by intelligence and reason is always in the same state, but that which is conceived by opinion with the help of sensation and without reason is always in a process of becoming and perishing and never really is.[7]

Plato recognized a fundamental distinction between knowledge and opinion: Opinion is often in error, but knowledge is infallible. He inferred that they cannot be concerned with the same objects. Opinion is concerned with the transitory, undependable objects of sense experience, whereas knowledge is concerned with the Forms. Plato did not agree with the skeptics who argued that you are totally ignorant of the sensible world because you lack knowledge in the strict sense of it. For Plato held that you could have justified opinions about sensible objects. Plato defends a *rationalist* theory of knowledge: It is only through the exercise of the rational faculty unaided by the senses that one achieves true knowledge of reality. Unfortunately, he was able to describe this process only in the suggestive, metaphorical language of the allegories of the sun, the line, and the cave. But he defends his rationalism in a negative way in the *Theaetetus* and *Sophist*, where he argues that the empiricist theories of the Sophist—that knowledge is sense experience or justified opinion about sensible things—commit the fallacy of self-refutation. To see that a statement is necessarily true is to recognize relationships between *timeless entities*, the Forms.

---

[6]Plato, *Laws*, 903c, *ibid.*
[7]Plato, *Timaeus*, 27d–28a, *ibid.*

PHILOSOPHER'S WORKSHOP

Plato's Sun, Line, and Cave Allegories

In Plato's *Republic* Socrates describes his attempts to make his view of reality comprehensible to a pupil, Glaucon, by using a series of allegories.

I said, "I must first come to an understanding with you, and remind you . . . of the old story, that many things are beautiful and many good and so we say of them individually that they *are*, and define them in speech."

"True," he said.

"And there is a beautiful itself and a good itself, and likewise for other things which we say are many; for they may be brought under a single Form which is called *what each thing is*."

"Very true."

"The many things, as we say, are seen but not known, and the Forms are known but not seen."

Socrates then develops the comparison between seeing and knowing. Seeing requires not only the power of sight and objects that can be seen, but also the sun as a source of the light by which these objects are seen. Plato develops an analogy in the intelligible world of Forms. Just as the eye depends upon the sun as a source of light in order to see visible objects, so the soul depends upon the Form of the Good as a source of truth and being in order to know the Forms.

"You know," I said, "that the eyes, when a person directs them towards objects on which the light of day is no longer shining, but the moon and stars only, see dimly, and are nearly blind; they seem to have no clearness of vision in them?"

"Very true."

"But when they are directed towards objects on which the sun shines, they see clearly and there is sight in them?"

"Certainly."

"And the soul is like the eye: when resting upon that on which truth and being shine, the soul perceives and understands, and is radiant with intelligence; but when turned towards the twilight of becoming and perishing, then she has opinion only, and goes blinking about, and is first of one opinion and then of another, and seems to have no intelligence?"

"Just so."

"Now, that which imparts truth to the known and the power of knowing to the knower is what I would have you term the Form of the Good, and this you will deem to be the source of knowledge, and of truth in so far as the latter becomes the subject of knowledge; beautiful too, as are both truth and knowledge, you will be right in esteeming this other nature as more beautiful than either; and, as in the previous instance, light and sight may be truly said to be like the Good, but not the Good; the Good has a place of honour yet higher."

Socrates now develops the contrast between the intelligible and the visible realm by means of a model: the divided line.

"You have to imagine, then, that there are two ruling powers, and that one of them is set over the intellectual world, the other over the visible. . . . Now take a line which has been cut into two equal parts, and divide each of them again in the same proportion, and suppose the two main divisions to answer, one to the visible and the other to the intelligible, and then compare the subdivisions in respect of their clearness and want of clearness, and you will find that the first section in the sphere of the visible consists of images. And by images I mean, in the first place, shadows, and in the second place, reflections in water and in solid, smooth and polished bodies and the like: Do you understand?"

"Yes, I understand."

"Imagine, now, the other section, of which this is only the resemblance, to include the animals which we see, and everything that grows or is made."

"Very good."

"Would you not admit that both the sections of this division have different degrees of truth, and that the copy is to the original as the sphere of opinion is to the sphere of knowledge?"

"Most undoubtedly."

"Next proceed to consider the manner in which the sphere of the intellectual is to be divided."

"In what manner?"

"Thus:—There are two subdivisions, in the lower of which the soul uses the figures given by the former division as images; the enquiry can only be hypothetical, and instead of going upwards to a principle descends to the other end; in the higher of the two, the soul passes out of hypotheses, and goes to a principle which is above hypotheses, making no use of images as in the former case, but proceeding only in and through the Forms themselves."

"I do not quite understand your meaning," he said.

"Then I will try again; you will understand me better when I have made some preliminary remarks. You are aware that students of geometry, arithmetic, and the kindred sciences assume the odd and the even and the figures and three kinds of angles and the like in their several branches of science; these are their hypotheses, which they and everybody are supposed to know, and therefore they do not deign to give any account of them either to themselves or others; but they begin with them, and go on until they arrive at last, and in a consistent manner, at their conclusion?"

"Yes," he said, "I know."

"And do you not know also that although they make use of the visible forms and reason about them, they are thinking not of these, but of the things which they resemble; not of the figures which they draw, but of the Square Itself and the Diameter Itself, and so on—the Forms which they draw or make, and which have shadows and reflections in water of their own, are converted by them into images, but they are really seeking to behold the things themselves, which can only be seen with the eye of the mind?"

"That is true."

"And of this kind I spoke as the intelligible, although in the search after it the soul is compelled to use hypotheses; not ascending to a first principle, because she is unable to rise above the region of hypothesis, but employing the objects of which the shadows below are resemblances in their turn as images, they having in relation to the shadows and reflections of them a greater distinctness, and therefore a higher value."

"I understand," he said, "that you are speaking of the province of geometry and the sister arts."

"And when I speak of the other divisions of the intelligible, you will understand me to speak of that other sort of knowledge which reason herself attains by the power of dialectic, using the hypotheses not as first principles, but only as hypotheses—that is to say, as steps and points of departure into a world which is above hypotheses, in order that she may soar beyond them to the first principle of the whole; and clinging to this and then to that which depends on this, by successive steps she descends again without the aid of any sensible object, from Forms, through Forms, and in Forms she ends."

"I understand you," he replied; "not perfectly, for you seem to me to be describing a task which is really tremendous, but, at any rate, I understand you to say that knowledge and being, which the science of dialectic contemplates, are clearer than the notions of the arts, as they are termed, which proceed from hypotheses only; these are also contemplated by the understanding, and not by the senses: yet, because they start from hypotheses and do not ascend to a principle, those who contemplate them appear to you to exercise the higher reason upon them, although when a first principle is added to them they are cognizable by the higher reason. And the habit which is concerned with geometry and the cognate sciences I suppose that you would term understanding and not reason, as being intermediate between opinion and reason."

"You have quite conceived my reasoning," I said; "and now, corresponding to these four divisions, let there be four faculties in the soul—reason answering to the highest, understanding to the second, conviction to the third, and perception of shadows to the last—and let there be a scale of them, and let us suppose that the several faculties have a clearness in the same degree that their objects have truth."

"I understand," he replied, "and give my assent, and accept your arrangement."

Socrates next develops the Allegory of the Cave.

"Behold! human beings living in an underground den, which has a mouth open towards the light and reaching all along the den; here they have been from their childhood, and have their legs and necks chained so that they cannot move, and can only see before them, being prevented by the chains from turning round their heads. Above and behind them a fire is blazing at a distance, and between the fire and the prisoners there is a raised way; and you will see, if you look, a low wall built along the way, like the screen which marionette players have in front of them, over which they show the puppets."

"I see." .

"And do you see," I said, "men passing along the wall carrying all sorts of vessels, and statues and figures of animals made of wood and stone and various materials, which appear over the wall? Some of them are talking, others silent."

"You have shown me a strange image, and they are strange prisoners."

"Like ourselves," I replied; "and they see only their own shadows, or the shadows of one another, which the fire throws on the opposite wall of the cave?"

"True," he said; "how could they see anything but the shadows if they were never allowed to move their heads?"

"And of the objects which are being carried in like manner they would only see the shadows? And if they were able to converse with one another, would they not suppose that they were naming what was actually before them?"

"Very true."

"And suppose further that the prison had an echo which came from the other side, would they not be sure to fancy when one of the passers-by spoke that the voice which they heard came from the passing shadow. To them, the truth would be literally nothing but the shadows of the images. And now look again, and see what will naturally follow if the prisoners are released and disabused of their error. At first, when any of them is liberated and compelled suddenly to stand up and turn his neck round and walk and look towards the light, he will suffer sharp pains; the glare will distress him, and he will be unable to see the realities of which in his former state he had seen the shadows; and then conceive some one saying to him, that what he saw before was an illusion, but that now, when he is approaching nearer to being and his eye is turned towards more real existence, he has a clearer vision, — what will be his reply? And you may further imagine that his instructor is pointing to the objects as they pass and requiring him to name them, — will he not be perplexed? Will he not fancy that the shadows which he formerly saw are truer than the objects which are now shown to him?"

"Far truer."

"And if he is compelled to look straight at the light, will he not have a pain in his eyes which will make him turn away to take refuge in the objects of vision which he can see, and which he will conceive to be in reality clearer than the things which are now being shown to him? And suppose once more, that he is reluctantly dragged up a steep and rugged ascent, and held fast until he is forced into the presence of the sun himself, is he not likely to be pained and irritated? When he approaches the light his eyes will be dazzled, and he will not be able to see anything at all of what are now called realities. He will require to grow accustomed to the sight of the upper world. And first he will see the shadows best, next the reflections of men and other objects in the water, and then the objects themselves; then he will gaze upon the light of the moon and the stars and the spangled heaven; and he will see the sky and the stars by night better than the sun or the light of the sun by day."

"Certainly."

"Last of all he will be able to see the sun, and not mere reflections of it in the water, but he will see it in its own proper place, and not in another; and he will contemplate it as it is."

Finally Socrates connects the cave with the preceding allegories.

". . . This entire allegory," I said, "you may now append, dear Glaucon, to the previous argument; the prison-house is the world of sight, the light of the fire is the sun, and you will not misapprehend me if you interpret the journey upwards to be the ascent of the soul into the intellectual world according to my poor belief, which, at your desire, I have expressed—whether rightly or wrongly God knows. But, whether true or false, my opinion is that in the world of knowledge the Form of Good appears last of all, and is seen only with an effort; and, when seen, is also inferred to be the universal author of all things beautiful and right, parent of light and of the lord of light in this visible world, and the immediate source of reason and truth in the intelligible; and that this is the power upon which he who would act rationally either in public or private life must have his eye fixed."

"I agree," he said, "as far as I am able to understand you."[8]

[8]*Republic*, Book VI, 507, 508, 514–16, 517, trans. Benjamin Jowett, with emendations.

33:2.6 *Ethics*   The hypothesis of the Forms also plays a central role in Plato's ethics and social philosophy. The Forms define the values that should direct individual action and community policy. Plato consistently attacks the popular theories that *pleasure* is the only value individuals should pursue (hedonism) and that the aim of society should be the utilitarian good of maximizing pleasure for as many people as possible (see Chapter 6). Plato argues instead that the good of the individual consists in personal virtue (Chapter 8). In the *Republic* he tries to show that virtue amounts to the same thing in the inidividual soul or in a social context and that it is intrinsically valuable in either place. Wisdom and courage are secured in the community when the enlightened philosopher-kings achieve insight into the realm of the Forms and consequently define policies which are supported by the warrior class. Self-control is the harmonious state in which all elements of society—leaders, warriors, and workers—agree as to who should rule and be ruled. Justice is the condition in which each social class performs its proper function and doesn't interfere with the others. Within the individual, self-control and justice are conditions of harmony and proper functioning of the parts of the soul: rational faculty, aggressive drives, sensuous desires. Virtue is thus a state of psychic equilibrium or mental health.

33:3.1 *The theory of Forms*   In the *Phaedo* Plato sets out two hypotheses: (1) "I hypothesize that there is the beautiful itself, the good itself, the large itself, and all the rest of them." (2) "Whatever else is beautiful apart from the beautiful itself, is beautiful because it partakes of the beautiful itself."[9] The Forms are real, and everything else derives its reality and nature from the Forms. These doctrines are central to Plato's solution to every philosophical problem. The Forms are central to a theory of meaning: To understand what a word like "equal" means

[9]Plato, *Phaedo*, 100 b/c, *ibid*.

is to grasp the Form of equality. According to Plato, a theory of language cannot explain how many things can share the same name, "equality," unless it assumes the *existence* of something, equality, which they share *in common*. Plato repeatedly argues that theories not making this assumption collapse in self-refutation. Moreover, as the firm objects of genuine knowledge, the Forms permit Plato to refute skepticism and relativism (see Chapter 22). They are the true realities, in contrast to the objects of sense experience which are in flux and merely becoming. They provide the rational basis for Plato's faith in the immortality of the soul and the omnibenevolence of God. They serve as ultimate values and principles of character.

33:3.2 *Plato's foundationalism*   Although Socrates often used contextualist methods, Plato's own philosophical approach was predominantly foundationalist, especially in the middle of his career when he wrote works like the *Phaedo*, the *Republic*, and the *Theaetetus*. He was inclined to work from self-evident "hypotheses" and follow them inflexibly, even when they led to extremely counterintuitive results. Examples of this foundationalism are the sharp dichotomies he drew between being and becoming and between knowledge and opinion. He maintains, in a self-consciously paradoxical way, that the objects of sense experience are not fully real; only the Forms are *"really* real." Sensible things are what they are only in a qualified way, as a stick is equal only in relation to a particular stick at a particular time for a particular observer and so forth; moreover, sensible things should not be said to *be* anything but only to *become* light or dark, hot or cold. Similarly, Plato denies what seems obvious, that you can entertain opinions and achieve knowledge about the same things. He argues that since only knowledge is infallible, knowledge and opinion must be mutually exclusive, and they have different objects. He thus denies that you can have any knowledge of the sensible world. He draws a sharp line between the body and soul, depicting them as locked in a fierce struggle for dominance. Closely related to this view is an emphatic repudiation of pleasure as a true measure of value. The only true value is the virtuous life, and the central virtue remains wisdom, which consists in understanding the Forms.

33:4.1 *Objections to the theory of forms*   Plato's theory came under attack from its very inception. Plato probably encouraged students and colleagues in his Academy to subject his views to searching criticisms, and the results seem to be recorded in the dialogue *Parmenides* and in the writings of his greatest pupil, Aristotle. Many questions were asked about the Forms that Plato had difficulty answering. The first problem was to explain the nature of a Form. At times they are treated like paradigms, ideal prototypes after which other things are modeled. It is easy to think of triangularity itself in this way, and beauty itself would be far more beautiful than any sunset or painting. But it is hard to view the most important Forms, like being, otherness, sameness, as such paradigms. It is easy to give examples of properties. It is extremely hard to explain what "a property" is. The second problem concerned the relationship between a Form and particular things. Plato liked to call a Form "one over many." He generally spoke of the many as "partaking" of the Form, but he recognized a problem in this metaphor: When many people partake of a pie, each of them gets a separate piece—but the Form is not divisible into pieces. However, if the indivisible Form were somehow "in" many things simultaneously, would not this be the impossibility of a thing being in different places at the same time? Aristotle also cast doubt on the use of the Forms in ethics. How could a "pattern" which is so remote from anything in human experience—being invisible, unchanging, indestructible, indivisible—serve as a guide for human actions?

33:4.2 *Plato's influence*   Despite these difficulties, Plato's philosophy has captivated countless thinkers. Contemporary mathematicians find Platonism especially appealing. Studies like mathematics and logic are different from empirical sciences like biology and astronomy, which study the nature and behavior of objects existing in space and time. Statements like "2 plus 3 make 5" or "The square of the hypoteneuse of a right triangle is equal to the sum of the square of the sides" do not just describe how physical things happen to behave. They seem to describe *timeless truths*. The truths of mathematics are not merely arbitrary conventions, for the mathematician is able to *make discoveries*. How is this possible? According to Plato, when mathematicians discover new theories, they are discovering relationships that hold between *timeless entities*, the Forms. Mathematicians are naturally sympathetic to this theory that there is a mathematical world of ideas out there waiting to be explored by them, a world different from the world of transitory sense objects.

Christian thinkers, like Augustine, reinterpreted the teachings of the Bible in terms of Plato's views of God, the soul, and spiritual salvation. Plato's portrait of an ideal society in the *Republic* has inspired an outpouring of utopian visions and revolutionary movements to implement them. Utopianism in all forms endorses the insight that an ideal may be better, and even more powerful, than anything in the real world.

EXERCISES for Chapter 33

1. Of the following statements, mark those T that correctly describe the philo-sophical concerns to which Socrates or Plato responded.
    A. Socrates wanted to justify the Sophists' view that morality is relative.
    B. Socrates wanted Athens to return to traditional religious beliefs and practices.
    C. Plato takes seriously the goal of self-knowledge.
    D. Plato thought of education as a nonphilosophical topic.
    E. Plato was concerned to show how knowledge is possible.
    F. Socrates wanted to find a rational, rather than a conventional, basis for morality.
    G. Plato had no interest in religious concepts.
2. In the Workshop in 33:3.2, Plato develops the analogy of the divided line. Each section of the line represents some form of mental activity.
    a. Describe and contrast the mental activity related to each section of the line.
    b. Plato contends that these four mental activities are focused on different kinds of objects. Describe and contrast them as Plato does.
    c. Briefly list the important functions Plato expects his analogy to serve.
    d. What sorts of limitations does Plato recognize that his philosophy has because of this reliance on analogy or metaphor?
3. Describe Plato's theory of the Forms in such a way as to outline how he uses it
    a. to characterize the relationship between the body and the mind or soul (33:2.3),
    b. to defend the thesis that human beings can have knowledge (33:2.5),
    c. to argue that there are truths of ethics (33:2.6).
4. Choose one of the topics below, and after consulting appropriate library research materials, write an essay
    a. examining Aristotle's criticism of the theory of Forms;
    b. describing Augustine's adaptation of Platonic ideas to a Christian con-text;
    c. comparing Descartes and Plato regarding skepticism, a mathematical model of knowledge, the possibility of knowledge, or mind-body dualism;
    d. comparing and contrasting the contextualism of Socrates as portrayed in Plato's early writings with the foundationalism Plato developed in later works.

SELECTED ANSWERS for Chapter 33

1. C, E, and F are true.
2. c. The general function of the analogy is to distinguish and characterize philosophical thinking, through which knowledge of the Forms is possible. Knowledge of the Forms is crucial for Plato since it is through such knowledge that he attempts to resolve many philosophical concerns.
   d. Plato's analogical language has left unresolved questions about the exact character of philosophical thought as he understood it, how such thought processes can be mastered, and how to be able to achieve agreement about one's conclusions when using analogical and metaphysical reasoning.

34

Thomas Aquinas

St. Thomas Aquinas (1225–1274) was one of the most gifted philosophers of the High Middle Ages. He was a dedicated Christian and a staunch champion of philosophy—a combination that created conceptual problems of great magnitude which he did not seek to escape either by rejecting human knowledge as false on religious grounds or by rejecting religion as irrational on experiential grounds. Rather he boldly faced the challenge of articulating an intellectual synthesis of the human knowledge available at his time and the religious beliefs of medieval Christianity. Aquinas was not narrow in his vision of the sources of wisdom; he enthusiastically embraced the philosophy of Aristotle which the Arabs had recently rediscovered. Since, for Aquinas, all truth is one, the revealed truths of faith and the human truths of philosophy must ultimately be reconcilable. In the final analysis the knowledge attained by human reason and observation must support and explain the sacred doctrine known through the eyes of faith. Aquinas's goal was to synthesize faith and reason, a contribution to the history of thought that has made him one of the leading philosophers in the history of Western thought and one of the most influential theologians in the Roman Catholic Church.

After reading Chapter 34 you should be able to

■ **State the major philosophical problems that Thomas Aquinas addressed.**

- **Describe how he used his methods to offer solutions to these problems.**
- **Address major criticisms and impacts of his philosophy.**

34:1.1 *Life and work*   At age five Aquinas entered the monastic school of the Benedictine monks near Monte Casino, Italy. During the Middle Ages, the monastic schools were centers of learning where children of the rich and noble families of Europe began their education. Later Aquinas studied at a university in Naples. Such universities were organized in the manner of medieval guilds. After serving an apprenticeship of study with a particular professor or master, Aquinas was awarded a baccalaureate degree. As a journeyman, he was permitted to defend various points of view during discussion sessions. Once he had demonstrated skills with "the tools of his trade," he was awarded the title of master. These tools were rhetoric (communication), grammar (writing and reading), logic (critical thinking), mathematics, music, and literature, and they were required for any advanced study in theology, law, or medicine. The sciences were not stressed, since they were only in their infancy.

Aquinas entered the renowned Order of Preachers (Dominicans) in 1244 and was sent to Paris and Cologne to study under the greatest European scholar of that time, Albert the Great. Albert had been chiefly responsible for promoting the study of Aristotle's works in natural science and metaphysics. These writings had recently been rediscovered and brought to Europe by Muslim and Jewish philosophers. Aristotle's ideas were feared by the intellectual and religious establishment and were in danger of being suppressed.

Aquinas studied theology and was awarded a position as professor in 1257. He spent the next twelve years teaching, preaching, and serving as an administrative consultant. From 1253 until his death in 1274 he wrote a number of lengthy and influential philosophical and theological treatises.

34:1.2 *Historical context* The flowering of European civilization during the High Middle Ages of the twelfth and thirteenth centuries had roots in both Greco-Roman culture and the Judaeo-Christian tradition. The culture of the West was shaped by the religion and language of Christian Rome, but Europe was now nurtured by a flow of new ideas from the Muslim cultures in the Near East and the Spanish peninsula and by trade with Syria, Palestine, and China.

The Catholic Church had dominated every aspect of European life during the High Middle Ages. The popes were stronger than emperors, kings, and nobles. They held several countries, including Hungary, Portugal, Poland, and Aragon, as fiefdoms. The clergy was responsible for many of the same charitable, educational, judicial, legislative, and social welfare activities that today are supported by governmental organizations. Bishops executed a number of civil as well as ecclesiastical duties, and ecclesiastical courts became involved in civil as well as religious cases. Virtually nothing happened without the involvement of the Church. So complete was its influence that in the popular mind treason and heresy were identical.

In the High Middle Ages Dante wrote the *Divine Comedy* in Italian, as national languages were emerging. Great Romanesque and Gothic cathedrals and palaces were erected. With the rise of universities came progress in philosophy, science, medicine, and law. The dominant world view was defined by *Scholastic philosophy*, which simply meant the philosophy taught at the established university schools. It was characterized by carefully worked out theses, detailed arguments, logical rigor, and the use of technical jargon and forms of argument. The intellectual ferment brought into Europe by the discovery of the Aristotelian writings created a great need for the establishment of a new intellectual synthesis to replace the disconnected myths and dogmas that represented the old orthodoxy.

Aquinas was controversial in his own time both for what he taught and for how he taught it. His style was to advance a thesis and to marshal all the known arguments, pro and con, relative to that thesis. Then he would evaluate and analyze each. Often he would reject all of them, only to advance his own new and stronger arguments. He invited the criticism of his students and colleagues, seeking always to strengthen his intellectual position in the light of these criticisms. Nevertheless, he piously cited an authority such as the Bible or a Church father in connection with those same conclusions.

THE ADORATION OF THE MAGI, *by Fra Angelico and Fra Filippo Lippi.*

Like the painting, Thomas Aquinas's philosophy aims to frame a synthesis of Christianity with classical antiquity.

34:2.1 *Aquinas's methods* He often relies on the method of explaining the difficult or unfamiliar case in terms of its similarities to and differences from the common or well-understood case. As a contextualist he tries to square the results of speculative reason with facts learned experientially, yet he is chary of accepting the common person's interpretations of those facts uncritically. In his dedication to observation and reason, he calls arguments based on authority the weakest form of intellectual defense. Thus, in an era dominated by myth and dogma, he risks immediate censure for his methods alone.

Following Albert the Great, Aquinas distinguishes between faith and theology and also between theology and philosophy. Those truths that can be known by the natural light of human reason are the truths of philosophy; those that can be known by revelation are said to be known through faith; and there are some that can be known through both means. Aquinas thinks that the existence of God is an example of a truth that can be known through both natural reason and revelation, whereas some of the dogmas of the Church (for example, the Trinity) can be known only by revelation. Theology, or "sacred doctrine" as he calls it, includes all that can be known about God by faith or by reason, including any information, experimental or conceptual, that supports what is known about God.

Thus, natural theology (what is known about God through reason alone) and revealed theology (faith) must be coherent if one is to preserve the intellectual unity of creation. Also what is known about the physical world through the emerging sciences ("philosophy of nature") must be reconciled ultimately with faith, for the universe is one, truth is one, and God created it all as a unified and ultimately comprehendible totality.

Aquinas shows contextualist tendencies, searching for the nuances of meaning in a term (see Exercises, Chapter 21) and for precise interpretations of crucial concepts. Often he responds to particularly puzzling questions that arise from the process of reconciling faith and reason. His contextualist approach emerges in his concern to show how one can prove that God exists by using the light of natural human reason, for he grapples with how to reconcile the existence of a good and moral God with evil, and how God guides our free will so as to achieve our ultimate happiness. This approach can be seen in his effort to understand God's freely created universe in terms of orderly change based on causal laws, or in his effort to understand human nature, and especially the human intellect, in terms of belief in the existence of the soul and immortality.

Throughout his work, he pursues subtlety and precision of expression. For example, he wants to solve the following paradox: If "God loves all people" is literally true, then God is an anthropomorphic being (a being that in its basic characteristics is humanlike). But God is a transcendent reality who in important respects is not humanlike. So the statement cannot be literally true; God does not *love*, in precisely the same sense of the word, as humans do. Nor does it help to say that God "loves" us in a completely different sense from that in which we "love" each other (as "bark" in different senses means the covering of a tree and the sound of a dog); for if there is no similarity between the two meanings, then the statement about God is meaningless. Since it disregards the normal meaning while specifying a new one it becomes useless as a tool for instructing the faithful or expressing the truth of one's religion.

This paradox results from the false dilemma of either taking every use of a word like "love" as having precisely the same meaning (as being a *univocal* use) or of taking each use as creating a new and unique meaning (as being an *equivocal* use). Aquinas solves this dilemma with the theory of *analogical meaning*. We speak analogically when we say "Humans can know danger" and "Horses can know danger." The abilities of animals and humans to "know" are *similar*, neither identical nor totally different. We speak analogically in a different way when we say "Liz is healthy" and "Liz's complexion is healthy." Here the second use of "healthy" is a derivative, analogical use of the term, because it means "*symptomatic* of what is healthy (in the primary sense)." Do you see how food is called healthy also by analogy to the primary meaning?

34:2.2 *Philosophy of nature* To understand God and the ways in which God provides for humankind with the totality of creation, Aquinas came to grips with the problem of understanding change and causality. Given the absence of the scientific knowledge we have today, he relies heavily on the philosophy of nature with which Aristotle explained the phenomenon of change. In every change there is an element of constancy and an element of alteration. For example, a lump of bronze is changed into a statue. Following Aristotle, Aquinas calls the constant element, the bronze, *matter*; but in the change another component, the shape of the lump of bronze, is replaced by a new shape. In general he calls the respect in which the thing changes its *form*. Thus, a bronze statue is the union of two metaphysical elements, form and matter. In a change, the form of a thing is replaced by a new form. Matter explains why we experience a certain sense of stability in change; form explains diversity.

Prime matter is the most basic type of matter, and substantial form is the most important type of form. In the case of living species, the substantial form determines the essential characteristics of the species. All individuals of a species thus have the same essential characteristics or *nature*; for example, all humans are rational (see Chapter 11). Particular differences between individuals are accounted for as differences in their *accidental* (nonessential) features, for example, hair color.

A full analysis of any change, such as the production of a bronze statue, must address four basic *causal* questions: What or who produced the change? Out of what material did the change emerge? What is the defining character (for example, shape) of that which has been produced by the change? and Why — for what reason — did the change occur? That is, to explain change one has to identify the *efficient, material, formal,* and *final* causes involved. Aquinas is especially interested in answering these questions in connection with human beings. He was especially interested in *human nature*, our substantial form, which is the formal and final cause of our biological generation and growth.

In trying to answer these questions Aquinas uses special methods. In the first place, you should not infer a being's *nature* until you have first identified all its *powers*. Thus you cannot make inferences concerning human nature as such until you have defined the faculties that exist at least potentially within each human being. Various potentials may be more or less fully actualized at different times in one's life. For example, all humans have the power to reason, but at times some do not. However, to understand what *powers* a being has you should observe the *activities* it exhibits. Thus, to know what it is to be human, you must first examine how humans behave. Because they see, hear, and so forth, they have powers of *perception*; because they reason, judge, and so forth they have the power of *intellect*; because they make choices, assert, refrain, and so forth they have the power of *will*.

Using his analogical methods Aquinas compares the perceptual and intellectual powers of human beings. In addition to our ability to judge and reason, our human intellect includes the power to form abstract concepts of the essential characteristics that individual things share. For example, you can form the intellectual concept of *weight* and conceive of it independently of any specific object, by observing that a variety of individual beings all have specific (yet different) weights and abstracting the concept of weight from those observations. In medieval philosophy these abstract concepts are called *universals* and are the subject of considerable controversy. For example, do they exist in the mind of God or are they the arbitrary creations of human beings? (This discussion is based in part on Plato's theory of Forms, which arises from similar considerations, and criticisms of his theory; see Chapter 33).

Aquinas attempts to avoid the philosophical extremes of having to postulate the existence of universals in God's mind and of denying any objective validity to them. Alternatively, he urges that the ways in which universals develop in the human mind are not arbitrary. Rather, the mind frames universals out of the comparisons it makes between individual things known to us through perception. In making these comparisons, the mind observes similarities, which are the qualities the individual things share with each other. Thus, although the mind is active in framing universals, it is not arbitrary but is guided by similarities in the things.

34:2.3 *Free will and soul*   These are very important parts of understanding human beings, especially in the contexts of responsibility for actions and belief in some concept of immortality. Thus Aquinas has to grapple with the problem of free will and the existence of the human soul. We use our power of will when we assent to statements and make choices. Aquinas holds that the operation of the will is in some things determined and in some things free. The human will is naturally and necessarily attracted to those objects that are intrinsically good, such as happiness, peace, justice, and perfection, when these things are understood as ends in themselves. In this respect the will is not free. However, people often do not accurately understand the connection between an end, happiness, and the means of achieving it. Thus, in another respect, some human actions are voluntary, and as such, are free. Selecting the *means* to a naturally determined end is often a free action, resulting from choices made after intellectual deliberation. Thus, even though the ends of action are determined, Aquinas argues that persons can reasonably be held morally accountable for their selection of means. Even though we cannot help but choose happiness, we freely choose how we shall try to achieve it, given what we understand our happiness to consist in.

𝒥 PHILOSOPHER'S WORKSHOP

Rational Disputation

Aquinas's style of writing tries to be rigorously logical, his concern not for literary elegance but for rational argumentation and proof. In this sample from his *Summa Theologica* he inquires into the issue of free choice.

Part I, Question 83

FREE CHOICE
(In Four Articles)

We now inquire concerning free choice. Under this head there are four points of inquiry: (1) Whether man has free choice? (2) What is free choice—a power, an act, or a habit? (3) If it is a power, is it appetitive or cognitive? (4) If it is operative, is it the same power as the will, or distinct?

First Article

WHETHER MAN HAS FREE CHOICE?

We proceed thus to the First Article: –

Objection 1. It would seem that man has not free choice. For whoever has free choice does what he wills. But man does not what he wills, for it is written (Rom. vii. 19): *For the good which I will I do not, but the evil which I will not, that I do.* Therefore man has not free choice. . . .

Objection 5. Further, the Philosopher [Aristotle] says: *According as each one is, such does the end seem to him* [Nich. Eth., III, 5]. But it is not in our power to be such as we are, for this comes to us by nature. Therefore it is natural to us to follow some end, and therefore we are not free in so doing.

On the contrary, It is written (Eccles. xv. 14): *God made man from the beginning, and left him in the hand of his own counsel;* and the *Gloss* adds: That is, in the liberty of choice.

I answer that, Man has free choice, or otherwise counsels, exhortations, commands, prohibitions, rewards and punishments would be in vain. In order to make this evident, we must observe that some things act without judgment, as a stone moves downwards; and in like manner all things which lack knowledge. And some act from judgment, but not a free judgment; as brute animals. . . . But man acts from judgment, because by his apprehensive power he judges that something should be avoided or sought. But because this judgment, in the case of some particular act, is not from a natural instinct, but from some act of comparison in the reason, therefore he acts from free judgment and retains the power of being inclined to various things. . . .

Reply Obj. 1. As we have said above, the sensitive appetite, though it obeys the reason, yet in a given case can resist by desiring what the reason forbids. This is therefore the good which man does not when he wishes—namely, *not to desire against reason,* as Augustine says. . . .

Reply Obj. 5. Quality in man is of two kinds: natural and adventitious. Now the natural quality may be in the intellectual part. . . . [From this fact], he naturally desires his last end, which is happiness. This desire is indeed a natural desire, and is not subject to free choice, as is clear from what we have said above. [Question 82, a.1 and 2.] Therefore this is in no way prejudicial to free choice.

The adventitious qualities are habits and passions by virtue of which a man is inclined to one thing rather than another. And yet even those inclinations are subject to the judgment of reason. Such qualities, too, are subject to the judgment of reason, as it is in our power either to acquire them, whether by causing them or disposing ourselves to them, or rejecting them. And so there is nothing in this which is repugnant to free choice.[1]

---

[1]*Basic Writings of St. Thomas Aquinas*, ed. Anton C. Pegis (New York: The Modern Library, 1945).

He takes our powers of voluntary decision-making and of contemplating universal ideas as evidence that human beings include an immaterial element—the substantial form that makes humans what they essentially are. For only the substantial form, considered abstractly, *could* be conceived of as immaterial and as distinct from prime matter. Another name for the substantial form of human beings is *soul*. Moreover, because the soul is immaterial and because each human consciousness appears as a unity (single personality), Aquinas infers that the soul is not divisible into parts. As such it is incapable of being corrupted (destroyed), and hence, by implication is immortal.

34:2.4 *Metaphysics* To come ultimately to as much of a philosophical knowledge of God as is possible one can begin by examining the created universe and discerning the relationships between beings of various kinds in order to discern the transcendental characteristics of being in general. Metaphysics is the study of being *qua* being (being as such). Being as such represents a unity of two metaphysical principles, *essence* and *existence*. Departing from Aristotle, Aquinas takes essence and existence as more basic than form and matter. We can find both essence and existence in all created beings, including angels; however, we find no primary matter in angels. Angels are immaterial beings of pure form. All beings are what they are, and as such can be thought of as unitary entities. Each can be understood as having a purpose (final cause) that gives it meaning. Further, each has an intrinsic desirability or goodness which attracts the will to at least some degree. Thus, Aquinas finds essence and existence to be preferable categories because they are more comprehensive. Each particular being represents (1) an internal unity, (2) an intelligible meaning, and

(3) an existential desirability. As such, being can be described analogically as (1) *one*, (2) *true*, and (3) *good*.

All beings can be arrayed in a spectrum, from those that have the fewest potentials to those having the most. Living beings fall on the top side of this spectrum, and inanimate objects (water, rocks, and so forth) are on the bottom. One can move up the spectrum to plants, animals, humans, and on to angels, at each level discovering a fuller range of potentials inherent in reality.

34:2.5 *God*   At the very top of the spectrum is God, pure actuality, ultimate perfection in all respects, pure existence. God's essence is purely and simply to be, to exist in the fullest possible way. What can be said of God can only be said by virtue of an analogy between God and other, less perfect forms of being. If they are one, true, and good, then God as pure actuality and infinite perfection exists as total unity, perfect truth, and ultimate desirability. If all being naturally tends toward the good, then all creation tends toward the ultimate good which is God. However, in this life our knowledge of God is necessarily imperfect; we know God in part by knowing that God is not limited in the ways that the beings we can experience in this life are limited, but that God infinitely magnifies their limited perfections.

In Aquinas's philosophy everything has a place in the spectrum of reality, a view that gives considerable integration to people's concepts of their places in nature and in society. Everything is understandable; everything has meaning and purpose. Starting from your ordinary experiences of the changeable characteristics of beings within this world, you can allegedly reason to the existence of the Perfect Being, which draws all to Itself, making understandable all that happens and all that is. One cosmological argument that Aquinas offers to defend the existence of God philosophically is quoted and discussed in Chapter 29. Aquinas identified five ways of expressing the cosmological argument: (1) The fact of motion can be explained only by positing a first mover, which is God; (2) the fact of physical change can be explained only by ultimately appealing to the existence of a first efficient cause of such change, which is God; (3) the presence of contingent and finite reality can ultimately be explained only by appeal to the existence of a nonfinite creative reality, which is God; (4) the differentials in the perfection, truth, and quality of different things can ultimately be understood only as analogous to the perfect truth and goodness of the Being that is called God; and (5) the purposefulness of individual events can ultimately only be understood in terms of purposes derived from God.

Aquinas responds as a contextualist to the problems of divine foreknowledge and evil (Chapter 28). He holds that divine foreknowledge is compatible with human freedom, arguing that God is constantly equally aware of the present and the future, thus accounting for foreknowledge. However, since seeing something happen does not make it happen, God's knowledge does not negate human freedom.

Human freedom is possible in part because our knowledge is not as complete as God's. An act is free insofar as it results from human knowledge presenting something to the will as a good end, as conducive to happiness. If we had perfect knowledge of God, we would understand God as the source of our ultimate happiness and necessarily be attracted to God. But free choice arises because the finite goods of this world are well known in comparison to our understanding of God. We often find that we have selected only an apparent good. Habits or personal virtues can internally guide us toward the real good, just as wise laws can serve as external guides. The natural law, "Do good and avoid evil," directs us toward self-preservation, toward securing the future by raising children, and toward rational social interaction in the community of other humans.

For Aquinas the issue of *God's freedom* is more serious than human freedom, given God's perfect and timeless knowledge. But since nothing could have caused God to create the universe, creation is conceived of as a result of and as evidence for God's freedom.

In responding to the problem of evil, he argues that evil is the negation of being, the absence of reality; for reality is essentially good. God allows this incompleteness of being, "evil," in order to permit the occurrence of several good results. If tyrants had not persecuted Christians, for example, there could have been no heroic martyrs. Moral evil results from human freedom and reminds us of the imperfection of created beings.

It is not clear, however, how he would handle the problem of determinism (see Chapter 18) had his philosophy of nature been like the scientific knowledge we have today. Nor is it clear how he should respond to cases of deliberate malice, like Lucifer's rejection of God, where apparently the will freely chooses an end known not to be good.

34:2.6 *Ethics* Aquinas derives his ethics from metaphysics and analogical interpretations of key terms like "good" and "law." A being's happiness is in the fulfillment of its own nature. Humans, then, naturally tend toward their own happiness, although they may be mistaken about what their happiness will ultimately turn out to be or about how it can be achieved. The law governing human ethical activity is that one should act in accord with reason, keeping in view the kind of agent one is, the station one occupies in life, and the relation of one's life in the total plan of reality. One should seek self-development and self-perfection through respecting others and practicing virtue.

The Natural Law (see 34:2.5) can be understood as the rational integration of one's life with God's eternal law as it is expressed in one's nature. You must do what is natural and appropriate to your essence. For example, you should satisfy your physical appetites in moderation, and you should perfect your intellect and powers of will. Applying this view, Aquinas defends Christian social values: He advocates monogamy and criticizes divorce on the grounds that the family represents a natural and reasonable kind of human society (organized, cooperative grouping).

34:3 World view The dominant themes characterizing Aquinas's thought are a concern for rationality, knowledge of one's place in the universe, and an honest assessment of one's abilities, intentions, and potentials. To act contrary to one's nature would be the ultimate error. Human nature is characterized primarily by intellectual and volitional powers. Thus, in developing institutions or recommendations for human living, one must always remember and respect the potential for rationality and voluntary choice in all human beings.

This world view strives for ultimate comprehensiveness with a fully developed metaphysics, epistemology, and value theory. It includes work on natural philosophy which moves toward the development of the natural sciences. It also includes work on the philosophy of law, philosophy of religion, and a number of other specialized areas within philosophy, such as logic and aesthetics. As indicated in Chapter 32, when one strives for comprehensiveness, one risks inconsistency. Aquinas's philosophy struggles to maintain consistency in developing a theory of the immortality of the soul and in reconciling human freedom with our experience of evil and the existence of God. His struggles against inconsistency appear even more heroic when one considers that he is concerned, not only to avoid contradiction within his philosophical thinking, but also to develop a philosophical system suitable for integration with "sacred doctrine" (theology). Moreover, he strives for wide applicability of thought, wishing to develop a philosophy that could genuinely service the advancement of religious understanding and the instruction of the faithful.

34:4 Criticisms and influence Aquinas was criticized roundly by his contemporaries for encouraging strange new intellectual activities (such as natural sciences) and for proposing potentially heretical doctrines. In 1277 a number of ideas fairly close to his own were condemned by the bishop of Paris, and this condemnation was not revoked for nearly

fifty years. Aquinas's philosophical ideas were criticized by later medieval philosophers, including influential thinkers such as Duns
Scotus and William of Ockham as well as those who followed the philosophical leads of Augustine and Bonaventure. These later philosophers criticized his proofs of the existence of God and rejected both
his theory of abstraction and his analogical method. However, since
about the sixteenth century his philosophical system, as handed down
both in original texts and through the revisions and rethinkings of
others, has become widely accepted in the Catholic Church as official
Catholic philosophy. In 1918 the Church revised its seminary code,
requiring from each candidate for the priesthood six years of study
based on the teaching of St. Thomas in philosophy and theology, although since the Second Vatican Council philosophical training in
more progressive seminaries has taken on a less rigidly Thomistic
structure.

In the seven centuries since Aquinas, a number of scholars have
studied his writings and reinterpreted his world view in an effort to
address social, theological, and philosophical issues and currents of
contemporary interest. Contemporary philosophers continue to study
his philosophy of language and his theory of mind, and Thomistic theologians are addressing the relationship between his world view and
the analyses of the human condition developed by other theologians,
by existentialist philosophers, and by social scientists.

EXERCISES for Chapter 34

1. Of the following statements, mark those *T* that correctly describe the philo-
   sophical concerns to which Thomas Aquinas responded.
   A. Thomas wanted to show how claims of religious knowledge are com-
      patible with the sciences of physics and chemistry.
   B. Thomas wanted to show the compatibility of religious (Christian) and
      philosophic (Aristotelian) truths.
   C. Thomas wanted to develop an integrated system of philosophic and re-
      ligious truths.
   D. Thomas wanted to distinguish faith as the sole basis for religious views
      from reason as the sole basis for philosophic views.
   E. Thomas was concerned about the sense and the degree in which hu-
      man beings could know things about God.
   F. Thomas tried to respond to a skepticism that no knowledge is possible.
   G. Thomas was concerned to synthesize two substantial systems of
      thought.
2. In the Workshop in 34:2.3 Thomas discusses whether or not human beings
   have free choice.

a. How do Objections 1 and 5 illustrate the relation Thomas strives to maintain between scripture and Aristotle?

b. What importance does Thomas, in arguing that people have the ability to choose freely, ascribe to the fact that people make judgments?

c. In the reply to Objection 1, Thomas says that sensitive appetite sometimes resists that which it obeys. How would you reply to the charge that this assertion is contradictory?

d. In the reply to Objection 5, Thomas says that a person does not choose happiness freely, but that a person does freely choose some individual thing which will give him or her happiness. To understand this view, notice the reasons Thomas provides for each assertion. Use these reasons to contrast the analogous meanings of freedom in the two assertions.

3. Describe Thomas's compatibilist synthesizing approach as he uses it

a. to argue that the essence-existence distinction is more fundamental than the form-matter distinction (34:2.4);

b. to show how talk about God can be meaningful, given both the difference between God and human beings and the fact that we are not directly aware of God through our sensory experience (34:2.1);

c. to provide a basis for rational decision-making in ethics (34:2.6).

4. Choose one of the topics below, and after consulting appropriate library research materials, write an essay

a. examining Ockham's critique of St. Thomas's natural theology;

b. describing both the positive and the negative impact of Thomas's philosophy on the development of the natural sciences;

c. examining later Thomistic responses to the problem of determinism;

d. examining the extent to which Vatican II modified the centrality of Thomas's philosophy for Catholic thought;

e. discussing the Natural Law approach to contemporary social and political problems, such as racism, ecology, war, and world hunger.

SELECTED ANSWERS for Chapter 34

1. B, C, E, and G are true.

2. b. What is based in judgment involves a reasoned comparison. It is therefore not an instinctive response.

c. When Thomas says that the sensitive appetite obeys, he means that it usually, normally, or properly — but not necessarily always — obeys.

d. Happiness is chosen naturally, that is, as a function of human nature. Thus "unfreely" here means "naturally." A particular happiness is chosen by a process of reasoning. Thus "freely" here means by the unconstrained use of reason.

35

![chapter ornament]

David Hume

"Human nature is the only science of man; and yet has been hitherto the most neglected."[1] David Hume registered this complaint because he perceived failure by philosophers to keep pace with the rapid advances of the natural sciences. In *A Treatise of Human Nature* Hume sought to apply what he called the "experimental method of reasoning" to traditional philosophical problems concerning reality, knowledge, and value. Thus, Hume brought empiricism to its most consistent and extreme expression, but he remained skeptical as to whether or not the traditional problems of philosophy could be solved. Hume exerted a powerful influence on the direction of philosophy, especially the English-speaking world in the twentieth century.

After reading this chapter you should be able to

- State major problems that Hume addressed.
- Describe how Hume used his methods to offer solutions to these problems.
- Address major criticisms and impacts of Hume's philosophy.

35:1.1 *A sometime philosopher* David Hume was born in Scotland in 1711. His controversial role in philosophy was belied by his appearance:

---

[1]David Hume, *A Treatise of Human Nature*, I,IX,VII, ed. L. A. Selby-Bigge (Oxford, Eng.: Clarendon Press, 1888) p. 273.

Rotund, cheerful, and easygoing, he never lost his harsh, Scottish accent. He early abandoned a career in law and decided instead to seek literary fame in France during the period of the Enlightenment, when intellectuals like Voltaire and Rousseau rose to great social heights by the power of the pen. Hume did not enjoy similar success. His *Treatise on Human Nature*, representing an investment of years of labor, "fell dead-born from the press." His skepticism and critical remarks about religion were unpopular. Hume's *Inquiry Concerning Human Understanding* and *Inquiry Concerning the Principles of Morals*, although shorter and more polished, did not help his reputation, and his attempts to secure a job as a philosophy professor were also a fiasco. Finally, he abandoned philosophy and became a librarian in Scotland. He contended that a philosophical skeptic would have nothing to fear from death, and true to his words, he died tranquilly in 1776.

35:1.2 *The context of the enlightenment* Hume had lived in England and France in a period of ferment, radical social change, and intellectual excitement. The Enlightenment involved new developments in the natural sciences and in social philosophy. Newton and Boyle had laid the foundations for physics and chemistry, and there was a general confidence in the ability of the experimental method to explain all phenomena in the natural world.

John Locke, a friend of Boyle's, had previously defended "the new way of ideas." Locke's thesis was that all knowledge was ultimately derived from ideas of sense experience. In the seventeenth century a French philosopher, René Descartes, had articulated a new method of philosophical analysis: techniques for achieving understanding and certainty by reducing complex concepts to simple ideas that would be "clear and distinct" (see Chapter 22).

All this interest in science and empirical investigations had important impact upon traditional philosophical concerns. For example, many traditional religious beliefs were intensely criticized. The new intellectuals discouraged belief in witchcraft and miracles as empty superstition. The Bible was criticized as self-contradictory and inconsistent with the discoveries of physics and astronomy. The onslaught of philosophical skepticism had left metaphysics in a shambles. Most of the skeptical arguments presented in Chapter 22 were vigorously articulated in the seventeenth and eighteenth centuries. The doctrine that nothing exists outside the reality of the mind (Chapter 16) was defended by Hume's predecessor, Bishop Berkeley. In the area of political and social philosophy, the new intellectuals were challenging traditional authorities. Theological skepticism naturally led to criticism of the divine right of kings, and thus the intellectual basis was being laid for the American Revolution and French Revolution of 1789.

35:2.1 *Hume's method*   As a young man, Hume believed that the empirical methods that had achieved revolutionary success in the physical sciences could be extended to the study of human nature. He hoped to apply this method in investigating the nature of the human mind, the motivational basis for human action, and the origin and rational basis of value and obligation. He argued that ultimately all scientific knowledge depends upon the science of man:

> 'Tis impossible to tell what changes and improvements we might make in these sciences were we thoroughly acquainted with the extent and force of human understanding, and could explain the nature of the ideas we employ, and of the operations we perform in our reasonings.[2]

Hume describes his work as "an attempt to introduce the experimental method of reasoning into moral subjects." And "moral subjects" are to be studied, like the physical sciences, as "matters of fact and existence." This method rests on his account of perceptions, which he divides into impressions and ideas.

> The difference betwixt these consists in the degrees of force and liveliness with which they strike upon the mind, and make their

---

[2]*Ibid.,* "Introduction," p. xv.

way into our thought or consciousness. . . . Those perceptions which enter with most force and violence, we may name *impressions;* and under this name I comprehend all our sensations, passions and emotions, as they make their first appearance in the soul. By *ideas* I mean the faint images of these in thinking and reasoning; such as, for instance, are all of the perceptions excited by the present discourse, excepting only, those which arise from the sight and touch, and excepting the immediate pleasure or uneasiness it may occasion.[3]

Hume makes the extremely important claim "that all our simple ideas in their first appearance, are derived from simple impressions, which are correspondent to them, and which they exactly represent." He also claims that all our perceptions are analyzable into *simple* impressions and ideas "such as admit of no distinction or separation." Thus, according to Hume, all contents of consciousness are ultimately derivable from simple experiences. On this basis he states his theory of meaning, which can be illustrated by an example. To teach a child what the word "scarlet" means is to give the child an *idea* of scarlet. To do this one produces the experience of scarlet in the child, ordinarily by showing the child a scarlet object, such as a ribbon. More complex expressions can be explained in terms of expressions whose meanings the child has similarly learned. Hume offers a very simple test for whether or not an expression is meaningful:

When we entertain . . . any suspicion that a philosophical term is employed without any meaning or idea (as is but too frequent), we need but to inquire, *from what impression is that supposed idea derived*? And, if it be impossible to assign any, this will serve to confirm our suspicion that it's meaningless.[4]

Hume offers a related theory of evidence. When you make a meaningful statement you must be able to determine whether it is true or false by reference to your experience. A statement not open to this sort of test contains "nothing but sophistry and illusion."

Hume adopts psychological methods for explaining why people combine ideas as they do. Through these methods he aims to explain the great uniformity that we find between different minds, cultures, and languages. For example, memory tends to preserve combinations of ideas in particular orders. More important, the faculties that govern us lead us to combine ideas as required at different times. "Here is a kind of *attraction*, which in the mental world will be found to have as

---

[3]*Ibid.,* I,I,I, pp. 1, 4.
[4]David Hume, *An Enquiry Concerning Human Understanding*, ed. L. A. Selby-Bigge (Oxford: Clarendon Press, 1888), Sec. II

extraordinary effects as [gravitational attraction] in the natural [world], and to shew itself in as many and as various forms." Hume described the *association of ideas* as "a gentle force, which commonly prevails, and is the cause why, among other things, languages so nearly correspond to each other."[5]

The association of ideas arises from three different qualities: *resemblance*, for example, you tend to recall your idea of scarlet when you encounter a new impression of a similar shade; *contiguity*, for example, when you have an impression or idea of an object such as the Statue of Liberty, you associate it with your idea of an object spatially or temporally near it, such as the World Trade Center; *cause and effect*, for example, your idea of rain naturally gives rise to the idea of clouds and frontal systems that cause it. You should note, however, that a psychological theory of why we hold the ideas we do and associate them as we do is not to be confused with a theory of *evidence*, which is concerned with whether or not we are justified in connecting ideas in the way that we do.

35:2.2 *Theory of knowledge* All our knowledge, according to Hume, is expressed in analytic or synthetic statements. Analytic statements, including those of mathematics and logic, state *"relations of ideas,"* which purport to be certain and ultimately based on intuition. We are able to compare our impressions and ideas in terms of resemblance, contrariety, quality, and quantity. Hume's *test* for truth or falsity in such statements consists in *whether or not we can imagine them as being otherwise*. For example, "When two numbers are so combined, as that the one has always an unit answering to every unit of the other, we pronounce them equal."[6] I cannot *imagine* a case in which each member of a set of apples has a member of a set of pears correspond-

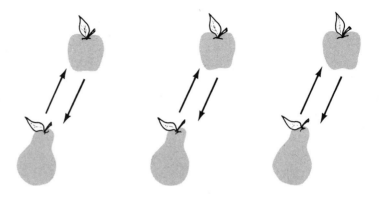

---

[5]Hume, *Treatise*, I,I,IV, pp. 12–13.
[6]Hume, *Treatise*, I, III, I.

ing to it and vice versa, but the two sets are unequal. This statement is analytically true, because you cannot *imagine* it being false. A statement is analytically false if you cannot imagine it being true.

Synthetic statements, in contrast, describe *"matters of fact,"* which are not necessary:

> The contrary of every matter of fact is still possible; because it can never imply a contradiction, and is conceived by the mind with the same facility and distinctiveness, as if ever so comfortable to reality. "That the sun will not rise tomorrow" is no less intelligible a proposition, and implies no more contradiction than the affirmation, "that it will rise."[7]

Hume claims that all our reasoning about matters of fact is founded on the relation of cause and effect, by which "we can go beyond the evidence of our reason and senses," for example, if you have impressions of heat and light and state, "There's a fire in here." These statements represent implicit inferences based on unstated assumptions.

(1) Experiences of heat and light are caused by fire. (Causal assumption.)
(2) I experience heat and light.
(3) Therefore, there is a fire. (Inference about matter of fact.)

35:2.3 *Analysis of cause and effect*   Since causality plays such an important role in our knowledge of fact and existence, Hume dedicated much effort to analyzing causality and to determining whether or not our concept of causation is really derived from experience.

---

[7]Hume, *Enquiry*, Sec. IV, Pt. I. Compare these definitions with those in 36:2.2 and in 3.3.3.

PHILOSOPHER'S WORKSHOP

Hume's Analysis of Causation

Hume here applies his method to the idea of cause and effect. (Review 35:2.1 in connection with this Workshop.)

To begin regularly, we must consider the idea of causation, and see from what origin it is deriv'd. 'Tis impossible to reason justly, without understanding perfectly the idea concerning which we reason; and 'tis impossible perfectly to understand any idea, without tracing it up to its origin, and examining that primary impression, from which it arises. The examination of the impression bestows a clearness on the idea; and the examination of the idea bestows a like clearness on all our reasoning.

Let us therefore cast our eye on any two objects, which we call cause and effect, and turn them on all sides, in order to find that impression, which produces an idea of such prodigious consequence. At first sight I perceive, that I must not search for it in any of the particular qualities of the objects; since, whichever of these qualities I pitch on, I find some object that is not possess'd of it, and yet falls under the denomination of cause or effect. And indeed there is nothing existent, either externally or internally, which is not to be considered either as a cause or an effect; tho' 'tis plain there is no one quality which universally belongs to all beings, and gives them a title to that denomination.

The idea then of causation must be deriv'd from some relation among objects; and that relation we must now endeavour to discover. I find in the first place, that whatever objects are consider'd as causes or effects, are contiguous; and that nothing can operate in a time or place, which is ever so little remov'd from those of its existence. Tho' distant objects may sometimes seem productive of each other, they are commonly found upon examination to be link'd by a chain of causes, which are contiguous among themselves, and to the distant objects; and when in any particular instance we cannot discover this connection, we still presume it to exist. We may therefore consider the relation of contiguity as essential to that of causation; at least may suppose it such, according to the general opinion, till we can find a more proper occasion to clear up this matter, by examining what objects are or are not susceptible of juxtaposition and conjunction.

The second relation I shall observe as essential to causes and effects is not so universally acknowledg'd, but is liable to some controversy. 'Tis that of priority of time in the cause before the effect. Some pretend that 'tis not absolutely necessary a cause should precede its effect; but that any object or action, in the very first moment of its existence, may exert its productive quality, and give rise to another object or action, perfectly contemporary with itself. But beside that experience in most instances seems to contradict this opinion, we may establish the relation of priority by a kind of inference or reasoning. 'Tis an established maxim, both in natural and moral philosophy, that an object, which exists for any time in its full perfection without producing another, is not its sole cause; but is assisted by some other principle which pushes it from its state of inactivity, and makes it exert that energy, of which it was secretly possessed. No, if any cause may be perfectly contemporary with its effect, 'tis certain, according to this maxim, that they must all of them be so; since any one of them, which retards its operation for a single moment, exerts not itself at that very individual time, in which it might have operated; and therefore is no proper cause. The consequence of this would be no less than the destruction of that succession of causes, which we observe in the world; and indeed the utter annihilation of time. For if one cause were contemporary with its effect, and this effect with its effect, and so on, 'tis plain there wou'd be no such thing as succession, and all objects must be coexistent.

If this argument appear satisfactory, 'tis well. If not, I beg the reader to allow me the same liberty, which I have us'd in the preceding case, of supposing it such. For he shall find that the affair is of no great importance.

Having thus discovered or suppos'd the two relations of contiguity and succession to be essential to causes and effects, I find I am stopt short, and can proceed no farther in considering any single instance of cause and effect. Motion in one body is regarded upon impulse as the cause of motion in another. When we consider these objects with the utmost attention, we find only that the one body approaches the other; and that the motion of it precedes that of the other, but without any sensible interval. 'Tis in vain to rack ourselves with farther thought and reflection upon this subject. We can go no farther in considering this particular instance.

Shou'd any one leave this instance, and pretend to define a cause, by saying it is something productive of another, 'tis evident he would say nothing. For what does he mean by production? Can he give any definition of it, that will not be the same with that of causation? If he can, I desire it may be produc'd. If he cannot, he here runs in a circle, and gives a synonymous term instead of a definition.

Shall we then rest contented with these two relations of contiguity and succession, as affording a compleat idea of causation? By no means. An object may be contiguous and prior to another, without being consider'd as its cause. There is a necessary connection to be taken into consideration; and that relation is of much greater importance, than any of the other two above mention'd.

Here again I turn the object on all sides, in order to discover the nature of this necessary connection, and find the impression, or impressions, from which its idea may be deriv'd. When I cast my eye on the known qualities of objects, I immediately discover that the relation of cause and effect depends not in the least on them. When I consider their relations, I can find none but those of contiguity and succession; which I have already regarded as imperfect and unsatisfactory. Shall the despair of success make me assert, that I am here possest of an idea, which is not preceded by any similar impression? This wou'd be too strong a proof of levity and inconstancy; since the contrary principle has been already so firmly establish'd, as to admit of no farther doubt; at least, till we have more fully examined the present difficulty.[8]

---

[8]Hume, *Treatise*, I,III,II, pp. 74–77.

Hume uses his method of identifying meanings to explain the statement "*C* causes *E*." When we say that fire *C* causes heat and light *E*, we express several relationships between the objects of the ideas of heat and light: (1) Heat and light are *contiguous* in space with fire, (2) the presence of fire is *prior in time* to heat and light, and (3) there is a *constant conjunction* of objects of this sort. We have in the past observed fire when we have observed heat and light. Hume denies that our idea of cause and effect involves the idea of a *necessary connection* between these events, for if two things are necessarily related, you cannot conceive of them as not being related. But our ideas of cause and effect are ideas of distinct events: You can conceive of a fire occurring that did not produce the effects of heat and light. For example, you can imagine lighting a match to a sheet of paper which burned with a cold, black flame.

Thus, according to Hume, the statement that *C* causes *E* really amounts to a description of our present and past experience. This view has important implications for the justifiability of our claims about causal relations. It also undercuts the rational basis of our statements about the relationship between matters of fact in different periods of time.

(1) Experiences of heat and light have been constantly conjoined with fire *in the past*.
(2) I experience heat and light *now*.
(3) Therefore, there's a fire there *now*.

Hume contends that we have *no good reason* to make this inference. The mere fact that *X* and *Y* have been related in the past does not, by itself, prove that *X* and *Y* will continue to be related. We would have good reasons if we could add the assumption:

(2′) The future will resemble the past.

Hume agrees that we all strongly believe statement 2′. But can you *prove* that the future will resemble the past? Because Hume can find no convincing proof, he is led to conclude that there is no *rational* basis for believing that it will and no rational basis for our causal inferences.

Hume believes that his *psychological* method can be used to explain *how* we are able to carry on this reasoning.

> When the mind, therefore, passes from the idea or impression of one object to the idea or belief of another, it is not determin'd by reason, but by certain principles, which associate together the ideas of these objects, and unite them in the imagination.[9]

---

[9]Hume, *Treatise*, I, III, VI, p. 92.

He claims that as a result of repeated experience, we become conditioned to expect certain results.

35:2.4 *The problem of the external world*   Hume's methods thus lead him to surprising results. He tries to extend the "experimental method," successful in the physical sciences, to the science of man itself. Scientists use empiricism to uncover the causes of natural phenomena, but Hume's empirical methods call into question the rational basis of our belief in causality. Hume is led to skepticism about the existence of the very world outside of the mind that is studied by physical scientists. Since our evidence consists exclusively of our experiences, we have no evidence for any causes outside of those experiences. Hume's inquiries lead to the skeptical result that claims about the intrinsic nature of reality, independent of human experience, cannot be confirmed by evidence and are, in fact, meaningless.

35:2.5 *Mind and self*   The problems Hume raises about the external world and the nature of physical reality were familiar to his predecessors. George Berkeley argued earlier that the supposition that physical objects exist outside of the mind is unsupported by any evidence and is, in fact, nonsensical. He argued instead that the only reality is the mind, which either produces or undergoes various experiences described in mental statements (see Chapter 16).

Hume's advance over his predecessors is to see that the empirical method raises exactly the same difficulties for a metaphysical belief in the *mind* as it had raised for a metaphysical belief in external material things. Since all the evidence we have for our statements consists in impressions, which are experiences of the mind, justifying and even conceptualizing belief in mind or self becomes problematic. Both idealists (Chapter 16) and dualists (Chapter 17) argue that because you think, you may infer your own existence as the thinking substance that underlies the thought. Hume argues, on the contrary, that all you really experience is thinking. The inference to a thinking entity that underlies or produces the thinking is just as problematic as the inference to an object outside of the mind supposedly producing perceptual experiences. Our memory and experience only reveal connections and associations between our experiences, not between our experiences and anything else, a mind, for example. Hume concludes that a consistent application of empirical method leads to the result that the existence of the mind, as such, is philosophically suspect.

35:2.6 *Hume's critique of religion*   Hume raises very similar skeptical difficulties about traditional philosophical proofs for the existence of God. He objects to proofs that God is a first cause of the universe.

Causal arguments should only relate things that are experienced and not try to connect experienced things with things outside the range of experience (see Chapter 29). The attempt to infer a supernatural cause of natural phenomena is suspect in the same way as metaphysical inferences about the external world, the existence of our own mind, or the existence of other minds outside our own. Hume applied empiricist methods of criticism to the argument from design and found it wanting (see Chapter 27). He also very powerfully expressed the problem of evil as an argument against God's existence (see Chapter 28).

35:2.7 *The "is" and the "ought"*   When Hume begins to apply his method to value statements or statements of obligation, he concludes that these statements are fundamentally different from other ones (see Chapter 5). He considers how evidence is related to the truth or falsity of different statements. A matter of fact, for example, "High levels of air pollution are correlated with lung cancer," can be supported by observation: We observe pollution and lung cancer and see whether or not they are, in fact, correlated. But you cannot present evidence in this way to support the value statements, "Pollution is bad" or "We really ought to do something about pollution." We don't observe pollution and badness and see whether or not they are correlated. Hume claims that a statement like "Pollution is bad" expresses a person's subjective response to pollution, an intensely negative response in this case, rather than describing matters of fact.

Hume does allow some role for reasoning in the value area, but he insists that reason "is and ought to be the slave of the passions." What he means by this statement can be illustrated with the example of pollution. Often we carry out reasoning of the following sort:

(1) We ought to remove any causes of cancer.
(2) High levels of air pollution cause cancer.
(3) Therefore, we ought to do something about eliminating air pollution.

Here we have rationally derived an ethical conclusion, but we have derived it from another ethical premise, namely, that "We ought to remove causes of cancer." This is an example of what Hume would describe as reason serving as a "slave" of the passions. Our negative reaction to cancer is expressed in the first premise, and the role of reason is to see that our passionate negative responses to cancer are carried out. According to Hume's psychological theory of motivation, whereas reason permits us to connect ideas in this way, reasoning will result in action (such as action to remove air pollution) only if we also have a passionate negative reaction (to cancer). Reason by itself does not produce any action. The ultimate motivation comes from the passions.

Hume contends that much work in ethics relies upon fallacious forms of reasoning. For example, the argument, "We ought to do something about stopping air pollution, because air pollution is a cause of cancer," is, as it stands, illogical. The argument can easily be made valid by adding the extra premise, as above, "We ought to eliminate causes of cancer." But now our conclusion, which contained the word "ought," follows only because we also have a premise that contains the word "ought." Hume claims: A statement containing the word "ought" cannot be logically derived from statements which contained words such as "is" rather than "ought." (Compare: How can you derive a conclusion about Frenchmen from premises dealing exclusively with Englishmen?) This is *the problem of the "is" and the "ought"*: Surely, no set of factual statements ("is" statements) can imply a value statement ("ought" statement.)[10]

35:3.1 *Hume's world view*   The question of whether or not Hume succeeded in his initial enterprise of developing an empirically based philosophical system comparable to Newton's physics is not easy to assess, because Hume was carrying out both a philosophical and a psychological endeavor. From the point of view of his psychology, he did indeed present a systematic account of various functions of reasoning, including mathematical reasoning, reasoning about cause and effect, moral reasoning, religious belief, and so forth. From the point of view of philosophical psychology, Hume represents a wholesale rejection of the traditional rationalistic views of the human mind, insisting that a large amount of our belief is based on custom, habit, and unreasoning passionate responses.

From the point of view of philosophy, however, there is hardly any system at all. In fact, Hume's results represent a complete collapse of philosophical system-building. There is skepticism everywhere: about our belief in an external world, about our belief in cause and effect, about the existence of our own minds, about religion, about the rationality of our confidence in scientific prediction, and a very deep skepticism about the power of rational thinking.

35:3.2 *Hume's foundationalism*   Hume has exerted a powerful influence over empiricist philosophers throughout the English-speaking world. One reason for this influence is that once a philosopher begins to work

---

[10]See Hume, *Treatise*, III,I,I. Perhaps you can find a counterexample to this assumption. Does anything normative follow from a sentence like "I promise to pay my debt" or from a statement like "Yesterday I did enter into a contract with you"?

in Hume's tradition, it is virtually impossible to escape it, for Hume's philosophical work involves two basic characteristics of all foundational systems. First, there is a belief in a fundamental set of basic statements—which are basically those that describe our impressions and ideas, the counterparts of what twentieth-century philosophers have called "sense datum statements" (see Chapter 23). Hume assumes to begin with that all our evidence consists exclusively in a description of our own immediate sense experiences. Second, Hume has a very narrow conception of the range of legitimate philosophical reasoning. This view is apparent in his criticisms of both cause and effect and reasoning to "ought" statements. In both cases he will not count as legitimate any conclusion that does not follow validly. It is not surprising, on the basis of these two foundationalist assumptions, that Hume is led to the skeptical conclusion that we can know nothing except for our immediate experiences and ideas.

35:4.1 *Hume's impact* A philosopher as profoundly skeptical as Hume was bound to be unpopular. His reputation as a freethinker on religious subjects made him controversial, and he made few friends with his quips, such as that the hardest miracle to explain is the fact that so many Christians believe in miracles. Hume had, however, an important immediate impact upon the development of philosophy, although it was essentially a negative one. Astute philosophers of the time recognized the magnitude of Hume's talents and sought to refute him. Another Scottish philosopher, Thomas Reid, attacked him from the vantage point of common sense, arguing that philosophers need not start from such a narrow base of evidence as Hume demanded.

Hume had a much more important impact, however, on the course of Continental philosophy. The reaction in Europe was not against his assumption about evidence, but against his assumption about the kind of reasoning that can be carried out from the type of evidence he allowed. The critical philosophy of Immanual Kant (see Chapter 36) and the idealist system of G. W. F. Hegel and other nineteenth-century idealists rejected the view that philosophical reasoning must be as narrowly deductive as Hume required. The nondeductive dialectical logic introduced by Hegel formed the basis for the philosophical and scientific views of Karl Marx (see Chapter 37).

35:4.2 *Hume in the twentieth century* Hume continued to exert an influence on nineteenth-century British thinkers, including John Stuart Mill, but toward the end of the nineteenth-century, idealism carried the day in England and the United States as well as in Europe. However, at about the turn of the century there was a sharp reaction in England against idealism, and many philosophers again became intensely interested in Hume. Not coincidentally, the twentieth-century philosophers reached skeptical conclusions regarding metaphysics, religion, and ethics, many of them regarding statements in these areas as "cognitively meaningless." Many contemporary philosophers who reject large parts of Hume's theory still regard his criticisms of causality and of the justification of scientific prediction as unanswerable. But probably the greatest value in Hume's philosophy lies in the fact that he was able to develop fully and fearlessly all the implications of his empiricist methodology.

EXERCISES for Chapter 35

1. Of the following statements, mark those *T* that correctly describe the problems to which Hume responded.
   A. Hume wanted to apply methods successful in astronomy and psychology to philosophical questions.
   B. Hume wanted to defend religion against rationalistic attacks.
   C. Hume was concerned to describe the actual functioning of the mind.
   D. Hume wanted to pursue the philosophical lead of Locke's new way with ideas.
   E. Hume wanted to defend a rationalistic approach to human knowledge.
   F. Hume wanted a clear description of human experience to serve as the foundation for whatever knowledge might be possible.
   G. Hume wanted to study the origin and rational basis of value and obligation.

2. In the Workshop in 35:2.3, Hume presents his analysis of causation.
   a. What argument does he give in the first paragraph for this method?
   b. What component ideas does he find involved in the idea of causation?
   c. Why is it troubling to Hume that those component ideas are not, together, identical with the idea of causation?
   d. Do you see a way of solving the difficulty?

3. Describe Hume's method of tracing ideas to their origins in experience in such a way as to outline his reasoning on the following topics:
   a. the existence of a (material, external) world beyond our impressions (35:2.4),
   b. the existence of a mind or self that has impressions and ideas (35:2.5),
   c. the nature of values and of moral judgments (35:2.7).

4. Choose one of the following topics, and after consulting appropriate library research materials, write an essay
   a. concerning what Kant thought correct versus what he thought incorrect in Hume's work,
   b. comparing Hume's understanding of simples and complexes with Russell's Logical Atomism.

c. comparing Hume's rejection of metaphysical ideas with the twentieth-century attack on metaphysics by logical positivism,

d. appraising the strengths and weaknesses of foundationalism in the light of Hume's foundationalism.

SELECTED ANSWERS for Chapter 35

1. C, D, F, and G are true.

2. a. The argument's conclusion is presented in the first sentence.

   b. Contiguity and succession.

   c. Hume assumes that the idea of causation is a legitimate one. Yet any legitimate complex idea, Hume assumes, is identical to a set of simple ideas which are included in our impressions. Hume is not inclined to doubt either of these assumptions even when the component ideas he finds within causation are not identical to it.

36

Immanuel Kant

The philosopher Nietzsche once with great irony praised Immanuel Kant for accomplishing a philosophical *tour de force*. "Kant," he said, "wanted to prove in a way that would dumbfound the common man that the common man was right; that was the secret joke of his soul." Kant sees himself defending the views of common sense, but his *Critique of Pure Reason* is one of the most difficult philosophical works ever written. Yet students who actually studied with Kant reported that his in-class discussions were by comparison a model of clarity. Unfortunately, that was before the age of the tape recorder. Despite its difficulty, Kant's *Critique* is regarded by most philosophers as one of the most important and most influential works on human thought ever written, containing a wealth of insight. Many philosophers today are basically Kantian. This chapter will introduce you to some important features of Kant's philosophy. After reading it you should be able to

- State the major problems Kant addressed.
- Describe how Kant used his methods to offer solutions to these problems.
- Address major criticisms and impacts of Kant's philosophy.

36:1.1 *Kant's life* The epitome of the ivory tower philosopher, Kant (1724–1804) dedicated his life almost exclusively to scholarly pur-

suits. He was born, reared, and educated in Prussia, northern Germany. He never married, and, being rather frail, did not indulge much in vigorous physical activity. He was regarded as a typically eccentric professor: People could, for example, set their watches by his daily rounds. His life-long dream, to become a professor at his alma mater, the University of Königsberg, was finally fulfilled when he was approaching 50. Although his earlier writings were respected by a limited circle, Kant did not publish his *Critique of Pure Reason* until he was 57. Not surprisingly, the *Critique* was greeted more with puzzlement than with instant admiration. Kant wrote a *Prolegomena to Any Future Metaphysics* to clarify his position in the *Critique*. His most important subsequent work was in ethics, especially his *Foundations of the Metaphysics of Morals*. On these foundations he soon erected his *Critique of Practical Reason* and the *Metaphysics of Morals*. Kant tried to avoid controversy during his life, and when his views on religion began to cause a stir, he became less outspoken at the request of the Prussian government. Nevertheless, his social views were rather liberal for his time.

36:1.2 *Reason under fire* Kant was a pivotal figure in the history of philosophy because he was able to appreciate fully the philosophical development that had been occurring over two centuries in two radically different traditions: the rationalist tradition of Descartes, Spinoza, and Leibniz, and the British empiricist tradition of Locke, Berkeley, and Hume. Rationalists from the time of Descartes to the time of Christian Wolff, an important figure in Kant's time, had been building systems attempting to justify all human knowledge in a foundationalist way. Although Kant was very sympathetic toward this enterprsie, he also appreciated the findings of the empiricist David Hume (Chapter 35), who had concluded that these rationalists' methods would not support the metaphysical conclusions they had drawn. Kant was grateful to Hume for arousing him from his "dogmatic slumbers." Berkeley and Hume had both argued that there is no basis whatever for supposing the existence of a world outside the mind. The whole physical world of space and time was either an illusion or a mental construct. According to Kant, the inability to establish the objectivity of the physical world was a "scandal to philosophy."

Kant professed to admire most two things: "the starry skies above and the moral law within."—which is a valuable clue to the problems that most concern him. He wished to validate the claims of reason in two crucial areas: He wanted to show that the natural sciences did have a firm foundation, that the scientific method was not vulnerable to skeptical objections; but he also wanted to safeguard the use of reason in the moral sphere, in ethics. He wanted to show that our moral judgments were as objective as the statements of science. This dual purpose in Kant, this recognition of the legitimacy of ethics as well as science, suggests already a strong *contextualist* tendency in his thinking. His writings attempt to substantiate his deep conviction that rationality in science and rationality in ethics need not conflict.

36:2.1 *Kant's method* Kant's arguments are exceedingly subtle and complex, so that there is wide disagreement among commentators about how to construe particular passages. There is general agreement, however, about his basic method, the use of *transcendental argument*. The basic strategy is to show that our experience would be impossible unless a particular disputed statement is taken to be true. This type of argument can be illustrated with a somewhat oversimplified example. Descartes had argued that there must be some kind of mind underlying the stream of conscious mental experiences, the way a pincushion underlies pins. But the skeptic, David Hume, argues that all we really perceive are the pins (our conscious experiences), never the supposed pincushion (mind) (see 35:2.5). What is your experience of your "self"? Have you ever perceived within yourself an entity which could be called an ego? Hume confessed that he never had, and doubted that anyone else had either. However, even Hume recognized that his skeptical position led to difficulty, for he had to recognize that he was just not a stream of disconnected experiences. Take the simple case in which you perceive something that you remember perceiving before. You say, "I am angry at my roommate. I (also) remember being angry at my roommate before. I was angry at my roommate before." These statements describe experiences that are connected with each other in an important way, for experience as we know it would be impossible otherwise. *Here* Kant's transcendental argument enters the picture: Our experience would be impossible if we did not *assume* that a basic *unity of consciousness* exists. We must take it as true that there is a self or a unifying subject of consciousness.

The strength of this type of argument is that it does not beg any questions against the skeptics, for it starts from exactly the same evidence upon which the skeptics base *their* arguments. But Kant also recognizes that transcendental arguments have important limitations, the conclusions of which only apply to our *experience* of things. They show how things must appear to us, if experience is to be possible, but they cannot be validly applied outside the bounds of how we experience or how things appear. They do not tell us how things must be "in themselves." The transcendental argument about the self shows only that there must be a unity *within* consciousness; it does not prove anything about any ego totally *outside* experience.

36:2.2 *Kant's theory of knowledge* Kant wants to establish the necessity of certain crucial statements that have been challenged by the skeptics. He begins by attacking the fundamental assumption of empiricism, that there are only two kinds of statements: *analytic* statements, such as "All bachelors are unmarried," and all the others, called *synthetic* (see 3:3.3 and 35:2.2). Hume argued that only analytically true statements were necessary and could be known with certainty, because they expressed certain relations between our ideas. Since part of what we mean by "bachelor" is "unmarried person," it is necessarily the case that all bachelors are unmarried. Kant agrees that there are analytic statements, which are necessarily true or false. Hume also denied that synthetic statements are necessarily true or false. These report "matters of fact" truly or falsely; they are not true or false in virtue of conceptual relations. To know synthetic statements like "Ducks swim faster than dogs," empiricists tell us to look to the facts. But Hume pointed out that the analytic-synthetic distinction, as he understood it, created obvious problems for a statement like "Every event has a cause." The statement is not analytic, like the statement "Every *effect* has a cause." Since "effect" is defined as "something having a cause," it is analytically true that every effect has a cause. However, because "event" is not so defined, "Every *event* has a cause" is a synthetic statement, and if so, it is not a *necessary* statement. Similarly, the statement "The future will resemble the past" is not analytic. Nothing in the definition of "future," "past," and "will resemble" makes this a necessary truth. However, because such statements form the bedrock of modern science, scientists *must* assume that they necessarily hold in order to apply the scientific method (see 35:2.3).

Against Hume, Kant argues that synthetic statements like these are necessary: Describing them as "synthetic a priori judgments," he defends them by transcendental arguments: Experience would be impossible without a unified consciousness. We could not have the complex awareness that we do of things in the world of space and time if our stream of consciousness were not unified. But we could not have this unity of consciousness unless our experiences were connected *in a regular way.* Our experiences can be connected in such a regular way only if they are governed by unified causal rules, such as the rule that something (a substance) continues to exist when unobserved, or the rule that the occurrence of an event of some type (the cause) is regularly followed by an event of another type (the effect). For example, the occurrence of a pin prick is regularly associated with the occurrence of pain. Thus we must take it as true that every event has a cause. Kant believes that he can thereby meet a skeptic like Hume on his own ground and establish the necessity of the existence of substances and of causes and effects. But since he is using transcendental arguments, their applicability is restricted to the bounds of experience. Kant believes that it is literally *meaningless* to try to apply the concept of substance or the concept of cause outside the realm of experience to any entity, such as God.

36:2.3 *Limits of human knowledge*   Kant distinguishes between *phenomena* and *noumena.* "Phenomenon" means literally "that which appears," and for Kant a phenomenon is any object of awareness. The noumenon, on the other hand, is the thing in itself, in contrast to the object of awareness. Kant's theory of phenomena can be understood by the following model: The mind is like a machine designed to process raw material into finished products. Raw experience flows into the mind, which receives the experience only when it has gone through certain filters. The filter our mind uses is the four-dimensional framework of space and time, without which experience would be completely incomprehensible to us. Thereafter, the raw material is subjected to the structuring activity of the mind, which organizes the data in terms of concepts such as cause and effect, substance and quality, and existence. The finished product of this process is the phenomenon, the basic constituent of human experience as we know it. How are the noumena or the things in themselves related to this complex process? Nobody knows. And nobody can, by definition, know. Presumably the raw experiences come in some way from things in themselves. We cannot even conjecture about how this happens.

If the mind is so active in filtering and structuring incoming data, how is objectivity possible? Kant's answer is that every human mind structures each human's experience in the same way. Therefore, your conception of cause and effect is no different from mine, and hence, it is possible for you to correct any errors that I might make in identifying causes of various phenomena. This similarity makes it possible for scientists to cooperate, for example, in discovering causes for diseases like lung cancer. This objectivity, however, applies only to phenomena; any attempt to prove conclusions about things in themselves must be fallacious.

PHILOSOPHER'S WORKSHOP

The Origin of the Natural Order

In his *Prolegomena to Any Future Metaphysics* Kant identifies the limits of his transcendental philosophy and the two chief questions that form its boundaries. He then points out that the source of the universal order of nature is, in actuality, the human mind.

This question—the highest point that transcendental philosophy can ever reach, and to which, as its boundary and completion, it must proceed—really contains two questions.

First: How is nature in the material sense, that is, to intuition, or considered as the totality of appearances, possible; how are space, time, and that which fills both—the object of sensation—possible generally? The answer is: By means of the constitution of our sensibility, according to which it is in its own way affected by objects which are in themselves unknown to it and totally distinct from those appearances. . . .

Secondly: How is nature possible in the formal sense, as the totality of the rules under which all appearances must come in order to be thought as connected in experience? The answer must be this: It is only possible by means of the constitution of our understanding, according to which all the above representations of the sensibility are necessarily referred to a consciousness, and by which the peculiar way in which we think (namely, by rules) and hence experience also are possible, but must be clearly distinguished from an insight into the objects in themselves. . . .

There are many laws of nature which we can know only by

means of experience; but conformity to law in the connection of appearances, that is, in nature in general, we cannot discover by any experience, because experience itself requires laws which are a priori at the basis of its possibility.

The possibility of experience in general is therefore at the same time the universal law of nature, and the principles of experience are the very laws of nature. . . .

Even the main proposition expounded throughout this section—that universal laws of nature can be known a priori—leads naturally to the proposition that the highest legislation of nature must lie in ourselves, that is, in our understanding; and that we must not seek the universal laws of nature in nature by means of experience, but conversely must seek nature, as to its universal conformity to law, in the conditions of the possibility of experience which lie in our sensibility and in our understanding. . . .

But we must distinguish the empirical laws of nature, which always presuppose particular perceptions, from the pure or universal laws of nature, which, without being based on particular perceptions, contain merely the conditions of their necessary union in experience. In relation to the latter, nature and possible experience are quite the same; and as the conformity to law in the latter depends upon the necessary connection of appearances in experience (without which we cannot know any object whatever in the sensible world), consequently upon the original laws of the understanding, it seems at first strange, but is not the less certain, to say: The understanding does not derive its laws (a priori) from, but prescribes them to nature. . . .

. . . [T]he understanding is the origin of the universal order of nature, in that it comprehends all appearances under its own laws and thereby produces, in an a priori manner, experience (as to its form), by means of which whatever is to be known only by experience is necessarily subjected to its laws. For we are not concerned with the nature of things in themselves, which is independent of the conditions both of our sensibility and our understanding, but with nature as an object of possible experience; and in this case the understanding, since it makes experience possible, thereby insists that the sensuous world is either not an object of experience at all or that it is nature [namely, the existence of things determined according to universal laws].[1]

[1]Immanuel Kant, *Prolegomena to Any Future Metaphysics*, Secs. 36, 38 trans. Lewis White Beck (Indianapolis: Bobbs Merrill, 1950), pp. 65–69.

36:2.4 *Critique of natural theology*   Kant was, therefore, highly critical of attempts to prove that God exists. "God" is understood to refer to some entity outside of human experience. The so-called ontological argument, or argument from perfection, involves a confused idea about the nature of existence. The word "exist" can only be used to assert that a phenomenon occurs in a given time. Thus, those who regard existence as if it were a quality or an intrinsic perfection of a thing in itself are confused about the meaning of the word (see Chapter 29). The first cause argument is also confused, because it involves speaking about a cause of the world, something outside of time. But the term "cause" makes sense only when it is applied to phenomena that are in a temporal order as given in experience. Kant rejected the claim that Christian orthodoxy could be rationally established.

Nevertheless, he believed that the distinction between a noumenal and a phenomenal realm left room for the possibility of faith in God's existence. Even though we are unable to demonstrate that God exists, nothing in our scientific knowledge rules out God's existence, because our scientific knowledge is completely confined to phenomena. Kant believed that when we rationally commit ourselves to the moral life we must suppose that reality is fundamentally in accord with our moral objective. This belief is truly a leap of faith, but not an *antirational* one (Chapter 30).

36:2.5 *Human nature*   Kant also makes a distinction between noumena and phenomena when he discusses the human self. He argues that one of the most important moral distinctions is that between persons and things: Persons have rights, whereas things do not, and humans are persons only because they have noumenal selves. Insofar as a human being is conscious of his or her duty in the world, he or she is not a phenomenon but a noumenon — not a thing but a person. This distinction is closely related to Kant's solution to the problem of free will. He contends that one's phenomenal self is totally determined by physical laws, but there is also one's noumenal self, one's true self. Freedom operates in a human being as a supersensible principle which is independent of nature and natural causality. Again, just as in the case of God's existence, Kant does not believe that the freedom of the noumenal self can be proved. Nevertheless, he does not believe that scientific knowledge, confined to phenomena, excludes it. We presume our freedom in making moral commitments. This second leap of faith is, in Kant's analysis, also compatible with scientific rationality.

36:2.6 *Kantian ethics*   Kant defends an ethic of duty (Chapter 7). Acting morally consists in acting on the basis of duties which are defined by principles of reason. The most important such principle is the *Categorical Imperative,* which requires that one act in accordance with the principles that can be applied consistently to everyone (see the workshop in 7:2.3).

Kant attempts to defend reason in ethics against Hume's skeptical attacks (35:2.7) on two different fronts. Kant tries to show that reason can establish the basic principle of morality, and he denies Hume's claim that reason is "the slave of the passions." Kant maintains that our sense of duty, based upon rational considerations, does lead us to act contrary to our passions and appetites. For example, the child of a slaveowner might reason to the conclusion that slavery is evil and then actively oppose it, even though he or she would only stand to lose through its abolition. When such a person acts in accordance with the dictates of reason, that person acts from a *good will*, and nothing else, in Kant's view, is good without qualification.

36:3.1 *Kant's system* Kant's system may be described as a contextualist attempt to reconcile the skeptic's demand for certainty and the rationalist's desire for a comprehensive understanding of knowledge, reality, and value. Kant believes that he can accommodate scientific method and principles within his system without sacrificing precision and certainty. He uses transcendental arguments to try to prove that certain statements are necessarily true even though they are synthetic. Traditional terms like "cause and effect," "substance," and "existence" are precisely defined as ways of organizing observable phenomena. A rational basis is also provided for ethical reasoning, and claims of science and ethics are reconciled in contextualist fashion. Kant's strategy is to distinguish between the phenomenal realm and the noumenal one, to confine our claims of knowledge to the former exclusively, and to claim that there is room in the latter to accommodate human freedom, immortality, and the existence of God.

36:3.2 *Criticisms* In criticizing Kant, philosophers generally distinguish between transcendental arguments as such and the particular ways that Kant uses them. The use of transcendental argument may in principle be acceptable, even though Kant made mistakes in using it. His worst mistake, in the view of many critics, is to reason from the premise that human experience could not exist without some rules (or others) for connecting our sensory inputs, to the conclusion that a certain set of rules is "objective" in the sense of being valid for all human beings. Kant's critics object that this is too rigid a view of such rules. It may be true that in having experience, each human being structures the raw material of perception in various ways, but it doesn't follow that all human beings share the same way of organizing experience. People of different cultures or races might turn out to structure their experiences in quite different ways. For example, people in a primitive culture might have a quite different view of causation from ours. They might view many phenomena as miraculous, as resulting from the arbitrary, unpredictable choices of the gods, rather than as determined by preceding events. Moreover, critics contend, the basic principles by which we organize our experience may be open to revision in light of new experience. For example, Kant assumes that our experience must be interpreted through the law of cause and effect, which means that there can be no event that was not determined by the preceding one. However, the development of quantum physics suggests that this principle is not universally applicable. An event at the subatomic level, such as the decay of a nucleus of a radioactive atom, is apparently not determined by preceding events. However, according to quantum mechanics, our experience is ultimately subject to *statistical* regularities; that is, subatomic events occur in certain predictable *patterns*. Thus, critics of Kant find that his use of transcendental argument to defend scientific reasoning introduces too much rigidity into scientific thinking.

Critics of his ethics also find unnecessary rigidity. Kant tries to found ethics entirely upon rational considerations, but critics deny that a satisfactory ethical system could be constructed as long as human desires and values are omitted in defining the basic principles.

36:4.1 *Kant in the nineteenth century*   Kant had a deep impact upon European philosophy, but not to his personal gratification because generally his arguments were not fully appreciated by his contemporaries. His distinction between the phenomenal and noumenal realm received the strongest criticism. On the basis of his transcendental method Kant argues that "percepts without concepts are blind; concepts without percepts are empty." He means that our conceptual apparatus is necessary to make our experience comprehensible, but this conceptual apparatus cannot be extended meaningfully beyond the bounds of sense. That is, a word like "exist" has meaning only when applied to experienced phenomena. Yet Kant proceeds to talk about the existence of things "as they are in themselves" rather than as they are experienced. To these critics, the claim that we can "postulate" the existence of God or the freedom of the noumenal self seems to be nonsense, on Kant's own principle. Therefore, the early critics rejected Kant's noumenal realm altogether as being unintelligible.

The result of rejecting "things in themselves" and confining philosophy to the phenomenal realm was a luxurious flowering of idealistic metaphysical systems. The presumption of idealism is that, ultimately, experience alone exists. First, Fichte and Shelling, and later, Hegel and Schopenhauer constructed elaborate idealistic systems. The enterprise was carried on by F. H. Bradley and McTaggart in Great Britain and by Josiah Royce in the United States. All these idealistic philosophers began their system-building with a careful criticism of Kant.

36:4.2 *Kant in the twentieth century* Scholars who have returned to Kant's writing, applying newer techniques of textual criticism and interpretation, have discovered that much of his thought had been misinterpreted or distorted by early critics. A large and influential movement, called Neo-Kantianism, arose in the late nineteenth and early twentieth century and spread to England and the United States from Europe. The Neo-Kantians defended Kant's use of transcendental argument. Transcendental arguments are widely discussed today by American and British philosophers, and their use forms the basis for the influential work of the contemporary British philosopher P. F. Strawson.

In this century Kant's work in ethics is also very influential. His method of analyzing ethical reasoning is of interest to Ordinary Language philosophers, and twentieth-century moral theorists have looked to him for insight into the logic of our moral language. The British philosopher R. M. Hare defends a basically Kantian view of moral principles. Thus, despite the difficulty and obscurity of Kant's philosophy, he is still a force to be reckoned with in our century.

EXERCISES for Chapter 36

1. Of the following statements, mark those *T* that correctly describe the philosophical concerns to which Kant responded.
   A. Kant was educated in a tradition skeptical of rationalism.
   B. Kant was scandalized that philosophy could find no adequate justification for simple claims of knowledge about the external world.
   C. Kant respected the force of Hume's skeptical arguments.
   D. Kant wanted to show how the existence of God could be proved.
   E. Kant was uninterested in problems of moral philosophy.
   F. Kant was sympathetic with the goals of rationalistic philosophers.
   G. Kant wanted to maintain the compatibility of scientific and moral truths.

2. In the Workshop in 36:2.3, Kant addresses the question, "How do we know that there are laws of nature?"
   a. What distinction does Kant make between empirical laws of nature and pure or universal laws of nature?
   b. What does Kant mean when he says, "The possibility of experience in general is therefore at the same time the universal law of nature . . ."?

    c. What argument does Kant outline in the paragraph beginning, "Even the main proposition . . ."?

    d. How do the reasons presented in the last sentence of the quotation support Kant's position?

3. Describe what a transcendental argument is in such a way as to outline how Kant uses this kind of argument to

    a. argue that the postulation of the existence of God is necessary (36:2.4),

    b. vindicate the claim to know that every event has a cause (36:2.2),

    c. justify the claim that persons have rights (36:2.5).

4. Choose one of the following topics, and after consulting appropriate library research materials, write an essay

    a. describing the influence of Kant on one of the idealist philosophers mentioned in 36:4.1,

    b. describing P. F. Strawson's use of transcendental arguments,

    c. comparing the ethics and the concept of freedom developed by R. M. Hare with Kant's,

    d. comparing Kant's and Heidegger's critiques of metaphysics.

SELECTED ANSWERS for Chapter 36

1. B, C, F, and G are true.

2. a. *Which* general scientific laws are true, Kant asserts, is an empirical question: Experiences of observation and testing are required to determine which lawlike statements are true. But *that* there are general scientific laws that are true, Kant asserts, is a pure, universal law of nature which can be known to be true independent of experience.

    b. Kant is insisting that human experience is possible if, and only if, there is a lawlike order in nature.

    c. Kant's premise is that universal laws of nature can be known a priori, that is, independently of experience.

    d. Kant feels that the strength of his argument rests in the fact that he is making no assertions about how things are independent of human experience but is, rather, making all his assertions about how things, as experienced, must be if they are indeed to be experienced.

37

![decorative chapter number 37]

Karl Marx

Karl Marx (1818–1883) viewed himself primarily as a scientific historian. He explained social, political, and cultural developments basically in terms of economic conditions, and he advocated revolutionary change in existing social institutions. His ideas have influenced large numbers of people in North America, Africa, and Europe and today dominate the political arena in much of South America, Eastern Europe, and Asia. This chapter sketches Marx's methods and shows their application to social and political perspectives. Then it traces some of the metaphysical and epistemological themes evident in his writing. After reading Chapter 37 you should be able to

- State major problems that Marx addressed.
- Describe how Marx used his method to propose solutions to these problems.
- Address major criticisms and impacts of Marx's philosophy.

37:1 *Life and times* Karl Marx was born in Treves, Germany, in 1818, into a family that converted from Judaism to Lutheranism when he was a child. He studied law, philosophy, and history, earning a doctoral degree in philosophy at the age of 23 from the University of Jena. In his youth he was influenced by the dialectical idealism of Hegel and the materialism of Feuerbach. Because he criticized religion, Marx

539

never found a teaching job in Prussia. He edited a controversial news-paper for two years, but was then expelled from Prussia. In Paris he met Friedrich Engels, who became his lifelong benefactor and collab-orator (1843). There he wrote his *Economic and Philosophical Manu-scripts* (1844), which give us insight into his analysis of the human so-cial condition and his arguments that the laissez-faire capitalism in the rapidly industrializing countries of Western Europe resulted in the exploitation of the working classes.[1]

Marx described capitalism in the following terms. By the mid-1840's the industrial revolution was coming into full flower and a new breed of capitalist was emerging. In addition to the traditional hard-working individuals who built a small fortune from humble begin-nings, there arose an increasing number of bourgeoisie capitalists whose riches derived not from their own labor but from fortuitous investments.

Governments tended not to control economic development in capitalist countries. As a result, claimed Marx, alternating periods of depression and inflation continually plagued the working classes.

---

[1]This work was not published in English until 1959, which suggests that criti-cism of Marxist thought dominant in English-speaking countries before that time may have been based on an incomplete understanding of Marx's total world view.

Economists assumed that there is "an invisible hand" by which each individual's pursuit of his or her own economic self-interest leads inevitably to the achievement of the collective economic well-being.[2] Marx saw this dominant economic myth as a tool whereby those in positions of economic advantage could maintain their subjugation and exploitation of people whose only economic asset was their personal labor. In Marx's view this exploitation contained the seeds of its own destruction, since the same economic conditions that made it possible would eventually lead to the revolutionary upheaval that would end it.

In 1845 Marx was expelled from France, but he continued his economic and historical studies in Brussels, where he first became acquainted with the working man's movement. He and Engels drafted the *Communist Manifesto* in 1848. It calls for an overthrow of capitalistic political and economic systems through unified revolutionary action. Expelled from Brussels, Marx finally settled in London in 1849 and spent the rest of his life studying and writing. In 1864 he organized the first International Workingmen's Association, but after eight years of factional strife between himself and the more anarchistic elements in the union, he disbanded the organization.

---

[2]The economic theories of Adam Smith's *Wealth of Nations* (1776) were especially influential in England and in other industrialized countries.

 **PHILOSOPHER'S WORKSHOP**

The Communist Manifesto

Many of the *Manifesto's* demands for social reform have been at least partially met in several Western nations, including our own. In our era of socialized capitalism, demands for a graduated income tax and free public education seem tame compared to how they appeared to European capitalists in the mid-nineteenth century.

Nevertheless, in the most advanced countries the following will be pretty generally applicable:

1. Abolition of property in land and application of all rents of land to public purposes.
2. A heavy progressive or graduated income tax.
3. Abolition of all right of inheritance.
4. Confiscation of the property of all emigrants and rebels.
5. Centralization of credit in the hands of the state, by means of a national bank with state capital and an exclusive monopoly.

6. Centralization of the means of communication and transport in the hands of the state.

7. Extension of factories and instruments of production owned by the state; the bringing into cultivation of wastelands, and the improvement of the soil generally in accordance with a common plan.

8. Equal liability of all to labor. Establishment of industrial armies, especially for agriculture.

9. Combination of agriculture with manufacturing industries; gradual abolition of the distinction between town and country, by a more equable distribution of the population over the country.

10. Free education for all children in public schools. Abolition of children's factory labor in its present form. Combination of education with industrial production, etc.

When, in the course of development, class distinctions have disappeared and all production has been concentrated in the hands of a vast association of the whole nation, the public power will lose its political character. Political power, properly so called, is merely the organized power of one class for oppressing another. If the proletariat during its contest with the bourgeoisie is compelled, by the force of circumstances, to organize itself as a class, if, by means of a revolution, it makes itself the ruling class and, as such, sweeps away by force the old conditions of production, then it will, along with these conditions, have swept away the conditions for the existence of class antagonisms and of classes generally, and will thereby have abolished its own supremacy as a class.

In place of the old bourgeois society, with its classes and class antagonisms, we shall have an association in which the free development of each is the condition for the free development of all.[3]

---

[3]Karl Marx and Friedrich Engels, *Communist Manifesto*, Part II, (Moscow: Foreign Language Publishing House, 1948).

Das Kapital (Capital), Marx's major work, was published in three volumes, two of which were edited by Engels and appeared posthumously. While he was alive Marx's writing was influential, but after his death, his work profoundly affected the course of human history, for it provided the guiding ideas of Lenin, Trotsky, Stalin, Mao Tse-tung, Fidel Castro, Che Guevera, and many other theorists and revolutionaries.

37:2.1 *Marx's method* Engels characterized Marx's method of inquiry as "scientific," partly because of Marx's concern to focus attention on the conditions that bring about social and political events and partly to contrast what Marx was doing with speculations of the philosophers of the time. "Philosophers have only *interpreted* the world differently: the point is, however, to *change* it."[4] For all their talk about high-sounding social ideals, philosophers, according to the young Marx, had failed to examine the actual causes of human suffering so that they could do something genuine to relieve it. Their highly rhetorical essays did little else than redefine and reclassify reality; they did not change it. Marx urged the realization that social existence has a practical nature: "Social life is essentially *practical*. All mysteries which mislead theory into mysticism find their rational solution in human practice and in the understanding of this practice."[5] With this view in mind, Marx articulated his criterion of truth. The speculations of mystics, theologians, and philosophers are hollow statements, for truth is not a question of theory but one of practice.

> The question whether human thought can achieve objective truth is not a question of theory but a *practical* question. In practice (Praxis) man must prove the truth, i.e., the reality, power and this-sidedness of his thought. The dispute concerning the reality or unreality of thought — which is isolated from practice (Praxis) — is a purely *scholastic* question.[6]

Marx would reject the foundationalist concern to base knowledge solely on incorrigible (undoubtable) statements and valid inferences from them (see 22:3.3). Rather he would embrace the contextualist approach of trying to reconcile theory with the multifaceted array of evidence gained from personal, social, and historical experience. Even the goal of logical consistency is less pure than that of achieving a comprehensive understanding of the human situation which is based on and proves itself accurate by appeal to social reality.

Following Hegel, Marx looked at human society as essentially organic.[7] Social development is not merely change, but progress toward continually higher levels of self-awareness and integration. However, this progress is not a smooth and undisturbed one, but rather its history is marked by significant upheavals and revolutions. Marx explained historical development in terms of Hegel's *dialectics*, the first law of which is that matter progresses through stages of thesis,

---

[4]Karl Marx, "Theses on Feuerbach," in Sidney Hook, ed., *From Hegel to Marx* (Ann Arbor Paperbacks, University of Michigan Press, 1962), p. 303.

[5]*Ibid.*, p. 298.

[6]*Ibid.*, p. 281.

[7]Others of quite different philosophical outlooks also take an organic view of society and human culture. A twentieth-century example is Bertolanffy, the noted systems theorist.

antithesis, and synthesis, always toward higher forms of integration. The synthesis emerges out of the tension that exists between the thesis and its negation (the antithesis). Accumulations of tension lead to qualitative jumps forward (the law of the transformation of quantity to quality) as the synthesis emerges. The synthesis then represents the union of the thesis and antithesis (the law of the union of opposites) and the expression of a higher stage of development.

Social "contradiction" is a key factor in applying the dialectic. A society contains a contradiction when divergent tendencies or forces within it conflict so deeply that the conflict can be removed only by the destruction of that society. In capitalist society the conflict between the possessors of wealth (the bourgeoisie) and the producers of value (the working "proletariate") is such a contradiction, as we shall see in 37:2.3. The irony is that capitalism cannot arise and exist without these two social classes, yet the conflict of the two classes will destroy it. Out of the destruction, a new, higher synthesis will emerge, the socialist society. Let us examine this process more closely.

37:2.2 *Alienation and exploitation*   Marx derives the concept of alienation from the philosophy of Hegel, in which it is an estrangement between objects or persons. Whereas many philosophers and poets have identified feelings of human alienation, few have tried to locate its source in the dominant economic system of the times. Marx, however, saw human alienation as arising fundamentally out of the capitalist mode of production. First, under capitalism the workers are alienated from the products they make. These products (chairs, automobiles, manuscripts) are owned by another, the capitalist, who decides what will happen to them. Second, laborers are alienated from their own labor activity. Under capitalism, work itself is bought and sold by the owners of the means of production; that is, along with potatoes and lumber, people, as labor, are bought and sold. As a related development, the workers are alienated from their fellow workers.

> From political economy itself we have shown that the worker sinks to the level of a commodity, and to a most miserable commodity; that the misery of the worker increases with the power and volume of his production; that the necessary result of competition is the accumulation of capital in a few hands, and thus a restoration of monopoly in a more terrible form; and finally that the distinction between capitalist and landlord, and between agricultural labourer and industrial worker, must disappear, and the whole of society divide into the two classes of property owners and *propertyless* workers.
>
> Thus we have now to grasp the real connexion between this whole system of alienation — private property, acquisitiveness, the

separation of labour, capital and land, exchange and competition, value and the devaluation of man, monopoly and competition – and the system of *money*.

We shall begin from a *contemporary* economic fact. The worker becomes poorer the more wealth he produces and the more his production increases in power and extent. The worker becomes an ever cheaper commodity the more goods he creates. The *devaluation* of the human world increases in direct relation with the *increase in value* of the world of things. Labour does not only create goods; it also produces itself and the worker as a *commodity*, and indeed in the same proportion as it produces goods.

This fact simply implies that the object produced by labour, its product, now stands opposed to it as an *alien being*, as a *power independent* of the producer. The product of labour is labour which has been embodied in an object and turned into a physical thing; this product is an objectification of labour. . . . The performance of work [is] a *vitiation* of the worker, objectification [is] a loss and *servitude to the object*, and appropriation [is] *alienation*.

So much does the performance of work appear as vitiation that the worker is vitiated to the point of starvation. So much does objectification appear as loss of the object that the worker is deprived of the most essential things not only of life but also of work.[8]

Labor activity becomes an object of value within the capitalistic system only if it can be marketed, and during the industrial revolutions the competition for jobs was especially severe. In the absence of organized labor unions as we know them today, individual laborers were in competition with each other. Someone was always willing to work longer hours or produce more products per hour for lower wages. Marx argued that as long as a relatively large and inexpensive labor force existed, or could be imported from other areas in a country's colonial empire, capitalists could maximize their profits by maintaining wages at a subsistence level. If workers demanded more than survival wages, the factory owner could replace them with desperate, unemployed persons willing to work for less. Because they are locked in a competitive structure, the workers are alienated from each other and unable to develop a social consciousness.

Marx also criticizes capitalism for exploitation. According to his labor theory of value, the value of a product is determined by the labor that goes into producing it. In a capitalist society the bourgeoisie owns the means of production as private property, and the working class (proletariat) sells labor to the bourgeoisie. The exchange value of a

---

[8]Karl Marx, "Economic and Philosophical Manuscripts," in *Early Writings*, ed. and trans. T. B. Bottomore and C. A. Watts (New York: McGraw-Hill, 1963), pp. 120–21.

commodity exceeds the price that the owner has paid the laborer for the work in producing it. This *surplus* of value is siphoned off as profit by the capitalists and used to increase their personal wealth and their capitalistic holdings. Thus, in capitalism, the bourgeoisie survive and grow rich off the labor of the economically suppressed class, the proletariat.

37:2.3 *Marx's interpretation of history*　According to Marx, the *economic laws* of the capitalistic system, not the hard-heartedness of individual capitalists, are responsible for the misery of the proletariat. These laws, which are revealed by a study of history, are not absolute laws for all time but only at one historical stage of human economic development. However, the economic factors governed by these laws determine the whole social, cultural, and political structure of society, according to Marx's economic interpretation of history.

Governments and laws exist in order to maintain the dominance of one economic class within society, which is the one that owns the means of production, whether it be land, factories, equipment, or raw material. Marx used his dialectical method to explain all of modern history as a series of struggles between different economic classes. For example, in the Middle Ages the aristocracy was founded on the economics of feudalism, but the developing bourgeoisie, or capitalist class, struggled against the nobles and finally overthrew them. The industrial revolution of the nineteenth century aggrandized the capitalists' position, but a new class, the proletariat, also began to develop and struggle against them.

Marx claimed that his dialectical method could be used to identify the contradictions within the existing system and to *predict* future developments. The competition between the capitalists would lead to cartels and monopolies. Big investors would swallow up the smaller ones, the numerous independent businesses giving way to a few powerful corporate giants. At the same time the numbers of the working class would be swollen by the addition of bankrupt businessmen and farmers. The proletariat, disciplined by hard work, overwhelmed by suffering and overwhelming in numbers, would rise up in revolution to overthrow the capitalists, who would be paralyzed by a worldwide depression. The ultimate triumph of the revolution was scientifically predictable and thus assured. Marx thought that nonviolent revolutions in democratic societies might be possible but that violence would probably be necessary in more autocratic regimes.

After capitalism, history would evolve into the "dictatorship of the proletariat." The victorious workers would take control of the means of production and would reorganize all social institutions to promote the era of a classless, *socialist* state or society. The workers would no longer be exploited for the benefit of those who did not participate in labor. The class struggles that had marked previous human history would be over because only one economic class would exist. Production and distribution under socialism would follow the rule, "From each according to his ability, to each according to his *work*."

As the socialistic society developed, individual socialist communities could become independent. A new rule would evolve to guide social interaction: "From each according to his ability, to each according to his *need*." It would no longer be necessary to suppress various economic classes, and eventually the state itself would dissolve, leaving a free association of producers which had conscious and purposive control of itself.

37:3.1 *Metaphysics*   Marx was mainly interested in economics and history. The implications of his views for other parts of philosophy were worked out as an orthodox Marxist ideology by Engels, Lenin, Trotsky, Stalin, Mao Tse-tung, and others. The Marxist metaphysics is monistic: Matter, the sole element, evolves toward ever-improved and more complex stages of self-expression. The dialectical network postulates that after periods of tension, matter surges forward in revolutionary leaps toward new and higher levels of integration. The accumulation of quantitative differences produces sudden qualitative changes once the internal contradictions of one mode of organization have reached a sufficient level of tension to bring about the qualitative leap forward. The emergence of *consciousness* from physical processes is explained this way: Mental events are epiphenomena, byproducts of complex material events. This view resembles the theory of *emergence* discussed in Chapter 15.

The same explanation applies to the organization of society. Thus it was possible for Mao Tse-tung to propose as government policy in the 1950's an effort at a "great leap forward" for all of China. Dialectical development necessitates that those deep-seated social conflicts ("contradictions") must somehow be resolved. Mao says:

> *War* is the highest form of struggle for resolving contradictions, when they have developed to a certain stage, between classes, nations, states, or political groups, and it has existed ever since the emergence of private property and of classes.[9]

37:3.2 *Ethics*   Orthodox Marxism has little to say about ethics as such because it is viewed as merely a tool in the class struggle. Human free-

---

[9]"Problems of Strategy in China's Revolutionary War," *Selected Works*, Vol. I (Dec. 1936), 180, cited in *Quotations From Chairman Mao Tse-tung* (Peking: Foreign Languages Press, 1972), p. 58.

dom consists in knowledge of the inevitability and inexorability of the socioeconomic process. Once you know and understand where history is leading, you can either accept the path of the future and strive to make the transitions occur more easily, or you can stand in opposition, which will ultimately prove futile.

37:3.3 *Religion*   Marxists are not interested in the speculative proofs of theologians, but in the social impact of religious *practice*. Religion is a "social product,"[10] growing out of human alienation. Through religion the exploited and alienated classes project their own best qualities onto God, a being external to themselves. Rather than helping them escape economic bondage, religion focuses their hopes on rewards in an afterlife and teaches acceptance of the present social order.

> Religion is one of the forms of spiritual oppression that everywhere weighs on the masses of the people, who are crushed by perpetual toil for the benefit of others, and by want and isolation. The impotence of the exploited classes in the struggle against the exploiters engenders faith in a better life beyond the grave just as inevitably as the impotence of the savage in his struggle against nature engenders faith in gods, devils, miracles and so forth. To him who toils and suffers want all his life religion teaches humility and patience on earth, consoling him with the hope of reward in heaven. And to those who live on the labour of others religion teaches charity on earth, offering them a very cheap justification for their whole existence as exploiters and selling them at a suitable price tickets for admission to heavenly bliss. Religion is the opium of the people. Religion is a kind of spiritual gin in which the slaves of capital drown their human shape and their claims to any decent human life.
>   But a slave who has realised his slavery and has risen up to fight for his emancipation is already only half a slave. The present-day class-conscious worker, trained by large-scale factory industry and educated by urban life, rejects religious superstitions with contempt, leaves heaven to the priests and the bourgeois hypocrites and fights for a better life here on earth.[11]

In practice the ethical and social mores supported by communist regimes tend to be conservative by Western standards. Given the goals of achieving social harmony, integration, cooperation, equality, and economic stability for the entire community, communist societies necessarily tend to promote virtues like perseverance, hard work,

---

[10]Marx, "Theses on Feuerbach," *op cit.*, p. 296.
[11]V. I. Lenin, *Selected Works* (New York: International Publishers Company, 1955), vol. XI, part III.

cooperativeness, and self-sacrifice. They tend to repress advocates of personal liberty, self-determination, and individualistic independence. The rugged individualism that characterized the adventurous capitalism of nineteenth-century and early twentieth-century America stands in contrast to the loyal cooperativeness sought by the builders of communistic societies. The major program for Marxism at this time is continuation of the revolution by preparing the social conditions necessary for its occurrence and by everywhere striving to prevent capitalist revisionism.

37:3.4 *Knowledge and truth*   Marx's epistemology has been elaborated recently by Marxists in the West such as George Lukacs. Our knowledge of ourselves and of the world is historically relative. No world view, according to Western Marxist thinking, can escape its historical relativity. The ideas we use to describe the world contain the hidden assumptions, the values, and the organization of our society. Even Marxism itself can be acknowledged to be historically relative. However (as was indicated in 37:2.1), social action provides the ultimate test for the claims of Marxism. The human spirit is itself conditioned by and emergent from human history and yet can subconsciously distinguish itself from its history. On the one hand, historical forces appear to be impersonal, uncontrollable, and inexorable in their movement. On the other hand, these forces are at bottom human ones, objectified and alienated from the human spirit. When the ultimate revolution occurs this alienation of the human spirit from itself will be overcome and dehumanizing institutions will be overthrown. Real self-knowledge is possible only as persons are able to see themselves beyond their alienation.

Both orthodox and Western Marxists hold that truth is a relative concept that is historically and socially determined. Each of us can know the truth only from our vantage point within that historical, social process. Knowledge progresses toward absolute truth, but because the progress is still occurring, knowledge at any time is not perfect. In this light intellectual attacks on Marxism, divorced from practical circumstances, are interpreted as blindly defensive reactions of bourgeois capitalists and revisionists, ignorant of the relativity of their own perspective.

37:4.1 *Criticisms*   Many of Marx's predictions about social change turned out to be false, for example, that the industrialized Western societies were most ripe for communist revolutions. As it turned out, communist regimes tended to take hold in relatively less developed societies with substantially agrarian and peasant populations. On the other hand, the industrialized societies socialized their capitalism, introducing stronger governmental controls on the economy. This sociali- zation was done by providing avenues for workers to own shares in the means of production through the purchase of stock and through participation in labor unions or other cooperative organizations (for example, mutual funds and pension plans) that essentially gave large percentages of the population an economic interest in preserving cap- italistic socialism.

The theory of the relativity of truth has often been criticized as an apparent excuse for less rigorous philosophical thinking. Even many orthodox Marxists have abandoned the dialectic as a tool for achieving precise understanding of empirical phenomena because it is scientifically dysfunctional. It serves better as an organizing princi- ple for action than as a tool for accurately predicting events.

Ironically, what Marx set out to develop as a nonideological, an- tiphilosophical theory of social and economic development has taken on the characteristics of a dogmatic, nonempirical ideology. Under many Communist regimes this has been manifested in a brutal intoler- ance for dissenting views. Yet Marxism remains immensely powerful as a world view that organizes thought and directs activity for millions of people throughout the world.

Marx's social philosophy has also been criticized by many liberal and libertarian philosophers for its devaluation of individual civil lib- erties and rights. In response to "From each according to his ability, to each according to his need," these critics object that this principle would make the productive members of society "slaves" of the non- productive members.[12]

37:4.2 *Maoism*   Probably the most influential and profound rethinking of Marx has been done by Mao Tse-tung (1893–1976). His achievement is all the more amazing if you consider the attitudes of Confucius (551–479 B.C.) and of classical China with which Mao had to merge Marxism to make it acceptable and applicable.

Mao became a Communist in the early 1920's. Intellectually, the first problem he confronted was Marx's view that urban, industrial workers would be the revolutionary class. Mao urged that the aliena- tion of rural, agricultural Chinese peasants paralleled that among the European proletariat. He then struggled against the Confucian view that society should look to its past for appropriate models of social re- lationships. The past, Mao said, revealed the contradictions of oppres- sive policies. Thus hope lies in the future—a Marxian idea with its

---

[12]See Robert Nozick, *Anarchy, State and Utopia* (New York: Basic Books, 1974), pp. 156–7, 172.

Western roots in the Old Testament—not in the Confucian veneration of the past.

Whereas Confucius saw human relationships as basically social and imbedded in mores and traditions, Mao saw them as fundamentally political—a struggle for power and authority. But where Marx saw himself as being able to gain a clear, abstract understanding of human needs and human history, Mao held to the more humble Confucian appreciation of the wisdom of the people. Accordingly, Mao himself, and all central government bureaucrats spent three months annually working in the villages and fields, learning from the people about their problems. Perhaps the people of China were following Mao Tse-tung even when in the mid-1960's the Red Guard in their anti-Confucian fervor were systematically destroying all ancient things—precisely because of the Confucian ideal of a leader's respect for his people which Mao so clearly exhibited.

EXERCISES for Chapter 37

1. Of the following statements, mark those *T* that correctly describe the concerns to which Marx responded.
   A. Marx wanted to expose capitalism as an oppressive force.
   B. Marx wanted to emphasize the importance of theoretical philosophical questions.
   C. Marx attempted to understand social movements dialectically.
   D. Marx thought it important to follow the lead of speculative idealists.
   E. Marx hoped to show that religion has great value because of the consolation it gives to the oppressed.
   F. Marx was concerned that human alienation should be understood and overcome.
   G. Marx assumed that class divisions are inevitable in human society.

2. In the Workshop in 37:1.1, Marx presents his understanding of political power.
   a. What, according to Marx, is political power?
   b. Is the use of political power ever justified?
   c. What, according to Marx, is the cause of social classes?
   d. What basis does Marx supply for asserting that classes will dissolve?

3. Describe Marx's concept of alienation in such a way as to outline how he uses it to
   a. develop his labor theory of value with the consequence that the working class is exploited (37:2.2),
   b. explain the meaning and existence of class tension,

    c. show the dialectical character of history (37:2.3),

    d. define social contradiction as a force leading to a transformation of quantity into quality (37:3.1),

    e. frame his concept of religion (37:3.3),

    f. base and justify the Marxist concept of the relativity of truth (37:3.4).

4. Choose one of the topics below, and after consulting appropriate library research materials, write an essay

    a. comparing the thought of Marx and Mao Tse-tung;

    b. describing contemporary Marxist responses to socialized capitalism;

    c. explaining the contemporary Marxist critique of "dialectic";

    d. appraising contemporary applications of Marxist thought to American minority groups or to third world countries.

SELECTED ANSWERS for Chapter 37

1. A, C, and F are true.

2. a. "Political power is the organized power of one class for oppressing another."

    b. Yes, but only by the oppressed, to resist and overcome oppression. (Note that, strictly speaking, such organization does not fulfill the definition of political power.)

    c. When one group of people starts to exploit another, the exploiters see that they share an interest in keeping the exploited servile and powerless. Social classes arise then as the exploiters see and act upon their common interest.

    d. Marx claims that classes will cease when the exploited have overcome the power of their adversaries to oppress them. (Thus Marx never shows why no new group of oppressors will arise.)

Index